HORSES

•THIRD EDITION•

A Guide to Selection, Care, and Enjoyment

HORSES

•THIRD EDITION•

A Guide to Selection, Care, and Enjoyment

J. WARREN EVANS

Texas A&M University
College Station, TX

W. H. FREEMAN AND COMPANY

New York

Library of Congress Cataloging-in-Publication Data

Evans, J. Warren (James Warren), 1938-
 Horses : a guide to selection, care, and enjoyment/ J. Warren Evans.—3rd ed.
  p. cm.
 Includes bibliographical references (p.).
 ISBN 0-7167-4255-1 (hardcover)
 ISBN 0-7167-4171-7 (paperback)
  1. Horses. I. Title

 SF285 .E933 2000
 636.1—dc21   00-042671

Printed in the United States of America

First printing 2000

Contents

PART III
USING AND ENJOYING THE HORSE

PART IV
BREEDING THE HORSE

Preface

The horse has served humanity in many different ways for centuries. Today, it serves primarily as a source of pleasure in technologically advanced nations, but still as a beast of burden and for draft power in underdeveloped countries. This book was originally written to provide people with an introduction to the basic principles of care and management of the horse so that their enjoyment of the horse will be enhanced, and the welfare of the horse will likewise be enhanced. The material presented throughout this edition reflects both our ever-increasing knowledge about horse care and training, and the advances in our understanding of disease prevention and control.

Aimed at the introductory equitation, horse management, and horse production courses taught at the undergraduate level, this book was also written to fulfill the need of the general reader seeking information about horses. The text assumes no knowledge of biology, chemistry, nutrition, physiology, medicine, or genetics; and every effort has been made to keep the technical vocabulary to a minimum and the exposition of concepts accessible to the lay reader.

Following an introduction that provides information on moral and legal obligations, costs, and benefits of horse ownership, the book is organized around five central themes. The first concerns the selection and purchase of a horse. Guidance is given in determining the kind of horse to purchase based on the owner's needs, locating a horse to purchase, and making purchase decisions. Some of the newer techniques used to determine differences that may affect performance have been added to this edition. Also, the latest information on disease prevention and parasite control programs has been included. The concluding chapter of this part includes details on numerous breeds and their characteristics. Photographs of current and successful representatives for many of the breeds have been updated.

The second part, on ownership responsibilities, discusses physical facilities, veterinary aid, and day-to-day tasks, such as feeding, handling, exercise, grooming, foot care, first aid, parasite control, and disease prevention. The proper planning and construction of the stable site, barns, fences, breeding facilities, and bedding are outlined. The important topic of fire safety is discussed in the context of physical facilities. The related issue of accident prevention is paramount in the discussion of proper methods of restraint, routine handling, and basic training. The chapter on nutrition has been expanded to include the relationship of nutrition to reproduction, as well as the concept of body condition scoring and its use in nutritional management. Practical approaches to the use of behavioral principles in managing and training horses have also been added.

Using and enjoying the horse comprise the third major theme. This part encompasses riding and driving, horse shows and races, rodeo, trail, and other sports events. Basic procedures and equipment for riding, driving, racing, and other equestrian activities are described in detail.

The fourth section of the book concerns reproduction and genetics. One chapter is devoted to breeding the stallion, and another to breeding the mare. The material on reproduction is unique in that step-by-step details are provided for successfully breeding and foaling the mare. Pregnancy care and various problems concerning foals are also discussed, in a separate chapter. The chapter on reproduction has been updated to provide the latest information on embryo transfer, computerized recordkeeping systems, care of the young foal, the use of ultrasound, and improved methods of estrous cycle control, including the use of GnRH and new artificial light program schedules. The segment concludes with a chapter on basic genetic principles for selecting and breeding superior horses.

The final section is a new chapter devoted to the business aspects of horse ownership. Hopefully, it will serve as a guide to the many aspects of business decisions that must be made concerning horse ownership and management for various uses.

For the more serious student of horse husbandry, numerous appendices contain detailed, technical information on ration formulation, semen evaluation procedures, and pregnancy determination. There are also glossaries of racing and rodeo terms, and addresses of breed associations and horse magazines. An extensive bibliography, organized by chapter, concludes the book.

If the reader increases his or her enjoyment of the horse and if the general care of horses is improved, I will have achieved my objectives in writing and revising this book.

Owning a Horse

Humans have been closely associated with the horse since its domestication in the Near East—where it was first used as a draft animal—between 4500 and 2500 B.C. And before that, the horse was a major source of food for us. By 1000 B.C., domestication had spread to Europe, Asia, and North Africa. After the development of machinery powered by fossil fuels, the horse was no longer a needed source of power in economically developed countries. In America, the horse population reached its peak in the early 1900s, declined until the 1950s, and regained a good deal of popularity in the late 1960s. Today, horses in the United States are mainly kept for recreational purposes. Because few people had contact with horses between 1900 and 1960, horse management skills were rarely passed to the next generation. Many American families are now having their first experiences with a horse or are relying on grandparents for assistance.

OWNERSHIP OBLIGATIONS

Uninitiated owners, lured by the horse's esthetic and athletic appeal, soon realize that owning such an animal is not like the romantic horse stories they read as children. As wonderful and rewarding as horse ownership can be, owning a horse involves a considerable amount of time, dedication, and hard work. Owners must be prepared to spend more time caring for the horse than riding it. A horse requires attention every day of the year when it is kept

1

confined. It must be fed, watered, groomed, have its feet cleaned, and be exercised. The owner must muck out and clean stalls daily and must take care of the tack and equipment.

OWNERSHIP COSTS

In addition to labor, the owner must be prepared to take care of the considerable financial obligations of horse ownership. Actual costs are not presented because they constantly change. The ensuing discussion calls attention to the many financial obligations that one assumes. Each cost must be calculated accurately to assess the total financial obligation of horse ownership. Before a horse is purchased, certain economic facts must be considered. The initial cost depends on several factors that determine the horse's value: its training, age, breed, and temperament. Other factors, such as color, conformation, manners, and soundness, also affect the decision to buy. All these factors are discussed at length in Part I, Selecting and Buying a Horse, Chapters 1–3.

One of the first considerations is the cost of stabling a horse. These costs vary depending on the use of a stall in a barn with or without adjoining paddock, pasture, or outside paddock. If the horse is kept at a commercial stable, there may be additional costs for labor, feeding, stall cleaning, and exercise. The costs for stabling vary quite widely depending on factors such as area of the country, location within an area (urban, suburban, or rural), quality of the facilities, and extra services provided. If one owns the facilities required to keep a horse, one must include the cost of construction or purchase, maintenance, electricity, taxes, interest on investment, and water expenses.

Estimated Annual Maintenance Costs

Horse	$5,100 (registered) or $2,336 (grade)
Acreage	9,975 (2 acres)
Barn/stable	3,907 per horse
Arenas, paddocks, and fencing	1,992
Trailer	715
Vehicle	2,973
Veterinary fees	87
Veterinary medications	53
Veterinary supplies	100
Grooming supplies	50
Hay and grain	841
Farrier	277

Clothing (riding/showing)	1,518
Saddles, tack	190
Insurance	460
Stable utilities	130

SOURCE: Indiana Horse Industry Survey and Texas Horse Industry.

Note: Call the United States Equine Marketing Association (703) 338-4642, for current and additional information.

Under confinement conditions, a horse consumes about 20 pounds of hay (9.07 kg) per day, or approximately $3\frac{1}{2}$ tons (3175 kg) per year. Depending on the horse and its intended use, you may need to feed grain as well. You must bed the horse's stall with straw, wood shavings, or other suitable material, and the bedding must be completely changed at least once a week. You will need the services of a farrier every 6 to 8 weeks to trim or shoe the feet. You will need veterinary services when an injury occurs, and a preventive medicine program to ward off common diseases and control internal parasites. Basic, necessary equipment for taking care of the horse must be periodically replaced. Tack is a necessary expense, as are appropriate clothes for riding and caring for the horse. If your horse is to be transported for trail rides or horse shows, you will need a trailer and a car or truck to tow the trailer. Special equipment for towing such as trailer hitches and mirrors are added expenses. If the horse requires training, you must hire a trainer or some additional help to complete the training process.

Owning horses entails certain risks and possible extensive liability. Therefore, people involved with horses need added insurance. (Many horsepeople fail to recognize the need for insurance or may have been misled to believe that additional insurance is not necessary.)

A limited number of companies offer horse mortality insurance. The large capital investment in a horse makes such protection especially prudent. You should discuss the conditions governing such policies with the underwriter. Humane destruction is sometimes necessary, but you must adhere to strict procedures to collect on the policy. The humane factor is the only consideration. A horse may not be destroyed because of injuries that merely prevent the performance function for which it is kept. Permission from the underwriter must be obtained, and it is usually given on the advice of a veterinarian.

In addition to the full mortality coverage, some companies offer a more limited peril policy covering fire, lightning, and transportation losses. The peril policy only covers loss from collision and/or overturn of the transporting vehicle. Losses are not covered for loading or unloading, van fits (the horse going berserk), or injuries received during sudden braking of the vehicle to prevent an accident. To cover these losses, a special accident policy must be obtained.

You must have liability insurance as protection against potential liability for injury to people and damage to property. There are some basic misconceptions about liability coverage for horses. The standard homeowner's or tenant's policy provides coverage only for a pleasure horse ridden on or adjacent to the owner's property, or in an area designated for pleasure riding. The policy does not provide protection once business pursuits begin, and that happens once a horse owner does anything other than pleasure riding, such as taking a horse to a public horse show and showing it, using the horse in a parade, renting the horse to someone else, or participating in a gymkhana (competitive performance events) or rodeo. This also means that the homeowner's policy does not cover race horses, brood mares, and breeding stallions (including shares in syndicated stallions). You need a special, private, saddle animal liability policy to cover off-premises events. Professional horsepeople engaged in the business of teaching people to ride, training, boarding, or breeding horses need a comprehensive general liability policy as well as an umbrella policy, which is an excess limit policy that picks up not only the horseperson's liability exposures as a business but also the vehicles that the person owns. The comprehensive general liability and umbrella policies have an exclu-sion clause that leaves one basic area for the professional horseperson: any animal in your care, custody, and control is excluded. Therefore, the pro-fessional needs a legal liability policy to cover horses that are the property of others and are in the insured's care, custody, and control for breeding, boarding, training, showing, or trucking. This policy pays for all legal obligations arising out of the insured's liability for all risks of physical loss, injury, or humane destruction to the horse in the care, custody, and control of the insured.

The professional horseperson who has farm and ranch employees may be subject to worker's compensation law requirements and may have to carry insurance to meet any liability covered by the law. Liability under worker's compensation law is without regard to negligence, and the employer must pay according to the law whether or not he or she was at fault.

There are also other forms of insurance. Most have to do with the reproductive status of a mare or stallion. Fertility insurance on stallions has become quite common with the advent of high price syndications. In utero policies are very popular with purchasers of mares in foal. Almost all breeding contracts state that the breeding fee is earned in full once the original owner who bred the mare has sold it. The purchase price of a mare in foal is determined in part by the foal she carries, and the purchaser is interested in protecting the investment. There are two basic conditions of in utero insurance: The policy does not indemnify the owner if abortion occurs as the result of multiple fetuses, or if a fetus is not in evidence for an autopsy report. Major medical policies that cover costs for medical treatment, including surgery, and surgical policies, which are more limited, are gaining popularity. Rising veterinary costs, particularly for emergencies, have made these policies important for the person on a limited budget. The policies usually have upper limits of coverage and deductibles, and one must carefully evaluate exclusions in the policy. Also, applicants should be prepared for a thorough investigation of their horse operations and management.

BASIC FACILITIES AND CARE

A horse is usually confined. Various types of facilities are suitable to keep the horse under confinement conditions. In most circumstances, a horse will be comfortable in an outside paddock that has a shelter to provide shade in hot environments or protection from wind in very cold climates. Details of stall construction and design are discussed in Chapter 4. Space must be available for tack and feed storage. An important consideration is adequate facilities for exercise: riding or exercising rings, or access to riding trails.

Many owners prefer to keep their horses at commercial stables, which range from a rented stall to elaborate equestrian complexes. When you select a commercial stable, you should consider several factors. Safety and cleanliness are very important. A clean stable is part of the disease and parasite control program. Manure should be removed from the paddocks and stalls at regular intervals (at least weekly) and stored in a compost pile. Removing trash and garbage helps control flies that carry diseases and parasites. No smoking should be permitted in the stable area, because it creates a fire hazard. Dogs should not be allowed unless the horses are accustomed to their presence. Equipment storage areas should be enclosed so that horses will not be injured by running into or stepping on the equipment. Fences should be safe for horses and kept in good repair. The stable area should be fenced to contain horses that accidentally get loose from owners. This can prevent accidents caused by the horses running out onto highways or streets and can prevent damage to neighboring property. Gates should open and close easily but should be constructed so that horses cannot open them.

Ask about the disease- and parasite-control program for the stable. Are all horses required to have the standard immunizations? Are flies controlled? Are stalls disinfected before a new horse is brought in? Is there a quarantine area in case a horse becomes sick?

Also examine the barn and other buildings for their general condition and maintenance. Is the electric wiring protected from horses and rodents chewing on them? Are the buildings clean? Have fire safety precautions been taken? Stalls should be the appropriate size for your horse and properly maintained. A source of clean water is essential. Clean and properly designed feed mangers are important for the horse's safety and to prevent digestive upsets. A good, absorbent bedding material helps maintain a clean, dry stall.

The nutritional program is important to the well-being of the horse. The hays and grains fed to the horse must be of good quality and stored in a clean area to which the horse cannot gain access. If the horse is kept at pasture, the pasture should be well maintained to provide quality forage. Overcrowded pastures decrease their quality and may be unsafe for your horse. Good stable managers keep horses that do not get along together in different pastures.

A well-managed and well-designed stable provides appropriate facilities in which to ride and exercise the horses, and to care for them. Areas to exercise horses during inclement weather are useful during certain periods of the year. Riding rings and access to riding trails should be conveniently located. The tack room should be secure and dry and have adequate storage room for your saddles and riding equipment. Rest rooms, drinking fountains, and telephones are convenient for riders.

Evaluate the knowledge and attitudes of the owners, boarders, and employees. Is the owner a knowledgeable horseperson? What is his or her reputation with the local farriers, feed store managers, tack shop owners, and horsepeople? Is he or she a good businessperson? What is the attitude of the stable employees toward the boarders? Are there enough employees working at the stable? What is the behavior of the boarders? Do they drink alcoholic beverages on the premises and use foul language? Are the boarders good horsepeople or do they abuse their horses? Is a trainer available to help you train your horse or to improve your skills with horses? If so, does the trainer have a good reputation? A veterinarian should be on call to the stable.

An examination of the horse often reveals if it is well cared for. It should not be too fat or too thin. Its coat should be in good condition and well groomed, and its feet should be properly trimmed or shod at all times.

BENEFITS OF OWNERSHIP

Horse owners and communities benefit from horses in several ways. Ownership and enjoyment of horses are not the exclusive privilege of the wealthy. In fact, 60 percent of all horse owners in the United States are among families with a below-average income.

Dealing with horses helps children develop a sense of responsibility. The urbanization and mechanization of agriculture have diminished the need for children to perform farm-oriented chores or to take care of animals. Taking care of, exercising, and riding one's own horse can play an important role in a child's training. Children also develop the discipline necessary to work with others by participating in mounted drill programs, horse-judging team contests, and U.S. Pony Club team competitions.

Riding is a sport in which the entire family can and often does participate together. A survey found that there are 2.9 riders per horse-owning family and that 80 percent of families that own horses have at least two people who ride. About 40 percent of horse-owning families own four or more horses. Trail rides frequently attract several members of the same family. Father-and-son teams in roping competition are quite popular. Riding horses provides relaxation and psychological benefits. And riding horses indirectly benefits those who never ride because horses help develop new trails and parklands used by backpackers and others.

Horse owners play a role in our nation's economics by contributing to the tax base of the community, state, and nation. Taxes collected from the horse industry amount to billions of dollars. Most of the obvious revenue is generated from parimutuel wagering and from real estate taxes on property devoted to the horse industry, but the hidden sources are just as important, such as taxes collected from the wages and salaries of people directly employed by the horse industry or by allied industries. Sales of horse-related clothing, tack, equipment, and so on are a source of tax revenue. Real estate taxes paid on land occupied by feed and equipment manufacturers and retailers, as well as transportation taxes on feed, equipment, and horses themselves, contribute to the economics of the horse industry.

Riding horses improves the rider's physical fitness. Because the improvement is painless, riders seldom realize that it is occurring, and unlike jogging, horseback riding is seldom boring. Thus, the horse quietly but efficiently helps solve a concern of many Americans today—maintaining physical well-being.

Disabled people can now enjoy riding horses. A horse can become an emotional outlet for them, and they gain a sense of freedom from restraints imposed by their handicaps. Many disabled children find it hard to relate to adults and able-bodied children, but they do not find it hard to relate to a pony. The pony or horse provides an exciting new and different learning situation for them.

Horseback riding by the physically disabled is now an accepted form of physical therapy to rehabilitate damaged muscles. Equestrian therapy for the disabled is developing all over the world. Starting in Europe, riding programs for the disabled have spread to countries such as Australia, New Zealand, Rhodesia, South Africa, Canada, Bermuda, and the United States.

Horseback riding has also become a recognized form of therapy for regaining mental health. Some benefits derived by patients are the conquering of fear and replacing it with self-confidence. Riding develops affection and companionship and a sense of mastery. It often helps overcome a feeling of inferiority and requires the patient to make decisions and act on them. Riding improves coordination and rhythm while providing a relaxing and stimulating form of exercise that creates a new interest.

CAREERS WITH HORSES

There is a wide variety of careers in the horse industry. Some involve working directly with horses, whereas others deal with goods and services needed by the horse industry. Some require extensive practical experience and knowledge of horses; others expect only general knowledge. Rates of pay are highly variable, but a significant percentage of people working in the industry make minimum or close to minimum wages. Some of the careers available in different areas of the horse industry are listed below.

Race track: clocker, racing secretary, veterinarian, trainer, exercise jockey, jockey, timer, identifier, groom, steward

Breeding farm: manager, groom, stud manager, broodmare manager, stall cleaner, stallion booking agent

Riding stable: manager, groom, stall cleaner, trainer, riding instructor

Training: trainer, assistant trainer, groom

Shows: secretary, announcer, judge, ring steward, jumping-course designer, groom, exercise person, professional trainer

Business: insurance, bloodstock agent for sales or purchasing, auctioneer, sales promotion and public relations staff, fitting sale horses, transportation, consultant, computers

Medical: veterinarian, veterinarian's assistant, hippotherapist

Therapeutic riding for the disabled: riding instructor, physical therapist, occupational therapist, speech therapist, educational specialist, program administrator

Breed association: executive secretary, editor and writer, registrar, field representative, show manager, public relations staff

Academic: 4-H and Cooperative Extension horse specialist, professor, FFA instructor, research technician

Law: specialist in equine law

Allied industries: sales for tack, trailers, and all horse-related equipment and supplies

HOBBY OR BUSINESS?

If one is entering the horse industry as a business entity, it is important to follow certain procedures that may be helpful if the business is challenged by the Internal Revenue Service under the hobby loss provision of the Internal Revenue Code. First, it is important to seek legal advice from an attorney and accounting information from a certified public accountant. To prepare for a potential challenge from the IRS, the following should be done at the initiation of the business and continued throughout the business. A separate checking account for the business should be established. A professional accountant should set up the accounting system and all of its parts. A business plan should be developed and periodically updated. Consultation with experts to solve problems, implement management policies, and provide advice before and after activities should be documented. Equally important is the maintenance of a log of the time spent on various horse activities. Visiting similar operations, attending association meeting and educational events, and studying the industry need to be documented. A change in management techniques to overcome problems or as a result of hardships should be recorded with the analysis of the situation resulting in the changes.

Part One

SELECTING AND BUYING A HORSE

CHAPTER 1

Considering Basic Factors

SEEKING HELP AND ADVICE

The novice or less experienced horseperson can get help from a variety of people in buying a suitable horse. Most novices consult a friend who is a horseperson before they talk to anyone else about buying a horse. The friend should be an accomplished horseperson, or the advice given may be based on myths and "folklore." Local 4-H Club horse leaders are an excellent source of information and help and have often previously helped new club members buy horses for projects. Most of the horses they find for their members are of the type suitable for novices. Some farriers are excellent horsepeople and sources of advice, whereas others only know how to shoe a horse. A local farrier with a good reputation may help in locating a horse because he or she is in constant contact with local horse owners. Members of local horse clubs may be willing to help a novice find a first, suitable horse. Ranchers can also help locate a horse because most keep horses. A local veterinarian who specializes in horses can be of help and should evaluate the horse for soundness and health. Professional help can be obtained from Cooperative Extension horse specialists, college animal science department faculty members who teach horse-related courses, and professional horse trainers.

The novice may want a trainer to work with a horse to correct deficiencies in its training or to help improve the novice's equitation or to prevent gross mistakes in training or riding. Disappointment usually awaits beginners who expect to become accomplished horsepeople without experienced horses and without the aid of a professional trainer. If novices want to break and train their own horses, they need a professional to watch and direct their efforts. Failure to do so usually results in injury to the novice or in an improperly trained horse. The trainer should be carefully selected. Most trainers are specialists—they usually train horses for specific types of performance. Select a trainer who specializes in the type of horse you want. The trainer should be as reputable and well known as you can afford. One who has had years of training and riding experience is usually the most desirable. Previous clients are the best references to check the trainer's reputation. Observe the trainers in action with their current students or horses. They should be kind, considerate, and in command of the situation at all times.

Financial arrangements should be discussed before you hire the trainer. If the trainer is to train the horse or help school the horse and rider, agree on a monthly rate, which should reflect the trainer's talents and ability to train horses and/or riders as well as his or her investment in facilities and equipment. There may be extra charges for grooming and for special training equipment. Some trainers require that the horse or rider be under their supervision for a minimum period. Ask how long each training session is and how regularly the sessions are given. You should be able to observe the training sessions for the horse, so that you will know the hand and leg aids used to ride the horse. It is better if the owner is trained at the same time as the horse so that the animal is not confused when the owner starts to ride it. The trainer should limit the number of horses being trained. Horses seem to learn best from short (20- to 30-minute), intense training sessions 6 days a week. An assistant trainer may do most of the riding, but the trainer should be riding and observing the horse at regular intervals. You should discuss the feeding program for the trainer's stable. The general condition and care of the horses in his or her custody should be evaluated. You should also discuss financial obligations for farriers and veterinary services as well as for expenses encountered if the trainer is to show the horse.

The trainer may want to inquire about the horse owner before agreeing to train a horse, select a horse to buy, or give the owner riding lessons.

LOCATING A HORSE TO BUY

Horses and ponies can be purchased in a variety of ways, each with advantages and disadvantages. Regardless of the way in which a horse is bought and sold, the buyer should be aware that dishonest people can calm horses and mask lameness with drugs. Also, many horses are sold by word of mouth, and facts about the horse become distorted and inaccurate after they have been passed through several people. However, information that comes from someone who is familiar with the horse can be useful. Databases kept by breed organizations can be accessed to get accurate information about a specific horse's performance and produce records.

Friends

Friends can be a source. But purchasing a horse from a friend can often strain relationships, because horses change their behavior in new surroundings and when they are ridden and cared for by new people.

Advertisements

Classified ads in newspapers or horse magazines can be an aid in locating a horse. These horses usually have some type of problem that makes the horse difficult to sell to people who are familiar with it. Problems are indicated by phrases such as "gentle but spirited" or "for experienced rider." Several Internet sites are used to advertise horses that are being sold privately or through auctions. It is a common business practice to advertise more expensive horses, those that have achieved a high level of performance, or those with performance potential. Thus, potential racing horses are highly advertised before an auction sale.

Dealers and Trainers

Local horse dealers keep a variety of horses. Most of these animals have some fault that the dealer can hide or has corrected so that he or she can sell the horse. Some horse dealers have the reputation of not being very honest. Honest horse dealers try to match a horse to the purchaser's needs and experience. A major problem horse dealers encounter is dishonesty by the person buying a horse. They try to impress the dealer or trainer by pretending to be much more advanced horsepeople than they really are. The end result is usually disappointment because the rider is overmounted. Many professional trainers keep horses that are for sale. They may belong to the trainer or to the trainer's clients. Horses should be purchased only from trainers who have a reputation for honesty. Trainers will make an effort to find an appropriate horse for someone who will take riding lessons from them and who will want the trainer to school the horse. They do expect to be compensated for their time and effort. A favorite mount being ridden by you and belonging to the stable where you are receiving instruction can be a safe purchase because you are familiar with the horse.

Farms

Breeding farms are good places to look for horses. A breeding farm offers the opportunity to look at horses that are typical of the breed you want. Breeding farms must sell horses that meet clients' needs, or they will have difficulty staying in business. Most breeders are interested in promoting their breeds and want to be sure that a client is satisfied with the horse. Satisfied clients are their best means of advertisement.

Auction Sales

Auction sales can result in bargains or headaches. There are several kinds of auctions, including local weekly, breed association, breeder, and specialty performance. Generally speaking, it takes an experienced horseperson to evaluate a horse being sold at auction because there is something wrong with most horses there, particularly the local weekly or monthly auction for all kinds of horses. Breed association auctions tend to be more reputable, and at some auctions only select horses for a given breed are sold. An auction where a breeder sells horses once a year can be a good source if the breeder has a reputation for quality. Some auctions specialize in specific types, such as race, cutting, roping, or polo horses. Quality Thoroughbred yearlings are sold at international markets such as those held at Keeneland, Saratoga, Del Mar, Hialeah, Deauville (France), Ballsbridge (Ireland), and Newmarket (England). International markets are also held for other breeds, such as the Arabian, Standardbred, and Quarter Horse. Buying and selling horses at auction is discussed in detail in Chapter 18.

EVALUATING THE HORSE AFTER ONE IS LOCATED

During the initial contact with the horse's owner or agent selling the horse, there are a number of questions one should ask. These questions allow you to determine if you want to take the next step and visit the horse. One should inquire about registered or grade, age, sex, health, personality, size, training, vices, loading and hauling, whether the horse has been kept in stall or in pasture, compatibility with other horses, period of time owned by the current owner, and approval for vet check.

During the visit to inspect the horse, evaluate weight, soundness, conformation, and personality, observe how it performs for the owner/handler, and watch how it performs for you. Have the owner/handler ride the horse and observe it during catching, leading, grooming, saddling, and while being ridden. If the horse is being bought for a specific purpose, be sure its ability is demonstrated. If you are still interested in the horse, the next step is to ride it and assess how the horse performs for you. Finally, check the registration papers and health certificates and arrange for a vet check. Prior to the vet check, one should negotiate the sales price. A sales contract should be prepared and signed by both parties to avoid future conflicts. Before taking the horse to where it will be stabled, obtain information about what it is accustomed to eating.

Most major breed associations maintain a database so that one can check the performance record, pedigree, and other information about specific horses. Some performance-based organizations such as the National Cutting Horse Association also keep performance records.

COST FACTORS

Many factors affect a horse's price. Before the selection process starts, potential buyers must decide how much money they can afford to pay for a horse and then try to find a suitable animal for that price. Be realistic in setting standards for a certain amount of money. The following discussion on selection details many of these factors. It is usually advisable to buy the best horse one can afford, because the costs of keeping a horse are the same regardless of its quality and value.

Breed

The breed and breeding of the horse influence its value. Grade horses are suitable for many purposes and are usually sold for less money than horses registered with a breed association. This is not always the situation, however, because some performance contests do not require a horse to be registered. Some grade horses are better performers and command the most money for that particular type of horse. Horses of fashionable, popular, or proven families within a breed registry usually command higher prices. Some may be of lower quality than other horses selling for the same price. The value of certain breeds varies depending on the locality. This is particularly true for breeds such as the Tennessee Walking Horse, Thoroughbred, and Quarter Horse. (Breeds are discussed more fully in Chapter 3.)

Sex

Sex of the horse influences the cost. A gelding, the most popular horse for riding and most performance contests, is generally more dependable and costs less than a mare or stallion. The better bred the horse is, the greater the price spread between the sexes. Well-bred stallions suitable for stud duty are quite expensive. Mares that will eventually be bred are worth more than geldings and are selected based on breeding potential as well as current value as a pleasure riding horse.

Training

Some of the most significant influences on price are the level and type of training and the horse's accomplishments. The horse's athletic ability increases its value. Many horses command very high prices because of their past, current, or potential performances or training for certain types of performance.

Age

The horse's age is a prime factor. Young, untrained horses sell for less because of the future investment in training and time that the owner must bear. There is always the possibility of injury or failure to reach the desired level of training. Horses that are 5 to 10 years old are usually higher priced than those younger or older. At this age, the horse is at its peak in training and performance. The younger horse requires more delicate and skillful handling than the older, more experienced horse. Therefore, the less experienced the horse, the more experienced the rider needs to be. An inexperienced rider can gain much experience by working with an older, well-trained horse.

Size

Size influences price. Ponies usually are cheaper because their utility will be limited to a few years before the child (or children) becomes too large. Small horses are priced about the same as average-size horses unless they are smaller than the minimal acceptable standards for the breed. Horses are measured in hands. A hand is equivalent to 4 inches (10.2 cm). The point of measurement is the distance from the highest point of the withers to the ground. Therefore, a 15-hand horse is 60 inches high (152.4 cm) at the withers.

Color

Some horsepeople are interested in certain colors and will pay a premium for them. These horses are used for show, parade, or breeding. If you will accept only a certain color for a specific purpose, the number of horses available for sale that meet your criteria will usually be very limited.

Conformation

Conformation of the horse and its soundness affect its value. Well-conformed horses almost always sell for more money compared with equivalently trained horses of poor conformation. Horses that are unsound for specific uses have a lower utility value. Blemishes detract from a horse's appearance and may decrease the value of horses used for show purposes. (Conformation and soundness are discussed fully in Chapter 2.)

Market Value

To help buyers form an opinion on value or costs for horses sold at auction, some breed associations and magazines publish the selling prices of the horses sold at various auctions.

Some breed associations and sales companies also publish annual analyses of all horses of a certain type or breed sold at auction during the year. Analyses such as those published by *The Bloodhorse* for Thoroughbreds is given by sire, by type of horse, and by specific auction. For a sire analysis (Table 1-1), data will often include the number of crops, foals, runners, winners, 2-year-old winners, stakes winners, average-earning index, comparable index, number of sales yearlings, minimum and maximum sales price, average sales price, and stud fee. For older stallions, their performance as a sire of broodmares may be given. This analysis may include the number of dams he sired and their produce records, including the number of foals they produced and the number of runners, 2-year-old winners, and stakes winners, and the percentage of runners, winners, and 2-year-old winners. The average-earnings index (AEI) and comparable index (CI) are also given. The average-earnings index of a stallion is a measure of how a stallion's progeny or his broodmares' progeny compare to the average of the breed during the years he had winners or his dams had runners. An average earnings index of 1.00 indicates progeny earning the average of all winners. The comparable index is a comparison of how a sire's progeny compares with progeny from the same mares when those mares were bred to other stallions. About 30 percent of all Thoroughbred stallions have a lifetime AEI higher than the applicable CI, which means they improve the mares' foals relative to the other stallions. By consulting these sources and attending a few auctions, you can determine the current market values for certain types of horses.

TABLE 1-1   Sire Record and Sales Statistics

MR. PROSPECTOR: 22 crops, 1049 foals, 829 rnrs (78%), 643 wnrs (63%), 174 2yo wnrs (24%), 165 sw (16%), 98 gsw (9%), 41 G1SW (4%), 4.32 AEI, 3.44 CI, 303 sale yrigs, avg $535,864, 13.8 TNA.

In 1998: 84 rnrs, 34 wnrs, $2,161,521, 52, 2yo, 4 2yo rnrs, 1 2yo wnr, 9 sw, stakes horses: SOUVENIR COPY (G3), CHESTER HOUSE, FAMILY CALLING, Hidden Reserve (G2), Prosperous Bid (G2), Golden Token (G3), Marie J (G3), Proud and True, Ikhteyaar.

1998 Sales Yearlings: 26 offered, 19 sold, avg $568,158, med $550,000, high $1,200,000, low $130,000, 9 colts avg $517,222, 10 fillies avg $614,000.

1998 Stud Fee: $200,000; 1996 Stud Fee: $200,000

SOURCE: *The Bloodhorse.*

Multiple Ownerships

Multiple ownership of a horse or horses has been popular in the horse industry. Popular stallions are usually syndicated because they are expensive to purchase and insurance is too high for one owner. Several people will buy shares that entitle them to breed one or more mares per share to the stallion each year. Groups of stallions and/or mares are also syndicated. Participation in a large syndicate allows one to spread the risk over a larger number of horses and to own higher quality horses. Syndicates are managed by a general partner, and the limited partners (syndicate members) have limited rights regarding management decisions. The success of the syndicate depends largely on the abilities of the general partner. Most syndicates are governed by the Securities and Exchange Commission, and detailed legal procedures must be followed.

GAITS

A gait is the horse's manner of moving its legs during progression. As a species, the horse is more versatile in selecting gaits than any other quadruped and uses several gaits unique to the species.

An understanding of gaits is important to detect lameness, to train a performance horse, or to cue a horse for a specific purpose. Of the several gaits that a horse can use to move, some are natural, others are "artificial or learned," that is, most horses must be trained to execute them.

Several terms and concepts are used to describe the various gaits. The left side of the horse is the near side, and the *right side* is the *off side*. Today, these two terms are not so commonly used. A foot (or two feet simultaneously) striking the ground constitutes a *beat*. The beats may or may not be evenly spaced in time. The *support sequence* is the sequence of the various combinations of feet that are touching the ground. A *step* is the distance between imprints of the two forelegs or two hindlegs. A *stride* is the distance between successive imprints of the same foot. During every stride, each leg goes through two phases: (1) the *stance* or *weight-bearing* phase and (2) the *swing* or *nonweight-bearing* phase. When horses are racing as trotters, pacers, or runners, the time required for the swing phase is almost constant, at about 0.32 seconds. Time for the swing phase appears to be independent of how fast the horse is racing; therefore, it takes about the same amount of time to prepare a leg for the weight-bearing phase regardless of speed or gait. Maintaining a constant swing during a race is important in keeping the horse sound. If the horse is unable to prepare its leg to begin the weight-bearing phase within the normal swing time, its leg structures are exposed to excessive concussive forces. When the leg is properly prepared for striking the ground, it is being retracted so that it strikes the ground at a relative forward speed of zero. If the necessary swing time is longer, the leg must strike the ground before being properly prepared and traveling at zero speed relative to the ground. The foot is thus pounded into the ground with excessive shearing force. This predisposes the horse to many pathological problems resulting from excess concussion, trauma, and strain. A horse's ability to maintain the swing time for a leg is affected by the amount of time that all legs are off the ground (airborne phase), the stance phase for all legs, and the overlap phase (when two or more feet are on the ground simultaneously). In examining the strides (Figure 1-1) of Secretariat (1973 Triple Crown winner of Thoroughbred racing) and Riva

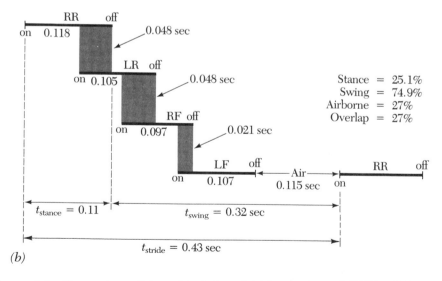

FIGURE 1-1   Comparison of the stride timing of *(a)* Secretariat and *(b)* Riva Ridge, to illustrate why Secretariat had a longer stride and ran faster. The graphs show the times at which each leg was placed on the ground or removed from the ground, the duration of the corresponding stance phases, the swing times, and the stride times. Read the succession of footfalls from left to right. The shaded regions show leg overlap. The percentages refer to percentage of the total stride time. (From Pratt and O'Conner, 1978.)

Ridge (1972 Kentucky Derby and the Belmont Stakes winner) during the running of the 1973 Marlboro Cup, in which both horses broke the world record for $1\frac{1}{8}$ miles (1.8 km), we can determine the effect of the overlap and stance phases. Secretariat ran faster because he spent less time with his legs in the stance and overlap phases; that is, his legs completed their ground contact quicker and more time was spent in the airborne phase.

Detailed analyses of gaits are made with the aid of computer-assisted three-dimensional motion capture. This procedure, which is becoming popular, allows a professional exercise physiologist or veterinarian to detect variances from normal gait and lameness. Often, the variances are not apparent to an observer simply watching the horse move. The analysis can be used to select high level performance horses such as those shown in dressage classes or race horses. It can also be used in a training program to detect and then correct subtle flaws in performance.

Natural and Artificial Gaits

Historically, six gaits of the horse were classified as natural: walk, trot, pace, canter, run, and back. Other gaits were said to be artificial. However, any gait that a horse will execute without training is a natural gait. For example, some Tennessee Walking Horses will execute the running walk without any prior training.

Walk

The several forms of the walk all show an even four-beat gait (Figure 1-2). The sequence of hoof beats is (1) left hind, (2) left fore, (3) right hind, and (4) right fore. Therefore, the sequence of beats is lateral in that both feet on one side strike the ground before the feet on the opposite side strike the ground.

Flat-Foot Walk

The ordinary walk is the most common form of the walk and is used by all horses. The flat-foot walk is the natural walk of the Tennessee Walking Horse. It is slightly faster than the ordinary walk.

Running Walk

The running walk is the fast walk of the Tennessee Walking Horse, faster than the ordinary or flat-foot walk. The hindfoot also oversteps the hoof print of the forefoot by as much as 50 inches (1.27 m) but normally about 12 to 18 inches (30 to 46 cm). The horse travels with a gliding motion, because it extends its hindleg forward to overstep the forefoot print. However, the regular four-beat rhythm is maintained. When executing the gait, the head moves up and down in rhythm with the legs. If the horse is relaxed while performing the gait, its ears flop and its teeth click in rhythm with the legs. The gait is easy to ride and not strenuous for the horse.

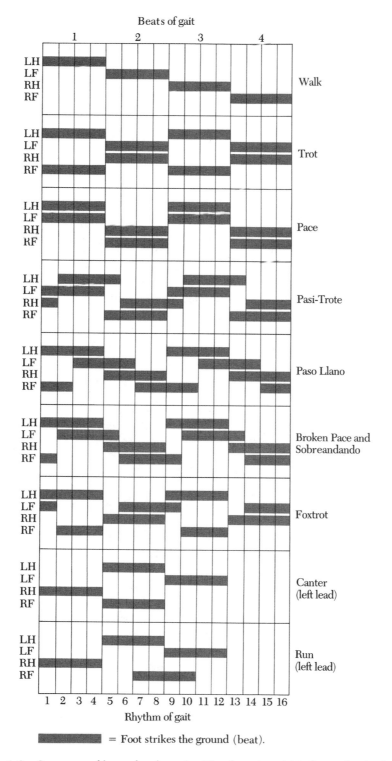

FIGURE 1-2   Sequence of beats for the gaits. Numbers 1 to 16 indicate the rhythm; LH = left hind; RH = right hind; LF = left fore; RF = right fore.

Rack

The rack is an even four-beat gait but is executed faster than the walk or running walk. The forelegs are brought upward to produce a flashy effect. The hind feet do not overreach the prints of the forefeet as far as they do in the running walk. In the show ring the rack is popular because of the speed and animation, but it is difficult for the horse to perform for extended periods. The excessive leg movement increases the amount of concussion and trauma to the forelegs.

Trot

The trot is a two-beat gait in which the paired diagonal feet strike and leave the ground simultaneously (Figure 1-2). Between each beat, there is a period of suspension in which all four feet are off the ground. There are three classifications of the trot. An *ordinary* trot serves as the basis of comparison. An *extended* trot is when the horse is trotting at speed and the length of the stride is extended. A racing Standardbred typifies the extended trot, although western pleasure and dressage horses are also expected to be able to extend their trot in the show ring. A *collected* trot is when the horse slows down and uses extreme flexion of the knees and hocks. The Hackney often characterizes the collected trot.

The two variations of the trot (two-beat sequence) each have four irregular beats. The foxtrot is one of the accepted slow gaits for a five-gaited horse. It is similar to the trot except that the hindfoot strikes the ground just before the paired diagonal forefoot. The paired diagonal feet leave the ground at the same time. When executing the *pasi-trote*, the Peruvian Paso horse allows the forefoot to strike the ground before the paired diagonal hindleg.

Pace

The pace is a two-beat gait in which the lateral limbs strike the ground simultaneously (Figure 1-2). There is a lateral base of support, and a period of suspension with all four feet off the ground occurs between each beat. Because the horse is shifting its weight from side to side, there is a rolling motion to the gait. A variation of the pace is the "stepping" or "slow" pace, which is the preferred "slow gait" for five-gaited show horses (Figure 1-2). It is the same as the *sobreandando* performed by Peruvian Pasos. The hindleg strikes the ground before the lateral foreleg so that the gait has four irregular-rhythm beats. In the takeoff, both legs leave the ground simultaneously.

The *paso llano* gait is also a broken pace, but the time between the hindfeet and the lateral forefeet striking the ground is longer than the sobreandando (Figure 1-2).

Canter or Lope

This gait is a three-beat gait in which the first and third beats are made by two legs striking the ground independently and the second beat is made by two limbs striking the ground simultaneously (Figure 1-2). The legs that strike the ground independently are called the *lead limbs,* and each bears the entire weight of the horse for a short period of time. Therefore, the lead limbs are more subject to fatigue than the other two legs. In the left lead, the sequence of beats is (1) right hindleg, (2) left hindleg and right foreleg, and (3) left foreleg. A period of suspension follows the beat of the left foreleg. If the horse is being circled to the left, it should be in the left lead to maintain its balance. If turned to the right, the horse should change leads to the right lead. The changes of leads occur during the period of suspension (Figure 1-3). When changing to the right lead from the left lead, the left hindleg strikes the ground after the suspension period. The paired diagonals—right hindleg and left foreleg—are the second beat, and the right foreleg is the third beat. Frequently, untrained horses switch leads behind

FIGURE 1-3   Correct change of leads in a canter. In the first sequence, the horse is in a right (off) foreleg lead with a left (near) hindleg lead. At S, the horse is in a period of suspension and properly changes leads at this time, coming down with right (off) hindleg lead and a left (near) foreleg lead, as shown by the second sequence of hoofbeats. (From Adams, 1974.)

but fail to do so in front, or just the opposite. This is called a cross-legged or dis-united canter, and it is very rough to ride.

Horses change leads at will when they are not under saddle. They must be trained to start in a desired lead and to change leads at the appropriate time while being ridden.

Run

The run is a four-beat gait (Figure 1-2), similar to the canter except that the paired diagonals do not land at the same time. The hindleg hits just before the foreleg. The lead limbs bear the full weight of the horse. In the left lead, the sequence of beats is (1) right hindleg, (2) left hindleg, (3) right foreleg, and (4) left foreleg. A period of suspension follows the four beats. If the horse changes leads, it will do so during the period of suspension. Because the legs bearing the weight of the horse become fatigued, the horse should change leads periodically when it is running. On the racetrack, the horse should change to the left lead as it goes around the turn and should change to the right lead along the straight portions to prevent excessive fatigue to the two lead legs.

Back

A horse backs by trotting in reverse, using a two-beat gait in which the diagonal pairs of legs work together.

Common Defects in Gait

There are several defects in the way that a horse may move its feet and/or legs while executing the gaits. Some defects are responsible for limb interference and may be severe enough to cause injury. Others are not serious but prevent the horse from giving its top performance. Some defects in the way of going are related to conformation; others are related to injuries, fatigue, or to improper shoeing and trimming of the feet. Some defects are obvious when the horse travels and some are not. The use of 3-D motion analysis can be used to detect defects that are not obvious.

Cross firing occurs when the inside of the hindfoot strikes the diagonal foreleg (Figure 1-4). It is generally seen in pacers that have long backs. A long back causes the horse to twist or swing its hindquarters. As the hindleg moves forward, it swings inward and strikes the diagonal foreleg, which is extended back under the horse's body.

Forging occurs when the toe of the hindfoot strikes the sole area of the forefoot on the same side (Figure 1-5). It usually occurs as the forefoot is leaving the ground. Overreaching is similar to forging except that the hindfoot comes forward more quickly and hits the heel of the forefoot before the forefoot leaves the ground. Both faults occur because the hindfoot breaks over and moves forward

FIGURE 1-4   Cross firing: hindleg strikes opposite foreleg.

too soon relative to the forefoot breaking over and leaving the ground (Figure 1-6). In many instances, forging and overreaching can be corrected by speeding up the breaking over and forward movement of the forefeet and retarding the hindfeet. This is usually accomplished by leaving the heels a little longer on the forefeet (increasing the angle of the hoof wall) and shortening the heels of the hindfeet. This changes the foot flight arc (Figure 1-7) and decreases the possibility of forging and overreaching. If necessary, the toes of the forefeet can be rolled to increase the ease of the forefeet breaking over (Figure 1-8). Also, trailers on the hindfeet will produce drag when the foot hits the ground, shortening the stride. Using heavier shoes on the forefeet than on the hindfeet carries the forefeet farther forward because of inertia and increases distance between the feet.

Interference occurs when one foreleg strikes the opposite foreleg. If the contact is very slight, it is called brushing. Interference is usually the result of poor conformation: toe-wide or base-narrow and toe-wide. The line of foot flight of horses that handle their forefeet in one of three basic ways is illustrated in Figure 1-9. At the left, the horse stands straight, breaks over straight,

FIGURE 1-5   Forging: toe of hindfoot strikes sole of forefoot.

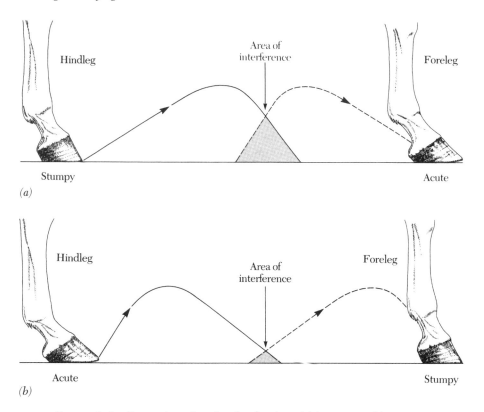

FIGURE 1-6   Corrective trimming for forging: *(a)* incorrect; *(b)* correct.

and has an absolutely straight line of flight. The horse in the center is toe-wide (toes out). The toe-wide conformation fault causes the forefoot to break over the inside part of the hoof wall, swing in an inward arc, and land on the inside part of the hoof wall. This type of movement is called *winging, winging inward,* or *dishing.* It may be prevented by corrective shoeing. The base-narrow, toe-wide conformation causes the forefoot to break over the outside part of the hoof wall and then wing inward. This fault almost always causes interference. The horse at the right in Figure 1-9 is toe-narrow (toes in); thus, its line of flight is more likely to be outward, and it will be a *paddler.* Although the way a horse stands in front usually provides a clue as to the anticipated line of flight of the front feet, this is not always a sure sign.

Paddling, or winging outward (Figure 1-10), is an outward swing of the forefeet. The feet break over the outside aspect of the hoof wall, move in an outward arc, and then land on the outside aspect of the hoof wall. Horses that are toe-narrow usually paddle.

Pounding is heavy contact with the ground and results in excess concussion trauma to the forelegs. Faults in conformation that shift the horse's center of gravity forward tend to make the horse's legs pound the ground.

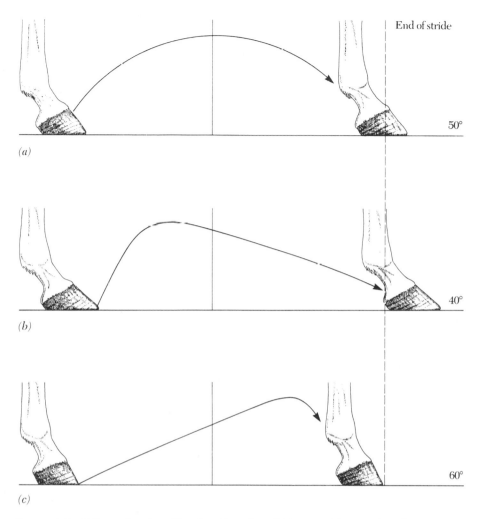

FIGURE 1-7 Effect of angle of hoof wall on foot flight arc: *(a)* normal angle;
(b) acute angle; *(c)* too much angle.

FIGURE 1-8 Rolled toe.

FIGURE 1-9   Lines of flight for the feet: *(a)* normal; *(b)* toe-wide; *(c)* toe-narrow. (From Harrison, 1968.)

Rolling is excessive movement of the shoulders from side to side. Horses that are wide between the forelegs and lack muscle development in that area tend to roll their shoulders. The toe-narrow fault in conformation also can cause rolling.

Scalping (Figure 1-11) occurs when the top of the hindfoot hits the toe of the forefoot right after the forefoot breaks over. As the area of impact moves

FIGURE 1-10   Paddling accompanies toe-in conformation. (From Adams, 1974.)

FIGURE 1-11   (1) Scalping; (2) speedy cutting; (3) shin hitting; (4) hock hitting. (From Harrison, 1968.)

up the hindleg, other terms are used to describe the defect. Speedy cutting occurs when the impact area is in the pastern and fetlock areas. Shin hitting occurs on the cannon bone, and if the hock is hit the fault is referred to as hock hitting. These defects in way of going are usually observed in racing trotters. As the speed of travel increases, the area of impact usually moves higher up the hindleg. Several faults in conformation predispose a horse to these defects in leg movement: short backs and long legs, leg weariness or hindlegs set too far under the body, short front and long back legs, and too long toes on forefeet.

A trappy gait is a short, quick, choppy stride. Horses that have short and steep pasterns and straight shoulders tend to have a trappy gait. It may indicate unsoundness, as in the case of navicular disease.

Winding is a twisting of the moving foreleg around in front of the supporting foreleg. The horse appears to be walking a rope. Horses that are wide in the chest tend to walk in this manner. It increases the likelihood of interference and stumbling.

TRAINING

Consideration of the type and degree of training of the horse by the potential buyer is critical. Beginning riders or horsepeople should select horses that are well trained for the purpose for which the animal is being bought. Older horses that are well schooled make excellent horses for beginners because their behavior and performance will probably remain the same for a long period of time. The beginner can make mistakes without spoiling the horse. Such a horse can be found at training stables or obtained from friends who have learned to ride it.

A beginner or intermediate rider should avoid buying a horse that is untrained or has only limited training. It takes years of experience before one is qualified to successfully continue a horse's training. Beginners have trouble knowing when to discipline a horse so that it associates the discipline with the mistake it made, knowing the fine line between discipline and cruelty, and knowing the fine line between kindness and permissiveness.

Intermediate riders may be successful in finishing the training required of a horse that has good basic training but needs additional experience and refinement of performance. The advice and help of a professional horseperson can keep the rider from making mistakes that would prevent the horse from reaching its performance potential.

A common mistake is buying a horse that is trained beyond the buyer's ability to ride it. Well-trained horses are sensitive to specific cues. Such a horse soon reverts to a lower level of training because it is constantly waiting for the right cues applied at the right time. When the right cues are not used appropriately, the horse becomes confused and does not know what to do.

Previous training should be compatible with the techniques used by the potential buyer. It is time-consuming and very difficult to retrain a horse to recognize a different set of cues.

Accomplished riders may wish to buy a horse and complete its training. They usually prefer to train their horses, because they do not have to buy someone else's mistakes. To train a green horse, the rider must have patience and training experience. Most important, the advanced rider must have sufficient time to train the horse. Irregular training schedules are a major cause of horses failing to become well trained and reach their performance potential. Riders who lack time, patience, and training experience should select horses that are well trained or at least have their basic training.

AGE

The desired use for a horse determines how old the horse should be. Generally, the best age at which to buy a horse is between 4 and 12 years of age. Before 4 years of age, the horse is not fully mature and is not ready for hard work and long hours of riding. Beyond 12 years of age, the usefulness of the horse is limited. There are exceptions, of course. The average horse lives about 24 years, but for most purposes has little practical value after 16 years of age. However, there are many horses that are serviceable in their early twenties. The Lippizaners of the Spanish Riding School frequently perform until the age of 24 and occasionally until they are 30. In some instances, an older horse or pony may be more desirable. Old age need not be considered if the horse is sound. A young child will probably become too large to ride a pony before an older pony must be retired because of age. A well-trained older horse serves its purpose for a person just learning how to ride. The inexperienced rider can learn a great deal about riding from an older, experienced horse. After 1 or 2 years, the rider will be ready for a different horse. Experienced riders buy horses at the peak of their physical development, because they will be exposed to strenuous exercise.

Most people make a mistake by buying a horse that is too young. The experienced horseperson can successfully train and handle a young horse. The inexperienced horseperson usually spoils the young horse, so it never reaches its performance potential. Parents often buy a weanling or yearling because they want their children to grow up with a horse, the rationale being that the children and the horse can learn together. The result is a poorly trained horse and numerous accidental injuries to the children and the horse or both.

Because the value of a horse depends largely on its age, familiarity with indications of age are extremely useful if the horse's registration certificate is not available or if it is unregistered. The teeth furnish the best index to the age of a horse, yet other general characteristics play an important role in determining or estimating age. In estimating the age of a young horse, size is a principal factor. In older horses, the sides of the face are more depressed, the poll is more prominent, the hollows above the eyes are deeper, the backbone becomes more prominent and starts to sag downward, the joints are more angular, and white hairs appear around the temples, eyes, nostrils, and elsewhere.

A horse that has been on the racetrack has a number tattooed inside its upper lip. Thoroughbred horses are tattooed according to a code. The letter indicates the year of birth (beginning with A in 1946 and I in 1980), and the four numbers are the last four numbers of the registration number. American Quarter Horses and Standardbreds do not have coded numbers.

Young horses are referred to according to their age. The young horse is referred to as a *foal* until it is weaned. The male horse is called a *colt* until it is 3 years of age, when it is called a *stallion*. Young female horses are called *fillies* until they are 3 years old, at which time they are referred to as *mares*. Some horsepeople refer to horses that are 6 months to 1 year of age as weanlings, 1 to 2 years as yearlings, and 2 years of age as 2-year-olds.

Teeth and Age

The order of appearance of the teeth and the way they are worn down are considered the most important and accurate cues for estimating the horse's age. However, the method is not absolutely accurate because the nature and quality of feed, environmental factors, heredity, and disease materially affect the wear of the teeth. A horse fed soft, succulent feed usually has a younger looking mouth. Horses fed hard feed or kept in dry, sandy areas of pasture may have mouths that appear 2 to 3 years older than normal. Consequently, one must consider all of these factors when examining the horse's mouth to estimate its age.

Up to 5 years, the age of the horse is commonly estimated by observing the appearance of the temporary and permanent incisors (Figure 1-12). Therefore, one must be familiar with the ages at which the temporary incisors

FIGURE 1-12   Positions and names of horse's incisor teeth: (1) upper central;
(2) upper intermediate; (3) upper corner; (4) lower central; (5) lower intermediate;
(6) lower corner.

appear and when they are replaced by the permanent incisors. Eruption of the
temporary premolars, the replacement of the temporary premolars by permanent premolars, and eruption of the molars are fairly accurate indications of
age, but are used infrequently. The ages at which various teeth erupt are given
in Table 1-2. The ages of 6 to 12 years are determined by the wear of the dental tables. Beyond 12 years of age, the length and angle of the incisor teeth and
Galvayne's groove are used to estimate the age.

To estimate the age of the horse, the horseperson must be able to distinguish between a temporary and a permanent incisor tooth and between the
presence and absence of a cup. The temporary incisor tooth has a more defined
neck where the crown and root meet at the gum line, is whiter in color, is more
rounded, and is not as long as a permanent incisor.

The appearance of the temporary incisors allows one to estimate certain
ages (Figure 1-13). The two central incisors on the lower jaw and/or two on
the upper jaw are present at birth or appear shortly thereafter. The intermediate incisors on the upper and lower jaws appear at 4 to 6 weeks of age. The
corner incisors appear at 6 to 9 months. A rule of thumb is that the incisors
appear at 8 days, 8 weeks, and 8 months. The temporary premolars are not
commonly used for estimating age because they are present at birth or appear
during the first couple of weeks. Therefore, the young horse has 24 teeth: 12
incisors and 12 premolars. Some young horses may have wolf teeth, which appear in front of the temporary premolars. A wolf tooth is a vestigial tooth and

TABLE 1-2   Average Times When Teeth Erupt

Deciduous	
Tooth	*Eruption*
1st incisor (or centrals)	Birth or first week
2d incisor (or intermediates)	4 to 6 weeks
3d incisor (or corners)	6 to 9 months
Canine (or bridle)	
1st premolar	Birth or first 2 weeks for all
2d premolar	premolars
3d premolar	

Permanent	
1st incisor (or centrals)	$2\frac{1}{2}$ years
2d incisor (or intermediates)	$3\frac{1}{2}$ years
3d incisor (or corners)	$4\frac{1}{2}$ years
Canine (or bridle)	4 to 5 years
1st premolar (or wolf tooth)	5 to 6 months
2d premolar	$2\frac{1}{2}$ years
3d premolar	3 years
4th premolar	4 years
1st molar	9 to 12 months
2d molar	2 years
3d molar	$3\frac{1}{2}$ to 4 years

SOURCE: Getty (1953).

has a very shallow root. It may not fall out prior to eruption of the second permanent premolar tooth (see section on care of teeth in Chapter 9).

At $2\frac{1}{2}$ years of age, the central incisors are replaced by permanent incisors. The permanent intermediate incisors erupt at $3\frac{1}{2}$ years of age; the permanent corner incisors, at $4\frac{1}{2}$ years. The canine teeth, commonly called bridle teeth, erupt in the interdental spaces at 4 to 5 years of age in male horses. They erupt in only about 20 to 25 percent of all mares. Table 1-2 shows the ages at which the permanent premolars and molars erupt. At 5 years of age, the horse is said to have a "full mouth." The mature male horse has 40 permanent teeth, and the mare has 36 to 40 teeth, depending on the number of canines present.

The cup in a tooth is shown in Figure 1-14. An outside layer of enamel covers the tooth. On the top of the tooth (table surface), the enamel extends inward, forming a pit commonly called the *cup*. The cup is filled with a variable amount of central cement. The inside of the tooth is filled with dentine. In the innermost part of the tooth, the pulp cavity contains the blood and nerve supply to the tooth. From the front of the tooth, the pulp cavity extends upward between the cup and front surface. The teeth of the horse continue to

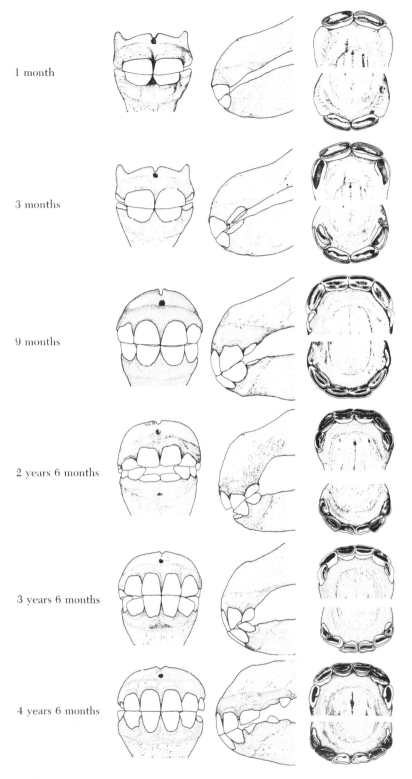

1 month

3 months

9 months

2 years 6 months

3 years 6 months

4 years 6 months

Figure 1-13   Guide to determining the age of a horse by its teeth.

34

6 years

7 years

8 years

10 years

13 years

17 years

FIGURE 1-13   *Continued*

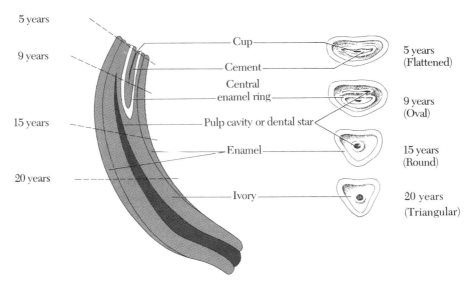

FIGURE 1-14   Anatomy of the horse's incisor tooth. A permanent middle incisor tooth at different ages and stages of wear. Changes in shape from oval to angular are shown in the cross-sectional views as wear progresses toward the root. (From Bradley, 1971.)

grow during its life but are continually being worn down. When the horse eats, a rotary grinding motion wears down the teeth. The table surface is worn down in a characteristic manner. First, the enamel on the table surface is worn off, leaving two rings of enamel around the outside edge and around the cup. As the wear continues, the table surface is worn down so that only the bottom of the cup remains. At this point, the cup is said to have "disappeared," even though the enamel from the bottom surface of the cup is still visible. Later, the enamel may completely disappear. When the cup disappears, the table surface has worn to the level of the pulp cavity. The pulp cavity is called the *dental star,* and appears at 8 to 10 years. It is first seen as a long, thin yellow line between the cup and the front of the tooth. As wear continues and the enamel on the bottom of the cup becomes dark, very small, and round, the dental star moves toward the center of the cup.

Between the ages of 6 and 12, the age can be determined by the presence or absence of the cups in the incisor teeth (Figure 1-13). Each year, the cups disappear from two of the incisors. At 6 years, they are absent from the lower central incisors. At 7, they are absent from the lower intermediate incisors, and at 8, they are absent from the lower corner incisors. Before age 9, the cups are present in all the upper incisors. At 9, the cups are absent from the upper central incisors, and at 10, they are absent from the upper intermediate incisors. When the horse is 11 or 12, they are absent from the upper corner incisors. At this age, the horse is said to be "smooth-mouthed."

Beyond 12 years of age, it is difficult to estimate the age of a horse and accuracy is decreased. In older horses, three indicators must be used: the incisive arcade, the table surface shape, and Galvayne's groove. When the incisors are viewed in profile, the incisive arcade—the angle formed between the upper and lower incisors—becomes more acute with age (Figure 1-15). In horses 20 years or older, the incisor teeth stick almost straight out. With advancing age, the table surface changes from a rectangular shape to a triangular shape (Figure 1-14). By the time a horse is smooth-mouthed, the table surfaces of the incisor teeth are very triangular in shape.

Galvayne's groove appears as a longitudinal depression at the gum line on the surface of the upper corner incisor at 9 to 10 years of age (Figure 1-15). The groove is recognized as a dark line. In some instances, it is hard to see, but it is always a darker color than the enamel. As the horse gets older, Galvayne's groove grows down the tooth. At 15 years, the groove is about halfway down the tooth. At 20 years, the groove extends the full length of the tooth. It then

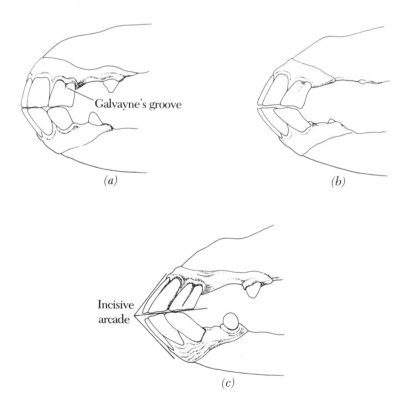

FIGURE 1-15   Profile of the upper corner incisor, incisive arcades, and Galvayne's groove; *(a)* 9 to 10 years—Galvayne's groove appears at gum margin; *(b)* 15 years—groove extends halfway down labial surface of incisor, *(c)* 20 years—groove extends entire length of labial surface. In profile, the incisive arcade (the angle between upper and lower incisors) becomes more acute with age. (Courtesy American Association of Equine Practitioners.)

starts to disappear at the gum line. At 25 years, it is absent from the upper half of the tooth and completely disappears by 30 years of age.

To examine the teeth, first stand to one side of the horse and separate the lips. Determine the incisive arcade, number of temporary and permanent teeth, and presence or absence of Galvayne's groove. If necessary, then examine the table surfaces. Place one hand on the horse's nose and grasp the tongue with the other hand. Remove your hand from the nose and use it to open the horse's mouth or to push the lips out of the way to look at the table surfaces of the upper and lower incisors.

TEMPERAMENT AND BEHAVIOR

The general temperament of the horse is an important quality. A good-tempered horse is obedient, intelligent, easy to train, courageous, confident, and calm. It is free of vices (bad habits) and easy to handle. Before buying, spend considerable time observing and handling the horse to evaluate its temperament. If possible, obtain the opinion of the previous owner, trainer, dealer, and breeder. A horse that has had several owners may have an undesirable temperament, particularly if it has had rough or inconsiderate treatment.

Compatibility of your personality with the horse's temperament should be considered. In most circumstances, opposite types of personalities are the most compatible. A nervous person may be just the stimulation needed for a placid horse to perform. And nervous horses usually are not so excitable when they are ridden and handled by someone who has a quiet, easygoing manner. Nervous people tend to make quick movements, which excite a nervous horse.

Hunters, jumpers, and stock horses need willingness and courage to perform successfully. Children's ponies or horses need to be gentle and obedient. A sluggish horse may not be obedient, and an inexperienced rider will not enjoy riding it because he or she will have difficulty getting the horse to move or preventing it from going where it pleases.

Temperament Types

Horses are like humans in that they all have personalities and temperaments. There are at least six general temperament types of horses: quiet, interested, nervous, extremely nervous, stubborn, and treacherous.

The *quiet* horse that is sluggish and has no interest in its surroundings is usually safe for the inexperienced horseperson. Because of its temperament, such a horse seldom advances to a highly trained state. It does not seem to care, and lacks the spirit and style for a well-schooled performance. The temperament of quiet horses makes them good for rental stables and for teaching beginners how to ride, because they are unconcerned about how a person moves or works around them.

The most desirable temperament trait is *interest* in its surroundings: the horse pays attention to what happens around it. When such a horse hears an unexpected noise or sees unexpected sudden movement, it responds by pricking its ears but does not shy or try to escape. These horses are usually easy to train and are willing performers. They have sufficient spirit to have animation and style in their performance. They are safe horses for beginners under the supervision of a knowledgeable horseperson or for the intermediate rider. When these horses are handled, they are sensitive to the handler's requests and respond calmly.

Nervous horses are easily excitable and shy away from strange objects, movement, and noise. They are safe horses for knowledgeable horsepeople. Nervous horses respond to training and are usually capable of reaching a highly trained state. One problem, however, is that they become excitable and flighty, and snort when they are exposed to new surroundings or unfamiliar objects. But as these horses get older and gain experience, their nervous dispositions improve.

The *extremely shy and nervous* horse is safe for only the very experienced horseperson who understands horse behavior. These horses shy at the least provocation, such as the slamming of a stall door, movement of a dog or cat, seeing a moving shadow, or any unexpected movement or noise. Frequently they try to escape without regard for the handler, even trying to run over or knock down the handler. They flee without concern for their own safety and run into fences, equipment, and buildings.

The behavior of a horse when it is around other horses should be carefully evaluated. Horses are usually stabled adjacent to other horses and kept together in larger paddocks. The horse that continually kicks and bites other horses or kicks the stall wall separating it from another horse is difficult to keep. On trail rides, it is a nuisance because it must be kept separated from the other horses to prevent accidents and injuries.

Horses with *stubborn* temperaments are difficult to train to be obedient. They are slow to learn obedience and require tact and patience by the trainer. When they get nervous or tired or are asked to perform quickly, they become sullen and refuse to work. Some of these horses reach a given stage of training and then seem to forget everything they learned. The trainer must start the training procedure all over at the beginning level.

A few horses have a *treacherous* temper and are very resentful. Treacherous horses can be divided into two types, based on underlying predominant motivation or emotion. Horses who behave treacherously because they have been severely or chronically abused are primarily motivated by extreme fear, and they usually will try to flee, escape, or otherwise avoid close proximity to a human if they see any way to do so—and sometimes even if they don't. If they cannot escape approach by a human, they bite, kick, or at least threaten such actions, or they bolt over the person. However, they give plenty of signs of what their intentions are. Such horses are usually labeled "hopeless" or "permanently messed up." They can be retrained if one understands equine psychology and training principles, is willing to commit indefinite patience to the project, and has good control over the horse's environment so that it is handled very consistently by all who come in contact with it. Most experienced horsepeople believe that training the treacherous horse is definitely not a project for a beginner, nor is it economical. Training this type of treacherous horse requires good fences, preferably a high-walled pen, and maybe even a restraining chute. But if the fear can be eliminated, the aggressive behavior is eliminated as well. Punishing these animals for aggressive behavior usually just convinces them even more that they have good reason to behave in such a manner, thereby making the behavior worse, not better. These types of treacherous horses need to be treated in a way that decreases their fear of humans and allows them to learn that people's behavior toward them is predictable and not harmful.

The second type of treacherous horse is the one that has learned to behave in this manner to get its way. This may be typified by the pony that has learned to intimidate a child (or the child's parents, if they are not experienced with horses), or a stallion who has learned to intimidate his handler. This type will suddenly bite or kick to avoid doing something (getting caught, being put back in a stall) or gain access to something (feed, open gate), but shows no extreme fear of people. Of the two types of treacherous horses, this one may be more truly treacherous, and perhaps more dangerous, as it is usually quite obvious that the first type is, indeed, dangerous, whereas it may not be immediately apparent that the second type is a threat. The second type should be punished immediately for behaving aggressively. All too often, the reason for the horse's behavior is that the handler is not experienced enough to immediately discipline the horse or to anticipate that the animal is about to misbehave. The handler may move away in fear or take a moment to regain composure. Then the handler begins repeatedly to strike the horse, jerk repeatedly on the lead shank, and/or scream in a fit of rage. By this time, already too much time has elapsed, and the horse fails to associate the punishment with the undesirable behavior, and excessive punishment could panic the horse. Then the horse gets even more treacherous. Usually only one strike or jerk on the lead shank, delivered as soon as the horse gives an indication of misbehaving, is the recommended punishment.

Agonistic Behavior

To be able to evaluate a horse's temperament accurately, we must understand normal and abnormal horse behavior. One of the best ways to judge a horse's "personality" is through its agonistic behavior, which relates to facial expressions, postures, vocalizations, and locomotor patterns that signify dominance, submission, or some intermediate status, or signify an escape pattern.

Agonistic behavior causes many problems for the horse owner because it is highly variable and can be very pronounced.

Dominance Hierarchies

Horses kept together form a dominance hierarchy, which is established by aggression. The introduction of two strange horses to each other usually results in a basic pattern. They approach each other with their heads held high, and they may "toss" their heads. The necks are arched, and the ears are pointed forward. They encounter each other face-to-face by smelling or exhaling at each other's nostrils. During the face-to-face encounter, they frequently squeal, rear up, and threaten to strike with their forelegs. They may continue to encounter by smelling each other's neck, withers, flank, genitals, and rump. The process may be interrupted by one horse laying its ears back, pivoting the hindquarter toward the other horse, and kicking out with one or both hindlegs. A squeal may or may not be emitted when the horse kicks. Sometimes, fighting between members of an established group and a newcomer can be avoided or at least minimized by first penning the newcomer adjacent to the group. This procedure, which requires fencing that is strong, safe, and of sufficient height, works best when the newcomer is obviously not going to be a strong contender for the top of the hierarchy.

Horses that are familiar to each other, but have been separated, greet each other by briefly smelling at the nostrils. Some very aggressive horses meet a strange horse by immediately laying their ears back, running at the other horse with their necks held low, heads extended, and mouths open, trying to bite. At the last moment, they may pivot their hindquarters and kick.

To establish dominance, a dominant animal threatens aggression or may fight the subdominant horse. It may be a traumatic experience, in which one or both horses are injured, or there may be little if any physical contact. Once the dominance hierarchy is established, only threats of aggression are necessary to maintain it, although fights occasionally occur. Threats of aggression are visual gestures that may be accompanied by sound. They are enforced by physical contact if necessary. The mildest threat is laying back the ears and looking at the subordinate horse. The most common threat is biting. The horse lays its ears back, exposes its teeth, opens its mouth, and nips in the direction of the other horse. About 30 percent of the bites are completed. Kicking threats are used less frequently than biting threats. In a mild threat, the horse may make a gesture to kick with one hindleg in a restrained manner. Serious kick threats are usually made by a squeal and a gesture to kick with both hindlegs.

Because submissive horses seldom challenge a dominant horse, the horses learn to get along together without very many injuries. From a management standpoint, the submissive horse must have adequate room for retreat and escape. When a new horse is introduced, the group should be observed until the dominance hierarchy is re-established. If serious fighting occurs, the new horse may have to be removed. Putting two boss mares together usually causes serious fighting.

Most dominance hierarchies are linear, but in some groups of horses they are more complex. If a complex hierarchy exists, one horse that is low in the order may be dominant over a horse that is at the top.

Young foals exhibit submissive behavior to older horses that allows the foals to move about in the herd. The foal extends its head, directs its ears sideways, and moves its lower jaw up and down. The foal also receives some protection from aggression by other horses when it is at its dam's side. Her position in the dominance hierarchy determines the amount of protection for the foal.

Social attachments occur between members of a group of horses. The social bonds may be at the family level or between horses that are not family members. A mare's reciprocal attachment with her foal begins about 2 hours after birth. The attachment continues to strengthen for a couple of weeks and then begins to weaken. By 6 months of age, the foal can be weaned with a minimum of stress if two or more foals are weaned together. Horses that are kept together for prolonged periods exhibit a preference to stay together. In a herd, some individuals form pair bonds. Some bonds are very strong and others very weak. When horses that have formed strong pair bonds are separated, they display considerable anxiety and call for each other by whinnying. This can cause problems when one is to be shown or ridden without the other present.

Epimeletic and Et-Epimeletic Behaviors

Epimeletic behavior is involved with giving care or attention. This is a very common type of behavior in horses because they seek care and attention from each other. Epimeletic behavior is displayed several ways.

During the fly season, horses stand head to tail and mutually fight flies for each other. They also practice mutual grooming, nibbling each other with the incisor teeth. The nibble areas include the neck, base of the neck, withers, back, and croup. Each horse seems to have a regular grooming partner. Mutual grooming is most frequent during the spring, when the winter coat is being shed, and during the summer, when horses stand under a shade. Licking another horse is usually limited to a mare licking the foal after parturition for about 30 minutes.

Mutual grooming behavior can be taken advantage of when handling horses. For example, it is wise to approach or try to touch a strange or untrained horse about the withers and other mutually groomed areas and then work toward other areas such as the head or legs.

Et-epimeletic behavior is the signaling for care and attention. It is used by all age groups and is most frequently observed when horses are separated from each other. A young foal becomes very nervous when separated from its dam and will nicker or whinny for her. Mares also call for their foals by whinnying, and they quietly nicker to a foal to indicate protection. Mature horses accustomed to being kept together become upset and call for each other when separated. If a strong pair bond has been formed, it may take 3 to 4 days for the horses to settle down after they are separated. During this time, they will repeatedly whinny for each other and be very nervous. At first, they may be excited enough to run over or through fences and other objects just to get together. Therefore, one must be careful about separating horses so that injuries and accidents do not occur.

Horses exhibit varying degrees of contactual behavior, although this type of behavior is not well developed. During inclement weather, they may huddle together. They will form a group when danger exists.

Other types of behavior, in addition to those resulting from interactions with other horses, may be useful in determining whether the horse is ill, eating properly, or normal. For example, horses become conditioned to being fed or exercised at a regular time. At feeding time or nearing a time when the horse is turned out for free exercise, the horse may start nickering. Some horses wait until they see their owner or handler. At other times, they may pay no attention to the person.

Investigative Behavior

A horse's first reaction to a strange object in its surroundings is to raise its head and investigate. If the object appears to be a threat, the neck remains raised (sometimes with a pronounced arch), ears directed forward, nostrils dilated, and tail slightly elevated. The horse may move about nervously with hesitant steps, while obviously prepared to run. It emits loud, explosive blows of air (snorts) through its nostrils. The horse may advance toward the object for further investigation or may decide to escape. Once it has decided that the object is not a threat, it resumes its prior activities but may continue to display a certain caution.

Other horses may respond to the cues given by the first horse to see the object. They usually react in a similar manner. If they are kept together in a large paddock or at pasture, they may move together to investigate it at a closer distance. If one horse decides to flee, the others usually follow.

Investigative behavior is the horse's inspection of its environment by use of the senses and movement. Horses are very curious about their environment and will use all the necessary senses to investigate it. When a horse is placed in new surroundings, it will investigate everything very thoroughly by use of its sight, smell, touch, hearing, and taste senses. Until the investigation is completed, the horse may be nervous and overreact to sudden noises or movements. When frightened, it may run into a fence or other object that it would usually avoid. If a new object is placed in its paddock, the horse normally cannot resist smelling, touching, tasting, and listening to the object. If not allowed to investigate, the horse will be apprehensive about it. Some horses must smell or touch new tack before it can be used on them without their becoming nervous. Investigative behavior can lead to accidents or other problems around a stable. While investigating a stall, a horse may learn to operate a latch and open the stall door. Horses can learn how to turn on water faucets and operate light switches because they play with objects during the investigation.

Most young foals go through a period during which they chew and taste anything that interests them. During this phase of investigative behavior, they may want to nibble on your hands or clothing. Normally they outgrow this phase without a lot of discipline, but such behavior can develop into a vice, so one must be careful to avoid the foal's nibbling or biting so that it does not become a bad habit.

Grooming Behavior

Horses maintain their hair coats by several methods. Besides mutual grooming, horses also groom themselves. They enjoy rolling in dry, fine soil such as sand and dust or in wet areas. Before rolling in a dry spot, they paw the area. After pawing, they lie down and roll on their backs. After they get up, they shake their whole body as if to dust themselves off. In fact, they do this after lying down for any reason.

Irritating insects cause horses to rapidly contract the superficial muscles on their trunks and forelegs. The muscle contraction causes rapid skin movements. They use their heads to displace insects on the foreleg, shoulder, and barrel areas. Insects on the belly are displaced with the hindleg, and the tail is used on the hindquarters. Itching is relieved by rubbing on a fixed object or by scratching itself. The head is used to scratch or bite the forelegs, sides, croup, and hindquarters. The hindfoot is used to scratch the head and neck.

Elimination and Ingestion

Eliminative behavior is associated with urination and defecation. All horses have the same characteristic stance while urinating. The neck is lowered and extended; the tail is raised; the hindlegs are spread apart and extended posteriorly. The flaccid penis is extended by the male. The mare contracts and relaxes the lips of the vulva, exposing the clitoris several times after each urination. The interval between urinations is usually 4 to 6 hours.

Most horses will urinate in a stall or trailer. However, some are reluctant to do so, and they should be allowed out of the trailer every 3 to 4 hours to urinate. If they are not taken out of the trailer, they start nervously moving around and may start kicking. They do not like to urinate on hard surfaces because the urine splatters on their legs. If they are kept in stalls or small paddocks, most horses will urinate in the same area because the area becomes soft and the urine does not splatter as much.

Defecation occurs about every 2 to 3 hours. To defecate, the horse raises its tail and may also hold the tail off to one side. Ponies almost always stop moving to defecate, whereas horses will defecate when they are moving about. Stallions prefer to defecate in a small area when kept in a stall or small paddock. They usually back up to the pile and then defecate. They avoid walking on the manure pile if they can. Mares and geldings tend to have no particular place to defecate and scatter the feces in the paddock. Therefore, it is harder to keep the bedding in their stalls clean.

In pastures, a stallion smells the area and walks on or backs up to it to urinate or defecate. Thus, a stallion wastes very little of the pasture areas. Because of the mares' and geldings' behavior, however, the defecation area may become larger. Horses refuse to eat grass growing in these areas, so the manure must be scattered over the pasture with a rake to prevent the formation of defecation and urination areas.

Horses usually defecate when they get nervous. Rope horses commonly defecate on entering a roping chute. Some horses defecate immediately upon entering a trailer or immediately after being unloaded.

Horses practice coprophagy—the eating of feces. Young foals will eat the feces of mares they are housed with. Adult horses will eat their own feces or the feces of other horses, a practice that does them no harm.

Ingestive behavior is the taking of food or water into the digestive tract. Foals may be stimulated to start eating solid food when they are only a few days' old. They start by nibbling on the feed and rapidly learn to eat it. If given the opportunity, horses prefer to eat small amounts of feed throughout the day. Horses kept at pasture are able to eat in this manner. Horses kept in stalls and small paddocks eat at the convenience of the owner or handler. Very few horses eat small amounts of their feed at one time so that it will last for a 24-hour period, unless the horse is fed ad libitum (freely; food is always available). If fed ad libitum, they usually overeat and may get digestive disturbances. Preventing overeating is an important aspect of horse management.

Horses graze by taking a bite of grass, taking one or two steps, and then taking another bite or two of grass. Therefore, they are moving about most of the time they are grazing, and they prefer to graze over a large area. If sufficient grass is available in the pasture, they eat the top part of the grass and leave the bottom portion. Typically, they graze down small areas in a paddock or small pasture and keep the grass at a minimum height. As the grass grows in these areas, it is succulent and high in quality. When the pasture has been overgrazed, the horse eats the grass down to the ground surface. Under these circumstances, horses will graze the defecation areas but are reluctant to do so unless the area has been harrowed routinely to prevent the accumulation of feces.

Some horses do not adjust to being kept in close confinement such as a stall for long periods of time. This may be because they have a strong desire to graze and move about, and short vigorous daily workouts may not accommodate their desire to walk around and graze for 8 to 12 hours each day.

Play

Horses enjoy playing. One of their favorite forms of play is running, either alone or in a group. When running alone, they frequently buck, slide to a stop in a corner, and jump and shy at familiar objects. When running in a group, they frequently push and nip other horses. They may chase each other. Two horses may be observed playfully nipping at and swinging their heads toward each other while rearing on their hindlegs and pawing at each other. This type of activity is also observed in young colts.

Horses also enjoy playing with objects they find in their paddock. They pick up small sticks and toss them about the paddock. They pick up and shake rags and pieces of paper. And they play with balls or other objects suspended in a stall to relieve boredom. They will play with a latch on a stall door or gate for long periods of time. They can even learn to open the latch.

The young foal plays during the first 3 weeks by running small circles around its dam. The circles get larger and the foal starts to play with other foals. They chase each other and frequently change roles of fleeing and chasing. Young foals will mount each other during play, which is normal play behavior that occurs long before either sex reaches puberty. Colts seem to mount more frequently than fillies. Play by young foals is "contagious" behavior that is very conducive to social facilitation. Peak periods of playtime are usually observed in the early morning or just before sunset. Absence of play at these peak playtimes may be the first indication that a foal is ill.

Mimicry

Allelomimetic behavior, or mimicry, is common among horses. They learn to copy the behaviors of other horses at a very young age. A young foal learns to chew on its tongue by watching its dam or another horse do so. A foal can become addicted to sucking air by observing a wind sucker. Wood chewing is rapidly learned from other horses. A horse that is difficult to catch because it runs away each time it is approached will be watched by other horses, who thus learn to run away. When one horse in a group decides to run and play, other horses usually join it. Therefore, it is important to separate horses with vices from other horses before the others learn to copy the undesired behavior.

Learning

The horse can be taught many different tasks. It usually excels at tasks that are athletic in nature, but it also has a good capacity for pattern discrimination learning. A horse first learns how to learn, and several factors influence this ability. The ability to learn how to learn is evident during pattern discrimination learning. It takes the horse numerous trials to learn to discriminate between the first two patterns. After it learns the correct response for a few patterns, fewer trials are needed to learn additional patterns. The horse can remember the correct response for several months. Once a horse has learned a specific type of athletic performance, it will remember it for years. After several years, the response may not be perfect, but the horse can then be retrained to reach a high level of performance much more quickly than it took for the initial training. More difficult maneuvers or tasks are forgotten at a faster rate than easier tasks.

A horse has the ability to learn temporal patterns very quickly. That is why they learn the wrong things so quickly when they are being trained. Thus, it is most important that reward/punishment is concurrent with targeted action. Also, training procedures or actions must be well planned and consistent. A trainer must avoid personal behavior patterns that may become cues to allow the horse to anticipate, establish, or follow particular actions that one does.

Early experiences affect the horse's ability to learn at a later time. Young foals can be taught to be led and handled. Early contact with humans under the proper environmental conditions results in a docile foal. Docility enhances later learning ability because the foal is not nervous about being handled. The docile horse pays attention to what it is being taught. But fear inhibits learning. Many people falsely believe that the only thing a horse really understands is fear and that the horse must fear them if they are to successfully and consistently control its behavior.

Sleeping and Waking

The way horses sleep and wake normally can help owners recognize abnormal behavior in illness. There are four recognizable stages in the sleep and waking cycle. Each has characteristic body and brain functions. The horse spends an average of 19 hours and 13 minutes awake. During this period, the horse is alert and active. It spends an average of 1 hour and 55 minutes in a drowsy state. Therefore, it is awake for an average of 21 hours and 8 minutes each day.

A horse sleeps for a total of about 2 hours and 52 minutes a day. There are two types of sleep: slow-wave and REM. Slow-wave sleep is characterized by slow, regular brain waves, as monitored by an electroencephalograph. The slow, regular brain waves indicate that the mind is not functioning, and slow-wave sleep has been called "sleep of the mind." During slow-wave sleep, the muscles are not fully relaxed. The horse may enter slow-wave sleep while lying down in the sternoabdominal position or while standing up. The horse can sleep standing up because it can lock its knees and hocks by using the stay apparatus, which is a series of tendons controlling leg flexion. The horse spends about 2 hours and 5 minutes per day in slow-wave sleep. This time is broken up into about 33 periods lasting 3.5 minutes each.

Between each period, the horse wakes up or enters a period of rapid eye movement (REM) sleep, characterized by irregular, rapid brain waves similar to the awake state. However, REM sleep is a deeper sleep than slow-wave sleep. The mind is very active, but there is almost a complete loss of muscle tone. During REM sleep, the horse usually is lying on its side with its neck and head extended and resting on the ground. During the time it drifts back into slow-wave sleep, it may go back to the sternoabdominal position, or it may continue to lie on its side. It is not known if the horse must be on its side to go into REM sleep. There are about 9 periods of REM sleep that last about 5 minutes each, so that the horse spends an average of 47 minutes in REM sleep.

Changes occur in body functions as the horse sleeps. As it enters the drowsy state, the heart rate, respiration rate, and muscle tone decrease. They continue to decrease as the horse enters slow-wave sleep. During REM sleep, there is a slight increase in respiration rate and heart rate, but the rates are less than during the drowsy state. Muscle tone continues to decrease and is minimal during REM sleep. The eyelids indicate the horse's state of alertness. They are partially closed during the drowsy state and are barely separated during slow-wave sleep. During REM sleep, they are fully closed.

The horse spends an average of 22 hours standing and 2 hours lying down each day. About 80 percent of the standing time is during the daylight hours. There are usually about 4 to 5 periods of recumbency each day.

The horse lies down by going through the same maneuvers each time. The hindlegs are brought under the body and the forelegs are directed back under the horse so that all four feet are close together. The head and neck are lowered. At this time, the horse may move around in a small area to decide exactly where it wants to lie down. The forelegs are flexed and the head is elevated as the horse touches the ground with its knees and sternum. Next, the hindquarters are lowered. Once down, the horse may lay on either side with its neck and head extended outward and resting on the ground. The legs are extended. The horse may rest in an asymmetrical sternoabdominal posture (right or left). When resting in this position, the legs are flexed and the limbs on the side the horse is lying on are underneath the horse. The horse rises from a lateral recumbency position to the sternal position by first extending its forelegs in front of itself. The forelegs are used to raise the forequarters off the ground. When the forequarters are raised, the flexed hindlegs are extended to raise the hindquarters.

Vices (Bad Habits)

Abnormal horse behavior can have a variety of causes. Some atypical behavior may indicate illness or injury. Other types are referred to as vices. Usually, a vice affects a horse's usefulness, dependability, or health. Vices such as charging, striking, kicking, biting, and bucking are aggressive vices directed against a handler and may cause injury to the handler. Some of the same vices may be directed against other horses and cause them injury. Flight responses such as rearing, balking, shying, halter pulling, and running away can injure the rider or handler. Stall vices may cause injury to the horse, may cause poor performance, or may waste energy. These vices include stall kicking, wood chewing, cribbing, weaving, stall walking, bolting food, pawing, tail rubbing, and eating bedding or dirt. Bad habits are difficult to eliminate and require a lot of thought and effort on the part of the owner or manager.

Abnormal behavior as a result of illness or injury is discussed in Chapter 9. Horses should be observed at least once or twice a day to determine if they are injured or sick.

Stall vices are sometimes called "nuisance vices." They usually arise out of boredom from lack of exercise or insufficient activity out of a stall. Horses that receive enough exercise seldom develop stable vices. Providing sufficient amounts of bulky food for the horse to nibble on all day gives the horse something to do, and horses prefer to eat frequently. Boredom can be eliminated by providing toys such as plastic jugs hung from the ceiling. A horse may toss or carry about short lengths of plastic hose or a small stick. Occasionally, a horse will carry a small rock around in its mouth to play with. Stable vices are contagious because horses mimic each other.

Other causes of vices are poor management, mishandling, or bad treatment at some previous time. Some people make a mistake of teaching a foal to do cute little things (such as nibbling tidbits from a hand) that cause the horse to lose respect for the horseperson when it grows up (such as biting).

The prospective horse should always be checked out for vices. Many vices can be detected by observing the horse in its stall or paddock, handling the horse, or riding it. When the horse is approached, it should not lay back its ears and threaten you with its mouth. By feeling all over the horse, you can detect any unusually sensitive areas. A tendency to kick can be detected when the horse lays back its ears and shifts its weight off the hindfoot nearest you.

Biting

Biting is a vice acquired as a result of incompetent handling. If a horse is consistently fed sugar cubes or other treats by hand, it learns to expect these treats when handled. It soon begins nuzzling the hands and nosing the pockets of the handler each time he or she is within reach. The nuzzling develops into a nip, because the horse is disappointed. Before long, the horse starts to bite very hard, which can cause injuries. To prevent development of this vice, all treats should be placed in the feed manger.

Rubbing a horse's nose while petting it also teaches it to bite. The horse should be petted on other areas of the body and only occasionally on the nose.

Once a vice is learned, it is difficult to eliminate. Some horses respond to being slapped quite hard on the side of the mouth or face. An effective way to retrain the confirmed biter is to use a war bridle (Chapter 6). Each time the horse attempts to bite, one or two quick jerks on the bridle punish the horse quite severely. This is continued until the horse associates the punishment with biting. If it persists, a wooden gag can be used. A block of hard wood, about

5 inches long (12.7 cm) and $1\frac{1}{2}$ inches square (9.68 cm^2), with a chain run through a hole drilled through the center long ways, is attached to the halter. The gag is adjusted so that it fits in the area of the bars. Each time the horse bites, the edges place pressure on the gums. It usually takes a few lessons to overcome most biting.

Bolting

Sometimes a horse bolts grain (gulps it down without chewing). This vice is undesirable because the whole grain passes through the digestive tract without being digested, leading to digestive disturbances such as colic. There are several methods to prevent bolting. The grain can be spread out in a large feeder with a flat bottom so the horse cannot get very much in its mouth with each bite. Large stones can be placed in the feed box so the horse must move the stones around to get to the grain, which slows down the rate of eating. The grain can be mixed with chopped hay to help induce chewing. Hay can be fed first, and grain can be fed after most of the hay ration has been consumed. The hay reduces the horse's appetite, so the horse is not inclined to eat as fast.

Attacking

Charging or savaging is a deliberate attack on a person. Not many horses are actually vicious, but they must be controlled. Stallions are prone to becoming unmanageable unless they are handled by a competent horseperson. The vicious horse must be taught to obey, or to suffer accordingly. However, it must become confident in the handler, so the training must not inflict pain. The most effective means is to humiliate the horse by either pulling it to its knees with a "running W" and holding it there until it becomes calm, or by laying it on the ground with a throwing harness and holding it down by restraining its head. This causes the horse no physical pain but does humiliate it. These procedures should be attempted only by competent personnel.

Cribbing

Cribbing is a vice in which a horse sets its upper incisor teeth against an object, arches its neck, pulls backward, and swallows large quantities of air. The vice leads to colic and other digestive disturbances caused by the excessive amount of air in the digestive tract. Most cribbers are hard to keep because of the digestive disturbances and the fact that they would rather crib than eat. Moreover, it wears off the front edges of the incisor teeth. Wind sucking is similar to cribbing, but here the horse does not set its incisor teeth on an edge of an object. These vices usually occur as a result of boredom or frustration.

There are several ways to prevent a horse from cribbing—punishment, medication, or surgery. However, once the vice is acquired, it is impossible to eliminate the habit if the opportunity to crib presents itself. Surgical procedures have been developed that stop some horses from cribbing. The most common preventive device is a neck strap that is placed rather tightly around the throat. When the neck is arched, the strap places pressure on the trachea, and the discomfort overrides the urge to crib. A spring-loaded strap that causes sharp, pointed nails to prick the horse when it arches its neck is more effective on those with a strong drive to crib. The straps cause the horse no discomfort when it is not trying to crib. There is some promising evidence that injecting the horse with a narcotic antagonist will stop cribbing for several months. Currently, medications are too expensive.

Fighting

Fighting is aggressive behavior by dominant individuals. Once the dominance hierarchy is established, there are seldom fights within the group. Sometimes two very dominant horses fight quite often because one is constantly challenging the other. In this situation, it is advisable to separate the horses before they injure each other.

Halter Pulling

Halter pulling can injure the horse's neck muscles—and the handler if the horse lunges forward after pulling back. After the horse pulls back one or two times and manages to break loose, it usually forms the habit. A confirmed halter puller breaks halters and lead ropes as it pulls back, and it can then escape. And, of course, a horse running loose around a stable can cause accidents. Three hitches are commonly used to overcome the habit. As soon as you discover that the horse is testing its halter when it is tied, tie a strong rope that the horse cannot break around the horse's throatlatch. Tie the rope with a bowline knot, so that it cannot slip and choke the horse. Run the rope through the ring in the halter and tie it to an immovable object. After the horse has been tied this way, it soon learns that it cannot break away and stops trying to do so. At this time, a lead rope can be used to tie the horse. However, if a horse has escaped several times and the habit is formed, more severe measures must be taken. A rope can be run around the horse's chest and placed just behind the withers. Secure the rope with a bow-line knot, and run the free end between the horse's forelegs and through the halter ring and tie it to an immovable structure. When the horse pulls back, it cannot tolerate the pressure being applied behind the withers. Some horsepeople prefer to place the rope around the horse's back in the area of the flanks. Form a small, stationary loop in one end and run the free end through it, between the front legs to the halter ring, and tie it so the horse cannot escape. As soon as the horse feels pressure around its body, it moves forward. After a few struggles and attempts to break away, it learns not to pull back. One must be careful that the equipment does not break, the structure the horse is tied to does not break, the horse does not jump or fall on the handler, and the horse does not hurt itself.

Kicking

The horse that habitually kicks at other horses or people is dangerous to own or to handle. The vice usually results from incompetent handling. As soon as a horse makes an attempt to kick, it must be corrected. If the horse is continually corrected in the formative stages, the vice can be eliminated. The confirmed kicker is difficult to correct, however. Handle such horses cautiously, so that you are never where the horse can kick you. A horse that kicks other horses should be tied up away from them and should be ridden at the back of a group of riders.

Many horses that kick acquired the vice because they were fed too much grain and were not exercised. At first they playfully kicked the wall. Later, the kicking became a habit. Stall kicking can cause serious injury to the hindlegs and hocks. Some horses kick the walls of their stable for no reason other than just to kick. Other horses kick the stable wall at feeding time to display their impatience. Some horses only kick at night; a light in their stall will stop the kicking. An uncongenial horse kept in an adjacent stall will provoke some horses to kick. Often, placing the horse in another stall solves the problem. However, it is difficult to correct a confirmed stall kicker. Padding the stall wall stops some horses, because the lack of resistance or noise when a pad is kicked removes the desire. A rubber ball or stick attached to the fetlock with an elastic band is an effective corrective device for some horses. When the horse kicks, the ball or stick sharply strikes the leg. Some horses simply cannot be corrected.

Pawing

Pawing the stall floor is more a nuisance than a serious vice. It wastes energy and digs holes into the floor that must be filled periodically.

Rearing

Rearing is one of the most dangerous vices a horse can have. When the horse rears up, the flailing forelegs can cause serious injuries to the handler, especially to the head. Such horses must be corrected with a lead shank or a whip by a knowledgeable trainer because of the seriousness of the vice. A horse that rears while being ridden should not be ridden by beginning or intermediate riders. An experienced trainer can usually find the cause and correct the vice.

Shying

Shying at unfamiliar objects makes a horse dangerous to ride for even the experienced rider. It is a long and difficult task to overcome the habit. The horse must continually be taken to new surroundings and over new trails until it learns that nothing will harm it.

Stall Walking

Stall walking is a nervous habit that wastes energy. Stallions often walk constantly or pace circles around the stall or paddock. Frequently, they start walking to work off excess energy and to calm their nervousness. Decreasing the energy content of the ration and giving regular exercise periods may eliminate the vice. Once horses start to stall walk, it is difficult to get them to stop. Placing a companion such as a goat, pony, or dog in the stall with them can be effective.

Striking

Striking with the forefeet is a dangerous vice, because the handler is always vulnerable to injury. While leading, grooming, and saddling such a horse, always remain alert and try to stay at the horse's side, not in front of it. Each time the horse attempts to strike, punish it with a war bridle or whip.

Tail Rubbing

Tail rubbing is usually started by horses whose tail areas are irritated by internal parasites, especially pinworms, or by a skin problem. Once the vice is acquired, the horse may continue to rub its tail even after the conditions that caused the initial irritation have been corrected. Tail rubbing is a common vice of Saddlebred horses that wear tail sets (device that trains the tail to stay in a certain position desired during performance events). To prevent the vice, a 2-inch × 12-inch board (5.1 × 30.5 cm) is used to construct a shelf that runs around the entire stall at a height just below the point of the horse's buttock. This tail board makes it impossible for the horse to rub its tail.

Horses' tails should be wrapped or protected with a leather tail guard when horses are shipped long distances in a van. If not, their tails will involuntarily be rubbed on the butt chain. One must be careful when wrapping a tail. If wrapped too tight, the blood circulation will be cut off and cause the hair to drop out or part of the tail to necrose.

Weaving

Weaving is a rhythmical shifting of the weight of the forehand from one forefoot to the other. This is a nervous habit that expends a tremendous amount of energy. It results from too much food and insufficient regular exercise. It is almost impossible to eliminate the habit once acquired. A stable companion or suspended play toy may be beneficial. Turning the horse out in a large pasture also helps. The vice is rapidly learned by other horses, so the weaver should be isolated from their view.

Wood Chewing

Wood chewing is one of the most common vices. All horse buildings, paddocks, and fences must be designed so the horse cannot chew them. It takes only a few hours for a horse to chew through a 2- × 12-inch board (5.1 × 30.5 cm). Some horses chew wood every chance they get; others chew wood only when the weather changes. The habit is dangerous to the horse because it can swallow splinters of wood. Also, it causes abnormal wear of the incisor teeth. The vice is expensive for the stable owner because of the need to continually replace badly chewed boards. Chemicals can be applied to wood to discourage the horse from chewing it or an electric fence wire can be used.

Other Vices

Many other vices can make it unpleasant to work with a particular horse. Some horses do not like to be groomed and will not stand still. Others do not like to be saddled and will jump around when the saddle is placed on their backs. A horse may inhale and hold the air while it is being cinched. After the horse is led around or ridden for a few minutes, the cinch can be tightened. Bucking is a serious vice that will get worse unless the horse is corrected by an experienced rider. Horses that are difficult to catch are a nuisance. All these vices detract from a horse's value and usefulness. If possible, one should avoid buying a horse that has one or several of them.

COLOR

The color of a horse is not normally a consideration in selecting most horses. However, it may be important if the horse is to be used for certain purposes. If a breed registry has certain qualifications for registration that are based on the color or color pattern, the color pattern is very important. The registration associations of Appaloosas, Paints, Pintos, Buckskins, and Palominos are based almost solely on color. Other breed associations, such as the American Quarter Horse Association, may disqualify for registration horses that have certain types of color patterns (see Chapter 3 on breeds and breed associations). Breeders must be knowledgeable about the inheritance of these color patterns, or they may produce individuals that cannot be registered. The color or color pattern of a horse may make it more or less desirable for certain types of performance classes where a horse's or rider's ability is judged, because some colors or color patterns seem to attract a judge's attention.

Finally, the color and color pattern of a horse serves as a basis for identification because it is one of the animal's most conspicuous traits (see Chapter 17 for information on the genetic inheritance of color and pattern).

Head Marks

The head markings of a horse usually consist of white hairs in specific areas. The most common head markings are illustrated in Figure 1-16. We lack knowledge concerning the inheritance of head markings. It is not clear

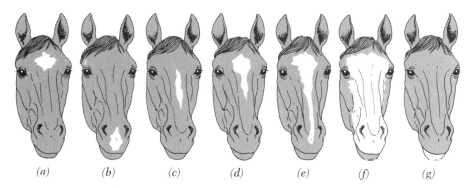

FIGURE 1-16   Head marks: *(a)* irregular star; *(b)* snip; *(c)* narrow stripe; *(d)* star and connected narrow stripe; *(e)* star and connected snip; *(f)* bald face; *(g)* chin spot. (Courtesy of Jockey Club.)

whether they are caused by dominant or recessive genes, although the chin spot is believed to be caused by two recessive genes.

Leg Marks

Common leg marks are shown in Figure 1-17. Very little is known about their inheritance. The distal spot is a small spot of dark hair that is located just above the coronary band in a white area. The marks are carried by a dominant gene.

Body Color

There are several basic body-coat color patterns and several variations. The inheritance of some coat color patterns is known, whereas knowledge of the

FIGURE 1-17   Leg marks: *(a)* coronet; *(b)* half pastern; *(c)* pastern; *(d)* pastern and part of ankle; *(e)* ankle; *(f)* white to above ankle; *(g)* half stocking; *(h)* three-quarters stocking; *(i)* full stocking; *(j)* heel; *(k)* outside of heel. (Courtesy Jockey Club.)

inheritance of others is only theoretical. It is difficult to predict the coat color of foals because the mode of inheritance is complex.

The black horse is a uniform black color on the body, mane, and tail. The uniform black color pattern is referred to as "jet black" if the coat color does not fade when the horse is kept out in the sun for several days. The black coat color of other horses fades in the sun to a "blackish bay" color pattern.

The bay color pattern is characterized by a black mane and tail, black points (black hair below knees and hocks, black muzzle, and black tips on the ears), and a reddish body. The color of the body may vary from a light to a dark reddish color. The dark reddish bay color is called a "blood bay." The basic color of the bay horse is black, but the black color is restricted to the mane, tail, and peripheral parts of the body. Some bay horses have zebra markings—a dark stripe down the back and extending down each shoulder and transverse bars on the forearm.

The seal-brown color is another modification of the black coat color. It is recognized by the brown hairs located in the flank areas, on the muzzle, under the eyes, and on the tips of the ears. A dark seal-brown horse may be difficult to distinguish from a black horse that fades in the sun. Those that have a lighter colored body area are easier to recognize and are normally called "brown" horses.

The chestnut or sorrel horse is another basic color pattern. The skin color is black or brown, and the hairs are red. The lighter colored horses are called "sorrel" horses, whereas the darker pattern is the "chestnut." The very dark red chestnut horse is called a "liver chestnut."

White horses are born and remain white throughout their lives. They have pure white hair, pink skin, and blue eyes. The white horse has a dominant gene for the white pattern. Two other white coat color patterns are modifications of the chestnut and black coat color patterns. The cremello pattern, a modification of the basic chestnut, is an off-white or cream-colored body and blue eyes. Some cremellos have a lighter mane and tail. The outlines of face and leg markings are evident. Perlino horses are modifications of the black coat color pattern. Their bodies are an off-white or pearl-white color. The mane and tail are a light rust color.

Grulla horses have black manes, tails, and peripheral parts like bay horses except the body is a dilution of the black hairs on the body to a sooty black.

The dun and buckskin color patterns are further modifications of the bay. The dun color is a modification of the dark bay, whereas the buckskin is a modification of the light bay color. Both color patterns are characterized by the black mane, tail, and legs. They may or may not have the dark stripe down the back, on the shoulders, and across the forearm. The buckskin color pattern has a light yellow body. The body color of the dun is darker than the buckskin and may be described as a dingy yellow. The mane and tail may not be as black in some dun horses.

The palomino color pattern is characterized by a yellow body color and a lighter mane and tail which may be almost white or flaxen.

The coat color of gray horses is characterized by white hairs mingled with hairs of the basic color. As the horse gets older, more white hairs appear in the coat. The foal may be born a solid color, or it may have a few white hairs in the coat. The skin is one of the two basic colors. Colored hairs are continuously being replaced with white hairs, so that older gray horses are almost white. When black horses with the gray gene have a higher proportion of black hairs than white hairs, the horse is referred to as an "iron" or "steel-gray" horse. Red grays are modifications of the bay pattern, and chestnut grays are modifications of the sorrel and chestnut colors.

The roan pattern is a mixture of white and colored hairs. The roan color is present at birth and does not change when the horse gets older. A blue roan is a mixture of white and black hairs. The roan pattern superimposed on the basic bay pattern is called a "red roan." Strawberry roans are sorrel or chestnut horses with white hair mixed in with the colored hairs. Unless one knows the pedigree or history of a gray or roan horse, one cannot tell them apart.

Paint and pinto horses have four color patterns. The main distinguishing character of these patterns is the white spotting. In the tobiano pattern, the white spotting crosses over the top of the horse's back and extends downward. The white extends from the belly and legs toward the back in the overo pattern. Horses with black pigmented skin and coat color are referred to as "piebald," whereas brown pigmented horses are called "skewbalds." There are piebald tobianos, piebald overos, skewbald tobianos, and skewbald overos.

Appaloosa horses have a variety of spotting patterns, but they must meet three minimum requirements if they are not spotted: mottling of the skin, striped hooves, and an unpigmented sclera (surface of the eyeball, except for the cornea). The mottled or particolored skin appears particularly on the nostrils, muzzle, and genitalia. The striped hooves have alternate vertical stripes of white (unpigmented) and dark (pigmented; black or brown) colors. White around the cornea of the eye is a white sclera.

There are many coat color patterns, and all have at least one of the three characteristics previously described. All of the spotting patterns are of two basic patterns. The leopard color pattern is a white coat with dark spots scattered over the horse's body. The other basic pattern is the blanket pattern in which a white blanket, usually containing dark spots, crosses over the horse's croup, loin, and/or back. There is considerable variation in the distribution of white hair and of spots from the classical basic pattern. In the mottled pattern, unpigmented hairs are grouped together into small, uneven areas of white that are not always continuous with one another. Pigmented spots may be found in the white areas. The pattern is usually located over the dorsal area. Speckled patterns are characterized by small clusters or specks distributed rather evenly throughout the pigmented area involved. Some horses have dark spots distributed over a colored coat pattern that contains no white areas. The Appaloosa may also have a white blanket that contains no spots.

The genetics of coat color inheritance is complex, and our knowledge is largely based on theory. The present concepts of coat color inheritance are discussed in Chapter 17 on genetics.

SEX

The sex of a horse influences its value and behavior and thus its desirability for certain potential uses. Some horsepeople prefer a mare because of her potential as a brood mare if she has good conformation and becomes well trained. Others do not use mares because of their behavior when they are in estrus. Before deciding to buy a mare to show in performance classes, it is advisable to determine her behavior during estrus. Some mares do not show the characteristic signs of estrous behavior unless they are actively teased by a stallion. Very seldom do their estrous cycles influence the performance of such mares. Other mares display estrous behavior when they are exposed to any strange horse. Their behavior does not allow them to be shown when they are in estrus. Some mares develop an erratic and sour disposition during estrus and are not attentive to the rider. If the mare will never be bred, she can be spayed (ovaries removed) to eliminate the mare's estrous cycle. The surgical procedure is simple, and the mare can be worked 10 to 12 days after surgery. Estrous behavior can also be controlled with the use of the oral progestin, Regumate®.

Only accomplished horsepeople should select stallions to be ridden or worked unless they are to be used for breeding. Their behavior usually causes problems and makes them difficult to handle unless the handler is competent.

Because of their aggressive sexual behavior, stallions must be kept separate from other horses. Their paddocks and stalls must be well made because most stallions will kick or run into them periodically to see if they can escape. It is difficult to haul them with other horses. If they are isolated in a trailer or van so they cannot see other horses, mentholatum can be rubbed in their noses to prevent them from smelling other horses and becoming aggressive. Some stallions are well behaved and have good manners because they have been competently trained and handled. However, if they are not continually corrected, they soon become difficult to handle. They should never be trusted, because even the most docile ones occasionally exhibit erratic behavior for a few moments. During these few moments, injuries can occur. Very few stallions consistently give a good performance when shown or worked.

Geldings—castrated male horses—are the most popular horses to ride and use because of their attitude. Their behavior is predictable and usually stays the same. They can be kept together or with other horses. Some geldings will mount and copulate with estrous mares, but most do not display any sexual behavior. Horses are gelded or castrated between birth and 2 years of age, but older stallions can be castrated. Colts that have poor conformation and/or a poor pedigree are gelded as soon as their testicles descend into the scrotum. The testicles may be descended at birth and, if not, usually descend by 10 months of age. Well-conformed colts may be given a performance test and are castrated if they do not perform or train as expected. Older stallions that do not produce quality foals should be castrated. Cryptorchids (only one or neither testicle descended into the scrotum) should be heavily discriminated against in breeding. They are referred to as "ridgelings" after they are 18 months of age. Ridgelings display intense sexual behavior and retain their stallion attitude for several months after castration. They are difficult to castrate, because a flank incision must be made.

PEDIGREE

One of the decisions the potential buyer must make is whether to buy a registered or an unregistered (grade) horse. Many grade horses are excellent horses and are suitable for many purposes. A large percentage of pleasure riding horses are unregistered, as are many horses used by riding stables and by ranches. Some horse shows or specific classes in a horse show do not require a horse to be registered. Some high-quality grade horses that have excellent performance records command a high price.

Breed associations have been formed to issue registration certificates and to maintain records of lineage and performance. Registration procedures continually change so that one must contact each breed association for correct forms and procedures. The stud books published by the breed associations give name, registered number, sire, and dam for all horses registered each year. Buying a registered horse has several advantages. The horse may have a performance record with a breed association, which is important in evaluating the horse for future performances or for possible value (prepotency) as a breeding animal. The horse's ancestors can also be evaluated in terms of their performance ability or ability to produce quality foals. For example, the following records can be obtained for horses registered with the American Quarter Horse Association: pedigree, racing activity, arena performance, dam's produce, and get of sire. Equine Line 2000, a part of Jockey Club Information Services, keeps racing records on Thoroughbred horses. For a fee, it will provide a five-cross pedigree by tracing the horse's ancestors in the *American Stud Book,* which is the record of foals registered by the Jockey Club. It uses other records to provide race records, produce records, crop analysis of sire, and domestic family histories. Their record service can provide a breeder's statistical report for all the racehorses that are racing and are bred by an individual, a monthly brood mare statistical report for all the foals of a mare that are racing, and a weekly stallion statistical report for all the horses a stallion has sired that are racing. Specialized reports can be obtained from the database.

Racing data for Quarter Horses and Thoroughbreds are published in the *American Racing Manual* and the *Chart Book.* The *American Racing Manual* is published yearly and contains the records of horses, owners, trainers, jockeys, breeders, stallions, yearling sales, stake race purse distribution, and many other statistical analyses. The *Chart Book* is published monthly and contains the official charts of all races run at recognized North American tracks during the month of issue. The charts can also be obtained on a weekly basis. The quality of a horse can be determined from these records, and a horse's pedigree can be a valuable aid for selecting young horses before they have had a chance to prove their performance ability.

Other breed associations keep similar data that is available to members or to the public for a fee.

IDENTIFICATION

When buying a horse, make sure that the animal being purchased is the same one described on the registration papers, or if it is not registered, make sure the horse is actually owned by the seller. There are numerous ways of identifying horses. A description of the color pattern(s) is found on the registration papers, but that offers little to identify solid colored horses. Photos of unique markings and patterns in a horse's hair, whirls, or cowlicks are effective in identification. Breed associations may require photographs to be submitted with registration applications. All race horses that have run in a race will have a number tattooed on the upper lip, and many horses have brands that are legally registered in the name of the owner with a breed association or the government.

The hot iron brand for horses has largely been replaced with the freeze brand, which is painless, does not scar or damage the skin, and produces a clear legible mark. By varying the application time, the hair will become white or absent since the intensely cold branding iron alters or destroys the pigment-producing follicle and/or the hair shaft follicle. The time that the iron is applied to the skin varies depending on the metal in the iron and the color of the horse. The correct time is determined by trial and error.

The procedure for freeze branding is as follows. The irons are chilled in liquid nitrogen until only very small bubbles rise. Hair is clipped from the brand site. The skin is soaked with alcohol to remove the skin oils and to aid in the transfer of cold temperature through the skin. While holding the horse still and immediately after soaking the skin with alcohol, the branding iron is applied to the brand site. The iron must be gently rocked back and forth and from side to side to ensure even contact. Sufficient pressure must be applied to indent the skin. Timing is critical, and the correct time must be determined for each set of irons (Table 1-3). The person applying the iron should indicate when the iron touches the skin and the person timing the procedure should indicate when to remove the iron. For a set of irons, the time for a "white hair" brand is about 8 to 12 seconds; for a hairless brand, about 15 to 20 seconds. After the iron is removed, a clear indented pattern should be evident. After 5 to 10 minutes, the brand pattern thaws and swells and will remain swollen for about 4 days. The superficial layer of skin sheds after 1 month and white hairs

TABLE 1-3 Freeze-Branding Times

	Nasco stainless steel branding irons	Nasco copper/brass branding irons
Dark-colored horses		
<8 months of age	8 seconds	7 seconds
>8 months of age	8 seconds	10 seconds
Light-colored horses		
<8 months of age	12 seconds	15 seconds
>8 months of age	12 seconds	15 seconds

appear after 2 months. A white hair brand is complete after 3 months. Arabian horses are freeze-branded under their mane with a code sequence consisting of date of birth, sex, and identification number.

Horses can be identified by microchip implants, which are tiny transponders encapsulated in biocompatible glass and placed in the horse's upper neck. Although this method is not visible, each implant has a unique code that can be read with a scanner. Implanting is simple, relatively painless, and does not change the horse's external appearance.

CHAPTER 2

Evaluating Conformation and Soundness

CONFORMATION

The light horse is used primarily for athletic purposes, whereas the draft horse is used for pulling power. The conformation, or physical structure, of a horse is related to the performance potential in that the relationships of the parts determine the way in which a horse moves. Different conformation types are suited to different types of performance. Variations of desired conformation are personal preferences in many respects, but there is a basic conformation that is desired for the light horse. Conformation determines the ease, freedom, and direction of leg movement. Limb interference can result from faults in the animal's basic conformation. Faults in conformation predispose a horse to certain unsoundnesses, discussed later in this chapter. Potential buyers can save much time by avoiding horses whose potentials are limited by faults in conformation.

To understand the basic conformation of a horse, one should be familiar with the nomenclature of the parts of the body and the bones supporting it (Figures 2-1 and 2-2). One should develop a logical procedure for examining conformation, to be followed for each horse that is evaluated.

The overall balance and symmetry of the horse should be evaluated from a distance (Figure 2-3). The measurements of Secretariat, winner of racing's Triple Crown in 1973, illustrate the unusual proportions in relation to his head, neck, shoulder, stifle, and waist; heart girth to the legs; and length to height. For the

FIGURE 2-1   General conformation and points of the horse: (1) forelock; (2) forehead;
(3) face; (4) bridge of nose; (5) nostril; (6) muzzle; (7) upper lip; (8) lower lip; (9) under
lip; (10) check, jaw, or jowl; (11) chin groove; (12) throatlatch; (13) jugular groove;
(14) neck; (15) poll; (16) crest; (17) withers; (18) back; (19) loin; (20) point of hip;
(21) croup; (22) buttock; (23) dock; (24) thigh; (25) flank; (26) stifle; (27) barrel;
(28) shoulder; (29) point of shoulder; (30) chest; (31) arm; (32) elbow; (33) girth;
(34) abdomen; (35) gaskin; (36) hock; (37) chestnut; (38) forearm; (39) knee;
(40) hoof; (41) cannon; (42) ergot; (43) pastern; (44) fetlock; (45) coronet.

standard horse, the length of the head is about the same as the length of the neck,
shoulder, waist, and front of stifle to point of the hock; the heart girth is about
the same length as the legs; and the height is about the same length as the horse's
length from shoulder to end of the croup. Some horses look as if they were made
up of parts from several different-sized horses; as a result, they are out of balance.
From a distance, observe the horse walking and trotting both toward and away
from you. This gives you the opportunity to observe faults in the horse's way of
going. Then observe the horse up close for a detailed examination.

Head

Generally, the horse's head is considered for its esthetic value. The exact shape
of the ideal head varies depending on the breed, but you should evaluate

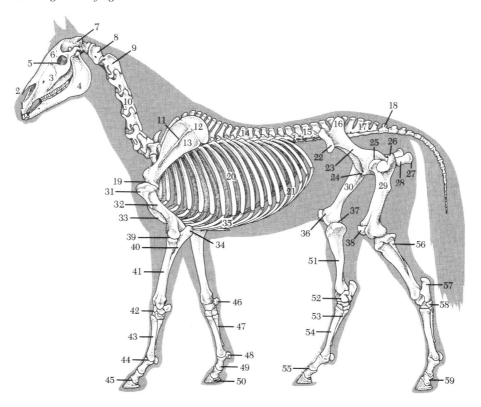

FIGURE 2-2   Skeletal system of the horse: (1) incisive bone (premaxillary); (2) nasal bone; (3) maxillary bone; (4) mandible; (5) orbit; (6) frontal bone; (7) temporal fossa; (8) atlas (first cervical vertebra); (9) axis (second cervical vertebra); (10) cervical vertebrae (there are seven of these, including the atlas and axis); (11) scapular spine; (12) scapular cartilage; (13) scapula; (14) thoracic vertebrae (there are usually eighteen of these); (15) lumbar vertebrae (there are usually six of these); (16) tuber sacrale; (17) sacral vetebrae (sacrum) (there are usually five vertebrae fused together); (18) coccygeal vertebrae; (19) shoulder joint; (20) ribs (forming wall of thorax: there are usually eighteen ribs); (21) costal arch (line of last rib and costal cartilages); (22) tuber coxae; (23) ilium; (24) pubis; (25) hip joint; (26) femur, greater trochanter; (27) tuber ischia; (28) ischium; (29) femur, third trochanter; (30) femur; (31) humeral tuberosity, lateral; (32) humerus; (33) sternum; (34) olecranon; (35) costal cartilages; (36) femoral trochlea; (37) stifle joint; (38) patella; (39) elbow joint; (40) ulna; (41) radius; (42) carpus; (43) metacarpus; (44) fetlock joint; (45) coffin joint; (46) accessory carpal bone (pisiform); (47) small metacarpal bone (splint bone); (48) Proximal sesamoid bone; (49) first phalanx; (50) distal phalanx (third phalanx); (51) tibia; (52) talus (tibias tarsal bone) (astragalus); (53) small metatarsal bone (splint bone); (54) metatarsus; (55) pastern joint; (56) fibula; (57) calcaneus (fibular tarsal bone); (58) tarsus; (59) middle phalanx (second phalanx).

(a)

(b)

FIGURE 2-3 *(a)* Secretariat's conformation versus *(b)* standard conformation. (Reprinted with permission from the February 1977 issue of *Horseman*. Copyright © 1977. All rights reserved.)

certain functional aspects. The head shape influences the visual field, balance, and respiratory function.

The ears should be clean-cut and alert, should curve around, and come to a fine point. Well-formed ears may indicate good breeding in grade horses. Ears spaced too far apart, droopy, or placed too close together are displeasing. Large ears are distracting and make the head look out of proportion. Alert ears mean the horse is attentive to its surroundings. Ear movement can indicate the horse's temperament. Horses with sour dispositions tend to pin their ears back. They usually do this before they bite, kick, or buck.

The head should be generally triangular from front and side views (Figure 2-4). From the side, the jaws should be deep, and the head should taper down to a reasonable-size muzzle. If the muzzle is too large, the horse's field of vision immediately in front will be limited. The head should not be too long or too short. Adequate length between the eyes and nostrils is important, because inspired air is heated or cooled before entering the lungs by the turbinates in the head, which are soft, bony structures well supplied with blood. Excessive head length tends to shift the horse's center of gravity forward. The heavy head is held out on the end of the neck, which acts as a long lever. Horses with excessively long heads also have a larger blind spot on the ground in front of them, due to interference with the visual field.

There should be adequate width between the jaws—three to four fingers—to provide adequate space for the trachea, which crosses the area.

FIGURE 2-4   Profiles of horses' heads: *(a)* good head, straight profile, Thoroughbred type; *(b)* good head, Arab type, prominent forehead but with dished profile below eyes, deep through jowl, small muzzle, eye typically low-set; *(c)* plain head, prominent forehead but no dish, and with "receding forehead"; *(d)* common head—Roman-nosed, same type as *(c)* but with arched nasal bone; *(e)* pony type of head—dished face (between eyes as well as the whole profile); *(f)* "camel" head, also called "elk-nosed"; *(g)* head as triangular as *(b)* but lacking the disk below the eyes; *(h)* "jug head," almost the same width from jowl to muzzle, high-set eye; *(i)* "platterjaw." (From Edwards, 1973).

The face shape from a side view varies from breed to breed. Arabian horses have the dish-shaped face that improves frontal vision. The convex shape, commonly called the Roman nose, impairs frontal vision. A straight profile is preferred for most breeds.

The head should be wide between the eyes and should taper down to the muzzle, giving a triangular impression. The eyes should be large, clear, and set out on the sides of the head. When the eyes are wide apart and set out on two corners of the triangle, the horse has the widest field of view. The "pig-eyed" horse has small eyes that are set too far back into the head. This impairs vision because the horse is "looking out of a tube" and finds it difficult to see behind. Impaired vision makes the horse nervous when something approaches it from behind because it cannot see what is approaching as well as can a horse with large, prominent eyes. Horses with slanted or "almond-shaped" eyes cannot see above and below their eyes as well as can horses with large, round eyes.

The horse should have large nostrils, and when the horse is working, the nostrils should flare out so that they do not restrict air flow into the respiratory system.

It is important to examine the horse's teeth. The upper and lower incisors, as well as the lips, should meet evenly. If the upper jaw is too long, giving the appearance of a parrot beak, the horse has an overshot jaw. The opposite condition, in which the upper jaw is too short, is an undershot jaw. Horses with these conformation faults have difficulty eating and require more careful management. The faults are inherited, so such horses should not be chosen as breeding stock.

Excessive wear on the front teeth may indicate that the horse has a vice. Horses that crib wear off the front edges of their incisor teeth. Playing with a chain used to lock a gate also wears off the incisors excessively.

Examine the head for melanomas, warts, and "ear tooth" that will be irritated by the bridle or halter. Melanomas are tumors of the pigment-forming cells in the skin of gray horses. They may be located across the forehead and behind the jaw on the throatlatch area. An "ear tooth," or dentigerous cyst, is a congenital defect involving the abnormal retention of a dental development structure that forms dental material. It may interfere with the bridle and/or may be a cause of drainage at the base of the ear.

The throatlatch area should not be too thick, and the angle should be wide and open (Figure 2-4). The trachea passes through the throatlatch area, and if the angle is too sharp it will be compressed when the head is flexed at the poll. Horses with a jaw that is too large ("platter jaw") have the same difficulty when flexing. Because of the discomfort, these horses do not make good performance horses, which must flex for a proper headset. Periodically, they throw their heads upward or stick their noses outward to relieve the discomfort. The classic Arabian horse has a slightly longer cervical vertebrae that typifies the open throatlatch and it can flex at the poll without discomfort.

Horses being selected for strenuous athletic performances should have their pharynx and larynx evaluated via endoscopy. Proper function of the epiglottis and muscles during swallowing and inspiration and expiration should be determined. Conditions such as displaced epiglottis and paralysis or slow movement of the muscles of the larynx should be avoided since they interfere with breathing. Unilateral or bilateral partial paralysis of the muscles will not allow the larynx to open fully to permit maximum air flow (Figure 2-5). Also, partial paralysis of the muscle(s) will further decrease airway space due to the vacuum effect of inspiration pulling them inward.

Neck

The neck should be moderately long and smooth (Figure 2-6). Proper length and weight contribute to the horse's balance and style. Flat, long, smooth muscles increase the ease and freedom of movement of the forelegs. The neck should grade smoothly into the shoulder and chest, but a definite line of demarcation should be evident. The swan-type neck is usually not discriminated against. The swan-type is a long, smooth neck that forms an S-shaped curve. This allows the horse to flex at the poll. The neck muscles are longer than usual and contribute to a smooth gait with a long stride because rotation of the shoulder is improved. Because of the flexation, the head is carried closer to the body, and the center of gravity or balance point is shifted posteriorly. This

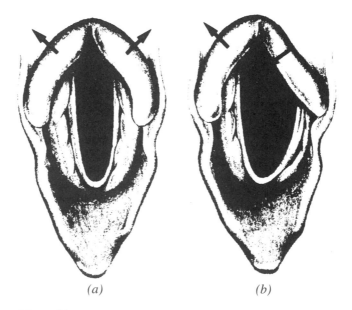

(a)   *(b)*

FIGURE 2-5   Normal larynx *(a)* and the effect of paralyzed or weak larynx muscles *(b)* on airway space. The paralyzed or weak muscle yields to the vacuum created during inspiration by moving inward, reducing the airway space and increasing air resistance.

FIGURE 2-6 Various types of necks and their attitudes when the horse is collected: *(a)* arched neck; *(b)* swan neck; *(c)* ewe neck; *(d)* "close-coupled" and upside-down neck. (From Edwards, 1973.)

lightens the forehand of the horse and reduces concussion and trauma to the forelegs. In contrast, a short and very thin neck that is placed high on the chest causes the horse to have shorter strides. Lack of muscle length inhibits the movement of the forelegs and makes the horse rough to ride. Most jumping horses have long necks, which enable them to raise their forelegs up high when they are folded.

The "upside-down" neck is characterized by excess fat deposits and heavy muscling on the underside of the neck. Horses with this type of conformation encounter two problems. Flexing at the poll causes discomfort, or the horse may not be able to flex sufficiently at the poll for the desired headset. The center of gravity is shifted forward so that the horse is predisposed to common unsoundness of the foreleg, such as ring bone, side bone, and navicular disease.

A cresty neck is the opposite of the upside-down neck. Excess fat deposits, located on the crest of the neck, can cause the crest to break or fall over to one side of the neck. The excessive weight on the forehand leads to the same problems as with the upside-down neck. Neither type of horse is well suited for performances that require fine control with reins, such as that required of the reined cow horse.

The "ewe-necked" horse has a sagging top line and bottom line neck profile. It has difficulty flexing at the poll. When such horses are stopped with a bit, they throw their heads upward. Therefore, they are unsuitable for performance classes, western pleasure, and reining.

Chest

Observed from the front, the chest should not be too wide or too narrow (Figure 2-7). Either extreme is a fault. If the chest is too wide between the forelegs, the horse will have a rolling or waddling type of gait and will usually paddle with its feet. A too-narrow chest causes leg interference when the horse travels, because the horse tends to crisscross its front legs. One cause of a narrow chest in front is that the shoulders may be set too far forward on the body. The American Quarter Horse usually has a definite V-shape between its forelegs because of its heavy muscles, but this V should not be too wide. The Thoroughbred does not have as much muscle, so it does not have as definite a V-shape.

Withers

The spiny processes of the thoracic vertebrae, located at the base of the neck and between the scapulas, form the horse's withers, which serve as a base of attachment for the muscles supporting the neck. They should be high enough to prevent a saddle from slipping to the side of the horse. Adequate height of the withers allows the horse to dorsiflex very easily since the withers act as a fulcrum over which the dorsal ligament works. If the withers are too high, the

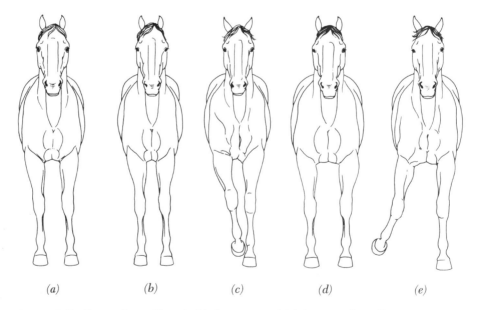

(a)   (b)   (c)   (d)   (e)

FIGURE 2-7   Front view of horse: *(a)* the proper width between legs allows correct straight forward movement of the legs; *(b)* the horse is too narrow, which may cause limb interference, as in *(c)*; *(d)* the horse is too wide in front; *(e)* some wide-fronted horses may paddle. (From Edwards, 1973.)

horse can easily be injured by a saddle. Withers that are too low are called "mutton withers" and predispose a horse to being clumsy and to forge. They restrict the rotational movement of the shoulder. There is usually a rolling motion to the way such horses move, so that the rider is shifted diagonally back and forth across the saddle. The saddle also tends to be displaced forward and can injure the horse. Mutton withers frequently accompany heavy front ends, shifting the center of gravity forward. This reduces the horse's athletic potential and usually shortens the length of stride. The withers should not be lower than the croup. This fault also shifts the center of gravity forward and makes it difficult for the horse to pick up its forehand and make maneuvers such as roll backs.

Shoulders

The ideal shoulder on a horse is long and sloping. Shoulder length is measured from the shoulder point to the top of the scapula. The ideal shoulder slope is 45°, but this is seldom seen (Figure 2-8). A 50° to 52° slope is considered quite good. The angle is measured at the intersection of (1) a horizontal line at the level of the shoulder point and (2) a line bisecting the scapula or shoulder blade. To judge the shoulder slope, look at the scapula, not at the shoulder point and the top of the withers. Some horses' shoulders are placed too far forward on their bodies, which gives the impression of long, sloping shoulders

FIGURE 2-8   Articular angles for a horse.

when in fact the shoulder is short and has a steep angle. The junction of shoulder and arm is one of the main concussion-absorbing mechanisms in the horse's foreleg. If the angle is too steep, the wear and tear on the leg increase as a result of the increased trauma. Horses with steep shoulders are predisposed to common unsoundnesses caused by poor concussion absorption. The horse is usually rough to ride because the concussion travels all the way up the horse's leg.

Shoulder length increases the stride length. A long shoulder means the muscles are working on a longer lever, giving more power and strength to the swing of the foreleg. Longer strides enhance the horse's running ability because a horse's forelegs strike the ground a fewer number of times in each mile. Therefore, horses with short shoulders are more prone to lameness over a period of years. In addition to absorbing concussion inefficiently, short, steep shoulders make a horse look out of proportion. They are usually accompanied by short, steep pasterns, so that the foreleg looks too straight vertically. The rotational movement of shoulders that have too steep an angle is retarded, so that the foreleg moves with less freedom and ease. Thus, on horses of the same size, the shoulder angle is more critical than the shoulder length to increase the length of the stride.

A long scapula is desirable because it increases the area for attachment of the muscles that tie the foreleg to the spine. These muscles form a sling-type arrangement suspending the horse's body between the horse's forelegs without a bony attachment (Figure 2-9). The suspension aids in absorbing concussion. Shoulder muscles should be flat and smooth, not thick and bulky.

Forelegs

Arms

The humerus, also called the arm, should be evaluated for slope and length. A long and steep angle for an arm results in a long stride and good forward movement. This conformation allows the horse to raise its knees well above its elbows and to easily fold the front legs when jumping. If the arm is horizontal and long, it will still have a long stride but the feet will travel close to the ground. Because a horse with this conformation can't raise its knees above the elbows and cannot fold the front legs adequately, it usually does not make a good jumper. In addition, the center of gravity is shifted forward and the horse stands with its front legs too far back under the body. Both conditions cause excess weight and strain on the front legs.

A short arm coupled with a steep slope causes a short stride but with high motion. However, a horse with this conformation can't get its knees above the elbows. Thus, it has a short, choppy gait. A moderate slope restricts the forward reach of the foreleg. If an arm is horizontal, the horse has no forward reach and keeps its feet close to the ground. Also, it can't fold its legs when going over jumps.

FIGURE 2-9   Muscular system of the horse: (1) facial nerve; (2) masseter muscle; (3) parotid salivary gland; (4) jugular vein; (5) splenius muscle; (6) sternocephalic muscle; (7) serratus ventralis muscle; (8) trapezius muscle; (9) brachiocephalic muscle; (10) deltoid muscle; (11) triceps muscle; (12) radial carpal extensor muscle (extensor carpi radialis muscle); (13) common digital extensor muscle; (14) ulnaris lateralis muscle; (15) lateral digital extensor muscle; (16) latissimus dorsi muscle; (17) serratus ventralis muscle; (18) pectoral muscle; (19) radial carpal flexor muscle (flexor carpi radialis muscle); (20) ulnar carpal flexor muscle (flexor carpi ulnaris muscle); (21) cephalic vein; (22) digital flexor tendons; (23) external abdominal oblique muscle; (24) gluteal muscles; (25) tensor fasciae latac muscle; (26) saphenous vein; (27) gastrocnemius muscle; (28) long digital flexor muscle; (29) digital flexor tendons; (30) semitendinosus muscle; (31) biceps femoris muscle; (32) long digital extensor muscle; (33) lateral digital extensor muscle; (34) Achilles' tendon (also called the "hamstring"), consisting of tendons of gastrocnemius, biceps femoris, and superficial digital flexor muscles attaching to calcancus.

The arms should operate in planes that parallel the body plane. If the elbow is set too close to the body—"tied in at the elbow"—the whole foreleg is rotated outward so that the horse stands toe-wide or "splay-footed" or "toe-out." The proper space between elbow and body is about the thickness of a human hand. If the elbow is pointed outward too much, the foreleg is rotated in, and the horse stands toe-narrow or "pigeon-toed" or "toe-in." The toe-narrow conformation fault is serious and is discussed more fully later.

The forearm should be long, with long, lean muscles that tie in close to the knee. This type of conformation allows long strides, particularly when the horse has a relatively short cannon bone. Long muscles work on a longer lever, which makes it easier to lift the foreleg and thus contributes to ease and freedom of movement.

Knees

A wide, flat, smooth, clean-cut knee is desirable. A large knee increases the supporting surface so there is less stress per unit of area. The knee should be centered on the radius, and the cannon bone should be centered on the knee. A common conformation fault of the knee is the "offset" or "bench" knee. The cannon bones are placed to the lateral side of the knee (Figure 2-10), causing an increased stress on the medial side of the knee, particularly on the medial splint bone. When "bench-kneed" horses are subjected to hard work, such as training, before the splint bone fuses to the cannon, the horse will tend to get splints. They result from irritation of the interosseous ligament attaching the splint bone to the cannon. After the splint bone fuses to the cannon, the splint bone cannot move, so no irritation occurs.

The "open-knee" fault in conformation (Figure 2-10) occurs when the knee joint bones are not large enough relative to the cannon and radius bones. A depression about the size of an index finger crosses the middle of the front surface of the knee. A horse is not criticized for having open knees until after it is 3 years of age, when the knee bones stop growing. Because the bones are small relative to the horse's size, they are subject to injury during exercise. Injuries result from greater than normal concussion per unit of cross sectional

(a)   (b)   (c)   (d)

FIGURE 2-10   Common conformation faults of the knee: *(a)* "bench" or "offset" knee; *(b)* tied in at knee; *(c)* chopped at knee; *(d)* open knee.

area. Excess concussion can stimulate excess bone growth, leading to unsoundness.

Cannon Bones

The cannon bone should be short, compared to the forearm, so that the knees and hocks are closer to the ground than in horses with long cannons. A relatively short cannon increases the horse's stability and length of stride. The cannon area should look refined and have thin skin. The outline of the cannon bone, tendons, ligaments, and blood vessels should be prominent. Although the cannon bone is round, it should appear flat from the side view because the superficial and deep flexor tendons are located posterior to the cannon. If the cannon bone is too small for the horse, it will look set too far under the knee when viewed from the side (Figure 2-10). This conformation fault is described as "chopped" at the knee. "Tied" or "constricted" at the knee describes tendons that are too small for the horse (Figure 2-10). Immediately below the posterior aspect of the knee, the cannon area is too small and is constricted. This fault predisposes a horse to problems such as bowed tendons when it is stressed during exercise.

Pasterns

Moderately long, sloping pasterns are desirable (Figure 2–11). If the pasterns are too long, the fetlock descends too much, which places excess strain on the deep flexor tendon, sesamoids, and suspensory ligament, and predisposes the horse to bowed tendons. Well-conformed horses are usually easy riding because the excess movement of the pasterns absorbs the concussion, whereas the horse with upright pasterns is rough riding because the concussion is inadequately absorbed. Upright pasterns predispose the horse to the common pathological problems resulting from the excess concussion—ring

FIGURE 2-11   Slope and length of the pasterns: *(a)* proper slope and length; *(b)* excessive slope; *(c)* not enough slope; *(d)* broken angle caused by excessive length of the toe; *(e)* broken angle caused by long heels; *(f)* broken angle caused by weak pastern.

bone, side bone, and navicular unsoundnesses. The pastern angle should be the same as the shoulder angle. Upright shoulders usually are accompanied by upright pasterns. If a horse has an upright shoulder but weak pasterns with too much slope, it is subject to tendon strain.

Length and slope of the pasterns affect the foot flight arc (Figure 2–12). The ideal arc is smooth, like a quarter of a circle. Pasterns with too much slope along with a long toe do not allow a smooth arc. As the foot breaks over the toe, it suddenly goes very high in the air and then coasts back to the ground. This type of forward movement stresses the tendons. With upright pasterns, the toes are usually shorter and the heels longer. The foot breaks over the toe very easily, with a gliding motion, comes to a peak, and then abruptly comes down, striking the ground with excessive concussion. Pathological problems often develop as a result of the increased concussion.

Feet

Observe the size and shape of the horse's feet carefully. Unsound feet usually mean the horse has no value except possibly for breeding purposes. Feet should be large but in proportion to the body. The feet are one of the main

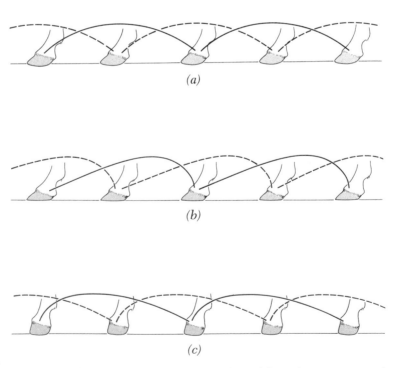

FIGURE 2-12   Foot flight arcs: *(a)* correct arc: balanced feet; *(b)* incorrect arc: long toes, flat heels; *(c)* incorrect arc: short toes, high heels.

concussion-absorbing mechanisms, and if they are too small, they suffer increased wear and tear. Very few horses have feet that are too large, but one of the traits that has been selected by breeders is small feet. Today, too many horses have small feet and develop foot unsoundness. The slope of the pasterns and the front of the hoof wall should be continuous (Figure 2-11). Improper foot care, leading to long toes, long heels, or short heels, causes the hoof wall angle to deviate from the pastern angle. These deviations stress tendons and suspensory ligaments. The hoof wall should be thick, free of defects, and open at the heel. The frog should be well developed and in light contact with the ground. Shallow heels indicate undeveloped digital cushions, and navicular disease may develop. The foot is discussed in detail in Chapter 8.

Front View

Viewed from the front, the forelegs should be straight (Figure 2-13). If two lines were drawn from the shoulder point to the ground, they should be parallel, bisect the forelegs, and strike the ground at 90° angles. Any deviations of the legs from these lines are conformation faults. The common faults are base-wide, base-narrow, toe-narrow, toe-wide, knock-knees and bowlegs, and rotation faults. Viewed from the side, a line should bisect the foreleg, touch the bulb of the heel, and strike the ground at a 90° angle. A deviation of the foreleg from this line is a conformation fault. Commonly observed faults are buck-knees, calf-knees, and camped out or under.

Base-Wide   The base-wide fault occurs when the distance between the center of the hooves is greater than the distance between shoulder points. Horses that have narrow breasts tend to be base-wide. The base-wide condition causes excess trauma to the medial side (inside) of the horse's leg, predisposing it to medial ring bone, medial side bone, medial splints, and navicular disease. When the horse travels, the foot breaks over the medial side of the toe, wings inward, travels back outward, and strikes the ground on the medial part of the hoof wall. If the horse is barefooted, the medial side of the hoof wall is worn down at a faster rate than the lateral side (outside) because the foot breaks over and lands on the medial side. Some horses are exceptions and may paddle when they travel.

If the horse is toe-wide and base-wide, the faults in way of going are exaggerated. Such horses have a greater tendency to wing inward and to interfere with the opposite foreleg. Often the horse just brushes the medial aspect of the opposite coronary band; this defect is recognizable by the hair being worn off in that area. In exaggerated cases, the opposite cannon bone may be struck during each step.

Base-Narrow   The base-narrow fault in conformation is characterized by the distance between the centers of the hooves being less than the distance between the shoulder points. When the horse travels, the foot may break over the center of the toe or over the lateral side of the toe. If the foot breaks over

FIGURE 2-13   Conformation defects in the front and rear legs and viewed from the front, rear, and side. (From *4-H Horse Judging Guide*, Cooperative Extension, Pennsylvania State University, University Park, Pennsylvania.)

the center of the toe, it almost always lands on the lateral side of the hoof wall first. The excess concussion on the lateral side of the foot and leg leads to concussion-related unsoundnesses on that side. If the horse is not shod, the lateral hoof wall wears off at a faster rate than the medial side.

Toe-Narrow   Frequently, the horse is toe-narrow (toe-in or pigeon-toed) as well as base-narrow. The foot breaks over the lateral side of the toe and lands on the lateral side of the hoof wall, predisposing the horse to unsoundness on the lateral side of the foot and leg. Such horses usually paddle when they travel. If the horse is toe-wide and base-narrow, the foot still breaks over the lateral side of the toe and lands on the lateral side of the hoof wall. This fault in conformation places the greatest strain on the fetlock and is considered the worst type of foreleg conformation. Because the foot breaks over the lateral side of the toe and lands on the lateral side of the hoof wall, the foot almost always wings inward; and because the forelegs are close together, there is almost always leg interference.

The toe-narrow fault shifts the center of gravity forward. The rider feels top-heavy, particularly when turning or working in circles. The horse does not respond to the bit as quickly as it should. If the condition is extreme, the horse shifts its weight from side to side in a rolling motion.

Toe-Wide   The toe-wide (toe-out or splay-foot) fault causes the foot to break over the medial side of the toe, wing inward, swing back outward, and land on the medial side of the hoof wall. The excess wear and trauma occurring on the medial side of the foot and leg predispose the horse to the unsoundnesses resulting from excess concussion. The toe-wide fault does not affect a horse's balance or its base of support. Such horses normally can perform quite well if there is no leg interference.

Knock-Knees and Bowlegs   Knock-knee and bowleg faults should be discriminated against because of the excess strain placed on the knee and lack of mobility of the leg.

Leg Rotation   Some horses have a straight leg down to the knee and then a rotation of the leg toward the inside or outside. Other horses have straight forelegs to the fetlock and then pasterns set so that they are rotated inward or outward. Both faults result in a horse that stands toe-wide or toe-narrow.

Buck-Knees   The buck-knee fault exists when the knees are in front of the line that bisects the foreleg. Other terms used to describe the condition are "goat knees," "over the knee," and "knee-sprung." A slight buck-knee is not too serious and seldom causes problems. Buck-kneed horses are clumsy and have a tendency to stumble, particularly if the toe is too long. The fault places an excess strain on the flexor tendons and on the sesamoid bone. Therefore, such horses tend to have bowed tendons and sesamoiditis. If the condition is severe, the horses' knees may shake and tremble when they stand.

Calf-Knees   One of the worst faults in foreleg conformation is the calf-knee. Here, the knee is behind the line that should bisect the leg and is in a compromised position when the foot strikes the ground. This causes excess strain on the knee, which breaks easily, particularly when muscles are tired and the knee goes farther backward. Such horses tend to chip their knee bones on the front edges as their knees move backward when their feet strike the ground.

Camped Out or Under   The "camped out in front" fault occurs when the forelegs are not placed squarely under the horse. They are placed on an angle so that the feet are too far forward. This condition is usually observed in horses that are foundered or have navicular disease. If it is their normal stance, they are usually poor athletes because they are unable to move their forequarters very easily.

The opposite condition is "camped under in front." When the legs are directed backward under the horse, it carries too much weight on the forehand. Such horses have shorter strides and a tendency to stumble because of a low foot flight arc.

Side View

After viewing the front legs, view the horse from the side to evaluate the body. The body should be properly balanced. The back and loin should be short and well muscled. The chest should be deep and full. Long, well-sprung ribs are desirable.

Back and Loin Muscles

Muscling in the horse's back and loin is important to support the weight of a rider (Figure 2-14). The loin has no support other than the vertebral column. Lack of muscling usually leads to a swayback or sagging back. Excessive length in the back and loin contributes to the swayback condition and affects the horse's gait. Long-backed horses have a rolling motion in their hindquarters and have a tendency to cross-fire—the hindfoot strikes the opposite foreleg. This is a problem in racing pacers. The roach-backed horse (with a convex back) is discriminated against because the back lacks flexibility. These horses have a short stride. They tend to overreach and to forge because the distance between the forelegs and hindlegs is shortened.

Chest and Ribs

The chest contains the lungs and heart. A deep, full chest provides adequate room for these vital organs. Horses that lack depth through the chest usually do not have endurance capacity. Well-sprung ribs protect the vital organs and serve as a point of attachment for muscles of the foreleg. Horses with flat ribs are referred to as "slab-sided" and lack chest capacity (Figure 2-15). This fault usually makes horses hard to keep. They require more feed to maintain body condition. Flat ribs are often associated with legs that are placed too far under the horse's body, so such horses are heavy on the forehand. The ribs

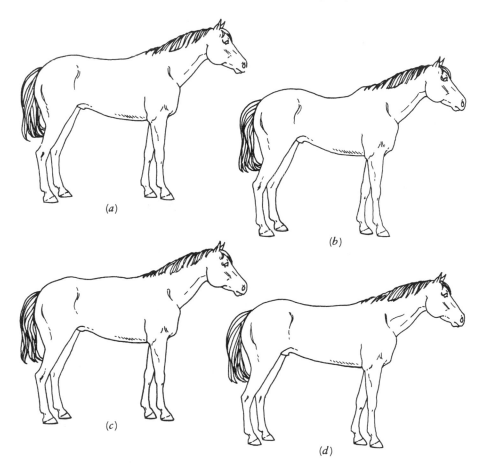

FIGURE 2-14   Side view of horse's back to evaluate conformation: *(a)* good top line; *(b)* sway back; *(c)* roach back; *(d)* long.

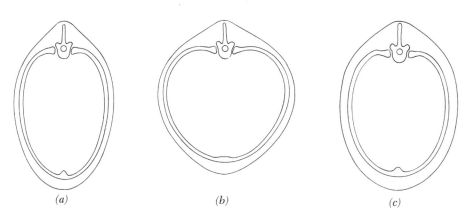

FIGURE 2-15   Cross-section of the thorax: *(a)* "slab-side"; *(b)* "round" cylinder; *(c)* ideal shape: large heart and lung capacity inside. (From Green, 1969.)

can be so arched that the horse becomes "barrel chested." It is difficult to keep a saddle on such a horse, and pressure from the saddle is not distributed over a sufficient surface area of the chest. The result can be sore spots on the back and sides. Look under the chest to determine if the horse has a prominent sternum, which may be irritated by the girth of a saddle.

Coupling

The junction of the loin with the hindquarters is the coupling. It should be heavily muscled and wide to provide a strong support for the loin. The coupling should be deep so that the horse is not cut up (lacks depth) in the flank. Depth in this area contributes to a large capacity for the digestive tract and gives the horse a long underline. Lack of depth in the flank should not be considered a fault with horses in excellent physical shape: Racehorses and endurance horses lack depth in the flank when they are well trained and fit. Horses lacking depth in the flank are sometimes described as "wasp-waisted" or "hound-gutted."

Hindquarters

The hindquarters are the propulsion mechanism of the horse. The croup should be long, fairly flat, muscular, broad, and have the tail set well on it (Figure 2-16). A long distance from the hip point to the hock, coupled with a desirable type of croup, allows speed and athletic ability.

The croup angle affects the movement of the hindlegs. A flat croup causes a long, flowing stride, and the foot stays close to the ground. A steep croup causes the hindleg to be driven into the ground. The steep croup is desirable for horses that need a quick start and will run for a short distance. Therefore, Arabian breeders want a fairly flat croup on their horses, whereas the calf roper wants a steep croup. If the croup is too flat, the hindlegs are carried too far behind the horse and limit its athletic potential. Racing Thoroughbred horses should be intermediate. Greater pelvic depth means a greater mechanical advantage for abdominal muscles which attach to the pubis, independent of slope, for flexion of the sacro-lumbar joint. The length of the croup, which is equivalent to the length of the pelvis, affects the length of the stride. Short croups are associated with short strides, and long croups with long strides. Placement of the acetabulum should be no farther back than 70 percent of the total pelvic length. If placed farther back, abdominal muscles must work hard to flex the sacro-lumbar joint and rotate the ischia forward. The sacro-lumbar joint should be placed as far forward as possible. Ideally, it should be on a line with the point of the hip. This conformation causes the horse to be short-backed and to have the greatest arc of rotation for the ischium.

The degree of muscling in the hindquarters depends on the breed of horse and its purpose (Figure 2-17). Horses that need power need larger muscles, and horses that work at speed need long, slim muscles. The width at the stifle

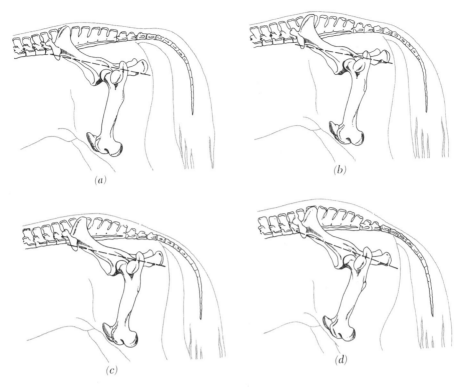

FIGURE 2-16   Relationship between slope of pelvis and the sacrum of Arabians.
(a) The so-called level croup desired in the Arabian horse. However, only the sacrum is
level (and even it has some slope) and the pelvis itself has just as much slant as the
"sloped" and "steep" (for an Arabian) croups shown in *(b)* and *(c)*. In *(b)*, the actual
position of the sacrum is the same as in *(a)*, but the crest of the ilium is higher and
somewhat farther back. This also has the effect of making the back appear longer. When
exaggerated in height, the crest of the ilium is very prominent and is termed the "jumping hump," because it is commonly seen in hard-conditioned jumpers and hunters. In
(c), the sacrum itself is straight; it slopes upward in *(a)* and *(b)*, while the topline thereof,
which of course makes the outline of the croup, slants down. This creates a "steep
croup," although the pelvis itself has the identical slope of *(a)* and *(b)*. Therefore, this
kind of slope would have no effect on speed or power compared to the other two, regardless of "raciness" a somewhat sloped croup may imply. Because of the angle of the
sacrum, the tail is set on much lower, further exaggerating the impression of sloped
croup. On the other hand, *(d)* shows the goose rump, common to draft horses. Here, the
pelvis itself is very slanted, and the sacrum follows suit, also slanting downward, with
tail very low set on. (From Edwards, 1973.)

should be greater than the width at the hip point when viewed from behind.
Lack of muscling makes the hip points wider, and such a horse is said to be
"rafter-hipped." Lack of croup muscling is described as "goose-rumped," and
such a horse lacks power and endurance. Thigh muscles need to be powerful.
Stifle muscles should be long, extending well down toward the hock. The
gaskin should be heavily muscled to the inside and outside of the leg, and the

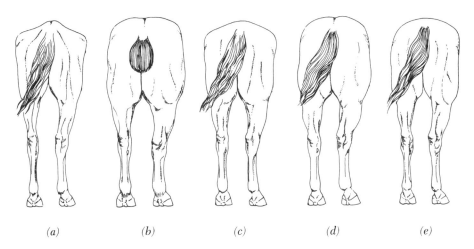

(a)   (b)   (c)   (d)   (e)

FIGURE 2-17   Muscling of the hindquarters: *(a)* peaked appearance of hips on emaciated horse, also showing wasted condition of thigh muscles; *(b)* the broad "double" hindquarters of a draft horse; *(c)* "rafter-hipped," "flat-hipped," or "ragged-hipped"—too flat across the top and with hip bones extending beyond the thigh muscles; *(d)* the "pear shape" desired in a Quarter Horse, with thigh muscles bulging well beyond the point of hip; *(e)* normal hindquarters, the croup well rounded from this rear view of the hips and is not to be confused with a "round croup" (apple rump) as viewed from the side. (From Edwards, 1973.)

muscles should be long. The gaskin muscling largely controls the course of the leg in forward movement, provided that the bone structure is well aligned. Excess muscling on one side or another causes the leg to move toward the side with the excess muscle.

The length and set of the femur, tibia, and cannon bones affect the horse's way of going and its speed. The femur is set to be inclined forward, downward, and slightly outward. It must be turned outward slightly to allow the stifle joint a full range of movement without interference from the abdomen. The tibia should be long for maximum development of speed. Tibia length increases the area for attachment of muscles that provide driving power for the hindquarters. A short tibia decreases the length of the stride.

Hocks

A good hock joint is wide and deep, well defined, and strong. The skin is fine textured and loose fitting, but the prominence and depressions are well marked. The angle or set of the hock is important. The angle when viewed from the side should be about 175° (Figure 2-8). If the angle is too large, the leg is said to "lack set." A straight hock increases trauma to the hock bones. Such a horse is predisposed to bog spavins, thoroughpins, and upward fixation of the patella. Too small an angle at the hock results in the sickle-hock type of conformation. This places an excess strain on the plantar ligament, which attaches just below the hock in the posterior surface of the cannon bone. The excess strain causes inflammation and enlargement of the plantar ligament at the point of attachment; this is referred to as a "curb." The sickle-hock conformation reduces stride length, and such horses tend to forge and overreach. Horses that must perform a lot of sliding stops are not discriminated against for a slight sickle hock, because the horse can get its hocks up under itself and can work. However, proper conformation is desirable since such horses are often unsound.

The hind cannon bones should be short, and they are larger than the front cannon bones.

Hindleg Faults

The set of the hindlegs should be viewed from the side and from behind (Figure 2-13). A line drawn from the point of the buttocks should touch the back of the hock, parallel the cannon, and strike the ground perpendicularly about 3 to 4 inches (76 to 102 mm) behind the heel. Several conformation faults can be observed from this view. The cannons of the sickle-hocked horse do not parallel the line but are directed forward at an angle to the line. Horses may be camped out or in behind. When the horse is camped out, the hindleg is posterior to the line; when camped under, the leg is anterior. The camped-out-behind fault prevents the horse from getting its legs under itself to move. Such horses cannot collect themselves. They tend to jab their legs into the ground and are unable to lift their bodies sufficiently to be good hunters and jumpers. If the horse is camped under behind, the distance between the fore- and hindlegs is decreased, and limb interference may occur. The fault may be associated with sickle hocks or a roached back.

From behind, lines dropped from the point of the buttocks to the hocks should bisect the hocks, cannons, and heels. Faults include base-wide, base-narrow, cow hocks, and bowlegs. Very seldom does a horse have the base-wide conformation behind. The base-narrow fault is common and increases the opportunity for hindleg interference. Excess muscling on the outside of the leg usually causes the horse to be base-narrow, which results in excess strain placed on the outer side of the leg.

The cow-hocked horse stands with hocks inside the two parallel lines, the hock points rotated inward, and base-wide and toe-wide feet. Cow hocks place an excess strain on the inside of a horse's leg, predisposing it to bone spavin. Power and movement in the hindquarters are lost, because the limbs move upward and outward, not straight ahead. Whenever a movement requires a straightforward thrust of the hindleg, the cow-hocked horse is limited. To a rider, the horse feels weak behind. The horse resents binding its joints and consequently develops bad habits such as rhythmic irregularity in gait, a high head carriage, and head tossing.

The horse is bowlegged behind when the hocks are wider than the two parallel lines. The points of the hock turn outward. As the horse moves, the hocks tend to rotate. The horse seems stiff in the hindquarters because it lacks flexibility. Any straightforward impulsion is impaired. It has weak hindquarters and fatigues quite easily.

One type of hindleg conformation that is not discriminated against and is preferable for many types of horses that are well-trained athletes is a hock turned inward so that the hindfeet are slightly toe-wide. The cannons are parallel and straight. This allows the horse to work off its hocks and to be collected, permitting maximum extension of the hindleg for long strides. The horse usually develops a good sliding stop.

BLEMISHES AND UNSOUNDNESSES

Before the horse is purchased, it should be evaluated for soundness. If possible, a veterinarian should make the examination. The veterinarian may have to use specialized equipment such as X-ray and ultrasound machines and computerized 3-D motion analysis to detect or verify some unsoundnesses that are not visually apparent. The word *unsoundness* is a general term that can mean anything from a slight injury to a defect that renders the horse useless. A horse may be sound for one purpose but unsound for another; for example, a crippled horse may be sound for breeding purposes but not for riding. Horsepeople refer to various defects as *blemishes* or *unsoundnesses*. A blemish is an injury or imperfection that affects the horse's value but not its serviceability. Injuries such as rope burns and insignificant wire cuts are normally classified as blemishes. An unsoundness is an injury or abnormality that affects serviceability. Most unsoundnesses drastically reduce the horse's value. In many instances, it is difficult to definitely classify a defect as a blemish or as an unsoundness. If the horse is sound for certain uses, a defect is a blemish. For another use, the horse may be unsound and of little value. At the time of an injury, the horse may be unsound but once the wound is healed, it is a blemish.

It is important for a horseperson to be able to recognize common blemishes and unsoundnesses, know their causes, and understand how they affect a horse's serviceability. When selecting breeding animals, it is extremely important to determine whether an unsoundness was caused by poor management, such as accidental injuries, nutrition, or strenuous training, or whether it was caused by faulty conformation. If it was caused by faulty conformation, do not use the horse for breeding.

Head

There are several unsoundnesses of the horse's head. Most are quite serious.

Blindness

Check for blindness in one or both eyes. The first indication that a horse may be blind is the way it walks. Blind horses hesitate before taking a step, and their ears move around more than normally. To verify blindness, move your hand close to the eye. If the horse can see, it will make a reflex movement.

Periodic Ophthalmia

Commonly called "moon blindness," periodic ophthalmia is characterized by a cloudy or inflamed condition of the eye. The eye goes through a series of recoveries followed by relapses. Each series becomes worse, eventually ending in blindness. At one time, the disease was believed to be the result of riboflavin (one of the B vitamins) deficiency. However, there are several other causes of moon blindness, such as leptospirosis, the parasite *Filaria equina* within the eye, reaction to systemic parasitism, or antigens developed as a result of repeated streptococcal infections. Moon blindness should not be confused with night blindness.

Night Blindness

Night blindness is faulty vision during the twilight hours and is caused by a vitamin A deficiency. Night blindness can be difficult to detect. It is usually evident if the horse is forced to move about during twilight hours in strange surroundings. It stumbles over unfamiliar objects or may bump into things as it moves around.

Poll Evil

Poll evil is an inflamed condition resulting from a bruise in the poll region, specifically the supra-atlantal bursa. The swelling usually contains pus. A veterinarian should treat it, because healing is very slow and difficult. It may break out again after it appears to be cured. The bruise is caused by someone hitting the horse between the ears with a whip or club, or by the horse accidentally bumping its head in a barn or trailer. It may also be caused by the horse hitting its head on the ceiling of a stall when the horse rears up. In some cases, it is caused by a bacterial infection by *Brucella abortus* and/or *Actinomyces bovis*.

Overshot and Undershot Jaw

As noted earlier, the overshot jaw, commonly called "parrot mouth," occurs when the lower jaw is shorter than the upper jaw (Figure 2-18). The opposite condition is undershot jaw. With either unsoundness, the horse has difficulty eating and requires extra care. Both conditions may be inherited, and

FIGURE 2-18   Side view of how teeth meet for *(a)* undershot jaws and *(b)* overshot jaws.

the overshot jaw is believed to be carried on a dominant gene. Breeding horses that are quite different in size can also result in the unsoundness.

Wobbler

"Wobbler" describes various conditions that affect a horse's coordination by their effect on the spinal cord. A so-called true wobbler is caused by spinal-cord compression in the neck, resulting from inflammation and/or bony abnormalities. The symptoms may appear at any time from birth to 3 or 4 years of age. In the early stages, it is difficult to recognize. It begins with incoordination of both hindlimbs. There is a gradual change in that the incoordination becomes worse. The signs of incoordination are dragging the toes of the hindfeet, and errors in the rate, range, force, and direction of movement. The symptoms may increase in severity until the horse falls down if it tries to make a sudden change in the direction of movement. It is a serious unsoundness because true wobblers do not improve. They are not safe for riding purposes because of their incoordination. The condition may be genetic, so it is doubtful that they should be used for breeding purposes. The syndrome can be corrected surgically in some horses.

Equine degenerative myeloencephalopathy (EDM) is a disease resulting in nervous system degeneration and is one cause of a "wobbling" syndrome. The onset of EDM has been correlated to a vitamin E deficiency during young horses' rapid stages of growth (see Chapter 5 for details).

Shoulders

Today you see very few horses with unsound shoulders. However, two conditions are worth mentioning.

Fistulous Withers

Fistulous withers are inflamed by bruising or by a bacterial invasion of the supraspinous bursa, caused by the same bacteria that can cause poll evil. In the past, the condition was caused by pressure from a horse collar, but today it frequently occurs as a result of a badly fitting saddle, usually a saddle with a low and wide gullet that is used on a horse with high withers.

Sweeny

Opinions vary regarding the true definition of a "sweeny," but the term actually applies to any group of atrophied muscles, regardless of location. Most people confine its usage to the shoulder muscles. Muscle, atrophy or degeneration results either from disuse or from loss of nerve supply. In "shoulder sweeny," the nerve crossing the spine of the shoulder blade has been damaged. It is usually easy to see, but in the early stages after the injury it may be difficult to see if no lameness is present. However, the horse's performance capability is limited when it needs the atrophied group of muscles. There is no known treatment, but nerve regeneration may occur, which usually takes a long time—at least 6 months. For cosmetic value, some unscrupulous horse traders inject irritants into the area to fill it with scar tissue so they can hide the unsoundness.

LEG UNSOUNDNESSES

The most common forms of unsoundness are leg unsoundnesses. Because most horses are kept for riding, leg unsoundnesses can cause considerable disappointment for the rider.

Forelegs

Bucked Shins

Bucked shins are a temporary unsoundness that occurs primarily in racing 2-year-olds and some 3-year-olds and in other horses that are trained hard (Figure 2 19). It occurs infrequently in older horses. Shins are usually bucked during the first few weeks of training when the horse is overworked. It is a very painful inflammation of the periosteum (bone covering) along the greater part of the front surface of the front cannon bone. The horse becomes quite lame and is extremely sensitive when the slightest pressure is applied to the shin. Bucked shins are caused by constant pressure or trauma to the periosteum, resulting from concussion during fast workouts or riding for too long a period before the horse is in good physical condition. The horse usually recovers

FIGURE 2-19   Unsoundnesses and blemishes: (1) bucked shins; (2) bowed tendon, (3) popped knee; (4) shoe boil; (5) wind puff; (6) sesamoiditis; (7) osselet; (8) high ring bone; (9) low ring bone; (10) splint; (11) broken splint bone; (12) side bone; (13) quarter crack; (14) stifled; (15) bog spavin; (16) bone spavin; (17) capped hock; (18) curb; (19) thoroughpin.

after 30 to 60 days' rest. If it becomes lame again after the rest, the lameness may be caused by "saucer" fractures of the front cannon bone.

Bowed Tendons

A bowed tendon is a result of a severe strain and/or wear and tear of the deep flexor and/or superficial flexor tendon (Figure 2-19). The tendon sheath separates from the tendon (attachments are torn) so that there is a hemorrhage inside the tendon sheath. There may also be some tearing of the tendon fibers.

Bowed tendons are commonly seen in the front legs of horses that work at speed. They usually occur when the horse is fatigued and its entire body weight is on one leg. Contributing or predisposing factors also include long, weak pasterns (the fetlock joint moves too far downward and stretches the tendon); long toes (this condition retards the breaking over the foot and consequently places a strain on the tendon); overexertion; fatigue; improper shoeing (cutting down heels and leaving toes long); muddy tracks (foot tends to slide rather than break over); weak tendons; blow (trauma); and pressure from a tight-fitting bandage that cuts off blood supply.

The condition primarily occurs on forelegs, but occasionally on a hindleg. It shows up as a thickened enlargement on the tendons that occupy the posterior space in the cannon regions—between knee and fetlock joints or between hock and fetlock joints. Only about 20 percent of these horses are sound for heavy work after they recover. Therefore, they are usually unsound for use as hunters, jumpers, cutting horses, or rope horses. The tendon is usually re-bowed when the horses are worked hard.

Ring Bone

Ring bone is new bone growth on the first, second, or third phalanx (Figure 2-19). It may occur on any foot, but is most common on the forefeet. It is caused by an excessive pulling on the ligaments of the coffin and/or pastern joints, trauma, a direct blow to the phalanges, concussion from constant work on hard surfaces or hard work over the years, or poor conformation, such as straight pasterns and toe-in or toe-out conditions. The periosteum (bone forming tissue) is disturbed, and new bone growth results. Ring bone is classified in two ways: (1) position on bones and (2) joint involvement. High ring bone appears on the lower end of the first phalanx and/or the upper end of the second phalanx. Low ring bone appears on the lower end of the second phalanx and/or the upper end of the third phalanx. The excess bone growth may be on either side of the bones or all the way around. Articular ring bone involves the joint surface of the pastern or coffin joints. Periarticular ring bone is around the joint but does not involve the joint surface. The following terminology is used to describe ring bone: periarticular, high ring bone; periarticular, low ring bone; articular, high ring bone; articular, low ring bone. Horses with ring bone often do not show very many symptoms. If there is no lameness, the enlargement may go unnoticed. In articular ring bone, there is always lameness, but in periarticular ring bone there is usually none. If the ring bone is high periarticular, the horse may never be unsound unless the ring bone becomes articular. Low ring bone is always regarded as unfavorable, because the animal travels on its heels.

Shoe Boil or Capped Elbow

Shoe boil or capped elbow is a soft, flabby swelling caused by an irritation of the elbow (Figure 2-19). There are two common causes: (1) injury from a long heel on a front shoe or the heel calk of the shoe, and (2) injury from contact with the surface the horse is lying on. It should be treated in the early stages by applying an irritant, such as a tincture of iodine daily, and by using a shoe boil boot or roll. The roll is strapped around the pastern and prevents the heel of the foot or shoe from pressing on the elbow while the horse is lying down. Long heels should not be left on front shoes.

Splints

Splints are abnormal or new bony growths on the cannon or splint bones (Figure 2-19). They are caused by a disturbance of the fibrous interosseous ligament between the second and third metacarpal bones, or between the third and fourth metacarpal bones; that is, a disturbance of the ligaments between the cannon and splint bones. This disturbance can be caused by excessive strain or by a blow to that area. Strain causes an increased blood supply to the area, which is stimulated to form new bone. The most common cause of splints is overworking young horses, which places too much strain on medial splint bones. Hard stops, fast turns, jumping on hard ground, and galloping on hard surfaces are particularly straining. Gaited horses with high action where the foot strikes the ground very hard (rack) are predisposed to splints. Horses with "bench knees" tend to develop splints because of the extra strain on the inner (medial) splint bone. Similar problems occur in all crooked legs: toe-in, toe-out, straight pasterns, and so on. Young horses in training should wear splint boots to protect their legs when they do turns and roll backs. Splints usually cause lameness only in the early stages. At first, the horse may walk sound but trot lame. A little later, it is also lame when it walks. There may be no swelling, but careful inspection will reveal a hot, painful spot in the splint area. In time, if not treated, the splint calcifies and a permanent hard lump appears. At that time, lameness disappears, and the lump is considered a blemish rather than an unsoundness. However, if it is the result of "bench knees" or other conformation faults, or if it interferes with a tendon or ligament, it is always an unsoundness. Do not confuse splints with a broken splint bone. They are not the same, but bony knots may be present in both. A broken splint bone is an unsoundness if it interferes with a ligament, tendon, or the carpal joint.

Wind Puffs

Sometimes referred to as windgalls or "puffs" (Figure 2-19), wind puffs are enlargements of fluid sacs located immediately around the pastern or fetlock joints in the front or back feet. They result from too hard or too fast work on hard surfaces or just heavy work. Very few old horses escape them. The size of a wind puff may be reduced by applying cold packs followed by a liniment, but the puff will reappear when the horse is exercised. Almost all roping horses, as well as other horses that have been used very hard, have wind puffs. Usually, they are not serious, and no permanent benefit results from treatment. They indicate that the horse has been worked hard for a period of time in its life.

Osselets

Osselets are inflammatory conditions around a fetlock joint (Figure 2-19). They result from strain or pressure on immature bones. Concussion is often a major cause, so horses with upright pasterns are predisposed to osselets, which are easy to recognize because there is a fairly well defined swelling on an area of the fetlock joint. If you touch it, it feels like putty or mush, due to hemorrhage, and fluid collects beneath the periosteum. The osselet may be warm or hot. The horse usually travels with a short, choppy stride and shows evidence of pain when the fetlock joint is flexed. An osselet usually affects the horse for several years because it is an arthritic condition.

Popped Knees and Hygroma

An inflammatory condition, popped knees usually have a sudden onset. They are caused by sprained or strained ligaments that hold the knee bones in position, or by damage to the joint capsule, followed by increased fluid within the capsule. Popped knees are most common in racehorses during hard training, but they may occur in other horses that are worked too hard. Trauma can lead to popped knees, as when a horse paws the stall or trailer and hits its knees. Horses hit their knees when they eat out of wide feed troughs or hang their heads over stall doors while stomping flies. Bad conformation, such as bench-knees or calf-knees, predisposes horses to the condition. Horses that have popped knees rarely regain a degree of soundness that allows them to race or work hard again. Often popped knees are associated with articular bone growth. Popped knees should not be confused with a hygroma, which is a fluid-filled swelling over the front surface of the knee caused by trauma. The fluid is not within the joint capsule.

Sesamoiditis

Sesamoiditis is an inflammation of the proximal sesamoid bones located at the back of the fetlock joint (Figure 2-19). It results from an unusual strain to the fetlock area and is common in racehorses, hunters, and jumpers. Sesamoiditis can be detected when the horse is moving. The horse will not allow the fetlock to descend to a normal level and shows that it is in pain. On closer examination, swelling is evident. If pressure is applied to the sesamoid bones, the horse will flinch. In chronic cases, the periosteum is disturbed and there is new bone growth.

Mud Fever

An inflammation of the superficial layers of skin accompanied by an exudation (discharge), mud fever is caused by the action of mud—exactly how, no one seems to know. It usually affects the limbs from the fetlock upward when they have been repeatedly splashed with mud, and is common in horses kept in a muddy paddock or pasture. The skin becomes thick, tender, and covered with scabs. When the scabs come off, the hair falls off with it. Mud fever is the reason for the old adage, "Don't wash off mud but allow it to dry and then brush it off." The problem seems to be aggravated by washing off the legs.

Feet

Contracted Heels

Contracted heels usually occur in the front feet but also in the hindfeet. The condition is characterized by drawing in or contracting of the hoof wall at the heels. Improper shoeing causes and/or aggravates it. Contracted heels can be caused by lack of pressure on the frog (if the frog is cut out each time the horse is shod). Another common cause is lengthening of the toe (long toes), because the slight expansion of the hoof is decreased or obliterated when the foot strikes the ground. The retraction force in the foot is greater, and the heels start to contract inward. In true contracted feet, the sole becomes abnormally dished. This puts pressure on the third phalanx and thus causes lameness. In some cases, the condition can be corrected in 1 or 2 years. A Chadwick spring can be used, the heels of the shoe can be slippered, or the hoof wall can be weakened with a rasp.

Corns or Bruised Sole

Corns are bruises of the soft tissue underlying the sole of the foot, marked by a reddish discoloration of the sole immediately below the affected area. They can be caused by fast work on rough, hard surfaces; flat soles; stepping on small, hard objects; and/or poor shoeing. If the shoes are left on the feet too long, the heels of the shoe are forced inside the wall and press on the sole at the angle of the wall and the bar. Usually, the working horse must rest until the bruise heals; in some cases, the condition may be chronic. Chronic lameness is usually caused by new bone growth on the third phalanx.

Laminitis, or Founder

Founder is an inflammation of the laminae of the foot characterized by a passive congestion of the laminae with blood. Severe pain results from the inflammation, which presses on the sensitive laminae. It can have several causes, but the common underlying cause is the release of endotoxins by gram negative bacteria:

1 Overeating can cause laminitis. Following consumption of an excessive amount of grain, changes occur in the pH of the gut contents, which kills certain types of gut bacteria. Endotoxins are released from the cell walls of the dead bacteria, causing the release of chemical mediators that result in changes in blood flow and clotting. These changes result in death of the laminae in the foot. The symptoms occur 12 to 18 hours after eating the grain. Immunization against endotoxins is recommended to help prevent laminitis.

2 Overwork or road founder is caused by concussion from a hard surface. If a horse is not conditioned to exercise, riding it for several hours may cause founder.

3 Water founder is caused by an overheated horse drinking large amounts of cold water. The cause in this case is not known. An overheated or hot horse should always be cooled out before it drinks.

4 Postparturient laminitis is caused by a uterine infection, and the fetal membranes may or may not be retained.

5 Grass founder is common among overfat horses that are grazed on lush pastures. The cause may be the same as for overeating.

6 Miscellaneous causes of founder include viral respiratory infections, drugs, eating black walnut shavings, and overeating beet tops.

All the feet are susceptible to laminitis, but the forefeet are more susceptible than hindfeet. If all four feet are involved, a standing horse carries its hindfeet well up under it and carries its forefeet posteriorly. It has a very narrow base of support. If only the forefeet are involved, the hindfeet are carried well up under the body and the forefeet are carried forward. The horse is obviously in pain and is reluctant to move. Heat is present over the sole, wall, and coronary band. You may observe muscle tremors, increased respiration, and fever. These are usually due to anxiety and pain. If your horse has acute founder, immediately call a veterinarian.

In chronic cases or after a severe case, several characteristics aid recognition of a foundered horse. The sole is dropped and flat and is usually very flakey. The hoof wall grows very rapidly. Because the heel grows faster than the toe, the feet may develop a long, curled-up toe.

A very heavy ring forms around the wall of the foot for the rest of the horse's life. A horse that has been foundered and cured almost always has rough rings around the hoof wall. (However, you can also detect different phases of nutritional status by looking at the rings on the feet. In this case, the rings merely indicate changes in the rate of hoof wall growth and should not be confused with founder.) In severe cases, separation of the laminae, rotation of the third phalanx, and penetration of the third phalanx through the sole may occur. Such horses are lame for the rest of their lives, as are those in which the third phalanx rotates but does not penetrate the sole. (Therapeutic shoes for the foundered horse are discussed in Chapter 8.)

Navicular Disease

An inflammation of the small navicular bone of the front foot, navicular disease is actually a degenerative and erosive lesion of the fibrocartilage surface of the bone that begins as an irritation of the navicular bone and deep flexor tendon, or a degeneration of the navicular bone. It is impossible to determine the exact cause. Some predisposing conditions are hard work, upright pasterns, and small feet. Trimming the heels too low on horses with upright pasterns increases the pressure of the flexor tendon on the navicular bone. Affected horses usually go lame, have a short, stubby stride, and usually point the lame foot when standing.

Treatment consists of special shoeing to make it easier for the foot to break over and to reduce the anticoncussive activity of the deep flexor tendon against the navicular bone. Raising the heels and rolling the toe allows the foot to break over faster and reduces concussion to the navicular bone. To further reduce trauma, bar shoes or pads are used. This type of correction tends to contract the heels by reducing frog pressure. The tendency for the heels to contract can be reduced by "slippering" (sloping) the heels of the shoe so that the wall slides outward as the foot strikes the ground. Wall expansion can be further aided by thinning the quarters of the wall with a rasp. If special shoeing does not help, the navicular nerve can be cut so the animal does not have any sensation in the foot. If you are buying a horse and want to see if the nerves have been cut, look for two small scars—$\frac{1}{2}$ to 1 inch (13 to 25.4 mm) long— above the bulbs of the front feet. These horses may well be useless for hard work because there is continual wear on the tendon, which may rupture, or the navicular may break. "Nerved" horses may be dangerous to ride because they cannot "feel" the ground. However, there are many horses that have been "nerved" and remain useful for many years.

Quarter Crack, or Sand Crack

A vertical split in the wall of the hoof is called a "quarter crack," or "sand crack," which may extend down from the coronet band or up from the hearing surface. It is located in the quarter part of the hoof (if it is located on the toe, it is called a "toe crack"). The condition results from the hoof becoming too dry and brittle, from an injury to the coronet band, from long hoof walls that start to split, or from not having the hoof wall surface level when shod. When it first starts, a crack can usually be stopped by burning a moon-shaped crescent at the tip of the crack, or by filing a groove across the tip. Cracks can be prevented by keeping the hooves flexible with plenty of moisture and hoof dressing, and by making sure the feet are trimmed or shod properly at regular intervals.

Severe toe, quarter, and heel cracks are frequent. Each crack requires individual corrective treatment and shoeing. The general principle is to use a toe clip on each side of the crack and/or lacing with wire or staples to prevent wall expansion and to lower the wall under the crack so the wall does not bear weight on the shoe. Plastics are often used to seal the crack and to keep the crack from expanding and contracting during foot action. There are many brands of hoof repair kits that can also be used to reinforce walls and rebuild hooves.

Quittor

A quittor, a deep-seated sore that drains at the coronet, causes severe lameness. The infection may arise from many causes—puncture wounds, corns, and so on. It may be a chronic inflammation of a collateral cartilage of the third phalanx that drains through the coronary band.

Scratches, or Grease Heel

Scratches (grease heel) are mangelike inflammations of the posterior surfaces of the fetlocks and are usually found in the rear legs. The condition is well named because there is a greasy, foul-smelling secretion. It is usually caused by filthy conditions or muddy paddocks. The skin becomes chapped, cracked, and infected. Grease heel can be corrected by clipping the hair very close, cleaning with soap and water, and applying an antiseptic.

Side Bones

Side bones are ossified lateral cartilages located immediately above and toward the rear quarter of the hoof head. They usually occur in the front feet. One or both sides of the foot, as well as one or both feet, may be affected. Lameness may or may not be present. Side bones usually develop from concussion—running or working horses on a hard surface, injury to the cartilage from a blow, or poor conformation that increases concussion. Toe-in or base-narrow conformation causes lateral side bones; toe-out or base-wide causes medial side bones. The horse may be lame during ossification but rarely after.

Thrush

Thrush is a disease of the frog caused by many organisms, of which *Spherophorus necrophorus* is the most common. It is found in any one or all of the four feet and is brought on by unsanitary conditions—the affected horse is usually standing in mud or on urine- or feces-soaked ground or bedding.

Thrush is also the result of failure to clean the feet regularly. There is a very offensive characteristic odor and a blackish discharge. The horse becomes lame if the sensitive structures of the foot become involved. Thrush is easy to cure by trimming away the affected part of the frog and by applying an antiseptic.

Sheared Heels

When one heel is higher (longer) than the other, there is an unequal distribution of weight that causes a shearing effect in the heel region above the cleft of the frog. Lameness results from pain associated with the pulling and shearing of the tissues. Proper shoeing over a period of time is required to bring the foot into balance.

Gravel

The word "gravel" is actually a misnomer for this condition. Foreign material such as rocks or gravel is not necessarily involved. Most gravels are nothing more than abscesses that occur between the sensitive sole, frog, or laminae and their insensitive or horny counterparts. Usually, the infections form as a result of bruises. The blood is not sterile, and an abscess forms. Dead tissue can act as the aggravating foreign material. In some cases, the white line cracks in a dry foot, and an infection is formed, which is the cause of gravel. When the infection shows up at the coronary band, it is not a piece of foreign material working out. Instead, pus from the infection follows the path of least resistance, which is up the laminae. Therefore, the pus migrates to the coronary band and forces its way out. There is a drastic improvement as soon as the pressure is relieved at the site of pus formation.

Onchomycosis (Seedy Foot, Seedy Toe, or White Line Disease)

Seedy foot is abnormal horn, stratum medium, usually at the point of the toes. It is a dead growth of the stratum medium and feels and looks almost like sawdust. Although it can be cut out, it grows back the same way every time, leaving a place for infection to enter the foot. In addition to causing unsoundness, the wall is weak and will not hold a shoe the way it should. The abnormal horn may be limited to the distal (~1 cm) part of the hoofwall or it may extend all the way to the coronary band. It is caused by a fungal infection. These fungi are keratinophilic and can be treated with bleach, DMSO, or specific fungicides. Environmental conditions such as excessive toe length, laminitis, poor hoof management, and poor hoof health predispose the wall to contamination by the fungi.

Hindlegs

Stifled

The horse's stifle corresponds to the human knee. A horse is said to be "stifled" when the patella of the stifle joint has been displaced. The patella usually moves upward and to the inside, but can be placed back in normal position. Older horses are normally not very sound once they are stifled. Young horses may recover and be sound after they get a little older and stronger.

Stringhalt

Stringhalt is an involuntary flexion of the hock during forward movement. It may affect one or both hind limbs. The true cause is unknown but has been blamed on nervous diseases or degeneration of nerves. Symptoms are quite variable. Some horses show mild flexion of the hock during walking; others show a marked jerking of the foot toward the abdomen. Some horses show signs with each step; others are spasmodic. The signs are usually exaggerated while turning and after the horse has had a rest. The important point is that the horse does not have good stability when making a turn. However, many stringhalted horses are serviceable and can gallop and jump perfectly satisfactorily. Unfortunately, the condition frequently gets worse with age.

Treatment is surgery to remove part of the tendon of the lateral digital extensor. Most cases then show some improvement.

Thoroughpin

Thoroughpin is a puffy condition in the hock web caused by trauma or tendon strain (Figure 2-19). Excess synovial fluid forms and accumulates in the tarsal (hock) synovial sheath, which encloses the deep digital flexor tendon of the hindleg. Normally there are no signs of pain, lameness, or heat. The condition can be determined by the puff's movement. When pressed, the puff will move to the opposite side of the leg. Thoroughpin can be treated by applying pressure and massaging, but these are not always successful. It is best to let a veterinarian treat the condition. If the condition is left untreated, the joint action is not influenced, and the horse is seldom unsound.

Bog Spavin

A filling of the natural depression on the front face of the hock, a bog spavin is a chronic distension of the joint capsule. In addition to the large swelling on the front surface of the hock joint, two smaller swellings are usually located on the back part of the joint, lower than the swellings of thoroughpin (Figure 2-19). The bog spavin, which is much larger than the blood spavin, is caused by faulty conformation (horses that are too straight in the hock joint suffer increased concussion and trauma to the hock joint) and by trauma (injury to the hock joint as a result of quick stops, quick turns, and so on).

A veterinarian can treat bog spavin that is caused by accidental trauma, such as the horse getting kicked by another horse. In this case, it is a blemish if no bone changes are present. Many horses with bog spavin work for years without lameness. However, it is extremely difficult to treat bog spavin that results from faulty conformation, because it recurs.

Blood Spavin

Blood spavin, an abnormally swollen vein on the front face of the hock, occurs just above where a bog spavin is located. Lameness, heat, and swelling usually accompany the condition. Actually, there is no agreed-on definition for a blood spavin. Many people refer to it as being the enlarged saphenous vein that crosses a bog spavin. No successful treatment is known.

Bone Spavin

A bone spavin is new bone growth on the inside (medial side) and upper (proximal) end of the third metatarsal or hind cannon bone and a couple of the bones of the hock (third and central tarsal bones) (Figure 2-19). The condition causes arthritis of the hock joint. Bone spavins are caused by the same conditions as bog spavin, except that the faulty conformation is sickle hocks or cow hocks, which stress the inside of the hock joint. Horses with narrow, thin hocks are predisposed to bone spavins. A very large bone spavin is usually referred to as a "jack spavin."

One symptom is pain when the horse flexes the hock joint; the horse therefore reduces the height of the foot flight arc. This causes the foot to land on the toe, so that the toe gets short and heels tend to get long. Also, the horse tends to drag its toes and roll its hips as it moves. These signs are caused by incomplete flexion of the hock.

Treatment for bone spavin is surgery by a veterinarian, but the horse will not recover completely.

Blind, or Occult, Spavin

Blind spavin is a disease originating in the hock joint and causing typical spavin lameness. However, there may be no outward palpable or radiological signs. The damage is usually to the articular cartilages. The horse is usually lame all its life.

Capped Hock

Capped hock, an enlargement at the point of the hock (Figure 2-19), is caused by bruising when the horse kicks a trailer or walls of the stall. It is unsightly but need not be considered serious unless it interferes with the horse's work. In the early stages of development, it can be reduced by daily painting with a tincture of iodine solution. Once the "cap" has set or become fibrous, about all that can be done is to give a series of blister therapy treatments and hope resorption takes place. It is often impossible to cure if the horse is a confirmed stall kicker.

Curb

Curb is a condition in which there is a fullness of the rear of the leg just below the hock, caused by an enlarged plantar ligament (Figure 2-19). Anything that increases ligament stress can cause curb, which thickens the ligament. Sickle hocks and cow hocks are conformation faults that often lead to curb. Sliding a horse too far when stopping it, or stopping it too suddenly in deep, soft ground strains the plantar ligament enough to "pop a curb." Firing and blistering are the usual treatments (firing is making a series of skin blisters with a hot needle over the area of lameness).

GENERAL UNSOUNDNESSES

Hernia and abnormal respiratory conditions are general unsoundnesses. They greatly lower the usefulness and value of a horse.

Hernia

A hernia is any protrusion of an internal organ through the wall of its containing cavity. Usually it involves part of the intestine passing through an opening in the abdominal muscle. Umbilical and scrotal or inguinal hernias are fairly common in young foals. They usually correct themselves; if they do not, surgery is delayed until after the foal is weaned.

Heaves, or Wind Broke

Horses with the heaves have trouble forcing the air out of their lungs during or after exercise, or after drinking cold water. The horse starts to expire, pauses, and then contracts its abdominal muscles forcibly. The jerking of the ribs is characteristic, as is the formation of the so-called heave line in back of the ribs.

A sequence of events usually precedes heaves. The condition actually results from a persistent cough probably caused by prolonged feeding of poor-grade roughage or of dusty feed, or by keeping horses in very dusty, confined conditions. The persistent coughing breaks down the alveolar walls in the lung, so that the lung loses elasticity. Thereafter, expiration is no longer passive, and the horse must force the air out.

A horse with the heaves is unsound for any strenuous or fast work. There is no satisfactory treatment. It is best to turn the horse out to pasture, only use it for light work, and keep down the dust.

Roaring

An animal that whistles or wheezes when its respiration is speeded up with exercise is said to be a "roarer." The whistling or roaring noise occurs only with inspiration, not expiration. Roaring can be caused by broken rings in the trachea or, as in most cases, by paralysis of the muscles that control vocal cord tension. Air passing through the sagging muscles makes them vibrate in such a way as to produce the noise. Once established, roaring usually gets worse. There are no known means of prevention, but about 90 percent of cases can be surgically corrected.

Thick Wind

Thick wind simply refers to any difficulty in breathing.

Photosensitization

During the summer, a condition known as photosensitization may be observed. It is an allergic reaction to light, particularly sunlight. Certain plants sometimes develop chemicals in their leaves that, when digested and absorbed by the horse, get into its bloodstream and eventually reach the skin cells. These chemicals cause the skin to have a severe allergic reaction when hit by light. Usually only unpigmented skin is involved, because dark skin contains melanin, a dark pigment that shields the skin against the sun's rays. When the horse is exposed to sunshine, the white or unpigmented areas become violently inflamed. Unpigmented hairless areas, being even more unprotected, are most severely affected. The owner is often puzzled by the pattern of the skin lesions, which so distinctly limits itself to the unpigmented skin. A sorrel or bay horse may have severe involvement of the blaze on its face, lips, and ankles on stockinged feet, whereas the rest of the body remains normal. In Paint horses, all the white areas may be severely inflamed, but the darker areas will be absolutely normal.

The skin looks as if it has been severely burned. It blisters, weeps, cracks, and may even slough off (die and fall away). In severe cases, the horse may be quite sick. In mild cases, the horse may not seem to notice the ugly lesions, but the owner surely will.

The feeds most likely to develop photosensitizing chemicals are the legumes, such as clover and alfalfa. Vetch has also been reported to cause the disease, as has puncture vine (*Tribulous terrestris,* often called "bull head" or "goat head"), which is common in the southwestern United States.

Common sense directs treatment of the horse. It should be promptly put in a dark stall and removed from the offending feed source. A laxative should be given to remove remaining feed from its digestive tract, and the diet should be changed. Although the disease is disfiguring and alarming, nearly all horses recover completely.

CHAPTER 3

Choosing the Breed

Many breeds of horses are found throughout the world. Various breeds were developed according to the needs and desires of horsepeople in each locality, or they developed naturally. The usual definition for a breed is a group of horses with certain distinguishable characteristics, such as function, conformation, and color. In 1935, Wayne Dinsmore of the Horse and Mule Association of America said, "A breed of livestock may be considered to exist when there are a substantial number of animals within a given species that possess certain common characteristics, differentiating them from others of the same species, with power to transmit said distinguishing characteristics with a high degree of certainty to their progeny. The distinguishing characteristics must have value or not enough breeders will participate in the production of such animals, nor will the work be continued with sufficient persistence to evolve a breed."

At some time in history, all horse breeds have been influenced by humans, and we have controlled the selection of breeding stock. It is interesting to trace breed evolution and see how a few horses have played a role in the development of almost all the breeds.

As early as the reign of King James I (1603–1625), Arabian horses were imported into England and were crossed with native light horses. During the reign of Charles II (1660–1685), the so-called Royal Mares were imported. Byerly Turk, Darley Arabian, and Godolphin Barb were brought to England between 1689 and 1728. These three stallions are the foundation sires of Thoroughbred horses. The descendants of Byerly Turk through Herod established one of the sire lines. True Britain descended from Byerly Turk and was the sire of Justin Morgan, foundation sire of the Morgan horse breed. From the Morgan, several other breeds developed. Allen F-1 was a grandson of a Morgan stallion and is recognized as the foundation sire of the Tennessee Walking Horse. The Morgan horse also contributed to the development of the Standardbred, Quarter Horse, American Albino, and Palomino breeds. Eclipse can be traced from Darley Arabian and is one of the sire lines of Thoroughbreds. Blaze, the foundation sire of the Hackney, and Messenger, the progenitor of the American Standardbred and American Saddlebred, were also descendants of Darley Arabian. The American Saddlebred stems from Denmark, who was a Thoroughbred and the sire of Gaines Denmark. Hambletonian 10, a great-grandson of Messenger, was one of the most influential sires of the Standardbred breed. Thoroughbreds have been very influential in establishing the American Quarter Horse breed.

LIGHT HORSE BREEDS

If you decide to buy or keep purebreds of a certain breed, you should join that breed association. Each association has rules that govern the registration, ownership transfer, and activities of the breed. Various records must be kept and submitted to the association at specified times. Failure to adhere to the rules of the association may result in fines or restriction of one's activities associated with the breed. The rules and procedures for conducting business with each association can be obtained by writing to each association (Appendix 3-1).

When you register a horse with a breed association, you must understand the type of registration certificate that has been issued. Some associations have more than one type of registration certificate. Some certificates restrict the horse's participation in various breed activities and the registration of foals the horse produces or sires. It is impossible to present here all the rules for the associations, and, furthermore, they change periodically. Therefore, you should obtain the rule books from the breed association in which you are interested.

The breed that a person chooses to buy, own, or breed is determined primarily by his or her interest in certain types of horse activities. Some breeds are versatile; others are suited for specific purposes. The more versatile breeds are more popular (Table 3-1).

American Quarter Horse

The American Quarter Horse originated in America during the colonial era, although an official breed association was not formed until the twentieth century (see Figures 3-1 and 3-2). Racing was popular with the colonists. The races were about a quarter mile in length. They were frequently run

Table 3-1 Foal Registrations, 1986–1997

Breed	1988	1989	1990	1991	1992	1993	1994	1995	1996	1997
Anglo & Half Arab	6,500	4,775	4,276	4,251	3,834	3,668	4,257	4,663	4,331	3,710
Appaloosa	12,317	10,746	10,669	9,902	10,033	9,079	10,104	10,903	10,067	11,030
Arabian	24,569	21,723	17,676	12,993	12,544	12,349	12,962	12,398	11,645	11,594
Hackney	866	779	809	731	464	701	790	620	666	797
Miniature Horses	3,986	4,636	5,760	5,278	6,500	6,500	6,500	12,700	7,983	8,274
Morgan Horse	3,803	3,732	3,618	3,392	2,408	3,120	3,038	3,053	3,053	3,415
National Show Horse	978	919	733	624	557	473	562	534	891	525
Paint	14,929	14,390	16,153	18,648	22,396	24,220	27,549	34,846	41,491	50,440
Palomino	1,747	2,080	1,598	1,564	1,358	1,671	1,664	1,493	1,493	1,684
Paso Fino	1,464	1,453	1,550	1,483	1,859	1,640	1,980	2,036	2,115	2,254
Quarter Horse	128,352	123,294	110,597	101,390	102,843	104,876	105,017	107,332	108,604	110,714
Racking Horse	4,475	2,951	2,616	2,823	3,897	3,922	2,823	2,731	2,498	3,487
Saddlebred	3,811	3,708	3,569	3,570	3,048	3,353	3,192	2,300	3,142	3,213
Standardbred	17,393	16,896	16,576	13,617	13,029	12,086	12,204	10,918	11,598	11,336
Tennessee Walker	8,983	8,850	7,972	7,852	8,123	7,510	7,856	9,450	10,991	12,256
Thoroughbred	49,219	48,218	43,571	37,442	37,915	35,405	37,940	35,200	35,400*	35,400*
Trakhaner	561	515	461	420	428	358	360	465	370	341
Total per year	283,953	269,665	248,204	225,980	231,236	230,931	238,798	251,642	256,338	270,470

* denotes estimated figures. SOURCE: American Horse Council and breed associations.

FIGURE 3-1   A painting of the "ideal" American Quarter Horse by Orren Mixer. (Courtesy American Quarter Horse Association.)

down village streets or along country lanes near the plantations. Horses that could successfully race for a quarter of a mile were known as "quarter pathers." As the frontier moved westward, the quarter pather moved with it to run on the newly established short racetracks. In addition to racing, these horses served several purposes. They were adopted by ranchers and cowboys to use with range cattle because they had an inherent "cow sense." Therefore, this type of horse was very popular in the Southwest during the late 1800s, and its popularity has continued to increase. The American Quarter Horse Association (AQHA) was founded in 1941 and has become the largest horse breed organization in the world. Over 3 million horses have been registered.

Two types of registration certificates are issued by the AQHA, so its Official Stud Book has two parts. The numbered section of the registry, which makes up the largest portion of registered American Quarter Horses, consists of horses registered from parents that are numbered American Quarter Horses. The second type of registration is the appendix listing of horses that have one parent that is a numbered American Quarter Horse and one parent that is a Thoroughbred registered either with the Jockey Club of New York City or any Thoroughbred it recognizes. An "appendix" horse may receive a

FIGURE 3-2   Wimpy, the first horse registered by the American Quarter Horse Association, painted by Orren Mixer.

number by fulfilling the requirements for a "register of merit," a record of outstanding performance.

Many breeds and types of horses played a role in the synthesis of the Quarter Horse. Several famous sires such as Steeldust, Old Billy, Shiloh, Yellow Jacket, Peter McCue, Little Joe, Traveler, and Copperbottom were responsible for the early establishment of the breed. Later, sires such as Doc Bar, Old Sorrel, Three Bars, Top Deck, Leo, King, Easy Jet, Dash for Cash, Impressive, and Go Man Go have left their mark on the breed. Wimpy, owned by the King Ranch, was the champion stallion at Fort Worth in 1941, and when the association was formed, he was given the registration number 1 (Figure 3-2).

Today there are many types of Quarter Horses because they are used for so many purposes. Because of the interest in racing created by the betting public and increased purses, some horses are bred primarily for speed. Others are used on ranches, so some breeders try to maintain the conformation and desire to work cattle. These types of horses are also shown in western event classes at horse shows. Other horse show classes, such as hunting and jumping, have resulted in Quarter Horses that have a Thoroughbred type conformation.

Arabian

The early history of the Arabian horse is obscure. Horses similar to the best Arabians were in North Africa more than 1,000 years before good horses were known in Arabia. They were apparently introduced to Arabia from Africa sometime between the first and sixth centuries. The Arabian proper is a descendant of the Kohl breed, and all Arabians descend from the five foundation mares known as Al-Khamesh (The Five). They were, according to legend, all owned by King Solomon about 1635 B.C. There are five great families of Arabian horses descending from Al-Khamesh: Keheilet Ajuz, with 37 subfamilies; Maneghi, with 4 subfamilies; Hadban, with 5 subfamilies; Jelfon, with 2 subfamilies; and Homdani, with 2 subfamilies. From Keheilet Ajuz come the most distinguished families. Darley Arabian descends from Keheilet Ajuz. The Arabians were bred as purebreds and also used to cross on native mares to improve or develop breeds in many localities.

The Arabian (Figure 3-3) was first imported to America in 1730. Since that time, a great number of horses have been imported from many countries.

FIGURE 3-3 Imperial Imdal, many times champion and Reserve National Champion Arabian Stallion, is by Ansata Imperial and out of Dalia. He is an Egyptian Arabian and stands at stud in Tennessee. (Photo by Polly Knoll courtesy Barbara Vallée, the owner.)

They have several distinguishing characteristics. Arabians are known for their endurance and tend to dominate endurance races and competitive trail rides. Their heads have a characteristic dished face. They are usually 14 to 15.2 hands tall and weigh 900 to 1000 pounds (408 to 454 kg).

The Arabian horse industry in Canada and the United States has three separate organizations not formally related, but all work closely together with many interlocking members. The first is the Arabian Horse Registry of America, Inc., which functions, as its name implies, strictly as a registry of all pure-bred Arabian horses in the United States. The registry was formed in 1908; before that time, the Jockey Club in New York City registered purebred Arabian horses to a limited degree. The International Arabian Horse Association was formed in 1950 with the moral and financial blessing of the Arabian Horse Registry, because they did not wish to go into promotional work or horse show activities or to establish member clubs. At that time, the Arabian Horse Registry was also the registering authority for all of Canada. In about 1960 or 1961, the Canadian Arabian Horse Registry was formed to operate in the same manner as the Arabian Horse Registry of America; that is, to register all purebred Arabian horses in Canada.

Shortly after the International Arabian Horse Association was founded, it was given the opportunity to acquire the Half-Arabian and Anglo-Arabian registries from a private party who had recently acquired them from the American Remount Association. These two registries then became part of International's operations, even though its primary members and promotional efforts are targeted toward the purebred Arabian horse, also including the Half-Arabian and Anglo-Arabian.

In the Half-Arabian Registry, the sire or dam must be a purebred Arabian registered either with the Arabian Horse Registry of America or the Canadian Arabian Horse Registry (Figure 3-4). The Anglo-Arab Registry registers foals by registered Thoroughbred stallions out of registered Arabian mares, foals by registered Arabian stallions out of registered Thoroughbred mares, foals by registered Thoroughbreds or registered Arabian stallions out of registered Anglo-Arab mares, and foals by registered Anglo-Arab stallions out of registered Anglo-Arab mares, registered Thoroughbred mares, or registered Arabian mares.

In 1973, International inherited the activities of the Arabian Racing Association of America. Arabian racing has taken place in several states, such as Nevada, Michigan, Delaware, Kentucky, New Mexico, Florida, Georgia, and California. This racing is in its infancy, but the interest among Arabian owners is increasing. International is keeping records of the performance of Arabians on the track.

Thoroughbred

The history of the Thoroughbred horse (Figure 3-5) began in England. The early racing stock, showing endurance but no speed, were native mares that

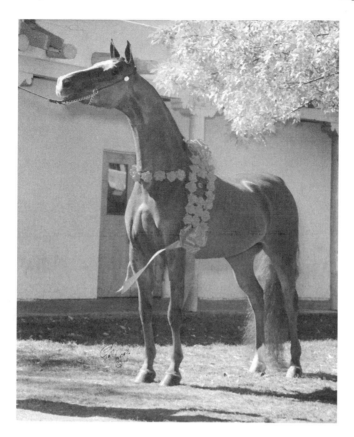

FIGURE 3-4   Dipsey Swivel, 1997 National Champion Half Arabian Mare, saddle type. She is by Erros Sultan's Secret Love, an American Saddlebred. (Photo by Polly Knoll.)

had been crossed with horses brought into England by the Romans and the French Normans (eleventh century). Oriental sires (Arabians, Turks, and Barbs) were used to try to improve the speed of the "Royal Mares," regarded by some as the foundation mares of the breed. However, it was not until Byerly Turk, Darley Arabian, and Godolphin Barb were imported that the Thoroughbred we know today was established as a refined running horse. Byerly Turk reached England in 1689 and was the first sire to have a significant effect on speed. Darley Arabian was imported in 1705 or 1706 and continued to improve the horses. Godolphin Barb arrived around 1728 to 1730. One of his fillies, Post, was sent to America in 1733, and because of his popularity as a racing sire, many of his offspring followed. All English and American Thoroughbreds trace their lineage in the male line from these three studs. The three foundation sires were Matchem, grandson of Godolphin Barb; Herod, great-great-grandson of Byerly Turk; and Eclipse, great-great-grandson

FIGURE 3-5   A. P. Indy (by Seattle Slew and out of Weekend Surprise), bred and raised by Lane's End, was champion 3-year-old colt in 1992 and Horse of the Year in 1992. He is one of the current leading sires of Thoroughbreds and stands at stud at Lane's End in Kentucky. (Photo by Tony Leonard, courtesy of Lanc's End.)

of Darley Arabian. Bulle Rock was the first Thoroughbred imported to America, in 1730. From that time, mares and stallions arrived from England to improve the U.S. running horse. The Thoroughbred has continued to be bred and selected to improve its speed and endurance.

Thoroughbred horses were first registered in England in the General Stud Book, the first volume appearing in 1793. All English Thoroughbreds must trace back to horses registered there. The American Stud Book, first published in 1873, was purchased by the Jockey Club in 1894 and continues to register American Thoroughbreds.

The Thoroughbred is one of the most versatile of horse breeds and has influenced the development of many other breeds. They are primarily running horses but are also used for hunters, jumpers, dressage, three-day events, cow horses, and so on.

Many famous racing horses have captured the hearts of Americans. Eleven horses have won the Triple Crown (the Kentucky Derby, the Preakness, and the Belmont Stakes) for 3-year-olds, including the first winner, Sir Barton, in 1919. After Citation won the Triple Crown in 1948, no other horse did so for 25 years until 1973, when Secretariat became the champion. Seattle Slew won in 1977, and Affirmed was the last winner in 1978. Other horses, such as Swaps, Round Table, Buckpasser, Man o' War, Forego, Kelso, Northern

Dancer, Dr. Fager, Alysheba, Cigar, Silver Charm, Victory Gallop, and Skip Away did not win the Triple Crown but compiled extensive race and/or sire records. Nasrulla, his son Bold Ruler, Northern Dancer, and Mr. Prospector are four stallions who have had a major impact on the breed during the second half of the twentieth century. Through the years the centers of racing have moved from colonial Virginia to California, Kentucky, Florida, and New York.

Most of the running Thoroughbreds are 15.1 to 16.2 hands high and weigh 900 to 1,200 pounds (408 to 544 kg). They have long, smooth muscles, short cannon bones, long forearms, long, sloping shoulders, and long distance from the hip to the hock.

Standardbred

The Standardbred breed (Figure 3-6) includes both trotters and pacers. They have a common history, and some Standardbreds have been successfully raced at the trot and pace. Speed at the trot and the pace is their most distinctive characteristic. The name *Standardbred* was derived from the original standard for speed, which was adopted in 1879. For a horse to be registered, it had to trot a mile in 2:30 minutes or pace it in 2:25. Since then, the standard has been lowered to 2:20 for 2-year-olds and 2:15 for older horses. The first 2-minute mile was recorded in 1897 by the pacer Star Pointer.

The past few years have witnessed major improvements in racetrack construction and maintenance, in sulky and harness design, and in the breed itself, with Niatross heralding a new era with a 1:49.5 time trial in 1980, the first mile less than 1:50 (see Appendix Table 12-15). All-time records for the fastest mile, most money won, and other statistics are given in Appendix Table 12-16.

The Standardbred, of American origin, traces back to horses imported from England, and can be traced directly to Darley Arabian; the most important stallions were Messenger and Bellfounder. The American influence came from the early days when the colonists selected horses that would travel long distances at the trot or pace. In the early history of the breed, three families were the most popular, the descendants of Messenger, Justin Morgan (the Morgans), and Grand Bashaw (the Clays). Hambletonian 10 was the most influential early Americanbred sire. He stood at stud 23 years and sired 1333 colts. Hambletonian 10 was linebred to Messenger, who appears four times in the third and fourth generation removed. Four sons of Hambletonian 10 established sire lines. In the early 1900s, four male trotting lines were prominent: Peter the Great, Axworthy, McKinney, and Bingen. More recently, Adios has exercised the most powerful influence on the breed. Currently, stallions such as Speedy Crown (Figure 3-6), No Nukes (Figure 3-7), Cam Fella, and Ambercrombie are dominant factors in racing pedigrees.

Since the early history of the Standardbred, several associations have maintained records. In 1870, the National Trotting Association was organized, followed in 1877 by the American Trotting Association. J. H. Wallace published the *American Trotting Register* in 1868, which was sold to the

FIGURE 3-6   Valley Victory, a top trotting stallion and 1998 leading money-winning sire of trotters, being driven by Steve Waller. He stands at stud at Southwind Farm in New Jersey. (Photo courtesy U.S. Trotting Association.)

American Trotting Association in 1891. The register was continued, and today all Standardbreds are registered in the *American Trotting Sires and Dams Book*. The official registry is maintained by the U.S. Trotting Association, which was formed in 1939 and is now closed. All registered foals must have registered parents. In addition, the United States Trotting Association has established rules that serve as a guide for Standardbred racing in the United States and Canada, licenses the majority of officials at harness racing tracks, maintains racing records, and promotes harness racing.

In addition to racing, Standardbreds are being shown as jumpers and pleasure horses and are being used in therapeutic riding programs for handicapped children. USTA sponsors the Standardbred Equestrian Program and maintains records of accomplishments for individual horses. The Standardbred Pleasure Horse Association is actively involved in sponsoring shows and activities.

FIGURE 3-7   Artsplace was 1998 leading money-earning sire of pacers and stands at stud at Southwind Farm in New Jersey. (Photo courtesy U.S. Trotting Association.)

Morgan

The Morgan horse breed (Figure 3-8) traces its history to Justin Morgan, foundation sire and foaled in 1789. Originally named Figure, the horse was taken to Vermont from Springfield, Massachusetts, and the new owner named it after himself. Justin Morgan was a small horse that stood slightly over 14 hands and weighed a little over 1000 pounds (454 kg). He gained a reputation over the years by pulling a log that a draft horse could not move, carried a president on a parade ground, and outran the best quarter-mile racehorse in central Vermont. He produced three stallions—Sherman, Kulrush, and Woodbury—that established him as a sire. Black Hawk, a grandson of Justin Morgan, produced Ethan Allan 50, champion trotter of the world.

The Morgan has always been a versatile breed. Originally they were developed as general-purpose horses for New England farms. Today they are used as working cow horses, trail horses, therapeutic riding horses, and youth horses and are shown under saddle, in harness, as jumpers, and as roadsters.

The Morgan Horse Register was formed in 1894 by Colonel Battell. Since then, the organization has undergone two name changes. The Morgan Horse Club took over the registry in 1927 and is presently named the American Morgan Horse Association, Inc. In 1907, the U.S. Morgan Horse Farm was

FIGURE 3-8   UVM Cantor, a Morgan stallion, was bred by the University of Vermont. (Photo courtesy American Morgan Horse Association.)

established in Weybridge, Vermont, to perpetuate the breed and was operated by the Department of Agriculture. The farm, a gift from Colonel Battell, was given to the University of Vermont in 1951.

The breed characteristics have changed little since Justin Morgan. They stand 14.2 to 15.2 hands and weigh 900 to 1100 pounds (405 to 495 kg). There are three major families in the breed: the Lippitt has the smallest numbers; the Government line is the most numerous family; and the Brunk family is the second most prominent family in modern Morgans.

American Saddlebred

The American Saddlebred horse was developed in Kentucky by pioneers who needed a utility horse. The breed traces back to natural English pacers, Galloway and Hobbie horses. It developed from the Thoroughbreds, Morgans, and Narragansett pacers and trotters, and was used for riding and driving, although some were used for plowing. One of the foundation sires for the breed is Denmark F.S., a Thoroughbred. Even though much of the development of the breed preceded Denmark, it was his mating to the "Stevenson Mare" that produced Gaines Denmark, through which over 60 percent of saddlers are traced. Nine other sires were important to the development of the breed and were recognized as Noted Deceased Sires in 1910. In 1991, the year of the ASHA Centennial, Harrison Chief was designated a foundation sire along with Denmark. The Chief family traces back to Messenger, the Thoroughbred who is considered the foundation sire of the breed. In 1891, a group of breeders met in Louisville, Kentucky, to form the National Saddle Horse Breeders' Association which was changed to American Saddle Horse Breeders' Association in 1899. Today the average height is 15 to 16 hands, and the average weight is 1000 to 1200 pounds (454 to 544 kg). Saddlebreds have short backs, flat croups, sloping shoulders, long arched necks, and long pasterns. They are used for riding, driving, hunting, jumping, parades, cow work, and show. They excel as show horses and are shown as three- and five-gaited, pleasure, and fine harness horses. The three-gaited horses are required to perform at the walk, trot, and canter, whereas the five-gaited horses are also shown at the slow gait, stepping pace, and the rack. They are judged on their action, conformation, performance, quality, animation, manners, and soundness. The five-gaited horse (Figure 3-9) is shown with a full mane and tail, whereas the three-gaited horse (Figure 3-10) is shown with a clipped mane. The fine harness horse is shown at two gaits, the walk and park trot. They are shown with

FIGURE 3-9   Perfect Prowler being shown by Frank McConnell in fine harness class. He was owned by Mr. Donald Rich. (Photo by Jamie Donaldson, courtesy American Saddlebred Horse Association.)

FIGURE 3-10   One for the Road, 1992 three-gaited world's grand champion owned by Crismont Manor Farm and shown by Randy Harper. (Photo by Jamie Donaldson, courtesy American Saddlebred Horse Association.)

an appropriate four-wheeled vehicle and carry a full mane and tail (Figure 3-11). Pleasure horses are shown with a full mane and tail.

Tennessee Walking Horse

The Tennessee Walking Horse (Figure 3-12) originated in the middle Tennessee bluegrass region. The breed had its beginning as the Southern Plantation Walking Horse. These horses were of mixed breeding, which included Narragansett and Canadian pacers as well as trotters and pacers. Later, other breeds

FIGURE 3-11 Roseland's Secret Rhythm, 1992 fine harness world's grand champion. He is owned by Dr. Helen Neave and shown by Mike Barlow. (Photo by Jamie Donaldson.)

such as the Thoroughbred, Standardbred, Morgan, and American Saddlebred were used in the area to produce horses. The horses that developed were utility animals, but they had a natural ability for an easy, gliding gait. In 1885, a cross between a stallion called Allendorf, from the Hambletonian family of trotters, and Maggie Marshall, a Morgan mare, produced Allan F-1, later recognized as the foundation sire for the Tennessee Walking Horse. Other bloodlines, such as the Copperbottoms, Gray Johns, Slashers, Hals, Brooks, and Bullett families, had already produced the Tennessee pacer prior to Allan F-1's arrival in middle Tennessee in 1903. However, it was the cross of Allan F-1 on the Tennessee pacer mares that produced the Tennessee Walking Horse as it is known today. Refinement of the style and conformation of the Tennessee Walking Horse was started soon after by the arrival of Giovanni. The Saddlebred stallion crossed quite well with the Allan F-1 mares to produce higher-quality horses.

In 1935, the Tennessee Walking Horse Breeders Association formed. When the stud book was established, 115 horses were selected as foundation stock. Almost every breed of horse in the United States was represented in the bloodlines of the foundation stock. The distinctive characteristic of the breed is the ability to do the running walk. The running walk is characterized as a four-beat gait in which all four feet strike the ground separately at regular intervals. The hindfoot overstrikes the footprint left by the lateral forefoot by 18

FIGURE 3-12   Generator's Santana, 1997 World Grand Champion Tennessee Walking Horse, owned by Castleman and Kilgore. (Photo by Stuart Vesty and courtesy of Tennessee Walking Horse Breeders' and Exhibitors' Association, Lewisberg, TN.)

to 50 inches (45.7 to 127 cm). This gives the horse a smooth, gliding motion that is comfortable to ride.

Gotland Horse

The Gotland is one of the oldest breeds of horses; it has a 10,000-year history on the Swedish island of Gotland in the Baltic Sea. Descendants of the Tarpans, the Gotland horses are called Skogsruss by the Swedes. Throughout history, they have been used for riding and as draft animals and carriage horses. In 1880, the Swedish government placed the Gotlands under strict government protection and supervision. At that time, some oriental horses were used in a crossbreeding program to expand the genetic base. Gotlands were imported to the United States in 1957 from Sweden and are registered with the Gotland-Russ Association of North America, Inc.

Gotlands are small horses ranging between 11.2 and 13 hands. Their size and temperament make them excellent youth horses.

Racking Horse

The Racking Horse Breeders' Association of America was formed in 1971 to register horses with the natural ability to perform the pleasure walk, slow rack, and fast rack. The rack is a four-beat gait in which the hindleg and its diagonal foreleg leave the ground simultaneously, but the hindleg strikes the ground prior to its diagonal foreleg. Its origins are within the Tennessee Walking Horse bloodlines.

Missouri Fox Trotting Horse

The origin of the Missouri Fox Trotter is obscure. The settlers that came from the mountains and plantations of Kentucky, Tennessee, and Virginia brought their saddle horses with them. Some of these horses could do the foxtrot, which was easy to ride, and the horse could travel long distances at the gait. The foxtrot gait is a broken trot in which the front foot strikes the ground prior to the diagonal hindfoot. The hindfoot glides forward of the print made by the lateral forefoot. Because the front of the horse is rising upward until the hindquarters are being lowered, the gliding motion gives the rider a comfortable ride. The speed of the gait is 5 to 8 miles (8 to 12.9 km) per hour.

In 1948, the Missouri Fox Trotting Breed Association was formed to preserve the type of horse that was developed from the settlers' foxtrotting horses after the infusion of Arabian, Morgan, American Saddlebred, Tennessee Walking, and Standardbred blood. Gradually sire lines developed, and the lines of the Diamonds, Copperbottoms, Brimmers, Red Bucks, Chiefs, Steel Dusts, and Cold Decks are recognized. In 1970, a rival association, the American Fox Trotting Horse Breed Association, was formed. Many foxtrotters are registered with both associations.

Lipizzan

Lipizzan horses trace their history back to the early 1560s when Arabian blood was infused with that of local Spanish horses. Maximilian II and his brother Archduke Charles established studs and bred the Lipizzan horses. All Lipizzans trace their family lines to six stallions that were used during the eighteenth and nineteenth centuries: Conversano, Favory, Maestoso, Neapolitano, Pluto, and Siglavy. In addition to the stallions, there are 18 mare family lines.

Gray is the predominant color as a result of selection over the years. Originally, all colors were represented. Lipizzans are known for their athleticism and are used exclusively by the Spanish Riding School in perpetuating the art of classical horsemanship. The Spanish Riding School is also the primary breeding facility for continuing the breed.

Morab

The Morab (Figure 3-13) is a breed created in 1973 with the formation of the Morab Horse Registry of America by Mrs. Irene Miller. After the decline of this registry, and of a successor organization, the International Morab Registry was formed and is the current registry. The first Morabs were probably bred in the 1800s by crossing the Arabian and Morgan breeds. Since then, many breeders have used the cross to produce good horses. The animals on which the Morab association and registry were established were selectively bred by Martha Doyle Fuller. The breed was perpetuated by Fuller, beginning in 1955, by crossing Morgan mares with Arabian stallions to produce distinct characteristics in the resultant foals. They stand 14.3 to 15.2 hands high and weigh 950 to 1200 pounds (428 to 540 kg).

National Show Horse

In 1981, the National Show Horse Registry was formed to create a new breed. Arabians and American Saddlebreds were crossed to form the foundation of the breed. The other primary purpose of creating the National Show Horse Registry was to broaden the base of the show horse industry and provide new incentives for showing horses.

FIGURE 3-13   Tezya, the first horse registered as a Morab. (Courtesy Morab Horse of Registry of America.)

Paso Fino and Peruvian Paso

The origin of the Pasos is in the Spanish provinces of Cordova and Andalusia. When the Moors invaded Spain, they brought Arab and Barb horses to the area. These animals were crossed with the native horses, which had remnants of the Andalusian breed. One strain to develop was the Spanish Jennet, which was noted for its comfortable saddle gait and for its ability to pass the gait on to its offspring. In 1492, Columbus took some horses of this descent to Santo Domingo. From this area, the Spanish Jennet horse with the saddle gait spread through the Caribbean, Mexico, and South America, and the Pasos developed from these horses. They have the common characteristic of the paso gait, a broken pace in which the paired lateral limbs leave the ground together, but the hindfoot strikes the ground prior to the lateral forefoot. This eliminates the jarring effect of the pace and makes the gait comfortable to ride. The exhibition of termino, which is the outward swing of the foreleg, is a desirable trait.

There are two registries for Paso Fino horses (Figure 3-14). In 1964, the American Paso Fino Pleasure Horse Association was formed; it registers purebred Peruvian Pasos. The Paso Fino Owners and Breeders Association also promotes and breeds Paso Fino horses. Most horses registered by these associations have come from Puerto Rico and Colombia.

Peruvian Paso horses (Figure 3-15) developed from Paso horses brought to Peru by the Spanish conquistadors. They were used by riders on long journeys between haciendas on the coastal plains of Peru. Two U.S. registries list Pasos imported from Peru. The American Association of Owners and Breeders of Peruvian Paso Horses was formed in 1967. They do not register horses

FIGURE 3-14 A Paso Fino being shown on lines for conformation and gait. (Courtesy Paso Fino Owners and Breeders Association.)

FIGURE 3-15   DHC Damisela, a Peruvian Paso, being shown by Michelle James to first place junior performance at Los Amigos Show, 1988. (Photo by Debbie Pye.)

with albino, tobiano, and overo color patterns. The Peruvian Paso Horse Registry of North America excludes the albino color pattern.

Galiceño

Galiceño horses (Figure 3-16) originated in the Galicia Province in Spain. They were brought to North America by Cortez in 1519 and were kept by natives in the coastal regions of Mexico. Even though purebred Galiceños never migrated north to join other American horses, they are the ancestors of countless Mustangs. In 1958, they were imported to the United States from Mexico, and in 1959, the Galiceño Horse Breeders Association was formed.

The Galiceños are small horses that are usually 12 to 13.2 hands in height and 625 to 700 pounds in weight (283 to 317 kg). They are used primarily by young adults for most types of performance events. Many of the Galiceños are recognized for their natural ability to perform the running walk.

FIGURE 3-16   Canta, a champion Galiceño mare. She was ridden by Shareen Allen of Kyle, Texas, to win the Highpoint Youth All-Around in 1977. (Photo by Falkner, courtesy Galiceño Horse Breeders Association.)

American Bashkir Curly

Horses with curly coats are an ancient breed and have been depicted in art and statuary in China as far back as AD 161. In Russia, they have been raised for centuries on the southern slopes of the Ural Mountains by the Bashkiri people, for whom they are named. The Russian Lokai breed also has individuals with curly coats, and some have Appaloosa markings. The milk from the mares is used for milk, cream, butter, and cheese. It is also fermented into kumiss, an alcoholic drink. The older animals are used for meat, and their hides are used to make clothes. The horses are also used for draft and transportation purposes.

In 1898, Peter Damele and his father found three curly-haired horses in the Peter Hanson Mountain Range in central Nevada. It is unknown how the horses got there, but since then, there have always been curly-haired horses on the Damele range. In 1971, the American Bashkir Curly Registry was formed to prevent their extinction in the United States.

Several characteristics differentiate these horses from other breeds: long, silky, curly hair (in waves or ringlets); some completely shed their mane and tail hair each summer; absence of ergots in some individuals; four black hooves; and five lumbar vertebrae.

Rocky Mountain Horse

In Spout Springs, Kentucky, on the farm of Sam Tuttle, the foundation horses for the Rocky Mountain Horse were bred. Most trace their lineage to the stallion Old Tobe. Prior to then, horses of this type were bred in eastern Kentucky. In 1986, the breed association was formed to track their lineage and supervise the growth and development of the breed. All horses must be examined for breed characteristics and approved prior to breeding. One of the requirements for approval is a natural ambling four-beat gait (single foot or rack).

REGISTRIES WITH COLOR REQUIREMENTS

Within breeds, many coat colors and color patterns or both are attractive to horse owners. People who found particular colors appealing established registries for these horses. The Palomino Horse Association of California was the first color breed association. Shortly thereafter, registries for color patterns such as Appaloosas, Albinos, Paints, Pintos, and Buckskins were established. Some registries only require color for registration; others have conformation standards. The color breeds do not breed true, with the possible exception of the overo color pattern.

American Albino

American Albino horses (Figure 3-17) as a color breed originated on the White Horse Ranch at Naper, Nebraska, in 1937 under the ownership of Caleb and Ruth Thompson. The foundation sire was Old King, who was milk-white in color with pink skin and brown eyes. Foundation mares were Morgans. Coloring is the primary requisite for registration. Horses must have snow- or milk-white hair with pink skin and brown, blue, or hazel eyes when born. They are not true albinos because they do not have pink eyes. The dominant white gene results in snow-white horses. Creme-colored horses are those with the gene(s) for dilution of the normal color patterns. To separate the dominant white from the creme-colored horses, the International American Albino Association has set up two separate registries. Creme-colored horses are registered with the American Creme Registry, and dominant white horses with the American White Registry. Both registries accept horses regardless of height.

FIGURE 3-17   American albino ponies in a field. (Courtesy White Horse Registry.)

American Buckskin

The American Buckskin Registry Association was started in 1963 to register Buckskin, Dun, and Grulla ponies and horses. In 1971, the International Buckskin Horse Association was formed as a forerunner to the International Buckskin Horse Registry, providing two registries for buckskin horses. The dilution gene(s) responsible for these color patterns was present in the Norwegian Duns and the Sorraia horses of Spain. The Spanish conquistadors brought horses with the dilution gene(s) to America, and thus the descendants of the Buckskin-colored horses (Figure 3-18).

The American Buckskin Registry Association describes four color patterns that are eligible for registration. Buckskin horses must have a body coat of some shade of yellow but not red. The points are black or dark brown. A dorsal stripe is not necessary. Dun horses have a yellow to nearly white body coat with dark points such as red, black, brown, and dark yellow. The mane and tail must be darker than the body. Grulla horses are smoky gray in color with no white hairs mixed in. A dorsal stripe must be present. Red Duns have a dun-colored body coat (flesh-colored or red). The points are dark red or red mixed with black. A dorsal stripe is necessary. Palominos and bays with dorsal stripes are not eligible for registration, nor are horses with blue eyes or white spots on their bodies. White markings are not allowed to extend above the hocks and knees except for face markings. Once eligibility for color is established, an inspector must approve the horse before registration.

The International Buckskin Horse Association describes five color patterns that are eligible for registration: Buckskin, Dun, Grulla, Red Dun, and Brindle Dun. Their ideal type is that of a western or stock-type saddle horse

FIGURE 3-18   Hank's Billy Van, a registered golden Buckskin. (Courtesy International Buckskin Horse Association.)

that is at least 14 hands. Since 1971, the association has registered over 19,500 horses.

Palomino

The palomino color pattern has been responsible for many myths and legends. The gold-colored horse appears in ancient tapestries and paintings of Europe as well as in Japanese and Chinese art of past centuries. However, the exact history has never been recorded.

Founded in 1941, the Palomino Horse Breeders of America, Inc. is a color and bloodlines registry for horses standing between 14 and 17 hands tall and exhibiting body color approximately that of a U.S. gold coin. The skin is dark colored without underlying pink skin or spots except on the face or legs. The eyes are black, hazel, or brown. The mane and tail must be white with not more than 15 percent dark, sorrel, or chestnut hairs. There are two basic divisions of Palominos registered with PHBA. The stock type is western horses predominantly represented by Quarter Horses; the pleasure type is exemplified by Saddlebred, Morgan, and Arabian horses. Individuals who own Palominos that are registered with the American Quarter Horse Association, American Morgan Horse Association, American Saddlebred Horse Associations, Arabian Horse Registry, International Arabian Horse Associations Jockey Club, and the Tennessee Walking Horse Breeders and Exhibitors Association have the option of filing for registration and participating with the PHBA. Palomino geldings and spayed mares with unknown parentage may also be registered based on color and conformation standards.

Palomino horses are also registered by the Palomino Horse Association and the Ysabella Saddle Horse Association. The Ysabella Association registers Palominos and sorrel horses with silver manes under their Gold Seal. Under their Silver Seal, they register white horses that have silver manes and tails and blue eyes. The Silver Seal Registry of the Ysabella Association is the major difference from the Palomino Horse Association. The Ysabella Association registers horses of the genotypes that can be used to produce the palomino color, whereas the Palomino Horse Association does not.

Paint, Pinto, and Spotted Horses

Three breed registries list horses with body markings of white and another color. These horses are described as being of the overo or tobiano pattern and of the piebald or skewbald color. The overo pattern (Figure 3-19) is any basic

FIGURE 3-19 The Midas Touch, a Palomino stallion with the overo color pattern; a supreme champion. (Photo by R. Yoeseh, courtesy W. G. Yoeseh.)

color with white body marks. The white usually does not cross the back between the withers and the tail. At least one and often all four legs are of the dark color. Head markings are often bald or apron- or even bonnet-faced. Irregular, rather scattered, and/or splashy white markings are on the body and are often referred to as "calico" patterns. The tail is usually of one color. The horse may be predominantly white or dark colored. The tobiano color pattern (Figure 3-20) is thought to be due to a dominant gene. The heads of tobianos are marked like those of a solid-colored horse and may have a star, a stripe, a snip, or a blaze. Generally, all four legs are white, at least below the knees and hocks. They usually have the dark color in one or both flanks. The spots are regular and distinct, often coming in oval or round patterns that extend down over the neck and chest, giving the appearance of a shield. A piebald is a black horse with white spots; a skewbald is any color except black with white marks.

FIGURE 3-20   Tobiano Paint horse stallion. (Photo courtesy American Paint Horse Association.)

In 1965, the American Paint Horse Association was formed to register, promote, and keep records on the Paint horse. The association was formed primarily because the American Quarter Horse Association does not register horses with white body markings. All registered Paint horses must be sired by a registered Paint, Quarter Horse, or Thoroughbred.

The Pinto Horse Association of America was formed in 1956 to register Pinto horses of various types. Some of the most popular types are stock, pleasure, saddle, and hunter. Because of the growing interest in ponies, the Pinto Horse Association has developed a Pony Registry for Pintos under 14 hands.

Appaloosa

The Appaloosa color pattern (Figure 3-21) dates back to prehistoric times. Drawings by early humans on the walls of caves in France depicted the pattern. Spotted horses later appeared in Chinese art dating from 500 BC and in Persian art of the fourteenth century.

During the exploration of western America, the Nez Perce were the only Indian tribe to have many Appaloosas. They bred their horses to a distinctive type. The breed nearly disappeared after the Nez Perce War of 1877, because

FIGURE 3-21 Registered Appaloosa with leopard pattern. (Photo courtesy Appaloosa Horse Club.)

the horses belonging to the tribe were sold. The spotted horses derived their name from the Palouse River, which drains the area that was home for the Nez Perce Indians. This area became known as the Palouse Country, and the spotted horses in the area were called Palouse horses. "A Palouse" horse became slurred to "apalouse" and later "apalousie." Finally, the horses were given their present name—Appaloosa.

Formed in 1938 by Claude Thompson, the Appaloosa Horse Club has been very active. In 1948, it held its first national show, which today draws over 2000 Appaloosa horses, making it one of the largest breed shows in the world. A racing program was developed in the early 1960s. Long-distance trail rides are also sponsored and are part of an awards program. Appaloosas are used for western events and cattle work as well as for hunters and jumpers.

In 1949, the stud book was closed to open registration of foundation stock. All Appaloosas are recognized by three color characteristics that separate them from other breeds. Their eyes are encircled with white (white sclera). The skin is mottled, with an irregular spotting of black and white. Hooves are striped vertically black and white. There are a variety of coat color patterns: black with white, containing black spots over loin and hips; black with white over loin and hips; blue or red roan; white with black spots over entire body; black with white spots over entire body; and black with white spots over the loin and hips. The Appaloosa Horse Club registers solid-colored Appaloosas, which are allowed to compete with horses possessing the color patterns.

"NATIVE" HORSES

American Indians caught some of the horses that escaped from the early Spanish explorers and subsequently bred them to form a type or breed of horse. The Appaloosa is a typical example of this horse type and became quite popular; the other types or breeds did not.

Spanish-Barb

The Spanish-Barb Breeders Association (SBBA) was formed in 1972 to perpetuate, through selective breeding and linebreeding, the few strains of true-blooded Spanish-Barbs bred for 50 to about 130 years by several dedicated people (see Figure 3-22). The SBBA foundation sires that represent the three major strains are (1) the Scarface horses, an isolated strain kept intact since the mid-1800s under the Romero family and presently owned by the Weldon McKinleys of New Mexico; (2) the Rawhide horses, representing a strain of Spanish-Barbs selectively bred for nearly half a century by Ilo Belsky of Nebraska; and (3) the "Buckshot" strain of isolated feral ancestry from the

FIGURE 3-22   Spanish-Barb stallion, Castile, owned by Judith L. Smith of Houston, Texas. (Photo courtesy Spanish-Barb Breeders Association.)

early 1920s. Standard height of the Spanish-Barb is 13.3 to 14.1 hands, and weight is 800 to 975 pounds (363 to 442 kg).

Chickasaw

After attacking de Soto's expedition in 1539, the Chickasaw Indians captured many of the horses that escaped. Chickasaw horses were used by the colonial Americans because they were all-around utility animals that were closely coupled and well muscled (Figure 3-23). They were about 13 hands 2 inches in height and were crossed with imported horses to produce some of the ancestors of the modern Quarter Horse. The Chickasaw Horse Association was formed to preserve the early Chickasaw-type horse.

Florida Cracker

Cracker horses descended from the horses brought into Florida by Ponce de León and other Spanish explorers as early as 1521. They were used to work cattle by Cracker people who derived their name from their use of loud cracking whips while working cattle. Over the years, they were used by Indians and

FIGURE 3-23   Chickasaw gelding. (Photo by Harris, courtesy Chickasaw Horse Association.)

early settlers and some escaped to form feral bands. A good percentage of them have a running walk and some have a "single-foot gait." Recently, a breeding band of mares and a stallion have been released on the Paynes Prairie State Preserve where free-roaming ones numbered in the thousands.

Feral Horses in America

Feral horses are those (or their immediate ancestors) that have been domesticated and freed. It is difficult to document how, when, and from where the first horses escaped or were stolen from the Spaniards and spread throughout America (Figure 3-24). They arrived with Columbus on his second voyage in 1493. During the early years of Spanish exploration, horses accompanied each voyage. Breeding farms established in the West Indies supplied the animals for the explorers. Indian tribes in Texas and New Mexico were probably the first to obtain horses, and by 1780 most tribes had them. Although no accurate estimates of feral horse numbers exist for the 1700s and 1800s, there were believed to be 2 to 5 million head. The greatest numbers occurred in the Southwest, especially in west-central Texas. Barbed wire and fencing reduced their numbers and shifted their range. At the end of the 1800s, most wild horse concentrations were found west of the Rocky Mountains. Presently, public land

FIGURE 3-24   The spread of the horse in America. (Adapted from Zarn, Keller, and Collins, 1977a.)

administered by the U.S. Bureau of Land Management and the U.S. Forest Service and located in California, Colorado, Idaho, Montana, Nevada, New Mexico, Utah, and Wyoming contains habitat for feral horses. About 30,000 feral horses are on these lands. Some have been feral for many generations; others have been recently released.

Out of public concern for the plight of feral horses (now referred to as Mustangs), Congress passed two federal laws to protect them. Public Law 86-234 prohibits pollution of water holes for trapping them and the use of aircraft or motorized vehicles to capture or kill them. Public Law 92-195 places feral horses and burros roaming on natural resource lands under the jurisdiction of the secretaries of the interior and of agriculture for protection management and control. It provides a penalty for harassing, capturing, killing, or selling them, as well as for processing them into any commercial product. There is a program under which individuals can adopt a wild horse and can keep it. The Adopt-A-Horse program began in 1973 as a humane way to distribute excess animals. In the mid-1950s, the Spanish Mustang Registry was formed to preserve a lineage of horses selected by Robert Brislawn from feral horses.

DRAFT HORSES

Draft horses were once used as war horses and as beasts of burden, and later for their pulling power. Thus, they were developed to be heavy (1500 to 2000 pounds, or 680 to 907 kg), to have a low center of gravity, to be wide, deep, compact, and strong, and to have large bones. In underdeveloped countries, they are still used for draft purposes when available.

Percheron

The Percheron (Figure 3-25) originated in the ancient province of Le Perche near Normandy, France. Percheron horses in the seventeenth and eighteenth centuries were smaller and more active than the modern Percheron. They were 15 to 16 hands and were for general use. In the nineteenth century, the French government established the Haras de Pin as an official stud stable to improve the breeding industry. The horses at de Pin were selected with great care and the breed was improved. In 1823 or 1824, the stallion Jean-le-Blanc was foaled and became the most famous Percheron sire. All of the modern Percherons trace their bloodlines to Jean-le-Blanc.

The French Percheron Society was established in 1833 to promote the purity of the breed, and the first registry of French Percherons was published in 1885. Because the Percheron was gaining popularity in America as early as 1850, the first U.S. stud book was published in 1876. In 1930, America held more registered Percheron horses than any other breed. The Percheron Horse Association of America is the oldest livestock breed association in the country.

The ideal Percheron has been described as a medium-size, heavy-boned, up-headed horse. Stallions stand 16 to 18 hands and weigh 1800 to 2300 pounds (816 to 1043 kg). Mares are 15 to 17 hands in height and weigh 1600 to 2000 pounds (725 to 907 kg). Larger Percherons may stand 19 hands and weigh 2600 pounds (1181 kg). They are predominantly black or gray in color. The Percheron is more refined and has more balance than some of the other draft breeds. Thus, they are frequently crossed with Thoroughbred horses to produce hunters and jumpers.

FIGURE 3-25 A Percheron stallion.

Suffolk

The Suffolk or Suffolk-Punch horse breed (Figure 3-26) was developed in East Anglia, in the counties of Norwich and Suffolk, England. The first English stud book was published in 1880, although horsepeople in the district had kept private records earlier. Crisp's Horse of Ufford, foaled in 1768, is the foundation stallion of the breed, and practically all Suffolk horses today trace to him in the direct male line. They are recognized as the only draft breed that breeds completely true to color—chestnut. Seven shades of the chestnut color are recognized. The horses are 16.1 hands in height, although some stallions are 17 hands.

The Suffolk was bred exclusively for farm work, not for city dray toil. They were popular during the 1930s, but the American Suffolk Association

FIGURE 3-26   Nortonean Ladyship, 1948, registered Suffolk mare bred by J. T. Thistleton-Smith, Fakenham, Norfolk, England. Imported by Upwey Farms, South Woodstock, Vermont, and owned by Mr. and Mrs. Lloyd B. Wescott, Clinton, New Jersey. (Courtesy American Suffolk Horse Association.)

ceased to function in the 1950s. However, in the early 1960s, when the draft horse made a recovery for show ring and pulling contest purposes, the association was revitalized.

Clydesdale

The native home of the Clydesdale (Figure 3-27) is southern Scotland, in the county of Lanark. Credit for establishing the breed is given to John Paterson, who imported a Flemish stallion, Locklyoch's Black Horse, dramatically improving the local horses. Not much is known about their development until 1780, when another stallion, Blaze, was imported from Ayrshire. In 1808, Glancer's dam was purchased. Most of the noted Clydesdale sires descended from Glancer. The first imports to North America were to Canada in 1842. It was not until the 1870s that they reached the United States from Canada and Scotland.

FIGURE 3-27   The Budweiser Clydesdale eight-horse hitch. (Courtesy Anheuser-Busch, Inc.)

The stallions weigh 1700 to 2000 pounds (771 to 907 kg) and stand about 16.2 hands. The mares weigh about 200 pounds (90.7 kg) less and are about 1 to 2 inches (25.4 to 50.8 mm) shorter. The horses are noted for the growth of long hair—"feathers"—on the back of the cannons. One problem with the Clydesdale is the difficulty in keeping its legs clean, dry, and free from disease.

The American Clydesdale Horse Association was formed in 1877 and maintains the stud book. Scottish Clydesdales were registered by the Scottish Clydesdale Horse Society, which was organized in 1878. Today, the Clydesdale Breeders Association of America maintains the stud book in America.

Belgian

Belgian draft horses (Figure 3-28) are native to Belgium. For centuries, the greater part of the Roman cavalry consisted of Belgian horses. No particular horses or individuals played a role in the development of the breed; instead, they were a product of their environment. They were improved as a breed after the government breeding stud at Tervueren was established in 1850. They were imported to America in 1866, but not in large numbers until the 1880s.

Belgians became popular because of their size, strength, endurance, and action. They weigh about 2000 pounds (907 kg) and are 16.2 to 17 hands tall. Records have been kept since 1866 by the National Draft Horse Society of Belgium and since 1887 by the American Association of Importers and Breeders of Belgian Draft Horses. In 1937, the name was changed to Belgian Draft Horse Corporation of America.

FIGURE 3-28   Belgian mare, Trixie du Marais. (Photo by Remsberg, courtesy Donald J. Wack.)

Shire

Shire draft horses (Figure 3-29) developed in the lowlands of east-central England. They have been known as the Great Horse, War Horse, Cart Horse, Old English Black Horse, Giant Leicestershire, Strong Horse, and, lastly, Shire horse. The early Shire horse was of mixed German, Flemish, and English origin. Robert Bakewell, father of improved livestock husbandry in general, improved the Shire breed during the mid-1700s. He imported large mares from Holland, crossed them with English stallions, and continued to breed the horses only if they met minimum criteria.

Shires were imported to Canada as artillery horses in 1836 and to the United States in 1853 as draft horses for farming. They did not become popular in America and were criticized for having straight shoulders and pasterns, feathers, and a sluggish temperament. They weigh about 2000 pounds (907 kg) and stand 16.2 to 17 hands.

FIGURE 3-29   Shire stallion, Ladbrook Aristocrat, owned by Fox Valley Draft Horse Farms, was the 1980 champion stallion at the 1980 National Shire Show in England. (Courtesy T. J. Smrt, Fox Valley Draft Horse Farms.)

Early records were maintained by the English Cart Horse Society, formed in 1878, and by the American Shire Association, formed in 1885.

HEAVY HARNESS OR COACH HORSES

There are several types of heavy harness horses: Hackney, French Coach, German Coach, Cleveland Bay, Yorkshire, Russian Orloff, and American Carriage Horse. They were primarily used to pull coaches. However, the Cleveland Bay (Figure 3-30) was used as a general utility horse, and the Hackney was used for park driving. Hackneys were first imported to the United States in 1879, and in 1891, the American Hackney Horse Society was formed.

FIGURE 3-30   Choc Dorton Yeoman, Cleveland Bay stallion imported to America from England in 1975. (Courtesy Cleveland Bay Horse Society of America.)

PONY BREEDS

Welsh or Welsh Mountain Pony

The original home of the Welsh pony (Figure 3-31) was in the rugged hill country of Wales. The severe winters required the development of sound, hardy, self-reliant ponies. They resemble a small Arabian in that they have fine features. Welsh ponies have been used to pull chariots, work in coal mines, work cattle, and serve as postmen's mounts. The ponies respond well to discipline and thus are ideal for young children.

Welsh ponies were imported to America in the 1880s. George E. Brown of Aurora, Illinois, brought in a large number between 1884 and 1910. Through his efforts and those of John Alexander, the Welsh Pony and Cob Society of America was formed in 1907. In 1946, "Cob" was dropped from the name, but reappeared in 1986. Welsh and English breeders formed their own registry in 1901. In America, their popularity declined during the Depression years but revived in the late 1950s and 1960s. Today, they are popular projects for 4-H, Vo-Ag, and Future Farmer club members. The registry

FIGURE 3-31   Rowfantina, 1991 national champion Welsh mare, owned by Jean Shemilt. (Photo by Bob Heidlage.)

contains ponies not exceeding 12.2 hands under section A, and those that are 12.2 to 14.2 hands under section B. The Welsh ponies of cob type under 13.2 hands are registered under section C and are a stronger counterpart of the Welsh pony. The Welsh Cob is registered under section D and exceeds 13.2 hands with no upper limit.

They are also crossed with other breeds to produce 13- to 14-hand ponies. These half-Welsh ponies can be listed with the registry. Because of the popularity of the crosses, the Cross-Bred Pony Registry was formed in 1959 to record the animals' pedigrees.

Connemara

The Connemaras are the largest of the pony breeds (Figure 3-32), from the west coast of Ireland. These rugged ponies developed in a harsh environment. At various times during their early history, Spanish, Arab, and French horses

FIGURE 3-32   Hideway's Grey—Tifferary, a 3-year-old Connemara gelding. (Courtesy Hideaway Farms.)

were bred to Connemara mares or stallions. In 1606, King James I was given a dark dun Connemara stallion as a gift, which sired other ponies, which he gave to King Philip of Spain.

In 1923, the Connemara Pony Breeders Society was formed in Ireland. By inspection, 9 stallions and 93 mares were admitted to the registry as foundation animals. Connemaras were first imported to America in 1951. By 1956, the interest was sufficient to form the American Connemara Pony Society.

Connemaras have been bred for utility. They are gentle and have good dispositions so they are desirable mounts for children. There have been several outstanding Connemaras. Nugget was one of the great show jumpers and Little Model had a distinguished dressage record.

Pony of the Americas

The Pony of the Americas (POA) is a small horse developed specifically for use by young people and families for better horsemanship, sportsmanship, and family fun (Figure 3-33). The breed was started by Les Boomhower of Mason

FIGURE 3-33   Pony of the Americas being shown in western pleasure class. (Photo by Jeff Kirkbride and courtesy Pony of the Americas Club.)

City, Iowa, as a cross of a Shetland stallion bred to an Appaloosa mare. The first foal was Black Hand No. 1. In 1955, the Pony of the Americas Club was formed.

POA horses must be 11.2 to 14 hands and must meet certain color markings. The horse must have Appaloosa coloring and characteristics and one registered POA parent to be eligible. In effect, the POA is a small horse with the Appaloosa color pattern. The POA blends features of Arabians, Quarter Horses, and Thoroughbreds as well as other breeds into the desired color pattern, size, and conformation.

Shetland

The Shetland pony (Figure 3-34) developed in the Shetland Islands, located 100 miles (161 km) north of Scotland and 350 miles (563 km) from the Arctic Circle. The ponies were living in this harsh environment when Norsemen arrived in the islands in about 1850. The breed is characterized by small size, shaggy winter coat, and conformation. The maximum height is 11.2 hands, but most are about 10 hands. Before refinement through selection in some countries, they had a draft horse conformation, so they were desirable for work in mines.

FIGURE 3-34 Shetland pony. (Courtesy Animals and Karen Tweedy-Holmes.)

They are registered with the American Shetland Pony Club, which was formed in 1888.

Norwegian Fjord

The Norwegian Fjord is Norway's oldest horse breed. The original Fjords migrated to Norway and the Scandinavian peninsula over 4000 years ago and were domesticated about 2000 BC. They have been selectively bred in Norway for over 2000 years. Selected breeding has increased their height to 13 to 14.1 hands. All of them exhibit the primitive or dun color pattern. It is thought that all present-day draft breeds in western Europe are descended in part from the Norwegian Fjord. Today, they are used for many pleasure horse purposes.

Other Ponies

Several other breeds of ponies have resulted from crosses of the main pony breeds and various types of horses. The Americana was started in 1962 by crossing Shetland and Hackney ponies to produce a Saddlebred type of pony. The Welsh Pony and Tennessee Walking Horse were crossed to originate the American Walking Pony in the 1950s. The smaller horses failing to meet minimum height requirements of the Saddlebred, Tennessee Walking Horse, and Quarter Horse are registered with the American Saddlebred Pony, American Walking Pony, and American Quarter Pony Associations, respectively.

MINIATURE HORSES

There are no breeds of miniature horses, as they are a "height breed." They are not dwarfs but small-size ponies and horses (Figure 3-35). The maximum height for registration by the International Miniature Horse Registry is 32 inches (813 cm). Tom Thumb measured 23 inches (58.4 cm), and Cactus measured 26 inches (66.0 cm) in height. They are being bred and shown by a number of breeders and owners. The famous Falabella horses of Argentina were first bred by the Falabella family in 1868. They were primarily selected from Shetland ponies and have developed a reputation for excellent conformation. The smallest miniature was 15 inches (38.1 cm) tall.

FIGURE 3-35   A champion miniature horse.

SPORT HORSE BREEDS

Andalusian

The Andalusian (Figure 3-36) originated in and gained its name from the Spanish province of Andalusia. The lineage of the breed traces to the Iberian horses of Spain and Portugal. The horses originating in Spain are referred to as Andalusians and those from Portugal are known as Lusitano. Both breeds are registered by the International Andalusian and Lusitano Horse Association.

Cave drawings in the Iberian Peninsula dating back 20,000 years depict horses similar to the Andalusian of today. Purity of the breed was maintained by Carthusian monks in the monasteries of Jerez de Frontera, Seville, and Castello. During early development, they were used as cavalry horses and were known as "the premier war horse." With the advent of heavily armored

FIGURE 3-36   Bruno, Andalusian stallion, was 1992 national champion stallion and 1992 three-year-old futurity champion. (Photo courtesy of the breeder and owners, Garrison Ranch, Thousand Oaks, California.)

knights, they were briefly displaced as the horse of choice for cavalries. Following the introduction of firearms, these horses again became the favorite of the new, rapid, and agile mounted armies. Later, they were used by royal courts and by riding academies. They gained a reputation for their accomplishments in dressage and high school riding because of their impulsion, forward motion, and agility. These characteristics led to their role in the development of the Lipizzaner of the Spanish Riding School in Vienna, German Warmbloods, Connemara, Cleveland Bay, and other breeds. In the United States, they compete in dressage, jumping, driving, trail, western pleasure, English pleasure, and parade classes.

They are characterized by their white or gray color (80 percent of breed), docile temperament, and strong build, and they stand 15.2 to 16.2 hands.

American Warmblood

The American Warmblood Registry (AWR) was established in 1981 to encourage the breeding of excellent sport horses. Horses in the AWR do not necessarily represent distinct breeds. The AWR registers European imports and their American offspring. Recognized for their athleticism and easygoing temperament, they have gained a reputation as a consistent performer in all sports competition except racing.

For quality control, selective breeding is practiced and AWR conducts annual inspections for grading and branding the horses it registers. Inspection of foals and young stock involves four stages: assessment of conformation; walk in hand; trot and canter at liberty; and an overall assessment and critique. Stallion inspection is to assess the horse as a potential breeding animal. They are inspected during 6 stages: preliminary walk and trot up and conformation; walk and trot on triangle and second conformation; trot and canter at liberty; free jumping; display under saddle; and final critique. Colts are tested as 2-year-olds and must return for a second inspection when they are 5 years of age. Mares may be inspected but inspection is not mandatory.

Holsteiner

The Holsteiner was developed in Germany in the area of Schleswig-Holstein and is one of the older horse breeds in the world. Originally, they were war horses carrying knights in armor. By interbreeding with Thoroughbreds, they were refined to their current status as very successful sport horses used for jumping, dressage, and driving.

The American Holsteiner Horse Association was formed in cooperation with Verband der Zuechter des Holsteiner Perfedes, the German association, and has the exclusive right to approve horses for breeding purposes and to maintain the breeding registry. A committee consisting of members of the association analyzes each horse presented for breeding purposes and determines acceptability. A point system is used to determine qualifications as a mare or stallion for breeding purposes. The criteria cover seven areas: type, top line, depth of body, front legs, hind legs, correctness of gait, and brilliance and impulsion. Each area of a mare is judged on a 9-point scale, with a maximum of 72 points. Qualifications for registry require a minimum of 39 points. A mare qualifying with 46+ points is classified as a "Premium Mare." A 10-point scale is used for stallions, with a minimum score of 47 points for registration. In addition, a stallion breeding awards program was established in 1992.

Trakehner

The Trakehner (Figure 3-37) was developed in the German province of East Prussia. Its name is derived from the main state stud (Royal Stud) at Trakehnen, which was founded by Friedrick Wilhelm I in 1732. The purpose of the Royal Stud was to breed light cavalry horses. During the eighteenth and nineteenth centuries, a significant infusion of Arabian and Thoroughbred bloodlines occurred. The stud at Trakehnen was evacuated five times during wars, the last evacuation in 1944. Fewer than 1000 horses survived to escape to the Baltic Sea, and were scattered over West Germany. Thus, the Trakehner

FIGURE 3-37   Trakhener stallion, Gaillard, being shown in dressage at the Intermediate 1 level. (Photo courtesy of J. L. Thornton, owner.)

began to be bred in West Germany. The Poles retained a large number of excellent Trakehners and continued a breeding program. The Soviet Union founded a breeding program with some of the horses that reached Mecklenberg following the evacuation, and from other studs. Always a riding horse, the Trakehner's primary use is for dressage, jumping, hunting, and 3-day eventing.

In 1974, the American Trakehner Association was formed to record, promote, and preserve the animal. The Official Registry Book has several divisions: full-Trakehner, Anglo-, Arab-, and part-Trakehner. Mares and stallions are also eligible to be registered in the Official Stud Book when they meet certain qualifications, such as minimum age (2 years for stallions and in the year in which they turn 3 for mares), minimum recommended height of 15.1 (mares) or 15.3 mandatory minimum (stallions) hands, and satisfactory appraisal, which includes pedigree, conformation, movement, gaits, temperament, and conformation to type. Stallions approved for breeding must pass a performance test by age 6 or within 2 years of their initial inspection, whichever is later. Stallions who fail to complete the performance test have their breeding approval withdrawn.

Hanoverian

The Hanoverian Horse originated in the Kingdom of Hanover, currently known as Lower Saxony, in Germany. Good war horses were produced in the area over 400 years ago. During the early period of horse breeding, no records were kept. Then in 1735, King George II of Great Britain established a stable of high quality stallions in Celle to improve the quality of horses, and records were kept of the breedings. However, the majority of foals raised in the area still resulted from privately owned stallions. Thus, to enhance the rate of improvement, a breeding license was required after 1844 and stallions had to pass a physical examination. In 1894, stallions were also required to have a well-established proven pedigree.

In 1867, horse breeders established the Society for the Improvement of the Hanoverian Horse, later merged into the Association of Hanoverian Warmblood Breeders, which controls the breed today.

Starting in 1928, all stallions that passed the required physical inspection were to undergo a training period, followed by a performance test, prior to issuance of a breeding license by the state. At the same time, the association started classifying mares as to their quality.

The American Hanoverian Society was founded in 1978 to adhere to highly selective breeding standards and to work closely with the German association. Mares must excel in type, conformation, temperament, and way of going to be listed in the stud book. "Elite Mares" must also pass a performance test demonstrating their qualities under saddle, cross country, and over jumps. These mares are entered into the Main Stud Book. Licensed stallions must also pass a performance test, which includes dressage, cross country, and jumping phases.

DONKEYS, ASSES, AND MULES (EQUUS ASINUS)

Donkeys

Donkeys and burros (feral donkeys) are used all over the world for a variety of tasks. Male donkeys are referred to as jacks, and a female donkey is called a jenny or jennet. In the United States, donkeys have enjoyed an increase in popularity and are used for riding, showing, driving, and packing, as well as for work. There are three American Donkey breeds registered with the American Donkey and Mule Association. The Standard Donkey is 36 to 48 inches tall; Large Standard, 48 to 56 inches; and Mammoth Jack stock (Figure 3-38) are 54+ inches for jennets and 56+ inches for jacks. They have a variety of coat colors, including spots. The American Council of Spotted Asses registers those with spots or "pinto" coat colors. One of their most recognizable characteristics are the large, long ears set on a relatively large head. Compared with those of horses, their hooves are smaller and the mane and tail have less hair.

FIGURE 3-38   Night Train, a Mammoth Jack. (Photo courtesy James and Christine Whitmire, owners.)

Miniature donkeys (Figure 3-39) are native to the Mediterranean islands of Sicily and Sardinia. Their average height is 32 to 34 inches at the withers, and they weigh 200 to 350 pounds. Maximum height for registration is 36 inches. An extra-small miniature is about 28 inches. Most miniature donkeys are gray-dun with a characteristic dark stripe down the back and across the withers. They can be registered with the National Miniature Donkey Association and with the Miniature Donkey Registry of the United States.

Mules

The mule (Figure 3-40) is a hybrid from the mating of a jack and a mare, whereas the hinny is a hybrid from the mating of a stallion to a jennet. Mules and hinnies are sterile. Male mules are referred to as horse or john mules, and female mules are known as mare or molly mules. The same terminology is used for hinnies.

FIGURE 3-39   Miniature donkeys owned by Judy Campbell.

FIGURE 3-40   Maynard's Miss Sheba, a mule that has been world champion. (Photo courtesy owners, Lloyd and Sarah Hawley.)

Mules are popular for many reasons and are used for many purposes throughout the world. Generally, they serve as draft animals, but in the United States they are used for recreational purposes—riding, driving, packing, and showing. Standard jacks are used to produce saddle mules and Mammoth Jacks are crossed with draft mares to produce draft mules.

Part Two
EXERCISING OWNERSHIP RESPONSIBILITIES

CHAPTER 4

Providing Physical Facilities

Stable management is among the important activities of a good horseperson. The building and facilities and their arrangement very much affect management efficiency. Carefully planned, well-designed facilities make horse care easier and add to the personal satisfaction and enjoyment of owning horses. In planning or inquiring about a facility for horses, you should (1) know what is needed, (2) know how to get it, and (3) keep within your budget.

Today most Americans live in or near large cities. Because of this urban background or, more exactly, the lack of a rural background, many people who buy a horse for the first time lack experience in handling and caring for large animals. Many new horse owners have virtually no conception of what are appropriate facilities for their situation or whether, in fact, they should have any facilities at all. Consequently, to make sure that they are at least meeting the minimum standards for horse housing, they may overbuild their facilities or construct poorly conceived, inadequately designed, or inappropriately located buildings.

First, the new owner must not forget the psychology of the horse. It loves to eat everything available, including wood and other types of material, and it likes to dig by pawing. Always keep in mind this fondness for digging, pawing, and eating wood when you think of constructing a facility for a horse.

PLANNING

The most critical step in establishing a good horse operation is the planning that precedes land acquisition and building construction. Planning is just as important for remodeling a facility as for buying something that someone else has built. If you plan to remodel, be sure to meet two criteria: (1) the remodeled facility should be at least as good as a new one, and (2) it should not cost more than a new building.

During the planning process, professionals can give advice and assist in evaluating specific needs and developing a specific plan. Professionals include the local county Extension Service agent, state Extension Service horse specialist, members of zoning boards, building inspectors, farm credit officers, accountants, insurance agents, certified Professional Animal Scientists, and builders and contractors. In addition, standardized plans and blueprints are available from many sources.

Identifying Needs

The first step in the planning is determining the number and makeup of the horse or horses to be kept. Make a very specific list showing the number of each kind or type of animal and how each one will be handled, managed, and housed. The list may be quite short (one or two riding horses) or quite extensive (a group including stallions, brood mares, and young stock such as are found on a breeding farm). It is extremely important to plan for expansion and future changes in the herd. A long-range plan allows better planning for facilities. Therefore, before establishing a new facility, set the ultimate goals of the entire operation and do not forget about future expansion and needs. Identifying these needs is very critical, and you must be able to tell the architect or builder what the horses need. Mistakes should be made on paper, not in the building.

Once the type of operation, the number of animals, and the future expansion of the herd have been determined, the next step is to decide on the type of facility needed to manage these horses. You must figure out the total amount of barn space required under a roof to stable and care for the animals. Consider basic space needs for stalls, traffic lanes, and storage of feed, tack, and equipment. Include special features such as wash racks, trailer storage, breeding area, show stable for selling horses, riding arena, rest space, and other areas needed under the same roof.

Also figure out the amount of space required under a roof for separate but associated buildings; for example, open shelters, riding arenas, sales barn, training barn, equipment storage, exercise area, hay and feed storage, office and lounge, and other areas, including living quarters if needed. You must decide whether certain areas should be placed under a roof or not. To make such decisions, consider the local climate, the location relative to homes, roads, and so on, and the requirements for the operation. For example, in a very cold, damp climate, horse and owner need an enclosed, perhaps even heated, grooming area. In a warm southern climate, a more open arrangement may be adequate. Having sufficient storage space enables the purchase of feed in bulk when prices are low.

Determine the amount of space you need for open and fenced areas, such as lanes and roads, outside lots and corrals, exercise areas, parking space for cars and trailers, other vehicles, and equipment, special events, and distance between buildings for a pleasing appearance, fire protection, and, most importantly, future expansion. If horses are to be boarded, you might want an area for a loading ramp. If horses are seldom trucked to or from the farm, the ramp may be unnecessary. A common mistake is lack of space to turn around trucks and trailers.

Carefully compare alternate housing arrangements and management methods and select those most suited to the situation. You may get ideas on horse facilities from publications, tours, visits to existing layouts, experienced horse owners, professional managers, farm advisers, and so on.

In your planning, investigate available methods for inoffensive manure storage and disposal. Assess fire protection and modify your plans accordingly, adding protection and fire controls if necessary. It is also important to find out what building codes, zoning regulations, and other local restrictions may affect development, construction, or use of the facilities. Finally, review your budget allocation, placing priorities on the necessities, conveniences, overall desires, and frills—in that order.

Then determine the size needed for the complete layout. Exclude family housing, large pastures, and crop or other land not directly associated with the stabling and facilities complex. Determine the size of the total layout based on the land area covered by the necessary buildings and the directly related open and fenced areas. This provides the basis for establishing how much land to buy or to make sure is available within a complex that is already built.

CODES AND REGULATIONS

The next step in selecting the area on which to build is to determine what effects various regulations and restrictions may have on the proposed stable. Depending on where you live, society places certain limitations on ownership, development, and use of property. This step is just as important whether you own the land or are considering it for purchase.

There are three types of codes and regulations. Generally speaking, building codes set construction standards, zoning prohibits the use of property for specific purposes, and sanitary or environmental regulations have to do with public health, related pollution, and pest control. Other restrictions may also limit the use of the property, including deed restrictions, easement, and covenants between property owners. Pay particular attention to the codes and regulations; it may save grief in the long run.

SITE SELECTION

Selecting a site for construction of a stable or a combination stable and riding arena involves some very elementary common sense. The most level site possible should be used for the barn or stable. The building site should be well drained, accessible, and have a slope of about 5 feet per 100 feet (1.5 m per 30.4 m) away from the building in all directions to assure good surface drainage. Topography particularly affects the cost of site development, and site preparation should be completed before building construction begins. Sites on steep slopes or rocky terrain and sites requiring considerable landfill are costly to develop and may make compromises necessary. Make sure that the property is not in a flood plain or other areas where high water could cause problems.

The first thing to consider is water supply. An adequate all-year water supply of the proper quality must be available at the site, either from a public water system or from convenient groundwater and surface water developments. Any needed well should be drilled before any other construction begins. Also keep in mind the distance water lines must go and the electrical supply available.

If at all possible, construct facilities away from distracting noise, offensive odors, and heavy traffic. Existing nuisances may affect use and enjoyment of the site, and nuisances that horses and horsepeople create may affect neighbors.

In larger operations, wind breaks may be important. Consider the natural protection from the elements provided by wooded areas, knolls, hills, and ravines.

Existing buildings may be a determining factor in site selection but only if their size, location, physical condition, and inside arrangement fit into the overall plan for horse facilities. The proximity of the barn in relation to residences and management of labor and the evaluation of the site in relation to ultimate use of the barn (private use, commercial stable, breeding operation, and so on) are important.

Esthetics are important, too. Appearance, personal taste, pride of ownership, and available funds may affect site selection. However, the horse-housing facilities should not overshadow the residence.

Building layout will probably be a deciding factor in selecting the site, and the site chosen may affect both layout and building style.

The size of the operation also affects site selection. In addition to room for the planned buildings, the site should provide space for other planned activities and areas. It should also provide for future building and paddock expansion; good traffic patterns; safe and convenient handling of animals, vehicles, equipment, and materials; and snow removal, if necessary. Farm-owned horses should be kept isolated from transient horses.

Horse facilities definitely need a good road to provide access in all kinds of weather. You must be able to get to the animals during inclement weather, and you may need to haul and/or feed horses in or out of the facility at such times.

The physical and social aspects of manure disposal can be a major problem, so be sure to follow local regulations on manure handling. It is essential to clean stalls, paddocks, and exercise areas of horses kept in confinement. Generally, spreading the manure and bedding on crop land is most satisfactory. If the location does not include fields where manure can be spread 365 days a year, you will need a manure storage area. Keep all manure storage and disposal areas well removed from streams or land that slopes directly into streams, and never spread manure on frozen land. Environmental regulations are usually strictly enforced.

In some areas, location of feed sources is important. Even saving $1 per ton (907 kg) of feed on hauling costs can make quite a difference over the years.

In most cases, it is less expensive to grade and prepare a site that satisfies a majority of factors than it is to pick a site that is level but doesn't meet any other factors. If the site must be graded, all the top soil should be removed. The construction pad should be higher than the surrounding areas outside the building for good drainage. The base or pad must be well compacted by the grading machine or the site must be graded well in advance of actual construction to allow rain to compact the area. Also, rain indicates low areas on the site that can be filled before construction begins.

BARNS

The function of a horse barn is to protect horses from temperature extremes and injury, keep them dry, and eliminate drafts. It should be easy for the operator to work in. Adequate barn space should be provided for the well-being of the animals and the convenience and safety of the people caring for them. There must be a sufficient supply of fresh air in both winter and summer. A barn should have sufficient light and be free from odors.

Functional Design

First decide on the functions that the proposed building should satisfy. Then choose a design that provides these functions. A common error is selecting a building that includes features that are not really needed. This drastically increases the cost of the building. For example, a covered exercise area costs nearly as much to erect as a building filled with stalls. If a training program requires the use of the exercise area, choose a design incorporating that feature. But if an exercise area is not needed, do not build one.

Barn styles are determined by the shape of the roof. The three shapes most widely used are the shed, gabled, and offset gabled (Figure 4-1). The once-popular gambrel, gothic, and monitor roofs, very much in evidence on old

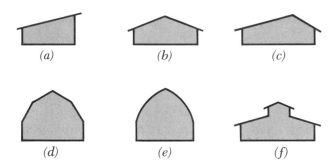

FIGURE 4-1   Barn styles: *(a)* shed; *(b)* gable; *(c)* offset gable; *(d)* gambrel; *(e)* gothic; *(f)* monitor. (Adapted from Blickle and others, 1971.)

barns, are used only occasionally on new barns. The trend is now toward one-floor structures with clear-spanned or post-beamed roofs (Figure 4-2). A one-floor structure eliminates or holds to a minimum costly overhead storage. One floor also permits lighter, less costly construction. However, it may be more economical to use overhead storage if ground space is at a premium. Clear-spanned roofs also add flexibility to buildings by making them more adaptable to other uses. The style you choose must first be utilitarian; esthetics are secondary.

Layout

There are many horse barn layouts. Basic designs incorporate one, two, three, or four rows of stalls (Figure 4-3). Most barns for housing one or two horses are of the one-row, porch-type construction. For more horses, stalls can be arranged around the sides of a large building, leaving an area in the center for riding or exercise (Figure 4-4). If the barn is smaller, a service alley may divide two rows of stalls. A large barn may have two such alleys (Figure 4-5). Alternately, the stalls can be grouped in the center with the exercise area around the outside (Figure 4-6), which is a popular racetrack layout. Simple facilities are shown in Figure 4-7. Choose the layout that will work best for your situation. The best way to do this is to study many of the available plans, visit other farms, and discuss the situation with people involved with similar requirements. Be critical about the layout and the building plans, because there are marked differences in the amount of floor space used to house horses. An eight-horse barn may be 10 × 92 feet (3.05 × 28 m). In this case, almost all of the floor space is used for housing. Another plan using a 50- × 24-foot (15.24- × 73.1-m) barn uses 80 percent of the area to house horses. Other plans use only a small percentage of space for horse housing.

Follow certain design tips when preparing or examining a barn layout. You need plenty of head room for the horse and rider if any riding is to be

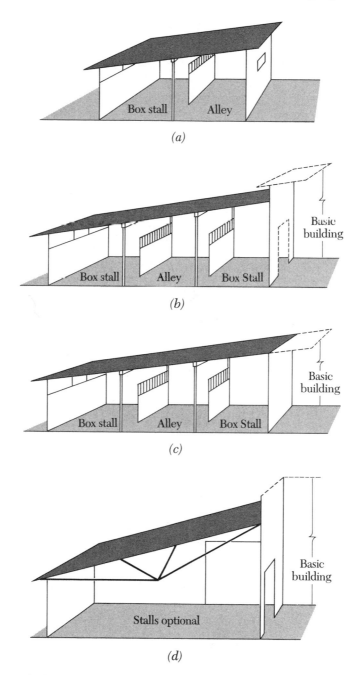

FIGURE 4-2   Shed roof options: *(a)* free-standing building (post and beam); *(b)* attached shed (post and beam); *(c)* roof extension (post and beam); *(d)* one-slope truss (clear span). (Adapted from Blickle and others, 1971.)

FIGURE 4-3 Gable roof options: *(a)* one row of stalls serviced from covered way (post—beam—wall); *(b)* one row of stalls serviced from enclosed alley (clear-span truss); *(c)* two rows of stalls serviced from outside (clear-span truss); *(d)* two rows of stalls serviced from center alley (clear-span truss); *(e)* two rows of stalls serviced from center alley (post and beam); *(f)* two rows of stalls serviced from center alley, mow over stalls (post and beam); *(g)* four rows of box stalls serviced from two alleys, two center rows of stalls back to back with mow above (post and beam). (Adapted from Blickle and others, 1971.)

FIGURE 4-4 Barn layout for two rows of stalls and center alley for inside service. (Adapted from Blickle and others, 1971.)

done in the area. Eight feet (2.4 m) of head room is the minimal acceptable height for an average horse. For a horse and rider, at least 12 feet (3.66 m) are needed. Ceiling height in stalls should be no less than 9 feet (2.7 m). Riding arena ceilings should be at least 14 feet (4.3 m) high. If jumping events or training are to be held in the arena, the ceiling should be at least 18 feet (5.5 m) above the ground.

The foundation is important. Regardless of the type of construction, whether wood, block, or steel, design an adequate foundation, with the bottom below the frost line. Poles should be sunk at least 3 feet (0.9 m) in the ground for stable areas, with a concrete pad below the poles. For arenas and

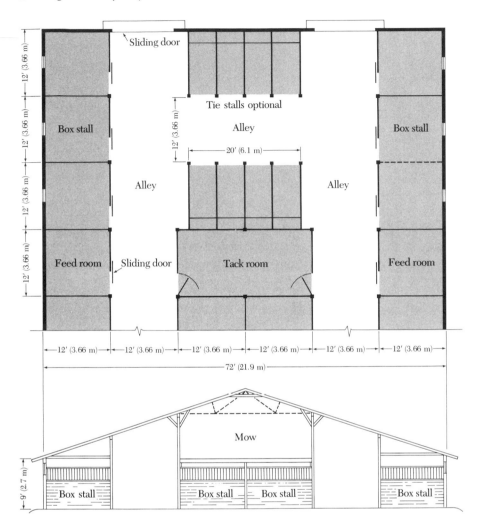

FIGURE 4-5   Barn layout for four rows of stalls and two alleys for inside service. (Adapted from Blickle and others, 1971.)

other large buildings, poles should be 4 feet (1.2 m) in the ground, with a concrete pad below. Moreover, one-quarter of the pole should be in the ground. For pole construction, the foundation of the building should consist of treated tongue-and-groove boards around the outer base of the building. These boards should be buried at least 2 inches (5 cm) below the surface of the building pad. Such considerations are particularly important for keeping the barn level so that the doors will work without difficulty and the walls do not crack.

FIGURE 4-6 Barn layout for two rows of stalls and two alleys for outside service. (Adapted from Blickle and others, 1971.)

Barn Exterior

The exterior walls can be of wood, block, steel, or aluminum. There are several points to remember in selecting the type of material. First of all, it should be durable—something that a horse cannot kick through or cannot eat through. Consider appearance and adaptability to changes in operation that require modifying walls for such things as doors and windows. Outside wooden walls of 4- × 8-foot (1.2- × 2.4-m) plywood sheets or tongue-and-groove material can be stained or painted for an excellent appearance. When aluminum expands and contracts with changing temperatures, it crackles. The

FIGURE 4-7   Barn layout to keep two horses, outside service: *(a)* basic facility; *(b)* one row of stalls, covered way. (Adapted from Blickle and others, 1971.)

noise bothers some horses and some people. Also, when the wind blows, aluminum can make an annoying noise.

The number, size, and types of windows depend on the operation and the owner's desires. If a window is to be opened so that the horse can hang its head outside, it must be carefully designed. Horses will chew the outside of the building. Also, wood sashes are not particularly good for horse barns. They are extremely difficult to protect from breakage by the horse and from chewing. However, a wood sash may be more attractive, depending on the type of exterior walls. Aluminum sliding windows are basically maintenance free, require no painting, and provide no surface that the animal can chew on. They are easy to protect from horses with bars, metal screens, or pipe. Horses cannot put their heads out through these windows. However, sliding windows allow only half the ventilating area, for the size of the glass, that other windows do.

There are at least four types of roofing: aluminum, metal, asphalt shingles, or wood shakes. All four are durable if properly installed. However, consider some minor characteristics when selecting the roof material. Aluminum and metal roofs may leak around the fasteners if they are not properly tightened. Many people now use screws rather than nails to hold aluminum and metal roof material to the frame. Then to expand facilities, the screws can be taken out and the sheets of aluminum or metal removed without damage. Also, sky-lights are usually easier to install on aluminum or metal roofs. Skylights of any kind should be put in the aisle, not above the stalls, because the light panels transmit heat. Skylights may also cause condensation problems, dark areas in arenas, and excess heat buildup in summer. However, they do cut down on the amount of electricity required to light the barn. With a shingle roof, conden-sation is not a problem. And the shingle roof system is warmer even without insulation.

Any door over 4 feet (1.2 m) wide should slide instead of hinge to elimi-nate warping and sticking. Doors should be sturdy and durable. They will be used often and should be very easy to handle. A Dutch door should have a metal covering over the top of the lower section to prevent chewing. Plan, con-struct, and use doors in such a way that they are not potentially dangerous to horses and people. And doors should be convenient. For example, double-aisle doors may be more convenient than a large single door, especially when chil-dren are to be opening them. One large door may be too heavy for a child to slide. If a horse is to be ridden through the door into the building, the door should be at least 12 feet (3.66 m) wide. Doors to accommodate trucks or other large equipment should be at least 16 feet (4.88 m) wide.

Barn Interior

The primary purpose of the barn is to modify the environment for the horse. Therefore, it should allow control of temperature, humidity, odors, light, ve-locity of air, and the amount of fresh air available.

Temperature and humidity are extremely important. A major problem in horse housing is moisture or condensation, which can be controlled in a prop-erly constructed facility. Horses, like other animals, produce heat and moisture. The moisture (2 gallons, or 7.6 liters, per horse daily) must be removed from the stable to prevent condensation and buildup of odors. Humid conditions contribute to respiratory diseases and cause odors to develop. Condensation on wood can accelerate the aging process by providing a good environment for growth of fungus and molds, which can cause wood to deteriorate rapidly.

Ventilation removes the moisture and odors and controls the temperature. It is important to install a ventilation system for the stable when the building is being constructed. This can be done by providing, in addition to doors, eave openings, ridge ventilators, and adjustable windows or wall panels in both uninsulated and insulated buildings used for cool housing. Ventilation fans, fresh air inlets, adjustable windows or wall panels, and supplemental heat can be installed in insulated buildings that are used for warm housing. As a rule, horse owners in mild or moderate climates can obtain adequate housing for their animals with uninsulated buildings; however, wood or masonry side walls and tight sheeting under the roof are desirable for some insulation.

If you must insulate a barn, make sure that water does not condense readily on the insulated surface (normally it does not). The roof should always be insulated, whereas insulation in side walls is desirable but not essential. Minimum insulation is equivalent to about $3\frac{1}{2}$ inches (8.89 cm) of fiberglass batts. Place a vapor barrier on the warm side to prevent or slow down passage of water vapor through the walls and ceilings. It must be installed between the insulation and the inside wall or ceiling lining. Many materials can be used as a vapor barrier; the most common is 4-mil polyethylene plastic.

Ventilating open-front buildings is rather simple. However, there must be good air movement during cold weather to prevent moisture from condensing on the underside of the roof and in hot weather to keep the inside temperature acceptable. Locate the building on a well-drained site with the open side away from prevailing winter winds. If drafts and snow blow-in are problems, close the front wall at each end and adjacent to solid partitions. Use spaced-board wind breaks at the end of the building. Install cross partitions from floor to roof in long, open sheds if indoor drafts continue to be a problem.

The box stall is the most important component of the barn, and the first consideration is size. A 10- × 10-foot (3.05- × 3.05-m) stall is the minimum, a 10- × 12-foot (3.05- × 3.66-m) area is more desirable, and a 12- × 12-foot (3.66- × 3.66- m) area is most desirable. Foaling stalls should be larger— 12 × 14 feet (3.66 × 4.27 m). Warmblood breeds and stallion stalls should also be 12 × 12 feet or 14 × 14 feet (4.27 × 4.27 m). Ponies need an 8- × 8-foot (2.4- × 2.4-m) stall. The stalls must be sturdy and free from sharp, projecting objects. Stall lining should be solid for 4 to 7 feet (1.22 to 2.13 m) above the ground. Bars ($2\frac{1}{4}$ inches, or 5.7 cm, between bars), heavy, woven wires, or expanded metal can be used above that point. Pressure-treated lumber is more durable than other kinds of lumber. Boards should be placed on posts so that the posts take the pressure, not the nails. Locate the feeders, waterers, and other stall equipment where the animal cannot injure itself (Figure 4-8). Most people prefer to put the water trough in one corner of the stall. The hay manger and feed box should be located across the front wall so that the grain or hay can be added without actually going into the stall.

The stalls should be lined with oak or some other durable material. The lining should be installed so that surfaces available for chewing are eliminated as much as possible. When installing linings, try to eliminate dead spaces between walls where rodents can nest.

The minimum ceiling height in stalls should be 9 feet (2.7 m). The stall floor is a major concern. In many instances, the existing soil can be used if it is acceptable. Clay can be added to stalls after construction. Concrete can be used if desired, but a drainage system should be built into each stall, and you will need to use deep bedding. Asphalt flooring has become quite popular and is very useful. The asphalt should be very porous; that is, the rocks used in the asphalt should be Nos. 1 and 2 grade. Resilient mats can be used to cover the stall floor. A specially compounded synthetic resinous material has been

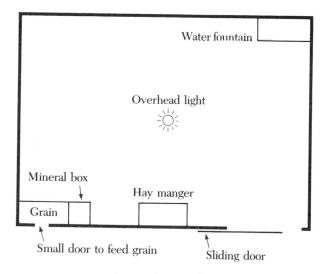

FIGURE 4-8   Stall layout.

developed that, when applied over an asphalt, concrete, or wood base, results in a smooth or textured, resilient, uniform, durable surface for use in stalls and wash racks. Rubber mats can also be used over a variety of floor surfaces to prevent pawing holes in dirt floors, provide a cushion over concrete or asphalt floors, and decrease the amount of bedding required.

Stall doors are one of the most important stall features to consider because they are used constantly and it is easy for them to get sticky and difficult to open. They should be at least 4 feet (1.22 m) wide. Sliding doors are more desirable because they are easy to use and do not pose any danger to horses or people. Doors that swing into the aisle can be dangerous to people, and those that swing inward can injure horses. Sliding doors can be solid or can have an opening on the upper section. The latch should require at least two types of movement to open. Moreover, it should be easy for the manager to look down the alley way and to check that all the stall doors are latched. The latches should be simple enough so that they do not bind and do not require frequent adjustment.

Aisle floors of asphalt or concrete are less dusty than dirt, but the surface should be coarse, not smooth. Make sure the surface is rough. If it is concrete, it should have a rough broom finish. The asphalt should be made with Nos. 1 and 2 grade stones. Rubber mats and rubber paving bricks are excellent and indoor–outdoor carpets have been used successfully on alley ways and grooming areas. Do not lay water lines under asphalt or concrete. They should be laid outside the building and then brought individually into each stall.

The most important aspect of the tack room is security. Installation of an automated security system utilizing motion, window and door open, and/or glass breaking detectors may prevent theft. Moreover, its size should fit the size of the stable. If possible, place the tack room between two stalls. Then small observation windows can be put in the walls adjacent to the stalls. These can be very useful when foaling mares, and so forth. The most common floor material in the tack room is concrete. The walls should be insulated if heat or air conditioning is to be installed. In damp areas, heat is desirable to keep the tack dry.

Grooming and washing areas depend on the type of facility and its primary function (Figure 4-9). They can consist of a single slab placed on the outside of a building where the water runs off, or they can be very elaborate. Elaborate indoor wash areas usually have hot and cold water, and also radiant heat lamps for drying purposes.

Barn lighting is extremely important. Lights should be shielded to prevent horses from breaking them. They should be evenly distributed in the alley way or aisle and in the riding arenas. If not, the horse will spook and try to jump the shadows. Fluorescent lights are cheaper because they produce $2\frac{1}{2}$ times the amount of light per watt of electricity. It is wise to be able to turn outside lights on and off from the house. Make sure there are sufficient outlets for clippers and other appliances. All electrical wire should be placed in conduits to protect it from rats and horses.

The feed room should be large enough to accommodate the size of the barn, especially if hay storage is not provided elsewhere in the building. The floor should be concrete. The feed bin should be rodent proof; in fact, the whole feed room can be made rodent proof by putting rat-proof wire mesh ($\frac{1}{4}$-inch $\times$ $\frac{1}{4}$-inch, or 6.4 mm, hardware cloth) behind all of the ceilings, floors, and walls. Organize the room so that it is easy to clean. This will also minimize the potential for rodent infestation. The door to the feed room should be large enough to allow feed bags, hay bales, and so on to be carried in. It should also be conveniently located so that it is easy to get the feed from the entrance

FIGURE 4-9   Wash rack. (Photo by W. Evans.)

to the feed room. In some operations, a door to the outside may be desirable for feed deliveries. If there are a large number of horses, you may want to have a bulk bin, which saves labor. It is much more convenient to store the hay on ground level than to put it into an overhead loft. If there is an overhead loft, some type of mechanized system is desirable to get the hay into it. Normally, it is cheaper to expand first-floor facilities than to build an overhead loft strong enough to support hay storage. One ton (907 kg) of hay requires 200 cubic feet (20.04 m^3) of space. The following formula determines the space needed to store 125-pound (56.7-kg) hay bales:

$$\frac{\text{Number of horses} \times \text{lb/day} \times 365 \times 200}{2,000} = \text{cubic feet required}$$

$$\frac{\text{Number of horses} \times \text{kg/day} \times 365 \text{ days}}{907} = \text{cubic meters required}$$

The space should hold hay for one year.

Each horse drinks 8 to 12 gallons of water per day (30.3 to 45.4 liters); therefore, the system must supply sufficient water for all the animals. It must also supply water for other necessary functions—wash rack, lawn, fire sprinkler system, and so on. Water should not move from one water fountain or trough to the next, because such systems spread diseases very rapidly. Decide whether to use automatic or individual waterers. This is a labor consideration. Decreasing labor requirements as much as possible means more free time to enjoy the horses. In commercial establishments, it also means money savings. Automatic water fountains should be easy to clean, have protected floats, and be designed so a horse cannot get its teeth stuck in them. They should have shut-off valves for emergency use.

Portable Barns and Equipment

Many portable barns and corrals are available, some inexpensive, others not. They offer advantages such as fast construction, low maintenance, and movability. You can buy single stalls and shelters or barns with many stalls, plus portable round corrals for training young horses, and a variety of other equipment.

FENCES

Many types of fencing are available to the horse owner, ranging from the standard post and rail and mesh wire to "high-tech" products. It is estimated that more than 50 percent of equine injuries are fence related. Fence construction and maintenance are expensive and time consuming, so it is important to consider fencing alternatives carefully.

Wood is the favorite material of many horse owners. When pressure-treated with copper-chrome arsenate preservative, it resists decay and termites. In diamond mesh fencing, heavy twisted horizontal cables on $4\frac{1}{8}$-inch centers with vertical wires are wrapped around each horizontal cable at $2\frac{1}{4}$-inch intervals to form a triangular or diamond pattern. No Climb horse fence is a rectangular shaped mesh. Both products aid in keeping out small animals, prevent feet and legs from getting caught in the fence, and discourage climbing by horse or person; they can be attached to any type of post. Sight boards are recommended as middle and top rails so horses can see the fence. High-tensile wire covered with a polymer to form a 5-inch band offers flexibility and low maintenance. Lumber permanently encased in a polyethylene sheath to prevent splintering, warping, termite damage, and a need for paint is produced in a variety of colors. Posts and boards can be sealed on both ends to protect them from moisture and insects. The boards can be sawed and nailed or screwed to posts. Electric power fencing is available as a tape made of polypropylene or polyethylene with tiny wires in it that conduct electricity. It is available in bright colors that horses can see. It is used to keep horses away from another fence or to define a temporary enclosure within a completely, permanently fenced area; it is not used for permanent fencing unless it is part of another fencing system. Many types of polyvinylchloride (PVC) fencing are available. They are tough, will not rot, and do not need painting.

Different manufacturers have incorporated specific design features the purchaser should be aware of. Rubber nylon fencing is composed of nylon reinforcement running through a cured rubber to form a band that does not expand or contract with temperature extremes. A woven polygrid fence is made in such a way that the joints of the junctions creating the grid do not fail under stress and will not cut a horse that runs into it; it has a high resiliency.

Five or six strands of polymer filament that is of high density and low expandibility form an effective horse fence. Galvanized steel fencing comes in long coils and requires special tools to form it into a board pattern. Metal rail fence is tubular and can be easily installed.

Chain-link fences are difficult to maintain because they are stretched out of shape by horses kicking and rubbing them. Precast concrete fences are strong, durable, maintenance free, attractive, and functional. Do not use rubber- or plastic-covered cable, as horses chew off the covering and the cables act like knives if a horse gets caught in them.

A horse fence should be at least 4 feet, 8 inches to 5 feet high (1.4 to 1.5 m). Horses like to play across fences, so barbwire should not be used along the top of the fence. A board covered with wire mesh or an electric fence wire across the top is best.

Gates in fences must be strong and designed for safety so that they do not sag and become difficult to open. For some reason, horses like to use the area around a gate as a rest area. Therefore, the gate should be made out of a material they cannot chew up. Gates should be designed so that a horse cannot get its foot caught, because horses tend to paw at a gate when they become anxious. The gatepost must be strong and set in the ground so it will not lean. Latches must be designed so that a horse cannot learn to open them.

BREEDING FACILITIES

Facilities for breeding are discussed in Chapter 15 on reproduction in the mare. In addition to the breeding area, palpation chutes, and teasing facilities, brood mare barns may be necessary. Usually sheds or open-front barns are sufficient to provide adequate protection for mares and foals.

Foals need creep feeders. In a stall, the creep feeder is designed so that the foal can eat the feed but the mare cannot (Figure 4-10). The bars across the top are adjustable so they can be opened up more as the foal gets larger. One

FIGURE 4-10 (Gro-Foal feeders by Paddock Products, 339 Bentleyville Rd., Chagrin Falls, Ohio.) Bars must be adjustable from $2\frac{1}{4}$ inches (5.71 cm) to fully open. Feed box is easily removed for cleaning.

of the problems with these types of creep feeders is that mares will lick at the feed and dribble saliva on it. In the pasture or paddock, the creep is fenced and must be close to the mare's feeding area. If it is not located properly, foals will not leave their dam to go to it. Creep feeders are dangerous because a foal can injure itself by trying to run in or out of it.

BEDDING

Bedding for horses should absorb urine (Table 4-1), and it should be free from dust and allergic materials, readily available, not palatable, and inexpensive. It should provide a comfortable bed and be easy to handle. Of the several materials used, barley and oat straw are the most common. The straw should be left in long lengths to keep it free from dust, even though the absorption capacity of chopped straw is much higher. If it is left long, the stable personnel can quickly separate the clean areas from the dirty areas in the stall, and thus less straw is used each day.

Wood shavings are preferred by many horse owners. To prevent respiratory problems, shavings must be free from sawdust. The softer woods have a greater absorption capacity. Shavings offer a definite advantage for people traveling to horse shows or sales because they can be purchased in bales. Do not use sawdust or shavings from nut-bearing trees such as black walnut. They are often toxic and can be fatal or produce laminitis-like symptoms if eaten.

Recycled newspaper that has been shredded and repulped to a cotton-like texture is an increasingly popular variation of wood by-products.

Rice hulls and peanut hulls provide excellent bedding when available. However, they do not absorb water, and the stall floor soon becomes saturated with urine.

Peat moss absorbs water quite well and absorbs odors, too. It is not palatable to horses so they won't eat it. Cleaning is easy since only the manure and wet spots need to be removed. It is not very flammable. However, the horse's feet must be kept clean to prevent foot problems.

Hemp chips made from the core of the hemp stalk have excellent absorbency, are virtually dust free, absorb ammonia, are easy to work with, and are not palatable to horses.

Sand is poor bedding. It absorbs very little urine, and horses that pick around in it for hay may develop sand colic. It is also quite heavy to handle.

The use of stall mats can reduce the amount of bedding required and can prevent a horse from pawing a hole in the stall floor. Mats can be used to cover dirt, wood, and concrete floors.

The average horse produces about 8 tons (7,257 kg) of manure per year. Because manure contains 60 percent water, 3.2 tons (2,903 kg) of dry manure must be disposed of annually. Bedding is usually disposed of at the

TABLE 4-1   Water Absorption of Bedding Material

Material	Lb water absorbed per 100 lb dry material
Straw	
Barley	210
Flax	260
Oat	
long	280
chopped	375
Rye	210
Wheat	
long	220
chopped	295
Wood Products	
Pinewood chips	300
Hardwood chips	150
Pinewood sawdust	250
Hardwood sawdust	150
Pine shavings	200
Other	
Corn stover	250
Corn cobs	210
Hay, chopped	200
Peanut hulls	250
Peat moss	1000
Sand	25

SOURCE: Ensminger (1969).

same site. To control internal parasites, pick up manure from stalls and paddocks at least once a week. To control flies and odors, pick it up daily. If it is not removed from the premises at the time it is picked up, the manure should be stored on a concrete slab. It will compost, and then it can be used for fertilizer. If it is to be spread on pastures, it should compost for at least 2 weeks to kill the larvae of internal parasites. The pile should be sprayed regularly to kill flies.

The location of the compost pit should be convenient to the stable area. For esthetics, it should be located out of sight. The pit should be accessible for easy loading into a truck when the compost pile is removed. If many horses are kept at the stable, a small tractor with a front-end loader is handy to haul manure.

Hydrated (slack) lime (calcium carbonate) sprinkled on the floor of a stall after the bedding has been removed is effective in reducing or eliminating ammonia odors. The lime must be covered with fresh bedding before the horse is returned to its stall. Lime dust can be harmful to the lungs so one must be careful when applying it. Other commercial products are available to reduce ammonia in the stall.

FIRE SAFETY

The problem of stable fires is acute, but the attitude of most people toward them is similar to their attitude toward car wrecks: they always seem to happen to someone else—that is, until they happen to you. Between 1960 and 1970, there were at least 140 reported stable fires in the United States. A total of 1400 horses were burned to death, and property damage amounted to $30 million. Today, fires are still a problem, as evidenced by the 1999 fire at Belmont Race Track. Therefore, preventing stable fires concerns all horsepeople. Fire risk–reduction factors include lightning rods, smoke detectors, resistant material used to construct the barn, location close to a fire station and fire hydrants, and protected electrical wiring.

Protecting a horse in a stall from the danger of fire is a totally different problem from fire prevention in a person's home. The horse is usually standing in some type of bedding that is kept dry. Oat straw develops a temperature of approximately 300°F (148.9°C) at the head of a fire approximately 1 minute after it ignites. Barley straw takes approximately 5 minutes to develop the same temperature. In other words, horses stand in material that develops as much heat and at the same rate as gasoline. All that is required to start a stable fire is a match or a spark.

A common problem is that there is usually only one door to the stall, so the horse cannot escape into the paddock. The size of the stall is approximately 10 × 10 feet or 12 × 12 feet (3.05 × 3.05 m or 3.66 × 3.66 m). Approximately 2 or 3 minutes are required for a straw fire in a stall to burn an area 10 feet (3.05 m) in diameter. By the time the fire covers an area 4 feet (1.22 m) in diameter, most horses have been injured. Their lungs are seared when the fire has covered an area 6 feet (1.83 m) in diameter. They start to suffocate when the area burned is 8 feet (2.44 m) in diameter and are dead by the time an area 10 feet (3.05 m) in diameter is burned.

If a horse is to survive, the fire must be extinguished in the stall within approximately 30 seconds. How does the horseperson cope with this special problem?

The most common answer is proper stable construction. Cement-block or metal barns or similar types of construction are meant to save the building, not the horse in an individual stall. If fire is to be prevented from spreading through a barn, some construction features are mandatory. Fire-retardant paints effectively delay combustion of wood framework inside the barn. Every third or fourth stall should have partition walls that extend to the ceiling to help delay the spread of the fire through the barn.

Sprinkler systems can also be used, but most sprinklers are not designed to put out a fire under the circumstances that exist in a stall. Automatic fire-extinguishing systems must meet at least two requirements to be used in a stable. They must not suffocate the horses when activated, and they must react within seconds after a fire starts. Most automatic sprinklers are designed to throw a circular instead of square pattern, so the spray must be strong enough to reach the corners of the stall. If a fog-type system is used, the fog must suffocate the fire to extinguish it, so the horse will suffocate with the fire. Water can cause extensive smoke formation, which in turn will suffocate the horse or at least cause lung damage. This can be prevented if the sprinkler is activated before the fire covers an area 1 foot in diameter. A thermal lag system with sensors located above the stalls takes 4 to 5 minutes to activate, which is too long. Now there are sprinkler systems that begin to operate approximately 5 seconds after a fire starts.

Of course, not all fires start inside a stall. A layer of chaff and dust, which covers the floor of many barn lofts, burns like gasoline. The loft and other storage areas of a barn should be swept regularly to remove dust. Periodically, the inside of a barn should be hosed down with water to remove all dust and cobwebs. This is just as important as keeping the alleys clean.

An adequate number of exits from the barn are necessary so that fire does not block the only exit. All exits should open into enclosed areas. In case of fire, the horses can be turned loose, but they must not flee the stable area. Fleeing horses may be killed by automobiles when they cross or travel down roads. They may also ruin other property such as lawns or crops. Also, adequate space between buildings will help prevent the spread of fire.

The stall doors should open by sliding. When horses flee through emergency exits, they can catch their hips and other parts on doors that open into stalls. When the doors slide open to one side, someone can run through the stable, opening all the doors and letting the horses out. Also, sliding doors cannot close accidentally. Because time is important in emergencies, stall door latches should be strong and easy for people to open. Latches with 2 or 3 movements make it difficult for horses to learn to open.

If a barn is constructed in this manner, all the stall doors can be opened by the rescuer on one trip through the alley. Horses that leave by themselves will be caught in the outside enclosed area. However, someone should prevent them from returning inside the barn because a scared horse likes to return to a familiar stall. Because of this trait, many horses will not leave their stalls unless they are led out. It may be necessary to cover their heads with a sack or something similar to prevent them from seeing the fire and smoke. They are easier to lead this way; if led any other way, they try to climb the back walls of their stalls.

All electricity in a barn should be turned off at night. The master switch should be located close to an entrance, so the lights can be turned on and one can see what is taking place inside the barn during an emergency. Flashlights and the bouncing, moving shadows and lighted areas they cause can frighten horses. Do not use flashlights unless absolutely essential. Electrical wire in a barn must be protected from mice and rats, which will chew the insulation off, leaving two bare wires that can easily start an electrical fire. At the same location as the electrical switch, which should be at an exit, keep a fire extinguisher available in case of a small fire. At this location also keep a water hose that can reach the length of the barn. This hose should remain attached to a water hydrant so that one can quickly get water to all parts of a barn. It is advisable to have a large pipe with adequate pressure to deliver a large stream of water through a fire hose positioned at the entrance.

As another protective measure, each stall should have a halter and lead rope hung on a hook beside it. Then you need not waste time taking a halter off one horse and putting it on another while rescuing horses. Time is of the essence.

People working at the stables should obey a strict set of fire prevention rules. Smoking should not be allowed in or adjacent to buildings. For convenience, large receptacles for disposing of cigarettes should be placed at building entrances. All electrical equipment should be in safe working condition and inspected regularly. Appliances such as hot plates, coffee pots, and radios should not be left unattended when in use and they should be used only in a special area. Inflammable materials such as lighter fluid, solvents, or cleaning fluids should not be used in the stable area. Gasoline should not be stored in the barn. The owner or manager should not tolerate rule infractions by employees or visitors. The rules must be rigidly enforced at all times.

DUST CONTROL

Dust originating from arenas, exercise paddocks, round pens, and hot walkers is annoying to neighbors and is not good for horses to breathe while being exercised. Excessive dust inhalation leads to respiratory problems such as heaves (see Chapter 10). Several products such as shredded rubber and microencapsulated sand and other soil additives are available to decrease dust. A water sprinkler system can also be installed and routinely used.

ARENAS

The placement and construction of an arena should be carefully planned since it can be the facility that gets constant use. Size, shape, and type of construction are determined primarily by the intended use. A dressage arena will be quite different from one used during riding and training of roping horses. Suitability of the soil is one of the first things to consider. Type of soil will determine softness and feel and how soon it can be used after a rain. If the soil needs to be improved, which materials should be added to prevent hardness can be decided and added to the soil prior to construction. At this time, it is much easier for large trucks to haul in the material and dump it. Dust control is a factor and may require addition of materials. Also, there are liquid materials that can be added by spraying. The base will determine drainage and any "mud holes" will develop in areas where the base is absent or changes. It may be necessary to remove the top soil and replace the base under it to get an even distribution of proper material. Manure management can be a problem and should be addressed early in the planning process.

Its design should include sufficient number and width of gates to move horses, people, and maintenance equipment in and out. Maintenance equipment such as tractors, harrows, roto-tillers, drags, and blades will be used to maintain the surface.

Lights are useful if horses are ridden at night. They should be placed high enough so they do not shine directly into the horse's and rider's eyes. Quartz lights are effective for outdoor lighting. Indoor arenas can be lighted with fluorescent lighting.

Placement of water sprinklers is always debatable and depends on the use of the arena. Sprinkler heads placed on top of the top rail or adjacent to it usually do not provide a uniform distribution of water on the surface. Muddy areas tend to form near the sprinkler heads. Pop-up sprinklers can be installed in the arena surface. Their circular pattern still will not evenly distribute the water. The pop-up heads always cause concerns about safety even though they are set in a rubber-topped housing that is even with the surface.

Installation of a sound system can be helpful when training young horses for "show ring noise." If horse shows are to be held in the facility, one set of speakers will be directed to the arena and another set will be directed to the warm-up area.

Indoor arenas under a roof are popular and provide many advantages over an outdoor facility. They are usually constructed of metal to provide a clear span. Overhead sprinkler systems can be used to help control dust.

Normally, it is well worth the expense of professional advice when constructing an arena. There are many subtle design features that must be incorporated such as traffic patterns for horses, equipment, automobiles, and trucks and trailers. Only an experienced professional will consider all of the desirable features to make it a user-friendly arena.

CHAPTER 5

Feeding

Nutrition is one of the most neglected aspects of horse care and management. Horses seem to suffer from two opposite extremes of malnutrition—either they are too fat or they are starving. An understanding of nutrient requirements, characteristics of common feeds, feeding management, and nutrient costs enables an owner to properly and economically feed horses.

ANATOMY AND FUNCTIONS OF THE DIGESTIVE TRACT

The digestive tract of the horse consists of the mouth, pharynx, esophagus, stomach, small intestine, large intestine, rectum, and anus (Figures 5-1, 5-2, and 5-3). The liver and pancreas are associated with the digestive tract and release part of their secretions directly into it. The functions of the digestive tract include prehension of food, mastication, digestion, absorption, and initial storage of the nutrients.

The lips of the horse's mouth are quite mobile and help in sucking and selection and prehension of food. They are very sensitive tactile organs. The hard palate, the upper part of the mouth, is a bony plate covered with a mucous membrane crossed by many ridges. It has a rich blood supply. The hard palate extends back to the soft palate. The tongue is an important tactile organ and is necessary for mastication and swallowing. It serves as a plunger to drive the food into the pharynx. Salivary glands—the parotid, mandibular, and

FIGURE 5-1   Sagittal section of the horse's head: (1) oral cavity; (2) nasopharynx; (3) oropharynx; (4, 5) laryngopharynx; (6) incisive part of mandible with first incisor; (7) incisive bone with first incisor; (8) incisive duct; (9) nasal bone; (10) osseous palate; (11) interparietal bone; (12) sphenoid bone; (13) sphenoid sinus; (14) ethmoid bone; (15) frontal bone; (16, 17) conchofrontal sinus, composed of (16) frontal sinus and (17) sinus of dorsal nasal cocha; (18) parietal bone; (19) tentorium cerebelli osseum; (20) occipital bone; (21) atlas; (22) axis; (23) funicular part of ligamentum nuchae; (24) rectus capitis dorsalis; (25) longus capitis; (26) longus colli; (27) sternohyoideus and omohyoideus; (28) nasal vestibule; (29) alar fold; (30) basal fold; (31) dorsal meatus; (32) middle meatus; (33) ventral nasal meatus, (34) nasal septum, almost entirely removed; (35) dorsal nasal concha; (36) conchal cells; (37) ventral nasal concha; (38) sinus of ventral nasal concha; (39) middle nasal concha, opened; (40) ethmoid conchae; (41) choana; (42) pharyngeal opening of auditory tube; (43) right gutteral pouch, opened; (44) epiglottis; (45) aryepiglottic fold; (46) arytenoid cartilage; (47) corniculate process; (48) cricoid cartilage; (49) entrance to lateral laryngeal ventricle; (50) thyroid cartilage; (51) cricothyroid ligament; (52) trachea; (53) upper lip; (54) lower lip; (55) labial vestibule; (56) sublingual floor of oral cavity; (57) frenulum linguae; (58) hard palate with venous plexus and palatine ridges; (59) apex; (60) body of tongue; (61) root of tongue; (62) genioglossus; (63) geniohyoideus; (64) hyoepiglotticus in glossoepiglottic fold; (65) basihyoid with lingual process; (66) soft palate with glands and muscles; (67, 68) rostral and caudal boundaries of intrapharyngeal opening; (69) free border of soft palate; (70) caudal end of the palatopharyngeal arch; (71) esophagus; (71) cerebrum; (73) cerebellum; (74) olfactory bulb; (75) optic chiasma; (76) brainstem; (77) spinal cord. (From Nickel and others, 1973.)

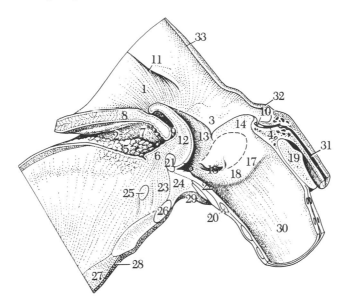

FIGURE 5-2   Sagittal section of the pharynx and larynx of the horse: (1) nasopharynx; (2) oropharynx; (3, 4) laryngopharynx; (5) root of tongue with tonsillar follicles (lingual tonsil); (6) glossoepiglottic fold; (7) palatoglossal arch; (8) soft palate; (9, 10) boundaries of intrapharyngeal opening; (9) free border of soft palate; (10) palatopharyngeal arch; (11) pharyngeal opening of auditory tube; (12) epiglottis; (13) aryepiglottic fold; (14) corniculate process of arytenoid cartilage; (15) entrance to lateral laryngeal ventricle, the broken line marks the extent of the ventricle; (16) median laryngeal ventricle; (17) vocal process of arytenoid cartilage; (18) vocal fold; (19, 20) cricoid cartilage; (21) thyroid cartilage; (22) cricothyroid ligament; (23) hyoepiglotticus; (24) fat; (25) hyoideus transversus; (26) basihyoid and lingual process; (27) geniohyoideus; (28) mylohyoideus; (29) sternohyoideus; (30) trachea; (31) esophagus; (32) caudal pharyngeal constrictors; (33) hyopharyngeus. (From Nickel and others, 1973.)

sublingual glands—produce saliva, which lubricates the food and contains amylase, a minor enzyme that helps digest carbohydrate. Each day as much as 10 to 12 liters (2.6 to 3.2 gal) of saliva are secreted. Teeth, discussed in Chapters 1 and 9, grind food, which increases the efficiency of digestion.

The pharynx connects the mouth with the esophagus and connects the nasal cavity with the larynx and trachea leading to the lungs. Both air and food pass through the pharynx, which directs them to their proper destinations. There are two cavities in the pharynx: the nasopharynx (part of the respiratory channel) and the oropharynx (part of the digestive tract). These two cavities are separated by the soft palate. The epiglottis passively covers the laryngeal opening during swallowing to prevent food or liquids from passing into the lungs. During inspiration or expiration of air, it rests against the upper border of the soft palate to close off the back of the oral cavity. Because of this arrangement, a stomach tube can be passed through the nostrils into the esophagus and stomach. Care must be taken not to pass the tube into the trachea. If liquids such as deworming medicines are passed into the lungs, the horse may suffocate or die from aspiration pneumonia.

The esophagus extends from the pharynx and opens into the stomach. It lies close to the skin on the bottom and left side of the neck. You can see the horse swallow because a muscular contraction moves the food. If a stomach tube is being passed, the operator should feel the tube as it moves down the esophagus, which joins the stomach at a very oblique angle. At the junction, there is a strong muscular sphincter and numerous mucosal folds. Because of the angle at which the esophagus enters the stomach and the strong sphincter, it is almost impossible for stomach contents or gas to be forced from the stomach into the esophagus. The stomach usually ruptures before stomach contents are forced into the esophagus. Therefore, the horse usually cannot vomit or belch. This is one reason horses are susceptible to colic and ruptured stomachs.

The horse's stomach is small for the size of the animal (see Figure 5-3). Its capacity is about 2.1 to 4 gallons (8 to 15 liters), about 10 percent of the digestive tract capacity. Because of its limited capacity, food does not stay in the stomach very long (less than 2 hours) before being forced into the small

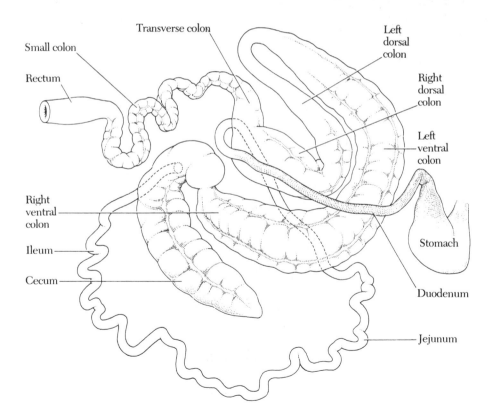

FIGURE 5-3 Digestive tract of the horse.

intestine. Even though frequency of feeding does not affect the efficiency of digestion, the size of the stomach does suggest other feeding management considerations. At least two feedings per day help to prevent overdistension of the stomach, colic, and founder (a lameness of the foot). In the natural state, the horse tends to eat small amounts continuously.

Some digestion takes place in the stomach as a result of gastric secretions and limited bacterial fermentation. Limited bacterial digestion of carbohydrates to lactic acid does occur.

The small intestine of the horse is composed of three parts that contain 30 percent of the digestive tract capacity: duodenum, jejunum, and ileum. The bile and pancreatic ducts open into the duodenum. Bile salts are secreted by the liver and are necessary to emulsify lipids (fats). The bile salts are secreted continuously into the digestive tract, because the horse has no gall bladder to store them. Pancreatic juice contains enzymes for protein and carbohydrate digestion. Intestinal cells also secrete digestive enzymes. The small intestine is the primary site of protein digestion and absorption of amino acids. About 60 to 70 percent of the protein eaten may be digested and absorbed before reaching the large intestine. Dietary protein content and quality are important for young horses.

Most soluble carbohydrates are digested in the small intestine. The end products are glucose and volatile fatty acids, which are absorbed and used for energy. The small intestine is also the primary site of fat digestion and absorption. Even though the horse has no gall bladder, it can still tolerate high-fat diets and can use dietary fat. Fats are a concentrated source of energy, and horses that have a high-energy requirement can efficiently use 10 to 15 percent fat added to the ration. Because of fat absorption in the small intestine, it is presumed that the fat-soluble vitamins (A, D, E, and K) are absorbed here, as are B vitamins. Most calcium, zinc, and magnesium are absorbed in the small intestine. And the same amount of phosphorus is absorbed here as in the large intestine.

The terminal end of the small intestine is the opening of the ileum into the large intestine. The opening extends into the large intestine because the ileum and the sphincter are very muscular. The muscular structure of the ileum allows the digesta to be forced into the large intestine even though the pressure may be higher there. Because the ileum prevents backflow of digesta and equalizes pressure between the large intestine and jejunum, colic can result when this sensitive equalization system malfunctions.

The large intestine, composed of the caecum and colon, has a large capacity. The caecum, a pouch close to the ileum, may hold as much as 18.5 gallons (70 liters) but normally contains about 7.9 gallons (30 liters). The ascending, or great, colon is composed of the right ventral colon, sternal flexure, left ventral colon, pelvic flexure, left dorsal colon, diaphragmatic flexure, and right dorsal colon. From a practical viewpoint, the great colon is in the form of two U-shaped structures that lay more or less on top of each other. The pelvic flexure is a constricted area where compaction of digesta often occurs. This, in turn, may result in colic. The left dorsal colon is smaller than the other three segments and is another problem area for colic.

The descending, or small, colon has a smaller diameter than the great colon. The small colon is shaped to form two rows of regular, almost semi-spherical sacs that form feces into the characteristic balls.

The large intestine serves as a fermentation vat. The microbial flora are similar to those found in cattle. These bacteria break down cellulose into volatile fatty acids: acetic, propionic, and butyric. Some soluble carbohydrates also reach the large intestine and are converted to volatile fatty acids. Fats are metabolized to volatile fatty acids. Bacteria synthesize amino acids in the large intestine. The amino acids are absorbed here, but the importance of their synthesis and absorption has not been fully evaluated. The bacteria are able to use some nonprotein nitrogen for protein synthesis, or at least increase nitrogen retention. A by-product of the microbial fermentation is methane. The caecum is the primary site of water absorption, but the large colon also plays an important role. B vitamins are synthesized by microflora in the large intestine, and some of them are absorbed.

The digestive tract ends in the rectum, which is 8 to 12 inches (20 to 30 cm) long, and the anus.

COMMON FEEDS

The common feeds fed to horses are usually classified into three categories—roughages, concentrates, and supplements. Roughages are high in fiber and relatively low in energy. They include pasture and hay, forage crops, and silage. Concentrates are low in fiber and high in energy. They include grains and some grain by-products. Supplements are used to balance rations, to make up for deficiencies in protein, minerals, and vitamins. Protein supplements are of plant or animal origin, whereas many minerals are available in organic or inorganic substances. Each vitamin has several good natural sources; in some instances, the horse can synthesize them.

Roughages

The most common forms of forage are pasture, hay, soilage (green chop), silage, and haylage. Pasture and hay are the two most common forages fed to horses. Silage and haylage are not routinely fed to horses. It is difficult to make silage and haylage without the presence of mold and toxic substances that can cause digestive upsets. Anaerobic conditions and a low pH are necessary to prevent the growth of mold.

Hay

The most common form of roughage given to the horse kept in confinement is hay, but it is difficult to produce or buy good-quality horse hay. There are many variables in hay production and an understanding of some of the general factors affecting hay quality will help you select high-quality hay.

Plant species affect certain qualities of good hay. Legumes are higher in protein, energy, calcium, and vitamin A than grass hays. Red clover is dustier and not as green in color as alfalfa. A mixture of legume and grass plants may be desirable for certain types of horses or geographical areas. Weeds are undesirable, because they add woody material that is low in acceptability and digestibility to the horse, and they have bad tastes and odors.

Growing conditions such as rainfall affect hay quality. Drought conditions result in stunted growth and fewer leaves. Excessive moisture often encourages diseases that attack and decrease leaves. Adequate fertility ensures a higher nutrient content, more leaves, and less fiber.

Stage of plant growth at harvest time affects nutrient content. As plants grow from the vegetative to the reproductive stage, their protein content, digestibility, and palatability decline. The ratio of stem to leaf increases, so the plant has a higher fiber content. For maximum nutrient content and good tonnage per acre, legumes are harvested when a few flowers start to appear in the field. Grasses are harvested when seed heads begin to appear. Grain hays are cut when the grain is in the soft-dough stage of development.

Weather conditions affect field-cured hay. The two most important curing conditions that reduce quality are rain and too much sunlight. Rain beats the leaves from the legumes, leaches out soluble carbohydrates, and packs the hay so it does not dry properly. The moisture content of hay should be about 12 to 18 percent, but it may extend up to 25 percent. If the hay is baled or processed before the moisture content is reduced to the acceptable limit, it will become moldy and have a musty, moldy odor. Mold can be toxic to horses. Preservatives can be applied to prevent molding and spoilage. One preservative has been successfully applied to alfalfa hay containing up to 30 percent moisture. Excessive sunlight bleaches the color out of the leaves, causing a loss of vitamin A. Therefore, hay should be dried as quickly as possible. If cured too slowly, hay begins to ferment and lose its nutrient content.

Harvesting procedures also affect quality. If hay is cut and placed in windrows, the stems should be crushed to aid drying. Crushing or crimping the stems may prevent the necessity of moving the windrow for proper drying. Excessive movement after the hay starts to dry shatters the leaves and mixes dirt into the hay. If hay is left in windrows too long, it dries too much, and the leaves fall off when the baler picks it up.

The above facts and the following criteria can help you select high-quality hay. Examine the hay for stage of plant maturity by looking for flowers or seed pods; there should be no mature seed or plants in full bloom. Estimate the percentage of leaves present. Leaves are the part of the plant that contain the highest percentage of nutrients, so look for a high proportion of leaves relative to stems. Stems are low in digestibility and quality. Determine what plants are in the hay and the relative proportions of each. A bright green color indicates a minimum amount of bleaching and loss of vitamin A. Discolored hay may mean it has been rained on and the nutrients leached out. The hay should have a good, clean smell to it. Moldy and dusty smells are undesirable. No foreign material should be present. Examine it for sticks, stubble, weeds, dirt, bottles, paper, and so on. These may cause mouth injuries or otherwise harm the horse, and you are purchasing them instead of quality hay. Economics are based on nutrient content, hauling, and storage costs. If hay is purchased in large lots, have samples of it analyzed by a commercial laboratory to determine nutrient content.

Alfalfa hay grown in the arid areas of the western and southwestern United States should be certified free of blister beetles prior to purchase. Because of their size, these beetles are very difficult or impossible to detect in alfalfa hay. They contain a toxin, cantharidin, which is an irritant that produces severe inflammation and blisters on body surfaces. Ingestion of several of the beetles may result in death. Symptoms for horses that have ingested these beetles include colic, increased temperature and heart rate, dehydration, and diarrhea. The lining of the esophagus and stomach become necrosed and sluff. The rest of the digestive tract and the urinary tract become severely irritated. Management procedures to reduce the potential hazard of contamination in the hay include spraying with an insecticide shortly before cutting, cutting prior to flowering since the beetles are attracted to flowers, and not crimping the hay at the time of cutting so that the beetles move out of the cut hay. Local county extension agents can provide information about areas of contamination.

Hay can be processed in several ways, but traditionally in bales. Each "three-wire bale" should weigh 125 pounds (56.7 kg), or 16 bales to a ton. A "two-wire bale" is much lighter. It varies in weight, but 66.66 pounds (30.2 kg) are standard. Thirty bales make a ton (907 kg). Hay can also be "cubed"—run through a press that makes small cubes about $1\frac{1}{2}$ inch square (3.84 cm^2) of varying lengths. Cubes and pellets require less storage space and are easy to carry to horse shows. There is practically no waste when they are fed. However, a horse takes 3 to 4 days to learn to eat them. Less time is spent eating, so the horse has more time to chew on fences, buildings, and so on. And there is always a slight possibility that a cube or pellets may lodge in the throat and cause the horse to choke.

Each kind of hay has certain characteristics that the horseperson should be familiar with. Many types of grass hays are fed to horses in the United States, including timothy, orchardgrass, smooth bromegrass, coastal Bermuda, oat, barley, prairie, tall fescue, and sudangrass. However, only a few are in widespread use.

Timothy hay once was one of the most popular horse hays and still is in some areas. It is easy to harvest as clean, bright hay free from mildew and mold. In some areas, it is quite expensive, because it must be shipped great distances. Timothy must be harvested in the pre- or early-bloom stage; afterward, the protein content rapidly declines. The second cutting is the best to feed; later cuttings are much lower in quality, and the first cutting is usually full of weeds.

Bermudagrass hay is used in the southern United States. Common Bermudagrass does not grow tall enough for hay production, but certain varieties of Coastal Bermudagrass can be used. The same stand of grass can be cut four to five times per year for hay. It is as nutritious as timothy hay. Its value can be increased by growing it with a mixture of legumes.

Prairie hay or *wild native hays* are suitable for horses if they are processed correctly. However, very seldom can one buy good-quality prairie hay outside of the Midwest. Most is made from poor-quality grass that is quite mature. It usually has lots of weeds and trash baled in it, such as foxtails, which cause mouth wounds and irritations. The protein content may be around 2 to 4 percent. In the Midwest, bluestems are normally grown with other grasses for hay production. Bluestems are highly palatable, provided they are cut before reaching full maturity and while still green.

Sudangrass hay (a sorghum) can be fed to horses and is popular in some areas. It must be cut in the early-bloom stage for maximum nutritional content. However, if cut earlier, it may contain large amounts of prussic acid, which is toxic to animals. The protein content is about 10 percent, and the energy content is about the same as for oat hay. Johnson grass, also related to the sorghums, makes good hay when cut at the early-bloom stage. Two or three cuttings can be made per year. It is usually grown in the southern United States.

Oat hay is an excellent feed for horses. The choice between alfalfa and oat hay depends on price per unit of energy or protein and on what kind of horse is being fed. Depending on its processing and the area in which it is grown, it can be low in protein and contain only marginal calcium, phosphorus, and carotene.

Barley hay is very similar to oat hay except it has barbed beards that cause mouth irritations and wounds. Do not use it for feed unless absolutely necessary. There are some smooth varieties that can be used for horse hay.

Legume hays most commonly fed to horses include alfalfa, clover, birdsfoot trefoil, and, to a lesser extent, lespedeza. High-quality legumes provide higher levels of energy, protein, calcium, and carotene than most grass hays.

Alfalfa hay is one of the best hays to feed horses. Several characteristics of alfalfa make it excellent. First, it is highly palatable. Most horses really enjoy eating alfalfa hay. In fact, they usually overeat and may get colic unless intake is restricted. Another reason to restrict availability is that it is high in energy—120 percent more energy per unit of weight than oat hay. Therefore, feed approximately 85 percent as much alfalfa as oat hay to get the same energy intake. It does not cause excessive sweating, as some horsepeople believe. However, the high-energy content may lead to overfeeding and to a fat horse. But it is safe as the only hay fed. Many people feel that alfalfa needs to be fed or mixed with another hay. It is not necessary to mix it, but it can be mixed to give a mature, nonworking horse more bulk. If fed to lactating mares or growing horses, it should not be diluted with other hay, because these horses need the high energy and protein content. It is high in good-quality protein—as much as 18 to 19 percent crude protein. People used to think that alfalfa would burn a horse's kidneys out, because an increased urine output high in ammonia results. The excess protein in alfalfa is converted to energy compounds, and nitrogen must be eliminated as ammonia. Alfalfa is a good source of vitamins A and B and, if sun cured, of vitamin D. The ratio of calcium to phosphorus is about 6:1 and must be considered when feeding young, immature horses. It is more laxative than grass hays but not enough to be of concern. Scientific evidence does not support the old idea that it is too laxative if cut before the late-bloom stage. It should be cut at early- to mid-bloom stage, when you can see a few blooms or flowers across a field. At the late-bloom stage, when the field is solid with flowers, the nutrient content of the hay has decreased considerably—as much as 5 percent.

The number of cuttings of hay from an alfalfa field each year will vary according to geographical location and irrigation practices. In California, five to eight cuttings may be obtained. In the Midwest, three to four cuttings are expected, whereas only two to three are expected in the Northeast. The first cutting will usually have more weeds and trash in it than later cuttings have. If several cuttings are obtained, the later cuttings tend to have more stems and fewer leaves. As the hay changes from fine to coarse stems, the nutrient content and palatability decrease.

Clover hays are nutritious and somewhat similar to alfalfa, because they are also legumes. Clover is difficult to cure unless mixed with grass hays, so pure clover hay is rare. There are five kinds of clover hays: red, common white, crimson, alsike, and ladino. White and ladino clovers are usually grown for pasture, not hay. The other three contain about 14 to 16 percent crude protein. Red clover causes "slobbers" in horses—excessive salivation that does not hurt the horse. However, the appearance of the horse may not be pleasing, and excess moisture in the feed box may result in moldy feed.

Another factor to consider when selecting a forage species to plant is forage acceptability, or the horse's preference. Horses are selective grazers and will express their preference when given the opportunity to select from a variety of forages. Grasses are considered more acceptable than legumes. In some Pennsylvania trials, Kentucky bluegrass was preferred over other grasses. In other tests, Timothy and smooth bromegrass were preferred to orchardgrass, tall fescue, reed canary grass, and meadow foxtail. Annual ryegrass was preferred over oats and wheat, and rye and triticale were least preferred. Of the annual clovers, crimson, berseam, and subterranean were highly palatable, but arrowleaf clover was unacceptable.

Pasture

Pasture is used as a source of roughage for horses kept in larger paddocks or in pastures. Many horses are kept on native pastures of grasses, legumes, and forbs. There are great nutrient content variations in annual pastures, depending on the type and the growing season. Early in the growing season, the green pasture is high in protein and energy on a dry-matter basis, but is high in moisture. Thus, as eaten by the horse, the percent protein and energy content is low. In fact, horses can starve while eating pasture that is 1 to 2 feet high (30.4 to 61.0 cm). Later in the season, the moisture content is lower and the nutrient content is higher. As the pasture continues to mature and weather, it becomes deficient in protein, energy, and other nutrients. A supplementation program must be considered for pastures during low nutrient periods. Irrigated pastures vary in quality depending on the pasture species and management. Irrigated pastures may supply all the required nutrients for some classes of horses.

Horse owners are somewhat limited as to the kinds of pasture grasses and legumes that can be grown in each geographical area. Certain species grow profusely, and others grow little or not at all. The horse owner should consult with the local Agriculture Extension Office for specific recommendations for specific areas. Generally, the pasture should be a mixture of one or two grasses with one or two legumes. The most common warm-season perennials used are Bermudagrass, Bahiagrass, bluestems, and native grasses. Common warm-season annuals include sorghum-sudan hybrids, sudans, and millets. Cool-season perennials are tall fescue, orchardgrass, timothy, smooth bromegrass, perennial ryegrass, and Kentucky bluegrass. Cool-season annuals include oats, barley, wheat, rye, pearl millet, and annual ryegrass. Legumes include alfalfa, clovers, and birdsfoot trefoil.

Before selecting grasses to plant, the horseperson must decide on the purpose of the pasture. It may be used primarily for exercise or to supply a significant portion of the daily nutrient requirements. Each grass has certain characteristics that make it desirable for the different uses. Kentucky bluegrass and white clover form a sod that is quite resistant to close cropping and trampling. Tall fescue is suited for areas that have a heavy traffic pattern, because it is most resistant to trampling. Birdsfoot trefoil is usually less stemmy than red clover and similar to alfalfa. Lespedeza contains tannins, which reduces its palatability.

Several management factors can improve forage production. Grasses respond to fertilization. The soil should be tested to determine the nutrient needs for optimum production and to allow meaningful decisions about fertilizers. The local county Agriculture Extension agent can be of help. The proper combination of fertilizers helps maintain the balance of grasses and legumes in a pasture. Irrigated pastures should be irrigated at intervals that do not allow plants to be stressed by lack of water. The amount of water will be determined by the kinds of plants and soil. Adequate drying time should be allowed to minimize trampling and plant injury.

Producing abundant, good-quality forage is possible only under proper grazing management. Pastures must be used in such a way that sufficient leaf area and root reserves are maintained. This is necessary for immediate regrowth. Minimum recommended grazing heights are bluegrass, 2 inches (5.1 cm); native meadow grass, 3 inches (7.6 cm); bromegrass, 3 inches

(7.6 cm); orchardgrass, 3 inches (7.6 cm); tall fescue, 3 inches (7.6 cm); Bermudagrass, 2 inches (5.1 cm); and small grains, 4 inches (10.2 cm). The pasture should be grazed evenly. If horses refuse to graze a certain area, moving the water supply, salt, or the feed supplement may be necessary to encourage its use. At regular intervals, the pasture can be clipped to a recommended minimum height. Grazing forage evenly is encouraged when the pasture is dragged with a chain harrow to scatter manure. Grazing pastures with both cattle and horses increases the uniformity of grazing.

There are other considerations for good pasture management. A large pasture is not as good as several small ones, for the latter allow rotational grazing and an opportunity to irrigate, clip, fertilize, and control weeds. Do not put the horses on the pasture before its growing season; give the forage a head start.

You can estimate the amount of pasture required per horse. The average mature horse consumes 2.5 percent of its body weight in dry matter per day. Therefore, a 1000-pound (454-kg) horse consumes 25 pounds (11.3 kg) of dry matter per day, or 750 pounds (340.2 kg) per month. Forage production varies from 1 to 10 tons (907 to 9070 kg) or more per acre each month. The local Agriculture Extension agent can provide data for a given area. A horse uses about 60 percent of the forage production. After taking into account the growing season for the pasture, you can calculate the number of horses per month per acre. The most common cause of pasture deterioration is overcrowding and overgrazing, so a minimum of 2 acres per mature horse and 1 acre per pony or yearling is necessary.

Pastures should be free from pits, holes, stumps, and other hazards that could injure the horse. Moles and gophers should be controlled to prevent tunneling.

Horses should be dewormed for internal parasites prior to turning them out on the pasture and at regular intervals thereafter. This prevents parasite buildup on the pasture.

Poisonous Plants

Poisonous plants (Table 5-1) can be a problem in pastures and in hays. Hundreds of plants are toxic to horses. You should be familiar with the ones that grow in your geographical area if you plan to pasture horses. Poisonous plants are frequently baled into hay along with the hay forage, so you must be able to recognize them when examining the hay prior to purchase or feeding. Horses also nibble on poisonous ornamental plants around stables or homes. All horsepeople should be familiar with the most common ones. If you suspect poisoning, call a veterinarian immediately.

Oleander is a common ornamental bush that is extremely poisonous to horses. They usually chew on the bush or prunings from it.

In hay fields, fiddleneck (*Amsinkia intermedia*)—also called tarweed or fireweed—and senecio are common. They contain toxic substances that cause

TABLE 5-1 Poisonous Trees, Plants, and Shrubs

Poisonous trees

Plant name	Symptoms	Comments
Black cherry, chokecherry, chokeberries	Uneasiness; staggering; breathing difficulty; mucous membranes turn blue; convulsions and rapid death	Shrubs with white flowers and red or black cherry fruit; commonly found along fence rows, thickets, and woodland areas; toxic agent is hydrocyanic acid produced in wilted or bruised leaves; most common danger is from branches blown down during storms or that have been pruned; death is usually so rapid that the animal is found with portions of the plant still in its mouth
Buckeye	Weakness; staggering; severe trembling and twitching of muscles; inflamed mucous membranes; dilated pupils; coma; death	Tree or shrub found in woods and along river banks in the East; seed is glossy brown with a pale scar; most danger occurs in spring and summer
Oak tree, acorns	Dullness; weakness, black pelleted manure followed by total constipation which is then followed by bloody diarrhea; frequent urination; dry muzzle; thin, rapid pulse	Common tree of varied heights found all over the United States; leaves and acorns contain tannic acid; especially toxic during spring and summer; heavy rainfall may soften fallen acorns and cause them to sprout, which makes them more tempting and palatable

Unusual poisonous plants

Plant name	Symptoms	Comments
Avocado	Severe, noninfectious mastitis; milk production is reduced; as inflammation subsides, no more milk is produced	Leaves, bark, and fruit are toxic
Blue-green algae	Abdominal pain; difficulty breathing; convulsions; death; survivors suffer liver damage and are sensitive to the sun	Some forms highly toxic to all animals; smaller animals at greater risk since they are more prone to drink from shallow water where algae blooms; animals must be removed from the water supply and water treated with algicides

	Paralysis and rapid death	No known treatment; animals are often found dead or paralyzed and near death
Wild tobacco		
Poisonous plants and shrubs		
Bladder pod	Inflammation of the intestines with yellowish diarrhea; frequent urination; short, rapid breathing; death	Tall plant common in the South; produces pods containing two poisonous seeds; especially poisonous in summer; necessary to prevent exposure and remove all plants and fallen pods
Bracken fern, brake fern	Progressive loss of condition, unsteady gait while walking, progresses to swaying, incoordination, and staggering; drowsiness; pressing head against solid objects; crouching stance with neck arched and feet wide apart; difficulty swallowing; between 7 and 20 days after first symptoms appear, horse lies down and is unable to rise again; death usually follows within a few days	Common to pastures and woodlands; has triangular shaped fronds and may reach a height of two to four feet; contains a toxin that destroys vitamin B; if caught in time, injections of thiamine may prove helpful; poisonings usually occur in early spring and late fall when the fern is the only greenery left in the pasture; also dangerous when dried; may be baled with hay; since symptoms take a while to show up, many horsepeople fail to believe that this plant is toxic; horse may be removed from the pasture before the symptoms become noticeable
Castor bean	Dullness; severe thirst; nausea; vision difficulty; incoordination; profuse sweating; watery diarrhea; heartbeat that shakes the entire body; colic pain; convulsions and death	Grown as an ornamental planting or weed along roadsides; palmlike leaves and pods containing "beans" are equally poisonous during all seasons; about 150 beans will kill a 1000-pound horse; symptoms often appear to go away, only to recur before the onset of death
Corn cockle	Inflammation of mucous membranes; diarrhea, vertigo; weak pulse	Has purple flowers, black seeds, and fine, white hairs on underside of leaves; seeds are the most poisonous part; sometimes harvested into grain
Death camas	Excessive drooling; staggering and incoordination; weakness; inability to stand; coma followed by death caused by heart failure	Resembles the onion with its bulbous root, except that it has flat leaves and no odor; most dangerous in early spring since it is one of the first plants to produce greenery when forage is scarce; also poisonous when cut and dried in hay

(continued)

TABLE 5-1 Poisonous Trees, Plants, and Shrubs (*Continued*)

Poisonous plants and shrubs

Plant name	Symptoms	Comments
Fly-poison	Excessive drooling; respiratory difficulty; weakness; death due to respiratory failure	Herb with a bulbous root that blossoms; poisonous year-round; an alkaloid that is found in woodlands and marshy pastures; also poisonous when cut and dried; there is no known cure
Indian hemp (dogbane)	Increased body temperature; sweating; ears and legs become cold; pupils dilate; linings of nose and mouth turn blue, soreness inside mouth; increased bowel action; weakness; labored respiration; coma; death	May grow as tall as 5 feet; stems contains milky, latexlike substance, leaves turn bright yellow during the fall; often found in sandy or gravelly soil along roadsides or in fields; extremely poisonous; as little as one half to one ounce can kill a horse; normally has a bitter taste, but some horses try it
Larkspur, dwarf larkspur, staggerweed	Small amounts cause loss of appetite; excitability; falling and staggering; constipation; large amounts cause slobbering; colic; bloating; straddled stance; convulsions and respiratory paralysis leading to death	Grows 1 to 3 feet high with blue or white flowers, often grown in gardens, but also in woodlands and along streams
Laurel, laurel cherry, rhododendron	Irregular breathing; drooling; grinding of teeth, staggering; blindness; stupor; paralysis; convulsions and death	Evergreen shrub with leathery, glossy leaves; generally found in acid soil, hilly pastures and rocky woodlands; animal eating 0.2 percent of its body weight can develop symptoms
Lupine	Nervousness; large accumulations of iron in the body, digestive disruption; weak heart; depression, liver damage; convulsions	Shiny green leaves and wide variation of blossom colors; often found in moist areas and foothills in the West; most dangerous from spring until first killing frost in fall; summer is the seed stage
Nightshade (also called nettles, Jerusalem cherries, poison berry)	Weakness; stupor, staggering; constipation or diarrhea, dilated pupils; muscle tremors; loss of muscular coordination and sense of feeling; cramps; convulsion; death from respiratory paralysis	Grows from 1 to 2 feet with white flowers resembling tomato plant flowers; has small, berrylike fruit that turns purplish-black at maturity; all parts are toxic; can be found in woods, fields, along fence rows, farm buildings, and in hay and grain fields

Plant	Symptoms	Description
Poison hemlock	Excessive drooling; loss of appetite; muscular weakness; muscular tremors; incoordination; dilated pupils; rapid pulse; pain; bloating; coma; death from respiratory paralysis	Common herbal plant with a purple spotted stem; leaves resemble parsley; root resembles a parsnip or pale carrot; people are often poisoned by mistakenly identifying the root as a parsnip; all of the plant is poisonous; common around farm buildings, roadsides, streams, fields, and ditches
Rattlebush	Rapid pulse; labored respiration; diarrhea; death	Common in the South; has orange blossoms and angled pods; most dangerous in the fall and winter
Rayless goldenrod	Tremors; dullness and depression; respiratory difficulty; death	Bushlike plant with many yellow flowers; grows readily in various types of soil; can be found around irrigation canals, pastures, woods, and fields; no known cure
Silverling	Paralysis and death shortly after ingestion; survivors suffer from weakness and depression	Woody plant from the sunflower family; bears whitish flowers; commonly found in open areas across the United States
St. Johnswort (also called klamath weed, rosin-rose)	Skin blisters; falling hair and scabs, dry skin with cracked open lesions, all caused by extreme sensitivity to sunlight on white skinned areas or unpigmented skin areas	Has small leaves and many yellow flowers; commonly found growing freely in meadows, pastures, and along roadsides; although not deadly, can cause severe skin disruptions in white-skinned animals
White snakeroot (also known as white sanicle, boneset)	Sluggishness; depression; incoordination; trembling; paralysis of throat muscles causing inability to swallow; nasal discharge and respiratory difficulty; death	Herb with tapering leaves and clusters of white flowers; commonly found in woods and shady pastures; poisoning usually occurs in late summer; if plants cannot be eradicated, horses should be removed from the pasture by late July
Yellow jessamine	Rigidity of limbs; lowered pulse rates; drop in body temperature; weakness; convulsions and death	Vine with yellow tubular flowers; toxin acts quickly

(continued)

TABLE 5-1 Poisonous Trees, Plants, and Shrubs (*Continued*)

	Poisonous plants and shrubs	
Plant name	*Symptoms*	*Comments*
Yellow-star thistle	Frequent yawning; stand in abnormal positions; wooden expression; flicking of tongue; paralysis of swallowing muscles causing inability to chew or drink; horse may lower head into water be unable to drink; death follows from starvation and dehydration	Has bright yellow flowers over dandelion-like leaves with cottony wool film over them; common in California, but found throughout the United States; most poisonings occur in late summer or fall; after onset of symptoms, the mortality rate is very high, since there is no known treatment; in areas infested with this plant, it is wise to remove horses from pasture altogether during the most dangerous season

Note: All horsepeople should contact their local Agriculture extension agents for a detailed list of poisonous plants in their regions.

SOURCE: *Horseman* (April 1992).

liver cirrhosis. The effects may not be noticeable until after prolonged feeding of the contaminated hay. Clinical symptoms include weight loss, jaundice, incoordination, depression, aimless wandering, colic, rectal prolapse, diarrhea, and anemia. There is no known treatment.

Yellow star thistle is also toxic to horses. The pattern of poisoning is unknown. Horses must consume at least 600 pounds (272 kg) during a 1- to 2-month period to produce the symptoms. After horses acquire a taste for it, they actively seek out the plant. Some clinical symptoms are being unable to swallow or grab food, pushing the head into water to drink, wrinkled skin around the mouth and nostrils, a wooden expression on the face, lips pulled over the teeth like a purse-string suture, tongue running in and out of the mouth, chewing movements with or without feed in the mouth, yawning, standing or walking around with head down, exhibiting depression, and not being able to close its mouth when attempting to graze. In most advanced cases, the horse starves to death. There is no treatment.

Avocado causes sensitive mastitis in mares and reduces milk flow. Damage usually is not permanent.

Sudangrass and hybrid sorghums are cyanogenic plants. Drought and freezing increase the hydrocyanic acid content in these plants, which cause death if ingested. The presence of lathyrogenis precursors in sorghum plants may indicate that these substances are responsible for cystitis syndrome, a peculiar affliction of horses that graze sudangrass pastures. Clinical signs include posterior ataxia, urine-stained hair and skin ulcerations in the perineal region, and frequent urinations. Reproductive consequences include abortion and fetal deformities.

Fescue pastures may be contaminated with a fungus that is seed-borne. Reproductive problems such as agalactia, abortions, retained placentas, and thick placentas may result from pregnant mares grazing fescue pastures infested with the fungus. Ninety days prior to parturition, pregnant mares should be removed from contaminated fescue pasture to prevent reproduction and lactation problems. A new drug, domperidone, is being used to successfully counteract the effects of fungus-infected fescue grass. Food and Drug Administration approval is required before it can be used by the horse industry.

Rye pastures and hay may contain the ergot sclerotia produced by the fungus *Claviceps purpurea,* which infects it during the flowering and seed-forming stages. Dallas grass may be contaminated with ergot, and Klein grass can cause liver damage.

Further information about poisonous plants can be obtained from the Agriculture Extension Service or by referring to Fowler (1963) and Kingsbury (1964).

Grains and Grain By-Products

The concentrate part of the ration contains the grains, which are higher in energy and lower in fiber than roughages. Many grains are fed to horses, the most common being oats, barley, and corn. Other grains such as wheat, sorghum (milo), and rye are not as popular because of their characteristics discussed below.

Oats

Oats are the most popular grain fed to horses. They are highly palatable, and very few horses refuse to eat oats. One characteristic that has made them popular with horsepeople is their fiber content—about 13 percent higher than corn or barley. This means they have more bulk per nutrient content, and the horse must eat more to satisfy its nutrient requirements. Bulk makes it more difficult for the horse to overeat and get colic or founder. Therefore, it is a safer grain to feed because of a wider margin for error by children, employees, or owners. Oats store quite well when they are harvested and dried properly. Kernels should be plump, heavy, and clean, and have a low ratio of husks to kernels, bright color, and clean smell. The weight of a bushel of oats can help determine if they are heavy and have a low ratio of husks to kernels. The heavier the oats, the more nutrients they contain per unit of weight. U.S. No. 1 heavy oats weigh 36 pounds (16.3 kg) per bushel, whereas U.S. No. 4 oats weigh about 27 pounds (12.2 kg) per bushel. The standard weight is 32 pounds per bushel. To decrease the percentage of husk, lower the fiber content, and increase the nutrient content per unit of weight; the ends of the kernel may be clipped. Clipped oats may weigh 42 to 50 pounds (19.1 to 22.7 kg) per bushel. Oats should be bought according to the least cost per unit of energy, provided they are clean and stored properly. Cleanliness is important; oats should be cleaned to remove dirt, weeds, other seeds, and broken kernels. Dust may indicate old oats and thus a decreased vitamin content or improper storage or cleaning. Dusty feeds lead to respiratory problems. Oats can be checked for dust by filling a can with them and pouring them back into the bin. A musty smell indicates that the oats have been stored with too much moisture and will spoil. They should not taste sour or bitter.

They may be fed whole or processed. Processing includes crimping, rolling, or crushing the kernel. There has been considerable discussion of whether or not oats should be processed. Whole oats are easily eaten and digested by the horse. However, it is desirable to process oats fed to young horses and to older horses with dental problems. If oats are processed, a slight crimp is sufficient. When the kernel coat is broken by processing, less chewing is required, and digestive juices have better access to the kernel. There seems to be a slight increase in digestibility after processing. However, with processing, the nutrients deteriorate faster during storage.

Barley

Barley is comparable to oats as horse feed except for some specific characteristics that influence how it is used. Generally, it is substituted for oats if its cost per unit of energy is less. Barley is lower in fiber than oats and is classified as a "heavy" feed. Barley has a greater energy density and weighs more per unit of volume (48 pounds per bushel, or 21.8 kg). The barley kernel is harder than the oat kernel, so it is usually rolled or crimped before feeding. If the barley (or other grain) kernel is crushed or ground, it is too heavy and can cause colic unless mixed with a bulkier feed such as wheat bran. Barley is evaluated the same way as oats to determine if it is of good quality.

Corn

Corn is one of the most energy-dense feeds; it contains a large amount of carbohydrate. Corn has a high energy content per unit of weight and a high weight per unit volume (56 pounds per bushel) (Table 5-2). Therefore, a given volume of corn contains approximately three times the amount of energy of an equal volume of oats. Because of its energy content, corn became known as "too hot" a feed for horses. However, if the horse is fed according to its energy needs, corn is an excellent feed. Horses that require a lot of energy for exercise and work are usually fed corn. It is one of the few grains that has any vitamin A value. Corn is low in protein and deficient in lysine, an essential amino acid.

Corn quality is judged by the moisture content and by the percentage of well-formed kernels. Very few damaged kernels should be present. Kernels should be well formed, plump, firm, and separated. There should be no insect damage or mold. Moisture content should be less than 14 percent. Because the kernel is high in starch, it ferments readily and becomes toxic. A musty odor indicates excess moisture.

Avoid feeding corn that is contaminated with fumonisin, a mycotoxin. A common soil-borne corn contaminant called *Fusarium moniliforms* flourishes in the tips of some field corn and produces the mycotoxin. Environmental conditions that lead to the mycotoxin production are not exactly known. Ingestion of the mycotoxin produces equine leukoencephalomalacia, commonly referred to as moldy corn poisoning. The condition is characterized by depression, incoordination, and loss of appetite. Some horses may become agitated and excitable; most die within 24 hours. To avoid feeding contaminated

TABLE 5-2 Volume, Weight, and Energy of Common Grains

Grain	Weight per bushel (pounds)	Weight per quart (pounds)	Volume per pound (quart)	Energy content, Mcal per pound	Mcal per quart
Corn, whole	54	1.7	0.6	1.82	3.09
Oats, whole	27–34	1.0	1.0	1.40	1.40
Milo, whole	54–56	1.7	0.6	1.60	2.72
Wheat, whole	60	1.9	0.5	1.76	3.34
Barley, whole	36–47	1.5	0.7	1.66	2.49

corn, do not purchase corn grown in areas where the mycotoxin has been currently found and inquire if corn that is being purchased is free of mycotoxin.

Corn can be fed while still on the cob, which can be used as a management technique for horses that bolt their grain. However, older horses and horses with bad teeth have difficulty eating whole corn. Whole ears keep longer than shelled corn but cost more to store. Many shelled corn kernels pass through the digestive tract without being digested, so it is best to crack or roll it before feeding. Cracked corn may be preferred; it allows the digestive juices to enter and increase the digestibility. Steamed rolled corn is a good feed. Ground or crushed particles are too small, pass rapidly through the small intestine, and ferment quickly in the hind gut. This may lead to colic if the horse is being fed a high-concentrate diet. Whole-ear ground corn can be fed because the cob maintains a high-fiber and low-energy content.

Other Grains

In addition to the commonly used grains, milo and wheat are also used in horse rations.

Milo is a high-energy grain fed to horses primarily in the Southwest. It is a very heavy feed and should be fed with a bulky feed to avoid digestive disturbances. Horses have difficulty chewing it unless it is cracked, rolled, or steam flaked. It may not be very palatable to some horses. The amount of rye included in a ration is generally limited to 33 percent because of its palatability.

Wheat is seldom fed except to very young horses. Most wheat is used for human consumption, and only the by-products of the milling process are available for horse feed. Wheat bran is the hard outer coating of the kernel. One popular way of feeding wheat bran is in the form of a mash. It is highly palatable to horses and is frequently used to add bulk. The content should be kept at 10 to 12 percent of the ration. It is also fed to increase the phosphorus content. Wheat bran has about 12 percent digestible protein. Wheat middlings are fine particles of the wheat kernel obtained during the milling process. Some wheat middlings or shorts are fed to horses, but they must be mixed with a bulky feed. They should be limited to 25 percent of the ration since it is a heavy feed.

Other Feeds

Molasses is a popular component of mixed concentrates and a by-product of sugar refining. Horses like its flavor, it is a cheap source of energy, and it reduces dust in the feed. The proportion of molasses generally should not exceed 10 to 12 percent of the ration; 5 percent is the most common proportion. Excessive amounts make the feed sticky and difficult to handle.

Beet pulp can be dehydrated and used as a source of roughage and energy. It is relatively high in energy and calcium, but low in protein, phosphorus, and

B vitamins. It contains no carotene or vitamin D. Brewer's yeast and dried brewer's grain are very palatable and are frequently included in commercial horse feeds. Brewer's yeast is a good source of B vitamins. Dried brewer's grains are a good source of protein and fiber.

Other by-product feeds that are used in horse rations include citrus pulp, hominy feed, feeding oat meal, oat mill by-products, rice polishings, soybean hulls, dried whey, dried brewer's grains, and dried distiller's grains and dehydrated brewer's yeast. Generally, they comprise only a small portion of a mixed feed. They are used for their energy, protein, vitamin, and mineral content.

Fats and oils are added to horse rations to increase the energy density and reduce dust. Horses with a high energy requirement generally benefit from the inclusion of lipids in the ration. They are the result of rendering or extraction processes of plant and animal material.

Supplements

Ration supplements are usually intended to increase nutritive value. There are four common types: protein, vitamin, mineral, and a combination of the three.

Protein

Adding a protein supplement is usually indicated when a horse has a high protein requirement. As previously discussed, horses that are growing, lactating, or in later stages of pregnancy have higher protein requirements. Additional protein may be required when horses are being fed a poor-quality roughage.

Protein is expensive, and many rations contain excess protein. The additional protein does not harm the horse because it is converted to energy. Excess nitrogen, a product of the conversion process, must be eliminated from the horse's body via urine, in the form of urea. This increases urine formation, and the urine has a strong ammonia smell.

Excessive feeding of nonprotein nitrogen sources such as urea can result in harmful ammonia toxicosis. Horses are more tolerant of urea than are cattle, and they tolerate up to 4 percent of the total diet.

Several feeds are commonly used as protein supplements: alfalfa, linseed, canola, soybean, and cottonseed meals; meat, bone, and blood meals; milk products; and dried brewer's yeast. Alfalfa meal and legume pellets are excellent sources of dietary protein for all horses. Of the three oilseed meals, soybean meal is the best protein source, particularly for young, growing horses. Soybean meal contains a better balance of the essential amino acids and has a higher lysine content compared with the other oilseed meals. Lysine is one of the limiting amino acids for growth. Cottonseed and linseed meals should not be the primary source of dietary protein unless they are fed in excess or supplemented with a lysine source. Modern methods of processing oilseeds extract a higher percentage of the oil. As a result, linseed meal is no longer fed to horses to enhance their coat, because the oil content in the meal is lower. Instead, add 2 to 3 tablespoons (28.6 to 42.9 ml) of corn or safflower oil to the ration each day to accomplish the same purpose. Cottonseed meal contains gossypol, which is toxic to pigs. However, mature horses can eat about 1.5 pounds (0.68 kg) per day without problem. Dried skim milk is an excellent source of dietary protein, particularly for young, growing horses (weanlings and yearlings), because it contains a high level of lysine.

Casein, fish meal, and meat meal are not widely used in horse rations. They are expensive and not readily available. Furthermore, meat meal is not very palatable and its high fat content may result in rancidity of the ration. If fish meals are used, they must be checked to see if they are contaminated with bacteria that cause diarrhea.

Vitamins

Vitamin supplementation is a very widespread mismanagement practice. If the horse receives sufficient vitamins from its ration or synthesizes them in its body, no vitamin supplement is needed. It is very uneconomical, and the horse derives no benefit from the excess vitamins. In fact, excess vitamins can greatly harm a horse. If a ration needs additional vitamins to balance it and to provide the daily requirements of the horse, several sources can be used. Supplementary sources of vitamin A are commercially synthesized vitamin A, fish liver oils, and liver meal. Carotene, a precursor of vitamin A, can be supplemented by adding dehydrated alfalfa meal, corn gluten meal, and good-quality hay. Fresh green forage such as pasture is an excellent source of carotene. Supplements high in B vitamins are dried brewer's yeast, animal liver meal, wheat germ, soybean oil meal, and dried legumes. The primary source of vitamin D is sun-cured hay and exposure to sunlight. Fish liver oils and irradiated yeast are excellent sources. Vitamin E is found in most feeds and seldom needs to be supplemented. Alfalfa pellets are a good source of vitamin E.

Injectable vitamins should be used only on the recommendation of a veterinarian to treat a disease or a deficiency.

Minerals

Mineral supplements are frequently needed to balance the mineral content of rations (see Table 5-3). The most commonly deficient minerals are calcium, phosphorus, sodium, chloride, and iodine. Salt (sodium chloride) and iodine requirements can be met by keeping iodized salt available to the horse in the form of a salt block or granules. There are many sources of calcium and phosphorus. The choice of which supplement to use depends on availability and cost. Ground limestone and oyster shell flour are good sources of calcium. Monosodium and disodium phosphates are good sources of phosphorus. Both calcium and phosphorus are supplied by steamed bone meal, dicalcium phosphate, monocalcium phosphate, and spent bone block.

TABLE 5-3 Composition of Mineral Supplements for Horses (100%-dry-matter basis)

Entry No.	Feed name	International feed number	Dry matter (%)	Protein equivalent (%) (N × 6.25)	Macrominerals (%)							Microminerals (ppm or mg/kg)							
					Calcium	Chlorine	Magnesium	Phosphorus	Potassium	Sodium	Sulfur	Cobalt	Copper	Fluorine	Iodine	Iron	Manganese	Selenium	Zinc
24	Phosphate, monobasic, monohydrate, $NaH_2PO_4 \cdot H_2O$; see also Sodium	6-04-288	97					22.50		16.68	1.55								
25	Phosphoric acid, H_3PO_4	6-03-707	75		0.05		0.51	31.60	0.02	0.04			10	10	3,100		17,500	500	130
26	Potassium bicarbonate, $KHCO_3$, cp[a]	6-29-493	99[b]		0.05				39.05										
27	chloride, KCl	6-03-755	100			47.30	0.34		50.00	1.00	0.45						600		
28	iodide, KI	6-03-759	100[b]						21.00						681,700				
29	sulfate, K_2SO_4	6-06-098	98[b]		0.15	1.55	0.61		41.84	0.09	17.35						710	10	
30	Selenium selenite, Na_2SeO_3	6-26-013	98[b]							26.60								456,000	
31	Sodium bicarbonate, $NaHCO_3$	6-04-272	100							27.00									
32	chloride, $NaCl$	6-04-152	100			60.66				39.34									
33	phosphate, monobasic, monohydrate, $NaH_2PO_4 \cdot H_2O$; see also Phosphate	6-04-288	97					22.50		16.68									
34	sulfate, decahydrate, $Na_2SO_4 \cdot 10\,H_2O$, cp[a]	6-04-292	97[b]							14.27	9.95								
35	tripolyphosphate, $Na_5P_3O_{10}$	6-08-076	96					25.00		31.00							40		
36	Zinc oxide, ZnO	6-05-533	100		0.02	0.015													780,000
37	sulfate, monohydrate, $ZnSO_4 \cdot H_2O$	6-05-555	99[b]								17.68						10	10	363,600

Note: The composition of mineral ingredients that are hydrated (e.g., $CaSO_4 \cdot 2H_2O$) is shown, including the waters of hydration. Mineral compositions of feed-grade mineral supplements vary by source, mining site, and manufacturer. Use manufacturer's analysis when available.

[a] cp = chemically pure.

[b] Dry-matter values have been estimated for these minerals.

SOURCE: *Nutrient Requirements of Horses,* 5th ed., National Research Council (1989).

The remainder of the minerals, referred to as trace minerals, are found in most natural feeds unless feeds are grown in areas of known mineral deficiency. A trace-mineralized salt block can be used if necessary. The local Agriculture Extension Service can provide information about trace mineral status of locally grown feeds.

NUTRIENT REQUIREMENTS

For normal body functioning, horses need six nutrients: water, carbohydrates, fats, protein, minerals, and vitamins. In addition to understanding which nutrients are required, the horseperson must understand the factors that regulate the amounts of required nutrients. These factors are growth, maintenance, reproduction, lactation, and work.

Water

The horse must have a source of fresh, clean drinking water. It drinks about 8 to 12 gallons (30.2 to 45.4 liters) per day during normal environmental conditions. Several factors control the amount of water each horse needs. One of the most important factors is dry-matter intake. Approximately 3 liters of water per kilogram of dry matter are required. During hot weather or when the horse is subjected to hard work, the water requirement is higher and may even double because of the water lost via sweating and respiration. Losses of 5 to 10 percent of body weight have been observed among horses during endurance rides. Pregnant mares require about 10 percent more water than do nonpregnant mares. Lactating mares require 50 to 75 percent additional water to replace that secreted in the milk.

The horse should have water available for drinking at all times. Some horsepeople prefer to water the horse in the morning and afternoon by placing water in the stall. Make sure the horse drinks enough to meet its daily requirements. Automatic drinking fountains ensure a source of fresh water but may get stuck open, flooding the stall.

During hot weather or while working, the horse should be allowed to drink frequently. This helps prevent overheating and keeps the horse refreshed. To prevent water founder, do not allow horses that are hot after being heavily exercised to drink too much cold water at one time (see the section on founder in Chapter 2). The horse should be cooled out and allowed to take a few swallows every couple of minutes while it is being walked around.

Horsepeople disagree as to the proper time of watering in relation to feeding. The horse can drink before, during, or after eating without any adverse effects on the horse or digestion.

Depriving a horse of water reduces its feed intake. After 3 to 4 days, the horse will eat very little, if any, feed. The feed reduction is accompanied by rapid weight loss. The weight loss is primarily due to dehydration and can be replaced in 3 to 4 days.

Water quality is important for horses. Common problems encountered are high salt content and pollution with disease organisms and toxic industrial wastes, including minerals. The safe upper limit of some mineral elements is given in Table 5-4. There are usually a number of local sources to test water and the Cooperative Extension Service can provide recommendations for having water tested.

Carbohydrates and Fats

The primary function of carbohydrates and fats is to provide energy. The expression *feed energy* denotes the value of feed for its greatest function, which is to furnish energy for body processes. There are several ways to express the energy content of feeds, but all rations are formulated for their digestible energy content or total digestible nutrient content. Gross energy—the total energy content of a feed—is determined by measuring the heat produced when the feed is ignited in a bomb calorimeter. Digestible energy is the gross energy of the feed minus the energy lost in the feces. Digestible energy (DE) is determined by digestion trials. Energy requirements are most commonly expressed as DE, the basis for all calculations in this text. Metabolizable energy (ME) is

TABLE 5-4 Safe Upper Level of Some Mineral Elements in Drinking Water for Horses

Mineral element	Safe upper limit (mg/liter)
Arsenic	0.02
Calcium	0.05
Chromium	1.0
Cobalt	1.0
Copper	0.5
Fluoride	2.0
Lead	0.1
Mercury	0.01
Nickel	1.0
Nitrate nitrogen	100.0
Nitrite nitrogen	10.0
Vanadium	0.1
Zinc	25.0

SOURCE: Adapted from National Research Council (1974).

a more refined definition of the amount of energy retained in the horse's body. Energy lost in the urine and gaseous products of digestion is subtracted from the DE value to obtain the ME value. Net energy (NE) is the energy actually used by the horse. The units to express these energy values are calories. A calorie is the amount of heat necessary to raise the temperature of 1 gram of water 1 degree Celsius; 1 kilocalorie (kcal) is 1000 calories, and a megacalorie (Mcal) is 1000 kilocalories.

Another method of expressing energy content of feed is total digestible nutrients (TDN), the sum of all the digestible organic nutrients retained in the horse's body. It is determined according to the same method as digestible energy but is expressed as weight or percent TDN. One pound of TDN is equivalent to 2000 kcal (1 kg TDN = 4410 kcal). Some feed tags give the TDN content.

Maintenance and Special Requirements

The requirement for energy varies according to the physiological state of the horse and its activity (Appendix Tables 5-1 to 5-8). The basic requirement for energy is referred to as the maintenance requirement. This is the amount of energy required to maintain a constant body weight during normal activities of a nonworking horse. The maintenance energy requirement of horses weighing up to 600 kg (1320 lbs) are estimated from the equation

$$DE \text{ (Mcal/day)} = 1.4 + 0.03 \text{ (kg body weight)}$$

The estimates for horses over 600 kg are from the equation

$$DE \text{ (Mcal/day)} = 1.82 + 0.0383 \text{ (kg body weight)} - 0.00015 \text{ (kg body weight)}^2$$

The two equations reflect the fact that horses over 600 kg are less active and require less energy per kilogram of body weight.

Appendix Tables 5-1 to 5-8 must be considered as a starting point when calculating a ration and feeding a horse. At first, it is best to feed the horse an additional 10 to 15 percent DE. This is necessary because the table values are estimated and allow no margin of error. They do not take into account an activity factor, environmental influences (cold weather), parasitism, or individuality. Some horses are "hard keepers" and require more energy. Others are "easy keepers" and require less energy than normal. If the horse starts to get fat, the amount of feed can be reduced, and vice versa. The most common problem is obesity from overfeeding, coupled with lack of exercise. The most noticeable effects of insufficient energy intake are loss of weight, loss of condition, and excessive fatigue.

Exercise

Exercise increases the DE requirement above the maintenance requirement. The DE requirements for work have been estimated by several methods. These estimates are influenced by a variety of factors such as condition, type of training, ability, weight of rider and tack, degree of fatigue, environmental temperature and humidity, and diet composition. For horses up to 600 kg body weight, estimates in Appendix Tables 5-1 to 5-8 are based on an increased requirement of 25, 50, and 100 percent above maintenance for light, medium, and intense work, respectively. Light work is typified by riding, such as showing or training for western and English pleasure and equitation, and for bridle path hack. Moderate work includes ranch work and short bouts of exercise like roping, cutting, barrel racing, and jumping. Intense exercise includes race training, polo, and polocrosse. For horses that are performing for long periods of time, energy requirements can be estimated by the equation

$$\text{DE (kcal/kg/hr)} = ([e(3.02 + 0.0065\ Y) - 13.92] \times .006)/0.57$$

where Y is the speed in meters per minute. Because of the factors previously discussed and individuality of horse and rider, it cannot be overemphasized that the estimates are indeed estimates and that owners must continuously monitor body condition of the performance horse to ensure that it is receiving adequate energy intake.

Reproduction

Reproduction influences the energy requirement. Stallions need more energy during the breeding season because their exercise increases. Semen production does not significantly increase the energy requirement. Pregnancy significantly increases the energy requirement only during the last 90 to 120 days of pregnancy (Appendix Tables 5-1 to 5-8). Prior to the last trimester of pregnancy, fetal growth is slow, and only 50 percent of fetal growth occurs over the long period of time. If the mare's weight increases 5 to 6 percent, the foal's weight should be normal. Under ideal management conditions, the products of conception are about 10 percent of the mare's weight. This means that the mare converted 5 percent of her body tissues to fetal tissue. If a mare converts slightly more than 5 percent of her tissue to the products of conception (loses a little more than 5 percent of her body weight), the foal's birth weight will be maintained; but the mare loses too much condition, which decreases her milk production and affects the foal's growth rate. If the mare loses too much body weight, the birth weight will be decreased, as will subsequent milk production.

Estimates of energy requirements for gestation were formulated by multiplying the maintenance requirements in Appendix Tables 5-1 to 5-8 by 1.11, 1.13, and 1.2 for months 9, 10, and 11 of gestation, respectively. There is a high correlation of body condition (amount of body fat) to reproductive performance of nonpregnant and pregnant broodmares. A body condition scoring system with scores ranging from 1 to 9 has been developed to appraise the degree of fatness and serve as a standard of reference (Table 5-5). The condition scores are based on visual appraisal and palpation of fat deposits (Figure 5-4). Pregnancy rates of mares entering the breeding season with a body condition score of 5 or greater, and maintained scores of 5 or greater, are higher. The number of estrous cycles bred per conception are lower and they start to cycle earlier in the breeding season. Mares with condition scores less than 5 have higher abortion rates, require more breedings per conception, and have lower conception rates. A common misconception has been that fat mares have lowered reproductive efficiency. Obese mares do not experience foaling problems nor are they difficult to breed as a result of increased body fat. However it is not recommended that mares be kept in an obese condition because of the susceptibility to other problems such as laminitis. Mares with body condition scores of 7 to 9 can lose body weight and still have high conception rates. Also, mares with condition scores of 3 and 4 that are gaining weight have higher conception rates than those that are maintaining a constant body weight and a condition score of 3 or 4. Thus, the body condition of broodmares is important and should be monitored regularly. During shipping or sudden decreases of temperature in cold weather, mares can rapidly lose body condition and abortion rate can increase.

Lactation

The lactating mare has the highest energy requirement (Appendix Tables 5-1 to 5-8). She needs enough energy for good milk production and to regain any body weight lost during gestation. Lactation can double the energy requirement, so the nutritional management of lactating mares is critical.

Milk production by mares tends to reach a peak at 2 months and then starts to decline. During the first 3 months, the amount of milk produced by the light horse breeds is about 3 percent of the mare's body weight; for pony mares, it is 4 percent. During the next 3 months, it is about 2 percent for the light breeds and 3 percent for pony mares. During the first 3 months, milk production is usually adequate to meet the foal's nutritional needs, but some mares produce an inadequate amount of milk.

Growth

The energy requirement for growth has not been established, because optimal growth rates have not been defined (Figure 5-5). Some horses may grow too fast in terms of body weight increases, which in turn may influence soundness and longevity. The recommendations in Appendix Tables 5-1 to 5-8 are based on the requirements for daily gain and for rapid and moderate growth,

TABLE 5-5 Description of the Condition Score System

Score	Description
1	*Poor.* Animal extremely emaciated. Spinous processes, ribs, tailhead, and hooks and pins projecting prominently. Bone structure of withers, shoulders, and neck easily noticeable. No fatty tissues can be felt.
2	*Very Thin.* Animal emaciated. Slight fat covering over base of spinous processes, transverse processes of lumbar vertebrae feel rounded. Spinous processes, ribs, tailhead, and hooks and pins prominent. Withers, shoulders, neck structures faintly discernable.
3	*Thin.* Fat built up about halfway on spinous processes, transverse processes cannot be felt. Slight fat cover over ribs. Spinous processes and ribs easily discernable. Tailhead prominent, but individual vertebrae cannot be visually identified. Pin bones not distinguishable. Withers, shoulders, and neck accentuated.
4	*Moderately Thin.* Negative crease along back. Faint outline of ribs discernable. Tailhead prominence depends on conformation, fat can be felt around it. Hook bones not discernable. Withers, shoulders, and neck not obviously thin.
5	*Moderate.* Back level. Ribs cannot be visually distinguished but can he easily felt. Fat around tailhead beginning to feel spongy. Withers appear rounded over spinous processes. Shoulders and neck blend smoothly into body.
6	*Moderate to Fleshy.* May have slight crease down back. Fat over ribs feels spongy. Fat around tailhead feels soft. Fat beginning to be deposited along the sides of the withers, behind the shoulders and along the sides of the neck.
7	*Fleshy.* May have crease down back. Individual ribs can be felt, but noticeable filling between ribs with fat. Fat around tailhead is soft. Fat deposited along withers, behind shoulders, and along the neck.
8	*Fat.* Crease down back. Difficult to feel ribs. Fat around tailhead very soft. Area along withers filled with fat. Area behind shoulder filled in flush. Noticeable thickening of neck. Fat deposited along inner buttocks.
9	*Extremely Fat.* Obvious crease down back. Patchy fat appearing over ribs. Bulging fat around tailhead, along withers, behind shoulders, and along neck. Fat along inner buttocks may rub together. Flank filled in flush.

SOURCE: Henneke et al. (1983).

taking into account the size of the horse relative to its expected final mature weight. Insufficient energy intake results in poor growth rates and an unthrifty appearance.

Feeding excess energy in the form of soluble carbohydrates for rapid weight gain has been associated with developmental orthopedic disease (see Chapter 16, Congenital Defects in Foals). Rapid growth in foals can be achieved without developmental orthopedic disease, by maintaining the proper ratio of protein and lysine to energy (see section on Formulating and Balancing Rations). Because lysine is apparently the first limiting amino acid in typical diets for growing horses, calculations from a number of research trials suggest the relationship between protein and lysine requirements and energy intake as shown in Table 5-6.

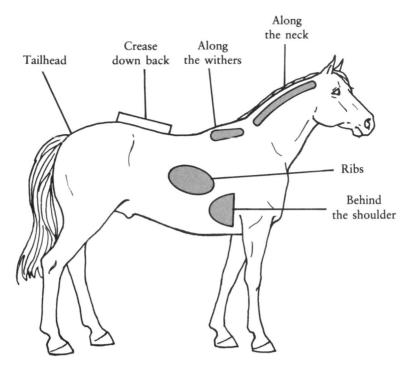

FIGURE 5-4 Visual appraisal areas used when determining body condition score.

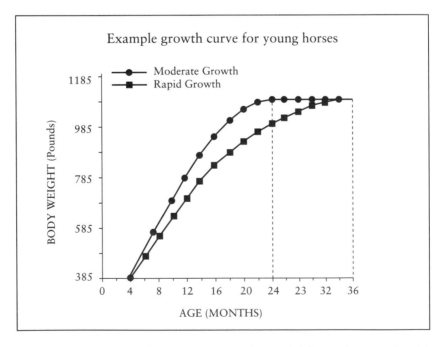

FIGURE 5-5 Example growth curves for young horses fed for moderate and rapid growth. (From Gibbs and Potter, 1993.)

TABLE 5-6   Relationship between Protein and Lysine Requirements and Energy Intake

	CP (g/Mcal DE)	DP (g/Mcal DE)	Lysine (g/Mcal DE)
Weanlings	50	30	2.1
Yearlings	45	27	1.9
2-year-olds	42.5	25.5	1.7

SOURCE: World Animal Science: C Production System Approach, Vol 7, *Horse Breeding and Management*, 1993.

The anticipated mature height of a foal is always of interest to a breeder. The mature height can be predicted with reasonable accuracy if the height at withers at birth is known. This method assumes normal growth and development, and neither breeding nor castration has an effect on the accuracy. However, some individual variation does exist and some bloodlines do mature earlier or later than the average. At birth, males have 61 percent of their mature height at the withers; at 12 months, 91 percent of final height; and at 24 months, 96 percent of final wither height. Females will have a higher percentage of height at birth (63 percent), at 12 months (92 percent), and at 24 months (97 percent).

Protein

Protein requirements of horses are expressed as crude protein (CP) or digestible protein (DP). Crude protein is a measurement of the amount of nitrogen contained in the feed, though not all the nitrogen is available to the horse in the form of protein. Digestible protein is the amount of available protein in the feed. The percentage of crude protein that is digestible varies from feed to feed and among classes of feed. About 70 percent of the CP in grass forage is DP, whereas it is about 85 percent for legumes and mixed rations.

Another factor that must be considered when protein requirements are discussed is protein quality. Protein is made of building blocks called amino acids. Some amino acids cannot be synthesized within the horse's body and are called essential amino acids. Nonessential amino acids can be synthesized from carbon skeletons resulting from carbohydrate and fat metabolism. The requirement for protein should really be expressed per amino acid, but the necessary research has not been performed. Protein quality indicates the amino acid balance of a feed. Good-quality protein has a balance of amino acids about the same as that found in the horse's body. Poor-quality protein is deficient in one or more essential amino acids. Protein quality is important because all the amino acids must be present and in the right amounts for protein synthesis to occur. If one amino acid is left out, synthesis cannot occur, and if one amino acid is not present in a sufficient amount, its deficiency limits the use of the other amino acids. To obtain the proper balance of amino acids, several feeds are usually combined to form a ration. This is important for young, growing horses.

Appendix Tables 5-1 to 5-8 list the requirements for protein. For horses kept on a maintenance ration, the CP should be kept at 7 to 8 percent (Tables 5-7A and 5-7B). Lower levels of CP are usually associated with low palatability of the ration and reduced food intake, body tissue loss, poor hair coat, and reduced hoof growth. Exercise does not increase the protein requirement beyond what would be supplied by the increased feed intake to meet the energy needs, provided the ration has a value of 40 g of CP per Mcal of DE. The same holds for the stallion. During the last 90 to 120 days of pregnancy, the mare's protein requirement increases to meet the needs of the rapidly developing fetus. About 60 to 65 percent of fetal development occurs during this period. The ration should contain 9 to 10 percent CP (Tables 5-7A and 5-7B) and a protein/energy ratio of 44 g per Mcal DE. Failure to supply adequate protein during gestation results in decreased birth weight and a loss in the mare's weight. During lactation, a ration containing 11 to 13.2 percent CP is required (Tables 5-7A and 5-7B). Growing horses appear unthrifty, have a high ratio of feed to weight gain, and have poor growth if their protein needs are not met. The rations for weanlings and yearlings should contain 13 to 14.5 and 11.3 to 12.6 percent CP, respectively. There is an optimum ratio of protein to energy for the growing horse. For weanlings, it is 50 g and for yearlings, it is 45 g crude protein/Mcal of DE per day (Table 5-7A). It is important that they be fed high-quality protein. Lysine, an essential amino acid, appears to be the most limiting amino acid for growth. Thus, the lysine requirement is 2.1 and 1.9 g/Mcal of DE per day for weanlings and yearlings, respectively. Dried skim milk and soybean and alfalfa meal are good sources of lysine. A mixture of feeds should be used for the young, growing horse to achieve the proper balance of amino acids.

The feeding of excess protein is a common problem encountered in the horse industry. Other than the increased cost of the ration, moderate excess does not appear to be detrimental to the horse. There is, however, an increased water requirement to rid the body of the excess nitrogen.

Vitamins

Vitamins are needed in exceedingly small amounts. They serve as catalysts for many transformations and reactions in the body tissues. Most vitamins act as coenzymes, which are small but essential parts of an enzyme that catalyzes some body process. Some vitamins can be synthesized in the body; others must be present in the diet.

Vitamins are divided into two general groups. Vitamins A, D, E, and K are soluble in lipids or lipid solvents and are referred to as fat-soluble vitamins. They are stored by the body in fat cells and in the liver. Thus, the horse can

TABLE 5-7A Nutrient Concentrations in Total Diets for Horses and Ponies (dry-matter basis)

	Digestible energy[a]		Diet proportions		Crude protein (%)	Lysine (%)	Calcium (%)	Phosphorus (%)	Magnesium (%)	Potassium (%)	Vitamin A	
	(Mcal/kg)	(Mcal/lb)	Conc. (%)	Hay (%)							(IU/kg)	(IU/lb)
Mature horses												
Maintenance	2.00	0.90	0	100	8.0	0.28	0.24	0.17	0.09	0.30	1830	830
Stallions	2.40	1.10	30	70	9.6	0.34	0.29	0.21	0.11	0.36	2640	1200
Pregnant mares												
9 months	2.25	1.00	20	80	10.0	0.35	0.43	0.32	0.10	0.35	3710	1680
10 months	2.25	1.00	20	80	10.0	0.35	0.43	0.32	0.10	0.36	3650	1660
11 months	2.40	1.10	30	70	10.6	0.37	0.45	0.34	0.11	0.38	3650	1660
Lactating mares												
foaling to 3 months	2.60	1.20	50	50	13.2	0.46	0.52	0.34	0.10	0.42	2750	1250
3 months to weaning	2.45	1.15	35	65	11.0	0.37	0.36	0.22	0.09	0.33	3020	1370
Working horses												
light work[b]	2.45	1.15	35	65	9.8	0.35	0.30	0.22	0.11	0.37	2690	1220
moderate work[c]	2.65	1.20	50	50	10.4	0.37	0.31	0.23	0.12	0.39	2420	1100
intense work[d]	2.85	1.30	65	35	11.4	0.40	0.35	0.25	0.13	0.43	1950	890

(continued)

TABLE 5-7A Nutrient Concentrations in Total Diets for Horses and Ponies (dry-matter basis) (*Continued*)

	Digestible energy[a]		Diet proportions		Crude protein (%)	Lysine (%)	Calcium (%)	Phosphorus (%)	Magnesium (%)	Potassium (%)	Vitamin A	
	(Mcal/kg)	(Mcal/lb)	Conc. (%)	Hay (%)							(IU/kg)	(IU/lb)
Growing horses												
Weanling, 4 months	2.90	1.40	70	30	14.5	0.60	0.68	0.58	0.08	0.30	1580	720
Weanling, 6 months												
moderate growth	2.90	1.40	70	30	14.5	0.61	0.56	0.51	0.08	0.30	1870	850
rapid growth	2.90	1.40	70	30	14.5	0.61	0.61	0.54	0.08	0.30	1630	740
Yearling, 12 months												
moderate growth	2.80	1.30	60	40	12.6	0.53	0.43	0.24	0.08	0.30	2160	980
rapid growth	2.80	1.30	60	40	12.6	0.53	0.45	0.25	0.08	0.30	1920	870
Long yearling, 18 months												
not in training	2.50	1.15	45	55	11.3	0.48	0.34	0.19	0.08	0.30	2270	1030
in training	2.65	1.20	50	50	12.0	0.50	0.36	0.20	0.09	0.30	1800	820
2-year-old, 24 months												
not in training	2.45	1.15	35	65	10.4	0.42	0.31	0.17	0.09	0.30	2640	1200
in training	2.65	1.20	50	50	11.3	0.45	0.34	0.20	0.10	0.32	2040	930

[a] Values assume a concentrate feed containing 3.3 Mcal/kg and hay containing 2.00 Mcal/kg of dry matter.
[b] Examples are horses used in Western and English pleasure, bridle path hack, equitation, etc.
[c] Examples are horses used in ranch work, roping, cutting, barrel racing, jumping, etc.
[d] Examples are race training, polo, etc.
SOURCE: *Nutrient Requirements of Horses*, 5th ed., National Research Council (1989).

TABLE 5-7B Nutrient Concentrations in Total Diets for Horses and Ponies (90%-dry-matter basis)

	Digestible energy[a]		Diet proportions		Crude protein (%)	Lysine (%)	Cal-cium (%)	Phos-phorus (%)	Mag-nesium (%)	Potas-sium (%)	Vitamin A	
	(Mcal/kg)	(Mcal/lb)	Conc. (%)	Hay (%)							(IU/kg)	(IU/lb)
Mature horses												
Maintenance	1.80	0.80	0	100	7.2	0.25	0.21	0.15	0.08	0.27	1650	750
Stallions	2.15	1.00	30	70	8.6	0.30	0.26	0.19	0.10	0.33	2370	1080
Pregnant mares												
9 months	2.00	0.90	20	80	8.9	0.31	0.39	0.29	0.10	0.32	3330	1510
10 months	2.00	0.90	20	80	9.0	0.32	0.39	0.30	0.10	0.33	3280	1490
11 months	2.15	1.00	30	70	9.5	0.33	0.41	0.31	0.10	0.35	3280	1490
Lactating mares												
foaling to 3 months	2.35	1.10	50	50	12.0	0.41	0.47	0.30	0.09	0.38	2480	1130
3 months to weaning	2.20	1.05	35	65	10.0	0.34	0.33	0.20	0.08	0.30	2720	1240
Working horses												
light work[b]	2.20	1.05	35	65	8.8	0.32	0.27	0.19	0.10	0.34	2420	1100
moderate work[c]	2.40	1.10	50	50	9.4	0.35	0.28	0.22	0.11	0.36	2140	970
intense work[d]	2.55	1.20	65	35	10.3	0.36	0.31	0.23	0.12	0.39	1760	800

(continued)

217

TABLE 5-7B Nutrient Concentrations in Total Diets for Horses and Ponies (90% dry-matter basis) (*Continued*)

	Digestible energy[a]		Diet proportions		Crude protein (%)	Lysine (%)	Cal-cium (%)	Phos-phorus (%)	Mag-nesium (%)	Potas-sium (%)	Vitamin A	
	(Mcal/kg)	(Mcal/lb)	Conc. (%)	Hay (%)							(IU/kg)	(IU/lb)
Growing horses												
Weanling, 4 months	2.60	1.25	70	30	13.1	0.54	0.62	0.34	0.07	0.27	1420	650
Weanling, 6 months												
moderate growth	2.60	1.25	70	30	13.0	0.55	0.50	0.28	0.07	0.27	1680	760
rapid growth	2.60	1.25	70	30	13.1	0.55	0.55	0.30	0.07	0.27	1470	670
Yearling, 12 months												
moderate growth	2.50	1.15	60	40	11.3	0.48	0.39	0.21	0.07	0.27	1950	890
rapid growth	2.50	1.15	60	40	11.3	0.48	0.40	0.22	0.07	0.27	17.30	790
Long yearling, 18 months												
not in training	2.30	1.05	45	55	10.1	0.43	0.31	0.17	0.07	0.27	2050	930
in training	2.40	1.10	50	50	10.8	0.45	0.32	0.18	0.0X	0.27	1620	740
2-year-old, 24 months												
not in training	2.20	1.00	35	65	9.4	0.38	0.28	0.15	0.08	0.27	2.380	1080
in training	2.40	1.10	50	50	10.1	0.41	0.31	0.17	0.09	0.29	1840	840

[a] Values assume a concentrate feed containing 3.3 Mcal/kg and hay containing 2.00 Mcal/kg of dry matter.
[b] Examples are horses used in Western and English pleasure, bridle path hack, equitation, etc.
[c] Examples are horses used in ranch work, roping, cutting, barrel racing, jumping, etc.
[d] Examples are race training, polo, etc.

SOURCE: *Nutrient Requirements of Horses*, 5th ed., National Research Council (1989).

maintain a reserve supply of the fat-soluble vitamins. The vitamin B complex and vitamin C belong to the water-soluble group. They are not stored by the body and must be ingested or synthesized daily.

Vitamin A

The functions of vitamin A are not fully understood, but deficiency and toxicity symptoms are well documented. One of the first deficiency symptoms is impairment of vision. Lacrimation—excessive watering of the eyes—is observed. This is in response to the cornea becoming too dry. The cornea can be damaged, and blindness can result. Night blindness is also observed. The horse has difficulty seeing when adjusting from bright to dim light. The skin becomes rough and dry, with a brittle hair coat. Skin lesions may develop that are difficult to heal. Poor hoof growth, digestive disturbances, impaired conception, and respiratory illness are observed.

Vitamin A refers to all the derivatives of β-ionone (except the carotenoids) that possess the biological activity of all-*trans*-retinol. One International Unit (IU) or United States Pharmacopeia (USP) of vitamin A activity can be derived from .0003 mg of all-*trans*-retinol. Provitamin A refers to the approximately 50 carotenoids that show biological activity of vitamin A of which all-*trans*-β-carotene is the most important one.

Vitamin A requirements of horses can be met by all-*trans*-β-carotene, which is found in all fresh green forages and is converted to vitamin A in the wall of the intestine. Carotenes are unstable in sunlight, oxygen, and high temperatures. About 90 percent of the carotene is lost when hay is left unprotected from sun and rain for 1 year. The carotene content also decreases when hay is properly stored, so that after 6 months of storage, a significant percentage of the carotene has broken down; after 2 years, only 10 percent remains. Fortunately, vitamin A is stored in the liver, and horses feeding on green forage can store 3 to 6 months' supply. Care must be taken not to oversupplement vitamin A, because toxicity causes bone fragility, hyperostosis, and exfoliated epithelium.

Vitamin A requirements can also be met by a derivative of retinol or by commercial forms of all-*trans*-retinol. All-*trans*-retinol palmitate and acetate are the two most commonly used forms.

Estimates of vitamin A requirements for all horses are: 30 to 60 IU of vitamin A activity as retinol or equivalent/kg body weight/day or 120 to 240 IU of provitamin A activity as carotene/kg body weight/day.

Vitamin D

Vitamin D is a common name that collectively refers to vitamin D_2 and vitamin D_3. Vitamin D is not a dietary requirement. The action of ultraviolet rays in the sunlight converts 7-dehydrocholesterol, a substance in the skin, to vitamin D_3, which is then absorbed by the body. Exposure to sun for

30 minutes per day is adequate to meet the daily requirement. The other source of vitamin D results from ultraviolet irradiation of ergosteral to ergocalciferol (vitamin D_2) after certain plants have been cut and exposed to sunlight. Thus, sun-cured hay is an excellent source.

The exact requirements for vitamin D have not been established. A deficiency symptom is rickets, but it is seldom observed. Oversupplementation is a common problem. Ten times the daily requirement of 2500 to 5000 IU (6.6 IU/kg or 300 IU/100 lb) for several months can lead to toxicity symptoms. Excessive calcium deposits develop in soft tissues such as the heart, muscle, and arteries. Once deposited, the calcium cannot be removed and bone abnormalities develop. Certain plants, such as day jasmine, contain toxic levels of vitamin D-like compounds. Excess amounts of the vitamin can be stored in the liver, so it is very seldom necessary to add vitamin D to the ration. Rations containing a maximum level of 2200 IU of vitamin D_3 per kg have been proposed by the National Research Council to be safe for long-term feeding (over 60 days).

Vitamin E

Vitamin E is the common reference to eight or more compounds that are quantitatively equivalent in biological activity to α-tocopherol. They are fat soluble, and their activity is expressed in International Units. Very little is known about vitamin E requirements. Current evidence indicates that total diets for foals, pregnant and lactating mares, and working horses should contain 80 to 100 IU per kg of dietary dry matter.

Because vitamin E functions as an antioxidant, vitamin E compounds are easily oxidized. Thus, the natural forms are unstable. Improper storage of feedstuffs leads to a rapid decrease in vitamin E content. High moisture content, which results in fermentation and growth of mold and grinding of grains, leads to a rapid decline. Commercial forms used to fortify rations are esterified chemically and are stable during storage. Following consumption, the ester links are broken in the digestive tract and the compound's biological activity is restored.

Vitamin E is found in green, growing forage, good-quality hay, cereal grains, and wheat germ oil. It has been synthesized, and α-tocopherol is used when a supplement is required. There have been many claims about the benefits of vitamin E, but few are based on scientific evidence. When combined with selenium, it has been an effective treatment for white muscle disease (degenerative skeletal muscles). It has been associated with muscle development, oxygen transport, red blood cell stability, and fertility. Vitamin E toxicity has not been observed in the horse.

Equine degenerative myeloencephalopathy (EDM) may develop during the rapid-growth stages in young horses that have some problem in transport or metabolic use of vitamin E. EDM can make the young horse unstable, lose coordination, be weak, and fall at any time. There may be a genetic basis for the disease. Therapeutic doses of vitamin E given between the ages of 2 and 18 months may reduce the symptoms.

Vitamin K

Vitamin K is actually a number of derivatives of naphthoquinone that are synthesized by the bacteria in the digestive tract and by plants. Thus, green feeds are good sources of vitamin K. Its major function is involved with blood clotting; although the dietary requirements for the horse are not known, a deficiency increases susceptibility to bleeding.

Vitamin C

Vitamin C is synthesized in the liver and is not a dietary essential. Toxicity has not been reported in the horse.

B Vitamins

The 10 vitamins known as the B complex are water-soluble. Their functions are better understood than those of the fat-soluble group. The B complex vitamins are synthesized by bacteria in the digestive tract and, except for vitamin B_{12}, are also supplied in adequate amounts in good quality forage. The only conditions in which supplementation may be necessary are heavy stress and heavy training and performance or when the horse is fed very poor quality roughages.

Most of the information about the B complex has been confined to thiamin, riboflavin, and vitamin B_{12}. Thiamin is involved with carbohydrate metabolism. A deficiency is manifested by loss of appetite. Three mg of thiamin per kg feed (approximately 1 mg/lb) meets the requirement. Vitamin B_{12} has received more attention than the other B vitamins because of its involvement with the synthesis of red blood cells. Considerable amounts of money have been spent on vitamin B_{12} injections to raise red blood cell counts, to no avail.

Minerals

Minerals are inorganic compounds that serve as components of body tissues and as catalytic compounds that trigger reactions in the body. They are generally grouped as macrominerals and microminerals (trace minerals). The macrominerals include sodium, chloride, calcium, phosphorus, sulfur, potassium, and magnesium. Their requirements are expressed as grams per day or a percentage of the diet. In contrast, the micromineral requirements are expressed as milligrams per day (mg/day) or parts per million (ppm) in the diet. They include cobalt, copper, iron, iodine, manganese, and selenium. Little is known about other minerals.

The intake of the major minerals must be closely monitored and controlled. Several factors control the intake. The soil content in a given area influences the mineral content of the forage. There are iodine-, magnesium-, and selenium-deficient soil areas in the United States and Canada. Horses consuming forage grown in those areas may need additional sources of the deficient mineral. The ratio of hay to grain and the type of hay fed is important because plants differ in mineral content. Quality of the feed is important, because improperly cured and stored feed has a lower mineral content. Failure to supply adequate amounts of minerals leads to deficiency symptoms, and excessive consumption can lead to pathological physiological problems.

Macrominerals

Sodium and Chloride

The sodium and chloride in salt play many roles in the horse's body, including maintenance of fluid balance, acid-base balance, normal flow of nerve impulses, and muscular movements. The requirement for salt has not been clearly established because of individual variation in the requirement and the influence of many environmental factors. Environmental temperature is one of the primary determinants of the salt requirement. Considerable amounts of salt are lost in sweat. The average salt requirement is about 25 grams per day. It can be provided in several ways, but horses should always have free access to salt, in block or granular form. It is a common practice to add 0.5 to 1 percent salt in a ration to supply most of the salt requirement. Free access to additional salt should still be provided. Horses regulate their salt intake and do not consume too much, provided they are getting an adequate supply of water. They may overeat salt if they have been deprived of it for extended periods, but with adequate water intake, the only result is a loose bowel. Other symptoms of salt toxicity are colic, frequent urination, weakness, and a paralysis of the hind limbs. Deficiency symptoms are depraved appetite (lack of appetite or none at all), rough hair coat, reduced growth, and reduced milk production.

Calcium and Phosphorus

Calcium and phosphorus are associated in their main function of aiding bone formation and maintenance. They also function in energy metabolism by serving as enzyme cofactors, nerve conduction, muscle contraction, and blood clotting. There are two important points to consider: the amount to feed, and the ratio of calcium to phosphorus content in the ration.

The absorption efficiency varies with age. It may be as high as 70 percent in young horses and around 50 percent in older horses. The concentration in the plasma or serum stays relatively constant because of close regulation by the body. Thus, the serum concentration is not a reliable indicator of the calcium status.

Mature horses need 20 to 60 grams of calcium (45 mg/kg or 2 g/100 lb body weight) and 15 to 40 grams of phosphorus (35 mg/kg or 1.6 g/100 lb body weight) per day, depending on their size and physiological state. Lactating mares and young, growing horses that are rapidly synthesizing bone require the most calcium and phosphorus. Pregnant mares also need more during the last trimester of pregnancy. Old horses need more calcium because they absorb less.

The calcium–phosphorus ratio (Ca:P) is an extremely important feature of horse rations. The ratio should be not less than 1.1:1, and the average ratio in milk and in growing tissues is 1.6:1. If the horse is fed a ratio less than 1:1 with adequate amounts of phosphorus, calcium is mobilized from bone and replaced with fibrous connective tissue. This is particularly evident in the head. "Big head" or nutritional secondary hyperparathyroidism is the name of the disorder. With a 0.8:1 ratio, it takes about 6 to 12 months for the symptoms to be manifested. If the ratio is 0.6:1, the symptoms occur much faster. The opposite situation is a high Ca:P ratio. Foals can tolerate a 3:1 ratio, and adult horses can tolerate a 6:1 ratio without adverse effects. However, excess calcium interferes with the use of magnesium, manganese, iron, and phosphorus. If excess calcium is fed for prolonged periods, bones may become brittle and dense. Inadequate amounts of calcium and/or phosphorus can lead to rickets, which is improper bone development.

Magnesium

The magnesium requirement is estimated at 14 mg per kg (636 mg/100 lb) body weight. The requirement is increased during growth, lactation, work, and the last trimester of pregnancy. Symptoms of a deficiency are hyperirritability, tetany, glazed eyes, and eventual collapse. The conditions are usually precipitated by some form of stress. In areas where grass tetany is common with grazing cattle and sheep, adding 5 percent magnesium oxide to the salt mixture helps protect horses. Seldom is it necessary to supplement magnesium to meet requirements.

Potassium

Horses consuming at least 50 percent of their ration as forage or hay should receive adequate amounts of potassium because it is readily absorbed from feeds. The requirement is about .4 to .8 percent in the ration. Foals on a high-grain diet may need additional potassium.

Sulphur

Sulphur requirements for the horse have not been determined. Apparently, the requirements for various classes of horses are met from the sulphur-containing amino acids of high-quality protein.

Trace Minerals

Iodine

The iodine requirement is about 0.1 parts per million (0.1 mg/kg) in the feed. In iodine-deficient areas, adequate amounts of iodine can be given by feeding the horse iodized salt. Deficiency and toxicity symptoms are very similar. Deficiency symptoms include goiter and foals born weak, hairless, or dead. A major problem is iodine toxicity. Oversupplementation of iodine by the use of some seaweeds or other sources can cause the development of goiter and weakness in newborn foals. Some foals may die soon after birth.

Iron

Iron requirements vary from 40 to 50 mg per kg of diet. Thus, the requirement is not significantly increased during growth, lactation, or pregnancy. Most of the iron in the body is contained in the red blood cells and in transport or storage forms.

Iron deficiency is not a problem in horses but is manifested by anemia. Trainers of performance horses have traditionally fed iron supplements to increase the oxygen-carrying capacity, but there is no scientific evidence to support this practice. Excess iron is toxic to the young foal and oral administration of digestive inocula containing supplemental iron can result in death.

Manganese

Requirements for horses are unknown but 40 mg per kg of diet is considered adequate. A deficiency of manganese may have a role in the development of limb abnormalities and congenital contractors, but there is still no evidence to support the theory.

Selenium

The requirement for selenium is estimated to be 1 mg per kg of diet. Selenium states can be evaluated by determining the mineral's concentration in the blood. Any manifestation of a deficiency is affected by the concomitant vitamin E status. Deficient animals may develop muscle degeneration—"white muscle disease." Symptoms include weakness and difficulty in suckling, swallowing, locomotion, and respiration. Selenium toxicity will occur if the feed contains 5 to 40 ppm of selenium. Toxic horses lose hair from the tail and mane, eventually become blind and paralyzed, and the hoofs may slough off. In certain selenium-toxicity areas in the United States and Canada, chronic toxicity, referred to as "alkali disease," may develop in horses.

Zinc

Many of the enzymes in the body that are associated with metabolism contain zinc. The exact requirements are not known, but approximately 50 mg per kg of dry matter is adequate for all horses. Toxicosis has been observed in foals grazed adjacent to a zinc smelter.

FORMULATING AND BALANCING RATIONS

A balanced ration is the amount of a mixture of feeds that provides the horse with its nutrient requirements for one day. A single feed may provide a balanced ration, or it may be necessary to mix several feeds to form a balanced and palatable ration. Rations can be formulated by trial and error, which is time-consuming, or by computer. The fifth edition of *Nutrient Requirements of Horses,* published by the National Research Council, includes a diskette with a ration formulation program. Details of the trial-and-error method of ration formulation are given in Appendix 5-1.

Rules of Thumb

You can formulate the initial ration in a crude manner by applying rules of thumb. One of the first rules concerns the amount to feed that the horse will consume. Feed consumption is related to body weight and to the use or physiological state of the horse (Table 5-8); for example, lactating mares consume more feed than an idle horse. Table 5-8 is only a guide, because horses vary considerably and nutrient content of the diet varies. Some horses have an excessive appetite, and their feed intake must be restricted; others must be encouraged to eat. The proportion of roughages to concentrate should also be considered (Table 5-8). Heavily exercised horses need a ration with a high-calorie density (Mcal/unit of weight), so they can consume enough feed to meet their energy requirement. If the energy density is too low, the horse develops a "potbelly" because of its large intake of roughage (Tables 5-7A and 5-7B). Growing foals need a high energy ration that contains adequate protein. Protein is also an important consideration in the initial stages of formulating rations for lactating mares and for mares in the latter stages of gestation.

Therefore, the initial concern when formulating a ration for idle and working horses is energy. For growing horses, it is protein; for lactating and pregnant mares, it is energy and protein.

Table 5-8   Expected Feed Consumption by Horses (% body weight)[a]

	Forage	Concentrate	Total
Mature horses			
maintenance	1.5–2.0	0–0.5	1.5–2.0
mares, late gestation	1.0–1.5	0.5–1.0	1.5–2.0
mares, early lactation	1.0–2.0	1.0–2.0	2.0–3.0
mares, late lactation	1.0–2.0	0.5–1.5	2.0–2.5
Working horses			
light work	1.0–2.0	0.5–1.0	1.5–2.5
moderate work	1.0–2.0	0.75–1.5	1.75–2.5
intense work	0.75–1.5	1.0–2.0	2.0–3.0
Young horses			
nursing foal, 3 months	0	1.0–2.0	2.5–3.5
weanling foal, 6 months	0.5–1.0	1.5–3.0	2.0–3.5
yearling foal, 12 months	1.0–1.5	1.0–2.0	2.0–3.0
long yearling, 18 months	1.0–1.5	1.0–1.5	2.0–2.5
2-year-old (24 months)	1.0–1.5	1.0–1.5	1.75–2.5

[a] Air-dry feed (about 90% DM).
Source: *Nutrient Requirements of Horses*, 5th ed., National Research Council (1989).

Rations

The ration should be as simple as possible. Rations for idle and for working horses are relatively simple (Table 5-9). They become more complex for lactating and pregnant mares because more nutrients are needed (Table 5-9). Rations for growing horses are more complex because higher quality protein is needed (Tables 5-10 and 5-11) and it is important to maintain proper nutrient-to-calorie ratios. The rations in Tables 5-9 to 5-11 are given as guides and should be modified depending on economics and the availability of ingredients.

Costs

One of the primary concerns about feed costs or economics of ration formulation is the cost per unit of energy. For example, the most economical hay for energy (comparing alfalfa with oat) can be calculated as follows. The first step is to determine the energy content of alfalfa hay and oat hay. Have the hay analyzed by a laboratory, or assume that it is of average composition and consult Appendix Table 5-9 on feed composition. Unless you are buying large quantities of hay, the published values for the composition of feeds are close

TABLE 5-9 Rations for Nonpregnant, Pregnant, and Lactating Mares (fed with timothy hay)

Ingredients	Nonpregnant or maintenance (%)	Pregnant (%)	Lactating[a] (%)
Rolled oats	40.0	40.0	40.0
Rolled corn	40.0	40.0	45.0
Wheat bran	10.0	10.0	5.0
Soybean oil meal	5.0	5.0	15.0
Molasses	4.5	3.0	3.0
Defluorinated phosphate	0.5	—	1.5
Dicalcium phosphate	—	2.0	0.5
	100.0	100.0	100.0

[a] Data from Hintz (1977).

enough. The average content of oat hay is 0.79 Mcal/lb (Appendix Table 5-9, entry 155) or 1580 Mcal/2000 lb (1 ton, or 907 kg). Alfalfa hay contains about 1.02 Mcal/lb, or 2.24 Mcal/kg (Appendix Table 5-9, entry 005), or 2040 Mcal/ton. For this example, figure alfalfa hay to be $82 per ton (907 kg) and oat hay to be $60 per ton (907 kg). Next, one divides the cost by amount of energy in 1 ton. The alfalfa hay costs 4.0 cents per megacalorie of energy ($82.00/2040 Mcal), and the oat hay costs 3.79 cents per megacalorie of

TABLE 5-10 Creep Rations for Foals

Example 1		Example 2	
Ingredient	(%)	Ingredient	(%)
Rolled oats	50.0	Rolled oats	23.0
Rolled corn	4.5	Rolled corn	37.4
Soybean oil meal	10.0	Soybean oil meal	33.0
Dried skim milk	5.0	Brewer's yeast	0.5
Dehydrated alfalfa	10.0	Molasses	3.0
Wheat bran	10.0	Dicalcium phosphate	1.0
Molasses	7.0	Ground limestone	1.0
Trace mineralized salt	1.0	Trace mineralized salt	1.0
Dicalcium phosphate	2.0	Vitamins A and D	0.5
Ground limestone	0.5		100.0
Vitamin premix[a]	0.5		
	100.0		

[a] 1×106 IU vitamin A, 1×105 IU vitamin D, 5×103 IU vitamin E, 0.5 g thiamine, 2.5 g niacin, 1 g pantothenic acid, and 2.5 mg vitamin B_{12} per pound (454 g) of premix.
SOURCE: Example 1, Baker (1971); Example 2, Tyznik (1975).

TABLE 5-11   Rations for Weanlings and Yearlings
(fed with alfalfa hay)

Ingredient	Weanling (%)	Yearling (%)
Rolled oats	40.0	50.0
Rolled corn	12.5	9.5
Rolled barley	10.0	13.5
Soybean oil meal	7.0	6.0
Dried skim milk	10.0	—
Dehydrated alfalfa	10.0	10.0
Molasses	7.0	7.0
Trace mineralized salt	1.0	1.0
Dicalcium phosphate	2.5	3.0
Vitamin premix[a]	0.5	0.5

[a] See Table 5-10 for formula.
SOURCE: Baker (1971).

energy ($60.00/1580 Mcal). At these prices, the alfalfa hay costs 5.5 percent more than the oat hay per unit of energy. To make the same calculations for another hay, substitute the cost per ton and divide by the megacalories.

To figure the cheapest source of energy from grains, the procedure is similar. If you consider $10.73/100 lb (or 45.4 kg) for rolled barley, $10.61/100 lb for rolled oats, and $9.70/100 lb for cracked corn, a typical calculation is as follows. Barley contains 1.49 Mcal/lb (Appendix Table 5-9, entry 025) or 149 Mcal/100 lb (3.26 Mcal/kg); oats contain 1.30 Mcal/lb (Appendix Table 5-9, entry 145) or 1.30 Mcal/100 lb (2.85 Mcal/kg); and corn contains 1.54 Mcal/lb (Appendix Table 5-9, entry 095) or 154 Mcal/100 lb (3.38 Mcal/kg). Dividing the cost per 100 lb by the number of megacalories per 100 lb, or cost per kilogram by number of megacalories per kilogram, we find the cost per unit of energy to be 7.2 cents, 8.2 cents, and 6.3 cents for barley, oats, and corn, respectively. Corn costs less than oats and barley, and barley costs less than oats based on the cost per unit of energy at the above prices. For this example, corn costs about 30 percent less per unit of energy than oats.

Commercial Feeds

When feeding commercial (premixed) feeds, you must be able to interpret a feed bag label to determine how much to feed. The information given on a feed bag label must meet certain state requirements. What you need to know to make a critical evaluation of your feeding program is not given on most labels. However, more and more feed companies are providing that information.

For the average horse owner, feeding commercially prepared feeds is the best option. Feed companies do a much better job of mixing a consistent product. Unless an owner has enough horses and good storage capabilities, custom mixing of rations may cause more problems than any possible cost savings that may be achieved.

Nutrient Analysis

In the United States, a basic nutrient analysis must be listed. It includes minimal amounts of crude protein and crude fat, and maximum amounts of ash (minerals) and crude fiber. Crude protein (not less than a given percent) merely informs you that a minimal amount of nitrogenous substances is present. It does not give an estimate of the digestibility of the crude protein. However, by looking at the list of feed ingredients, you can determine if the sources of protein are highly digestible or not. Protein quality is not given; you must estimate it by "reading between the lines." Protein quality refers to the balance of amino acids that make up the protein. As tissues or protein compounds are formed in the horse's body, they are made up of specific percentages of each amino acid. For the protein to be formed by the horse's body, all the amino acids must be present at one time. Therefore, a low-quality protein in a feed means that the protein has a low percentage of one or more amino acids (improper amino acid balance) in relation to the total amino acid content. That is, one of the protein building blocks required by the horse to build the given protein(s) is limiting the amount of the given protein(s) that the horse's body can build. For example, one of the amino acids that is low in cottonseed meal is lysine.

The crude fat content indicates the minimum amount of fat in the feed. The fat and fatty substances include the fat-soluble vitamins (A, D, E, and K) and fat that is added to keep the "dust content" under control and/or increase the energy density of the ration. Fats are concentrated sources of energy and provide about twice the energy that carbohydrates do on a weight basis. The guaranteed maximum amount of crude fiber indicates if the feed is a concentrate feed (low in fiber) or a roughage feed (high in fiber). Most important, no estimate is given of the amount of the fiber that can be digested by the bacteria in the horse's digestive tract. How much of the fiber passes through the horse? If the crude fiber content is known, the digestible energy content (Mcal/lb) can be estimated, i.e., $4\% \simeq 1.7, 6\% \simeq 1.6, 8\% \simeq 1.5, 10\% \simeq 1.4$, and $12\% \simeq 1.3$. The ash content is what is left after a sample of the feed is completely burned. It is an estimate of the mineral content. However, a horseperson needs to know how much of each mineral is present. Is the calcium–phosphorus ratio about 1.5 to 1? Quite frequently on some tags, the nitrogen-free extract (NFE) is also listed. The NFE is an estimate of the more readily available carbohydrate content of the feed. If the TDN (total digestible nutrients) is listed, the energy content of the feed can be calculated. One kg of TDN is equivalent to about 4410 kcal (1 lb TDN is about 2000 kcal).

In Canada, feeds are tested for protein, fat, fiber, calcium, phosphorus, selenium, and vitamins A, D, and E.

Ingredients Listing

A second federal regulation in the United States, but not in Canada, is that all ingredients must be listed. Although the percentage of each ingredient is not given (because the feed company would be giving you their formula), by knowing the ingredients, one can estimate protein quality and the digestibility of the feed. You should also visually examine the feed to be sure that the ingredients are of high quality and not moldy or damaged. The list must include any "fillers." The ingredient list is important if your horse is allergic to a specific ingredient or becomes allergic to the feed, because the veterinarian needs to know what the horse has been eating. Vitamin and mineral supplements that are added must be listed.

Other Considerations

A third federal requirement is feeding instructions. They are usually quite simple and recommend a given amount of the feed to various classes of horses (pregnant, lactating, and so on) as part of their overall feeding program. Any cautionary measures must also be listed.

A final consideration is the company that produces the feed. It makes no difference if it is large or small, known or unknown, as long as it produces a quality product.

FEEDING MANAGEMENT

Feeding horses is still an "art" that is acquired from experience. A knowledge of the nutrient requirements and the composition and use of the common horse feeds serves as basic information. The individuality of horses and their behavior makes it difficult to feed them to maintain the proper body condition and obtain maximum performance. A certain amount of skill, sound judgment, or experience is necessary for feeding horses well.

Most horses are kept in individual stalls or paddocks. From a management standpoint, this is important if one wants to obtain maximum performance from a horse or maintain an optimum condition. Some horses digest and use nutrients more efficiently than do others. The "hard-keeping" horse is inefficient. Both types must be fed individually, or they will become fat or too thin.

The following topics are discussed to give the horse owner or manager the basic or practical aspects of feeding management. Some of the discussions dispel false information that has been passed around for several generations.

When considering feeding management, it is important to be sure the horse is receiving regular exercise, has its teeth examined routinely, and has a parasite control program. These factors have a direct influence on efficiency of feed utilization and digestive tract dysfunction.

Group Feeding

Group feeding works with some groups of horses, but several management practices should always be used. Adequate feeder space should be available if only a single trough is used. Group feeding is not advisable for mature horses without close monitoring, because most horses are individualistic in their eating habits. Aggressive horses eat more than their share, and timid horses do not get enough. A more satisfactory situation is to provide feeders for each horse, separated by at least 50 feet (15.24 m). This allows a timid horse to eat without undue harassment. Group feeding of young foals usually works without too many difficulties, provided adequate feeder space is available. Feeder design is important. The trough should have no sharp edges or projecting points. If the trough is too wide (front to back), the horse will bump its knees when eating the feed on the far side of the trough. Injury to the knees frequently leads to the unsoundness referred to as popped knees. A narrow trough is preferred. However, overly aggressive eaters cannot be fed from narrow troughs. The grain must be spread out over a larger area so they cannot get a mouthful each time. They are thus forced to take small amounts each time and eat more slowly. Small rocks or other obstacles that cannot be swallowed can be placed in the trough to force the horse to pick the grain from around them. Small salt blocks are excellent for this purpose. Preventing the horse from bolting its feed may prevent indigestion, colic, and founder.

Group feeding of high-performance horses is not advised. The nutrient intake of high-performance horses must be carefully regulated, which is extremely difficult with group feeding.

Feeding Facilities

Hay can be fed from a manger, hay rack, or net, or from the ground. Placing the hay on the ground is discouraged because it becomes contaminated with dirt, feces, and urine. The horse wastes more of the hay by walking on it and scattering it about the stall. Parasite control is more difficult because the horse may ingest the parasite eggs in feces. The hay manger, net, or rack should not be placed so high that the horse must reach up to eat, because hay particles and foreign material fall into the eyes and cause irritation.

Feed troughs and hay mangers and racks should be cleaned regularly. Moldy and spoiled hay or grain can cause colic and other digestive disturbances. Fecal contamination of feeding areas and water troughs should be removed as soon as possible. And dusty feed can lead to heaves or to pulmonary emphysema.

Appetite: Timid Eaters and Off Feed

Timid horses or finicky eaters must be encouraged to eat, and it can be a real challenge to get some horses to consume their daily ration. These horses should be fed individually, in an environment where they are not afraid to eat and where they are not disturbed by other horses or by people. Fresh carrots, apples, lettuce leaves, or molasses can be sprinkled on the ration to get the horse to eat it. Selection of the hay and feed is important. Alfalfa hay may be more palatable to the timid eater than grass hay. Commercial feeds with a higher molasses content may stimulate consumption. Generally, it is a trial-and-error process until you determine which feeds are more palatable to the timid eater. A change in the quality of the hay or concentrate portion of the ration may reduce intake. Moldy feeds are not very palatable to horses. The appetite of some horses is stimulated by grazing green pasture for a couple of hours per day or adding sliced carrots or apples to their ration. Their teeth should be inspected for hooks (see Chapter 9, Dental Care). Occasionally, an inadequate source of clean, cool water causes the problem.

When a horse suddenly quits eating, one must determine the cause. Usually, sick horses quit eating or dramatically reduce their feed intake. Mouth or tongue injuries may be involved as well as a tooth problem. Tooth or teeth problems may require special feed processing.

Horses, such as race horses, that are being heavily exercised to maintain physical fitness over extended periods may become "track sour" and quit eating. Some will respond to thiamin supplementation when a couple of tablespoons of brewer's yeast is sprinkled on the ration. Warm bran mashes during the winter months will also stimulate some horses to eat.

Feed Processing

Digestibility and/or palatability of some feeds are improved by processing. Horses with teeth problems or old horses may require their hay to be chopped, and all grains to be cracked or rolled so they can chew their ration.

Barley, milo, rye, and wheat should be routinely processed (see section on Grains and Grain By-Products). However, one must realize that processing will lead to a faster deterioration of carbohydrates, and processed feed will not store as long. Pelleted feeds have several advantages: ease of transportation; the horse cannot sort out ingredients; the feed can contain more economical sources of fiber and energy; less wastage by the horse; reduced dust; uniform distribution of ingredients including supplements; decreased storage space; and ease of handling.

There are, however, disadvantages to feeding completely pelletized rations. More serious than the increased cost of the ration, the two most serious disadvantages are the speed of consumption and development of bad habits (chewing wood and other horses' tails). The rate of consumption can be slowed by spreading the pellets over a larger surface area or by placing rocks in the feed trough, forcing the horse to eat around them. The development of extruded feeds has offered another means to decrease the rate of consumption and decrease the digestive upset associated with it. Feeding the roughage as hay or pasture along with the pelletized concentrate portion of the ration will usually eliminate wood- and tail-chewing vices.

Feeding Times

Feed horses at the same time each day. Horses form habits, and they anticipate being fed at regular times. Failure to feed regularly results in bad eating habits such as eating too fast or going off feed.

Feeding Frequency

The frequency of feeding is important. Mature, idle horses can be fed once a day, but it is preferable to feed all horses at least twice daily at close to 12-hour intervals. Hay and grain should each be given in equal parts morning and night. Horses that are being exercised heavily or expected to be in the best physical condition should be fed three times per day. Working horses should be fed 2 hours prior to work and at least 1 hour after hard work. This gives the horse time to digest part of the ration before work and to cool out and relax after work before eating. Some horsepeople prefer to feed one-half of the grain in the morning prior to work, one-fourth of the grain at noon, and one-fourth of the grain and all the hay at night to hard-working horses.

Age

Age affects the way horses should be fed. Young foals should have the opportunity to eat a mixed concentrate ration within a few days after birth. One method is to place the ration in a box adjacent to the mare's feed trough. The box contains spaced rods above the feed so that the foal can pass its mouth between the rods to eat. This prevents the mare from eating the foal's ration. If several mares are kept together, a creep area can be placed in the large paddock or pasture. The creep enclosure allows only the foals access to the feed. Foals are creep fed until they are weaned. It is best to wean at least two foals at a time and place them in a box stall. During and following weaning, they should have free access to their ration unless it causes digestive disturbances, in which case access should be limited. Yearlings and 2-year-olds are managed as mature horses, because their feed is restricted but meets their requirements.

A decision must be made as to whether young horses are to be fed for moderate or rapid growth. Either way, the young horse can be fed to produce a mature horse that is sound for work and reaches its maximum mature height. In addition to feeding an adequate supply of major nutrients, the diets must be formulated to contain the correct ratios of protein, calcium, phosphorus, and other minerals and vitamins to the amount of energy. Inadequate concentrations of protein, minerals, and vitamins relative to the energy concentrations may cause developmental orthopedic disorders.

Pregnancy

There are three management aspects of feeding a pregnant mare. One is the maintenance of body condition. Mares entering the breeding season should be in a moderate to fleshy condition (body condition score greater than 5). During periods of stress, a condition score of at least 5 should be maintained. During short periods of stress, such as very cold weather, a mare may decrease her body fat, resulting in a lower body condition score of 2 points within a couple of days. Mares foaling in a thin condition have impaired reproductive performance even when fed to meet the energy requirements for lactation. They should be fed to regain a body condition score of 5 or better as soon as possible. Daily amounts of feed required for the lactating mare to gain weight can be dangerous to feed. Good nutrition is critical during the 18- to 35-day period after breeding to aid in preventing early embryonic death. Mares on a poor-quality diet have normal fetal growth to day 25 of pregnancy, but resorption will occur within the next 6 days. If their nutrition regimen is increased on day 18 and extended through day 35 after breeding, the chances of fetal resorption are much lower.

From an economic standpoint, maintenance of mares in moderate to fat condition is usually cheaper than trying to increase the weight of thin mares during the breeding season. It requires more energy to add fat to a thin mare than to maintain the mare in a body condition score of 6 or 7. Because thin mares arriving at a stud farm stay at the farm for a longer period of time than moderate or fat mares, board and breeding charges are higher than feed costs to maintain them in the proper condition. During the last trimester of pregnancy, the mare should be fed adequate amounts of nutrients to allow normal fetal development and a gain in body weight of 5 percent (see earlier under Reproduction). During lactation, mares must be fed to regain any body condition lost during pregnancy and to meet the demands of milk production. Orphan foals are a special problem and are discussed in Chapter 16.

Care must be taken in feeding old horses. They need high-energy feed that is easy to digest. Good-quality leafy hay should be fed, and you may need to chop it. The grain ration should be crimped to aid digestion. Old horses require more energy to perform work than do younger horses and thus need more feed per unit of body weight. Frequently inspect and care for their teeth and keep their parasite load to a minimum.

Ration Changes

Change rations gradually over a period of about 1 week. Sudden changes may cause colic, going off feed, loss of condition, and digestive disturbances. One method is to replace 25 percent of the ration with the new ration every 2 days so that it takes 6 days before the horse is eating 100 percent of the new ration. Horses being turned out to pasture should be turned out for 30 minutes the first day and then for increased amounts of time so that after a week, they are left out. This procedure is particularly critical when pastures are lush and green.

Horses returned home from sales or strenuous performance training should be brought down gradually. Their ration and amount of exercise should be reduced over a 2-week period.

Rations must be closely controlled for horses subjected to strenuous daily exercise when the horse is given a day off or when it gets very tired. Azoturia, or "Monday morning sickness," is caused by feeding the grain portion of the ration on a horse's day of rest. (See Chapter 10 for full discussion of azoturia.)

Time of Watering

A horse may consume water before, during, or after eating without influencing digestibility. If possible, it is best for the horse to have water available at all times. After exercise, when the horse is hot, the horse should be allowed to only drink small amounts until it cools out. This is to prevent the development of laminitis.

Roughage Requirements

Horses require a minimum of 1 percent of their body weight in roughage per day. When smaller amounts are fed, digestive dysfunction may occur. Colic and enterotoxemia are typical problems.

Use of Cattle and Swine Feed

There are two major concerns when horses are fed cattle feeds. Monensin, an antibiotic, improves the feed efficiency in cattle but causes sudden death or delayed cardiac circulatory failure in horses. Salinomycin is also added to cattle rations to improve feed efficiency. It is extremely toxic to horses, causing death or colic, dehydration, muscle spasms, and ataxia. Lincomycin, an additive in swine rations, causes founder, diarrhea, and death when consumed in small amounts.

Feeding Fat

The energy density (Mcal/kg) of a feed can be increased by the addition of various fats and oils produced from rendering and extraction processes. In addition to their energy value, they help reduce dust. Normally, 1 to 3 percent fat additives are used in commercial rations. Levels of 10 percent are well tolerated by horses. The high level can be used for horses that have a high energy requirement and are timid eaters by top-dressing the ration with the fat. Adding fat also spares glycogen utilization during exercise, thus perhaps increasing endurance.

Obese and Thin Horses

One of the most common forms of horse malnutrition is being too fat. Horsepeople may overfeed their horses out of kindness. Often, overfeeding is coupled with lack of exercise. The weight of a horse can be monitored periodically by weighing it on a scale or by estimating its weight by measuring its heart girth with a calibrated tape. "Weigh tapes" are supplied by several feed companies. They are fairly accurate ($\pm$ 10 percent) and indicate if a horse is losing or gaining weight over a period of time. A formula to estimate body weight is

(heart girth $\times$ heart girth $\times$ body length)/330 = weight in pounds.

Heart girth is the circumference at the highest point of the withers. Body length is measured from point of the shoulder straight back to the point of the buttock (around to back side of horse). The condition score system can be used and horses maintained between condition scores of 4 to 6. The concept is explained earlier under Pregnancy.

Prolonged fasting is not a recommended practice for weight reduction in horses, because hyperlipemia may be induced. This condition is characterized by high concentrations of lipid in the blood. In severe cases, the animal will not start to eat again after food is offered. It may die unless treated properly with glucose and insulin.

Thinness in horses is caused by poor-quality feed, inadequate amounts of feed, internal parasites, poor teeth, milk production, pregnancy, and excessive work. These conditions can usually be corrected by increasing the energy intake. If not, the horse may be sick or have a metabolic disorder.

Feed by Weight, not Volume

Horses should be fed by weight of the feed, not by volume (see Table 5-2). Nutrient content must also be taken into consideration. Changing from a coffee can of oats to a coffee can of corn increases the energy intake two- to threefold. Therefore, an adjustment in volume (actually, weight) must be made to keep from giving the horse excess energy.

Depraved Appetite

Horses kept in close confinement tend to crave unnatural feedstuffs, particularly if they are bored with their surroundings. Those fed pelleted or cubed rations tend to chew on wood and eat hair and dirt. Chewing wood can be alleviated by placing the horse in a stall or paddock where no wood is exposed. Exposed wood can be treated with chemicals. Exercise reduces time spent chewing wood. Excessive consumption of sand or dirt can result in sand colic, an accumulation or impaction of sand in the caecum or colon that prevents the passage of digesta. Horses that graze pastures grown on sandy soil are prone to sand colic. Young foals chew the tails of their dams or other horses. This can be prevented by rubbing some bone oil on all the horses' tails that are exposed to the culprit. Isolation is usually easier. Coprophagy (eating feces) is commonly observed in horses. Young foals seem to do it more often than mature horses. It can result in eating the eggs of internal parasites.

Other Factors

Parasite control (see Chapter 10) is an important part of feeding management. Internal parasites decrease digestive efficiency and cause digestive disturbances such as colic and diarrhea. External parasites can annoy horses and cause extra energy expenditure to escape or fight them by running, stomping feet, or continually switching tails.

Feed should be stored in rodent-proof bins. Galvanized garbage cans with lids are excellent for storing one to two sacks of grain. Rodents eat the grain out of grain hay and leave the bales as straw. They can be prevented from living and breeding in stored hay with new chemicals that are available.

Exercise (at least 30 minutes per day) is important to maintain muscle tone, stimulate appetite, and help prevent digestive disturbances.

Dental problems can lead to improper mastication and digestive disturbances. Teeth should be inspected at regular intervals (at least yearly) for abnormal wear (hooks) and for broken teeth.

Treats such as carrots, apples, commercial treats, and sugar cubes are given to horses by some horsepeople. Sugar is never recommended. Other treats should be placed in the feed trough, or else the horse will develop bad habits. If fed from the hand, horses look for treats when they are handled, constantly nibbling at one's hand, shirt pocket, or pants pocket. Although horses enjoy them, treats play no role in the nutritional program.

CHAPTER 6

Handling, Training, and Conditioning

HANDLING

Horses form habits rather quickly, and improper handling leads to undesirable behavior patterns. Once these are established, the horse is not as much fun to work with and may be unsafe to work around. Horses that are trained by competent horsepeople learn to be handled in certain ways. If not handled according to their expectations, they become confused and/or frightened. For full enjoyment, owners should become familiar with accepted and safe procedures for handling horses.

Catching and Haltering

Catching a horse the proper way prevents it from becoming hard to catch. When approaching the horse, you must make it aware of your presence. If the horse is daydreaming or focusing its attention on something else, it may be startled when it realizes you are about to catch it. Speak to the horse to make it aware of your presence. Approach the horse at an angle, from the side (Figure 6-1). Never approach it directly from the front or rear, because if it is startled it may kick or run over someone. A horse cannot see well directly behind and may not recognize what is approaching unless it turns its head. On reaching the horse, allow it to smell a hand and then rub it a couple of times with

FIGURE 6-1 Approaching a horse to catch it.

the back of your hand on the neck or shoulder. Do not try to rub the horse's nose. Once a horse learns this routine, it will let you approach and halter it without any difficulty.

Some horses are hard to catch, a habit that may be classified as a vice and that is hard to cure. They are usually hard to catch because of fear, resentment, or just plain habit. To overcome fear of being caught, the horse must be handled often, and the experience should be pleasant. It is best to handle a horse properly at birth, imprinted, so that it trusts whoever will handle it. The experience can be made pleasant by grooming and talking to it until it relaxes and accepts a person's presence. You can also feed it a few bites of grain from a bucket after it is caught. Most horses will come to you after you catch them a few times and then give them some grain. A horse should never be allowed to eat the grain before being haltered so that it will never learn to play the game of taking a bite and then refusing to be haltered. If this procedure does not work, the horse should be kept confined in a small stall or paddock where it cannot escape from being caught. It should be caught, haltered, and rewarded several times a day until it becomes easy to catch.

Horses should never be chased so that they run. If they run, they are or have become afraid. After they learn the habit of running away, they usually have to be run into a small paddock before they will let someone catch them.

Horses that resent how they are used once they are caught become difficult to catch. Some common causes of resentment are long, hard, confusing training sessions, exhausting rides for poorly conditioned horses, painful wound doctoring, and abuse. Most horses that have been injured and require injections or painful treatments become hard to catch. Prevent this by catching the horse several times between each treatment session and giving it a pleasant experience by grooming or feeding it. With a varied routine, it will not know what to expect each time it is caught and will not become bored. The horse that resents being caught and tries to kick can be dangerous. Such horses usually watch you approaching them and try to keep their heels directed toward you. As soon as they shift their weight so they can kick, slap them across the croup. Such horses can be taught to face you by hitting them below the hocks with a whip. As soon as they face you, speak to them in a calm voice and approach. In a few sessions, they will always face someone who approaches them.

The horse that is hard to catch only because of habit can be retrained by isolating it and catching it several times a day. After it is caught for a few minutes and given a pleasant experience, it soon forgets about running away. Once the horse discovers that being caught is part of its daily routine and is usually pleasant, it looks forward to being caught and handled.

Do not place the halter on the horse as soon as you rub its neck. This gives the horse an opportunity to escape. Place the lead rope around the horse's neck before slipping the halter on its head so the horse cannot escape.

Keep the halter in good repair so the horse cannot break it easily after being tied up. Do not leave a halter on a horse turned out in the paddock or confined in a stall unless it has a safety release buckle. Horses can easily get the halter hung up on something and have an accident. When a horse scratches its head with a hindfoot, the foot can get caught in the halter and this can lead to injury or death. A safety release buckle can release the halter when sufficient pull is applied. A horse should never be tied up and left unattended. If it decides to pull back and "have a fit," it can break its neck or damage neck muscles. And it may throw itself down and hang itself.

One of the most successful methods of training a horse to let you catch it and remain calm while you work with it takes advantage of psychology. The horse is taken into a round corral. A longe whip or a rope is the only equipment needed. The horse is made to trot and to canter around the round corral and made to reverse directions several times. When the horse tries to stop, it is kept moving for another couple of trips around the round corral. Then stop the horse by stepping in front of it and then back out of its space. Take a step toward the horse. If it moves, force it to canter again and to reverse directions until it wants to stop and it no longer carries its head looking outward toward the round corral fence. After you allow it to stop, approach the horse head on. After repeating this procedure until it lets you rub its forehead, step back a couple of steps. If the horse does not follow, send him around the ring for longer than he wants to canter. Then repeat rubbing the forehead and stepping back until the horse follows you. Very soon, he realizes that it is easier to allow you to approach, stand still, and then follow you than to run away from you. Next, rub all over its body when you approach and it stands still. If it does not stand still, send him around the corral again. When it stands still, the lesson is completed. It may need to be repeated two or three consecutive days until the horse will approach the trainer when he/she enters the round corral. At this point, the horse has realized that it is not going to be punished by working when it stays close to the trainer. This method of training is the one of choice by 4-H Club advisors and other knowledgeable trainers.

While working a horse in a round corral, there are some basic principles that need to be followed to make each session productive and efficient. The trainer works along an imaginary line that is parallel to the horse and about 12 to 15 feet from it. Body position is used to cue the horse. A longe whip held in the off hand can be used to reinforce body position cues. The neutral body position is standing quietly at the point of the horse's shoulder with the shoulders parallel to the horse's body and at a distance of 12 to 15 feet. To cue the horse to move forward, the trainer turns his/her shoulders to face the direction in which the horse is being cued to move. Initially, it may be necessary to step sideways and toward the horse's hip to get it to move. If it is still reluctant to move forward, step slightly back of the line to the horse's hip and wave the whip toward the hocks in the direction the horse is to move. The goal over 2 or 3 sessions is to get the horse to move as soon as you move your shoulders and if you want it to speed up, you move toward the hip. You may want to teach the horse verbal cues for walking, trotting, or cantering. As the horse gets tired and wants to stop before being cued to stop, it may be necessary to keep it moving forward with the whip being moved along or being flipped behind the horse. To slow the horse down, step sideways toward the shoulder. In the early stages of training, it may be necessary to take a step toward the head and reinforce the cue with the whip being placed in front of the horse. By stepping a step or two beyond slowing down the horse, it can be cued to stop. Early in the initial training session, the horse may turn instead of stopping. By immediately going across the round corral and repeating the cue, the horse will understand that it is to stop and not turn. Usually the horse must be cued several times in a row before it will learn the cue to stop. When the horse stops, one should step back out of the horse's space. It is important for the horse to remain stopped with its body parallel to the round corral. Later, you will cue it to come forward. To turn the horse, start by having your shoulders parallel to the horse's body and then take a step to get in front of the line to the horse's head. Next, take a step in toward the horse and turn your shoulders in the direction for the horse to turn.

It is important to read the horse's body language while it is being trained in a round corral. Horses use multiple cues and each horse may use a different cue. Stress is usually indicated by the ears being pointed backward and held tightly, by tension in nostrils, flared nostrils, increased respiration rate, high and stiff head carriage, wringing tail, choppy gait, increasing or decreasing its gait speed, and focus of its eyes. As the horse relaxes, its ears move forward, the head comes down, muscle tension relaxes, and gait has an even rhythm and speed.

Leading

Walk beside a horse when it is being led (Figure 6-2). The proper position for the handler's shoulder is between the horse's head and shoulder, with the hand placed about 12 to 18 inches below the lead shank ring. Fold and place the lead rope in the hand opposite the one with which you are leading the horse. Never coil the

FIGURE 6-2   Correct position to lead a horse.

lead rope around your hand because an injury will result if the horse suddenly bolts and runs away. If you lead the horse from in front, the horse's feet will strike the back of your feet or legs. Also, if the horse goes too far forward, you cannot control it, and it can easily run away or run around the handler. And you are vulnerable to kicks from a hindleg when the horse passes by you.

A horse can be led from either side, but it is customary to lead it from the left side. On a trail, you must sometimes lead from the right side.

Turn the horse to the direction opposite to the side from which you are leading it. This way, you walk around the horse. If you turn the horse toward you, it may step on your feet.

If a horse fails to start forward when you cue it to move forward, you can turn it sharply to one side and lead it a few steps forward. You cannot pull horses that fail to move forward, because they are too strong. Some horses will not move forward when you face them. If so, pass a rope around the horse's buttocks and pull it to encourage forward movement. If a horse rears up while being led, release the lead rope from the hand adjacent to the halter. This will prevent the horse from lifting you off the ground or throwing you down. Immediately move to the side of the horse to avoid its flailing front legs. From the side, you can pull the horse down. Some horses prance around or get nervous while being led. They will step on your feet unless you extend your elbow and place it against the horse's neck. The procedure used to catch a horse can also be used to train it to lead properly. Each time the horse does not follow you properly, send him around the round corral. Eventually, it will follow you everywhere without the use of a halter.

When you remove the halter, the horse should face you. Do not let it bolt away once the halter is off. Make sure the horse does not turn and run, kicking as it passes by.

Restraint

There are several methods of restraint, and each use depends on specific needs. The safety of the horse and handler should always be considered. Accidents are common during restraint procedures.

Tying

Horses can be tied with the lead rope to hitching rails or posts. The horse should be tied with a quick-release knot so that it can be released in an emergency (Figure 6-3). It should be tied about the same height as the withers, and the rope should have 12 to 18 inches of slack in it. Tying this short prevents the horse from getting a front leg over the tie rope. Cross-tying restricts movement more than a single rope. Two tie ropes are used to cross-tie the horse. The ropes are usually anchored about 6 to 8 feet off the ground and are long enough to allow the horse to stand with its head about level. The ends anchored to the wall or posts are tied with quick-release knots.

The horse may be tied without a halter. Use a bow-line knot on the end placed around the horse's neck so that it will not slip and choke the horse (Figure 6-3).

Release the tie rope before removing the halter. Failure to do so may cause the horse to pull back and break the halter. The horse may become a habitual halter puller once it does this a few times.

Hobbles

When a horse will not allow someone to hold up its leg while being shod or will not remain still while a leg is being treated for an injury, a variety of hobbles can be used to restrain the horse. Restraining hobbles should seldom be used, but should always be properly used. They do not absolutely immobilize a horse but are usually more humane than a big battle with the horse. All horses should become accustomed to being hobbled.

First, lift one of the horse's front legs off the ground. If the horse is easy to handle, an assistant may be able to hold the leg. When no assistance is available or if the horse struggles, you can tie up the leg with a strap or soft cotton rope at least $\frac{1}{2}$ inch in diameter (see Figure 6-4). Lay the strap across the pastern in front and then cross it behind. Lift the leg and secure the rope or strap around the horse's forearm. A different technique is used on

(a)

(b)

(c)

(d)

Crown knot on end

Overhead knot

(e)

FIGURE 6-3   Knots. *(a)* The square knot is useful for tying two ends of the same rope together. *(b)* The bow-line knot will not slip. Every horseperson should be able to tie it. To tie, make a loop over the standing line. Take the free end and run it under and up through the loop. Now bring the end around the standing part and back through the top of the loop. Tighten the knot by pulling the standing part while holding the end loop. *(c)* Use the sheet bend knot for tying together two different ropes of two different diameters; this knot will not slip. *(d)* Use the slip knot to tie a horse to a post or ring. It is easy to tie and can be quickly untied by pulling on the free end of the rope. *(e)* Use the honda knot to tie a small loop in the end of a rope so that the loop will not slip.

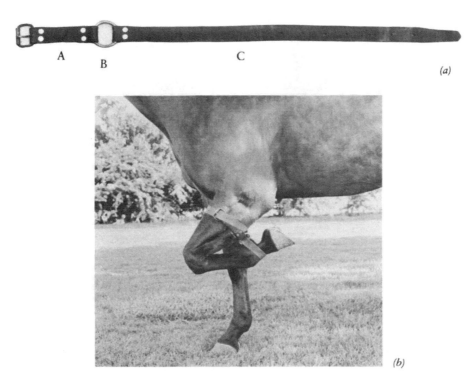

FIGURE 6-4   *(a)* Front leg strap: (A) 6.5 inches (16.5 cm); (B) 3.5-inch ring (8.89 cm); (C) 31.5-inch (80-cm) strap is 2 inches (5.08 cm) wide. *(b)* Front leg tied up. (Photos by W. Evans.)

horses that refuse to let their legs be lifted. Tie a 25- to 30-foot (7.62- to 9.14-m) cotton rope around the horse's neck just in front of the withers with a bowline knot. Wrap a short strap with two rings in the ends around the pastern. The free end of the rope is passed through the rings and then through the loop around the neck. This forms a pulley system to hoist the leg.

To lift a back leg, use a 25- to 30-foot (7.62- to 9.14-m) cotton rope ($\frac{3}{4}$-inch diameter) and strap with two rings to form a "sideline." If the horse tries to kick or is a confirmed kicker, apply the sideline as in Figure 6-5. Lift the foot until the horse cannot get it closer than 4 to 6 inches to the ground (101.6 to 152.4 mm).

You can use the tail tie method with horses that do not offer much resistance (Figure 6-6).

Hock hobbles are used to prevent the horse from kicking with the hindfeet. However, they are usually only used on breeding farms to hobble mares during the breeding process (Figure 6-6).

(a)   (b)

(c)   (d)

(e)   (f)

FIGURE 6-5 Tying up the hindleg of a problem horse with a pastern strap and a long line *(a)* Equipment: (A) 30 feet of $\frac{3}{4}$-inch soft cotton rope (9.14 m of 1.9-cm rope); (B) 8-foot lead rope with snap; (C) pastern strap. *(b)* A long line is tied around the neck with a bowline knot, and the free end is passed through one ring of the pastern strap. *(c)* The horse has stepped over the rope with one hindleg. *(d)* The rope is above the hock, and the free end has been passed through the other ring of the pastern strap. *(e)* The pastern strap is placed in position by pulling on the free end of the rope. *(f)* The leg is held up, and the rope is tied off with a quick-release knot. (Photos by W. Evans.)

FIGURE 6-6   Back leg held up with tail tie and pastern strap by pulling rope over the horse's croup. (Photo by W. Evans.)

Western hobbles (Figure 6-7) are used to keep a horse from walking very fast. They are used to keep horses from running away from camp on trail rides or if they are ground tied. The hobble consists of two straps that encircle the pasterns and are joined together with a short strap or chain. In an emergency, you can make one by opening up a burlap bag and rolling it across the diagonal, like a bandanna. Wrap it around one pastern and twist and tie it around the other.

Twitches

For generations, various types of twitches have been used to restrain horses (Figure 6-8). The simplest twitch is grasping the upper lip of the horse and rolling it upward. The skin on the shoulder area can be grasped and rolled with the hand. An ear twitch is applied by grasping the ear, placing the wrist and forearm against the horse's head, and pulling outward. The ear should never be twisted or bent double and twisted. If possible, one should avoid the ear twitch because it makes horses head shy.

(a)   *(b)*

FIGURE 6-7   Hobbles: *(a)* two types of western hobbles; *(b)* horse hobbled with western hobble. (Photos by W. Evans.)

    More severe twitches include the types that are loops placed around the horse's upper lip and tightened. A chain or rope is used to form the loops, and a handle is used to twist the loop. The twitch may injure the horse's teeth, gums, and inner lip. If the horse jerks its head or rears, the handle of the twitch becomes a lethal club, so you must be very careful when using this type of twitch.

    The Wilform twitch is a square frame with a movable bar across the center. A screw ring tightens the bar on the horse's upper lip.

    The Kendal twitch is one of the safest lip twitches for the horse and handler (Figure 6-9). Two aluminum bars are slightly flared on one end to form a loop and are hinged together like pincers; a cord at the other end of the bars is wrapped around the bars which fastens the twitch quickly and safely. The cord is then snapped to the halter. The smooth bars do not injure a horse's mouth, they allow some blood circulation, and are not as dangerous to the handler if the twitch is thrown off.

    All lip twitches should be snug enough for restraint but not too severe. They should not be left on too long, because they cut off blood circulation.

FIGURE 6-8   Twitches: *(a)* chain; *(b)* Kendal. (Photo by W. Evans.)

FIGURE 6-9   Kendal twitch on upper lip. (Photo by W. Evans.)

War Bridles

Horses that are difficult to control while being led can be restrained with a war bridle (Figure 6-10a). The simplest war bridle is formed by tying a honda in the end of a rope and then forming a loop. The loop is placed over the poll and across the gum of the upper incisor teeth. Sharp, quick pulls on the loop are used to correct or restrain the horse. Similar results can be obtained by using a leather halter and a lead shank (stallion lead shank) with a chain and snap on the end. The chain is run through the ring on the left side of the halter, across the gum, through the ring on the right side of the halter, and snapped to the upper ring on the halter (Figure 6-10b and d). If the chain is passed through the mouth (Figure 6-10b, c, d) or over the nose (Figure 6-10e, f, g), it will not be as severe. The latter three methods are frequently used to restrain stallions. A less severe use of the chain is to pass it over the nose and snap it under the chin (Figure 6-10g) or just to snap it under the chin (Figure 6-10g).

Chemicals

Many tranquilizers are effective for horses. However, they should be used only under the direction or supervision of a veterinarian, because horses do not always react as expected. They may go berserk and seriously injure themselves and handlers.

(a)

(b)

(c)

(d)

FIGURE 6-10   War bridles and chains: *(a)* rope loop over poll and through the mouth; *(b)* chain across gum; *(c)* chain in mouth (left side view); *(d)* chain in mouth (right side view); *(e)* chain over nose (left side view); *(f)* chain over nose (right side view); *(g)* chain over nose and under chin; *(h)* chain under chin. (Photos by W. Evans.)

(e) (f)

(g) (h)

FIGURE 6-10 *Continued*

SAFETY

Observe all safety precautions while working with horses. Most accidents happen with horses that are very gentle. The person handling the horse forgets how horses react to a situation, so he or she suffers an injury when the gentle horse reacts. Following are a few safety rules you should always observe.

Actions

Your actions around a horse reflect your ability and confidence in handling it. Remain calm and confident at all times. Nervous handlers usually make a horse become nervous and unsafe.

Never tease or unduly punish a horse. A teased horse may develop dangerous habits for the rest of its life and may lose all respect for its handler.

If you must punish a horse, do so at the instant of its disobedience. If you wait, even for a minute, the horse will not understand why it is being punished. Control your temper at all times, but let the horse know that you are its firm, kind master.

Know the horse's temperament, reactions, and peculiarities. If the horse is unfamiliar to you, ask about the horse before working with it.

Clothes

Wear footgear that protects your feet if the horse steps on them and from being injured by nails and other small objects around the stables and barnyard. Boots or hardtoed shoes are preferable. Never wear tennis shoes or moccasins. Never go barefoot, because infectious organisms such as tetanus are prevalent around barns, corrals, and fences. Gloves safeguard against cuts, scratches, splinters, and rope burns.

Catching and Releasing

Be careful when approaching a horse to catch it so that the horse does not kick or run over you (see first section in this chapter). It is not safe to leave a halter on a loose horse. When you must do so, check the halter daily or make sure it has a safety release. Some halter materials shrink, so be certain to check the fit. A loose horse may catch a foot in the halter strap or may catch a halter on posts or other objects.

Use judgment when turning a horse loose. It is generally safest to lead the horse completely through the gate or door and then turn the horse around, facing the direction of entry. Make the horse stand quietly while it is being released. Then release the lead strap or remove the halter or bridle. Avoid letting a horse bolt away when released because it may kick as it wheels around or runs by.

Leading

The proper position for leading a horse is described earlier. When leading a horse, avoid using excessively long lead ropes that may become accidentally entangled. When using lariats or longe lines, watch out for the coils. Never wrap the lead strap, halter shank, or reins around your hand, wrist, or body. When leading, tying, or untying a horse, avoid getting your hands or fingers entangled, and also be careful not to catch a finger in dangerous positions in halter and bridle hardware, including snaps, bits, rings, and loops.

Be extremely cautious when leading a horse through narrow openings such as a door. Be certain you have firm control and step through first. Step through quickly and get to one side to avoid being crowded.

A horse is larger and stronger than a person. If it resists, do *not* get in front and try to pull. Have someone walk behind the horse and tap it with a whip or try to push it to the side to get it moving again.

Tying

Tie or hold horses when working around them. Always tie a horse in a safe place—with a halter rope, not the bridle reins. Be certain to tie the horse to a strong, secure object so that the rope will not break or come loose if the horse pulls back. Use a quick-release knot (Figure 6-3) so you can release the horse in an emergency.

Never tie the halter rope below the level of the withers, and tie it short enough to prevent the horse from stepping over the halter rope. Tie the horse a safe distance from other horses and from tree limbs or brush where the horse may become entangled.

Working Around the Horse

Work around a horse from a position as near the shoulder as possible. Also, stay close to the horse so that, if it kicks, you do not receive the full impact. Stay out of kicking range whenever possible. When you go to the opposite side of the horse, move away and go around it out of kicking range. Let the horse know where you are by talking to it or rubbing your hand on it as you move around it.

Never stand directly behind a horse to work with its tail. Stand off to the side, near the point of the buttock, facing to the rear. Grasp the tail and draw it toward you.

A good horseperson always lets a horse know what he or she intends to do. When picking up the horse's foot, for example, do not grab the foot hurriedly. This startles the horse and may cause it to kick. Learn the proper way to lift the feet.

A horse should be trained to be workable from both sides, even for mounting and dismounting. Some horses become very irritable and nervous when they are worked on from the right side.

Be careful not to drop grooming tools underfoot while grooming. Place them where they will not trip you and where the horse will not step on them. An accidental slip or stumble can result in injury.

Bridling

When bridling, protect your head from the horse's head. Stand close, just behind and to one side (preferably the left side) of the horse's head. Use caution when handling the horse's ears.

Maintain control of the horse when bridling by refastening the halter around the neck.

Adjust the bridle to fit the horse before riding it. Three points to check are the placement of the bit, the adjustment of the curb strap, and the adjustment of the throatlatch.

Saddling

Before saddling the horse, check the saddle blanket and all other equipment for foreign objects. Be certain the horse's back and the cinch or girth areas are clean. Foreign objects will make a horse buck or will cause saddle sores.

Bridle reins, stirrup leathers, headstalls, curb straps, and cinch straps should be kept in the best possible condition; the rider's safety depends on these straps. Inspect them frequently, and replace any strap when it begins to show signs of wear (cracking or checking).

When saddling to ride western style, it is safest to keep the off-cinches and stirrup secured over the saddle seat and ease them down when the saddle is on. Do not let them swing wide and hit the horse on the off-knee or belly—this hurts the horse and causes it to shy.

Swing the western saddle onto the horse's back easily, not suddenly. Dropping the saddle down too quickly or hard may scare the horse. You do not need to, and should not, swing the saddle into position. Lift it and place it into position.

Pull up slowly to tighten the cinch. Check the cinch three times: (1) after saddling, (2) after walking a few steps (untracking), and (3) after mounting and riding a short distance.

When using a double-rigged western saddle, remember to fasten the front cinch first and the rear cinch last when saddling. Unfasten the rear cinch first and the front cinch last when unsaddling. Be certain that the strap connecting the front and back cinches (along the horse's belly) is secure. The back cinch should not be so loose that the horse can get a hindleg caught between the cinch and its belly.

When using English equipment, "run up" the stirrups immediately on dismounting. Dangling stirrups may startle or annoy the horse. When fighting flies, the horse may catch the cheek of a bit or even a hindfoot in a dangling stirrup iron. Dangling stirrups can also catch on doorways and other projections while you are leading the horse. After running up the stirrups, immediately bring the reins forward over the horse's head. In this position, they can be used for leading.

Fasten accessory straps (tie downs, breast collars, martingales, and so on) and adjust them after the saddle is cinched on. Unfasten them first before loosening the cinch.

Mounting

Never mount or dismount a horse in a barn or near fences, trees, or overhanging projections. Sidestepping and rearing mounts have injured riders who failed to take these precautions. A horse should stand quietly for mounting and dismounting.

Riding

Until you know your horse, ride only in an arena or other enclosed areas. Do not ride in open spaces or unconfined areas until you are familiar with the horse. When the horse is full of energy, exercise it on a longe line or ride it in an enclosed area until it is settled.

Keep the horse under control and maintain a secure seat at all times. Horses are easily frightened by unusual objects and noises that may catch the rider unaware.

Spurs can trip you when you are working on the ground. Take them off when not mounted. Wear neat, well-fitted clothing that will not snag on equipment. Belts, jackets, and front chap straps can become hooked over the saddle horn. And wear boots or shoes with heels to keep your feet from slipping through the stirrups. Wear protective headgear appropriate to the activity in which you are engaged, especially in any form of jumping.

Keep the horse's feet properly trimmed and/or shod. Long toes predispose a horse to stumble and to fall.

There are certain safety precautions to remember when trail riding. First, if you plan to ride alone when trail riding, tell someone where you are going and approximately when you expect to return.

Ride a well-mannered horse. If a horse becomes frightened, remain calm, speak to it quietly, steady it, and give it time to overcome its fear. Then ride or lead the horse past the obstacle.

Courtesy is the best safety on the trail. Do not play practical jokes or indulge in horseplay. Never ride off until all riders in a group are mounted. Ride abreast or stay a full horse's length from the horse in front to avoid the possibility of a rider being kicked, or the rider's horse being kicked. Never rush past riders who are proceeding at a slower gait, because to do so startles both horses and riders, and often causes accidents. Instead, approach slowly, indicate a desire to pass, and proceed cautiously on the left side.

Hold the horse to a walk when going up or down a hill. Allow a horse to pick its way at a walk when riding on rough ground, or in sand, mud, ice, or snow where there is danger of slipping or falling. Use extreme caution at wet spots or boggy places. Walk the horse when approaching and going through underpasses and over bridges.

Select a riding location with care. Choose controlled bridle paths or familiar, safe, open areas. Try to avoid paved or other hard-surfaced roads. Walk the horse when crossing such roads. In heavy traffic, it is safest to dismount and lead across.

If it is necessary to ride on roads or highways, ride on the side required by law. State laws vary as to which side of the road you should ride on. Ride on the shoulders of roads or in ditches, but watch for junk. Riding at night can be a pleasure but is more hazardous than daytime riding. Walk the horse; fast gaits are dangerous. Wear light-colored clothing and carry a flashlight and reflectors when riding at night. Check details of your state's regulations.

When riding on federal or state lands, seek advice from the forest or park officials. Know their rules concerning use of the trails and their fire regulations. Obtain current, accurate maps and information on the area. Become familiar with the terrain and climate. Be certain the horse is in good physical condition and that its hooves and shoes are ready for the trail.

Avoid overhanging limbs. Warn and watch the rider behind you if you encounter one. Watch the rider ahead so that a limb pushed aside does not snap back and slap your horse in the face.

Learn to handle a rope before carrying one on a horse. Always use caution when working with a rope if the horse is not "rope-broken." Never tie the rope "hard and fast" to a saddle horn while roping from a "green" horse.

GENERAL EXERCISE

Lack of adequate exercise is one of the most common types of horse mismanagement. Horses need to be exercised for at least 30 minutes each day to maintain some muscle tone. Those that stand in a stall or small paddock and are not exercised become bored. Boredom leads to the common stall vices of weaving, cribbing, chewing wood, and stall walking.

There are several ways of exercising a horse that is not kept in a paddock large enough for free exercise.

Exercise Methods

Hot Walker

A horse can be placed on a "hot walker." A mechanical hot walker (Figure 6-11) keeps a horse moving in a small circle. A properly designed hot walker has several safety features. It must be difficult to pull over, so it must be properly anchored to the ground. The arms should be high enough to keep a horse from bumping its head. The drive system should contain a "slip-gear," so the rotation of the arms will stop if a horse falls down. Most of the good hot walkers have two forward and two reverse speeds. For each direction, one speed is for a slow walk and the other is for a fast walk or slow trot.

Horses should not be left on a hot walker too long at one time or they get bored. An exercise period of 30 minutes is usually sufficient. If left on it too long, some horses develop the habit of pulling back to get it to stop.

Treadmills

Treadmills are also used for horses that receive no other exercise or as part of a conditioning program for performance horses (Figure 6-12). Treadmills are constructed so that a continuous belt is driven by an electric motor. The belt runs over a series of closely spaced steel rollers. Treadmills can be positioned so that the horse is moving up an incline of up to a few degrees (5 to 7°). It is an excellent method of providing exercise and developing muscle tone.

FIGURE 6-11   Mechanical "hot walker" used to exercise a horse. (Photo by W. Evans.)

FIGURE 6-12   Horse being exercised on a treadmill. (Courtesy Horsey, Inc., manufacturer of Anamill Treadmill Conditioner, West Lake Rd., Vermillion, Ohio 44089.)

Longeing

Longeing is another method of exercising the horse without riding it (Figure 6-13). To longe a horse, one needs a 20- to 30-foot (6.1- to 9.1-m) longe line and a longe whip. The longe line is made from flat, braided nylon webbing about an inch wide. It has a swivel snap at one end. The longe whip has a stiff or slightly flexible 5-foot (1.5-m) handle and a 4- to 5-foot lash (1.2- to 1.5-m). If one is available, use a longeing cavesion, which has a ring on the nose piece to attach the longe line. If not available, attach the longe line to the bottom ring of an ordinary halter.

. To train the horse to longe, it should be trained in a round corral or small corral. The first lesson is to get the horse to walk in a small circle around you. Position the horse next to the wall of the round corral, stepping toward the

FIGURE 6-13   Horse being exercised on a longe line. (Photo by W. Evans.)

horse's hindquarters, and tapping it lightly with the whip to encourage it to move forward. As you tap the horse with the whip, give the voice command "Walk." As soon as the horse learns to go in one direction, teach it to go in a small circle in the opposite direction. This can usually be accomplished in one lesson. Starting with the second lesson, allow the horse to go in a larger circle, but within reach of the whip. After it makes a few rounds walking in one direction, teach it to stop. Give the voice command "Whoa," and place the whip in front of the horse. Do not let the horse stop and turn to face you. This teaches them to stop and turn on their forelegs. Later, it is difficult to train them to stop and pivot on their hindlegs. The third lesson is to train the horse to reverse directions. After the horse is stopped by the voice command "Whoa," approach it, give the voice command "Reverse," turn it around to the opposite direction, and give the voice command "Walk." The horse should learn how to reverse in a few repetitions. In later lessons, you can teach it to trot and canter. When cantering, the horse must be using the correct lead. After each good performance, the horse should be rewarded with a good pat on the neck.

Two mistakes are often made while training a horse to longe. One mistake is to let the horse approach you. While longeing, it should never come toward you or face you. It should be taught to keep its side toward you. Facing you usually results from the second common mistake—pulling on the longe line. By using voice commands and the whip, you never have to pull on the longe line.

Driving

Another form of exercise for the young horse is driving. The horse is worked with driving lines to teach it the basic commands while it is still too young to be ridden. Driving horses is discussed in Chapter 11.

Riding

Riding the horse is the most common method of exercise, because most horsepeople like to ride. The horse should be ridden at least 30 minutes per day, at least 5 to 6 times per week. A common mistake is to ride the horse for several hours on a weekend and not ride it during the week. This is hard on a horse because its muscles are not in physical condition and its bones are not used to the concussion trauma. Horses that are to be used or exercised very hard for long periods need to be conditioned over a period of time.

CONDITIONING FOR PERFORMANCE EVENTS

Conditioning is not difficult or stressful for the horse if the trainer takes certain precautions. Working with a horse in poor physical condition requires that you start the conditioning slowly and increase in intensity as the horse's muscular, respiratory, and cardiovascular systems become conditioned. If the program is too strenuous at the beginning, the horse's muscles become sore and lameness may develop because the bones are not accustomed to the stress of concussion.

Program

When developing a training or conditioning program, the main objectives are to mentally and physically prepare the horse for the rigors of competition, condition muscles, tendons, and bones to decrease the chance of injury, increase the working capacity so the horse can work longer, harder, and faster, and better perform and be consistent in specific tasks. Specific goals are defined—i.e., successfully completing a given type of performance such as running a given task in a specific time. Different types of performances require different energy demands, biomechanical functions, thermoregulation, and conditioning strategies for adaptation. The starting point for a conditioning program is defined, so that the trainer knows the current physical condition and can develop the program from that point. Thus, one needs to determine the physiological values such as normal temperature, heart and respiration rates, the conformational problems that lead to unsoundness or limit performance potential, unsoundness such as heat in joints, and previous conditioning programs.

There are four parts or phases of a conditioning program to develop the horse's skills and its energy-utilizing capabilities: base conditioning, development of stamina, development of sharpness, and competitiveness and rest. Base conditioning is long, slow distance training to develop aerobic capacity and condition bones, tendons, ligaments, and feet. The purpose is to lay a solid foundation for later strenuous exercise. Aerobic conditioning of the cardio-vascular system takes 30 days or slightly longer. It takes about 100-plus days to condition the skeleton and muscle systems.

Development of stamina requires slow work at aerobic capacity with hill or incline training for muscle strength. This phase takes 4 to 6 weeks.

Sharpness and competitiveness take varying periods of time depending on the performance objective. For race horses, it would be development of speed.

Rest days are a critical phase. The number of rest days per week (normally 1 or 2 days) depends on how strenuous the competitive task is.

Writing a training prescription for each day of training until the performance event is the next step in the conditioning process. The prescription will entail making decisions about a specific amount of work to be done including number of repetitions during each work bout. It is typical for disruptions to occur so the prescription is modified or reviewed on a regular basis. Also, it will contain the method(s) to be used to evaluate progress.

Concepts with which the trainer must be familiar include metabolic specificity, mode of activity specificity, muscle group specificity, motor skills, progressive loading, heart rate monitoring, preparation for and ending the exercise bout, and dealing with environmental factors.

Aerobic metabolism occurs when sufficient oxygen is available to metabolize energy sources. When exercising at a slow pace, the conditioned horse is able to exercise for long periods using aerobic metabolism without the buildup of metabolic products such as lactic acid. For quick short bursts of intense exercise, phosphagen is utilized. It is stored in muscles, does not require oxygen, and will last only 20 to 40 seconds. Anaerobic metabolism is utilized when oxygen availability is not adequate, so the horse utilizes glycogen and ATP stores. This process is inefficient and produces lactic acid. Usually, the horse can use this source for about 3 minutes before becoming fatigued.

Mode of action specificity means that the horse must be trained for a specific activity. Thus, a cutting horse cannot be trained on a treadmill. It would never learn how to work the cattle. Also, it would not be using the muscle groups that would be utilized when going through the maneuvers to hold the cow. Therefore, each muscle group must be trained for its function during the performance movements and repetition of the activities results in efficiency. Specific movements are also learned so motor skills develop and must lead up to the final performance at a competition.

For physical conditioning to occur, the concept of progressive loading is used to increase the workload as the horse becomes conditioned. As soon as the horse can handle the workout, the workload is increased. One must be patient and not rush a conditioning program to prevent excessive fatigue, injury, and loss of willingness to work. The time to increase the workload is recognized by a plateau in recovery time and when performance has become very consistent.

Overloading the cardiovascular system is accomplished in several ways: changing the rate of performance by working the same distance but faster; increasing the number of repetitions or performances; decreasing the duration of rest periods so that complete recovery does not occur; and varying the amount of work done, whether in total time or distance. The muscular system is overloaded in other ways: changing the length of contraction, for example, from trot on bare ground to trot through cavaletti (a series of long poles laid on the ground or slightly elevated above the ground) to stretch the muscle; varying the force of contraction along a higher cavaletti or steeper incline on the treadmill; and altering the rate of contraction with faster pass-through jumps or by increasing the number of cavalettis per given distance.

A heart rate monitor is used to follow the heart rate response during the work bout and during recovery. Heart rates over 150 are required to stress the system and heart rates between 150 and 200 are typical working rates. Heart rate will increase with the amount of work done, but as the horse becomes conditioned, the steady state heart rate for a specific amount of work will decrease and the rate of heart rate recovery will be faster.

Prior to exercising the horse, it is "warmed up" to stretch and relax muscles and to increase muscle temperature and blood flow to increase oxygen transfer efficiency. After exercise, it is "warmed down" or cooled out to allow time for metabolites of exercise to clear the blood system, which prevents muscles from getting tight and sore. Cooling down is probably more important than the warmup period.

A horse needs the opportunity to adapt to all the environmental factors that it will encounter during a performance. If the performance will be in an arena with people hanging over the rail and clapping, and loud speaker systems making loud noise, the horse needs to adapt to this prior to the event and be conditioned to stay mentally focused.

Recognition of excess physical stress resulting from overwork is critical to any conditioning program. Excessive fatigue during a work bout or immediately after it can be recognized by an increasing heart rate or when recovery rate suddenly becomes longer. Respiration becomes shallow and regular. Hydration needs to be monitored by the "pinch test," "capillary refill time," and sweating rate. Lack of coordination occurs, a signal that injury may occur if the work bout continues. Heat stroke may occur when the heat load is greater than the horse's ability to reduce it. Synchronous diaphragmatic flutter or "thumps" may occur. Exercise-induced pulmonary hemorrhage is recognized by presence of blood in the nostrils after exercise. Stress accumulated over a period of time is usually manifested by an attitude change. Horses lose their desire to work. Most horses will "go to the wall" (maximum all-out effort resulting in excessive muscular, cardiovascular, and respiratory stress) only so many times in a given period of time. This varies with individual horses. Decreased stamina and fatigue are two other symptoms of accumulated work stress. Psychic stress is recognized by depressed appetite, diarrhea, and muscle tremors. Race horses that return from a hard race and fail to eat usually need extra rest over the next few days. Those that clean up their feed are normally ready to resume their normal conditioning program.

Cardiovascular Responses to Exercise

During an exercise bout, the heart rate increases from the resting rate to a peak after about 30 seconds, then it declines and levels off to a plateau as exercise continues (Figure 6-14). Peak values will be affected by intensity of exercise and excitement. The steady state heart rate, or plateau, will depend on physical condition and the stress of exercise. After exercise, the heart rate will rapidly decline for 2 to 5 minutes and then gradually decline to the resting value. The recovery time is the time from cessation of exercise until resting heart rate is attained. It is also affected by environmental factors.

The heart rate response to varying work loads for a horse in a given state of physical condition is shown in Figure 6-15. Increasing work loads result in increasing peak values and increasing steady state values up to the maximum heart rate of 200 to 220. Heart rate response to repetitions for a poorly and a well-conditioned horse is given in Figure 6-16. In a horse lacking condition, each repetition results in higher peak and steady state values. In the well-conditioned horse, the peak and steady state values remain about the same for each repetition until fatigue starts to occur. Then, the values start to increase and recovery takes longer. Effect of training is shown in Figure 6-17. Resting heart rate does not change as the horse becomes conditioned. As the work load increases, the steady state heart rate curve is shifted to the right—lower heart rate for a given work load. Maximum heart rate does not change, but the load required for the maximum is increased.

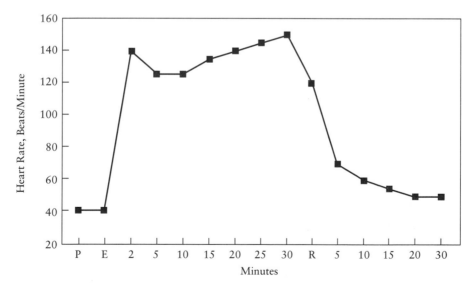

FIGURE 6-14   Heart rate response to exercise. P = prior to start of exercise. E = start of exercise. R = recovery starting at 2 minutes after cessation of exercise.

FIGURE 6-15   Heart rate responses to increasing work loads. P = prior to start of exercise. E = start of exercise. R = recovery starting at 1 minute after cessation of exercise.

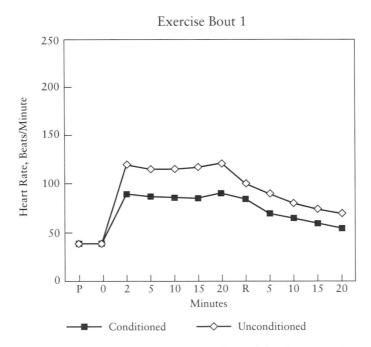

FIGURE 6-16   Heart rate response to repetitions of a work load in a poorly conditioned horse and a well-conditioned horse. P = prior to exercise. R = start of recovery period.

Exercise Bout 2

Exercise Bout 3

FIGURE 6-16   *Continued*

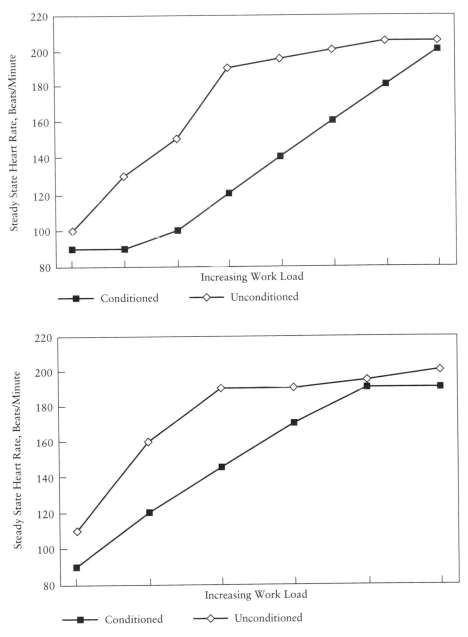

FIGURE 6-17   Effect of increasing work load on maximal and steady state heart rates in a horse that is not conditioned, and in one that is conditioned.

Heart mass or size will increase during conditioning, but the change is minimal. Training will increase cardiac output after about 12 weeks, but the change is minimal. It is more affected by the work bout since it is the volume of blood pumped each heartbeat times the heart rate. During exercise, there may be a six-fold increase. Coupled with the increased cardiac output, the spleen contracts to increase the number of circulating red blood cells. There is an increase in blood flow to skeletal muscles. Training increases the number of capillaries surrounding muscle fibers and red blood cell transit time through the capillaries to increase oxygen uptake by the muscles.

Respiratory Responses to Exercise

Very little adaptation to exercise occurs in the respiratory system. Rate is coupled to stride frequency.

Bone Response to Exercise

One of the least understood concepts in horse training is bone remodeling during conditioning. There are three zones of work load for bone. In zone 1, the bone is not stressed enough for any training effect. The architecture of the bone does not change. In zone 2, a training effect occurs and is the zone of fatigue. It takes about 120 to 130 days for the bone to remodel itself during stress. Zone 3, or the overload zone, is where the bone is overloaded to the point of failure. The overload can be a single incidence or it may occur over time as a result of accumulated micro damage.

To prevent failure or bone damage, a trainer must be careful during the 130-day period not to overload and go into the overload zone. It is during the later part of the 130-day period that most race trainers start asking a young horse for some speed in their work bouts. The bone is porous and injuries can occur. Thus, it is best to get bones adapted to exercise prior to the start of cardiovascular training.

Conditioning Program for Competitive Trail Ride

It takes about 10 to 12 weeks to condition an average horse for a 25- to 50-mile (40.2- to 80.4-km) competitive trail ride. A typical training schedule that has been used to successfully train several competitive trail ride and endurance horses is:

Week 1: Walk the horse every other day on level ground for 2 hours.

Week 2: Walk the horse every other day on level ground for 3 hours.

Week 3: Walk and trot the horse every other day on level ground for 2 hours. Gradually increase the trotting to 50 percent of the time. However, the trotting periods last for 5 to 20 minutes.

Week 4: Walk and trot the horse every other day on level ground for 3 hours. Gradually increase the trotting until the horse can trot for a full 30-minute period.

Week 5:   Walk the horse up hills every other day for 2 hours. Go slowly, but make the horse keep moving. During conditioning, never stop for a rest during a climb; stop only when you reach the top.

Week 6:   Walk the horse up the steepest hills you can find every other day for 3 hours.

Week 7:   Trot the horse up hills every other day for 2 hours. Gradually increase the trotting to 50 percent of the uphill work.

Week 8:   Trot the horse up hills every other day for 3 hours. Trot as much as possible.

Week 9:   This is the weekend before the ride. Saturday, ride 20 miles (32.2 km); Sunday, ride 15 miles. Ride at a good, steady NATRC (North American Trail Ride Conference) pace. Trot the levels and walk the ups and downs at a good fast walk.

Let the horse rest the balance of the week.

Week 10:   Go to the ride.

Evaluation of Condition and Stress

When training a horse for long physical performances, the trainer should be able to evaluate pulse and respiration rates and recognize thumps, dehydration, and azoturia.

Evaluation of the pulse (*P*) and respiration (*R*) is necessary to prevent stressing the horse beyond its physical condition and to recognize when the horse becomes conditioned. The methods for determination are discussed in Chapter 10. A well-conditioned horse has a resting pulse of 35 to 40 beats per minute and a respiration rate of 12 to 25 per minute. The *P:R* ratio should be 3:1 or 2:1. As the horse exercises, both *P* and *R* increase, but the ratio is maintained in a well-conditioned horse. While working, the pulse rate usually ranges between 75 and 105 but may increase to ~175 during heavy workouts. The respiratory rate increases to 24 to 36. At the end of an exercise period, the rates recover rapidly—within 5 to 10 minutes in a well-conditioned horse. Horses in poor condition do not recover for 30 to 45 minutes. When the *P:R* ratio decreases at elevated levels, it indicates a stress condition of such magnitude as to make further exercise totally inadvisable. For example, at rest a horse may have a pulse rate of 36 and a respiration rate of 12 (a 3:1 ratio). After severe exercise, the horse may show a *P* of 120 and an *R* of 60 (a 2:1 ratio). A well-conditioned horse may recover during a 45-minute rest period to a *P* of 60 and an *R* of 30 or, again, the 2:1 ratio. Should a horse under the same set of circumstances show a *P* of 85 and an *R* of 80 or 90 (a 1:1 ratio), a potentially dangerous level has been reached, and the horse probably should not be allowed to continue to exercise. Many trainers also share the opinion that a horse whose pulse does not drop to 70 or below after a 45-minute rest period is not in good physical condition.

Horses often become dehydrated on long trail rides unless a deliberate effort is made to keep them hydrated. Water is lost from the horse's body in several ways, but during strenuous exercise the primary loss is from profuse sweating. The water loss upsets the water and electrolyte (salts) balance of body tissue. Failure to replenish water and electrolytes leads to disturbance of body functions, weakness, and death.

Dehydration is easily recognized by two methods. One method is to pick up a fold of skin at the point of the shoulder and release it. Normally, the skin flattens out immediately. If the horse is slightly dehydrated, it takes about 5 seconds for the skin to flatten out, and if there is moderate dehydration, it takes about 10 seconds. When the horse is severely dehydrated, the skin does not flatten out, the eyes look sunken in, and no saliva is being produced. Another method is to determine the blood capillary refill time. This is done by opening the upper lip of the horse and pressing the thumb against the gum until the gum turns white (no blood present) under the thumb. On release of the thumb, blood quickly returns to the area. If the horse is dehydrated, the refill time may be 10 seconds, the membranes are dry, and the gum is usually bluish in color, which indicates a lack of oxygen.

Prevent dehydration by making sure the horse has adequate water and that the lost electrolytes are replaced. Prevention starts with a good, balanced diet and free access to salt (sodium chloride) during the training period. During an endurance ride or long training rides, allow the horse to drink at every opportunity to do so. Electrolyte therapy may be required. There are numerous types of electrolyte combinations and methods of administration. Their use for an individual horse should be discussed with a veterinarian who is familiar with the problem.

Heat stroke or heat exhaustion can occur in the stressed horse whose body fails to regulate his temperature in response to heat and/or exercise. Heat stroke usually develops in poorly conditioned horses that are subjected to overexertion in hot, humid climates. Heat stroke is characterized by depression, weakness, lack of appetite, refusal to continue to work, dehydration, and increased respiration and heart rates. Rectal temperature may rise to 106–110°F. The sweating response may be exhausted so that the skin is dry and hot. These symptoms may lead to incoordination, collapse, coma, and death. Overheating can also occur in horses that are being transported in enclosed trailers during the heat of the day or that are stabled in hot, poorly ventilated quarters. If overheating is observed, the body temperature should be lowered as quickly as possible by bathing with cold water and ice packs applied to the legs, face, and neck. In severe cases, the rectum can be packed with ice or cold-water enemas given. Fluid therapy may also be required.

Sweat evaporation is the primary cooling mechanism for horses. Anhidrosis is a failure of the sweating mechanism and can lead to hyperthermia in the exercising horse or, during hot, humid conditions, in the nonexercising horse. Anhidrosis is also referred to as nonsweating or "dry coat syndrome," and "blowing off" or "puff disease." The onset of anhidrosis appears to be precipitated over time by heat stress in a humid environment. It occurs primarily in year-round hot, humid climates such as the Gulf states. It affects horses of all ages, colors, and breeds and is equally prevalent in horses at all levels of exercise. The cause is unknown. When it occurs, one must be careful to keep the horse cool to prevent excessive hyperthermia, collapse, and death.

Fatigue can lead to "exhausted horse syndrome," which consists of depression, lack of interest in food or water even though dehydrated, high pulse and respiratory rates, irregular heartbeat, absence of gut sounds, and diminished anal tone. In addition, colic or synchronous diaphragmatic flutter (SDF) may be observed. SDF is recognized as a twitch or spasm in the flank which may be severe enough to produce a thumping sound. Fatigue resulting from short-term, maximal exercise is primarily due to a depletion of energy stores, whereas long-term, submaximal exercise leads to water and electrolyte loss and depletion of energy stored. The electrolyte losses in sweat include sodium, potassium, chloride, calcium, and magnesium. A veterinarian should treat the horse to restore fluid volume and electrolytes.

Exercise-induced pulmonary hemorrhage (EIPH) is bleeding from the lungs post-exercise and is a common problem among horses that run at maximum speed. About 9 percent of race horses show blood from the nostrils after racing, but endoscopic examination indicates bleeding farther down the respiratory tract in approximately 50 percent of Thoroughbreds, 35 percent of Standardbreds, 11 percent of polo ponies, and 13 percent of upper-level three-day event horses. Over 3 races, 80 to 90 percent of all race horses will exhibit EIPH. It is most likely due to pulmonary hypertension which occurs in response to maximum exertion during racing. Pulmonary hypertension is sufficient to rupture capillaries in the respiratory tract. However, there is some evidence that underlying respiratory disease may also be a cause via compromised lung performance. The bleeding results in irritation and inflammation which in turn causes fibrosis and a new network of capillaries. Very mild bleeding seems to have minimal effect on performance, whereas more profuse bleeding reduces racing performance. Treatment with the diuretic Lasix may or may not reduce the incidence of EIPH in a horse.

TRANSPORTATION

All horses should be trained to load into a trailer. Horses that refuse or are difficult to load cause accidents, injuries, and bad experiences. A horse usually refuses to enter a trailer because it fears an unfamiliar trailer or remembers a bad experience while loading. Prior planning prevents poor performance when a horse must be loaded and transported.

Trailers

There are many types of trailers to haul horses. Most are the bumper-hitch type, but the gooseneck type is also popular. Gooseneck types extend over the rear of the truck and hitch to the truck over its rear axle. Single- and two-horse trailers are usually of the bumper-hitch type but are available as goosenecks. Four-horse and larger models are usually goosenecks. The advantages of the gooseneck for larger trailers are weight distribution, ease of handling, radius of turns, and safety. The weight is distributed on the vehicle in front of the rear axle, instead of back on the bumper, where heavy weight tends to pick up the nose of the towing vehicle, which encourages fish tailing. The towing vehicle and trailers should be compatible in terms of size, weight, and towing class to provide stability, power, safety, and control. Towing vehicles that are too light, too narrow, or lack sufficient horsepower are a hazard on the road. If the towing vehicle is used frequently to pull a trailer, it is advisable for it to be equipped with enhanced engine and transmission cooling systems, heavy duty flasher, and a class IV trailer hitch receiver. When you are purchasing the vehicle, the following checklist should be discussed with the vehicle dealer to see if it meets your needs: horsepower, cooling systems, suspension, tow rating, torque rating, electrical systems, transmission, brakes, power train/axle ratio, gross vehicle weight rating, gross axle weight rating, and gross combination weight rating. The trailer should be of adequate height, width, and length. Allow at least 10 inches of clearance above the horse's head when it is standing at rest. There should be 3 to 6 inches of clearance from side to side and from front to back so the horse is not in constant contact with the walls and butt bar or chain. All interior and exterior features such as lights, windows, latches, knobs, vents, and hardware should be sturdy, smooth, protected, or recessed and "horse proof."

Rear doors can be hinged or have loading ramps, or have combinations of the two. A hinged door is preferable if the step up is not too high. It is more difficult to train horses to go up a loading ramp. They may step off the edge of it and injure their legs. If the horse will only load by someone leading it into a trailer, an escape door may be advisable.

The wheel wells should be located on the outside of the trailer. Trailers are equipped with electric or hydraulic brakes. The tires should be 6- or 8-ply for added protection.

The partition that separates the horses should be carefully considered. You may need a full-length partition or one that extends just below the hips. If the trailer is not full width, a full partition makes it difficult for the horse to keep its balance, because it cannot spread its legs. This causes some horses to try to "climb the sides" of the trailer on turns. Most horses ride better and are more comfortable with the partial partition. However, a full divider will prevent horses from stepping on each other.

In large trailers, the horses may ride so that one is hauled directly behind another. They may all face forward, or some may face backward, opposite the direction of travel. Others are hauled while standing in a diagonal position in the trailer. Position seems to make no difference to the horse.

Before loading and transporting the horse, inspect the trailer and towing vehicle for safety. The trailer ball should be the proper size and tightly secured to the hitch. The electrical connections should be working, as should all directional and turn signals, running and stop lights, and the brakes. Manure and urine left too long in the trailer eventually rots out the wooden floors. Clean them out, and check the floor boards for rot. A rubber mat provides a firm foothold and prevents the horse from slipping down. All door and window latches should work properly and be securely fastened. Butt chains should be present and secure. A properly inflated spare tire, lug wrench, and trailer jack should be in the trailer or towing vehicle. Tires should be properly inflated and checked for abnormal wear, tread depth, and dry rot. Wheel bearings should be serviced yearly or every 10,000 miles (16,090 km). Safety chains should be in working condition. Vents should be properly adjusted for adequate ventilation.

Before hauling a horse, the driver should be experienced with towing trailers or should pull the trailer around to get the feel of how it influences the towing vehicle. For the safety of the horse, execute turns more slowly and less sharply than when not pulling a trailer. Avoid sudden stops. Moreover, it takes a longer distance to stop a rig, to start moving, and to reach a desired speed. Backing a trailer is tricky and requires practice. If only one horse is being transported in a two-horse trailer, the horse should be hauled on the driver's side. This way, if the outside wheel drops off the shoulder, there will be less chance of the trailer turning over. For easier towing, each trailer has a recommended height between the tongue and the ground.

Loading

A well-trained horse will go into a trailer without any hesitation but other horses can be loaded only with great difficulty. There are several methods of training horses to load or loading a stubborn horse.

One way to train a green horse to be loaded is by teaching it to longe with a whip. While learning to longe, the horse should learn the voice commands "Whoa" and "Walk." The horse should respect the whip. To load the horse, position a tandem trailer so that the right rear door will open adjacent to a smooth fence or wall. Lead the horse to the trailer and allow it to examine it for a few minutes. As soon as it becomes accustomed to the trailer, load the horse as follows (Figure 6-18). Position the horse facing the open trailer and between you and the fence or wall. Hold the lead shank in your left hand, stand at the horse's shoulder, and hold the whip in your right hand. Guide the horse's head with your left hand. Give the horse the command to walk. If it does not step forward, give the command again and tap the horse on the croup with the whip. Constantly tap the horse with the whip until it goes into the

FIGURE 6-18   Training a horse to load into a trailer. (Photo by W. Evans.)

trailer. The wall on the horse's off side prevents it from moving or swinging around to the right. If the horse tries to move around to the left, you can apply the butt of the whip firmly to its ribs. If the horse attempts to back away, apply the whip more firmly. If the horse attempts to rear, apply the whip across the withers and back. Each time the horse moves forward, stop tapping with the whip, as a reward. Give the horse the command to walk; if it does not move forward again, apply the whip. As soon as one foot is placed in the trailer, praise the horse but do not allow it to hesitate too long or it will back out. A little more pressure from the whip usually gets the horse to move all the way in. The butt chain should be secured immediately and the door closed. Praise the horse and allow it to quiet down for a few minutes. Then unload it, making sure it does not bump its head on the top of the trailer. During the first lesson, load and unload the horse at least six times. Repeat the lesson for a couple of days or until the horse walks immediately into the trailer. The first two or three times the horse is hauled should each last only 15 to 30 minutes.

The spoiled or stubborn horse can be very difficult to load, and more drastic procedures may be necessary. One procedure can be to tie two longe lines to the halter, pass them through the ring in the front of the trailer and back alongside the horse. Cross the lines behind the horse just above its hocks. One person pulls on each line, and an assistant taps the horse on the croup with a whip. This way, the horse cannot back up. Another method is to place a lip chain on the horse. If it refuses to follow you into the trailer or backs up, give it a jerk on the lead shank. The horse soon learns that it must move forward to get away from the pressure of the lip chain.

One of the more successful and less traumatic ways to train the stubborn horse to load is to use the psychological principle discussed for catching a horse. This method avoids use of the whip and unnecessary harsh punishment. When the horse refuses to go into the trailer, it is backed up a couple of steps and longed at the canter until it does not want to canter any further. Give the command to "Whoa" and then immediately give the horse an opportunity to go into the trailer. If it refuses, repeat the procedure. Eventually, you will be able to lead it into the trailer. Each time the horse approaches the trailer and moves closer to entering it, let it stand for a moment. Then ask it to move closer. If it refuses, then it is longed. Be sure to longe the horse in both directions and make it change directions. When the horse does load into the trailer, let it stand there and rest for a few minutes. Repeat the loading several times until there is no hesitation to enter the trailer. When asking the horse to load into the trailer, use the same voice command or cue each time.

Horse Safety Precautions

Protecting the horse during hauling is a wise safety precaution. Helmets that attach to the halter can be used to protect the top of the horse's head. It may also be advisable to wrap the tail to prevent it from being rubbed out by the butt chain or top of the rear door. The method for wrapping the tail is discussed in Chapter 7 on grooming.

The front and hindlegs can be protected by shipping boots or by wrapping the legs with track bandages. Be sure to follow correct procedures, or the legs will be injured by lack of blood circulation. First, wrap a piece of padding (such as rolled cotton, sheet cotton, or quilts) around the leg. Prepare the track bandage by rolling it up with the ties on the inside of the roll. They will be at the end when unrolled. Place the end of the track bandage about halfway up the cannon and roll it toward the back of the leg. Roll it around the back, toward the front of the leg, and to the back again. Wrap it down the leg so that each wrap overlaps the previous wrap by about 1 inch. Wrap the leg down to where one wrap is taken around the pastern, wrap back up the leg to just below the top of the cotton or quilt, and then back down to the center of the leg. Tie the bandage off on the outside of the leg. It should be tied firmly but not too tightly. If the leg is cushioned by the cotton or quilt and part of the cotton or quilt is left extending beyond the wrap, the circulation should not be cut off.

Prior to trips lasting 6 or more hours, all immunizations should be current since suppression of the immune system occurs during these trips.

Commercial Transportation

There are a large number of commercial carriers that transport horses by van and/or by air. Commercial carriers must be licensed by the federal Department of Transportation and registered with the Interstate Commerce Commission.

The Department of Transportation performs routine compliance inspections for maintenance logs for the tractor trailers and checks insurance records. A commercial carrier is required to have insurance in every state in which it operates. Drivers for commercial carriers are required to take physical exams at the request of the Department of Transportation. Members of the National Horse Carriers Association have higher safety standards than federal standards.

Communications between drivers and office personnel is greatly enhanced for the commercial carriers that utilize satellite tracking systems, on-board fax machines, and cellular telephones. Some vans have a video system to monitor the horse's activities in the van.

Transportation by air is a common practice for performance or sale horses that are traveling long distances both domestic and international. International air transportation arrangements are usually made by a shipping agent such as Mersant International. The shipping agent takes responsibility for quarantine, passports, health records, vaccinations, insurance, and health examinations. There are a number of government regulations that apply when a horse crosses international boundaries and they are different for each country. See Chapter 18 for details regarding import and export regulations.

Avoiding Travel Fatigue

When horses are transported for more than 14 hours to a destination, steps should be taken to reduce travel fatigue. Every 4 to 6 hours, the horse should have a rest period during which it is walked for exercise and allowed to drink and eat. On longer trips, overnight stabling may be required or is certainly desirable for performance horses. The Nationwide Overnight Stabling Directory and Equestrian Vacation Guide is a source for finding overnight stabling in the United States and Canada.

TRAINING

Behavior is a combination of both genetics and environment. Nature versus nurture is an old controversy that has been well investigated by proponents of both views. Certain behaviors can be attributed to genetics; others have been varied greatly with environment. Psychologists have been more concerned with environment basically because of their interest in human behavior, which lends itself to manipulation by environment more than genetics. However, the animal breeder has an opportunity through selective breeding to cause many genetic effects on behavior, and the field of behavior genetics has become more popular in recent years. B. F. Yeates, retired horse specialist with the Texas

Agricultural Extension Service, describes in the following pages the application of principles of psychology to horse training.

Environmental Influences

Horse training deals with the modification of behavior, and most of the principles of learning are applicable to horses. When training begins, the horse has a certain operant level of performance, which the trainer must determine and then begin to modify. The behavior must be modified progressively to achieve a desirable performance. At this point the genetic potential of the horse has already been determined, and the horse should be capable of reaching the desired level of performance. What the trainer has to manipulate is the environment. The trainer should divide the environment into stimuli and reinforcement, and use them relative to the desired response. Responses, stimuli, reinforcement, and their relationships to each other are fundamental to the psychology of training. The aspiring trainer must develop a clear understanding of each.

Responses

The term *response* refers to specific parts of behavior. Responses are the acts or movements that the horse makes. Training involves teaching the horse to make the desired response. On occasion, the term will be used when referring to major maneuvers such as stopping or jumping. However, for the most part, responses should be thought of as smaller segments of major maneuvers, and major maneuvers should be regarded as many responses chained together. The trainer must learn to identify these smaller segments and know how to put them together for the major maneuvers. The initial reaction of the horse to bit pressure is a response that, properly reinforced, will eventually be part of a stop, which is a major maneuver.

Stimuli

Stimuli are divided into conditioned and unconditioned categories depending on their natural effect on the horse. If a stimulus can naturally cause a response with no practice, it is said to be unconditioned. Few of these are used in horse training. A stimulus that has been learned through practice is said to be conditioned. Many of these are used in horse training and are known to horsemen as cues. Most cues are learned; very few stimuli will naturally cause the response sought in training.

Basic Cues

Since few of the cues used in training are natural and for the most part must be learned, the trainer starts with basic cues, which are the closest to being natural. These cues practically show the horse what to do. They are very obvious and readily learned. Direct rein pressure response is obvious because the horse is shown the direction in which it is supposed to go, and the horse can learn this quickly. But if these obvious cues were all that the horse ever acquired, it would not be considered very highly trained.

Presenting New Cues

Using basic cues, the trainer will advance the horse to new cues. This is accomplished by pairing the new cue with the more basic one in the daily training routine. The rate at which the horse learns is affected by how these two cues are paired.

The new cue should always be presented first, followed by the old cue that the horse knows. For best results, allow no time lapse between the two cues. After the new cue is presented, the old cue should be paired close enough to slightly overlap the new. For example, in teaching a horse the neck rein, the basic cue of the direct rein (direct pull on the rein to turn the horse's head) is introduced first. Once the horse has learned to respond to this cue, the bearing rein (rein placing pressure on the neck) is introduced. The bearing rein means nothing to the horse in the beginning, but by following its presentation with the direct rein, the horse soon learns to make the same response to the bearing rein. Assuming that from early training the horse knows the cue "Whoa" to mean stop, the command can enhance learning to stop in response to bit pressure; that is, pull on the bit (new cue) and, while pressure is still intact, say "Whoa" (old cue). The horse should learn to stop from the pressure quickly and efficiently with this method. The trainer continually uses this method to teach the horse less obvious cues, but it will be successful only if the horse has learned the old cue well. The old cue must reliably cause the response before it can be used in acquiring a new cue. For example, if the bit is getting the correct response, then leg pressures may be introduced.

Teaching a horse to make a response to a combination of cues using different sensory modalities is also common practice. This method has the advantage of presenting a stronger stimulus to the horse and helps to make certain that the horse gets the message.

Presenting Specific Cues

The horse can receive stimuli through its sensory systems in many ways, but a person's best communication with the animal seems to be through its senses of touch and hearing. Common stimuli (cues) used in horse training are pressure and voice commands. Pressure is used on the nose by bosals (see section on bits and bitting), in the mouth by bits, on the neck by reins, and on various parts of the body by feet and legs. But a horse makes greater use of its hearing than touch or sight. Therefore, voice commands should be utilized where possible.

Indiscriminate presentation of cues will only confuse the horse. Cues must be specific so that the horse can identify them and separate them from the other things that are happening. It takes ability and skill to deliver specific identifiable cues to the horse. This helps to explain why some horsepeople can train better than others. Good horsemanship is a must. A rider cannot flop and fall over a horse and then expect to apply discriminate and specific cues that the horse can identify.

When teaching a horse to respond to cues, the trainer should start with the most basic cues; present new cues; present new cues to be learned just prior to the old cues; and be very specific in presenting the cue.

Reinforcement

It is doubtful that any learning can be accomplished without reinforcement, which means that certain events are capable of strengthening responses to certain stimuli. Reinforcement can be divided into two broad categories: primary and secondary.

Primary and Secondary Reinforcers

Primary reinforcers have natural reinforcing properties for the horse. Feed is a primary reinforcer in that the horse naturally appreciates feed, so it can be used to strengthen certain behavior. Only a few primary reinforcers are used directly in training.

Secondary reinforcers are acquired over a period of time. It can be said that they are learned. General acts of kindness to the horse can acquire secondary reinforcing properties. Learning that the training period will end if it performs well is secondary reinforcement for the horse. There are many examples, and they are all distinguished from primary reinforcements in that they are learned. A horse trainer who can condition a horse for secondary reinforcement has another good tool with which to work.

Positive and Negative Reinforcers

Reinforcers, whether primary or secondary, can also be divided into two general types: positive and negative. Positive reinforcement, often referred to as reward training, is not always readily apparent to the horse, such as a pat on the neck or a spoken word. How rewarding are these? Any rewarding effects would have to be of an acquired or learned nature. An untrained horse would not appreciate them until they are associated with primary reinforcers such as food and water.

Many experienced horsepeople report good results from reward training. But because it is nearly always secondary or acquired reinforcement, and sometimes so vague, it is difficult to observe. The presence of the trainer or the sight of a working ring or a riding trail may have acquired reinforcing properties to the horse. Positive reinforcement may indeed be a valuable asset, and there is too much evidence of results obtained from reward training for the trainer to ignore its effects.

Negative reinforcement is aversive stimuli that the horse will work to avoid or to get rid of if given a choice. There are at least three different methods of conditioning with aversive stimuli—punishment, escape, and avoidance.

Punishment is a type of negative reinforcement characterized by the horse making a response in the absence of a cue and then being punished contingent upon the response. The aim here is not to teach a new response, but to weaken or eliminate a response that the horse has already acquired. Traditionally, horsepeople use this method to break bad habits or try to correct some vices. The intensity of punishment is critical. Light punishment does not break a habit but merely suppresses it. This is why horsepeople do not generally recommend that horses be gently pecked on for correction. There is much variation between individual horses concerning punishment. A light tap with a bat may mean practically nothing to one horse and may be fairly severe punishment for another. To be most effective, punishment must cause the horse to select a desirable alternate habit that leads to reward.

With *escape*, the second method of negative reinforcement, the aversive stimuli is applied with no cue and independent of what the horse is doing. The execution of a specific response by the horse is necessary for the termination of the stimuli. When a spur is pushed into a horse's ribs to get it to move, the horse is making an escape response that will result in the spur being removed.

Avoidance is the third method of conditioning with aversive stimuli and is characterized by the horse first being given a cue. If the response is correct, there is no punishment; if the response is incorrect or latent, aversive stimuli is applied. This method is the most used negative reinforcement in horse training. The sharp and precisely trained horses that perform with almost imperceptible cues are actually making avoidance responses, and it is the threat of aversive stimuli that keeps them sharp. A well-trained horse will require very little negative reinforcement, as it has learned to make the correct response on cue.

Neck reining is actually an avoidance response. The horse moves from the bearing rein pressure because the threat of the direct rein is always there. Backing on light mouth contact is also avoidance conditioning, as the threat of hard pressure on the mouth is always present. This is an example of a stimulus being a cue at one intensity and negative reinforcement at an increased intensity. Such practice is common for many stimuli and is used by horsepeople quite frequently. A horse moves from slight heel pressure because failure to do so has been followed by a hard kick.

Contingent Reinforcement–Alternate Response

For any reinforcement to be most effective, it must be contingent; that is, it must be given immediately with relation to the response. Contingencies between response and reinforcement are limited with reward. However, with negative stimuli there are many more possibilities, such as the three methods discussed above. Contingent punishment enables a horse to know what response is being punished, whereas noncontingent punishment will cause horses to have a general fear, and all behavior will be abnormal.

Another important aspect of negative reinforcement as a training tool is the availability of alternative responses. This means that when a horse is punished for making a wrong response, the trainer should make sure that the desired response is available. Without available alternative responses, it is difficult to permanently change behavior with any kind of aversive stimuli. When alternate responses are available and the punishment is contingent on the behavior being reinforced, punishment is more effective than any other method in causing one habit to be abandoned and another adopted.

The effects of contingent punishment and alternate response can be seen very clearly in the training of cutting horses. The horse must be trained to move with a cow and to make hard stops and turns on its own with only the cow as its cue. When the cutting horse makes a bad turn, it needs correcting immediately; this is usually done with a spur or a sharp pull on the bit. The more contingent this punishment is with the bad turn, the quicker the horse learns to make the correct movement. However, it should be noted that the alternate response (a correct turn) is available.

Abnormal behavior as a result of overly severe and noncontingent punishment can also be seen in the cutting horse. Punishment of this kind causes the horse to watch the rider much more than the cow and to be more prone to make mistakes. Many cutting horse trainers today are relying more on reward training and less on punishment, but they have learned that any punishment used must be contingent and must always allow for the alternate response.

Good trainers by necessity are also good riders because they must be skillful enough to administer contingent punishment. The knowledge of contingent punishment, plus the skill to administer it, are key differences between good and mediocre trainers. Many novice horsepeople are not contingent with their punishment. In many instances, a barrel racing horse will be punished after a run is over because it failed to turn the first barrel correctly. But the horse does not know why the punishment is being administered, and certainly at this point it cannot make the alternate response of turning the barrel correctly. This kind of punishment will only make the horse dread the entire ordeal. The correct way to administer the punishment is to run the horse several times at home, beginning slowly, then gradually increasing the speed, and administering the punishment when the horse first makes the wrong move around the barrel. It would be more effective to administer no punishment at all than to administer noncontingent punishment. A sharp trainer would let the mistake pass but be alert for its future occurrences, and then try to administer the punishment contingent upon the act.

Punishment must be administered with care so that it will not become re-inforcement for bad behavior. If the trainer inflicts punishment on a horse that causes it to become so unmanageable that the punishment ceases, the unmanageable behavior is then reinforced by the cessation of the punishment. Every time this particular punishment is initiated, the unmanageable condition will reappear. No punishment should be given until all consequences have been considered and there is assurance that control of the horse can be maintained and the desired response is evident.

Schedules of Reinforcement

Schedules refer to when and how often a horse is reinforced. Schedules of reinforcement have a direct effect on horses being trained and on already trained horses that are being ridden. Early training when all behavior is being taught for the first time is called the *acquisition* phase. During acquisition, most desirable responses are reinforced. This continuous reinforcement will result in faster learning by the horse. During this phase, the trainer continually either rewards or punishes the horse for every response it makes to the cues given. If the cues are presented without any reinforcement, the learned responses will gradually diminish. Eventually the horse will make no correct responses, and this is called *extinction*.

Continuous reinforcement during acquisition and no reinforcement resulting in extinction are the two extremes in reinforcement schedules. Between these extremes on some intermittent schedule is where most older trained horses are reinforced to keep them performing correctly. Intermittent schedules of reinforcement mean that the horse is not reinforced after each response, but is reinforced at irregular intervals. This change from continuous to intermittent reinforcement is usually a gradual transition as the horse progresses in training. The common occurrence is that as the horse progresses, the trainer applies less reinforcement, which means that the trainer is not reinforcing every response and is moving toward an intermittent schedule.

It is important that a horse be trained with intermittent reinforcement because this will help resist extinction. In other words, a horse trained on an intermittent schedule will perform longer with no reinforcement than a continuously reinforced horse. This is what is referred to as a finished or fully trained horse.

Many times the finished horse is presented as one that requires no reinforcement, implying that this horse will perform indefinitely to its cue, and there is nothing more to do than present the cues. This is not true. If there is no reinforcement, the horse will cease to perform as it was trained, regardless of the cues given. However, this horse can be ridden for a period by a novice rider who lacks reinforcing ability, and the horse will still respond to cues. Eventually, however, the novice rider must learn the reinforcement for the horse or a more experienced rider will have to ride the horse again. Horsepeople are referring to this situation when they talk about "getting a horse tuned up."

A horse that requires continuous reinforcement is not a well-trained horse. In fact, it is still in the acquisition phase. Horsepeople should try to advance the horse to intermittent reinforcement by not applying any more reinforcement than is necessary after the original acquisition phase. This horse should appear to perform indefinitely with only the presentation of its cues. The amount of reinforcement necessary should be so minimal that it goes unnoticed by the average horseperson.

The principle of extinction is also used to good advantage in horse training. Horsepeople are speaking of this principle when they advise to ignore certain acts of the horse and the horse will quit doing them. In other words, do not reinforce those acts and they will extinguish themselves. Another problem arises when a horse is first being reinforced for its responses. Very seldom are its responses so accurate that there are not some undesirable actions being made at the same time. So the horse is not sure which response was reinforced. It may take several trials of contingent reinforcement for the undesirable behavior to extinguish itself as the desirable behavior becomes stronger. The trainer should be aware of what is happening to the horse and should be tolerant during these stages.

Shaping

The psychological term analogous to training is *shaping*. This means that behavior is shaped by reinforcing each successive approximation of the desired response. Trainers use different techniques, but each will try to get a horse to first do something similar to the desired response and will progressively reinforce more desirable behavior. The importance of recognizing small responses is paramount at this point. The trainer must recognize and be able to apply reinforcement to these small responses as he or she builds up to greater things. That first step taken backward, properly reinforced, can lead to a good backing horse.

A rollback is a difficult maneuver to teach a horse. It involves a series of movements that are not all accomplished in one day's training. The trainer will usually start by teaching a stop; then a side pass or some other maneuver designed to get the horse moving laterally, especially in the front; then go to some short pivots; and eventually put it all together into a rollback. All along the way, the trainer applies reinforcement to any behavior that approximates the desired one. However, the trainer must expect more from the horse during each series of trials before reinforcing it, or no progress would be made.

Massing of Trials

Massing of trials, or prolonged practice, has proven to be an inefficient learning method. Fatigue comes into play, and horses that have been overworked to the point of fatigue will learn at an inefficient rate.

During the very early stages of training, it may be necessary to bring about light fatigue in order to get control of the horse. After this initial period, the trainer will enhance learning by using shorter training periods. This is not to say that the horse cannot be ridden for longer periods of time, but rather that specific practice for certain maneuvers should be shortened. An example might be riding the horse for 1 hour, but practicing rollbacks or jumps for only a few minutes. There might be more than one short practice session during each ride divided by periods of relaxation or simple riding.

Inhibition

An intervening variable between a stimulus and a response, often seen with repeated practice, is inhibition. This variable is inferred from observed behavior and is used in a theoretical sense only, with no physiological reference. Suppose animals were allowed 100 free-choice trials down a T-maze. The outcome would probably be 50 to the left and 50 to the right. But if we closed the right side and kept only the left side open for 100 additional trials and then opened up both sides again, we would probably expect all the horses to go left because of the extra practice in that direction. What would actually happen, however, is that all the horses would go right. Eventually, they would again go in a fifty-fifty choice pattern. This is the influence of inhibition, which can be seen in horse training. What a horse has learned on one side, it must also learn on the other. Consequently, training must be directed at both sides or in both directions. Repeated trials to one side may only cause the horse to be inhibited from actually going in that direction. To balance the effects of this phenomenon and still train both sides, the trainer should periodically work both sides of the horse with increased concentration on the problem side.

Effort and Effects on Learning

The more effort required of a horse to make a particular response, the harder it will be for the horse to learn that response. The time and number of trials (amount of practice) required to learn a response will increase as the amount of effort required increases. For horse show purposes, it usually takes less time to train a pleasure horse than it does a reining or jumping horse. The amount of effort required to perform the tasks accounts primarily for the time difference. Extinction of the responses will also be faster when the response is difficult. To horsepeople, this means that a reining horse will become untrained more easily than a pleasure horse.

Many of the tasks for which horses are trained do require great effort. Horses that have greater athletic ability should learn faster than those with less ability because less effort will be required to do the tasks. The trainer should be aware of the effort required for each task and should realize that some horses with less ability will learn slowly and may never learn to perform the task well. In many cases, the behavior that is learned does not come as easily for the horse as it does for some animals. The porpoise has been trained to do many things that are quite remarkable and make the animal appear very intelligent; however, much of the required behavior for those tasks is easy for that particular animal.

Many of the tasks that horses are asked to do today are far removed from their natural behavior in the wild state. Untrained horses in pastures do not perform sliding stops, hard rollbacks, high obstacles jumps, or hacking. The most used natural behavior of the horse is locomotion, or, more specifically, its natural instinct of flight. Consequently, it is not hard to teach a horse to run; any novice can do it, although it may be difficult to get the horse to run well. People need to realize that this is a natural instinct when training timed-event horses. It will not be hard to teach a horse to run, but it will be difficult to teach the hard turns, flying lead changes, and stops. For this reason, the training of the timed-event horse should concentrate on these hard-to-teach maneuvers. A trainer has not accomplished much by getting the horse to run; this is easy, or cheap, behavior.

Intelligence

Most horse trainers associate intelligence with anything that relates to mentality. There are many different kinds of intelligence and there is no one general measure of it. All animals do not excel at all measures of intelligence, which indicates that some have different abilities for different kinds of activities.

Intelligence is usually associated with the ability to reason; in this category, the horse makes a very poor showing relative to other animals. In problem-solving intelligence tests, the horse will place low, but so will the dog. Rats, cats, monkeys, and birds commonly show a higher intellect in these tests. Even though some horsepeople would be hard to convince, the donkey possesses a great deal more reasoning power than does the horse.

But this apparent lack of reasoning does not necessarily condemn the horse to a state of helplessness; there are other things for which it is well equipped. The horse actually learns quite well, but it is not very adept at integrating a lot of different information for a common solution. The horse can best be evaluated on problems that allow it to use its skills of locomotion. Learning new tasks are not difficult for the horse if the cues involve its stronger senses. The great performance horses seen in the arena are examples of the high degree to which these senses can be developed. As early as the nineteenth century, some famous cases were recorded in the history of animal psychology of the horse's ability to respond to stimuli almost too weak to be perceived.

The successful horse trainer must be aware of limitations in the horse's intellect and must train more toward its positive assets. The greatest asset of the horse is its ability to learn and discriminate between the slightest of cues. Regardless of how intelligent a horse may appear when working, the trainer must remember that somewhere behind the performance are cues that the horse has learned. It did not logically decide what was desired; it responded to the stimuli of cues.

Training Summary

The factors concerning horse training discussed here are not all-inclusive, but they are the common factors encountered daily in training routines. On occasion, the trainer may apply all these principles almost simultaneously. Horse trainers may not recognize all the principles by the names given them, but if the trainer is successful, he or she is using most of them.

Most of this information is presented to support one concept: A cue is presented to signal a desired response, and this association is strengthened by reinforcement. The following guidelines are suggested for horse trainers:

1 Learn to recognize and appreciate small responses in the learning phase.

2 Learn how to start with basic cues and advance to harder ones.

3 Be specific and consistent in the presentation of all cues.

4 Be contingent with all reinforcement.

5 Provide alternate responses when using punishment.

6 Learn to shape behavior by reinforcing approximations of the desired response.

7 Advance to intermittent schedules of reinforcement.

8 Do not try to train with negative reinforcement only; it has too many pitfalls and can cause too many ill effects.

9 Learn how to use positive reinforcement—try to develop secondary positive reinforcement.

10 Do not expect the horse to have powers to reason that are not common to it.

Effects of Early Experience

An animal's ability to learn, to solve problems, or to survive the effects of severe stress are greatly influenced by the characteristics of the environment in which it was raised during very early life. These effects are environmental; however, because they are accomplished prior to training, they affect trainability in much the same manner as heredity. Early stimulation has been administered before birth, after birth but before weaning, and after weaning.

Continuous stimulation, such as greatly varying the environment where animals live (enriched, deprived, or isolated), and discontinuous stimulation, such as shorter periods of daily handling, have both been investigated. It appears that from before weaning through a portion of the yearling year, the horseperson may be able to further influence a horse's learning ability by the kind of environment provided.

The effects of early experience have been well documented in the research literature and are shown to influence many behaviors in addition to those noted here. For horsepeople, this is another opportunity, but one without direct guidelines. Early experience has not been scientifically studied in the horse. Such things as critical time, type, or stimulation, and how to effectively manipulate this stimulation to later change the desired adult performance have not been determined.

In general, horses of today are said to be more docile, intelligent, and tractable than those of 30 years ago. Some of this change is probably due to heredity, but it can more easily be accredited to increased handling of horses at earlier ages. Horses that have been trained only as adults are wilder and much less tractable than those with established human contacts in early life. Docility enhances learning in that there are fewer distractions. A social relationship between horse and handler can be established much more easily at an early age. Most recommendations for breaking and training horses encourage the handling and preparation for riding to begin as early as possible. Halter breaking can start prior to weaning, followed by activities limited only by the horse's physical capabilities.

CHAPTER 7

Grooming

Grooming is an essential part of caring for a horse. It is important for the health, hygiene, and appearance of all horses. Daily grooming is the only way to remove dust, dirt, grease, scurf, and dead cells from a horse's skin. Proper grooming stimulates blood circulation and helps maintain muscle tone. Grooming brings out natural oils in the skin and distributes the oil over the hair coat, giving it a glossy sheen. The time spent grooming gives the horseperson and horse time to get to know each other. As the horse becomes accustomed to being groomed, it will relax and become less nervous when handled. While grooming, you can inspect the skin for wounds, cuts, and parasites and inspect the feet for puncture wounds, foot disease, and loose shoes.

BASIC GROOMING

The basic equipment for grooming a horse consists of a hoof pick, rubber curry comb, dandy brush, body brush, mane and tail comb, and a grooming cloth (see Figure 7-1).

Routine grooming usually starts with the feet. Pick the feet up and clean with a hoof pick (see Chapter 8). Remove dirt, manure, and other foreign material from the sole and from the crevices between the frog and base. Clean the feet by working the pick from the heel area toward the toe. If you pull the hoof pick from the toe toward the heel, the hoof pick may become lodged in dirt and if the horse pulls its foot away, the point of the pick may be driven into the sole or frog when the foot strikes the ground. You can remove dirt on the bulbs of the heel with a stiff brush.

287

FIGURE 7-1　Basic grooming tools: *(a)* storage box; *(b)* hoof pick; *(c)* sweat scraper; *(d)* mane comb; *(e)* scrubber; *(f)* rubber curry; *(g)* wash bucket; *(h)* sponge; *(i)* dandy brush; *(j)* body brush; *(k)* shampoo; *(l)* rubber wash mitt; *(m)* rubbing glove for insect repellent. (Photo by W. Evans.)

Use the rubber curry comb to remove mud and loosen matted hair, dirt, and scurf. Use it in a small circular motion, beginning on the neck and working toward the rear. If you use the rubber curry comb on the head and on the legs below the knees and hocks, do so with caution. It is uncomfortable to the horse when it is used over bony areas. After every few strokes, clean it by tapping it against your heel, the floor, or a post.

The dandy brush has long, stiff bristles and is used to remove deep-seated dirt and scurf. Use it with short, deep strokes in the direction that the hair lies. You can use the dandy brush on the head and below the knees and hocks to remove dirt. However, horses with thin, sensitive skin object to it; you can use a soft body brush or grooming rag on such horses. After brushing the horse with the dandy brush, use the soft body brush to remove surface dirt and dust. This brush is soft enough to be used all over the horse. Brushing in the direction the hairs lie gives the coat a sleek look because it spreads natural oils from the skin. Some grooms prefer to vacuum the horse to remove the dirt after the dandy brush. After vacuuming, a soft brush is used to bring the oils to the surface of the coat.

After brushing, rub the horse with a grooming cloth (usually made of linen, flannel, or terry cloth). Any soft, absorbent cloth is suitable. Some horses are very sensitive to brushing and may prefer that they be rubbed with the grooming cloth.

When the horse's coat is clean, no white or gray debris appears on your fingers when you run them against the hair.

In Europe, grooms massage the horse with a wisp to help maintain muscle tone. Make a wisp from grass or timothy hay. Lay some hay out in a narrow row on a floor. Twist a handful of hay on one end of the row to form a rope $\frac{1}{2}$-inch thick (13 mm). Twist the hay until a 6- to 7-foot rope is formed (1.83 to 2.13 m). Fold one end of the rope to form two loops. Each loop is about a foot long and is on each side of the long free end. Braid the two loops and the free end. Finally, pass the free end through what remains of the loops. Trim off the bristles, and cut off the excess tail of the free end of the rope. A good wisp lasts 3 to 4 weeks. To wisp the horse, hold the wisp in your right hand and a clean towel in your left hand. Strike the muscles on the neck, shoulder, barrel hindquarters, and hindlegs. As the wisp hits, the horse's muscle tenses. Then immediately wipe the muscle with the towel in one motion, in the direction of the hair. This wiping causes the muscle to relax. For a good massage, hit each area about 40 to 50 times.

Clean the eyes and nose with damp sponges. A separate sponge should be used to clean the dock.

After the body and legs are cleaned, brush the mane, forelock, and tail with the dandy brush. Some horsepeople prefer to use a mane comb, but it tends to break off or pull out the mane and tail hairs. Groom the tail by separating the hairs with the fingers, and then brush each section to remove dirt.

BATHS

Periodically, you may need to give the horse a bath to keep its skin and coat clean. Some horsepeople do not believe horses should be bathed, but many horses are given a bath after each strenuous exercise period. It is true that bathing removes the natural oils from the skin and hair.

Before giving a horse a bath, be sure the horse will have enough time to dry before being stabled for the night. The temperature should be at least 50°F (10.6°C) or the horse may catch a cold.

Use a gentle liquid soap or a gentle hair shampoo in warm water that is not supposed to remove natural oils from the hair. You can hose the horse off to get it wet. Start washing at the neck behind the ears and work toward the horse's tail. Wash its face with a wrung-out sponge, and make sure no water gets in the ears. Always wash under the horse's tail. During hot weather, when horses perspire a lot, a skin irritation can develop under the tail. Clean the mane and tail with a soapy brush, and wash the tail in a bucket of soapy water. Rinse with clear water, making sure that no soap remains. Then rinse with ordinary hair conditioner, which will allow you to remove the tangles easily. Remove excess water from the coat with a sweat scraper to help dry the horse. As the horse dries off, brush it with a soft body brush to keep the hairs lying down. After the horse is dry, brush and rub it vigorously to bring the natural oil up into the coat. Adding fat to the ration helps maintain oil in the skin and coat.

Clean the penis sheath of stallions and geldings periodically to remove dirt, grease, and debris. Part of the debris is smegma, which consists of a fatty secretion and dead cells. The sheath should be cleaned at least once a year. The stallion or gelding must be trained so that you can pull the penis out of its sheath for cleaning. If the horse refuses to allow this, a veterinarian can administer a tranquilizer. Wash the penis and inside of the sheath with a warm, antiseptic soap solution. Make sure that all the folds in the sheath are thoroughly cleaned. The end of the penis around the urethra should be carefully cleaned, because this area tends to accumulate dirt and debris. After the sheath has been thoroughly cleaned, it is important to remove all soap by rinsing with clean, clear water. Failure to remove all the soap may result in a skin irritation. If the sheath and penis were very dirty and had a large accumulation of scales, apply a little mineral oil after drying the sheath.

During inclement weather, instead of bathing the horse, it can be cleaned with hot towels soaked in hot water containing baby oil. By leaving the hot towel on the area for a moment, the steam will raise the dirt to the surface and then it is wiped off with the towel. This also keeps the hair and skin moist.

Horses that have lots of white on their body or that are gray in color may require special treatment of the bath water. There are compounds for maintaining and enhancing the gray coat. Other compounds are used for white areas. On the legs, corn starch is used to keep the socks extra white. They are usually used on show horses. Baby oil is used on the muzzle and around the eyes to enhance the presentation of show horses.

BLANKETING

Blankets are kept on horses for a variety of reasons. Most horses shown at halter or in performance classes are blanketed all the time to protect their coats. In summer, sun bleaches the coat, leaving it an undesirable color. In winter, blankets keep the horse warm so that it does not grow a heavy coat of hair. Blankets help keep the hair clean. A cooling or summer sheet is placed on some horses such as racehorses while they are being cooled out after exercise, to prevent them from cooling out too fast.

Have blankets fit so that they are cut back behind the withers. This prevents the wither mane from being rubbed off by the edge of the blanket. Also, take care to prevent the tail from being rubbed out by the blanket. If you use a hood to cover the neck and head, it should be lined with linen to prevent rubbing out the mane.

Some horses like to pull their blankets off. You can prevent this by placing a bib on the halter or by placing a cradle on its neck.

TRIMMING

There is a traditional way to prepare each breed of horse for various performance events. The rule book of the American Horse Shows Association describes how horses must be presented for each class. Minor fashionable modifications do occur, and one must be aware of them.

Horses being prepared for sale or to be shown at halter may need a full body clip if they have been at pasture or have been neglected. Clip the horse at least 1 month before being shown, to allow the hairs to even up and the "clipped look" to disappear. Do not clip a horse that you cannot protect from extreme weather.

When preparing a horse to be clipped, allow it to become accustomed to the clippers and the noise they make. Horses are very sensitive about having their ears and heads clipped, so be extremely careful when clipping these areas. Before clipping, give the horse a good bath. Dirt and oil dull the clipper blades. Also, clean, dry hair is fluffy and stands up, allowing a clean, close cut. Cut the hair in the opposite direction of its natural lay. Be careful on the flanks and belly as well as on cowlicks and swirls because the natural lay changes direction. Keep the head of the clippers as flat as possible. A No. 10 blade in an Oster clipper cuts the hair the right length on the body.

There are some problem areas in clipping. On the flank, make one cut from the top of the swirl downward through the center. Then cut the hair toward this center cut. At indentations such as in a muscle or other area where skin is folded, stretch the skin tight to avoid cut marks. Clip the elbow by having someone lift the foreleg, stretch the skin, and move the skin around as you cut. To clip below the knee, flex the foreleg, and take care to clip the grooves around the tendons. Clip the inside of the leg by standing on the opposite side of the neck and clip downward to get any hair that sticks up. Then clip a line horizontal to the mane. The hairs around the tail head are clipped square across where the tail joins the body by going from one side across to the other.

After the horse has been completely clipped, give it another bath and dry it. Inspect the horse for tracks left by the clippers and remove them. Tracks result from dull blades or blades that get too hot.

Remove the hair from the ears of most performance horses. Clip them with a fine blade. Cut the hair against its natural lay. After removing the inside hair, pass the clippers from the tip of the ear to the base on both inside edges of the ear. Then run the clippers along the edge. Remember that clipping the inside of the ear removes part of its protection against insects.

In addition to full body clips, there are various patterns for partial body clips, depending on how the horse is used. Horses can be partially clipped so that they do not get too hot, sweat excessively, and catch colds from taking too long a time to cool out. Working stock horses, trail horses, and hunters may have their bodies clipped and the legs unclipped. The unclipped portion of the legs can be curved downward from front to rear rather than left straight across. Leave the legs unclipped to protect them from brush and other obstacles on the trail. For hunters, leave the legs and a saddle patch unclipped (Figure 7-2).

FIGURE 7-2   Body clip for hunter.

MANES

How long to leave mane hair depends on the type of horse. To roach (cut or trim) a mane or cut a bridle path, clip the mane very short. A bridle path is normally about 6 to 8 inches long (152 to 203 mm) starting from the poll, but may be only $1\frac{1}{2}$ to 2 inches (38 to 51 mm). For manes that are short rather than full and loose, pull the hair rather than cutting it. To shorten and thin a mane, comb the hair with a mane comb. Grasp the ends of the long hairs with one hand and back comb the remainder of the hairs. Pull the long hairs out. Continue until the mane is thin and has the proper length. If the mane will not lie down or if some of it hangs on both sides, you can train it to lie flat by wetting and braiding it.

The manes of some horses, such as hunters and jumpers, are braided (Figure 7-3). First, collect the necessary tools: a pail of water, mane comb, scissors, a large blunt needle (yarn needle), and heavy thread that is the same color as the mane. Pull the mane to a length of about 4 inches (102 mm). Divide the length of the neck to allow 15 to 17 braids. Braid a short-necked horse with 17 braids to make the neck appear longer. Braid a long-necked horse with 15 braids to make the neck appear shorter. The braids should be the same size and evenly spaced. Dampen each section with water so that you can hold the hair

FIGURE 7-3 Braiding the mane: *(a)* length of mane is divided into braids; *(b, c)* each length is braided; *(d–h)* braids are tied and folded under; *(i)* braided and tied mane; *(j)* braided mane.

and make a tighter braid. Starting at the poll, comb each section, divide it into three equal parts, and braid it. To make the braid lie flat against the neck, apply more tension to the hairs underneath than on top. Fold the ends of the braid under and secure with needle and thread. Next, bring the braid up almost to the crest of the neck and sew it in place with a few stitches. Cut off the excess thread. The last section to be braided is on the withers where the saddle touches. Brush the remaining hair smooth.

FIGURE 7-4   Braiding the tail: *(a–g)* tail hairs are braided as shown by diagrams; *(h–i)* two ways of finishing off the end of the braid (each number refers to a strand of tail hairs).

Fine harness horses, ponies, Tennessee Walking Horses, and five-gaited saddle horses display their stable colors as ribbons braided into the forelock and in the upper lock of the mane. Braid the upper lock with a fine braid that is left to fall free down the neck. The rest of the mane is full and loose.

The forelock is prepared in different ways depending on the type of horse. You can clip it the same way the mane is roached, leave it loose, or braid it. A colored ribbon can be braided in.

TAILS

The tail may be clipped or left long, full, and free flowing. Thoroughbreds, Arabians, and five-gaited horses have full, long tails. Quarter Horse tails are frequently pulled so they are shorter and thinner.

To pull and thin a tail, remove the tangles by combing and brushing. Pull the longer hairs one or two at a time with a quick, jerking motion of the fingers. Pull the short hairs around the root of the tail to remove the bushy effect. After pulling the short hairs, bandage the tail with damp tail wraps to make the hair lie close to the tail.

Braiding the tail is more difficult than braiding a mane. After removing all the tangles, dampen the tail hair near the croup with water. Then braid the tail to the end of the tail bone (see Figure 7-4). For a neat job, keep each section of hair snug and straight. The braid should be uniform in size. At the end of the tail bone, simply braid out the last strands. Then tuck this end braid under the tail braid and secure it or coil and sew it in place. Sew the initial braid in place with heavy thread and a large, blunt needle.

A "mud tail" is braided to keep the tail clean during rainy weather or to make a hunter with a short tail presentable. Braid the tail as just described, but make one large braid with the hair below the end of the tail bone. Then coil the large braid, if it is not too large, and sew it in position. You can sew it on top of the braid extending down the tail bone. It must be carefully sewn or it will fall down.

After braiding the tail, wrap it in a damp tail wrap to get all the hairs to lie flat (otherwise they get fuzzy). Use extreme caution when wrapping a tail. A tail wrap that is too tight cuts off blood circulation, and the horse will lose its tail. Wrap the tail by starting next to the croup. Each wrap around the tail overlaps about one-half the width of the preceding wrap. Tie off the wrap below the end of the tail bone. Each wrap should be snug enough to hold it in place but not tight enough to damage the tail roots. To help hold the wrap, a couple of short hairs can be bent over a wrap and then covered with the next wrap. This prevents the tail wrap from sliding downward and becoming loose enough to fall off.

CHAPTER 8

Caring for the Feet

Caring for the feet is one of the most important but often neglected parts of horse care. Neglecting the feet often leads to problems that prevent the horse from working. Diseases such as thrush and scratches develop rapidly in feet that are not cleaned regularly. Hooves that are not regularly trimmed grow too long, and hoof cracks and contracted heels may develop. Other unsoundnesses of feet and legs can be caused by poor foot care.

HOOF HANDLING

Confined horses should have their feet cleaned and inspected daily. The feet must be raised and held properly, or the horse will be uncomfortable and try to pull away. When you approach the horse to lift one of its feet, make the horse aware of your presence. A calm, deliberate approach gains the horse's confidence and keeps it from becoming frightened or excited. Raise and hold each front foot in position as shown in Figure 8-1. Stand facing the rear of the horse and beside the front leg. Place the hand next to the horse on its shoulder and move the other hand down the leg so that the horse knows its leg is being handled. Grasping the leg suddenly may startle the horse and make it shy away. Move your hand down to grip the pastern. As you do so, press the shoulder with your other hand so the horse will shift its weight to the opposite leg. When the weight is shifted, lift the foot off the ground and place it between your legs just above your knee. To hold the foot securely in a position

(a)

(b)

(c)

FIGURE 8-1   Lifting and holding forefoot: *(a)* One hand on the shoulder causes the horse to shift weight to the opposite leg so the foot can be picked up with the other hand. *(b)* Foot is held up in preparation of restraining it. *(c)* Proper position for holding the foot. The farrier's toes are pointed inward, and the pastern is gripped above the farrier's knees. (Photos by W. Evans.)

that is comfortable for both you and the horse, turn your toes in, turn your heels out slightly, flex your knees, and bend your back forward. This position forces your knees together to grip the horse's foot with a minimum of effort. While shoeing or trimming the feet, you may need to take a forefoot forward to work on it. This procedure is illustrated in Figure 8-2. First, hold the foot up with your hand. Then take one step back toward the horse's head. Turn your body so that you step back under the horse's neck, in line with its front and back legs. Swing the leg and rest the foot between your knees. To work on

(a)

(b)

(c)

(d)

FIGURE 8-2   Taking forefoot forward: *(a)* Holding foot by the toe—called the "home position." *(b)* The farrier turns toward the horse and changes hands, holding the foot while taking the foot forward. *(c)* Foot held to work on its medial side. *(d)* Foot held to work on its lateral side. (Photos by W. Evans.)

the opposite side of the foot, turn initially to face the horse, swing the horse's leg forward, and grip it. Instead of resting the foot on your legs, you can use a foot stand or stall jack (see Figure 8-12j on page 312). Be careful when using a foot stand to prevent the foot from sliding off and striking your own foot. The stand helps prevent excessive back strain while working on the foot. Raise and position a hindfoot as shown in Figure 8-3. While standing and

(a)   (b)

(c)   (d)

FIGURE 8-3   Lifting a hindfoot: *(a)* One hand is placed on the hip to shift the horse's weight to the opposite leg, while the other hand grips the pastern and lifts the foot. *(b)* Hindfoot is brought forward. *(c)* The farrier steps under the hindleg. *(d)* Correct position for holding the hindfoot. (Photos by W. Evans.)

facing toward the rear of the horse and standing forward of the hindleg, place the hand next to the horse on its hip, and move the other hand down the hindleg to the fetlock. While gripping the back of the fetlock, use the other hand to push against the horse's hip. As the horse shifts its weight to the other leg, pull the hindleg forward. As the leg is raised up, step forward and under the raised foot. The hand you used to push on the hip now grasps the toe of the foot so that you can correctly position the foot on your outside knee. Hold the foot low to the ground. The hind cannon should be about perpendicular to the ground. To take the hindfoot forward, follow the procedure illustrated in Figure 8-4.

(a)

(b)

(c)

FIGURE 8-4   Taking a hindfoot forward: *(a)* From the "home position," the toe is held with one hand. *(b)* The farrier turns in between the horse's body and leg to work on the lateral side of the foot. He supports the foot on the inside of the leg just above the knee. *(c)* To work on the medial side, the farrier turns facing the horse and positions the foot. (Photos by W. Evans.)

By taking the hindleg forward, you can rasp (file) the sides of the hoof wall. Grip the toe, step backward, and turn so that your back is next to the horse's abdomen. Bring the foot forward and rest it between your knees. To work on the inside part of the hoof wall, step back and turn to face the horse's abdomen. Then place the foot between your knees.

Horses must be trained to have their feet handled. Young foals are trained by getting them accustomed to having their legs groomed. When they no longer pay attention to their legs being brushed, lift each foot off the ground and hold it for a couple of minutes. Someone may have to hold the foal's head while someone else lifts the foot. It is often easier to lift the feet if you back the foal into a corner. After you can lift the feet and hold them in position without the foal struggling and the foal feels comfortable, lightly tap the feet to accustom the foal to the shoeing hammer.

Older horses may develop bad habits that hinder holding and working with their feet. Restless or nervous horses may become excited if they are not handled very often and are taken out of familiar surroundings. Allowing the horse to "settle down" before handling its feet usually makes it more cooperative. It may be necessary to let its companion horse stand nearby. If a horse tries to lean on the person holding its foot, it should be disciplined by quickly dropping the foot so the horse must catch its balance or by letting it lean against a sharp object.

Some horses will not allow their feet to be raised or held. There are several methods to restrain their feet (see Figures 6-4 and 6-5 in Chapter 6 on handling). A nose twitch can be applied to the horse that continually takes its feet away from a handler (Figure 6-8).

Horses that bite should be held by someone or tied with a short lead shank. If a horse tries to kick or strike the handler, someone should always hold the horse's head. If the horse continues to strike deliberately or kick, it should be disciplined with a whip.

DAILY CLEANING AND INSPECTION

A horse's feet should be cleaned every day. Use a hoof pick (Figure 7-1) to clean the dirt and debris from the bottom of the foot. Run the pick from the heels toward the toe to avoid puncturing or bruising the sole or frog if the horse pulls its foot away and slams it to the ground. Clean the frog area thoroughly, particularly between the frog and bars. Failure to keep the foot clean can lead to thrush, a disease caused by a bacterium that lives in the absence of oxygen. The organism is usually present in manure. Manure packed in the sole area presents the proper conditions for the bacteria to grow, multiply, and attack the foot. The signs of thrush are a very foul odor and usually a blackish discharge. If thrush is present, clean the foot with soap and water, using a toothbrush or other similar brush. After the foot is thoroughly dry, apply a germicidal preparation such as Koppertox or a 7 percent iodine solution. Thoroughly clean and treat the foot daily until the disease is cured. It may be necessary to trim the affected part of the frog to remove the diseased tissue.

After cleaning the foot, you should inspect it for puncture wounds, bruises, loose shoes (if shod), abnormal growth, uneven wear, and abnormal hoof conditions. Hoof moisture must be maintained or the hoof wall will become dry and brittle and will start to crack. Moisture is continually being lost from the hoof wall by evaporation. This moisture is replaced by blood and lymph from the coriums of the foot and by environmental water conducted up the hoof wall by osmotic and capillary action. Moisture balance is maintained by the waxy hoof varnish (*stratum tectorium*) on the outside of the hoof wall, which reduces evaporation loss. Usually this varnish wears off of the lower part of the hoof wall. The tubules that form the hoof wall are very dense and flat at the surface to retard moisture loss. Conditions that lead to dry hooves are stabling in dry, dusty, and sandy paddocks; dry bedding; careless rasping of the hoof wall; and application of most commercial hoof dressings. The hoof needs water for moisture, and the best way to help water enter the foot is to stand the horse in a pool of water or clean mud for 20 minutes daily for several days or to pack the feet in wet, clean clay. To stimulate increased blood flow and hence moisture, massage the coronary band for a few minutes each day. Exercise also increases the blood flow to the foot. After the proper amount of moisture is present in the hoof, applying an oil base hoof dressing helps prevent moisture loss. Products with neatsfoot and cod liver oil, pine tar, petroleum compound, and turpentine as their main ingredients are the best for hydrating the hoof wall. Pine tar will hydrate a hoof wall to 100 percent hydration. Products whose primary ingredients are lanolin, stearates, lactates, and glycerine are also good for hydration.

Abnormal hoof growth can be caused by founder (excessive growth) or by injury to the coronary band (defects in hoof wall). The feet of a foundered horse need special care (see Chapter 2). Defects in the hoof wall as it grows can lead to unsoundness, particularly if the wall splits and the sensitive structures are irritated. Factors that affect hoof growth are age, season, irritation, or injury of sensitive structures, front versus hind, neurectomy, and nutrition. As horses get older, the rate of growth decreases. Hoof growth is approximately 0.6 inch (15.5 mm) per month for nursing foals, 0.5 inch (11.5 mm) per month for weanlings, and 0.34 inch (8.5 mm) per month for mature horses. Growth is most rapid during spring and slowest during summer and winter. Injury to the sensitive structure of the foot increases the growth rate of the hoof wall, as does neurectomy. The hindfoot grows about 12 percent faster than the front foot for young foals, but the difference decreases with age. The level of feed intake is the only nutritional factor demonstrated to significantly affect rate of hoof growth. Adequate intake of a balanced ration encourages maximum hoof growth. Feed supplements are merely a waste of money if a balanced ration is being fed.

Bruises on the sole are indicated by a red or yellowish-red discoloration that is sensitive to tapping or pressure. Severe bruises may require the attention of a veterinarian.

TRIMMING

Most horses that are shod need their feet trimmed every 6 to 8 weeks. Some horses that are kept unshod wear off the hoof wall at a faster rate and need their feet trimmed at longer intervals of time.

Failure to properly and regularly trim the feet causes foot problems. The toe grows at a faster rate than the heel, so the toe tends to curl upward as the foot gets too long. This causes the heels to contract. The hoof wall starts to split and crack, and the angle of the pastern is changed, which affects the foot flight arc. A long toe inhibits the foot from breaking over at the toe and may cause forging, overreaching, and scalping. Long toes may cause other limb interferences and faulty gaits.

The tools needed to trim a horse's foot are illustrated in Figures 8-11 and 8-12. The rasp is 14 inches long (0.36 m) and has two sides. One side has larger teeth and is used for rasping down the hoof wall. Use the side with small teeth for the final dressing. Some rasps have regular file teeth on one side to file sharp edges off of horseshoes. Use hoof knives to trim out the dead sole and to trim the frog, and use hoof nippers to cut the hoof wall.

To trim the foot, use the following procedure. First watch the horse move and look for limb interference and faults in way of going. Observe the overall conformation to see if the horse is predisposed to a faulty way of going. Observe the position of the feet when the horse is standing squarely on them.

Examine the feet to determine conformation and balance of the foot. Determine foot balance by sighting across the foot from heel to toe. Both sides of the hoof wall should be equal in length (Figure 8-5). Faults in conformation and in the way of going cause uneven wear on the sides of the hoof wall. Horses that stand toe-wide (toe-out) and wing-inward when traveling wear down the inside wall faster. Toe-narrow (toe-in) and wing-outward horses wear down the outside of the hoof wall faster. If not corrected when the hoof is trimmed, the uneven wear will accentuate the fault in conformation and/or way of going.

If the horse is shod, remove the old shoes (see the section on shoeing later in this chapter). Remove the dead sole from the sole area with the hoof knife. Only the dead sole should be removed; stop when the sole is thin enough to be flexed by pressure applied with the thumbs. The remaining sole is $\frac{1}{4}$ to $\frac{3}{8}$ inch thick (6.3 to 9.5 mm). Removing too much sole leaves insufficient protection for the underlying sensitive structures. If the sole is extremely hard, use a sole knife to chisel it out. Trim the bars level with the

FIGURE 8-5   Foot balance. The opposite heels and opposite quarters should be equal in length. The hoof wall should be flat all the way around.

sole to prevent them from being broken or torn, and trim the frog to remove ragged edges and loose pieces. The frog should be trimmed so that it almost touches the ground when the horse stands on a hard surface. Removing too much frog interferes with normal functioning. The frog is sloughed off and replaced about twice a year. Frogs of neglected feet can often be pulled off, because they are in the process of sloughing. The frogs of feet that are well cared for may not slough because they are continually being trimmed. Trim the hoof wall with hoof nippers. Make the first cut at the toe. Be sure to cut the hoof wall flat, not on an angle. Keep the line bisecting the angle of the two handles perpendicular to the hoof wall surface. Continue the cut around the hoof wall to both heels. After trimming the hoof with nippers, check the balance of the hoof wall—both sides should be of equal length. Rasp the hoof wall level with the coarse side of the rasp. Check the balance again. If it is balanced, use the fine side of the rasp to smooth the surface and remove the sharp edge around the hoof wall.

If the foot is now properly shaped and the angle of the hoof wall is correct (50 to 55 degrees), nail the shoe on. The angle of the forefeet should be the same as the angle of the shoulder, and the angle of the hindfeet should be 2 to 3 degrees greater. If the foot is to remain unshod, round off the outer edge of the hoof wall (about one-half the thickness of the wall) to prevent pieces of the wall from chipping off.

Some feet are not shaped normally and must be shaped with the rasp. Any outward distortions ("flares") are removed. The rasped area must be blended into the slope of the undistorted upper part of the wall (Figure 8-6).

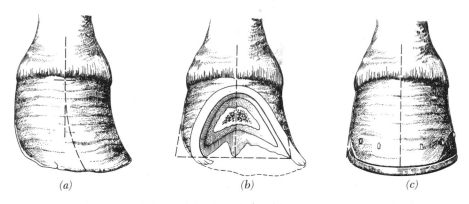

FIGURE 8-6   Principles of shaping the foot: *(a)* rough untrimmed foot; *(b)* diagram of trimming; *(c)* trimmed and shod. (From Butler, 1985.)

ANATOMY AND PHYSIOLOGY

Anatomy

The external structures of the foot are shown in Figure 8-7. The shape of the hindfoot is slightly different from that of the forefoot. The toe of the hindfoot is more pointed, and the sole is more concave. The internal structures are illustrated in Figures 8-8, 8-9, and 8-10.

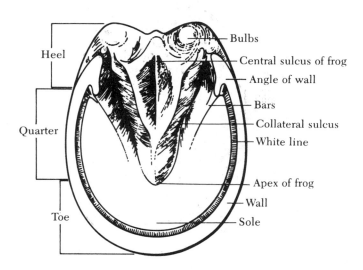

FIGURE 8-7   External structures of normal forefoot. (From Adams, 1974.)

Skin
Tendon of common extensor
Bursa
Capsule of fetlock joint
Cavity of fetlock joint

8 9
1
10
6
7
11   12
2
13   Middle sesamoidean ligament
Digital synovial sheath
Cavity of pastern joint
Superficial sesamoidean ligament
Deep flexor tendon
Distal end of digital sheath

Cavity of pastern joint
Cavity of coffin joint
Corium of periople
Periople
Coronary corium
Wall
Laminae

14
14
17
15   16
4   5   18

Digital cushion
Frog

Deep flexor tendon
Corium of sole
Sole

FIGURE 8-8   Sagittal section of digit and distal part of metacarpus of horse: (1) metacarpal bone; (2) first phalanx; (3) second phalanx; (4) third phalanx; (5) distal sesamoid bone; (6) volar pouch of capsule of fetlock joint; (7) intersesamoidean ligament; (8–9) proximal end of digital synovial sheath; (10) ring formed by superficial flexor tendon; (11) fibrous tissue underlying ergot; (12) ergot; (13, 14) branches of digital vessels; (15) distal ligament of distal sesamoid bone; (16) suspensory ligament of distal sesamoid bone; (17) proximal end of navicular bursa; (18) distal end of navicular bursa. The superficial flexor tendon, behind (9), is not shown. (From Getty, 1953.)

Hoof Wall and Laminae

The bulk of the hoof wall is composed of keratinized epithelial cells, which are arranged in tubules that run from the coronary hand to the ground surface. These tubules are formed from papillae that project from the coronary band (coronary corium). A tubule is formed around each of the papillae. The centers of the tubules are filled by a cementlike substance of loosely packed cells called *intertubular horn*, which holds the tubules together. Tubules toward the outer surface of the hoof wall are flattened and packed closely together, which helps retain hoof moisture. The cells that form the intertubular horn, located next to the outside surface of the hoof wall, contain pigment. The same cells adjacent to the white line do not contain pigment.

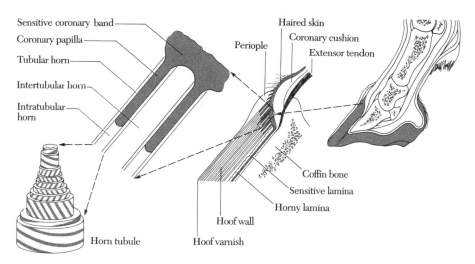

FIGURE 8-9 Magnified diagrammatic section of papillae of the coronary band and horn tubules of the hoof wall. (From Butler, 1985.)

FIGURE 8-10 Diagrammatic representation of the cross section of the interlocking of the sensitive and horny laminae, showing the relative size of the horn tubules of the hoof wall. (From Butler, 1985.)

The outer surface of the hoof wall is covered by the periople and the stratum tectorium (a varnish-like substance). The periople extends below the coronary band for approximately $\frac{3}{4}$ inch except at the heels, where it covers the heels and blends in with the frog. The periople protects the junction of the hoof wall with the coronary band. The underside of the periople flakes off, and this material forms the stratum tectorium, which therefore extends from the periople to the bottom of the hoof wall. Friction from dirt, grass, and so on usually wears off this thin layer of cells so that the stratum tectorium is usually not present on the lower part of the hoof wall.

The insensitive laminar layer forms the inner surface of the hoof wall. This layer intermeshes with the sensitive laminae that cover the surface of the third phalanx. The sensitive and insensitive laminae are composed of primary leaves. There are about 600 primary leaves in each hoof. Each primary leaf has about 100 secondary leaves that run parallel to the primary leaves. The sensitive and insensitive laminae intermesh or interlock to hold the hoof wall to the third phalanx. The third phalanx is actually suspended from the inside of the hoof wall. Therefore, the weight of the horse is not exerted on the sole surface but is borne by the hoof wall. The laminar arrangement allows the weight to be distributed over a large surface area.

The white line of the foot is the area where the laminae intermesh. It is composed of sensitive and insensitive laminar leaves and the interlaminar horn produced by papillae at the base of the leaves of the sensitive laminate. This combination of structure gives it a yellowish color. It should not be confused with the white (unpigmented) area of hoof wall tubules adjacent to the white line.

The hoof wall is thickest at the toe and becomes thin at the quarters. At the angle of the wall, the wall is reflected forward to form the bars of the foot. The bars serve as a brace structure to prevent overexpansion of the hoof wall.

Sole

The sensitive sole (sole corium) covers the bottom of the third phalanx. Papillae similar to those of the coronary band form the horn tubules that compose the sole. The sole has self-limiting growth in that flakes of it slough off after it gets about as thick as the hoof wall. The sole varies in thickness from about $\frac{3}{8}$ inch (9.5 mm) adjacent to the hoof wall at the toe to about $\frac{1}{4}$ inch (6.03 mm) at the heel area. The sole is concave at the ground surface. This shape, in conjunction with the continual scaling or sloughing, prevents the sole from bearing weight. The sole is easily bruised, and bruises occur frequently when the sole bears weight.

Frog

The frog is the elastic, wedge-shaped mass that occupies the area between the bars. The bottom surface is marked by a depression called the *central sulcus* or *cleft*. Internally, the frog stay is formed as a result of the wedge shape. The point of the frog toward the toe is referred to as the *apex*.

The horny frog is produced by the papillae that project from the surface of the sensitive frog (frog corium). Horn tubules produced by the sensitive frog are not completely keratinized, so they remain more elastic. Elasticity is enhanced by greasy secretions from the fat glands that pass from the digital cushion into the frog. The moisture content is about 50 percent, which also helps to maintain a pliable condition.

Coriums

Five coriums of modified vascular tissue furnish nutrition to the hoof. The perioplic corium, within the perioplic groove in the coronary band, serves the periople. The coronary corium, responsible for the growth and nutrition of the bulk of the hoof wall, lies within the coronary band. Because the coronary band is responsible for wall growth, injury to the coronary band is quite serious and usually leads to a defect in wall growth and structure. The laminar corium is attached to the top of the third phalanx and bears the sensitive laminae. Consequently, it transports blood and nutrition to the sensitive and insensitive laminae as well as to the white line. The sole corium, on the lower surface of the third phalanx, nourishes the sole. The frog is nourished by the frog corium.

Digital Cushion

The back half of the foot contains the digital or plantar cushion. This fibroelastic, fatty cushion acts as a shock absorber for the foot.

Bones

Three bones are located in the horse's foot: the second phalanx (or short pastern), the third phalanx (or coffin bone), and the navicular bone. The third phalanx is located mainly to the front of the hoof and slightly to the outer side of the hoof. It is the largest bone in the foot, is quite porous, and resembles a miniature foot in shape. The second phalanx is partly in the hoof and partly above it. The navicular bone is the smallest bone of the foot and increases the articulatory surface and movement of the distal interphalangeal (foot or coffin) joint.

Lateral Cartilages

The lateral cartilages are attached to the wings of the third phalanx. They rise above the coronary band and extend approximately one-third of the way around each side of the hoof from the heel.

Physiology

The structures of the foot work together to absorb concussion when the foot strikes the ground. As the foot strikes the ground, the heels are expanded by frog action. The frog is pushed upward but primarily flattens out. Because of its wedge shape, the frog stay forces the digital cushion upward and outward on both sides of the foot. Movement of the digital cushion presses on the lateral cartilages, which in turn move outward. The lateral cartilages compress the blood veins draining the foot. Compression of the blood veins forces blood toward the heart and also causes blood to pool in the foot. The pooled blood then acts as a hydraulic cushion that absorbs concussion. To aid further in concussion absorption, the third phalanx descends slightly and the sole yields slightly. The laminae also help absorb shock. In addition, the navicular bone helps absorb concussion as a result of its placement in the coffin joint. As the weight is transferred from the second phalanx to the navicular bone, the navicular bone yields slightly before the weight is transferred to the third phalanx. The deep flexor tendon supports the navicular bone. The remainder of the concussion is absorbed at the pasterns, knee, and shoulder.

SHOEING

Horses have been shod for centuries; the oldest shoes, found in ancient Celtic villages in France, date back to AD 700. Horses are shod for a variety of reasons, usually to protect the hoof wall from excessive wear and from damage, to increase traction, and to correct gaits or prevent limb interference. Shoeing must be done properly if the foot is to function normally. Therefore, it is important to understand the anatomy and physiology of the foot before one learns how to shoe. Also, one should be under close supervision by an instructor while learning how to shoe a horse.

Equipment

The basic horseshoeing tools are shown in Figure 8-11. In addition, the other tools used by farriers are shown in Figure 8-12.

A leather apron is worn for protection against nail cuts and burns if a forge is used. For safety reasons, strings are used on the apron, tied so they can be quickly released if a horse hooks a nail in the apron and starts kicking. The strings should be long enough to be crossed behind and in front and then tucked under on the sides. Use the hoof or farrier's knife to remove dead sole scales, trim the frog, and cut out corns. Such knives are available with a wide or narrow blade, with one or two sharp edges, and for use by the left- or the right-handed farrier. Initially,

FIGURE 8-11   Basic tools of shoeing: *(a)* apron; *(b)* hoof pick; *(c)* hoof knife; *(d)* nippers; *(e)* "pull-offs"; *(f)* rasp; *(g)* driving hammer; *(h)* clinch block; *(i)* clinch cutter; *(j)* tool box; *(k)* rounding hammer; *(l)* anvil. (Photos by W. Evans.)

FIGURE 8-12   Other tools for shoeing: *(a)* fullering iron; *(b)* nail or alligator clinchers; *(c)* sole chisel or knife; *(d)* pritchel; *(e)* shoe spreader; *(f)* tongs; *(g)* hoof level; *(h)* divider; *(i)* hardy; *(j)* stall jack; *(k)* portable coal-burning forge—(1) crater, (2) twyer ball, (3) slide, (4) pipe leading from fan, (5) draft.

learn to use a knife with a single-edged wide blade. If the sole is too hard to cut out with the hoof knife, use a sole knife (sole chisel) to chisel out the sole. To keep the edges of the hoof and sole knives sharp, first clean the sole of all rocks and dirt with a hoof pick. Sharpen knife edges with a tapered, flat oilstone.

Use the blade end of a clinch cutter or buffer to cut or straighten out clinches (bent-over nails) before removing the shoe. After the shoe is removed and the nails cut off, use the pritchel end to take seated nails out of the shoe.

Two types of hammers should be kept as part of the basic equipment: the rounding hammer for shaping shoes on the anvil to fit the horse's feet, and the driving hammer for driving nails and forming and finishing clinches. Use the claw end of the driving hammer to wring (twist) off the nails. Driving hammers can be bought in different weights such as 10, 14, or 16 ounces. The 14-ounce hammer is most commonly used.

Cutting nippers have two sharp edges and are used for removing excess hoof wall. Some farriers prefer a hoof parer, which is similar to the nippers but

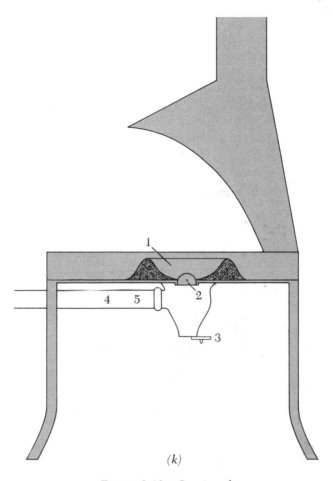

(k)

FIGURE 8-12   *Continued*

has a blunt edge and a sharp edge. Farrier's pincers, commonly called the "pullers," are similar in shape to cutting nippers but are used to pull shoes or nails from the foot and may be used to clinch the nails. Usually, a clinch block or an alligator clincher is used to set the clinches. If the pincers are used as a clinch block, they are closed, and the backside of the jaw is held against the nail. A crease nail puller is used to pull out nails from the crease in a shoe.

If a forge is not available to shape shoes, use a shoe spreader to spread the heels of the shoe. Use a rasp fitted with a handle to level the bearing surface of the foot and finish the clinches. Use the rough side for rasping the hoof, and the smoother side for final leveling and for finishing the clinches. In the final leveling process, use a hoof leveler to determine the angle of the wall and to determine if the foot is level. The length of the wall is usually checked with the hoof calipers or a divider to make sure both feet are the same and are of the proper length.

Keep the tools just described in a shoeing box so they are handy for work on a horse's feet. The anvil is the farrier's workbench and is used in many ways to prepare the shoe properly. Normally, the anvil weighs 80 to 125 pounds (36.3 to 56.7 kg). The farrier's anvil has a thinner heel and a longer, more tapered horn than the blacksmith's anvil. The horn may have a clipping block to draw out clips. The face or flat area has a hole for the hardy and one or two pritchel holes. The hardy is used for cutting hot metals, such as the heels of the shoe. It is also used to cut blank bars to the proper length to be made into shoes. A pritchel is used to expand the nail holes in a shoe or to remove nails that are broken or cut off even with the web of the shoe. The stall jack is a handy tool used by farriers to shape aluminum plates when shoeing racehorses so that the foot does not have to be put down during the process.

Most competent farriers are skilled in the use of a forge to make and shape shoes. At one time, the coal-burning forge was the most common, and portable ones can be carried in a pickup truck. Today, most farriers use gas forges. The gas forge keeps the temperature constant and will not burn up a shoe that is left in the forge too long. Coal-burning forges require the use of a fire shovel to add coal and a fire rake to remove clinkers (melting metal particles that bind burned coal into larger masses). Farrier's tongs are used to handle the shoes in the forge and while shaping hot shoes. A fullering iron is necessary to crease a hand-forged shoe or to repair damaged creases during shaping.

In addition to the shoeing tools, some other equipment may be needed. The farrier must carry a halter and lead rope to use on horses when the owner is not present. In some areas where horses are kept together in large numbers and are not handled regularly, a catch rope is necessary. A knee strap 2 feet long (61 cm) is handy to hold up a forefoot of a problem horse. Often a horse will stand if a twitch is applied to the muzzle. A couple of long, soft ropes may be used to tie up a hindfoot or tie down a vicious horse. If it is necessary to tie up a hindfoot, a 12-inch (30.5-cm) strap with dee-rings in each end will prevent a rope burn around the pastern (see Figure 6-5). Some horses kick, thus requiring the use of a hoof hook to pick up a hindfoot.

If a person shoes horses all day, a 14-inch-high (35.6-cm) foot stand can prevent excessive back strain. However, such stands are not safe to use around nervous horses and they teach young horses to lean on the farrier. A farrier who can properly handle a horse's foot seldom uses a foot stand.

A 5-inch (12.7-cm) vise is useful, particularly when filing the heels or turning calks on a shoe. A crease nail puller is used to grasp a nail head seated in the crease and enables the farrier to pull out the nail. Nail cutters are used to cut off the ends of the nail to the same length before they are clinched. This is important if the horse is to be shown.

Shoes

The shoe selected depends primarily on the intended use for the horse. Other factors influencing the selection are types of terrain, need for traction, way of going, and conformation. A typical shoe and its parts are shown in Figure 8-13. Shoes may be custom-made by a farrier, but most shoes are keg

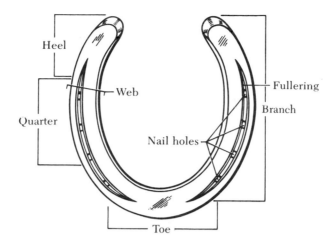

FIGURE 8-13   Ground surface view of a horseshoe.

(machine-made) shoes (Figure 8-14). A variety of kinds and sizes of keg shoes are used. Machine-made "hot shoes" are made with long branches so they can be cut off at the proper length or so that heel calks can be made. A forge is required to shape them. Machine-made "cold shoes" are designed like machine-made "hot shoes" but have shorter and finished heels. They are fitted without a forge. Because they are more difficult to shape and to properly nail on the foot, they are not used very often by skilled farriers, who prefer the "hot shoe." The Diamond brand bronco and saddle horse shoes are examples of machine-made "cold shoes." These shoes are popular because they are shaped and ready to be used without much alteration for a good fit. Racehorses are shod with aluminum or steel plates. Barrel racing and polo horses are shod

FIGURE 8-14   Basic types of shoes: *(a)* aluminum racing plate; *(b)* shoe for hot shoeing; *(c)* cold shoe or ready-made shoe for cold shoeing. (Photo by W. Evans.)

with polo or rim shoes. Reining horses are shod with sliding plates. Calks and toe grabs can be added to the shoes to increase traction and help prevent limb interference. Shoes are made in front or hind patterns and shapes. Draft horses, mules, and ponies require different patterns and shapes.

The size of the shoe needed for a foot is determined by the size of the hoof, the position of the nail holes, and the length of the shoe heels. The last nail hole on a front shoe should not be behind the widest part of the foot. Nails placed too far back inhibit expansion of the heels. In the hindfoot, the last nail may be a little farther back. The branches must be long enough to support the entire hoof wall. If they are too long on the forefeet, a hindfoot may overreach and pull the front shoe. If too short, the heels of the horse will grow out beyond the heels of the shoe, and the heels of the shoe will rest on the sole, producing corns.

The most commonly used shoes are keg (ready-made or cold) shoes that are presized and made to be fitted "cold." There are several types and manufacturers of keg shoes. The saddle horse and bronco shoes (sometimes referred to as western, or cowboy shoes) (Figure 8-15) made by Diamond or similar shoes made by others are used on most pleasure horses and on working cow horses. The bronco shoe is available in several sizes to cover the range of light horse hoof shapes. Standard Diamond brand shoe sizes range from the No. 000, which is $4\frac{13}{32}$ inches long (11.2 cm) and $3\frac{5}{8}$ inches wide (9.2 cm) for the plain bronco, to the No. 3, which is $6\frac{5}{32}$ inches long (15.6) cm and $5\frac{9}{16}$ inches wide (14.1 cm). The No. 1 shoe fits the average horse. In another size system, used by the Multi-Products Company, the No. 3 is equivalent to the Diamond No. 00, the No. 6 is equivalent to the Diamond No. 1, and the No. 9 is equivalent to the Diamond No. 3. The No. 4 is slightly smaller than the Diamond No. 0, and the No. 5 is slightly larger than the Diamond No. 0. The No. 7 is slightly smaller, and the No. 8 is slightly larger than the Diamond No. 2. These so-called half-sizes almost completely eliminate the necessity to shape standard shoes to obtain a good fit. Diamond brand pony shoes come in two sizes, No. 2 and No. 0.

FIGURE 8-15   Keg, cold, or ready-made shoes: *(a)* plain; *(b)* heeled, with heel calks; *(c)* heeled and toed, with heel and toe calks.

Keg shoes are also classified as plain, heeled, or toed and heeled (Figure 8-15). The heeled shoes have heel calks, and the heel and toed shoes have heel and toe calks. Calks increase traction on slick, soft, or rough terrain. To form the calks on keg shoes which do not have them, heat the shoe with a forge and bend the end of the heel back against the heel. If toe calks, or "toegrabs," are required, they must be welded to the toe. They also come in different weights—plain and light.

Mule shoes are a variation of keg shoes and are similar to bronco shoes. However, their sizes are slightly different, and they are shaped to fit a mule's feet (Figure 8-16).

Plates are a type of keg shoe used on racehorses. Steel plates are very seldom used on running horses because aluminum is lighter. They are available in two sizes—light or heavy—and can be obtained with a variety of combinations for toe and heel calks (Figure 8-17). Aluminum racing plates (Figures 8-18 and 8-19) weigh 2 to 3 ounces (0.7 to 1 mg). The front plates can be obtained plain, which means that there are no calks on the plate. A standard toe has a toe calk. If the toe calk is lower than the regular height, it is a low toe plate. Heel calks on the front plates are referred to as "jar calks." Hind aluminum racing plates are also available with various toe and heel calk combinations. The heel calk on a hind plate is referred to as a "block" or "sticker," depending on its shape. The sticker, or "mud-calk," is set across the heel, whereas the block is set lengthwise. Blocks cause a horse's hindfeet to break over faster, thus preventing the track surface from burning the ergot area. Stickers increase the traction on muddy tracks.

Polo shoes (Figure 8-20) differ from cowboy shoes in that the inside rim on the web is raised above the outside rim. This shape increases traction, prevents sliding, and enables the foot to roll over faster. Polo horses and western barrel-racing horses make many turns at high speeds. The polo shoe allows the horse to pivot on the shoe and maintain a toe grip regardless of where the foot breaks over. Barrel racing shoes have a high outside rim to help prevent sliding when the horse goes around the barrel.

(a)   *(b)*   *(c)*

FIGURE 8-16   Shapes of pony and mule shoes (Diamond Brand): *(a)* plain mule shoes; *(b)* heeled mule shoes; *(c)* plain pony shoes.

FIGURE 8-17   Shape of steel racing (running) plates: *(a)* plain; *(b)* block heels toed.

Farriers modify shoes with the aid of a forge. Toe and/or heel clips (Figure 8-21) can be drawn on shoes to help hold the shoe in position. They are essential for horses that have weak hoof walls and whose hooves do not hold nails very well. Gaited and walking horses need toe and heel clips to help hold the extra-heavy shoes. Horses that must stop and turn suddenly or horses working in mud are difficult to keep shod unless toe and heel clips are added to prevent the hoof wall from sliding off or pulling off the shoe and tearing out the nail holes. They can also support the hoof wall in the areas of cracks.

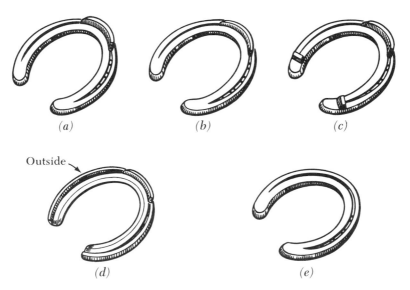

FIGURE 8-18   Aluminum racing plates for front feet: *(a)* regular toe; *(b)* low toe; *(c)* jar calk; *(d)* level grip or outside rim; *(e)* queens plate—flat (no calks).

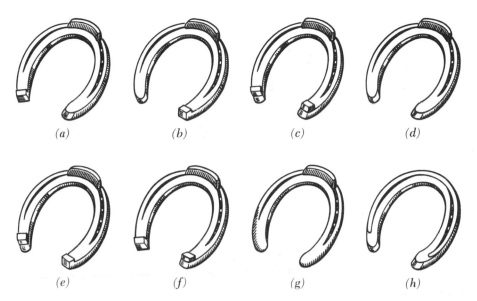

FIGURE 8-19   Aluminum racing plates for hind feet: *(a)* right sticker or mud calk; *(b)* left sticker or mud calk; *(c)* block heel; *(d)* plain heel; *(e)* left block and sticker; *(f)* right block and sticker; *(g)* level grip or outside rim; *(h)* queens plate—flat therapeutic (no calks).

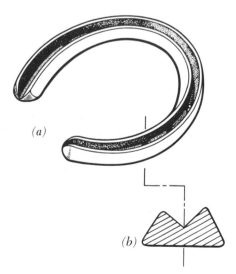

FIGURE 8-20   *(a)* Polo shoe; *(b)* cross section of polo shoe, showing that the inside rim is higher than the outside rim.

(a)   (b)

FIGURE 8-21   *(a)* Toe clips; *(b)* heel clips.

Borium (a metal alloy) can be applied to horseshoes with an oxyacetylene torch to improve the grip and life of the shoe. The roughened surface increases grip on ice, pavement, and dry grass. Borium is harder than any substance except diamonds, so it doubles or even triples the life of the shoe. Application of borium is particularly important before long trail rides over rough terrains; it should also be applied to the shoes of pack horses and mules.

During the past two centuries, new technology in farrier science has been limited to the development of aluminum, plastic, rubber, urethane, and new styles of steel horse shoes. All of these shoes must be nailed to the hoof wall. However, the GLU-STRIDER and Dalric horseshoes—a new concept—are glued to the outer surface of the hoof wall (Figure 8-22). The purpose of these shoes is therapeutic; they are not designed to replace the conventional shoe.

Horseshoe Nails

Horseshoe nails (Figure 8-23) are made so that one side of the shank is flat and the other concave, with a bevel near the point. The head of the nail is tapered and roughened on the same side as the bevel. Horseshoe nails differ according to size and head shape. The most commonly used sizes are 4, 5, and 6, but sizes range from 2 to 16 (small to large). After being driven, a regular head does not fit completely into the fullering. The city head fits into the fullering and is used for racing plates. Nails with regular heads are used when the shoes are reset and when the nail holes are slightly larger. Sharp, beveled heads, called frostheads, are used to increase traction on icy surfaces. Nails with countersunk heads can be obtained but are seldom used except for handmade shoes. Use a pritchel to open the nail holes in a shoe before driving the nails (Figure 8-12).

FIGURE 8-22   GLU-STRIDER therapeutic shoe: *(a)* Parts consist of pad and main shoe structure. *(b)* Shoe being shaped to fit the pad with special tools. *(c)* Shoe being glued to the hoof wall. (Courtesy of GLU-STRIDER.)

Shoeing Procedure

First, remove the old shoes (Figure 8-24). To do so, cut the clinches by placing the sharp edge of the clinch cutter under the clinch (bent-over nail) and striking the cutter with the driving hammer. After the clinches are cut or

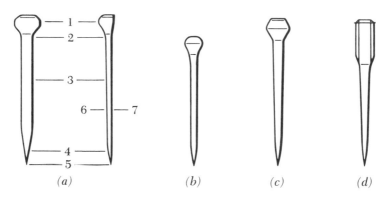

FIGURE 8-23   Horseshoe nails: *(a)* parts—(1) head, (2)neck, (3) shank, (4) bevel, (5) point, (6) inner face, (7) outer face; *(b)* city shape; *(c)* regular shape; *(d)* frosthead shape.

straightened out, remove the shoe with "pull-offs." Insert them under one heel of the shoe and rock them forward and toward the center of the toe. Repeat the procedure for the opposite side. Then gradually work the pull-offs toward the toe until the shoe is removed.

Examine the shoes for abnormal wear, and give the horse the same preliminary examination as for trimming the feet. As previously described, trim the feet and select the appropriate shoe. Then shape the shoes to fit the horse's feet. Using a forge to heat the shoe so it can be shaped more easily is called "hot shoeing." In cold shoeing, the shoe is shaped without heat. The only advantage of a forge is to make shaping easier. The shoe must be flat after it is shaped so the surface touches the hoof wall all the way around and does not rock on the foot. Each high spot causes excess pressure, which in turn cracks the hoof wall. The shoe fits the foot if the outside edge of the hoof wall is flush with the outer edge of the shoe except at the heels. Shoes should be about $\frac{1}{16}$ to $\frac{1}{8}$ inch (1.6 to 3.2 mm) wider at the heels to allow for normal heel expansion when the horse moves. The inside edge of the shoe should not press on the sole. Heels must be long enough to cover the foot buttress, but not long enough to be stepped on by the other feet. Nail holes should be in a position so that the nails can be properly placed and directed.

Nailing the shoe on the foot is the next step (Figure 8-25). Most shoes have four nail holes in each branch, but three nails are usually enough. Four nails are used if the horse is worked heavily, or at speed, or ridden in rough country. After positioning the shoe on the foot, drive the first nail. Any nail can be driven first, but one of the two center nails in either side is usually the best choice. The point of the nail should exit the hoof wall about $\frac{3}{4}$ inch (19.1 mm) above the ground surface. Hold nails so that the bevel side faces the center of the foot and the flat side faces the outside surface of the hoof wall. Point the nail toward the point where it should exit, and drive it with the driving hammer. Light taps with the hammer drive the nail deeper; a sharp blow

FIGURE 8-24 Cutting clinches and removing the old shoe: *(a)* cutting clinches; *(b)* inserting pull-offs under one heel; *(c)* inserting pull-offs under the opposite heel and rotating pull-offs toward the toe; *(d)* pulling the shoe off. (Photos by W. Evans.)

(a)   (b)   (c)

FIGURE 8-25   Nailing on the shoe: *(a)* Start nail in one of the center nail holes; it should exit about $\frac{3}{4}$ inch from the ground surface of the hoof wall. *(b)* Bend the nail over.*(c)* Insert the nail between the jaws of the hammer and wring off. (Photos by W. Evans.)

causes the nail to exit. Therefore, hit the nail head with a sharp blow just before it is $\frac{3}{4}$ inch (19.1 mm) into the hoof wall. Immediately after the point exits and the nail is driven completely in, bend it over and wring it off with the claws of the hammer. Drive in the remaining nails and cut them off. Remove and reposition nails that are driven in too far or not far enough. Take care not to drive a nail into the sensitive tissue (such an accident is called "quicking"). If this does occur, remove the nail and treat the wound with an iodine solution. The horse should have been immunized against tetanus; if it has not, give it a tetanus antitoxin injection for protection.

Form the clinches by holding the clinch block under the nail and hitting the nail head a couple of times with the hammer (Figure 8-26). If the nail stub places too much pressure on the hoof wall, the hoof wall will tear or crack. The stub should project about $\frac{1}{16}$ inch (1.6 mm) from the wall before forming the clinch. Cut clinches to their final length with pull-offs or a pair of nail cutters. If necessary, rasp them to the proper length. After forming the clinches, rasp the hoof wall lightly immediately under the nails to remove the burr of horn that appears under the nails. Then bend the clinches flat against the hoof wall by hitting them with a hammer or by using the clinchers.

Evaluation

After the farrier has completed work, the job should be evaluated by considering several points (Figure 8-27). Examine the feet first while they are on the ground. The feet should be the same size. The angle of the hoof wall should be the same as the pasterns and the shoulder. The toe should not be "dubbed off," and the branches should extend about $\frac{1}{16}$ inch (1.6 mm) out from the heels

(a)

(b)

(c)

FIGURE 8-26   Forming clinches: *(a)* Hold the clinch block under the end of the nail and strike the nail head with a hammer to bend the nail and form a clinch. *(b)* Rasp the hoof wall lightly under the bent nail to clear the hoof wall. *(c)* Bend the clinch over with a clincher (or hammer). (Photos by W. Evans.)

to allow for expansion. Shoes should be the right length. The foot should be in balance with the leg and be properly shaped. Clinches should be about $\frac{3}{4}$ inch above the hoof wall ground surface, and they should be evenly spaced. The hoof wall should not have been excessively rasped except for necessary corrective shaping of the foot. The entire surface of the web should be in contact with the surface of the hoof wall; that is, there should be no space between the shoe and hoof wall. Then lift the foot off the ground and examine it. The nails should have been driven home, and the frog should have been trimmed, but not excessively.

Finally, observe the horse moving to make sure it is not lame and has no defects of gait caused by shoeing.

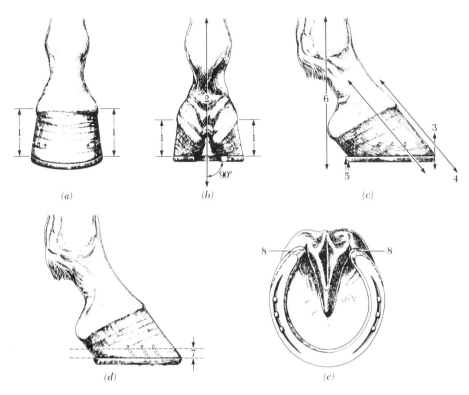

FIGURE 8-27   Properly shod foot. *(a)* Front view: 1's are equal length. *(b)* Back view: 1's are equal length; 2 is at right angles to the ground surface. *(c)* At 3, shoe is even with the edge of the hoof wall. Heel of the shoe extends up to $\frac{1}{4}$ inch (6.4 mm) beyond the heel of the foot at 5. Hoof wall has proper angle at 4 and is continuous with the slope of the pastern. Line 6 bisects the leg, touches the bulb of the heel, and is perpendicular to the ground surface. *(d)* Nails exit (7) $\frac{3}{4}$ to 1 inch (19.1 to 25.4 mm) above the shoe and are in a straight line at 7. Drive nails parallel to tubules in the hoof wall. *(e)* Shoe extends beyond the heels and extends about $\frac{1}{16}$ inch (1.6 mm) from the hoof wall at 8.

CORRECTIVE TRIMMING AND SHOEING

Corrective trimming and shoeing are used to change the way the foot travels or lands, to avoid limb interference.

Foals

Many faulty positions of stance or incorrect ways of going in young foals can be helped or corrected by proper trimming of the feet. Corrective trimming for young foals is based on three principles.

First, adequate exercise is important if the foal is to be straight-legged when it matures. Support muscles increase in size and strength as the body size increases. However, when foals are kept in close confinement, the muscles required for shoulder propulsion and rotation are not used as much as they should be to stimulate normal development. Consequently, these muscles shrink and weaken as the foal grows, allowing the legs to become base-wide. Then the feet become toed-out and the inside hoof wall is worn off because the foot rolls over the inside wall. To prevent this sequence, foals should be kept where they have room to run and play, or they should be vigorously exercised for a few minutes every day.

Second, pressure across the growth plate or epiphysis of the leg bones influences the rate of bone growth. Unevenly distributed pressure across the epiphyseal plate causes improper bone growth. The objective of corrective trimming for young foals is to evenly distribute pressure across the epiphysis and, when necessary, to redistribute pressure to stimulate or depress bone growth to strengthen the leg. In the toe-wide (toed-out) stance, excess pressure is occurring on the lateral (toward the outside) side of the epiphysis, and less pressure is occurring on the medial (toward the center of the horse) side. Excess pressure decreases bone growth and less pressure increases it so that the medial side of the bone grows at a faster rate than the lateral side. The condition worsens if the feet are not correctively trimmed.

Third, corrective trimming must begin when the foal is a few days old and the hoof wall is hard enough to trim. All corrections must be accomplished before the epiphyseal plate closes for a particular bone. Radiographic data indicate that the epiphyses of the first and second phalanges close at approximately 9 months (Figure 8-28). The epiphysis at the distal end of the cannon bone closes at 9 to 12 months. Most of the remaining bones' epiphyses close at 1 to 2 years.

Glue-on shoes, BABY-GLU and Dalric, have been developed and, because they are not nailed on, can be used on very young foals to prevent excessive hoof wear that would lead to an imbalanced foot. These shoes have many possibilities for treating foals with angular limb deformities.

A foal can be born with a "club foot," or flexural deformity, as a result of uterine malposition or genetic defects. Acquired "club foot" can result from injuries after birth, improper nutrition, neglected foot care, or pain. When severe pain occurs, the horse might seek relief by not flexing the leg, which in turn causes the digital flexor tendon to contract. This, in turn, causes the horse to walk on its toes or to knuckle over at the fetlock joint. Correction of the "club foot syndrome" requires accurate diagnosis of the underlying problem by a veterinarian and a prescribed series of treatments. The severity of the club foot is graded 1 to 4, with 4 being severe, and the treatment plan varies according to severity. Those classified as grade 1 respond to treatment of lowering the heels and application of a toe tip shoe. This realigns the hoof pastern axis and stretches the deep digital flexor tendon. Progress should be monitored at two-week intervals. Without treatment, the performance potential for a horse is diminished, and with treatment, it is usually still diminished.

Epiphyseal Line	6 months	9 months	12 months	18 months	2 years	2½ years	3 years
Foreleg							
First phalanx (proximal)	▬						
Second phalanx (proximal)	▬						
Third metacarpal bone (distal)		▬					
Radius (distal)						▬	
Radius (proximal)				▬			
Ulna (proximal)						▬	
Ulna (distal to distal radial epiphysis)	▬						
Humerus (distal)				▬			
Humerus (proximal)					▬		
Humerus (lateral tuberosity)						▬	
Humerus (medial epicondyle to discal epiphypsis of humerus)	▬						
Hindleg							
First phalanx (proximal)	▬						
Second phalanx (proximal)	▬						
Third metatarsal bone (distal)		▬					
Tibia (distal)				▬			
Tibia (proximal)						▬	
Tibial crest							
United with proximal tibia		▬					
United with tibial shaft							▬
Fibula (distal with tibia)					▬		
Femur (distal)					▬		
Os calcis	▬						

Age during which closure usually takes place ▬▬▬▬

FIGURE 8-28   Closure of epiphyseal plates. Age of epiphyseal closure is based on Quarter Horse and Thoroughbred breeds, both male and female. The age of epiphyseal closure given here is based on radiographic determination, which will be earlier than actual closure determined histologically. (From Adams, 1974.)

Mature Horses

The hoof wall grows at the rate of $\frac{1}{4}$ to $\frac{1}{2}$ inch (6.4 to 12.7 mm) per month. Therefore, the hooves should be trimmed or shod every 6 to 8 weeks. They need to be trimmed more frequently if they are growing abnormally fast, such as after founder, or if they show uneven wear. Horses that wear their hoof walls unevenly usually have crooked feet or legs. Uneven wear of the hoof wall accentuates faulty conformation and way of going. Keeping the hoof wall level does not correct the fault in mature horses, but it may prevent leg interference. Quite often, corrective trimming only requires rasping down one side of the hoof wall until it is level with the opposite wall.

The outside wall wears down at a faster rate than the inside wall of base-narrow and toe-in or toe-out horses. Consequently, the inside wall must be rasped level with the outside wall. Remove additional hoof wall if the wall is too long after it is leveled. Horses that are base-wide and toe-out or toe-in wear the inside wall at a faster rate. If the horse only toes out, the inside wall wears faster; if it toes in, the outside wall wears faster.

The toe of the hoof wall grows faster than does the heel. A long toe decreases the expansion of the wall when the hoof strikes the ground. Because the contraction is greater than the expansion, the walls contract inward. Contracted heels put excess, painful pressure on the third phalanx. Failure to trim long hooves leads to contracted heels, faulty gaits, and limb interference. Long toes and low heels inhibit the foot rolling over during forward motion and may cause forging, overreaching, and scalping.

The basic principle of corrective shoeing is to trim the foot level and then to apply corrective shoes to improve the faulty gait. Drastic changes in the flight of the foot and leg can put excess strain or pressure on other bones and structures of the foot and leg. The new stresses can cause pathological changes, so use the least severe corrective measure.

Several horses may share the same defect in way of going, but each horse may require different corrective measures. The initial step is a visual inspection of the horse's way of going. Note any "breakover" and "landing" areas of the hoof wall. In the base-narrow, toe-in fault in foreleg conformation, the foot breaks over and lands on the outside wall, and if the horse is unshod the outside wall will be worn down. The inside wall must be lowered to level the foot, and then several corrective measures can be used to force the foot to break over the center of the hoof (see Figure 8-29). One of the simplest and mildest methods of correction is to put on a square-toed shoe. Other measures, such as an outside half rim (outside rim) shoe, calks, a calk at the first outside nailhole, or a lateral toe extension, encourage the foot to break over the toe. If the horse is base-narrow but toe-out, the foot will break over the outside of the toe, wing inward, and land on the outside wall. Successful correction methods to encourage the foot to break over the center of the toe include outside half rim shoes, square-toed shoes, outside toe extensions, and half shoes on outside wall.

Horses with a base-wide, toe-out conformation tend to break over and land on the inside aspect of the toes. Correct the fault by modifying the shoe to make it difficult for the foot to break over the inside of the toe but easier to break over the center of the toe. Several modifications, such as heel calks, square toes, or bars across the breakover points, force the foot to break over the center of the toe. Base-wide horses that have their toes pointing the

FIGURE 8-29   Corrective and therapeutic shoes: *(a)* half-rim shoe; *(b)* square toe; *(c)* calk at first outside nail hole; *(d)* heel calks; *(e)* lateral toe extension; *(f)* shoe with trailer; *(g)* half shoe; *(h)* bar across breakover point; *(i)* rolled toe; *(j)* bar shoe; *(k)* skippered heels; *(l)* Chadwick spring.

opposite way (that is, toe-in) land on the inside wall. To improve their way of going, the inside branch of the shoe must be raised.

Cow-hocked horses tend to break over the inside toe and thus strain the inside of the hock. This fault in conformation is particularly straining when the horse makes a sliding stop. The main objective in correcting the fault is to force the hindfoot to break over the center of the toe, by braking the inside of the hoof when it lands and by rotating the toe inward. A lateral extension toe or a short inside trailer usually accomplishes the objective.

The stance of a sickle-hocked or camped-under horse can be improved by shortening the hind toes if they are too long. This correction causes the hindlegs to move backward. The opposite effect can be accomplished for the camped-behind horse by lowering its hind heels if they are too long.

Other less obvious faults in conformation may lead to faulty gaits. Forging and overreaching result when the hindfoot breaks over faster than the forefoot in such a way that the toe of the hindfoot strikes the sole of the heels of the forefoot. Horses that have short backs and long legs, or short forelegs and long hindlegs, or that stand under in front or behind tend to forge and overreach. The corrective measure is to speed up the breaking over of the forefoot and retard the breaking over of the hindfoot, and/or increase the height of the forefoot flight. A variety of corrective measures can be used. The fault can be corrected in some horses by rolling the toes (and shoes) of the forefeet and leaving the toes of the hindfeet slightly longer than usual, or by placing heel calks on the hind shoes. In extreme cases, a $\frac{1}{2}$-inch (12.7-mm) bar can be welded across the heel of the front shoes and across the toe of the hind shoes.

When the toe of the forefoot strikes the hairline of the hindfoot ("scalping"), rolling the toe enables the forefoot to break over faster and may prevent contact. The same corrective principle and objectives apply to horses that scalp and/or hit their shins as to horses that forge and overreach.

Pacers that toe-out in front and toe-in behind tend to cross-fire. To prevent the hindfoot from hitting the opposite forefoot, all feet must be shod to encourage breaking over the center of the toe. Corrective measures include those discussed earlier for correcting the front toed-out and hind toed-in conditions.

Interference usually results when a horse is base-wide or base-narrow and has a toed-out conformation in the forelegs or is cow-hocked in the hindlegs. Correction of these conditions has been previously discussed and applies also to interference.

A farrier often encounters horses with pathological conditions that require therapeutic shoeing. The most common conditions are contracted heels, ring bone, side bone, navicular disease, toe or quarter cracks, and founder.

There are several ways, or combinations of ways, to re-establish proper foot function in a horse with contracted heels. Frog pressure can be increased with a bar shoe so that the bar maintains constant pressure on the frog. Other types of shoes include shoes with skippered (beveled) heels or a Chadwick spring to force the wall outward. The expansion process should be gradual, but additional expansion aids can be used; for example, cutting a horizontal groove below the coronary band, cutting several vertical grooves in the quarter area, or thinning the wall at the quarters with a rasp.

Horses with acute laminitis or chronic founder are shod with a heart-bar shoe developed by Burney Chapman. The shoe is designed to place pressure on the frog just behind the apex. The inner rim of the shoe is concaved to prevent sole pressure. The toe is rolled to allow the foot to break over easier. Resectioning the hoof wall of the chronic foundered foot provides relief for the horse and allows the re-establishment of normal laminar relationships.

Horses with ring bone have impaired or no action of the pastern and/or coffin joints. The objective of correction is to enable the foot to break over more easily so that the required action of the joint or joints is reduced. The simplest corrective measure is to roll the toe. When side bone is the problem, the action of the coffin joint needs to be decreased, so rolling the toe is helpful. To restore the ability of the foot to expand and relieve pain if the horse is lame, thin the quarters of the wall.

The objective of corrective shoeing for a horse with navicular disease is to make it easier for the foot to break over, and to reduce the anticoncussive activity of the deep flexor tendon against the navicular bone. Raising the heels and rolling the toe let the foot break over faster and reduce concussion to the navicular bone. To further reduce trauma to the area, use a bar shoe or pads. This type of correction contracts the heels because frog pressure is reduced. The tendency for the heels to contract can be reduced by slippering the heels of the shoe so that they slope to the outside. This causes the wall to slide outward as the foot strikes the ground. The expansion of the wall can be further aided by thinning the quarters with a rasp.

When shoeing a horse with flat feet, trim the sole slightly but do not trim the frog. Prevent the sole from dropping farther by making sure that the shoe covers the entire wall and white line and covers only a small part of the outside edge of the sole. Pads are usually necessary to prevent sole bruising.

Toe, quarter, and heel cracks are quite frequent. Each crack requires individual analysis with regard to the corrective treatment and shoeing. The general principle is to use a toe clip on each side of the crack to prevent wall expansion and to lower the wall under the crack so the wall will not bear weight. Plastics may be used to seal the crack and prevent expansion and contraction of the crack during foot action.

CHAPTER 9

Recognizing Illness and Giving First Aid

There are several components to a successful health care program for the horse. One is prevention of injury and sickness. This is accomplished by parasite and disease control, immunizations, teeth and foot care, safety, exercise, keeping accurate records, and other measures. When an injury or a disease occurs, the horseperson must know proper procedures for immediate care of the horse and where to obtain assistance. Most importantly, the horseperson must recognize symptoms that indicate a horse needs medical attention.

RECOGNIZING ILLNESS

Horses must be observed at regular intervals—at least daily—to determine if they need special attention. Certain vital signs should be checked for horses that appear to be sick: temperature, heart rate, respiration, gut sounds, mucosal color, and skin pliability. In addition to the vital functions, feces, urine, appetite, depression, nasal discharge, coughing, swelling, and behavior should be monitored.

Other signs can indicate illness. Rapid weight and appetite losses indicate a sudden change in health and are usually the first signs of illness. The horse may become depressed and isolate itself from other horses.

Respiration

The normal respiration rate for a horse is 8 to 16 respirations per minute. To determine the respiration rate, watch the nostrils or the flanks. Nostrils flare and contract with each breath, and the abdomen rises and falls with each breath. Any type of distress increases the respiration rate. If the respiration rate exceeds the heart rate, the horse has a serious problem.

Temperature

Normal body temperature for a horse is 100°F, or 38°C. It does vary from 99.5°F (37.5°C) to 101.5°F (38.6°C) for normal horses. It also varies during the day for the same horse. Internal and environmental factors can increase body temperature. Exercise, excitement, and hot weather raise temperature, as will pain and illness. A fever is classified as mild (102°F, or 38.9°C), moderate (104°F, or 40°C), or high (106°F, or 41°C). If it exceeds 106°F (41°C), the chances of recovery are low, and the horse needs immediate veterinary care. A low temperature may be observed in horses that are in shock. The increased body temperature is also classified as continuous (constant), remittent (marked increases and decreases), intermittent (normal periods between marked ups and downs), and recurrent (long periods of increased temperature followed by long periods of normal). When you describe a horse's condition to a veterinarian, he or she will want to know the temperature and its classification.

To take the temperature, use a veterinary thermometer. It contains a loop on one end to which an 8-inch (203-mm) string with an alligator clip or clothespin on the other end can be attached. Shake the mercury level down to below 95°F (35°C) before inserting the thermometer. Coat the thermometer with a small amount of lubricant such as petroleum jelly for easy insertion. Raise the horse's tail and insert the thermometer bulb end first about 75 percent of its length into the anus with a rotating motion. Attach the alligator clip or clothespin to a few tail hairs to prevent the thermometer from being lost in the rectum or from being broken if it falls out. After at least 2 minutes, remove and read the thermometer. Clean it in cool, soapy water and dip it in alcohol before storing or using it again. Digital display thermometers immediately record the temperature.

Heart Rate

Heart rate or pulse varies with the age of a horse. Normal mature horses have a pulse of 28 to 40 beats per minute. Newborn foals have 80 to 120; foals, 60 to 80; and yearlings, 40 to 60. To determine an accurate pulse, the horse should be calm, rested, and relaxed. Many things increase heart rate, such as exercise, fright, excitement, and hot weather. Illness causes pulse rates of 80 to 120 for a prolonged period of time.

Pulse rates per minute are determined by counting the pulse for 30 seconds and multiplying the value by 2. It may be necessary to determine 15-second rates, but in this case several determinations should be used, because pulse rates can vary widely over short time periods.

To determine the pulse, press your fingers against an artery. Each throb is a pulse or heartbeat and is the increased pressure in the artery caused by the heart contracting and forcing blood into the arteries. There are several locations where the pulse can be felt (see Figure 9-1), but practice is usually necessary to feel it easily. If a stethoscope is available, listen to the heart beat by monitoring the chest. Trainers use electronic heart-rate monitors during exercise bouts to monitor the heart rate so that the degree of fatigue can be determined.

Skin and Mucous Membranes

Skin pliability is a test for dehydration. Normally, the skin is pliable and elastic. If you pick a fold of skin up on the neck and release it, it quickly returns to its original position. But if the horse is dehydrated, the skin returns slowly and tends to stay in a fold. Other signs of dehydration are loss of moisture on mucous membranes and dull, sunken eyes.

FIGURE 9-1   Points at which the horse's pulse can be felt and taken: (1) the inner surface of the groove under the lower jaw (external maxillary artery); (2) the hack edge of the lower jaw (the cheek), four inches below the eye (facial artery); (3) under the tail, close to the body (medial coccygeal artery); (4) point where heartbeat can be monitored with stethoscope; (5) inside the left elbow, up and forward, against the chest wall (heart); (6) the inside of the foreleg (median artery); (7) behind the carpus, or knee (digital artery); (8) medial or lateral pastern (digital artery).

The color of the mucous membranes and the rate of capillary refill (rate of return of blood to the area) give an indication of the quantity and condition of the circulating blood. These signs help determine the presence of anemia, colic, congestion, and shock. Several mucous membranes can be checked: the gums, the inside lips of a mare's vulva, nostrils, and conjunctiva should be pink. A fire-engine-red color usually denotes illness. Anemia causes a pale color, and lack of circulation causes a bluish-purple color.

Determine capillary refill time by pressing your thumb on the horse's gum and then releasing it. It should take about 2 seconds for the blood and normal color to return to the area. Longer capillary refill times indicate dehydration or a circulatory problem.

Excreta

Normal urine from a horse is yellow to brown in color. The cloudy color is caused by calcium carbonate crystals. The longer the time period between urinations, the cloudier the urine. It is somewhat viscous because mucus and cellular debris are present. Normally, an average-size horse produces about 5.5 quarts (or 3.5 liters) each day.

Reduced urine volume may mean the horse is dehydrated. Other abnormalities that should be checked for are difficulty in urinating (straining), free blood present in urine, or coffee-colored urine. These conditions should be called to the attention of a veterinarian.

Examine the feces for consistency, and determine the frequency of defecation. Most horses defecate about every 2 hours, but if excited they defecate very frequently. Failure to defecate usually indicates a disorder such as impaction, colic, or severe dehydration. Normal feces are tan or yellow to dark green in color. The fecal balls should be well formed and not too hard or soft. Loose stools may mean a disorder, and diarrhea can lead to severe dehydration in a short period of time (2 to 3 hours in a severe case). Severe diarrhea is very serious in a young foal.

Gut sounds can help you diagnose a sick horse. The sounds can be heard by placing an ear on the flank area or using a stethoscope in the same area. The sounds are caused by the normal contracting and relaxing movements of the digestive tract during the digestion process. It requires considerable practice to gain experience in distinguishing excessive from normal gut sounds. Listen to several normal horses as a basis for comparison. Absence of gut sounds is usually more critical than excessive sounds.

RECOGNIZING LAMENESS

Lameness can be identified by using several diagnostic aids. Because lameness is caused by pain, the site of the pain must be located by visual inspection, manipulation, pressure, and checking for swelling, rapid pulse, and heat.

Several symptoms of lameness should be taken into account during a visual inspection. If the pain is severe, the horse may hop around on three legs and may refuse to place weight on the affected leg when standing still. If the pain is not very severe, only a disturbance of the gait will be observed. The horse may step short with the affected leg rather than take a full-length step.

Two of the most useful signs are a bobbing of the head or hip. With a front leg lameness, the horse will bob its head upward when the lame leg strikes the ground during the trot. Have the horse trot around you on a level surface in a 20- to 30-foot radius (6.1 to 9.1 m) and watch the head movement. A sound horse will carry its head steady without any up and down motion when it is trotting.

With a hindleg lameness, the horse extends its hip upward as the lame leg strikes the ground during the trot. To observe this, stand behind the horse and have it trot away from you.

Often, a lame leg can be identified by comparing pulse strength. An inflammation makes the pulse in the affected leg stronger than in the unaffected leg. Make the comparison several times to take into account shifts in body weight.

Manipulating the legs and their joints may evoke a response to the pain caused by the pressure or tension placed on the damaged area. The knee and hock joints and the joints located below them can easily be manipulated. Pressure is a useful tool during the manipulation because it aggravates the injury. Starting at the knee or hock, use your hands to circle the leg and place pressure on all the parts of the leg. As you feel the leg, check for swelling, heat, and abnormalities. Compare each leg with the opposite leg. Examine the knee by flexing and probing it with your fingers. Thoroughly examine the back of the leg for tendon problems. When examining the hindleg, increase pressure slowly to discourage the horse from kicking. While you are applying pressure, the horse's behavior may indicate pain by withdrawing the affected part, putting the ears back, jerking the head, and grunting.

Flex tests place pressure on the hoof and fetlock, knee, elbow, and shoulder in the foreleg and the hoof and fetlock, stifle, and hip joints in the hindleg. The flex tests produce pain from an injured joint that will be noticeable when the horse trots away from you immediately afterward. To test the hoof and fetlock joints in the foreleg, grasp the toe of the foot with one hand and the front of the knee with the other hand. Flex the hoof toward the knee for about 30 seconds. For a knee flex test, fold the front leg in a "V" and apply upward pressure on the cannon bone for about 30 seconds. Flex the elbow by facing the horse, grasping the leg behind the knee, and pulling the leg upward until the horse's forearm is at least parallel to the ground. For a shoulder flex test, lift the forefoot up about knee high, grasp the knee, and rotate the leg toward the horse's belly. For a hock flex test, face the hindleg, grasp the hack of the cannon and fetlock, and draw the leg up toward the stifle. Hold this position for about 1 minute. Test the hind fetlock and foot joints by grasping the toe and rotating the foot upward while pushing down on the point of the hock with the other hand. Flex the stifle by facing the side of the hindleg, grasping the leg in the hock, and pulling the leg upward and back. The hip flex is difficult. Pick up the hindleg and extend it toward the horse's elbow without bending the hock joint too much.

VETERINARY ASSISTANCE

It is important for horsepeople to be acquainted with a veterinarian and use his or her services when needed. The ability to obtain the services of a veterinarian during an emergency or when such aid is indicated pays dividends because properly treated horses recover faster. If you suspect illness but cannot diagnose it, call a vet immediately. The veterinarian may use other diagnostic aids, including nerve blocks, X-ray, Faradism, hoof testers, and wedge tests. Many illnesses that require a veterinarian also require first aid before he or she arrives, and every horseperson should be skilled in giving first aid.

FIRST AID

Confined horses are accident prone because of their behavior patterns, negligence in stabling, and subjection to stresses and strains beyond their capabilities. Horses protect themselves by running away from adversaries or frightening situations. In so doing, they frequently try to run through or over obstacles in their path. Their means of immediate defense is to kick other horses, stall walls, people, and so on. Horses are inquisitive and may paw at objects or may stick their legs through fences, holes in the stall wall, or pieces of equipment. As a result, they frequently cut themselves or receive puncture wounds. The frequency of injury increases when they are kept in surroundings with protruding nails, sharp edges, barbwire, miscellaneous junk, and other dangerous objects. And many common unsoundnesses result from injuries from stresses and strains beyond a horse's capacity. Horses forced to run too far and too often, jump too many or too-high fences, and stop too quickly damage tendons, ligaments, muscles, and bones.

First aid is the emergency treatment you give a horse until the services of a qualified veterinarian can take over. In many instances, the horse must be transported to a veterinary hospital. The following sections discuss first aid procedures commonly employed to prevent further injury to the horse and to reduce pain.

Be prepared for emergencies by keeping a first aid kit readily available. First aid kits should be kept at all stables and carried in every horse trailer or van. Kits that fit on the back of a saddle should be carried on trail rides. First aid kits are commercially available, but can also be ready made by buying the necessary supplies. A commercially available kit from Springbrook Forge (Figure 9-2) contains a shoe puller and spreader combination (also used for cutting nails and wire); a wide Frost hoof knife; hack saw; rasp; handmade rope halter, braided and spliced; a lead; aluminum humane twitch; straight forceps; bandage scissors; twelve cotton leg wraps (30 inches × 36 inches, or 76.2 × 91.4 cm); latex tubing tourniquet; twelve 3-inch (76.2-cm) kling gauze rolls;

FIGURE 9-2   Equine first aid kit. (Courtesy Springbrook Forge.)

a roll of 3-inch (76.2-cm) sterile cotton; twenty-five 5-inch × 9-inch (12.7-cm × 22.9-cm) surgical pad dressings; toppers; fifty 4-inch × 4-inch (10.2-cm × 10.2-cm) surgical sponges; four track bandages with tie tapes; 1-inch (2.54-cm) porous adhesive tape; a 5-inch × $5\frac{1}{2}$-inch (127-mm × 139.7-mm) natural sponge; a 4-inch (10.2-cm) elastic bandage; 1 pint (0.47 liter) of surgical soap; a tube of Vaseline; a self-tying canvas poultice boot; a large container of poultice powder; 1 pint (0.47 liter) of alcohol; 1 pint (0.47 liter) of iodine; soft nail brush; 5 yards (4.6 m) of 4-inch (10.2-cm) Vetrap bandaging tape (two rolls); stream spray eye wash; 1 pint (0.47 liter) of soluble salts; veterinary thermometer with ring top and clip case; reusable containers for medicines, pills, and salves; $\frac{3}{4}$-inch (19-mm) poly-ethylene plastic electrical tape with dispenser; flashlight with batteries; vinyl ex-amination gloves; plastic aprons; revolving leather punch; steel storage box ($26\frac{1}{2}$ inches × $18\frac{1}{2}$ inches × $10\frac{1}{2}$ inches, or 67.3 cm × 47.0 cm × 26.7 cm); first aid in-struction booklet; and a Kidde triclass fire extinguisher with a clip attachment out-side the kit (with a limited 2-year warranty).

Cuts and Tears

Wounds require immediate first aid treatment. The seriousness of a wound de-pends on its location, depth, type of cut or tear, amount of tissue damage, and type of tissue affected. All serious wounds should be treated by a veterinarian.

Proper wound treatment before the veterinarian arrives enhances veterinary services and the healing process.

Emergency Treatment

First, bleeding must be controlled. Blood from a severed artery spurts and is bright red. Venous blood is dull red and flows rather than spurts. Direct pressure controls bleeding for almost all injuries. Very seldom, if ever, is a tourniquet needed. Pack gauze into large or deep wounds and apply pressure until the bleeding stops. Apply direct pressure on a wound by firmly pressing a sterile pad over the wound and holding it in place by hand or by a tight bandage. As soon as the bleeding stops, a tight bandage should be removed. Cuts in the coronary band are serious and need immediate treatment by a veterinarian. The bleeding can be controlled by pressure.

Bleeding or loss of blood seems to panic most horsepeople. A 1000-pound (454-kg) horse has about 50 quarts of blood and can lose about 10 percent of its blood before the loss becomes critical. Rapid blood loss is critical; a horse can tolerate slower blood loss. If you find an injured animal that has been bleeding for some time, evaluate it for shock. If there has been excessive blood loss, the inside of the mouth will feel cold to the touch and the gums will be pale. Other signs of shock include an inability to stand and profuse sweating. Do not move the horse, but cover it with blankets.

The second step is to clean the wound with warm water and a mild soap. Remove all dirt and foreign matter. The best way is to use a squeeze bottle or a hose with running water to clean the wound. If these methods are unavailable, use gauze. Rubbing and swabbing wounds cause further tissue damage, so just press gauze on dirt to remove it. Do not use cotton, because pieces of it will remain in the wound. Peroxide, irritating disinfectants, or other cleaning agents cause further tissue damage and slow healing. The hair should be clipped or shaved from the edges of the wound, but this can be delayed until the veterinarian arrives.

The third step is to immobilize the wound to prevent further damage. Hold the horse at halter or place it in a box stall. Keep it from chewing the wound or the bandages. A neck cradle prevents chewing of most wounds. Cayenne pepper or hot-pepper sauce applied to a bandage discourages the horse from chewing it.

If the wound must be sutured, the veterinarian should do so within 12 to 24 hours for best results. The quicker the veterinarian arrives, the better the chances of successful suturing.

The fourth step is to prevent infection. The procedure should be under the supervision of a veterinarian. Systemic antibiotics may be necessary, or a nonirritating wound dressing may be used (Table 9-1). Clean and treat minor skin wounds with nitrofurazone.

The fifth step is to bandage the wound to protect it from dirt or other irritation. The bandage may help decrease movement of the wound and allow a

TABLE 9-1   First Aid Treatments

Wounds and injuries	Medication and treatment recommended	Medication not to use
Minor scrapes or abrasions	Vaseline, Corona, or Topazone spray	
Minor skin scratches	Furacin solution or Topazone	
Rope burn Superficial	Furacin solution or powder, or Topazone	
Deep[a]	Furacin or Dermafur salve and bandage	Astringents or caustics
Small skin wound, left open	Furacin solution or powder or Topazone	Astringents or caustics
Large skin wound, to be sutured[a]	Furacin or Dermafur under bandage	Astringents or caustics
Large skin wound, left open[a]	Furacin powder or Topazone spray	Astringents or caustics
Jagged skin wound, to be sutured[a]	Furacin or Dermafur salve and bandage	Astringents or caustics
	Furacin solution or powder if not able to bandage	
Jagged, deep muscle wound, to be sutured[a]	Furacin or Dermafur salve and bandage	Astringents or caustics
	Furacin solution or powder if not able to bandage	
Deep open wound, over 48 hrs old[a]	Furacin powder or Topazone	Astringents or caustics
Open wound Healed to skin level	Furacin powder or Topazone	Astringents or caustics
With proud flesh[a]	Tissue should be trimmed flat; caustic powder	Tissue stimulants
Puncture wound In soft tissues	Furacin solution or powder	Astringents or caustics
In hoof	Kopertox or tincture of iodine or Betadine	Caustics
Minor wound to hoof coronary band	Kopertox or Topazone	Caustics
Minor sprain or swollen leg	Cold water or ice and supportive bandage-aspirin twice daily in grain (50–60 g/1,000 lb, or 50–60 g/454 kg)	Heat applications, such as liniments, sweats, leg paints, or blisters

[a] Wound should be under the care of a veterinarian.
SOURCE: Naviaux (1974).

faster healing process. However, bandaging is dangerous unless done properly. An improperly applied bandage aggravates the original damage or creates serious new problems. Bandaging is a basic skill that requires practice, and all horsepeople should be familiar with the process (see the next section).

The final step is to prevent tetanus by immunization. If the horse has not been immunized, tetanus antitoxin should be administered. A tetanus toxoid booster may be given if it has been 8 to 12 months since the last toxoid booster or since the two tetanus toxoid vaccinations.

Bandaging

When bandaging a leg, apply the medication and cover it with a nonstick surgical pad. Telfa or Adaptic squares are excellent. Hold the pad in place with a primary wrap such as kling gauze. Always apply padding over the primary wrap to permit even pressure without hindering circulation. There are many different commercial padding materials. Rolled cotton, quilted leg wraps, and baby diapers are excellent. The final wrap is used to hold up the padding, and can be an adhesive and elastic-type bandage or a nonelastic, nonadhesive bandage. Vetrap and Ace bandages are elastic, and the traditional track bandages are nonelastic.

The proper way to wrap an injured foreleg below the knee or hock is shown in Figure 9-3. Before starting the leg wrap, lay out all materials within easy reach. Apply medication to the nonsurgical sterile pad used to cover the wound. Hold the pad in position by wrapping the leg with kling gauze, which is very elastic and does not restrict blood circulation. Stretch the kling gauze just enough to hold the pad in place. Start the wrap about 3 to 4 inches (7.6 to 10.2 cm) above the wound and extend it 3 to 4 inches below the wound. Each wrap overlaps the previous wrap about one-half the width of the gauze. Do not tie the primary wrap off; leave the end free. Apply the padding to the leg, placing the edge of the padding on the side of the leg to start the wrap and also finishing on the side. Starting on the front of the cannon bone or on the tendons can cause injury. Padding should be $\frac{1}{2}$ to 1 inch thick (1.27 to 2.54 cm). After the padding is on, apply the final wrap by starting just below (1 inch) the upper edge of the padding and wrapping downward to within 1 inch of the lower edge. Wrap the leg upward again and then finish by taking a couple of wraps downward. When making the wraps, keep the pressure uniform and use an even overlap.

Wounds on the forearms of horses are difficult to bandage (Figure 9-4). The bandage is easy to apply but it easily slips off because the forearm tapers. Apply two or three long strips of adhesive tape vertically to the horse's leg so that the ends extend below the knee. Put the Telfa pad with medication over the wound and wrap it with kling gauze. Sheet cotton can be wrapped around the leg. Apply an elastic wrap plied over the cotton and incorporate the ends of the tape into the elastic wrap. Pressure from the bandage holds the tape to the horse's leg, which helps hold up the bandage.

FIGURE 9-3   Bandaging a leg below the knee or hock: *(a)* injured leg ready for routine dressing; *(b)* applying medicated covering and primary wrap together (note hand position); *(c)* progressive turns of the primary wrap spiraling downward; *(d)* turning back up the leg, well below the injury; *(e)* upper limit of the primary wrap, well above the injury; *(f)* finished primary wrap; *(g)* applying padding to relieve tension; *(h)* end of padding carefully smoothed for finishing off; *(i)* securing end of the self-adherent stretch bandage with a second turn; *(j)* successive turns of final spiraling downward; *(k)* all the way up and back to the center, unrolling final turn for application without tension; *(l)* pressing final wrap so that it adheres to itself. (From *Equus Magazine.* Copyright © 1978. Gaithersburg, MD 20760.)

FIGURE 9-4   Bandaging the foreleg: *(a)* wound is ready for dressing; *(b)* apply adhesive tape; *(c)* apply medicated pad and wrap with primary wrapping; *(d)* wrap cotton around leg; *(e)* apply elastic wrap. (From *Equus Magazine.* Copyright © 1978. Gaithersburg, MD 20760.)

Bandages over the knee and hock joints are more difficult to apply. The same principles as the simple leg wrap apply; however, be very careful not to place pressure where bony prominences are situated just under the skin. Otherwise, the skin will be damaged.

The proper way to wrap the knee is shown in Figure 9-5 and to wrap the hock in Figure 9-6. Start the knee wrap by placing the medicated surgical pad on the wound and taking two or three wraps above the knee with kling gauze, continuing in a figure-eight pattern until about a dozen wraps around the knee are completed. Then apply a final adhesive elastic wrap. Start the final bandage by spraying tincture of benzoin on the hair above the knee to aid in sticking the adhesive wrap to the skin. At 6 to 8 inches (15.2 to 20.3 cm) above the primary wrap, start the elastic final wrap and take two wraps around the leg. Use moderate tension as you start wrapping downward. As you continue wrapping down the knee, do not cover the bony prominences on the inside and at the back of the knee. Continue wrapping until you have applied four layers of final bandage. Apply the last two wraps without tension so the adhesive will stick and not come loose.

FIGURE 9-5   Bandaging the knee. The steps are shown in succession; see text explanation. (From *Equus Magazine.* Copyright © 1978. Gaithersburg, MD 20760.)

When bandaging the hock (Figure 9-6), do not cover the point of the hock and the bony protrusion on the inside of the leg right above the hock. Start the primary wrap above the hock and take a couple of wraps. Start wrapping downward by dropping below the point of the hock. About two layers of primary wrap are sufficient. After spraying the area above the primary wrap with tincture of benzoin, start the final bandage about 6 to 8 inches (15.2 to 20.3 cm) above the primary wrap. Spiral the wrap downward, and do not use tension over the Achilles tendon. After about three wraps, place two soft rolls of gauze or toweling on each side of the Achilles tendon so that they fill up the holes just above the point of the hock. The rolls should avoid tension being placed on the Achilles tendon. Continue by covering the rolls, spiraling

FIGURE 9-6   Bandaging the hock. The steps are shown in succession; see text explanation. (From *Equus Magazine*. Copyright © 1978. Gaithersburg, MD 20760.)

downward and then back up to the top. A couple of wraps with electrician's tape will hold the loose end of the bandage.

Three other types of bandages are used. The shipping bandage protects a horse from leg injury during transport and provides support to prevent excess strain and "stocking up." Exercise bandages are used for support while the horse is being worked. Stable bandages are also used for support.

Apply the exercise bandage in almost the same way as the bandage for an injury to the leg above the fetlock and below the knee or hock. The medicated pad and primary wrap are not used. Because less padding is necessary, the proper tension applied to the wrap is critical to prevent injury. Extend a stable bandage down just below the fetlock. Start a shipping bandage below the knee or hock and cover the rest of the lower leg, including the bulbs of the heel. Before using stable, exercise, or shipping bandages, rub a leg brace, consisting of 50 percent veterinary absorbine and 50 percent alcohol, on the legs to stimulate circulation.

Healing

As cuts and tears heal, proud flesh may develop. This is granulation tissue formed to fill in the wound space. The excess granulation tissue bulges above the skin surface and inhibits the growth of the edges of skin, so the wound heals slowly. Proud flesh can be removed by surgery or by caustic chemicals like silver nitrate or copper sulfate. Use caustic chemicals with caution.

Punctures, Burns, and Abrasions

Puncture wounds are caused by sharp, protruding objects and are usually deep and penetrating. They should be attended by a veterinarian because of the danger of tetanus. If necessary, treat them by stopping the bleeding and then irrigating with hydrogen peroxide. Normally, the next treatment step is to clip the hair around the area and to make sure the wound can drain. Routine care during healing consists of daily cleansing and irrigation with hydrogen peroxide. Nail punctures in the foot need veterinary attention. The veterinarian may enlarge the hole to provide drainage and fill the hole with iodine. Bandage the foot to keep it clean.

Burns are treated with tannic acid jelly. If the burn must be cleaned before the veterinarian arrives, use gauze soaked in saline solution: 1 teaspoon (4.9 ml) table salt per pint (0.47 liter) of water.

Abrasions can be treated with a coating of Vaseline if only the hair has been rubbed off. If some bleeding and oozing of serum occurs, wash the abrasion with an antiseptic solution, and apply nitrofurazone. Treat minor rope burns as abrasions, but deep rope burns need attention by a veterinarian.

Wound Treatment—"Don'ts"

There are some "don'ts" for wound treatment as discussed by J. L. Naviaux (1974):

1 *Don't* apply any astringent or caustic, such as gentian violet, tincture of iodine, copper sulfate, or alum, to any fresh wound more severe than a superficial scrape, abrasion, or scratch.

2 *Don't* apply *any* medicine to a wound that will need to be sutured unless it is recommended by your veterinarian to be used as a first

aid until he or she arrives. Washing it with a mild soap and water is safe. Peroxide can irritate the tissues and should not be used in a wound to be sutured.

3   *Don't* apply a salve, such as Vaseline, corona, or nitrofurazone, to any open deep wound, because salve accumulates dirt and debris.

4   *Don't* wash a wound frequently with water, peroxide, or any liquid as this slows healing and stimulates growth of proud flesh.

5   *Don't* wrap a leg without good padding under the bandage, because an unpadded bandage can cut into the leg and/or restrict blood circulation. This is especially true for young foals.

6   *Don't* leave a stretch bandage on for more than 24 hours. Daily removal is necessary to ensure proper circulation.

7   *Don't* use sugar or salt water in the eyes. Fresh water or boric acid rinses are safe.

Other Emergency Situations

In addition to wounds, other situations require first aid.

Electric Shock

A horse found dead in the pasture may have been killed by electric shocks or lightning. The teeth are usually tightly clenched, and there is rectal bleeding. The mouth may be full of fresh feed. If still alive, the horse may be in shock, unconscious, or dazed. A weak pulse and convulsions are typical, and veterinary treatment is indicated. Survivors frequently have impaired vision, bad coordination, or paralysis. Full recovery may take months.

Eye Injuries

Failure to treat eye injuries can lead to permanent damage and blindness. Wash the eye with clear water in a squeeze bottle or syringe to remove dirt and debris. Foreign bodies that will not wash out but are not imbedded in the eye can be removed with a wet, cotton-tipped applicator. If the eyeball has been penetrated, keep the horse in a clean, dust-free stall until a veterinarian arrives. Any eye inflammation needs veterinary diagnosis and treatment.

Bruises

Bruises are common injuries, because horses frequently kick each other. As soon as a bruise occurs, treat it with cold packs or cold water from a hose. If blood vessels are damaged, a hematoma ("blood blister") will form under the skin. After a day or two, the hematoma can be treated with hot packs and massaged with witch hazel. After a couple of weeks, a veterinarian may drain it. It usually takes 1 to 2 months for the hematoma to disappear. Large hematomas need the care of a veterinarian.

Sprains and Strains

Sprains and strains result when a muscle has been pulled or twisted. There may be a partial rupture of the ligaments and tendons. These injuries need immediate medical attention by a veterinarian. Rest the horse and restrict its movement until it is treated.

Saddle Sores

Saddle sores are frequently encountered when horsepeople use poorly designed and poorly fitted saddles or when insufficient padding is used under the saddle. Minor saddle sores are swollen, tender areas. First aid is rest and cold water or ice packs to reduce swelling. If the area is raw, zinc oxide salve or gentian violet may be helpful. Continued use of the horse under similar conditions can lead to large open wounds, requiring a veterinarian's help. They can be treated with nitrofurazone. If a saddle sore develops on a trail ride or camping trip, cut a hole in a sponge saddle pad to prevent continued damage to the tissue.

Heat Stroke

In hot, humid weather, horses may suffer heat stroke when being exercised. The symptoms are rapid breathing, weakness, dry skin, and no sweating. First aid consists of immediately lowering the body temperature. Place the horse in a cool place and spray with cold water. In extreme cases, use ice packs and place ice in the rectum. It may be necessary for a veterinarian to restore lost body fluids.

Severe Chilling

Horses are very tolerant of extreme cold, but young foals can become chilled. They should be placed under heat lamps and can be given a warm water enema.

Snake Bites

In some areas, snakes frequently bite horses on the head, neck, and other body parts. The only first aid treatment is to make sure that the swelling does not obstruct the airways. It may be necessary to pass a rubber hose down the trachea. All snake bites should be attended by a veterinarian, but almost all horses survive even if left untreated.

Fractures

All fractures are serious, but many can be repaired with sophisticated surgical techniques and equipment. It is important that the fracture not be made worse than it is. Do not move the horse, and call a veterinarian to make a temporary splint before moving the horse to a veterinary hospital. Successful treatment usually depends on immediate and continued immobilization during healing. Fractures in the pastern area always have a poor prognosis even though the area can be immobilized, because large calcium deposits usually develop and cause lameness. Fractures in heavily muscled areas are very difficult or impossible to immobilize. Euthanasia is often recommended for horses suffering such fractures.

If a veterinarian cannot arrive in a few minutes, immobilize the leg fracture with a pillow. Wrap the pillow around the leg as tightly as possible and wrap it tightly with bandages. Place two sticks along the leg and wrap them tightly to give extra stiffness. If the splints are properly applied, the horse can then be moved to a veterinary hospital.

Lameness

First aid for the acutely lame horse with injured and inflamed tissue must be given before the veterinarian arrives. Applying cold is an accepted means of first aid, because it reduces pain, swelling, hemorrhage, and inflammation. Cold constricts the blood vessels, which in turn reduces blood flow to the area. Use cold treatment as soon as possible and only during the first 24 to 48 hours after an injury. There are several ways to apply cold, such as running water from a hose, ice packs, or standing the horse in a cool stream or a bucket of cold water. Apply cold for 20 to 30 minutes and then allow an hour before starting another treatment. If the treatments are too long or too often, the opposite effect is obtained—pain, swelling, and inflammation increase.

Heat is used to increase the blood supply to an area by dilating blood vessels and increasing their permeability. If infection is present, do not use heat because it allows the infection to enter the bloodstream and spread to other parts of the body. Heat can be applied with a heat lamp, warm water, a hot water bottle, liniments, and poultices. Heat is usually applied on the advice of a veterinarian.

Massage also increases blood flow and reduces tissue swelling. Increased blood flow pulls excess fluid in the tissue into the bloodstream, which carries it away. Soaking the injury in an epsom salts solution (2 cups epsom salts per gallon of water) draws the excess tissue fluid out of the tissue and reduces swelling. Poultices work on a similar principle and effectively draw fluid out of puncture wounds.

Older injuries require different treatment. A common treatment is the use of a counterirritant. Its purpose is to convert an old chronic injury into an active form to begin an active healing process. There are several types of counterirritants that vary in strength. Braces (such as Absorbine) are mild forms and are usually used after a workout. They produce mild heat. Tighteners are a little stronger than braces but are still mild counterirritants. These drug mixtures reduce fluid filling in a joint or tendon sheath and are used after hard workouts to reduce swelling of the lower legs. Tighteners are applied with a massage—which may be the most beneficial part of the treatment. Liniments are mixtures of drugs that increase blood flow to an area by producing mild heat. There are many types of liniments, and the advice of a veterinarian is helpful in choosing one. Sweats cause an accumulation of moisture on the skin. Wrapping the area with plastic after applying the sweat increases its effectiveness. Sweats should never be used without the advice of a veterinarian. Blisters and leg paints produce a profound counterirritation. They are used for bowed tendons and chronic bone unsoundnesses. Their effectiveness is debated among veterinarians because the effect may be limited to the skin. Firing is another means of producing counterirritation; it involves piercing various parts of the horse's leg with a red-hot iron or needles, and may be used on splints, bowed tendons, osselets, ring bone, and sesamoiditis. Some people feel that the rest following the treatment is the most beneficial aspect of many treatments.

Drugs are also used for therapy. Some antiinflammatory drugs are useful while others only serve to mask a lameness. Masking a lameness usually leads to more serious consequences that could have been avoided by resting the horse.

DENTAL CARE

Proper dental care for the horse is a necessary part of the grooming and health care program. Bad teeth or other dental problems result in poor mastication (chewing), which may cause colic. Some horses with painful dental problems may refuse to eat and will rapidly lose body weight. You can recognize problems in the early stages of development, because the horse may tend to wallow the feed around in its mouth before it swallows and a lot of feed may fall out of its mouth. There may also be clumps of hay in the horse's mouth a couple of hours after it has eaten.

The teeth of young horses grow about twice as fast as those of mature horses until the horse is about 5 years old. Therefore, the teeth of young horses should be examined every 6 months. The teeth of mature horses should be examined at least yearly. Examine the teeth by opening the mouth and pulling the tongue out to one side. With a flashlight, examine the incisors and the molars on that side. Then pull the tongue to the other side of the mouth to see the remaining molars. Some horses resist the procedure; use a mouth speculum (Figure 9-7) to examine their teeth (but avoid being hit if the horse swings its head).

FIGURE 9-7   Equipment needed to float the teeth: *(a)* mouth speculum; *(b)* floats; *(c)* bucket of warm, soapy water. A flashlight is also helpful for examining teeth. (Photo by W. Evans.)

One of the most common dental problems is "hooks," or sharp edges on the molars that develop because the upper and lower molars do not meet evenly (Figure 9-8). The upper molars are set slightly wider than the lower molars. The horse chews in a circular grinding motion, which causes the inside edges of the upper molars and outer edges of the lower molars to wear off at a faster rate than the rest of the top surface. Sharp edges develop on the outside edge of the upper and the inside edge of the lower molars. Hooks can cause mouth sores by striking the opposite gums and can cut the cheek or tongue. A horse with a sore mouth eats poorly. Remove the sharp edges with a special rasp called a float (Figure 9-7). Floating is an easily learned process. The supplies needed are floats, mouth speculum, flashlight, and a bucket of warm, soapy water. When floating teeth, take care not to hit the gums or the back of the jaw. This hurts the horse, which will flinch and pull away. Floats of various shapes are made for upper and lower jaws and have a fine and coarse side. The fine side is used for the final dressing. Use warm, soapy water to keep the floats warm and clean.

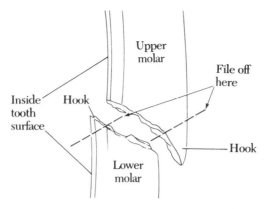

FIGURE 9-8   View of upper and lower molars in need of floating, looking at the left jaw toward the rear of the horse's mouth.

Wolf teeth are small teeth located in front of the premolars. There may be one to four wolf teeth in the horse's mouth. Normally, only the upper wolf teeth erupt. If not removed, they can cause dental problems. A bit hitting the wolf teeth can be very painful to the horse. A horse with sore wolf teeth may carry its head to one side to escape pressure from the bit. If a wolf tooth is broken off, a chronic sore may develop, and it is almost impossible to use a bit until the problem is corrected. The lower wolf teeth usually do not erupt, but the bulge they make can bruise and become sore.

Wolf teeth are poorly developed and can be removed easily. However, those broken off below the gum margin can be difficult to pull out. The upper wolf teeth are lost at 5 to 6 months of age, but all young horses' mouths should be examined for wolf teeth before training. Older horses that sling their heads or carry them off to one side when wearing a bridle should be examined for wolf teeth or a broken wolf tooth.

The canine teeth of older horses may grow too long and strike the opposite gum, causing sores. A veterinarian can clip them to correct the problem. Sharp edges that develop can be dressed with a float.

The tooth opposite a tooth lost by accident or surgery can hinder chewing. Because it is not worn off by an opposed tooth, it may become too long. Rasp the tooth off at about 6- to 12-month intervals to keep it from getting too long. A too-long tooth can be clipped off.

Temporary teeth that fail to fall out may cling to the gum when they are being replaced by permanent teeth. These so-called caps interfere with the horse's ability to chew. Until the horse is 5 years old, the molars must be checked every 6 months to make sure the caps fall out. If they do not, pull them off.

Molars may wear unevenly so that they do not meet and cannot grind properly. Affected teeth can be floated. Usually, the correction is made in two to three steps at 6-month intervals unless only a minor correction is required.

CHAPTER 10

Knowing About Parasites and Diseases

Two major concerns of horse owners are to keep the parasite infestation of their horses to a minimum and to keep their horses from getting common communicable diseases that can be prevented by immunization and a disease prevention program.

PARASITES

Parasites are small organisms that live on or in a host organism and derive their food from it. Parasites can be beneficial (such as symbiotic cecal bacteria) or detrimental to the horse. Our primary management concern is to control harmful parasites, which can lower efficiency, performance, and digestion and can even kill a horse.

The symptoms of parasitism may develop slowly and may not be recognized by the person who works with the horse every day. Typical symptoms are weakness, unthrifty appearance (poor body condition), emaciation, "potbelly" (large, distended abdomen), tucked-up flanks, rough hair coat, and slow growth. The horse may seem lazy and lose its desire to perform. Some symptoms of acute parasitism are colic, diarrhea, cough, and lameness. These symptoms are discussed for each parasite.

354

Two types of parasites infest horses—internal and external. Internal parasites spend part of their life cycle in their host; external parasites live on and/or derive their food from their host.

Internal Parasites

Many internal parasites affect horses, mules, and donkeys. From a management standpoint, they are generally classified as roundworms and insects with an internal stage of development. There are six groups of roundworms: Ascarids, small strongyles, large strongyles (bloodworms), threadworms, pinworms, and stomach worms. Insects that have an internal stage of development in the horse are stomach bots and cattle grubs. To minimize parasitism, the life cycle must be broken. An understanding of the life cycles can help you to make management decisions.

Ascarids

Commonly called large *roundworms,* Ascarids (*Parascaris equorum*) are among the largest parasites that live in horses. They grow 12 to 15 inches (30.5 to 38.1 cm) long and are about the diameter of a lead pencil. Ascarid infestation is primarily a problem in young horses, because older horses develop an immunity to them. The Ascarid life cycle (Figure 10-1) starts with mature female worms laying eggs in the digestive tract of the horse. The eggs pass out of the horse in the feces. After the eggs are outside the horse for about 2 weeks, they develop to an infective stage. The eggs are swallowed by the horse as it eats grass, feed, or feces, and drinks water. Once inside the horse, the eggs hatch into larvae. These larvae burrow into the wall of the small intestine and then enter the bloodstream, which carries them to the liver and heart. They migrate through the liver and heart to the veins that drain these organs and then travel to the lungs. They are coughed up from the lungs and swallowed. They reenter the digestive tract and mate, and the female produces eggs.

Ascarids damage the liver, heart, and lungs. In the bloodstream, they can block small capillaries and other blood vessels. Heavy infestations of mature worms can block the small intestine, causing colic. The intestine may rupture, causing peritonitis and death. Coughing due to lung migrations and accompanied by copious mucoid nasal secretion is a common clinical sign in infected foals. The usual clinical signs during heavy infestations which occur at about 10 to 12 weeks of age are a rough hair coat, poor appetite, and pot belly.

Ascarid eggs are very resistant to environmental conditions and can live for years before being eaten by a horse. Therefore, paddocks, stalls, and pastures easily become very contaminated with eggs.

Managerial control of Ascarids requires clean stalls for foaling, preventing fecal contamination of feed and water troughs, frequent manure removal from paddocks, proper manure disposal, and frequent treatments with

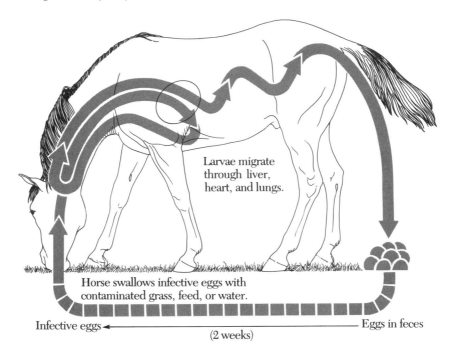

Larvae migrate
through liver,
heart, and lungs.

Horse swallows infective eggs with
contaminated grass, feed, or water.

Infective eggs ←——————————————————— Eggs in feces
(2 weeks)

FIGURE 10-1   Cycle of infection by large roundworms.

anthelmentics (deworming chemicals). The primary objective is to keep the environment relatively free from egg contamination. This is critical, because once the infective egg is swallowed, the larvae travel their migratory route before they return to the digestive tract and can be killed by drugs (deworming medicines). Deworming the foal at 2-month intervals beginning at 2 months of age keeps the number of mature worm females and the number of eggs passed in the feces to a minimum. It also allows the foal to build up an immunity to them. If the foal has a heavy infestation, it is advisable to deworm with a partial dose so that not all the worms are killed at one time and block the intestine.

Older horses usually develop a resistance to Ascarids by the time they are 4 to 5 years old. The continuous feeding of one of the deworming medicines will control the infestation in young horses, but it may be a disadvantage when the horse matures. It will not have developed the natural immunity to them.

Strongyles

Of the many parasites affecting horses, the most serious threat to the horse's health is the strongyle. Approximately 54 species of strongyles (either large or small) infest horses. Three species of large strongyles (*Strongyloidae*, *Strongylus equinus* and *Strongylus vulgaris*) do the most harm to horses. The small strongyles (cyathostominae) are much less pathogenic. Severe infestations of both types are common in horses grazed on permanent pasture.

Symptoms of severe infestation are grouped under the condition known as *strongylosis* and include low appetite, anemia, emaciation, rough hair coat, sunken eyes, digestive disturbances, and "tucked up" appearance. Sometimes the horses have posterior incoordination.

The life cycle (Figure 10-2) of this parasite has some unique, important features. The eggs are laid by adult worms in the intestine. They pass out in the feces and hatch into larvae in 1 to 2 days. Larvae feed on manure and continue to develop. After about a week, the larvae become infective, move up on the blades of grass, and the horse eats them. Once inside the horse, they migrate to various organs and tissues where they do extensive damage. After the young adult worms return to the small intestine, they attach themselves to the gut wall, feed on the gut lining, reach maturity, and lay eggs. The life cycle of the small strongyle is different from that of the large strongyle in that the larvae penetrate the large intestine and become encysted. After 1 or 2 months, the larvae emerge and return to the lumen where they mature. Simultaneous emergence of large numbers can cause the symptoms described above. Normally, they are not a problem when low numbers energe.

Large strongyles cause arterial damage and the development of small blood clots in the arteries. After the artery becomes damaged, aneurisms develop and can burst. When the aneurism bursts, the horse bleeds internally and dies. Blood clots may break loose and become lodged in smaller arteries,

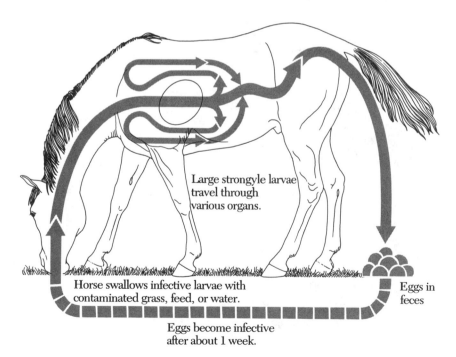

Large strongyle larvae travel through various organs.

Horse swallows infective larvae with contaminated grass, feed, or water.

Eggs in feces

Eggs become infective after about 1 week.

FIGURE 10-2   Cycle of infection by large strongyles or bloodworms.

blocking the blood supply to a particular organ or tissue. Frequently, the blood supply to parts of the digestive tract is blocked, leading to colic and necrosis of the affected part. When the blood supply to muscle groups is partially blocked, the horse may become lame.

Strongyle control is based on the life cycle. The larvae become infective after about 1 week outside the horse, so manure must be removed at least weekly and preferably twice weekly. Outside, infective strongyle larvae are not as resistant to the environment as Ascarid eggs and usually cannot live beyond 1 year, so pasture rotation or resting the pasture for a year helps control them. Grazing the pasture with cattle or sheep, which are not harmed by them, also helps remove the larvae. Routine deworming with appropriate drugs must be used to keep larval numbers to a minimum and to minimize damage to the intestinal mucosa.

Pinworms

Pinworms do not cause much damage to the horse and their life cycle is simple (Figure 10-3). The mature worms live in the colon of the large intestine. One quite small species, *P. vivipara*, completes its entire cycle in the host. The species *Oxyuris equi* is much larger—up to 3 inches long (7.6 cm). The eggs of *O. equi* are laid in the large colon and pass out in the feces, or the female worm may crawl out the anus and deposit the eggs on the skin around the

Horse swallows eggs mixed with grass, feed, and water.

FIGURE 10-3   Cycle of infection by pinworms.

anus. This causes an itching sensation, so the horse rubs its tail on fences, stall walls, posts, and so on. The eggs are quite sticky and yellow in color. They stick to stall walls, feed mangers, buckets, and other equipment. Therefore, the environment becomes contaminated with eggs and increases the opportunities for reinfestation through water and feed. Pinworms are controlled by manure removal and medication. To avoid egg contamination, cloths or sponges used to clean the perianal region should not be used to clean the mouth and nostrils of the horse.

Threadworms

Foals are particularly susceptible to threadworms (*Strongyloides westeri*). The infestation can become severe in a short time, because the life cycle can be completed within 2 weeks. Infestation occurs from the dam's milk as early as 4 days after foaling and from penetration of the skin by larvae in the bedding. Control requires daily removal of feces from the stall and keeping mares relatively free of parasites.

Threadworms are one cause of "foal heat scours" in the young foal. Heavy infestations occur at about $1\frac{1}{2}$ to 2 weeks and last for about 10 weeks; lighter infestations last another 20 to 30 weeks. They usually disappear at about 6 months of age when the foal acquires an immunity to them. Their life cycle is complicated in that it can follow one of two pathways. Larvae can come from parthenogenesis or from mating of free living forms. Because of the 2-week life cycle, large infestations occur very rapidly.

Onchocerca

Commonly called neck threadworms (*Onchocerca cervicalis*), they are a common parasite in horses. The adults live in the connective tissues and release microfilaria, a larval form, into the blood. These larvae concentrate at the skin and are transmitted to other horses by biting flies. Severe infestations cause allergic reaction in the skin, usually along the ventral midline, shoulders, and face. Symptoms include hair loss, redness, ulcers, and scabs. When treated with ivermectin, the only deworming medicine that kills them, the condition temporarily increases because treatment kills microfilaria, causing an enhanced reaction. Adults continue to live for several years so only the buildup of microfilaria is controlled.

Stomach Worms

Stomach worms (*Habronema muscae* and *Draschia megastoma*) attach themselves to the stomach wall or they may be free. Their life cycle (Figure 10-4) must be taken into account for management practices. The eggs are laid in the stomach and pass out in the feces. The maggots of flies that breed in horse

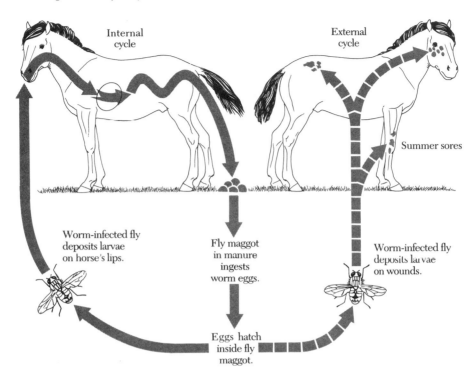

Internal cycle

External cycle

Summer sores

Worm-infected fly deposits larvae on horse's lips.

Fly maggot in manure ingests worm eggs.

Worm-infected fly deposits larvae on wounds.

Eggs hatch inside fly maggot.

FIGURE 10-4   Cycle of infection by stomach worms as internal and external parasites.

manure eat the eggs. The worm egg hatches and stays inside the fly maggot until an adult fly is formed. The larva leaves the fly when it is feeding around the liquid secretions of the horse's lips. The larvae are swallowed and go to the stomach, where they mature and lay eggs. They can cause stomach inflammations and colic. Controlling stomach worms requires manure removal, fly control, and deworming medication.

Stomach worms (*Habronema muscae*) are responsible for a condition known as "summer sores." When the fly is feeding around the edges of a wound, the larvae leave it and enter the wound but are unable to complete their life cycle. Therefore, they remain as larvae for 6 to 24 months. The sore becomes a granulomatous mass and is very difficult to heal. Chronic sores that fit this description should be treated by a veterinarian. The treatment of choice for larvae and adult worms is ivermectin.

Stomach Bots

Three species of bots, or botflies, affect horses (see Figure 10-5). Parts of their life cycle are similar in each species and others are different. The adult botfly resembles a bee. They do not feed and are an energy-consuming stage

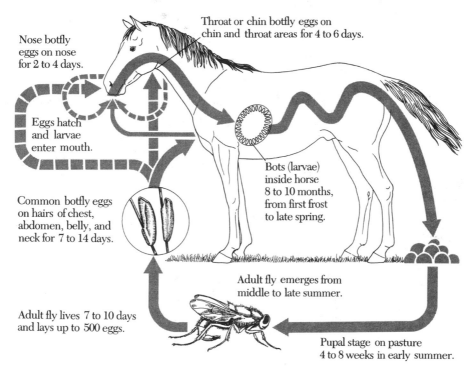

Nose botfly eggs on nose for 2 to 4 days.

Throat or chin botfly eggs on chin and throat areas for 4 to 6 days.

Eggs hatch and larvae enter mouth.

Bots (larvae) inside horse 8 to 10 months, from first frost to late spring.

Common botfly eggs on hairs of chest, abdomen, belly, and neck for 7 to 14 days.

Adult fly emerges from middle to late summer.

Adult fly lives 7 to 10 days and lays up to 500 eggs.

Pupal stage on pasture 4 to 8 weeks in early summer.

FIGURE 10-5   Life cycle of horse botflies.

of the life cycle. Botflies are active from the first part of the summer until the first hard frost in winter.

Common botflies, *Gasterophilus intestinalis,* start their life cycle by laying eggs on the hairs of the horse's legs, chest, belly, and neck. Eggs on the hair are yellow and can be easily seen. About 1 to 2 weeks after they are laid, the eggs can hatch, but only when exposed to moisture, warmth, and friction. These conditions are created when the horse licks the area; when the eggs are licked, they immediately hatch and enter the mouth, burrow into the tongue, and are eventually swallowed. Inside the stomach, they grow to maturity attached to the stomach lining. On maturity, they detach themselves from the stomach and pass through the digestive tract and out the anus. During the movement, they change to a pupal stage. Once outside, they burrow into the ground. Adult flies develop in the pupal casts and emerge during warm weather. Therefore, the cycle takes 1 year.

The throat or chin botfly, *G. nasalis,* has a different life cycle from the common botfly in that the eggs are laid around the chin and throat. Their eggs incubate in 4 to 6 days and hatch without any stimulation. The larvae then crawl inside the mouth and enter the gum tissue around the teeth. They leave the mouth and enter the stomach and first part of the small intestine. The remainder of the cycle is similar to the common botfly.

The third botfly is the nose botfly, *G. hemorrhoidalis*. It lays black eggs in the area of the nostrils and lips. Eggs hatch in 2 to 4 days without stimulation and burrow into the inner lip membranes. After 5 to 6 weeks, they enter the stomach.

Bots cause stomach damage and can block the entrance into the small intestine, causing colic and rupture of the stomach. Most horses have a few bots, which will not cause problems. To control or prevent heavy infestations, the life cycle must be broken by killing the flies, removing the eggs, and deworming. Botflies may be killed by sprays, but it is difficult to control them this way. Once the eggs of the common botfly are laid, they can be removed from the hairs by scraping them with a knife or sandpaper. For effective control, they should be removed at least twice a week. If there are large numbers of common bot eggs on the horse, they can be induced to hatch by washing them with warm water (110° to 120°F, or 43.3 to 48.9°C) containing an insecticide. Washing the eggs once a week will hatch and immediately kill them. However, the empty yellow eggs will remain on the hairs. The horse should be treated with an anthelmintic (deworming) medication at least twice yearly and preferably four times a year. At the end of the botfly season, after the first hard frost, deworm the horse to remove internal bots. The frost should kill the botflies, and no new larvae should enter the horse. The second time to deworm the horse is in the spring, to kill any larvae that were in the tissues at the previous treatment and to prevent any live pupae from passing out in the feces. For more effective control, deworm the horse two more times, during the middle of the winter and summer.

Tapeworms

Tapeworms, *Anoplocephala perfoliata*, *Anoplocephala magna*, and *Paranoplocephala mamillana*, infest horses, but the horse normally does not show clinical symptoms. The frequency of infestation is usually quite low, but some local areas have a high rate of infestation.

The life cycle begins with terminal tapeworm segments detaching and passing out in the feces. Upon drying, the segments burst and release the eggs. Oribatid mites ingest the eggs and the mites are ingested during grazing. The mite continues to be the host until the infective cysticercoids mature at 2 to 4 months. Maturity of the parasite is reached after several months. Adult tapeworms are primarily confined to the cecum and may form clusters that are attached around the ileocecal valve.

No specific dewormer has been approved by the Food and Drug Administration for treatment of equine tapeworm infestations. However, scientific studies have demonstrated that infestations can be controlled by administration of pyrantel pamoate at a dosage of 13.2 mg/kg body weight or 2.64 mg/kg of pyrantel tartrate on a daily basis in the feed. They are effective at twice the normal dosage to control infestations with a single dose.

Cattle Grubs

The larvae of heel flies, which are cattle parasites, can also cause problems in horses. The flies lay their eggs on the lower extremities. Larvae hatch and enter the horse through the skin. After a long migratory period, they emerge on the back of cattle by cutting a hole in the skin. The horse is the wrong host, so they cannot complete their life cycle and thus appear as hard knots on the neck, back, and withers. If the grub is mashed, a sore will form that takes a long time to heal. Sometimes it is best to have a veterinarian remove the grub before it becomes a sore.

Lungworms

The lungworm, *Dictyocaulus arnfieldi*, occurs primarily in donkeys as the natural host and infestations are very common. The infestation rate in horses is very low, 2 to 3 percent, and usually occurs when horses are grazed with donkeys on the same pasture. Persistent coughing is the usual sign of a heavy infestation.

Controlling Internal Parasites

The main features of a parasite control are as follows: include all horses in the program; deworm all new horses upon arrival; regularly deworm mares prior to foaling; and periodically examine feces.

A number of management practices should be followed to control internal parasites, feed horses from mangers and troughs rather than from the ground. Prevent fecal contamination of feed and water. Water should be fresh and not from stagnant water holes.

Remove manure from stalls and paddocks at least weekly. If possible, twice weekly or daily removal is preferred. Scatter manure in pastures grazed by other species with a harrow to dry out the feces and expose eggs to the environment.

If pastures are used, temporary pastures that are plowed up or rotated yearly are preferred over permanent pastures. The more space that is available per horse, the less chance it will have to eat contaminated forage. Treat all horses with an anthelmintic before putting them at pasture.

Keep the general area clean and free from materials that encourage fly populations. Clean stalls daily to remove feces. This helps control flies. Compost the material removed from the stalls and all manure. The heat generated during composting kills the eggs and larvae. Regularly deworm all horses. Eight classes of dewormers have been developed (Table 10-1). Only one class of dewormer, avermectin, has been found to control all types of the common internal parasites consistently and safely in all classes of horses. Otherwise, a combination of dewormers is necessary. Generally, one of the organophosphates effective against bots is used in combination with one of the other

TABLE 10-1 A Guide to Dewormers

Product	Class	Active ingredient	Form	Stomach Worms	Intestinal threadworms	Onchocerca	Bots	Pinworms	Ascarids	Strongyles	Tapeworms	Lungworms
Equimectrin Paste	Avermectin	Ivermectin	paste	★	★	★	★	★	★	★		★
Rotectin 1 Paste	Avermectin	Ivermectin	paste	★	★	★	★	★	★	★		★
Zimectrin Paste	Avermectin	Ivermectin	paste	★	★	★	★	★	★	★		★
Eqvalan Liquid	Avermectin	Ivermectin	liquid	★	★	★	★	★	★	★		★
Eqvalan Paste	Avermectin	Ivermectin	paste	★	★	★	★	★	★	★		
Panacur Paste	Benzimidazole	Fenbendazole	paste					★	★	★		
Safe-Guard Paste 10%, 92 gm	Benzimidazole	Fenbendazole	paste					★	★	★		
Anthelcide EQ Equine Wormer Suspension	Benzimidazole	Oxibendazole	liquid				★	★	★	★		
Quest 2% Equine Oral Gel	Milbemycin	Moxidectin	paste	★			★	★	★	★		
Rotectin 2 Paste	Pyrimidine	Parantel Pamoate	paste					★	★	★	H	
Alfalfa Pellet Horse	Piperazine	Piperazine	pellet					★	★	★		
Benzelmin Paste	Benzimidazole	Oxfendazole	paste					★	★	★		
Benzelmin Suspension	Benzimidazole	Oxfendazole	liquid					★	★	★		
Equi-Phar Horse & Colt Wormer	Pyrimidine	Pyrantel Tartrate	pellet					★	★	★		
Horse Care Horse & Colt Wormer	Pyrimidine	Pyrantel Tartrate	pellet					★		★		

Product	Drug Class	Active Ingredient	Form									
Panacur Granules	Benzimidazole	Fenbendazole	granules			★	★	★				
Panacur Paste	Benzimidazole	Fenbendazole	paste			★	★	★				
Panacur Suspension	Benzimidazole	Fenbendazole	liquid			★	★	★				
Piperazine–17%	Piperazine	Piperazine	liquid			★	★	★				
Piperazine–34%	Piperazine	Piperazine	liquid			★	★	★				
Pip-Pop 320	Piperazine	Piperazine	liquid			★	★	★				
Purina Colt & Horse Wormer	Pyrimidine	Pyrantel Pamoate	pellet			★	★					
Safe-Guard Paste 10%, 25 gm	Benzimidazole	Fenbendazole	paste			★	★	★				
Strongid Paste	Pyrimidine	Pyrantel Pamoate	paste		H	★	★					
Strongid T	Pyrimidine	Pyrantel Pamoate	liquid		H	★	★					
Wonder Wormer for Horses	Piperazine	Piperazine	powder			★	★					
Anthelcide EQ Equine Wormer Paste	Benzimidazole	Oxibendazole	paste			★	★	★				
Strongid C	Pyrimidine	Pyrantel Tartrate	pellet			★	★					
Strongid C 2X	Pyrimidine	Pyrantel Tartrate	pellet			★	★	★				
Anthelban V	Pyrimidine	Pyrantel Pamoate	liquid			★	★	★	★			
Equi Aid CW	Pyrimidine	Pyrantel Tartrate	pellet			★	★	★				
Ivercide	Avermectin	Ivermectin	liquid		H	★	★	★		★		
Kaeco Horse and Colt Dewormer	Pyrimidine	Pyrantel Tartrate	pellet			★	★				★	
Manna Pro Foal and Horse Pellet Dewormer	Pyrimidine	Pyrantel Tartrate	pellet			★	★					
Phoenectin	Avermectin	Ivermectin	liquid	★		★	★	★				★

H = high doses are required and a veterinarian should be consulted before use.

compounds that are generally effective against the other common internal parasites. The efficacies of the commonly used dewormers are given in Table 10-1. Be careful when administering dewormers to young foals and pregnant mares. Some are safe and others are not.

New drugs are continually being produced, and you must be aware of their use and efficiency in killing internal parasites. There are several ways to deworm horses. A veterinarian can pass a stomach tube and administer a combination of drugs. This method is effective because the dose can be given quickly so that the concentration is sufficient to kill the worms. However, today, very seldom is it necessary to deworm a horse via a stomach tube since other methods are as effective and there is less chance of complications. Paste deworming is popular because of its effectiveness and ease of administration and because there is less chance of injury. The individual horse owner can obtain and administer the paste. Liquid ivermectin for horses is as effective and further reduces chance for injury when it is squirted in the back of the mouth. However, this route of administration has not been approved. Feed additives can be used, but palatability can be a problem. Some horses refuse to eat their feed containing the medicine.

Continual feeding of a deworming pellet containing pyrantel tartrate can be used to keep horses relatively parasite free except for bots and Onchocerca. This procedure is still controversial since two species of small stronglyes and one species of large stronglyes are unresponsive to pyrantel tartrate's action. Periodic deworming with another anthelmintic such as ivermectin is advised to get the broad spectrum of parasites.

A number of small strongyle species have developed resistance to benzimidazole compounds. Thus, one must be careful about the buildup of resistant populations to dewormers.

For large horse farms, it may not be economical to routinely deworm horses at predetermined intervals. Fecal examinations can be made and the horses treated when the average egg count indicates the need. Trained personnel are necessary to determine fecal egg counts, but the individual horse owner can check for strongyle eggs. The procedure is to put a fresh fecal ball in a quart jar. Place the jar, with a loose lid on top, in a dark room at room temperature for a week. Drops of condensed moisture should develop on the sides of the jar. If, on daily examination, the walls are dry, add 10 to 20 drops of water to the jar. At the end of a week, strongyle larvae will be visible with a hand lens in the moisture drops if the horse has the parasites. A heavy strongyle infestation will be evident because of the large numbers of the larvae, giving the inside of the jar a frosted appearance. With training by the local veterinarian, egg counts can be made by a horse owner (Figures 10-6 and 10-7). The sugar flotation test is easy to use. Weigh a piece of feces (about one-quarter of a fecal hall) and place it in 20 cubic centimeters of a solution of equal parts sugar and water. Stir the solution until the feces is in suspension. Strain the mixture through a piece of gauze or a tea strainer. Let the fluid portion sit for 15 minutes, and then put a few drops on a microscope slide for 15

FIGURE 10-6 Procedure of determining fecal egg count. (A) Components include *(a)* bottle of flotation media; *(b)* flotation screen for vial; *(c)* fecal scoop; *(d)* vial to mix feces and flotation fluid; *(e)* microscope slide; *(f)* fecal sample in zip lock bag; and *(g)* disposable sleeve for collecting fecal sample. (B) Two to three grams of feces are placed in vial that has been filled about half full with flotation media and mixed. (C) Flotation screen is pressed down to lock screen on the vial. Flotation media is added until a convex meniscus is formed on top of the screen cylinder. (D) A microscope slide is placed on top of the meniscus and allowed to stand for at least 15 minutes while ova float through the screen and adhere to microscope slide. The slide is gently removed and a cover slip is placed on it. Under low power magnification, ova are located with a microscope.

minutes. Count eggs with a microscope and a 100 or 200× lens with a 10× objective lens. Counts of over 1000 per gram of feces indicate that large numbers are being passed daily. The count should be around 50 or less under a good parasite control program. Commercial kits are available and are inexpensive to use (Figure 10-6).

  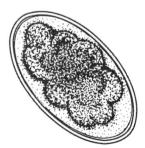

FIGURE 10-7 Strongyle eggs as viewed under microscope. For color images, see http://www.cvm.okstate.edu/~users/jcfox/htdocs/clinpara/lecture.htm and http://www.missouri.edu/~vmicro/byhost/equids.edu.

External Parasites

In addition to internal parasites, many external parasites also annoy or harm horses. Control of external parasites involves extermination on the horse and, at the same time, control in the surrounding environment. It is desirable to use products formulated to kill the external parasite by combining an insecticide and a growth-regulating chemical.

Ticks

Three kinds of ticks commonly infest horses. The winter tick is widely distributed in the northern and western states. Pacific Coast ticks are found primarily in coastal areas. Spinose ear ticks occur in the arid and semiarid regions of the West and Southwest. Horses grazed on pasture normally acquire heavy tick infestations. Frequently, the ticks go unnoticed on a horse with a long winter hair coat. The first visible symptoms are rubbing, itching, or biting of the affected areas. Ear ticks may cause drooping ears, head shaking, moist exudate, or excessive wax secretion from the ear.

Tick removal is important because heavy infestations of winter ticks can cause weakness, emaciation, loss of appetite, anemia, and a general state of poor health. Pacific Coast ticks transmit many diseases, such as Rocky Mountain spotted fever and Colorado tick fever. It only takes a few of these ticks to cause paralysis. Ticks transmit piroplasmosis and African horse fever.

Many insecticides are available for tick control (Table 10-2). The entire horse can be sprayed with either emulsifiable concentrates or wettable powders. An excitable horse can be sponged off. In 2 to 4 weeks, repeat the process. Single ticks can be removed by swabbing them with cotton soaked in alcohol or chloroform. Because ticks breathe through spiracles or holes on their abdomens, they are suffocated by the alcohol or chloroform.

Areas where horses are confined that become infested with ticks should be sprayed with insecticide. Surfaces such as the underparts of feed troughs, corral posts, stall walls, barn walls, and tree trunks should be carefully sprayed. Areas where horses congregate and stand, such as under shade trees or loafing sheds, should also be thoroughly sprayed.

Lice

Two kinds of lice infest horses: the sucking louse and the biting louse. Their life cycles are similar, but the sucking louse probably does more damage. Sucking lice can live only a few days after removal from their host. Their eggs—commonly called nits—are laid on the hair and are firmly attached to it. After 10 to 20 days, they hatch. The newly hatched nits reach sexual maturity and lay eggs when they are about 11 to 12 days old. Thus, their life cycle is 20 to 30 days. Infestation usually shows up in the winter, when the animals have long hair. Lice spread quite quickly by direct contact and through hair left in grooming equipment. The biting louse lives by feeding on the external layers

TABLE 10-2 Parasite Control for Horses (Nonfood Use)

Horn flies, stable flies (treat during warm months when abundant)
Lice (treat during fall and early winter, with repeated application in 10 to 14 days if necessary)

Chemical formulation and concentration			Application method	Amount	Remarks
Ciodrin®[a]	Aerosol	2%	Mist spray	Direct application	Apply to areas where flies congregate (head, neck, withers). Repeat as necessary.
Coumaphos (Co-Ral®)	WP[b]	25%	Hand wash or spray[c]	$\frac{1}{2}$ lb/25 gal water, or 226 gm/94.6 liters (0.06%)	Do not use in conjunction with internal medications, especially phenothiazine, natural or synthetic pyrethroids and their synergists, or with organic phosphates. Repeat as necessary. Apply to areas where flies congregate (hand, neck, chest, withers).
	EC	11.6%		$\frac{1}{2}$ qt/25 gal water, or 226 gm/94.6 liters (0.06%)	
Dichlorvos (Vapona®)	EC	20–24% (2 lb/gal)	Hand wash or mist water, spray	$\frac{1}{2}$ oz/1 qt or 14 gm/ 0.75 liter (0–5%), $\frac{1}{2}$ oz/animal	Apply to forehead, neck wither, or chest areas where flies congregate. Repeat as necessary.
Lindane[d]	WP[d]	25%	Hand wash or mist spray	4 oz/25 gal water, or 113 gm/94.6 liter (0.03%)	Do not treat overheated or sick animals.
Malathion	WP[b]	25%	Hand wash or spray	1 lb/25 gal water, or 454 gm/94.6 liters (0.12%)	Do not treat overheated or sick animals.
Methoxychlor	EC	5%	Hand wash or spray	1 pt/1 gal water, or 0.47 liter/3.78 liters (0.7%)	Do not treat overheated or sick animals.

(continued)

TABLE 10-2 Parasite Control for Horses (Nonfood Use) *(Continued)*

Horn flies, stable flies (treat during warm months when abundant)
Lice (treat during fall and early winter, with repeated application in 10 to 14 days if necessary)

Chemical formulation and concentration		Application method	Amount	Remarks
Pyrethrins + Synergist (Piperonyl butoxide)	EC	Hand wash or spray	0.1% +1%	Full strength	Do not treat overheated or sick animals.

Face flies[e] (treat during warm months when flies are abundant)

| Stirofos (Rabon®) | Smear | Wipe on | 1% | Direct application | Apply to areas where flies congregate (face area; under eyes, atop nostrils in line to forehead). Repeat as necessary. |
| Coumaphos (Co-Ral®) | Dust | Dust bags | 1% | Add 2 to 3 lb dust/bag (0.9 to 1.3 kg). Recharge as necessary. Do not allow more than 1 oz (28.4 gm)/ head-day use. | Coumaphos dust may be in dust bags made from narrow-gauge burlap sacks and grommeted at open end for hanging from a chain or board; placement depends on number of horses, size, and habits. In some instances dust transferred to homemade bags hung like punching bags may prove more effective. Also pour dust into sack and apply by hand. |

Screwworms (*treat when present*)

Ciodrinsa[a]	Aerosol	2%	Thoroughly mist spray wounds and surrounding area with not more than 2 oz (56.8 gm).	Direct application	Repeat once weekly until wound is healed.
Coumaphos (Co-Ral®)	Dust	5%	Thoroughly dust wounds and surrounding area.	Direct application	
Lindane[d]	EQ 335 smear		As directed on label	Direct application	
Romnel (Korlon®)	Spray	2.5%	Spray, dust, or smear	Spray, smear or dust into and around wounds. Use as directed.	
	Dust bottle	5%			
	Smear	5%			

Spinose ear tick (treat when abundant; may be present all seasons, particularly in spring and fall)

Ciodrin®[a]	Aerosol	2%	Mist spray or dust into ears as deeply as possible.		Repeat as necessary.
Coumaphos (Co-Ral®)	Dust	5%			
Romnel (Korlon®)	Smear	5%	Smear into and around ears. Use as directed.		Repeat as necessary.

(continued)

TABLE 10-2 Parasite Control for Horses (Nonfood Use) (*Continued*)

Chemical formulation and concentration		Application method	Amount	Remarks
Ticks (treat when abundant)				
Coumaphos (Co-Ral®)	WP[b] 25%	Hand wash or spray	1 lb/25 gal water or 454 gm/94.6 liter (0.12%)	See instructions given for horn flies.
	EC 11.6%		1 qt/25 gal water, or 0.75 liter/94.6 liters (0.12%)	
Lindane[d]	WP[d]	See instructions given for horn flies.		
Malathion	WP[b]			
Botfly eggs (on body, lips, and jaws of animals)				
Coumaphos (Corrals)	WP	See instructions given for horn flies. Hand wash using warm water.		Wipe body hair areas, lips, or jaw regions where botfly eggs are observed. Refer to remarks given for horn flies.
Lindane[d]	WP			
Malathion	WP			

[a] May be sold in combination with or without 0.25% dichlorvos (Vapona®) and/or pyrethrins + synergist.

[b] Wettable-powder formulations are preferred over emulsifiable-concentrate solutions because of certain solvents contained in EC formulations, which even upon dilution with water may cause hair damage and skin irritation to some horses.

[c] Hand washing or sponging may be more desirable than spray applications because some horses become excitable and difficult to control when sprayed.

[d] Restricted material. A permit is required to purchase, apply, and possess this material.

[e] These flies are extremely annoying to horses, congregating mainly on muzzles and eyes. They closely resemble the common house fly, which is more numerous on horses having access to pasture, open rangeland, or when in confined conditions (pens) when these are adjacent to pastured cattle. Animal sprays do not give satisfactory control of the face fly, and because the fly concentrates on the face, frequent use of face smears, or daily dust-bag use by horses offers more promise of satisfactory control.

SOURCE: Bushnell and others (1976).

Note: Formulas to Calculate Insecticide Dosages:

1. To prepare a spray of certain percentage strength from a wettable powder (WP), use

$$\frac{\text{gal spray needed} \times \% \text{ spray recommended} \times 8.3*}{\% \text{ of WP}} = \text{lb WP to add}$$

Example: 100 gal of 0.25% coumaphos is needed from a 25% WP package

$$\frac{100 \times 0.25\% \times 8.3}{2} = \text{lb to add}$$

2. To prepare a spray of certain percentage strength from an emulsifiable concentrate (EC) use

$$\frac{\text{gal spray needed} \times \% \text{ spray recommended} \times 8.39}{\text{lb active ingredient-gal in EC} \times 100} = \text{gal EC to add}$$

Example: 100 gal of 0.06% coumaphos is needed from a 11.6% EC can (1 lb active ingredient/gal);

$$\frac{100 \times 0.06 \times 8.3}{1 \times 100} = 0.49 \text{ gal} = 2 \text{ qt to add}$$

Various emulsifiable concentrates usually contain the following lb active ingredient/gal:

Less than 20	= 1 lb
21–25	= 2 lb
40–45	= 4 lb
50–57	= 5 lb
58–67	= 6 lb
72–80	= 8 lb

(There are exceptions to this, so be sure to read the insecticide label.)

*8.3 = density in lb/gal for water. If mixing insecticide in #2 fuel oil for backrubber, use 7.3.

of skin, hair, and exudates. Sucking lice actually penetrate the skin and suck blood. The itching sensation causes the animal to rub, bite, and kick. If lice are present in large numbers, the horse's coat becomes rough and patches of hair are rubbed off.

Lice can be seen by pulling a tuft of hair and holding it up to the sunlight. Treatment consists of applying an insecticide, which will also kill mites and ticks (Table 10-2). One treatment usually suffices, but it is best to give another treatment about 10 to 14 days later to get the ones that hatch out after the first treatment.

Mites

Mange or scabies of horses is a specific skin disease caused by small mites that live on or in the skin. There are three types of mites—sarcoptic, psoroptic, and chorioptic.

The sarcoptic mites penetrate the upper layer of the skin and form burrows in which to mate and lay eggs. This causes irritation and itching. Each female forms a separate burrow and lays 10 to 25 eggs. The eggs hatch in 3 to 10 days. The young mites begin laying eggs in new burrows when they are 10 to 12 days old. The average life cycle is 14 to 15 days. The first symptoms are intense localized itching. Later on, blisters and nodules form, break, and discharge serum. The first lesions usually form on head, neck, shoulders, flanks, and abdomen but spread to the whole animal.

Psoroptic mites do not form burrows but live in colonies on the skin surface. The female lays about 24 eggs that hatch in 4 to 7 days. They reach maturity and lay eggs 1 to 12 days later. They have a 2- to 3-week cycle. Psoroptic mites spread faster than the sarcoptic variety. They usually start in the mane and tail. They puncture the skin for food and secrete a poisonous substance into the wound. This causes itching, inflammation, formation of vesicles, and exudation of serum.

Chorioptic mites are usually found below the hocks and knees. They live on the surface and cause symptoms similar to psoroptic mites. The horse tries to relieve the irritation by pawing, kicking, and biting its lower limbs.

Treatment for mites requires a thorough weekly application of an effective insecticide (Table 10-2). Dusts are not effective for the sarcoptic mites, because the insecticide must penetrate into the burrows.

Chiggers

Chiggers, commonly called redbugs, may also infest horses. Massive infestations cause severe dermatitis. They can be controlled by application of a detergent wash containing an insecticide (see Table 10-2).

Gnats

Several species of blood-sucking gnats that feed on horses are widely distributed throughout the United States. Some black fly species are attracted to the horse's ears, where they suck blood and cause irritations and tissue damage. Lesions resulting from the bites make the ears very sore. Other species attack the head, neck, and belly. As a result, when horses are feeding, they toss their heads, swish their tails, twitch their skin, and restlessly move about their paddock. Other species of gnats are small and difficult to see. Their bites are painless but later cause itching. The horse loses hair where it rubs and scratches.

Gnats are difficult to control so sprays, wipe-ons, or smears must be used daily (Table 10-2). It may be necessary to have the horse wear an ear net if the ears get very sore and there are many gnats.

Mosquitos

Mosquitos should be controlled because they are a vector for transmitting "sleeping sickness" viruses. Their biting annoys horses, and skin reactions may develop. Large populations of mosquitos are usually found close to their water-breeding sources. However, wind can carry them several miles. To control them, eliminate standing water or treat the water areas with insecticides. Look for standing water in old containers, water troughs, plugged rain gutters, low spots in corrals and pastures, ditches, irrigated pastures, creeks, tree holes, and poorly covered septic tanks and drains.

Flies

Several species of flies annoy horses and must be controlled. House flies transmit stomach worms. They feed and lay their eggs in waste matter such as manure, bedding, wet feed, and decomposed plant material. Stable flies are vicious biters and suck blood. They also transmit stomach worms. Their eggs are laid in horse manure and piles of decomposed plant matter. Face flies are pests to horses grazing with cattle. They irritate the mouth, eyes, and nose by sucking mucous secretions. Their control is difficult because repellants and contact insecticides do not last long enough. Fly masks can help keep face flies from the eyes and general face region. Screwworm flies lay their eggs in fresh wounds. The larvae develop in the wound and feed on the tissue; large sores develop as a result. In areas where screwworm flies are a problem, inspect horses frequently for minor cuts and abrasions. The navel cords of newborn foals are prime targets, and blowflies lay their eggs on the vulva after the mare has foaled.

Fly control on horse ranches is based on reducing natural fly attractants, eliminating breeding areas, and chemical (Table 10-2) or biological control. Eliminate attractants and breeding grounds by practicing manure and water management and general farm sanitation. Remove manure from stalls and paddocks daily or at least twice weekly. It should be composted, taken to a sanitary landfill, or spread very thin on a field. Avoid accumulations of manure, bedding, and/or feed with water. No part of the water supply system should leak, and water should not accumulate around water troughs. General farm sanitation requires prompt removal of all animal and vegetable matter. Remove garbage, spoiled feed, afterbirths, and so on, as quickly as possible.

There are several ways to control flies chemically. The choice of the appropriate insecticide and method of application depends on the fly population and physical facilities. Persistent insecticides can be applied to surfaces in the stable area. Large populations can be reduced quickly with quick-knockdown insecticides. Baits can be used around areas that tend to attract flies. Space sprays or fogs can be used in enclosed areas to quickly kill large numbers if no residual effect is necessary. Automatic spray systems on timers are effective.

Finally, biological control by the use of fly predators such as parasitic wasps is effective, economical, and labor saving. A major benefit of biological control is that it avoids the adverse side effects of chemical controls. Many of the chemicals are toxic nerve poisons that accumulate in fat deposits of horse and human bodies; for example, DDT and organophosphates.

DISEASES

The ability to recognize diseases or disease symptoms is important because the symptoms indicate the need for veterinary services. A knowledge of the common diseases, their means of transmission, and ways of prevention enables the horse owner to mount an effective disease control program. (See Table 10-3 for a summary of infectious diseases and Table 10-4 for a summary of vaccines for infectious diseases.)

Common Diseases

Anthrax

Anthrax is an acute infectious disease caused by bacteria—*Bacillus anthracis*. There are two routes of infection—ingestion or biting insects. Horses eat anthrax spores during droughts when the pastures are overgrazed or after a flood that spreads the spores. Spores resist environmental conditions and live for several years. The ingested spores cause colic, enteritis, and septicemia. Horses also eat the feces of infected animals or contaminated feed and feed products. Biting insects transmit the disease, and the symptoms resulting from insect bites include fever, hot and painful edematous swelling of the throat, lower chest, abdomen, prepuce, and mammary glands. The symptoms last 48 to 96 hours. Treatment is usually not successful or necessary because mortality is very high. In areas where anthrax is a problem, it can be prevented by annual vaccinations. If a horse dies from anthrax, bury the carcass at least 6 feet deep. Flesh eaters can spread the disease, so dispose of the carcass immediately.

TABLE 10-3   Summary of Infectious Diseases

Disease	Cause	Primary characteristics	Prevention	Treatment
Influenza	Myxovirus	Fever of 101–105°F (38.3–40.5°C), watery nasal discharge	Vaccinate; isolate new animals; test kit	Good nursing care
Strangles	*Streptococcus equi*	Fever of 103–105°F (39.4–40.5°C); enlarged lymph nodes, nasal discharge—watery at first, then purulent	Isolate new animals; vaccinate all animals	Antibiotics
Pneumonia	Virus or bacteria	Fever of 102–105°F (38.9–40.5°C); chest pains, lung congestion, difficulty in breathing	Good management; avoid chills and stress, provide proper ventilation	Antibiotics when cause is bacterial
Rhinopneumonitis	Herpes virus	Fever of 102–106°F (38.9–41.1°C); coughing, clear nasal discharge; abortion primarily in last third of gestation	Vaccinate	No treatment
Viral arteritis	Herpes virus	Fever of 102–106°F (38.9–41.1°C); abortion	Vaccinate	Good nursing care

TABLE 10-3 Summary of Infectious Diseases (*Continued*)

Disease	Cause	Primary characteristics	Prevention	Treatment
Equine encephalo-myelitis	Virus	Brain lesions, drowsiness, fever; lower lip drops; difficulty in walking	Vaccinate	Good nursing care
Equine infectious anemia	Virus transmitted in blood of infected horses	Fever of 104–108°F (40–42.2°C); weakness, jaundice, edema of ventral abdomen	Use of Coggins or test to detect carriers	No treatment
Tetanus	*Clostridium tetani*	Muscular rigidity; prolapse of third eyelid	Tetanus toxoid or antitoxin	Mortality rate is high
Anthrax	*Bacillus anthracis*	High fever, edema about throat, lower neck, and chest; lasts approximately 48–96 hours	Vaccinate—only in an epidemic area	Antibiotics, antianthrax serum
Piroplasmosis	Protozoans	Fever, depression, anemia, tearing eyes and swollen eyelids	Tick control	No treatment
Potomac horse fever	*Ehlichia risticii*	Depression, anorexia, and fever of 102–108°F (38.9–42.2°C) followed by diarrhea	Vaccination and detection kit	No treatment

TABLE 10-4 United States Department of Agriculture Licensed Biologicals for Use in Horses

Anthrax
  Anthrax Spore Vaccine (Colorado Serum)
Botulism
  Bot Tox-B (Neogen)
E. Coli
  E. Colicin-E (Equilabs)
  Equine Coli Endotox (Grand)
Ehrlichia risticii (Potomac Horse Fever)
  Mystique (Bayer Corp.)
  PHF-Vax (Schering Plough)
  Potomac (Equilabs)
  PotomacGuard (Fort Dodge)
  PotomacGuard (Franklin)
  RM Equine Potomavac (Merial)
Ehrilichia risticii (Potomac Horse Fever) and Rabies
  Mystique II (Bayer Corporation)
  RM Equine Potomavac + Imrab (Merial)
Ehrilichia risticii (Potomac Horse Fever), encephalomyelitis (Sleeping Sickness), and Tetanus Toxoid
  PHF-Vax + 3 (Schering Plough)
  PotomacGuard EWT (Fort Dodge)
  PotomacGuard EWT (Franklin)
Ehrilichia risticii (Potomac Horse Fever), encephalomyelitis (Sleeping Sickness), and Influenza
  PHF-Vax + 4 (Schering Plough)
Equine Encephalomyelitis (Sleeping Sickness)
  Encephaloid IM (Fort Dodge)
  Encephaloid IM (Franklin)
  Encephalomyelitis Vaccine Eastern and Western (Colorado Serum)
  Encevac with Havlogen (Bayer Corporation)
  Triple-E (Fort Dodge)
Equine Encephalomyelitis (Sleeping Sickness) and Tetanus Toxoid
  Cephalovac EWT (Boehringer Ingelheim)
  Cephalovac VEW (Boehringer Ingelheim)
  Double-E (Fort Dodge)
  Encephalomyelitis Vaccine Eastern & Western with Tetanus Toxoid (Colorado Serum)
  Encevac-T with Havlogen (Bayer Corporation)
  Equiloid (Fort Dodge)
  Equiloid (Franklin)
  EWT (Shering-Plough)
  Tetmune EW (Pfizer Animal Health)
  Triple-E T (Fort Dodge)
Equine Encephalomyelitis (Sleeping Sickness), Influenza, and Tetanus Toxoid
  Double-E FT (Fort Dodge)
  Encevac TC-4 with Havlogen (Bayer Corporation)
  Equi-Flu EWT (Boehringer Ingelheim)
  Equi-Flu VEWT (Boehringer Ingelheim)

continued

TABLE 10-4   United States Department of Agriculture Licensed Biologicals for Use in Horses (*Continued*)

EWTF (Schering-Plough)
Flumune EWT (Pfizer Animal Health)
Fluvac EWT (Franklin)
Fluvac EWT Plus (Fort Dodge)
RM Equine EWTF (Merial)
Triple-E FT (Fort Dodge)

Equine Encephalomyelitis (Sleeping Sickness), Influenza, Rhinopneumonitis, and Tetanus Toxoid
Double-E FT + EHV (Fort Dodge)
Triple-E FT + EHV (Fort Dodge)

Equine Influenza
Equicine II with Havlogen (Bayer Corporation)
Equ-Flu (Boehringer Ingelheim)
Flumune (Pfizer Animal Health)
Fluvac (Franklin)
Fluvac Plus (Fort Dodge)
Inflogen-3 (Fort Dodge)

Influenza and Rhinopneumonitis
Equigard-Flu (Boehringer Ingelheim)
Fluvac EHV 4/1 (Franklin)
Fluvac EHV 4/1 Plus (Fort Dodge)
Inflogen-3 + EHV (Fort Dodge)
Prestige II with Halvogen (Bayer Corporation)
Rhino-Flu (Pfizer Animal Health)

Rabies
RM Imrab 3 (Merial)
RM Imrab Bovine Plus (Merial)
Rabguard-TC (Pfizer Animal Health)
Rabvac 3 (Fort Dodge)

Rhinopneumonitis
Equigard (Boehringer Inglheim)
EquiVac EHV 1/4 (Fort Dodge)
Pneumabort-K + 1b (Franklin)
Pneumabort-K + 1b (Fort Dodge)
Prestige with Havlogen (Bayer Corporation)
Prodigy with Havlogen (Bayer Corporation)
Rhinomune (Pfizer Animal Health)

Rhodococcus Equi
Polymune-R (V.D.I.)

Rotavirus
Equine Rotavirus Vaccine (Fort Dodge)

Salmonella
ENDODERUM (Immvac)
ENDOVAC-Equi (Immvac)

Streptococcus spp (Strangles)
Strepguard with Havlogen (Bayer Corporation)
Strepvax II (Boehringer Inglheim)
Pinnacle I.N. (Fort Dodge)

Tetanus Antitoxin
   Tetanus Antitoxin (Colorado Serum)
   Tetanus Antitoxin (Fort Dodge)
   Tetanus Antitoxin (Merial)
   Tetanus Antitoxin (Professional Biological)
   Tetanus Antitoxin Equine Origin (Equilabs)
   Tetnogen-AT (Fort Dodge)
Tetanus Toxoid
   Super-Tet with Havlogen (Bayer Corporation)
   Tetanus Toxoid (Fort Dodge)
   Tetanus Toxoid (Franklin)
   Tetanus Toxoid-Concentrated (Colorado Serum)
   Tetanus Toxoid-Concentrated (Professional Biological)
   Tetanus Toxoid-Unconcentrated (Colorado Serum)
   Tetguard (Boehringer Ingelheim)
   Tetnogen (Fort Dodge)
Viral Arteritis
   Arvac (Fort Dodge)

Note: New vaccines are continually being developed and made available to veterinarians and horse owners.

SOURCE: *Compendium of Veterinary Products*, 5th edition, 1999.

Botulism

Botulism is caused by a neurotoxin produced by the anaerobic bacterium, *Clostridium botulinum* and is one of the most potent toxins known to man. Horses are particularly susceptible and death rates of 70 to 90 percent occur when it is not treated. Of the eight toxin types, Type B accounts for most cases and Types A and C account for the remainder.

Symptoms include flaccid paralysis of the muscles by interfering with the neuromuscular junction. Initially, the symptoms are loss of tail and tongue tone, inability to swallow, weakened gait, decreased eyelid tone, decreased bowel sounds, sweating, shaking forelegs, colic, bloating. Horses are able to chew at a slow rate but feed drops from their mouth. As the disease progresses, the horse lies down and has increased heart rate and decreased respiratory rate. Death results from respiratory failure. In young foals, the disease is called "shaker foal syndrome." It normally occurs at about 2 to 8 weeks of age. The young foal trembles when it is standing, has difficulty breathing, difficulty swallowing, and tongue paralysis. Milk dribbles from the mouth when it suckles.

Botulism is contacted in three ways. Ingestion of the toxin is the most common and occurs via contaminated feed and water. Feed contaminated with decomposing carcasses of birds and other small animals or through improper storage of hay or silage products is the most common source. It can occur through entrance into a wound that provides an anaerobic environment. Foals contract it through the entrance of the dead tissue of the umbilical stump. Treatment consists of removing the source of poisoning and administering an antitoxin. Vaccination of mares 30 days prior to foaling will prevent the disease in foals, and vaccination of adult horses with the 3-shot sequence and an annual booster will protect them against Type B.

Equine Encephalomyelitis

The common name for equine encephalomyelitis is "sleeping sickness." This disease results in degeneration of the brain's vascular system. It is caused by several different viruses, each located within a given geographical area. The three most common virus types are Eastern (EEE), Western (WEE), and Venezuelan (VEE). Viral transmission is primarily by mosquitos. Wild birds serve as the principal reservoir for the virus, even though it is also carried by wild rodents and other animals. People and horses get the disease but do not transmit EEE and WEE to other people or horses. VEE can be transmitted from human to human or horse to horse by moisture in the breath.

Early symptoms include high fever for 1 to 2 days, restlessness, and nervousness. Brain lesions form, and the horse becomes drowsy, holds its head low, has droopy ears, and may walk around aimlessly. This is followed by paralysis and possibly death within 2 to 4 days after the first symptoms are noticed. Mortality for WEE is about 20 to 30 percent. Horses that recover are seldom useful because of the brain damage suffered. EEE and VEE have mortality rates of 70 to 90 percent.

All three types of sleeping sickness can be prevented by yearly vaccinations. Vaccine is available to the horse owner at tack shops and animal care centers. There is no treatment for the diseases.

Equine Infectious Anemia

Equine infectious anemia (EIA) is a viral disease that has received considerable attention by horsepeople ever since a means of detecting carrier animals was developed. The disease affects less than 1 percent of the horse population. It takes three forms—subacute (chronic), acute, and inapparent (in carriers). The forms differ widely in their impact on the horse.

The temperature of an acutely infected animal rises to 105 to 108°F (40 to 42.2°C). The horse appears depressed, becomes weak, and loses appetite and weight. Fluid (edema) may collect under the skin, in the legs, chest, and abdomen. Membranes lining the natural body openings may be congested and yellow in color. There is a marked drop in the number of red blood cells (anemia). The horse usually dies in a few days.

Subacute forms are less severe, so the horse survives. The chronic form is sometimes classified as subacute. Such horses may display acute symptoms at any time or periodically.

An inapparent carrier usually shows no symptoms of EIA except that it may be unthrifty. Such horses react positively to the test for EIA. The virus can be transmitted by some of these horses by various means. About 85 percent of positive reactors are inapparent carriers.

The disease is primarily transmitted from acute and subacute cases to other horses by biting insects (primarily horse flies) and contaminated syringe needles. Therefore, insect control and use of sterile or disposable needles is important to prevent spread of the disease. There is no immunization for protection against EIA in the United States, nor is there a treatment. However, a vaccine has been developed in China.

The current recognized test for EIA is the agar-gel immunodiffusion (AGID) test developed by Dr. Lee Roy Coggins. It is not for the EIA virus but for antibodies developed to fight the disease. A horse that reacts positively to the test is classified as a carrier of EIA. The test is very accurate and demonstrates whether the horse has been infected with EIA virus. A more recent test, enzyme-linked immunosorbent assay, is being adopted as the official test. Many states have regulations concerning positive reactors and require tests before horses are shipped into the state.

Equine Protozoal Myeloencephalitis

Equine protozoal myeloencephalitis, EPM, is a neurological disease caused by *Sarcocystis neurona*, a protozoa. The parasite is ingested by the horse from infested food or water. Horses are dead-end hosts for the parasite and cannot spread it. Food and water become contaminated by the feces of opossums carrying the protozoa. The opossum get the protozoa from eating dead carcasses of birds that serve as the reservoir.

Only a small percentage of horses become sick after ingesting the parasite. Symptoms include anything from dragging a toe, incoordination, or drooped eyelid to complete recumbency and death. Most horses display an asymmetric incoordination. Blood tests detect antibodies to the *S. neurona* but do not indicate if the horse will develop the disease. Exposure to the protozoa can result in a positive test. Presence of antibodies in the cerebral spinal fluid along with neurological signs are positive indicators of the disease. The protozoa can remain in the horse's body for years without causing the disease, but stress may trigger clinical signs in infected horses. The horse can be re-infected over and over again. Treatment protocols are being developed and are based upon the use of diclazuril.

Influenza

Two specific type viruses—myxovirus A/Equi and myxovirus A/Equi 1—are responsible for most cases of influenza (flu). About 48 hours after exposure to the virus, symptoms develop, including fever (101 to 106°F, or 38.3 to 41.1°C), cough, runny nose, depression, and loss of appetite. Flu is quite common where large numbers of horses are congregated for shows, rodeos, and sales. The virus is spread by water droplets moving through the air. A coughing horse can spread the virus as far as 35 feet (10.7 m). It settles on feed and in water troughs and is ingested. It is inhaled in water droplets. Flu is not fatal and only causes temporary incapacity. However, if the horse is not rested and is exposed to bad weather, serious secondary complications may arise.

Horses bought at sales should have their temperature taken a couple of times per day for about a week after they are brought home. A rapid rise in temperature is the first sign of flu. The horse can be immediately treated and isolated to prevent the flu from spreading. All horses should be vaccinated against influenza and booster shots given annually. Horses that are constantly being shown or exposed to large groups should be given booster shots at 3- to 6-month intervals.

There is a test kit available to veterinarians so they can determine if the horse actually has the flu and not a disease with similar symptoms.

Lyme Disease

First recognized in 1975, Lyme disease is known to exist in North America, Europe, and Asia. Areas characterized by high humidity and dense vegetation are ideal for vectors of the disease, which affects a wide variety of birds and mammals, including man. Deer ticks are the primary vector, and the black-legged tick and the western black-legged tick are also associated with the disease. Although Lyme disease is a year-round threat, most cases occur in May through August in the North Central and Pacific coast states. Symptoms include fever, lethargy, lameness, joint swelling, loss of appetite, and eye problems. Control is with an insecticide to kill the deer ticks on horses and other animals and in the stable area.

Piroplasmosis

Piroplasmosis, discovered in the United States in 1961, is a tick-borne disease caused by either of two protozoans that invade the red blood cells. The tick attaches itself to the horse, the protozoan leaves the tick and enters the bloodstream and red blood cells, multiplies, and ultimately destroys the cells. The released protozoa enter other red blood cells and multiply. Symptoms include fever, depression, anemia, thirst, tearing eyes, and swollen eyelids. The urine is yellow to reddish in color. Mortality rate is 10 to 15 percent. Prevention consists of tick control and sterilizing all needles and medical instruments.

Pneumonia

The all-inclusive term *pneumonia* refers to any lung inflammation. Pneumonia can be caused by a bacterium, a virus, or a combination of the two. The symptoms are fever (102 to 105°F, or 38.8 to 40.5°C), nasal discharge, loss of appetite, difficulty in breathing, chest pains, and lung congestion. Prompt treatment by a veterinarian is usually successful. However, in some circumstances treatment is useless. Foals that have combined immunodeficiency disease (CID) (see Chapter 16) die after they contract adenoviral pneumonia.

Pneumonia can develop in a horse as a result of liquid being passed down a stomach tube inadvertently placed in the trachea. Therefore, stomach tubes should be passed only by trained personnel.

Potomac Horse Fever

Potomac horse fever was discovered in 1979. Outbreaks seem to occur near large rivers. It was originally described for horses dying along the Potomac River, which flows through Washington, D.C. It occurs between May through October and at random among horses. Caused by an organism in the richettsiaceae family, *Ehrlichia risticii,* this fever is transmitted by ticks. Symptoms include initial mild depression, refusal to eat, mild temperature, and cessation of all gut sounds. Some horses will have colic. Within 24 to 48 hours of cessation of gut sounds, a profuse projectile diarrhea begins, which may last for up to 10 days. Laminitis develops in one in four horses stricken with this disease. Severe symptoms prior to diarrhea usually result in death. Treatment is not successful in 30 percent of clinical cases. Tick control will help decrease the prevalence of the disease. All horses should be vaccinated in problem areas; a test kit to detect the disease is available.

Rabies

Rabies is common among horses in some areas. The presence of a rabid animal on the premises and fresh wounds on the muzzle, face, or lower limbs usually indicate that exposure has occurred. Quarantine the horse and closely observe it for 3 to 6 months. Exposed animals should be immediately treated by a veterinarian. Initial signs of rabies include personality change, lack of appetite caused by inability to swallow, and incoordination. Some horses with rabies do not become vicious. Others are very vicious and must be destroyed. In problem areas, horses should be vaccinated against rabies.

Rain Rot

Rain rot or rain scald is an infectious skin disease caused by *Dermatophilus congolensis,* an organism that lives on the skin surface. It is particularly prevalent in humid climates during the fall and spring after prolonged rainfall. For the horse to contract the disease, several conditions must exist. First, the fungal organism in the form of a spore must be present on an infected carrier animal or piece of tack. Second, there must be extreme moisture, such as heavy rainfall. Third, heavy hair coats retain the moisture and aid the spore in growing. Fourth, the horse's skin has been damaged by a cut, scrape, or insect bite which allows spores to enter the skin. Once the disease occurs, it is recognized by tufts of matted, crested hair on the withers, back, croup, and rump. Serum oozes from the skin. The lesions may follow the pattern of water runoff in the coat. If it occurs at the back of the fetlock, it is known as greased heels or dew poisoning.

Rain rot is spread through the use of contaminated grooming equipment or by horses' rubbing on infected fences and stalls. Control is therapeutic bathing with an antiseptic shampoo (Betadine, Chlorhexadine, or phenol), treatment with penicillin, and dry shelter. All grooming equipment should be disinfected with a bleach solution (1:20 with water).

Ringworm

Several kinds of fungi cause ringworm. They are spread by direct or indirect contact with contaminated stalls, feed, mangers, gates, and grooming equipment. Some types can be spread to other animals, including people. Each type of ringworm requires a certain type of treatment, so a veterinarian should take skin scrapings, identify the type, and then prescribe appropriate treatment. A diagnosis of ringworm can usually be made from its appearance. Small, reddish, round lesions appear, covered with small scales. The hair breaks off just above the skin level. Older lesions may heal in the center, but the edges are quite active.

Rhinopneumonitis

Rhinopneumonitis is a viral infection passed from horse to horse and is similar to flu. It affects horses of all ages. The respiratory symptoms are usually quite mild. Body temperature may increase 1 to 2°F (0.6 to 1.1°C), nasal discharge is clear and thick, and the cough is shallow. There are four strains but two strains of equine herpes viruses, EHV-1 and EHV-4, are primarily responsible for rhinopneumonitis in the horse. EHV-1 causes abortions or stillborn foals. Abortions normally occur during the last trimester of pregnancy and may occur as long as 4 months after the respiratory symptoms. Occasionally, EHV-1 may attack the central nervous system, causing ataxia (inability to walk or stand). Severe cases of the neurologic type usually result in death. EHV-4 is most frequently associated with upper respiratory disease in young horses and rarely with abortion.

Two vaccines have been developed against viral rhinopneumonitis. One containing inactivated or killed virus is recommended for use in pregnant mares to prevent abortion and for respiratory illness in all horses. The other vaccine is a modified live virus product and is an aid in prevention of the respiratory form of infection. Immunity or protection provided by both types of immunization is not 100 percent effective or of long duration. Neither vaccine seems to protect against the neurologic form.

Strangles

Strangles, also called *distemper* or *shipping fever,* is a highly communicable disease caused by a bacterial infection. The bacteria *Streptococcus equi* causes the lymph glands in the jaw and throat to become infected and swollen. The incubation period is about 3 weeks. Symptoms are fever of 103 to 104°F (39.4 to 40°C), nasal discharge, cough, swollen lymph glands, and difficulty in swallowing. The lymph glands may abscess and burst. Severe cases may result in abscesses forming in other organs of the body. Treatment consists of penicillin injections by a veterinarian and good husbandry (clean water and feed; clean, dry stall; and quiet surroundings).

Once strangles bacteria are present in an area, they persist for years. Horses are exposed and develop the disease, so it is a common problem of stables that have a transient trade or of horse traders. To avoid strangles, all horses should be isolated when they are first brought to the premises. Quarantine sick horses so that no feed buckets, equipment, or personnel handle the sick animal and then other horses unless first disinfected. After the horse recovers, thoroughly disinfect the area and all its contents. If the stall floor is dirt, the disinfectant must penetrate at least 6 inches (15.2 cm).

Horses should be vaccinated (intranasal) against strangles and given a yearly booster. When possible, the best procedure is to avoid contact with horses that have the disease. After recovering, horses develop varying degrees of immunity to it. If they have it again, the severity is greatly reduced, and many horses develop a lifetime immunity.

Tetanus (Lockjaw)

Tetanus is a serious disease caused by a wound infection by a bacterium called *Clostridium tetani.* The bacteria are unique in that they grow in the absence of oxygen and light. Tetanus bacteria spores are present in most soils. These spores are dormant and resist heat, cold, and dryness for several years. When the spores are carried into a wound on the end of a nail or in dirt and when the right conditions exist, they change back to a normal bacterial cell. The bacteria produce toxin that affects the nervous system. The initial symptoms, which occur about 7 to 10 days after the infection, are stiffness in all four legs, stumbling when walking, and cocked-out ears. The third eyelid may cross the inside aspect of the eye, or it may flip across the eye when the horse is startled. In 2 to 3 days, the horse is unable to walk and stands like a "sawhorse." The ears are cocked-out and the tail raised and held out behind. Muscle spasms and twitches occur. All muscles seem to contract. If the horse falls down, it will be unable to rise.

Treatment should be by a veterinarian, but few horses recover. Prevention is by two means. All horses should be immunized against tetanus with tetanus toxoid and given booster shots at recommended intervals. If the horse has not been protected by immunization and sustains a wound, tetanus antitoxin gives temporary protection for 2 to 3 weeks. Tetanus antitoxin should be given within 24 hours after an injury occurs. Young foals can be immunized by tetanus antitoxin after birth or by boosting the mare's immune system with tetanus toxoid about a month before foaling. Sufficient antibodies are produced and secreted in the milk to protect the foal.

Vesicular Stomatitis

Basic information about vesicular stomatitis is as yet unclear. It is not known where the virus reservoir is, or what causes the outbreaks. First signs of the disease are increased salivation and fever, followed by blistering around the hooves, mouth, nose and/or teats. Secondary effects are decreased appetite and bacterial infections that may lead to death. It normally runs its course in less than a month and is seldom fatal. However, outbreaks of the disease have occurred in several states and all horses in the area are immediately quarantined. The closing of borders has economic consequences for the whole horse industry.

Viral Arteritis

Viral arteritis is an upper respiratory disease that resembles rhinopneumonitis and influenza. Symptoms include a fever (102 to 106°F, or 38.8 to 41.1°C), nasal discharge, edema or swelling of the lower legs, conjunctivitis, and, in some horses, a hivelike rash. The symptoms are more severe than for influenza and rhinopneumonitis, but mortality is usually very low. The virus also causes abortions in about 50 percent of affected pregnant mares.

The disease is highly communicable for 8 to 10 days from an infected horse and is spread by inhalation of respiratory droplets from infected horses or through the veneral route. Perpetuation of the virus is by carrier stallions who asymptomatically harbor and persistently shed the virus in semen. After exposure, horses acquire a natural immunity. Vaccination has been successful in eliminating acute cases. Mares vaccinated 21 days before breeding are protected when bred to a shedding stallion. Stallions testing seronegative are protected after vaccination. Annual booster vaccinations are required for continued protection.

Warts

Warts frequently appear around the lips and muzzles of horses as well as the underparts such as the inside of the thighs and on the prepuce. One wart or masses of them may be present. They usually cause no harm unless they are irritated by tack. They will spontaneously disappear in 3 to 4 months if they are not treated. They are transmitted to humans and other horses because they are caused by a virus. A vaccine is available for treatment.

Metabolic and Other Diseases

Azoturia and "Tying Up" Syndrome

Azoturia and "tying up" syndrome are two metabolic disorders involving various muscles of the horse. Azoturia is frequently called "Monday morning disease" and is technically known as paralytic myoglobinuria. The circumstances under which it occurs are as follows: the horse is being exercised regularly, and typically it is being fed a ration high in grain; the horse rests for 1 or 2 days and eats its full ration during that period; the horse returns to work, and shortly thereafter symptoms of the disease appear—signs of muscle stiffness, tremors, and pain. If exercise continues, the severity increases. In advanced stages, the horse is unable to move and may fall down. Anxiety causes profuse sweating. The urine becomes reddish-brown to almost black. The change in urine color is caused by the release of myoglobin (red pigment in muscle tissue) when the muscle fibers break down. All movement should be stopped and a veterinarian called.

To help prevent azoturia, reduce the amount of grain or do not feed grain on rest days. Horses that "tie up" should receive less grain if they have been receiving large amounts. Other preventative measures include vitamin E and selenium therapy. However, none of these procedures will prevent tying up in all cases.

There are two categories of tying-up. Sporadic tying-up occurs in horses that have been exercising all their lives but suddenly endure an episode of stiffness and muscle cramping. Environmental influences cause damage to normal muscle. It is normally the result of overexertion, strenuous endurance rides, severe training programs, or dietary imbalance of electrolytes or carbohydrates.

Chronic tying-up occurs in horses that have an intrinsic abnormality in muscle function. The most common cause is an inherited abnormality in muscle energy regulation called polysaccharide storage myopathy (PSSM) which closely resembles azoturia. It is due to a recessive trait. There is a rapid uptake of sugar into the muscle and the accumulation of an abnormal form of sugar—a polysaccharide. Horses can start showing symptoms at any age. The severity and frequency of tying-up can be reduced by feeding grass or oat hay as the roughage and feeding a fat-supplemented grain ration at minimal amounts. Daily exercise is most important for performing horses. Keeping stress to a minimum by using regular routines is also helpful.

Colic

The term colic is used to describe a number of painful digestive disturbances with many different causes. Improper feeding practices such as abrupt changes in the horse's feed or overfeeding concentrates without providing adequate fiber commonly cause colic. One of the overwhelming causes is parasites. The bloodworm *Strongylus vulgaris* migrates through the circulatory system, causing arterial damage and blood clots. When blood clots block the flow of blood to part of the intestines, irreparable damage occurs. Roundworms may block the intestine and prevent the movement of digesta through the tract. Twists may occur in the long digestive tract, which causes part of the tract to necrose. Therefore, the extensive folding and length of the digestive tract make the horse vulnerable to colic. Infections with bacteria and viruses may cause enteritis and colic.

The symptoms of colic are essentially the same regardless of the cause. Heart rate and body temperature increase. Sweating may occur and may become very profuse as the pain increases. The horse will be restless, paw the ground, try to roll, frequently get up and down, bite its abdomen, kick at its abdomen, refuse to eat, may or may not drink water, show a change in feces, or fail to defecate for several hours. The pain is caused by the digestive tract becoming stretched by gas or digesta accumulation, inflammation resulting from blockage of blood supply or blood leaking into the peritoneal cavity, or muscle spasms in the gut wall.

Because colic is the number-one killer of horses, it is a serious problem. Prompt action is essential to successful treatment. Professional assistance is necessary whenever abdominal pain is moderate to severe; abdominal distension is present; temperature, pulse, and respiration have increased; the color of the mucous membranes darkens, or no feces have been passed for 24 hours. Treatment may be as simple as a mild analgesic or walking the horse around, or it may be complicated and involve surgical correction.

The incidence of colic can be reduced by good feeding management practices, by a well-planned and well-executed internal parasite control program, and by keeping stress to a minimum.

Heaves

The common names for pulmonary emphysema are "heaves" and "broken wind." It can be caused by an allergic reaction to milk, by chronic cough in dusty surroundings, or by eating dusty hay. The condition is characterized by a chronic cough, difficulty in forcing air out of the lungs, possible nasal discharge, unthriftiness, and lack of stamina. Heaves cannot be cured, but relief from the symptoms can be obtained by proper management precautions. One of the most obvious visual signs is the marked jerking of the flanks to force the air out of the lungs. Extensive use of these muscles causes the formation of a "heave" line in the flank area. Air must be forced out of the lungs because the alveoli, small air sacs in the lung, have lost their elasticity. Because expiration is passive, the air will not move out of the lung after the elasticity is lost. Lack of stamina results from a decreased ability to get oxygen to the tissues.

To prevent heaves or to manage the horse with heaves, never feed moldy or dusty feed. Keep bedding as free as possible of dust. Avoid keeping the horse in confinement conditions where dust is a problem. Horses should be kept at pasture if possible. Severe cases render the horse useless for anything except breeding purposes. Horses with mild cases can be used for pleasure if they are not strenuously exercised.

Melanomas

Melanomas are benign growths that occur on the tail and anus and on the head of gray or white horses. They are usually rare in horses 6 to 7 years old, but about 80 percent of gray horses over 15 years old have them. They start out about the size of BB shot and gradually increase in size. There is a treatment that is successful for most cases and some tumors can be surgically removed. New ones may appear at a later time. They can become malignant and invade vital organs, causing death. The major problem is interference with tack, particularly on the head. Treatment with cimetidine will reduce the size or lead to disappearance of most melanomas.

Disease Prevention

Disease prevention is an important part of managing a horse farm or keeping a pleasure horse healthy. The age of the horse affects the efficiency of the program. Young foals are not capable of developing antibodies very efficiently until they are about 3 months of age, when passive immunity acquired from the mare begins to decline. Therefore, they should not be immunized until they are 3 months of age unless a high incidence of disease persists. Then one may start immunizing them at 6 to 8 weeks of age. All horses should be immunized against tetanus, influenza, rhinopneumonitis, and sleeping sickness (EEE, WEE, and VEE). It may also be advisable to immunize against strangles, viral arteritis, anthrax, botulism, Potomac horse fever, and rabies, depending on the circumstances. New vaccines are being routinely developed (see Tables 10-4 and 10-5). Each has specific instructions that must be followed. Thus, it is not possible to give specific vaccination schedules that will remain current.

Each farm or stable should have an isolation area where incoming horses can be kept for 2 to 3 weeks for observation. The incubation periods for most diseases are less than 3 weeks. Horses that become sick should also be isolated to prevent the spread of communicable diseases. The tools and equipment used to take care of a sick horse should not be used for other horses until they have been decontaminated. They can be washed in disinfectants but a veterinarian should choose the disinfectant, depending on the disease. The stall area should be decontaminated. After all dirt and debris are removed, a thorough scrubbing with water and soap followed by a thorough application of moist steam under pressure is an excellent method because it kills all disease organisms except some spores. Steam cleaners can be rented from local tool rental agencies. If such cleaners are unavailable, the stall can be sprayed with a disinfectant such as one of the phenolic germicides or hypochlorites. Each disinfectant has limitations as to which bacteria, fungi, spores, and viruses that it will kill, so a veterinarian should be consulted for the exact product to use.

TABLE 10-5   Manufacturer Index for United States Department of Agriculture Licensed Biologicals for Horses

Bayer Corporation Animal Health P. O.Box 390 Shawnee, KS 66201	IMMVAC 6080 Bass Lane Columbia, MO 65201
Boehringer Ingelheim Vetmedica, Inc. 2621 North Belt Highway St. Joseph, MO 64506	Merial Limited 2100 Ronson Road Iselin, NJ 08830-3077
Colorado Serum Company 4950 York St., Box 16428 Denver, CO 80216	Neogen Corporation 628 Winchester Rd. Lexington, KY 40505
Equilabs 20927 State Route K St. Joseph, MO 64503	Pfizer Animal Health Group Whiteland Business Park 812 Springdale Drive Exton, PA 19341
Franklin Laboratories P.O. Box 717 Fort Dodge, IA 50501	Professional Biological Company 4950 York Street, Box 16428 Denver, CO 80216
Fort Dodge Laboratories 800 Fifth St., N.W. Fort Dodge, IA 50501	Schering-Plough Animal Health Corporation 1095 Morris Ave. Union, NJ 07083
Grand Laboratories, Inc. 1447 140th Street Larchwood, IA 51241	Veterinary Dynamics Inc. 1535 Templeton Road Templeton, CA 93465

Bedding and manure that is removed should be burned. Aborted fetuses should be removed and buried.

Rats and mice must be controlled because they are a source of contamination. All grain and feed bins should be rodent-proof. Flies and other insects serve as vectors of disease and must be controlled.

Records of all vaccinations, treatments, health care, wormings, hoof care, and dental care should be maintained for all horses. Review them periodically to make sure that each horse is receiving appropriate care.

Part Three

USING AND ENJOYING THE HORSE

CHAPTER 11

Riding and Driving

Riding and driving a horse, popular means of recreation, are discussed in this chapter. Horses are ridden several different ways, such as western, forward ("English-style"), sidesaddle, or saddle seat. Each method of riding was devised to meet a particular purpose or obtain a particular type of performance. Driving horses is also becoming increasingly popular. A large recreational industry has developed, including riding stables (both private and public), breeding farms, training facilities, tack manufacturers, clothing companies, transportation, and so on. There are organizations that promote safe riding and certify riding instructors. The CHA was formed in 1967. Their goal is "to promote safe, supervised riding experiences in basic horsemanship for groups and/or children." To accomplish their goal, CHA sponsors instructor certification clinics and certifies instructors. They provide a number of instructional manuals for a variety of horsemanship programs that help standardize group riding programs. The North American Riding for the Handicapped Association certifies therapeutic riding instructors and accredits therapeutic riding centers that meet safety standards.

RIDING EQUIPMENT

To ride or drive a horse successfully and safely, one must become familiar with the necessary equipment for various methods of riding and driving.

Western

Saddles

The western saddle was developed because horsepeople who spent long hours riding needed a comfortable saddle for the horse and for themselves, and a strong saddle that could hold a roped steer. The basic western saddle is shown in Figure 11-1. In selecting a western saddle, one of the main considerations is the seat, which should be flat, not built up in front. A seat that is built up in front prevents the rider from sitting forward over the horse's center of gravity. The rider then sits too far back on the loins of the horse, which fatigues the horse too quickly. The placement of the stirrup leathers determines the position (forward or backward) of the legs and feet and thus determines balance when riding. Many saddles are made with the stirrups too far forward, which also puts the rider's legs too far forward.

The tree is the basic unit of the saddle. Saddle trees (Figure 11-2) are made of fiberglass, aluminum, or wood covered with rawhide. The way a saddle fits on a horse's back is determined by the width and height of the gullet and the flare of the bars. Gullet height and width are important in determining what type of horse the saddle tree will fit. A low, wide gullet will probably rub

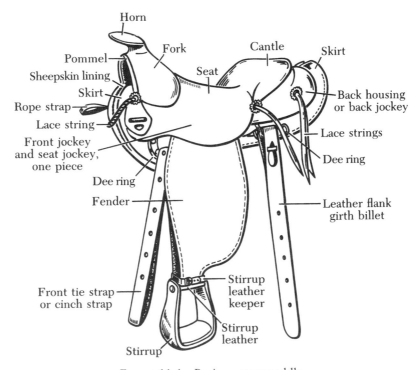

FIGURE 11-1   Basic western saddle.

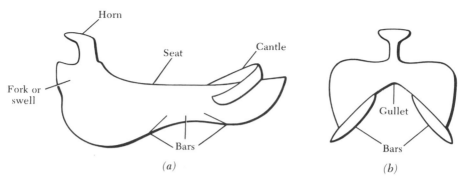

FIGURE 11-2   *(a)* Side view and *(b)* front view of a western saddle tree, around which the rest of the western saddle is built. (From Hyland, 1971.)

against the withers of a narrow-chested, high-withered horse, whereas a narrow or regular-width gullet will not fit down on a wide-backed horse. The bars of a saddle tree must have the proper angle and "twist" to fit a horse. The bars must be long enough so that they do not irritate the back over the loin. Longer bars give more bearing space on the horse's back and distribute the rider's weight more evenly. These factors often determine the difference between a low-cost saddle that causes saddle sores on the shoulders and back, and a good, usable saddle. The size of the tree determines the size of the finished saddle. The average size of a tree is 15 or $15\frac{1}{2}$ inches (38.1 or 39.4 cm) measured from where the seat joins the fork to the inside of the cantle after the saddle is completed. The saddle is rigged as centerfire, $\frac{5}{8}, \frac{3}{4}, \frac{7}{8}$, or full, depending on the position of the front cinch ring (Figure 11-3). The centerfire-rigged saddle is rigged with a single cinch. Cowboys

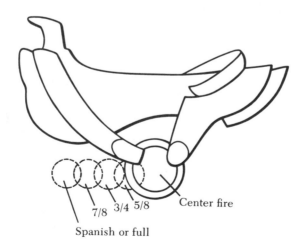

FIGURE 11-3   Single rigging position of a western saddle. (From Hyland, 1971.)

found that such saddles tended to tip and slip forward when they roped cattle, so the front cinch was moved forward and a flank cinch was added (Figure 11-1). Today, most saddles are rigged double—full or three-quarters. Western saddles weigh approximately 40 pounds (18.5 kg) but may be lighter or heavier. The saddles used by single-steer ropers take a great deal of strain and weigh 43 to 45 pounds (19.4 to 20.4 kg).

Pads

Western saddles require a pad between the saddle and the horse's back. These pads are made of a variety of materials (Figure 11-4). Those made of synthetic material can be washed and kept clean quite easily. Pads made from the material used to make orthopedic hospital pads have become very popular. The "hair pad" has been a standby over the years. It does cake with dirt when it is wet with sweat, but the dirt can be brushed out. Failure to clean hair pads results in a bruised or irritated area on the horse's back. Wool blankets are used on horses that are not worked very hard and are ridden for short periods.

New types of pads are being developed and marketed that consist of energy-absorbing cores covered by leather or synthetic materials. The SaddleRight™ pad consists of a $\frac{3}{8}$-inch-thick pad of high-density/high-tech

FIGURE 11-4   Four types of western saddle pads: *(a)* hair; *(b)* orthopedic; *(c)* wool; *(d)* SaddleRight™. (Photos by W. Evans.)

open-cell urethane with a $\frac{1}{8}$-inch-thick strip of even higher-density urethane laminated onto the outside of the base pad across the area where the bars of the saddle sit. Encased in a leather, felt, or leather and felt cover, the pad is meant to be used over a thin, sweat-absorbing cloth pad. The urethane, used in the space shuttles to prevent vibrations, was developed to instantly rebound to its shape despite millions of compressions. If fitted properly on the horse's back, it helps prevent back injuries.

Bridles

Western riders use a bridle composed of a set of reins, a bit, and a headstall (Figure 11-5). The type of rein varies with the use of the horse. Braided rawhide reins with a romal are quite popular with many riders. Rope horses are usually ridden with a single closed rein. The split reins are an old standby used on ranch, pleasure, and show horses. Many variations of headstalls are used. The simplest headstall consists of a leather strap that goes over the poll and is split so that it encircles one ear. Other types of headstalls have a browband and/or throatlatch to keep the headstall in the proper position on the horse's head.

Forward

Saddles

Forward saddles (Figures 11-6 and 11-7) are made in three basic designs. The "flat saddle" is the general-purpose saddle for all-around riding and for dressage. The seat of the flat saddle is a little deeper than that of the show saddle used for saddle seat equitation. In recent years, however, many forward seat riders have opted for the "forward seat" or "jumping" saddle. The flaps are cut well forward and may incorporate padded knee rolls to help the rider when going over jumps. The forward seat saddle may be cut back. The third type, the "show saddle," has a flat seat that causes the rider to sit back toward the cantle. The flaps are straight down, and usually the pommel is cut back. Show saddles are used in saddle seat classes and for saddle-bred and gaited horses that are ridden with long stirrups. These saddles are measured from the front end of the pommel (at the screw) to the top of the cantle. The average rider takes a 20- to 22-inch (50.8- to 55.9-cm) saddle (Figure 11-8).

The girths that hold the forward-type saddle on the horse are made of several types of material. Sturdy, washable cotton webbing or folded leather are the most popular. A tubular, sheep-wool girth cover can be slipped over the girth to prevent chafing.

If the girth is not sufficient to hold the saddle in position, a breastplate is attached to the sides of the pommel and to the girth. Breastplates are

FIGURE 11-5   Three types of bridles. *(a)* Use the Weymouth bridle, composed of snaffle and curb bits with double reins, in showing three- and five-gaited horses. *(b)* Use the pelham bridle, a single-bitted, double-reined bridle, on hunters, polo ponies, and pleasure horses. *(c)* Use the one-ear or split-ear bridle on working stock horses (horses that work cattle); the type shown has a roping rein and a curb bit.

(a)

(b)   *(c)*

FIGURE 11-6   Basic types of forward-seat saddles: *(a)* dressage saddle; *(b)* general purpose forward-seat saddle; *(c)* show saddle. (Photos by W. Evans.)

frequently used on hunters. A plump-bellied pony may require a crupper under the tail to prevent the saddle from slipping forward.

Stirrup leathers for forward-type saddles are sold separately. To keep the stirrups adjusted to the same length, the holes must be punched at exactly the same length on both stirrups. Leathers should be switched from one side of the saddle to the other quite regularly because mounting tends to stretch them.

Stirrup irons must be approximately 1 inch (2.54 cm) wider than the rider's foot. Many novice riders use safety stirrups (Figure 11-9) because they automatically open if the rider falls. Rubber stirrup treads are quite popular

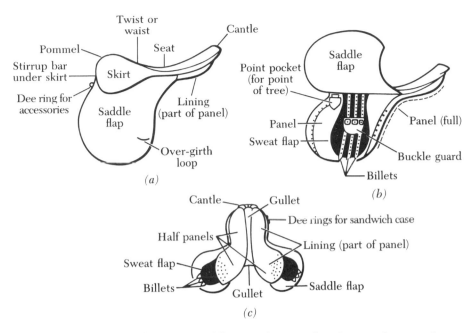

FIGURE 11-7   Forward (hunt seat) saddle: *(a)* side view; *(b)* side view, flap raised; *(c)* saddle flap.

FIGURE 11-8   Measure forward-seat saddle from the front end of the pommel (at the screw or headpin) to the top of the cantle to determine the size.

FIGURE 11-9 Safety stirrup for the forward-seat saddle. The pressure from a fall disengages the heavy rubber band, thus releasing the rider's foot.

but are dangerous to use because the rider's foot does not slip out of the stirrup as easily when an accident occurs.

Pads

Saddle pads or "nunnals" are not necessary for English-type saddles, but they are used by many horsepeople, particularly during ordinary riding. The pad is attached to the saddle by running the billets through two straps. Pads are usually made of sponge rubber, synthetic fibers, sheepskin, or felt (Figure 11-10). They absorb sweat (thus protecting the saddle) and protect the horse's back and withers.

(a)   *(b)*

FIGURE 11-10 Forward saddle pads: *(a)* felt; *(b)* orthopedic. (Photos by W. Evans.)

Bridles

English bridles (Figure 11-5) come in a variety of types, depending on the use of the horse and type of bit it needs. The so-called pelham bridle is composed of a double set of reins, the pelham bit, cavesson, headstall, browband, and throatlatch. It is commonly used on hunters, polo ponies, and pleasure horses. The Weymouth bridle is used to develop flexion while maintaining the head carriage induced by riding the horse into the bradoon (small ring snaffle). Consequently, it is used on pleasure, three-gaited, and five-gaited horses.

The cavesson (noseband) can be used with a bridle to prevent the horse from evading bit action by opening its mouth (Figure 11-5). The effectiveness of the noseband can be increased by dropping the chin portion forward and under the mouthpiece of the bit and moving it to cross the chin groove.

Endurance and Competitive Trail Riding

Saddles

On endurance or competitive trail rides, most riders use western and forward seat saddles. However, special saddles have been developed to meet the needs of these performance events (Figure 11-11). Modifications of the McClellan saddle have been popular (Figure 11-12). Most are equipped with

FIGURE 11-11   Endurance saddle designed by Sharon Saare for American Saddlery of Chattanooga, Tennessee.

FIGURE 11-12   McClellan saddle. (Courtesy R. A. Woodworth.)

a crupper and/or breastcollar to prevent the saddle from slipping backward or forward on the horse's back. The cinch must be positioned far enough behind the horse's elbow to prevent galling the horse behind the front legs, so western saddles are rigged with a three-quarter rigging. The saddle horn of western saddles is in the rider's way and prevents one from riding a horse properly up steep inclines, so it is usually removed.

Pads

Endurance and competitive trail riders use typical western and forward saddle pads. Good-quality pads and blankets are very important to prevent back sores. The padding must be thick and heavy enough so that it will not wrinkle. When actually competing, most riders have enough saddle pads so that they can start out with a fresh, dry pad after each veterinary check. They are transported by the rider's crew.

Bridles and Bits

Almost all types of headgear are used by trail riders. Although it is not advisable, some people ride with only a halter. The bridle and bit should be simple but should allow easy control of the horse and enable it to drink easily out of shallow streams.

Other Equipment

Riding long distances requires equipment for the horse's and rider's safety and comfort. Water canteens are usually carried in warm climates. If water is not available for the horse, the crew may have to carry water to the rest stops. A small pouch attached to the saddle is handy to carry a flashlight, Chapstick, sun lotion, salt tablets, gloves, sunglasses, and a snack. A water sponge, hoof pick, and a rubber boot (in case of a lost shoe) are carried for the horse.

Bits and Bitting

Bitting a horse has traditionally been done by trial and error and probably will continue to be. Each person has a different sense of touch for a given horse's mouth with a particular bit. You may have to use a different bit on the horse to obtain maximum performance. Riders with "light hands" may use a harsh bit with a punishing effect, but beginning riders or riders with "heavy hands" need to use a bit that does not punish a horse. Similarly, each horse may require a different bit for maximum performance because of differences in jaw width, tongue thickness, head length, and amount of pressure applied by the bit to specific areas.

A bit must fit the horse's mouth so that the horse is comfortable. Bit selection also depends on the horse's training and temperament and on the kinds of riding the owner does. The wrong bit can decrease control or delay training. Proper selection requires an understanding of the types and uses of bits.

Types

Bits are classified as hackamore, curb, and snaffle (Figure 11-13). Forward seat (English) and western riders are acquainted with the many types and uses of snaffle bits. Western riders use curb bits that have many variations, whereas English riders use kimblewicks (commonly called "kimberwickes"), curbs, and pelhams. The snaffle bit comes in a variety of forms (Figure 11-14) and is used for many purposes. The common feature of all snaffle bits is that the mouthpiece is jointed or straight, with rings for the reins at both ends. The rings on the ends of the mouthpiece may be of four types: round, egg butt, racing dee, or full check. The snaffle is a mild bit, and the severity is regulated by the circumference of the mouthpiece; that is, the smaller the circumference, the more severe the bit. Twisted mouthpieces also increase the severity of the bit and, if used improperly, can ruin the bars of a horse's mouth. The pull of the rein exerts a direct pull on the horse's mouth equal to the force exerted by the rider. Therefore, lowering a snaffle in a horse's mouth from the correct position of one or two wrinkles at the corners of the mouth increases its severity. The round rings must be large enough not to pull through the mouth. Quite often the lips are pinched by the rings. To prevent this, the racing dee and egg butt snaffles have metal casing around the joints. The full cheek snaffle has two small bars inside the rings that prevent the rings from sliding into the mouth and that serve as a steering aid for the young horse.

(a)

(b)

(c)

FIGURE 11-13   Three basic types of bits: *(a)* hackamore; *(b)* curb; *(c)* snaffle.

The hackamore bit (Figure 11-13) is often confused with a hackamore (Figure 11-15). Hackamore bits do not have mouthpieces; they are used on horses that will not accept a bit or that have mouth injuries that would be irritated by a mouthpiece. Many hackamore bits have long shanks, and thus a great deal of pressure can be applied to the nose and chin groove without much pull on the reins.

A true hackamore (Figure 11-15), derived from the Spanish word *jaquima,* is used to start young horses in training. The hackamore is used to apply a direct pressure on the nose and chin with the bosal. Bosals can be made of any of several materials such as rope, horsehair, or leather, but a braided rawhide bosal with a rawhide core is preferred. The bosal must fit closely around the horse's nose and low near the soft cartilage. The bosal is held in place with a headstall and a fiador. The fiador (Figure 11-15), which is a small double rope attached to the heel knot, passes over the poll and serves as a throatlatch. The mecate (Figure 11-15) is a soft, large-diameter rope that is easy to grip and is long enough

FIGURE 11-14   Types of snaffle bits: *(a)* jointed mouth; *(b)* flat ring, Y, or W twisted wire snaffle; *(c)* jointed mouth, German egg butt snaffle; *(d)* jointed mouth, twisted egg butt snaffle; *(e)* rubber-covered racing dee snaffle; *(f)* egg butt fullcheek snaffle; *(g)* Australian loose-ring or Fulmer snaffle; *(h)* metal mullen mouth egg butt snaffle; *(i)* soft rubber mullen mouth full-spoon check snaffle. (From DuPont, 1973.)

to form a lead rope after the continuous rein is adjusted so that it reaches the saddle horn. Attachment of the mecate to the bosal forms the lead rope knot. The size of the bosal is adjusted by the hackamore knot (Figure 11-16) so that a slight lift to the heel knot causes the cheeks of the bosal to apply pressure to the chin. The heel knot should be heavy enough so that chin pressure is relieved as soon as rein pressure is decreased. Both reins of a hackamore are used simultaneously in the early stages of training so that the horse learns to respond to a direct rein and a bearing rein. The direct rein applies lateral pressure to the horse's head, and the bearing rein applies pressure to the side of the neck. Later, only a bearing rein is used.

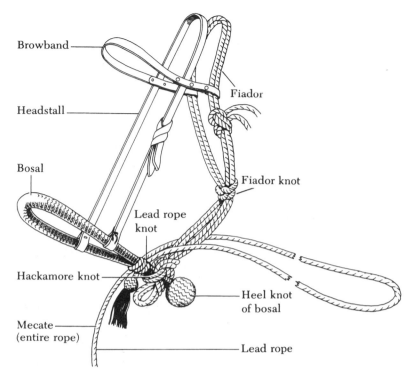

Browband

Headstall

Bosal

Hackamore knot

Mecate
(entire rope)

Fiador

Fiador knot

Lead rope
knot

Heel knot
of bosal

Lead rope

FIGURE 11-15 A hackamore (jaquima) with a fiador.

The kimblewick bit (Figure 11-17) is similar to a snaffle bit except that there are loops or slots at the top of the rings for attachment of the bridle and a curb chain. The kimblewick uses single reins that exert light pressure on the mouthpiece. Increasing the pull on the reins causes the dee rings (see Figure 11-14c, d, e, and h) to act as short shanks and apply curb chain pressure. The curb pressure is not severe because of the short lever action of the dee rings and because the rider does not have much control over the amount of curb action.

To gain greater control than that provided by snaffle and kimblewick bits, English-style riders use the double-reined pelham bit (Figure 11-17). One set of reins attaches to rings that pull on the mouthpiece, and the other set is attached to rein loops on the ends of shanks. Pulling on both reins simultaneously or on the shank rein gives snaffle action. Pulling only on the curb rein activates the curb action, which also applies pressure to the curb chain groove and on the poll. The pelham bit is popular because it is easy for a rider to learn to use.

The double bridle allows the English-style rider to use snaffle and curb action either simultaneously or separately. The two bits, called a Weymouth set (Figure 11-18), are composed of a bradoon (small ring snaffle) and a curb. They are used primarily on dressage and gaited horses and sometimes on hunters.

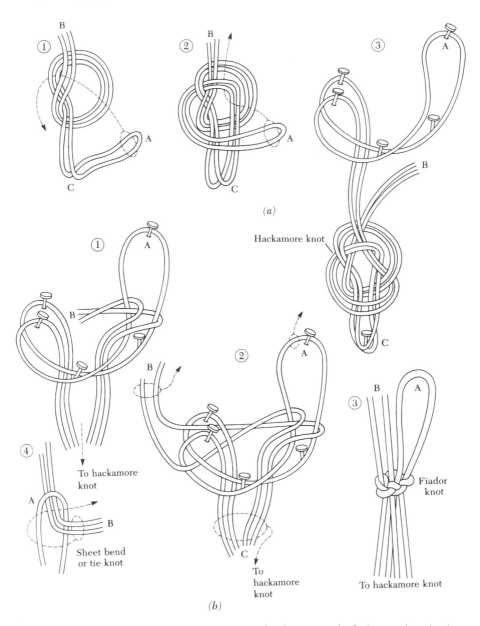

FIGURE 11-16   Steps in preparing *(a)* jaquima (hackamore); *(b)* fiador; and *(c)* lead rope knots for a jaquima.

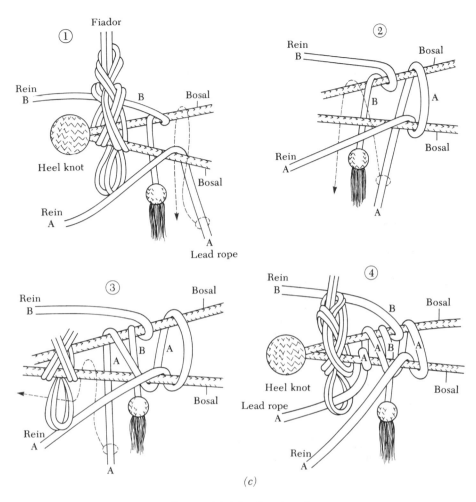

FIGURE 11-16 *Continued*

Curb bits for western riders come in numerous shapes and combinations of mouthpieces and shanks. The basic curb bit is shown in Figure 11-20. The distance between the center of the mouthpiece and the center of the bridle loop should be $1\frac{7}{8}$ to 2 inches (4.8 to 5.1 cm) for proper bit action. The distance between the center of the mouthpiece and the center of the rein loop (shank length) determines the leverage or amount of pull from the reins that is exerted on the bit. The shanks of most curbs are 5 to $5\frac{1}{2}$ inches long (12.7 to 14 cm). Mouthpieces are $4\frac{1}{2}$ to 5 inches long (11.4 to 12.7 cm). Solid mouthpieces usually have a rise (port) in the middle that relieves part of the tongue pressure and applies pressure to the roof of the mouth. The "halfbreed" has a high port ($1\frac{1}{2}$ inches maximum, or 3.8 cm) with a roller in it. The curb chain must be kept fairly tight to prevent the port from injuring the roof of the mouth. Most horses play with the roller with their tongues and, in so doing, keep their mouths moist. Quite

FIGURE 11-17   Pelham and kimblewick (kimberwicke) bits: *(a)* mullen mouth egg butt steel pelham with lip strap; *(b)* loose-ring, fixed port mouth steel pelham; *(c)* mullen mouth, sliding cheek, Tom Thumb pelham; *(d)* jointed mouth steel pelham; *(e)* hard nylon Tom Thumb pelham with converter straps; *(f)* steel kimblewick. (From DuPont, 1973.)

often, rollers and the ports of bits are covered with copper, which increases the flow of saliva to keep a horse's mouth moist. The spade bit (Figure 11-19) is very severe ($3\frac{1}{2}$-inch port, or 7.8 cm) and must be used with a tight curb chain and very light rein pull. The spade bit also has a roller (cricket) and springs.

Bit Action

A bit and bridle can exert pressure on one location or on a combination of several different locations on a horse's head. The shape, weight, and size of the mouthpiece and the thickness of the horse's tongue determine the amount of pressure exerted on the tongue. A common mistake is to use a thick mouthpiece on a thick-tongued horse so that the animal cannot comfortably close its mouth. When the mouth is closed, too much pressure is applied on the tongue by the mouthpiece so that the horse wants to keep its mouth open. The curb chain applies pressure to the curb chain groove. Proper adjustment for different types of bits is necessary for proper action. A "halfbreed" bit with a roller or a spade bit requires a tighter

FIGURE 11-18   Weymouth set: *(a)* flat ring bradoon; *(b)* sliding cheek curb; *(c)* leather curb strap; *(d)* double-link curb chain; *(e)* single-link curb chain; *(f)* wide, single flat-link curb chain. (From DuPont, 1973.)

FIGURE 11-19   Santa Barbara *(a)* silver-mounted spade bit and *(b)* spoon spade mouthpiece.

curb chain than does a curb bit. This limits the rise of the port, avoiding possible injury to the roof of the mouth. Curb chains that are too loose pinch the corners of the mouth when the reins are pulled tight and do not give the desired pressure on the chin groove. A general rule is that you should be able to insert two fingers between the curb chain and the chin groove.

The bars carry the weight of a snaffle bit primarily when the bit is passive, unless the horse properly flexes its head at the poll to relieve the pressure. The curb bit presses on the bars when the curb chain becomes tight. Because of the fulcrum action of the mouthpiece, most curb bits exert some pressure on the poll right behind the ears when the reins are pulled. The pressure results from movement of the curb strap loop forward and downward. Bridle adjustment varies the amount of pressure applied by a curb bit to the poll (a loose bridle applies less pressure). The lips receive pressure at the corners of the mouth and over the bars which they cover until heavy pressure is applied to a curb or snaffle bit. The amount of pressure applied to the roof of the mouth is controlled by the type and movement of the curb bit port. As previously discussed, the curb chain adjustment limits the rise of the port. Certain types of bits, such as the hackamore bit (Figure 11-13), apply pressure to the nose.

The balance or collection of a horse can be controlled to a certain extent by the bit it carries. With curb bits, the ratio of the distance from the curb strap loop to the mouthpiece and from the mouthpiece to the rein loop (Figure 11-20) controls the horse's balance. A horse that is heavy on the forehand (that is, its center of balance is too far forward) will pick up its head, bring in its nose, and flex at the poll so that the center of gravity is shifted backward when the ratio is increased (for example, increased from $1:1$ to $1:3$). In contrast, a horse with a sensitive mouth performs much better for a heavy-handed rider when the ratio is decreased and less pressure is applied for a given pull on the reins.

1⁷/₈–2 inches (4.76–5.08 cm)

5–5½ inches (12.7–14.0 cm)

FIGURE 11-20 Curb bit.

Martingales

A standing martingale keeps a horse from carrying its head too high (Figure 11-21). It attaches to the noseband, is supported by a neck strap, and is connected to the girth. A running martingale (Figure 11-21) works on the mouth to keep the head low. The reins are run through the rings on the end of the straps, which change the direction of the rein pull. It is used to get the proper headset during training and to correct a horse that throws its head upward. The Irish martingale (Figure 11-21) is a leather strap with rings at each end. It links the reins together in front of the horse's neck to prevent them from being flipped over onto the same side of the neck during a stumble or other sudden, unexpected movement of the horse's head. It is merely a safety device and does not affect a horse's performance.

Care, Storage, and Cleaning

Saddles

Saddles and other tack are expensive and require adequate care if they are to have a long and useful life. A few minutes of care after each ride can keep tack in excellent condition. Soft, pliable leather is comfortable for the horse as well as for the rider. Cleaning leather that is exposed to sweat, moisture, and dirt with saddle soap prolongs its usefulness. Cleaning after use also allows an opportunity to inspect the saddle and tack for damage and excessive wear.

Every 3 to 6 months, the saddle and all tack should be stripped, thoroughly cleaned with saddle soap, and preserved with neat's-foot oil. Commercial preparations combine neat's-foot oil with other compounds to form an excellent preservative and waterproofing compound. During these two to four

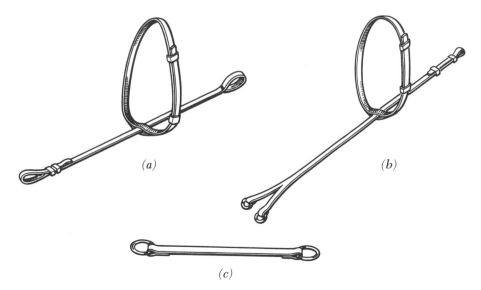

(a)   *(b)*

(c)

FIGURE 11-21   Martingales: *(a)* standing; *(b)* running; *(c)* Irish.

cleanings each year, give all tack components a thorough safety inspection. Clean the sheepskin of western saddles with a brush. Dirty, lumpy sheepskin causes saddle sores. Remove excess dirt from tack by soaking in warm water and castile soap. After the dirt is soft, remove it with a stiff brush. Allow the leather to dry partially, but wipe it with neat's-foot oil while it is still damp. Usually two or three coats of neat's-foot oil are needed to restore it to a usable condition. You can rejuvenate old, dried, cracked leather by applying warm neat's-foot oil at least once a day over a period of several days.

The saddle and other tack should be stored in a dry room because moisture and mildew cause rapid deterioration. To keep saddles and other tack clean, the room should be free from dust and a dust cover placed on the saddle. The room should be free of rodents and insects. Rodents chew on leather to obtain salt and can ruin a great deal of tack in a short time. Store saddles on saddle racks to prevent the tree from being damaged and to keep the sheepskin clean. Place the cinch straps and cinch across the seat, or hang them from the saddle horn. Store forward seat (English) saddles on a rack with the irons slid up the stirrup leathers next to the saddle flap. Place the girth over the seat so that the saddle is ready to be placed on a horse.

Clean saddle pads and blankets with a brush after drying. Dirty blankets frequently cause saddle sores. The new synthetic pads are machine washable and are easy to keep clean.

Bridles

Clean the leather parts of the bridle in the same manner as described for a saddle. When the bridle is thoroughly cleaned, remove the metal components, if possible, and clean them with warm water and soap. Clean sterling silver parts with any of a variety of commercially available compounds.

It is important to hang the bridle over a round rack that is approximately 4 inches (10.2 cm) in diameter and similar to a coffee can, to keep the headstall in the proper shape. Bridles and reins that are hung over nails tend to crack and develop weak spots.

Bits

You can clean bits with a damp cloth. If you remove a bit from a sick horse, boil it in water before using it again. This helps prevent the spread of disease. Vaseline prevents bits that are not made of stainless steel from rusting. Other types of oils leave a bad taste in the horse's mouth even after they are wiped off.

RIDING

Saddling

Before the saddle is placed on the horse, make sure the horse's back and cinch areas are clean and all the hairs are lying in their natural direction. Check the saddle blanket and all other equipment for foreign objects.

Forward

With the forward saddle or hunt seat (Figure 11-6), lay the girth (leather strap that goes under the belly) across the seat and pull the stirrups up high before placing the saddle on the horse's back. A saddle pad is not necessary, but if you use one, connect it to the saddle before saddling up. Place the saddle and pad gently on the horse's back from the near (left) side and just behind the shoulder blades. Then move the saddle back approximately $1\frac{1}{2}$ inches (38.1 mm) so that the hairs are straightened. Never move the saddle forward because if you do the hairs become ruffled and will cause saddle sores. Next, pass the girth—attached to the off (right) side billets (Figure 11-7)—under the horse's belly. Pull the girth up and buckle it to the near (left) side billets. Before tightening the girth enough to ride, smooth out all skin wrinkled under it and lead the horse around briefly. Then tighten the girth enough to keep the saddle in position during the ride. Adjust the stirrup leathers on a hunt seat saddle for proper length, and pull the stirrups up high again until you are ready to mount. The stirrup length should be such that the stirrup iron reaches the armpit when you extend your arm with the fingertips touching the stirrup buckles. Some people adjust (shorten or lengthen) their stirrups to a position in which the iron hits just below the ankle bone. A riding instructor may suggest changing the standard stirrup length to improve the rider's position.

Western

To saddle a horse for western riding, place the saddle pad on the horse's back in front of the withers. Then prepare the western saddle (Figure 11-1) by placing the cinches and right stirrup across the seat. Grip the saddle by the pommel and cantle and place it gently on the saddle pad and horse's back just behind the shoulder blades. Move the saddle and pad backward to a position where the bars will not rub the shoulder blades. After lowering the cinches and right stirrup, cinch the saddle up, but not too tight. If the saddle has front and back cinches, tighten the front cinch first to prevent the horse from bucking the saddle off. After walking the horse around, tighten the cinches.

Before using a saddle on a horse, determine if the saddle fits the horse or, in some instances, if the horse fits the saddle. A saddle that does not fit the horse can cause sores but usually causes skin and muscle damage. The pain from an incorrectly fitting saddle will most likely affect performance. During riding, you may notice tail swishing and ear pinning, not traveling straight, stumbling and tripping, and resistance to work or training. To find out if the saddle fits, the following steps are suggested. First, place the saddle, without any padding, far forward on the back, and slide it back into the place it is usually fastened. Before doing up the girth, run a hand under the saddle. If at any point it becomes difficult or impossible to slide the hand between the horse and saddle without lifting up the saddle with the other hand, that part is putting excessive pressure on the horse. Now fasten the girth just tight enough to take the slack out of it, but not tight enough to mount. Stand to one side and look down the gullet (the "backbone bridge") from the front (withers) end. You should be able to insert two fingers between the withers and the gullet at the top; there should also be space on either side of the withers. The padding of the bars should rest $\frac{3}{4}$ inch (19 mm) below the side edge of the withers. Again standing to the side, look through the gullet from the back (loin) end. There should be $\frac{1}{2}$ inch (12.7 mm) of clearance between backbone and bars on either side, and the tree must not touch the spine. Face the saddle from the side, and grab the pommel with one hand and the cantle with the other. Rock the saddle, front to back, exerting moderate pressure. If either end rocks up more than 1 inch, the tree is too hollow for that back; in other words, that saddle belongs on a horse that is more swaybacked. If there is no motion at all as you rock, the saddle is too flat and the horse's back too hollow. The saddle is resting only on its ends, not putting any pressure at all on the center of the back. Now look under the back of the saddle again, this time at the padding on the bars. The center of the padding should be resting on the back muscles. If the inner edges of the bars are the only parts touching the horse, the saddle is too flat and broad and the horse will wind up with pressure injuries along either side of its spine. If the outer edges touch, the saddle is too narrow—or else the horse is too fat.

With the saddle still in the position of normal use, look at where it bears on the withers and shoulder blade region. If the bars touch the shoulder blade, the saddle is placed too far forward. Rotate the shoulder blade by extending the horse's foreleg. Although the edge of the scapula may rotate under the saddle, it should not make contact.

Now, with an assistant, tighten up the girth and get into the saddle (or have a friend of your approximate build mount up). Repeat all the tests: there should still be daylight through the gullet, you should be able to tell where most of the pressure from the bars is bearing, and the saddle should not rock with the rider's weight in riding position. Put a hand between the saddle and the shoulder blade; as the foreleg is extended, there should not be severe pinching as the hand is run under any part of the saddle as you ride. If it pinches the hand, it is pinching the horse.

Several signs of an improperly fitting saddle may appear after a horse has been ridden. The horse shows pain when the saddle is placed on its back and may sink its back down sharply. The horse may also do this when it is mounted. Some horses will not stand still while saddled and will move with a very stiff gait. Both reactions indicate pain from pressure on the back. You can locate tender spots by rubbing a hand over the back—the horse will flinch. After a saddle is removed, dry spots in the middle of a large sweaty area indicate that pressure has prevented the sweat glands from functioning in that area. When the pressure is removed, the area fills with fluid (edema). If you see dry areas, replace the saddle and loosen the cinch slowly during the next 2 hours. Failure to immediately replace the saddle results in dry, crusty skin and hair falling out. Frequently, the hair is white when it grows back. Any swelling, broken hairs, or bald spots indicate scalding and/or abrasion. Scalding is an irritation or burning of the skin caused by a saddle or piece of tack chafing a sweaty hide. Abrasion curls or breaks off the hair. The spontaneous appearance of wrinkles in an area indicates that the skin is losing elasticity because of excess pressure on that area from the saddle.

Riders need to know what size seat they need in a saddle. The most common fault is having the seat too small for the rider. This forces the rider to sit at the back of the saddle which puts excessive pressure on the horse's back.

Bridling

After saddling the horse, bridle it. When bridling a horse, hold the crown (Figure 11-22) in your right hand. As your right hand pulls the bridle upward, your left hand guides the bit into the horse's mouth. If you bang the teeth with the bit during a few bridlings, the horse usually becomes head shy and hard to bridle. If the horse does not open its mouth for the bit, insert your thumb and forefinger between the bars, and the horse will usually open its mouth. After inserting the bit in the mouth, adjust the bridle so that there are one or two wrinkles at the corners of the mouth. Adjust the throatlatch strap, if present, so that you can insert three or four fingers between it and the horse's jaws. The noseband (English bridle) and curb strap must also be properly adjusted for the horse (see the section on bitting). When removing the bridle, place your left hand on the horse's face to keep its nose down and tucked in, so the bit will not hit the teeth when you remove it.

Follow several safety precautions when bridling the horse. Protect your head from the horse's head. Stand in close, just behind and to one side (preferably the

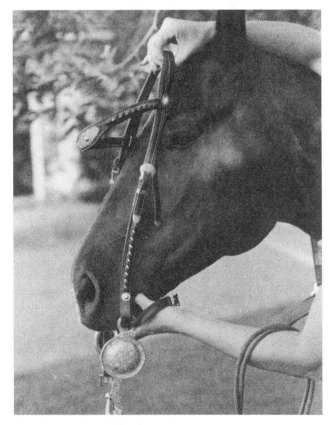

FIGURE 11-22 Bridling a horse with a curb bit. Place the bit in its mouth by holding it with your fingers and pressing on the bar of the mouth with your thumb. (Photo by W. Evans.)

left side) of the horse's head. Handle the horse's ears carefully. Maintain control of the horse when bridling by refastening the halter around its neck. Adjust the bridle to fit the horse before riding it. Check the placement of the bit, the adjustment of the curb strap, and the adjustment of the throatlatch.

Western Riding

Mounting

A western horse is customarily mounted from the near (left) side. However, all horses should be accustomed to being mounted from the off (right) side because some conditions preclude mounting from the near side. Grip the reins properly in the left hand, which also grips the mane in front of the saddle. When mounting, face the rear of the horse and place your left foot securely in the left stirrup. With your right hand, grip the saddle horn, and swing your right leg over the saddle. The right leg swing should be close to the saddle, your left toe should not hit the horse, and your left knee should not exert excess pressure on the horse's side. Then place the right foot in the right stirrup. A horse should stand quietly for mounting and dismounting. To be certain of this, you may have to control its head through the reins. On cold, frosty mornings when horses feel good and may buck, or when mounting horses that may buck, pull the horse's head toward you with the reins in your left hand to prevent the horse from bucking until it is mounted. The procedure for dismounting is opposite from the procedure for mounting.

Before riding the horse, adjust the stirrups for length. Each person needs a different length stirrup to maintain the proper position, but a general rule is to adjust the stirrup so that it strikes 1 inch (25.4 mm) above the ankle bone. If the rider stands up in the saddle, there should be a 4-inch (101.6-mm) clearance between the crotch and saddle.

Never mount or dismount a horse in a barn or near fences, trees, or overhanging projections. Side-stepping and rearing mounts can injure riders who fail to take these precautions.

Position

After learning to mount and dismount, the rider's next consideration is position. You must have good position to control the horse and to be able to use the riding aids. A rider with good position is graceful and relaxed when the horse is in motion. Each rider usually modifies the basic position slightly, and the positions that are popular in the show ring are different in different parts of the country. The American Association of Health, Physical Education and Recreation (Division for Girls' and Women's Sports and the Division of Men's Athletics) lists four elements of good position: it (1) allows unity of horse and rider, (2) is nonabusive to the horse, (3) ensures security for the rider, and (4) permits the effective use of aids or controls. Proper riding position is shown in Figure 11-23. Flex your ankles and turn your toes outward approximately 30°. When your ankles are flexed so that your heels are down, your ankles can act as shock absorbers. Drop the weight of your body into your heels. The inside area of the ball of the foot is slightly lower

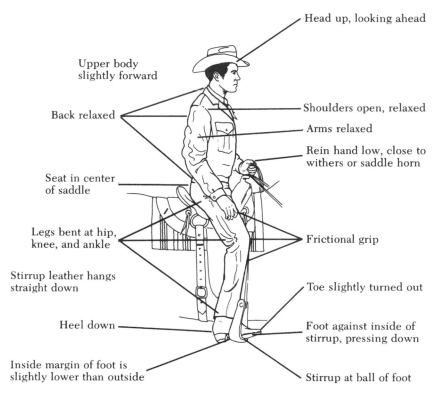

Head up, looking ahead

Upper body slightly forward

Shoulders open, relaxed

Back relaxed

Arms relaxed

Rein hand low, close to withers or saddle horn

Seat in center of saddle

Legs bent at hip, knee, and ankle

Frictional grip

Stirrup leather hangs straight down

Toe slightly turned out

Heel down

Foot against inside of stirrup, pressing down

Inside margin of foot is slightly lower than outside

Stirrup at ball of foot

FIGURE 11-23   Basic position for western riding. (From Shannon, 1970.)

than the outside area. For a good position that allows you to be balanced, rest the ball of your foot on the stirrup treads, and make sure the inside of the ball of your foot is lower than the outside (Figure 11-24). This foot position, with your toes turned out slightly, keeps the inner side of your calf in close contact with the saddle fender for good frictional grip. To aid in shock absorption, flex your ankles so that your heels drop downward. When your body weight is carried by your heels, the stability of your lower leg increases. Complete the positioning of your lower leg by keeping the inside of your calf in contact with the saddle so that your leg, from the knee down, allows the stirrup to hang vertically. You can thus use your lower leg efficiently and effectively to signal the horse.

One of the most common mistakes made by beginning riders is keeping the ankle stiff. The concussion, rather than being absorbed by the ankle, is transferred upward, and the rider bounces in the saddle. The bouncing irritates and tires both the horse and the rider. Flex your knees to help absorb concussion and to slightly grip the saddle. Keep the inner surfaces of your thighs flat against the saddle to complete the leg-gripping action.

To keep your balance on a horse, relax your hip joints and keep them mobile. This allows the upper part of your body to adjust for changes in speed and direction. Maintain three-point contact between the rider's seat and saddle (that is, at your two seat bones and your crotch).

FIGURE 11-24   Frictional grip: thighs, knees, and calves held in contact with the horse by weight flowing into the heels. The rider's weight is supported by the crotch and seat bones. Hold the inner surface of your thighs flat against the saddle, and position your knees and lower thighs against the fender of the saddle and barrel of the horse. The inner surface of your upper calves is in contact with the barrel of the horse; the lower part of your legs does not grip below the knee. Use the lower leg to signal the horse to indicate the movements you desire. Position the ball of the foot in the stirrup in such a way that the inside margin is lower than the outside margin, and position the foot against the inner curve of the stirrup. (From Shannon, 1970.)

Keep your back straight except for a slight arch in the small of your back. Tilt your upper body slightly forward to maintain balance and to align with the horse's center of gravity. Keep your shoulders open and even. Hold your head erect, and look straight forward.

For the right-handed rider, allow your left arm to drop naturally beside your body. Your left hand holds the reins (Figure 11-25) just above the saddle horn. Wrist and finger motion and carriage are important to obtain proper response from the horse. Hold your wrist straight but relaxed. To feel the horse's mouth, keep your fingers relaxed and "soft." A rider's lack of self-confidence or nervousness is quickly transmitted to the horse via the rider's hands. The style of holding the reins varies from locality to locality and under different conditions. Some styles are shown in Figure 11-25.

Carry your right arm in a relaxed position, resting on your thigh or holding the romal (Figure 11-26).

FIGURE 11-25   Proper way to hold reins during western riding: *(a)* free hand holding the split ends of the reins or romal; *(b)* reins in one hand; *(c)* reins passing down through the thumb and index finger; *(d)* reins separated by the little finger; *(e)* reins separated by the index finger. (From Shannon, 1970.)

As the speed of the horse increases, increase your frictional grip of the thighs, knees, and calves and tilt your upper body forward to maintain balance. If your upper body gets behind the center of gravity of the horse and you do not shift more weight into your lower leg, you lose balance, control of the horse, and effective, efficient use of the riding aids. Most riders also feel that, with speed, it is easier to carry the free forearm parallel to their belt.

FIGURE 11-26   Position for free hand during western riding: *(a)* holding split reins or romal (juniors); *(b)* on thigh; *(c)* at belt. (From Shannon, 1970.)

FIGURE 11-27   English equitation—mounting, correct seat, and dismounting: (a) prepare to lead; (b) stand at horse's head; (c) mount, first step; (d) mount, second step; (e) position right foot; (f) address the reins; (g) position hands; (h) basic position in saddle; (i) ready to ride; (j) prepare to dismount; (k) dismount; (l) step down. (From Bradley and Hardwicke, 1971.)

FIGURE 11-27 *Continued*

Forward Riding

Mounting

The sequence of mounting the horse for forward riding is shown in Figure 11-27. Address the reins (pick them up and adjust them) and hold them with the bight (loop) on the right side. Stand facing the rear of the horse and just forward of its shoulder, and place your left hand on its withers. Use your right hand to position your left foot in the stirrup. After positioning the stirrup, grip the off side of the cantle with your right hand. To gain momentum to swing up, take one or two hops on the right foot. Swing your right leg over the horse's hips, and ease into the seat. Position your right foot in the stirrup. In general, dismounting is a reversal of mounting. After swinging your right leg over the horse's hips, step down or slide down, depending on your size and the horse's size. Immediately on dismounting, "run up" the stirrups. Dangling stirrups may startle or annoy the horse. Horses can catch a cheek of the bit or even catch a hindfoot in a dangling stirrup iron when fighting flies. The dangling stirrup can also catch on doorways and other projections while you are leading the horse. After running up the stirrups, immediately bring the reins forward over the horse's head. In this position, they can be used for leading.

Position

The basic position (Figure 11-27) is described as follows by George H. Morris, former United States Equestrian Team member. Place the ball of your foot in the middle of the stirrup with your heel down and just behind the girth. When you turn the toe out (to a maximum of 18°), your calf and inner knee bones establish equal contact with the horse. Your thighs grip the saddle with the same pressure as your calves and knees. Sit forward in the saddle as close to the pommel as possible and as far from the cantle as possible. Carry your upper body erect but relaxed. An imaginary plumb line should be able to fall from your ear, to your shoulder, down through your hip bone, to the back of your heel. Carry your head so that you are looking directly ahead. Do not carry your shoulders forward or backward. Position your hands so that there is a direct line between your elbow and the horse's mouth. Your hands should be flexible, held above and slightly in front of the withers. Your thumbs should be 2 or 3 inches (50.8 to 76.2 mm) apart and as straight as possible. The correct position of the reins is illustrated in Figure 11-28.

When the horse is in motion, your body is farther forward so that your center of gravity is also shifted forward. This allows the rider to follow the motion of the horse. The faster the motion, the farther forward your body is shifted.

Saddle Seat

Mounting

The sequence of mounting the horse is discussed in the previous section on forward riding (Figure 11-27).

Position

Your seat and hips should be underneath, in a balanced position. Each leg should be in the middle of the saddle skirt with the stirrup leather under each

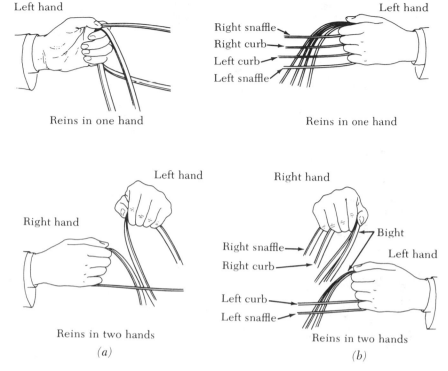

Left hand

Right snaffle
Right curb
Left curb
Left snaffle

Left hand

Reins in one hand

Reins in one hand

Left hand

Right hand

Right hand

Bight

Right snaffle

Left hand

Right curb

Left curb

Left snaffle

Reins in two hands

(a)

Reins in two hands

(b)

FIGURE 11-28   Methods of holding the reins for forward-seat riding: *(a)* single-rein bridle, *(b)* double-rein bridle.

knee (Figure 11-29). The lower half to two-thirds of the calf of your legs should be slightly out from the horse's side. Each stirrup should be at a right angle to the horse and flat across the ball of your foot. Stirrup length is correct when the stirrups strike your ankles (Figure 11-29) when feet are free of stirrups and the leg is hanging naturally. Keep your heels slightly down, a little lower than the toes. Turn your toes out about 15°. You should be able to look down and see your toes. A line perpendicular to the ground can be drawn through the middle of your head, through your shoulder, side, and ankle. Your arms should hang in a natural position from your shoulders. Do not tuck them in too tight. Your elbows should not come back past the sides. Hold your shoulders square with your head, and hold your neck erect. Your hands hold the reins as in Figure 11-28. Hand position depends on the height of the horse's head carriage. Keep your hands low if the horse carries its head low. When the horse trots or canters, your basic position changes a little so that you can follow the motion of the horse. You should post at the trot, on the correct diagonal. When the horse trots to the left, rise as the right foreleg goes up. When traveling to the right, post on the left diagonal. As the horse's foreleg moves downward, move downward. The purpose of posting on the correct diagonal is to allow the horse to keep its balance.

Some common errors while riding saddle seat are made with the hands and/or legs. Holding the reins too long forces the rider to use excess arm

(a)   *(b)*

FIGURE 11-29   Correct and incorrect leg positions for saddle seat equitation.
(a) Correct position. With your legs hanging free, the stirrup should be ankle
height. With your feet in the stirrup, your knees should rest on the stirrup
leather. Your calves should be just slightly out from the horse's side. Swing your
heels down and out to achieve the proper contact, with the inside thighs and
knees on the saddle. *(b)* Incorrect position of foot—toe is turned out and ankle
is bent in an unnatural position. (Photos by Jennifer Barron, courtesy of Quarter
Horse Journal.)

motion to control the horse. If the stirrups are too long, the rider's legs are
forced too far forward and the seat moves to the back of the saddle. Riding
too far forward in the saddle forces the legs behind the center of balance and
tips the shoulders forward.

Sidesaddle

Mounting

Pick up the reins with your right hand, which also holds the riding crop.
While holding the reins and crop, grasp the pommel of the saddle. Stand fac-

ing the front of the horse with your right shoulder next to the horse (Figure 11-30). An assistant slightly stoops in front of you. Place your left foot in the assistant's hands and your left hand on the assistant's shoulder or on the pommel. Flex your left leg and spring up sideways onto the flat of the saddle. Lift the right knee over the horn.

To dismount, place the reins in your right hand, and remove your left foot from the stirrup. Bring your right leg up over the pommel and to the left so that you are sitting facing your left. With your right hand, grip the top of the pommel as you dismount lightly and land facing the horse's head.

(a)

(b)

FIGURE 11-30   Mounting the sidesaddle: *(a)* with an assistant to give a leg up; *(b)* from the ground or with a mounting block. (From Floyd, 1979a.)

Position

Your left leg should hang perpendicularly from the knee. Depress your left heel, and hold your foot parallel to the ground (Figure 11-31). Sit erect in the middle of the saddle with your back slightly hollowed and perpendicular to the horse's back. Hold your arms naturally by your sides with your hands positioned a few inches apart (Figure 11-32). Hold your hands as low as possible, just above your knees.

Post when riding at the trot. To keep from bouncing off the saddle, hold your left foot parallel to the horse, which keeps your knee close against the saddle and prevents your leg from moving around.

DRIVING

There has been a rapid increase of interest in driving horses, which is an enjoyable way to exercise a horse. Many types of harnesses and hitches can be

FIGURE 11-31   Proper leg position for riding a sidesaddle.

FIGURE 11-32   Proper hand position and way to hold reins while riding sidesaddle.

used and, although complete description is beyond the scope of this book, some of them are discussed in this section.

Harnessing

A popular and common harness is the single fine harness. The basics for "putting to" in fine harness are as follows. When driving a heavy vehicle, the horse should wear a collar; a light vehicle may be driven with a breastcollar. Collars come in two types: (1) the Kay or closed collar is usually used with a fine harness, and (2) the open collar opens at the top and is closed with a strap (Figure 11-33). A collar must fit the horse so that it lies comfortably and flat on the shoulders with enough room at the bottom to allow a hand to pass freely between the collar and neck. Morgan horses usually wear a 21- or 22-inch (533.4- or 558.8-mm) collar. Determine the size by measuring from the inside, top to bottom (Figure 11-33). Place a Kay collar on the horse by slipping it over the horse's head. Turn it upside down so the head will pass through it. You may need to stretch open the sides. Then rotate and place it in the proper position. Fasten the hames in their grooves in the collar, with the leather strap on top and a kidney link on the bottom. The harness' saddle back band, bellyband, girth, crupper, loin strap, and breeching are in one unit that is placed on the horse's back (Figure 11-34). Place the saddle in the center of the back, and hang the breeching down around the horse's hindquarters so it rests about a foot below the dock. Place the tail through the crupper. Then

FIGURE 11-33   Way to measure a horse collar. The collar is of the open type. (Photo by W. Evans.)

move the saddle forward until the back strap is tight and the crupper is under the root of the tail. Take care that no tail hairs are between the crupper and the tail, because they will irritate the horse. The saddle should be resting so that the elbows do not rub on the girth. Tighten the girth and buckle it. Attach a martingale to the bottom of the collar, pass it between the forelegs, and fasten it to the girth. Pass the reins through the saddle pad terrets and the hame terrets and leave them hanging until the horse is bridled. When you place the bridle on the horse, it should be tight enough so that the bit makes one to two wrinkles in the corner of the mouth. This prevents the winkers (blinkers) from bulging out when the reins are pulled. Adjust the winkers so that the eyes are in the middle of them. Connect the reins to the bit. Two common driving bits are the snaffle and the Liverpool (Figure 11-35). Attach the overcheck to the saddle ring.

After harnessing the horse, hitch it to the vehicle. Keep the horse still by cross-tying it or by having an attendant hold its head. Always draw the vehicle to the

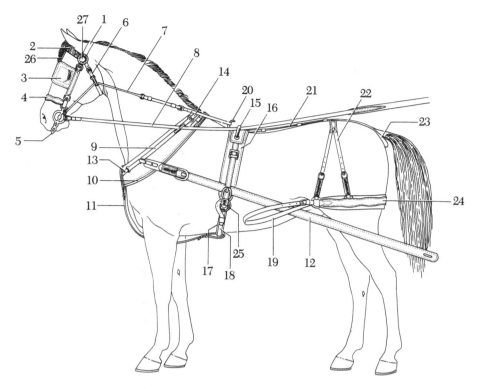

FIGURE 11-34   Single surrey harness: (1) headpiece; (2) browband; (3) winker (or blinker); (4) noseband; (5) Liverpool bit; (6) throatlatch; (7) bearing rein; (8) rein; (9) hame; (10) collar; (11) false martingale; (12) trace; (13) bottom hame strap; (14) top hame strap; (15) terret; (16) saddle; (17) girth; (18) bellyband; (19) breeching strap; (20) saddle hook; (21) back strap; (22) hip or loin straps; (23) crupper; (24) breeching; (25) tug; (26) winker stay; (27) rosette.

horse. With the shafts held high, draw the vehicle into position and place the shafts in the tugs. Uncoil and attach the traces to the vehicle. Next, fasten the breeching to the vehicle so that if the vehicle moves forward about 6 inches (15.2 cm), the breeching will take hold and keep it from striking the horse's hindlegs. Then pass the bellyband over the traces and fasten it around the shafts. Tighten it, but not as tightly as the girth. The shafts should be free enough to move slightly up and down.

To unhitch the horse, reverse the procedure. Be sure to move the vehicle away from the horse so that the horse does not step on the shafts. Also, take care not to drop the shafts and strike the horse's legs or feet.

Driving

The whip (driver) mounts the vehicle from the off (right) side and sits on that side. As you prepare to mount, hold the reins in your right hand and transfer them to

FIGURE 11-35   Liverpool bit for fine harness horse.

your left hand immediately on entering the vehicle. Hold the reins so that the near-side rein lies on your index finger and the off-side rein goes between your index and middle fingers (Figure 11-36). Keep equal tension on the reins. To turn the horse, apply pressure to one of the reins by moving your wrist. Some horses require you to use both hands when turning. Carry a whip in the right hand, holding it at the balance point. Most whips are about 6 to $7\frac{1}{2}$ feet long (1.8 to 2.3 m).

FIGURE 11-36   Correct way to hold harness reins and whip.

CHAPTER 12

Showing and Racing

Of the 7 to 8 million horses in the United States, 80 percent are used for nonprofessional purposes. The amateur owners and their enjoyment of the horse are the foundation on which our pleasure horse industry is built. At no previous time in U.S. history have so many people used the horse for recreational purposes. Interest in racing, rodeo, horse shows, endurance rides, competitive trail rides, cutting horses, polo, combined training, gymkhana, and fox hunting has continued to increase during the past few years. The following sections describe the most popular ways that horsepeople enjoy their horses.

HORSE SHOWS

The Association of American Horse Shows, Inc. was founded in New York City in 1917. In 1933, its name was changed to the American Horse Show Association, changing again shortly thereafter to its present title, the American Horse Shows Association (AHSA). The AHSA has grown steadily since its inception, but its growth has been phenomenal since 1960. The AHSA has 26 breeds and disciplines, over 70,000 individual members, and more than 2,600 member competitions per year. The AHSA Rule Book has become the definitive guide to equestrian competition, and is so universal that its specifications are enforced even at most unrecognized competitions. The awards program is one of the most extensive in the sports world.

In addition to sanctioning various types of horse shows, the AHSA keeps all records, licenses judges and stewards, handles disciplinary matters, awards annual prizes, and compiles the annual rule book of the horse show world.

There are two types of membership in the AHSA—show and individual. Show memberships contain the following classes: regular show, local show, combined training event, dressage competition, driving competition, honorary show, group, and affiliated. Individual membership consists of senior-active, life-sustaining, junior-active, athletic, and individual group. The selection of each type of membership is governed by specific rules.

The AHSA is a member of the Fédération Equestre International (FEI), the world governing body of equestrian sports. The FEI is the certifying agency for equestrian athletes for the Olympic Games and other international competitions. Exhibitors competing at FEI-sanctioned events must comply with the veterinary regulations of the FEI. Their regulations are basically a no-foreign-substance rule: no drug or medication is to be administered to a horse or pony in the time before a competition such that it, or a metabolite or derivative of it, might be present in the animal, might be detectable in its blood or urine sample, or might have any effect on its performance at the time of competition. Exhibitors must be aware that some normal feedstuffs contain trace amounts of several substances that might be detected in a urine sample. Acceptable trace limits for these substances have been established and this information is available to competitors. One must be careful about feeding treats that contain caffeine or other common drug-related compounds.

Horses are shown in many divisions under the auspices of the AHSA: Arabian, children's junior and hunter, combined training, Connemara, dressage, driving, equitation, Hackney, hunter breed, hunter division, hunter pony, jumpers, Morgan, National Show Horse, parade, Paso-Fino, reining, roadster, Saddlebred Horse, Shetland, vaulting, Welsh, and western. Each breed has specific classes, and there are open shows where the horse can be of any breed or nonregistered. Some of the most popular classes are equitation, hunter, jumper, western, gaited, roadster, and halter.

Halter Classes

Most halter classes are judged on type, conformation quality, substance, and soundness. Some breeds are also judged on disposition, manners, and action. Each breed organization has specific guidelines that are used by the judge. There are classes for certain ages and sex such as weanlings, yearlings, fillies, colts and stallions (Figure 12-1), mares, and geldings. Horses are also shown in breeding classes, such as produce of dam (two animals from the same dam), get of sire (three animals by the same sire, as in Figure 12-2), and sire and get (sire and two of get).

Equitation Division

The equitation division is divided into three classes: hunter, saddle, and stock seats. Only the rider is judged in equitation classes. Therefore, any horse suitable for a particular style of riding and capable of performing the class routine is acceptable.

FIGURE 12-1   Doubley Impress, 1992 American Quarter Horse Association high point halter stallion, owned by Roy and Malia Donn. (Photo by Don Schugart.)

FIGURE 12-2   Get-of-Sire Class at Dixie Cup Morgan Classic. Sire is UVM Promise, and the get are TVM Majesty and TVM Emperor. (Photo by Madeder, courtesy Tennessee Valley Morgan Horse Farm.)

In hunter seat equitation, the rider uses a forward saddle with knee rolls (Figure 12-3). At horse shows, the class may or may not be over obstacles. If the class is over obstacles, their number, designs, and height depend on the class of the entries. In nonjumping classes, the entries are required to perform at the walk, trot, and canter, and to execute individual figures. Competitors in the saddle seat division ride a flat English-type or forward-seat saddle (Figure 12-4). They are required to demonstrate the walk, trot, canter, and individual tests. Individual tests may include a figure eight at trot or canter, a serpentine at trot or canter, a change of leads, and other specified performances. Stock seat equitation is quite different from hunt and saddle seat equitation in that the rider uses a western stock saddle (Figure 12-5). In stock seat equitation competition, the horse and rider are scored as a team. The rider is scored on seat, hands, performance of horse, appointments of horse and rider, and suitability of horse to rider.

Western Division

The western division is composed of working cow horse, trail, western riding, and pleasure horse classes. Horses may be of any breed or combination of breeds as long as they are at least 14.1 hands, serviceably sound, and of stock horse type. Riders must be dressed according to specific rules about western attire.

Working Cow Horse

Working cow horse competition consists of two mandatory phases, the reined work and the cow work (Figure 12-6). In the reined work, every movement of the horse is controlled and the horse must be willing to be guided and

FIGURE 12-3   Hunter seat equitation. Toni Dirschel Werk riding Mr. Jutona, an AQHA gelding. (Courtesy T. Dirschel Werk.)

FIGURE 12-4   Kathleen Daly riding Ahu Pzazz in a saddle seat equitation class. (Photo by Fallaw, courtesy K. Daly.)

controlled with little or no apparent resistance. They perform a precise pattern of movements including stops, spins, rollbacks, circle, back ups, hesitations, lead changes, and run downs as in Figure 12-7. The purpose of the cow work phase is to demonstrate the horse's ability to control a cow—hold, drive, rate, turn, and overall contain and dominate a cow (Figure 12-8).

Trail

Trail horses (Figure 12-9) are required to work through and over obstacles that might be found on the trail, at a walk, jog-trot, and lope. They must work on a reasonably loose rein and without undue restraint. Tests include crossing bridges, mounting and dismounting, carrying objects from one part of the arena to another, backing through obstacles, and riding through water or over other types of obstacles. Trail horses are usually required to allow the rider to open a gate, pass through it, and close it while maintaining control. Performance and manners are scored 70 percent; appointments, equipment, and neatness are scored 20 percent; and conformation is scored 10 percent.

FIGURE 12-5   Pass to the Stars, 1992 American Quarter Horse Association high point western pleasure horse, owned by William and Sandy Stevenson of Renfrew, Pennsylvania. (Photo courtesy W. and S. Stevenson.)

Pleasure

In the popular western pleasure horse class (Figure 12-5), horses are required to be shown at a flat-footed four-beat walk, easy-riding two-beat trot, and three-beat lope. They must work both ways in the ring on a reasonably loose rein and be able to extend the gaits. The horses are also required to back in a straight line. Finalists in a class may be required to do further ring work. They are judged on performance (60 percent), conformation (30 percent), and appointments (10 percent).

Western Riding

Western riding is a competition in the performance and characteristics of a good, sensible, well-mannered, free and easy moving horse. A class is judged on riding quality of gaits, flying changes of lead, response to rider, manners, and disposition for 70 percent; appointments, equipment, and neatness for 10 percent; and conformation, 20 percent.

Jumper Division

The jumper division of the AHSA is very popular. Jumping horses may be of any breed, height, or sex. In this division, unsoundness does not penalize an entry

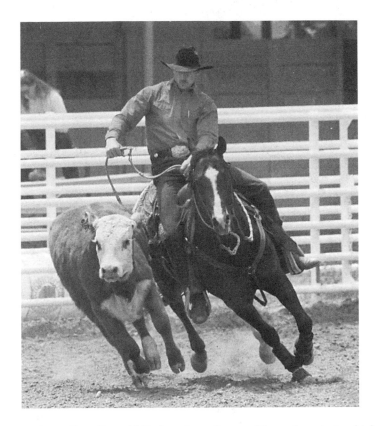

FIGURE 12-6   Stage Four Doc, 1992 American Quarter Horse Association high point working cow horse, shown working a cow. He is owned by Thelma Gutierrez. (Photo by J Bar D Studios.)

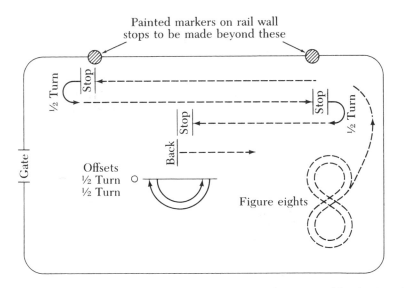

FIGURE 12-7   Stock horse dry work patterns as previously suggested by the American Horse Shows Association.

FIGURE 12-8   Burnt Girl, being ridden by Bobby Ingersoll in a jaquima class. (Photo by Fallaw, courtesy B. Ingersoll.)

FIGURE 12-9   April, owned by J. Sprafka and being shown by Maggi McHugh in a trail horse class. (Photo by Fallaw, courtesy M. McHugh.)

unless it is sufficiently severe that entering such a horse is considered an act of cruelty. Each horse is classified as preliminary, intermediate, amateur-owner, junior, or open, depending on the amount of money or points the horse has won. An amateur-owner jumper is any horse that is ridden by an amateur owner or an amateur member of the owner's immediate family. The horses are required to go over a course that should allow the exhibitor a fair opportunity to demonstrate the horse's capabilities and training. Each course must be carefully designed to fit the capabilities of the horses to be exhibited. Ideally, the faults should be evenly distributed over the course after the first or second jump, which is a single jump. A reasonable percentage of the horses should be able to negotiate the courses without faults, and, if no horse has a "clean round" (no faults), the course is too severe a test. Variation of obstacles on the course is important; however, they must be fair, "jumpable" tests of a horse's ability. The jumper is scored on a mathematical basis according to the number of penalty faults. Disobedience, falls, knockdowns, touches, and time penalties are considered penalty faults. Refusals, run-outs, loss of gait, and circling are disobediences. The horse is said to refuse when it stops in front of an obstacle to be jumped, whether or not the horse knocks it down or displaces it. When a horse evades or passes an obstacle to be jumped or jumps the obstacle outside its limiting markers, the horse is penalized for a run-out. Gait is lost when it loses forward movement after crossing the starting line. A penalty is also given if the horse crosses its original track between two consecutive obstacles anywhere on the course. A horse is penalized if it falls on the course. Knockdown faults are given when any part of an obstacle that establishes the height of the obstacle is lowered, whereas touching any part of the obstacle is considered a touch fault. The horse with the best score wins the class. If a tie for first place exists, a jump-off is held over the original course but a different sequence of obstacles. At least 50 percent of the obstacles can be raised 6 inches (18.7 cm) for each clean round.

Hunters, Hunter Breed, and Hunter Pony Divisions

The hunter division of the AHSA is open to all horses of either sex (Figure 12-10). This division is usually divided into green, regular, amateur owner, adult amateur, or miscellaneous classes. A green hunter is a horse in its first or second year of showing at regular member competitions or combined training/eventing events that require horses to jump 3.5 feet or higher, whereas a regular hunter is a horse of any age that is not restricted by the number of years shown previously in any division. Ponies must not exceed 14.2 hands. Breeding classes are judged on conformation, quality, substance, way of moving, soundness, and suitability to become or, in the case of sires and dams, apparent ability to produce or beget hunters. Conformation classes are judged on conformation, way of moving, and soundness. Depending on the class, conformation may count toward 25 to 60 percent of the total score. Working and

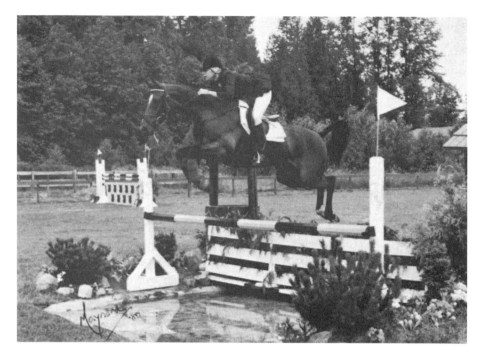

FIGURE 12-10   Shannon Oldham going over a jump in a hunter class. (Photo by Maynora, courtesy S. Oldham.)

amateur-owner hunters are judged on performance and soundness. Conformation and working hunters are exhibited over a course with obstacles that are between 3 feet 6 inches (1.07 m), 3 feet 9 inches (1.14 m), and 4 feet (1.22 m). The fences usually simulate obstacles found in the hunting field, such as natural postand rail, stone wall, white board fence or gate, chicken coop, aiken (parallel bars with brush in the middle), oxer, and hedge. Hunters should keep an even hunting pace and have good manners and style. They are also scored on faults and way of moving over the course, as well as soundness. Faults include falls, touches, knockdowns, and disobediences. Cause for elimination includes three refusals, off course, jumping a fence before it is reset, bolting from the ring, and fall of horse and/or rider.

Saddlebred Horse Division

Classes for three-gaited and five-gaited horses are offered within the saddlebred horse division (Figure 12-11). The horses must be registered with the American Saddlebred Horse Association or the Canadian American Saddle Horse Registry. Three-gaited horses are required to be shown at the walk, trot, and canter. Five-gaited horses must also be shown at a slow gait (slow pace or

FIGURE 12-11 Having a Good Time, American Saddlebred Three-gaited Pleasure Horse of the Year in 1977, being shown by Sue Camins. (Photo by Inman, courtesy S. Camins.)

foxtrot) and the rack. Horses are worked both ways in the ring at all gaits. Finalists are usually requested to do further work as directed by the judge. Gaited horses are shown in any bridle that suits the horse except a snaffle bit and with a flat, English-type saddle. The exhibitor wears informal dress during morning and afternoon classes and dark-colored riding habit with accessories during the evening classes. For formal wear, women usually wear tuxedo-style jackets with matching jodhpurs, whereas men usually wear dark suits. Both wear saddle derbies or silk top hats.

Saddle horses are also shown in breeding classes and are judged on conformation, finish, soundness, and natural action. In the fine harness section, they are shown with an appropriate vehicle, usually a small buggy with four wire wheels and no top. The horses are shown at a walk, the park trot, and "show your horse." A variety of other classes are offered.

Roadster Division

Horses shown in the roadster division of the AHSA may be of any breed (Figure 12-12). The only qualifications for the horse shown in this division are that it be a standard or of standard bred-type, of attractive appearance, balanced in conformation, and good manners that make the horse a safe risk in the ring. The horse must also be serviceably sound. Horses are shown as bike roadsters or road wagon roadsters. Some horses can be shown in either class, but the road wagon roadster is larger than the bike roadster. Roadsters are shown at a walk, slow jog trot, fast road gait (also a trot), and a full speed trot. When working in the show ring, the roadster has animation and brilliance. When asked for speed, this horse maintains form and shows full speed. The gait must be even and smooth at all times, particularly in turns. The exhibitor in the bike class wears his stable colors and a cap and jacket that match. In the road class, the exhibitor wears a business suit and hat. There are many types of classes in this division.

Three-Day Events

The three-day competition demands extensive training and devotion to horsemanship (Figure 12-13). Originally a trial for cavalry patrol mounts, it became

Figure 12-12   Cedar Creek Beydala, bred and owned by Cedar Creek Farm, being shown in a park harness class. (Photo by Moseder, courtesy R. M. Burger.)

FIGURE 12-13   Shannon Oldham taking a jump during a three-day event. (Photo by Maynora, courtesy S. Oldham.)

a recognized form of equestrian competition in 1912, when it was included in the Olympic Games. It is now defined as "the most complete combined competition, demanding of the rider considerable experience in all branches of equitation and a precise knowledge of the horse's ability, and of his horse a degree of general competence resulting from intelligent and rational training."

On the first day of the three-day event, the dressage test is given to show off a horse's gymnastic development—a series of movements designed to show the horse's fitness, precision, suppleness, and sensitive obedience. Each movement is marked by judges. The dressage test was originally designed to show the horse's capability on the parade ground. The horse must perform in close formation maneuvers and must perform various movements involved with reviewing troops.

The endurance test is held on the second day. It tests the speed, endurance, and jumping ability of the true cross-country horse. At the same time, it demonstrates the rider's knowledge of pace and the coordination of effort between horse and rider. The test is composed of four phases.

Phase A: The first phase is the roads and tracks, in which the horse must cover a given distance over country roads and tracks at the trot or slow canter. It serves as a warm-up period.

Phase B: At the finish of the course (Phase A), the horse must immediately start the steeplechase. In this phase, the horse must negotiate a course of fences at an average speed of 24 miles (38.6 km) per hour.

Phase C: The third phase is another roads and tracks course to allow the horse to relax and recover. After Phase C, the horse is given a 10-minute rest and is examined by a veterinarian for soundness and condition.

Phase D: The last phase is a cross-country obstacle course which is $2\frac{3}{4}$ to 4 miles long and comprised of 24 to 36 fixed and solid obstacles. It is ridden at a good gallop.

The test given on the third day is show jumping. Its object is to prove that, on the day after a severe test of endurance, the horse has retained the suppleness, energy, and obedience necessary to continue in service.

Combined Driving

As performed, combined driving is a relatively new sport. The rules were approved in 1970 by the FEI, and the first recognized international competition was held in Switzerland the same year. Since then, more than 17 countries hold national championships. In the United States, the American Driving Society sanctions competitions.

Combined driving is an adaption of the ridden three-day event and is designed to test the versatility of the horse and driver. Combined driving competition consists of one to three distinct tests taking place on separate days during which the competitor drives the same horse throughout and may only compete with one entry. During the dressage phase, the horse and driver are judged on the level of training and style and flexibility exhibited during the set movements of the test. The second day is the marathon, which tests the stamina, endurance, and agility of driver, crew, and horse over a 26-km cross-country drive. The third day is devoted to the obstacles: the vehicles wind through a course of obstacles requiring speed and changes of direction. The officials for combined driving include a technical delegate representing the American Driving Society, ground jury (official judges), and a scorer.

Gymkhana

Gymkhana events or games and pattern racing on horseback are held by many riding clubs, 4-H Clubs, and other interested horsepeople. They are very popular with children but are also enjoyed by many adults because they are competitive and require harmony between rider and horse. The rules of gymkhana events may be established by the contestants, or they may be closely governed by breed or horse show organizations. The standard gymkhana events are keyhole race, figure-eight stake race, cloverleaf barrel race, quadrangle stake competition, pole bending, hurry scurry competition, figure-eight relay race, rescue race, and speed barrel race. In the gymkhana riding competition, the horses are shown on the rail after they have completed a cloverleaf barrel competition pattern.

Barrel Racing

Barrel racing is a standard gymkhana event. The rules vary depending on the organization that sanctions the gymkhana. The standard positioning of the three barrels and the distance between them is illustrated in Figure 12-14. The event is sometimes called "cloverleaf barrel racing" because the race pattern resembles a cloverleaf. The rider's horse has a running start when it crosses the starting line. Knocking over a barrel or failing to follow the prescribed course results in a time penalty or disqualification. The horse and rider with the fastest time win the race.

Pole Bending

Pole bending is a timed event in which the horse must travel a pattern around six poles (Figure 12-15). The 6-foot-high (1.83-m) poles are set on top of the ground, and if a horse knocks down a pole it is disqualified. There are two types of patterns that can be used. In one pattern (Figure 12-16), the six poles are placed 20 feet (6.1 m) apart in a straight line. The timing line is perpendicular to the line of poles and located even with Pole 1. The horse crosses the timing line, bends between the poles, circles Pole 6, returns through the course by bending between the poles, and crosses the timing line. In the other pattern (Figure 12-16), the poles are 21 feet (6.4 m) apart and the timing line

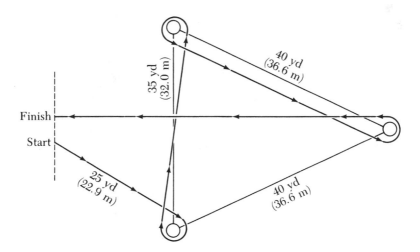

FIGURE 12-14   Cloverleaf barrel racing pattern.

FIGURE 12-15   Jackie Holley riding Shotgun around a pole to win the singlestake championship, California Gymkhana Association. (Courtesy C. Holley.)

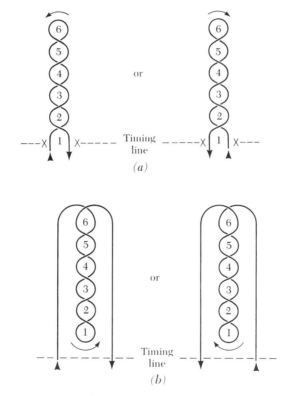

FIGURE 12-16   Pole-bending patterns. *(a)* Poles are 20 feet (6.1 m) apart; *(b)* poles are 21 feet (6.4 m) apart.

is 21 feet from Pole 1. The horse crosses the timing line, moves parallel to the line of poles, makes a 180° turn around Pole 6, passes between Poles 6 and 5, bends through the poles to Pole 1, circles Pole 1, bends through the poles to Pole 6, makes a 180° turn around Pole 6, and moves parallel to the line of poles to cross the finish line.

Keyhole Racing

The keyhole race is run over a course that is laid out with a limed keyhole on the ground. The throat of the keyhole (4 feet wide and 10 feet long, or 1.2 m wide and 3.05 m long) is perpendicular to and faces the timing line. The center of the keyhole (20 feet in diameter, or 6.1 m) is 100 feet (30.5 m) from the timing line. The horse crosses the timing line, enters the throat of the keyhole, goes to the center of the keyhole, makes a 180° turn in either direction, and returns across the timing line. The horse is disqualified if it steps on or over the limed keyhole at any point, or if it fails to turn around in the center of the keyhole.

Figure-Eight Stake Racing

Young riders find the stake race a challenge during their early stages of learning to ride. The rider has to run a figure-eight pattern around two upright markers that are 125 feet apart, or 38.1 m (Figure 12-17). If an upright marker is knocked down, the entry is disqualified.

Other events, such as quadrangle stake, scurry, figure-eight relay, rescue, speed barrel, and potato race competitions, are also exciting, and a successful competitor requires a well-schooled horse.

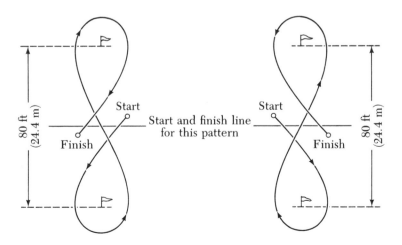

FIGURE 12-17   Figure-eight stake race pattern.

DRESSAGE

Dressage (pronounced drə-säzh′) is a system of skilled horsemanship that draws its foundations from the earliest link between rider and animal. Dressage teaches a horse to be obedient, willing, supple, and responsive (Figure 12-18). It is a complex activity that nonetheless emphasizes fundamentals, combining the best of sport and art. The principles of dressage first appeared in a book written by the Greek statesman and general Xenophon in 400 B.C. The philosophy he expressed is still current in today's dressage riding: "Anything forced and misunderstood can never be beautiful. If a dancer were forced to dance by whip and spikes, he would be no more beautiful than a horse trained under similar conditions." Similarly, the American Horse Shows Association states:

> The object of dressage is the harmonious development of the physique and ability of the horse. As a result it makes the horse calm, supple, loose, and flexible, but also confident, attentive, and keen, thus achieving perfect understanding with his rider.
>
> These qualities are revealed by: a) The freedom and regularity of the paces; b) The harmony, lightness, and ease of the movements; c) The lightness of the forehand and the engagement of the hind quarters, originating in a lively impulsion; d) The acceptance of the bridle, with submissiveness throughout and without any tenseness or resistance.
>
> The horse thus gives the impression of doing of his own accord what is required of him. Confident and attentive, he submits generously to the control of his rider, remaining absolutely straight in any movement on a straight line and bending accordingly when moving on curved lines.
>
> His walk is regular, free, and unconstrained. His trot is free, supple, regular, sustained, and active. His canter is united, light, and cadenced. His quarters are never inactive nor sluggish. They respond to the slightest indication of the rider and thereby give life and spirit to all the rest of his body.
>
> By virtue of a lively impulsion and the suppleness of his joints, free from the paralyzing effects of resistance, the horse obeys willingly and without hesitation and responds to the various aids calmly and with precision, displaying a natural and harmonious balance both physically and mentally.
>
> In all his work, even at the halt, the horse must be "on the bit." A horse is said to be "on the bit" when the hocks are correctly placed, the neck is more or less raised and arched according to the stage of training and the extension or collection of the pace, and he accepts the bridle with a light and soft contact and submissiveness throughout. The head should remain in a steady position, as a rule slightly in front of the vertical, with a supple poll as the highest point of the neck, and no resistance should be offered to the rider. The horse shows cadence when its movements are well marked, rhythmic, and harmonious.

Dressage competitions are held in 65.6 × 131.2-foot (small) or 65.6 × 196.8-foot (standard) arenas (20 × 40 meters or 20 × 60 meters). The smaller arena may be used for tests through the second level. Depending on the size, the

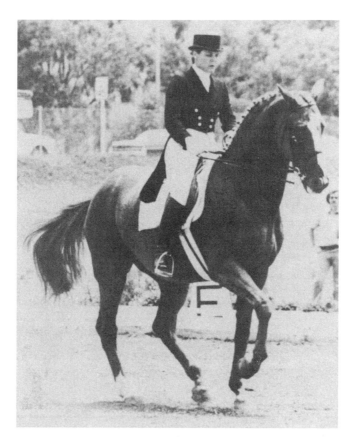

FIGURE 12-18   Hilda Gurney on Keen, 1976 Olympic Gold Medal winner in the dressage competition. (Courtesy USDF.)

arenas are laid out according to Figure 12-19. Letters identify specific parts or areas of the arena. Horses and riders are tested at several levels depending on their abilities: training, first, second, third, fourth, Prix St. Georges, Intermediate, Intermediate 2, Grand Prix, and Grand Prix Special. A typical test for third level is given in Table 12-1. The terms used to describe dressage movements are noted in Appendix 12-2.

United States Dressage Federation

The United States Dressage Federation (USDF) is a nonprofit educational organization founded in 1973 by a group of dedicated dressage enthusiasts from across the country.

The USDF seeks to promote and encourage a high standard in dressage, primarily educating its members and the general public. This goal is advanced by

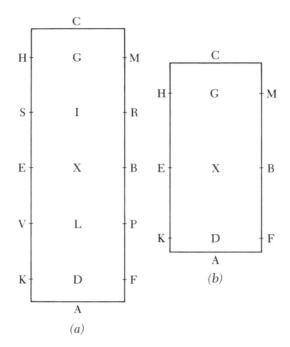

FIGURE 12-19   Dressage arenas. *(a)* 65.6 × 196.8 feet (20 × 60 meters); *(b)* 65.6 × 131.2 feet (20 × 40 meters).

the USDF's national publicity program and its growing network of over 90 member organizations situated in all areas of the United States and divided into 9 national regions. There are more than 20,000 USDF members and over 400 USDF-recognized dressage competitions. These competitions vary from 1-day, 1-judge affairs with 50 riders to shows lasting several days with several judges and 200 to 300 riders completing 700 to 800 tests. The USDF has a number of award programs for riders, horses, and shows.

Rider Award Program

The general requirements for the rider award program are:

1   Riders must be members of the USDF (individual or participating) at the time their scores were earned.

2   Scores are cumulative and need not be earned in one year. Any number of horses may be used.

3   Only scores from USDF-recognized competitions are counted. Riders are personally responsible for notifying the USDF of scores, using official rider award report forms available from the USDF.

4   To assure accuracy in recording, scores should be reported no later than September 30 of the award year in which they were earned.

TABLE 12-1 Typical Third-Level Test

Purpose: The third-level tests are of medium difficulty and are designed to determine that the horse has acquired an increased amount of suppleness, impulsion, and balance, so as to be light in hand and without resistance, enabling the rider to collect and extent its gaits. In addition, third-level tests require that the proper foundation for the collection has been attained; the horse shows a distinction between the paces.

Conditions:
1. To be ridden in a plain snaffle with a dropped noseband; regular cavesson, flash noseband, or crossed noseband, made entirely of leather, are mandatory.
2. Arena size: 20 × 60 meters (65.6 × 196.8 feet).
3. Time allowed: 9½ minutes.

Exercise	Letter in arena	Test	Directive ideas	Points	Coefficient	Total	Remarks
1	A X	Enter, collected trot Halt, salute; proceed collected trot	Straightness on center line; transitions; quality of halt				
2	C HXF F	Track left Medium trot Collected trot	Quality of turn at C; straightness; quality of trot; transitions				
3	K–X	Half-pass right	Quality of trot, lateral movement		2		
4	X X C	Circle right at 8 M Straight ahead Track right	Quality of trot; roundness, size of circle; straightness				
5	MXK K	Extended trot Collected trot	Straightness; quality of trot, transitions				

(*continued*)

TABLE 12-1 Typical Third Level Test (Continued)

Exercise	Letter in arena	Test	Directive ideas	Points	Coefficient	Total	Remarks
6	F–X	Half-pass left	Quality of trot, lateral movement		2		
7	X	Circle left 8 M, proceed straight ahead	Quality of trot; roundness, size of circle, straightness		2		
	C	Track left					
8	E	Turn left	Quality of turns, halt, rein back				
	X	Halt, rein back 4 steps, proceed collected trot					
	B	Turn right					
9	F	Collected walk	Quality of walk, transitions				
10	K–R	Extended walk	Straightness; quality of walk, transitions		2		
	RMC	Medium walk					
11	C	Collected walk	Quality of walk; execution of movement				
	H	Turn left					
	Between G and M	Half-pirouette right, proceed collected walk					
12	Between G and H	Half-pirouette right, proceed collected walk	Quality of walk; execution of movement				

No.	Letter	Movement	To be judged	Coeff.
13	G	Collected canter, right lead	Calmness, smoothness of depart	
14	M–F F	Medium canter Collected canter	Straightness; quality of canter, transitions	
15	A L–R	Down center line Half-pass right	Straightness; quality of canter, lateral movement	2
16	M	Simple change of lead	Calmness, smoothness of change	
17	H–K K	Extended canter Collected canter	Straightness; quality of canter, transitions	
18	A L–S	Down center line Half-pass left	Straightness; quality of canter, lateral movement	2
19	H	Simple change of lead	Calmness, smoothness of change	
20	M B X G	Collected trot Turn right Turn right Halt, salute Leave arena at free walk on long rein at A	Quality of trot, transition, turns, halt	

Collective marks:

			Coeff.
Gaits (freedom, regularity)			2
Impulsion (desire to move forward, elasticity of steps, suppleness of back, engagement of hindquarters)			2

(continued)

TABLE 12-1 Typical Third Level Test (Continued)

Exercise	Letter in arena	Test	Directive ideas	Points	Coefficient	Total	Remarks
			Submission (attention, confidence; harmony; lightness, ease of movements; acceptance of bridle, lightness of forehead)		2		
			Rider's position, seat; correctness, effect of aids		2		

Further remarks:

Subtotal _____
Errors (− ___)
Time faults (− ___)
Total points _____

Time: Minutes _____ Seconds _____

Scoring: 10, excellent; 9, very good; 8, good; 7, fairly good; 6, satisfactory; 5, sufficient; 4, insufficient; 3, fairly bad; 2, bad; 1, very bad; 0, not performed or fall of horse or rider.

Penalties: $\frac{1}{2}$ point for each commenced second of overtime.

Errors: First error, 2 points; second error, 4 points; third error, elimination; leaving arena, elimination.

Maximum points possible: 330.

SOURCE: The American Horse Shows Association (1986).

(The USDF award year is from October 1 to September 30 of the following calendar year.)

5   If two or more judges are scoring one ride, the average of their scores counts as one.

6   Only scores earned riding AHSA tests will be counted.

The Qualified Rider Award is given to riders with 4 scores earned at a minimum of two different competitions under four different judges for 4 different rides. On completing the requirements, the rider receives a certificate and a patch to be worn on a warmup jacket or other apparel.

The Bronze Medal Rider Award is given to riders with six scores of 60 percent or better, from two different judges for two different rides each at the first, second, and third levels.

The Silver Medal Rider Award is given to riders with four scores of 60 percent or better, from two different judges for two different rides each at the fourth level and Prix St. Georges.

The Gold Medal Rider Award is awarded to riders completing four scores of 60 percent or better, from two different judges for two different rides each at Intermediate I and/or II and Grand Prix.

There are award programs for riders over 50 years of age (Vintage Cup Awards), junior/young riders under 21 years of age, adult amateur awards, and the Master Challenger Award for riders 60 years of age or older.

Horse of the Year Awards Program

The requirements for the USDF Horse of the Year awards are:

1   Scores are recorded from results submitted directly to the USDF by USDF-recognized competitions.

2   Only scores earned from currently approved FEI, AHSA, or USDF tests ridden in USDF/AHSA recognized competitions count toward awards.

3   Scores are recorded only for USDF-registered horses owned by participating or business USDF members. Membership number and horse registration number should be included on entry blanks. If the horse is owned by more than one person, or by a stable, at least one of the owners must be a participating member.

4   No scores are recorded for the horse until it is registered.

To qualify, the horse must have a minimum of eight scores earned at four competitions under four different judges, with scores of at least 55 percent.

Awards are given as follows: 25 at the first level, 25 at the second level, 10 at the third level, 25 at the fourth level, 25 at Prix St. Georges, and 15 at each level for AHSA International 1, AHSA International 2, Intermediate I and II, and Grand Prix. Also, there are Freestyle and All-Breeds awards.

VAULTING

Vaulting traces its origins to Roman games, which included acrobatic displays on cantering horses. Modern vaulting became recognized when it was included in the 1920 Olympic Games. In the U.S., the American Vaulting Association was founded in 1966 and competitions were sanctioned in 1969. In 1983, vaulting became one of the equestrian disciplines recognized by the Fédération Equestre International; and the first FEI World Vaulting Championships were held in Switzerland in 1986. The FEI also published the rules for competition.

Vaulters are judged on both freestyle (Kur) routine and on a series of compulsory exercises. All exercises are performed to music on the moving horse. There are seven compulsory exercises that are performed in two sets (4 and 3) separated by a dismount. During team competition, each team member performs the first set and then all perform the second set. Another way of separating the exercises is by classification. Static exercises are the basic seat, flag, and stand. The other four (vault-on, mill, scissor, and flank) are considered dynamic. The first round of compulsory and the freestyle exercises are performed with the horse moving counterclockwise, and the second set is performed with the horse moving to the right. Scoring for the freestyle is based on degree of difficulty, composition, and performance.

RACING

Racing horses has been a popular activity for many centuries. Its history traces from the domestication of the horse to the early Olympiads, and finally to modern racing. Racing consistently draws more spectators than almost any other sport. The racing industry currently involves several types of horses: Thoroughbreds, Quarter Horses, Standardbreds, Arabians, trotting ponies, Appaloosas, Paints, and mules.

Types of Races

A horse can enter several types of races, depending on its ability. The types of races to be run each day are determined by the racing secretary of the racetrack, and the horses that meet the conditions of the race may be entered by the trainers. The types of races and the conditions of each race are published every few days in the "condition book."

A stakes race is a top-quality race in which the owners pay nominating fees, entry fees, and starting fees. In addition, the racetrack may add money to the purse to guarantee a certain value.

In handicap races, the racing secretary takes entries, evaluates the horse's past performance, and assigns weights to be carried so that all horses have an equal chance of winning. The horses with better records or potential carry more weight than those with poorer records. Their purse value is determined by nomination and starting fees and by added money. Fees are not paid when the race is an invitational handicap race.

In allowance races, the eligibility and the weight a horse carries are based on the number of races or amount of money the horse has won. A basic weight is assigned for the race, and horses with poorer records are given weight allowances. An allowance can be an invitational race.

In claiming races, all horses entered are for sale at the price they are entered. They may be claimed or purchased by any owner who has started a horse at that race meeting. The claiming race is a method of classifying horses in order to produce races involving competition of equal quality.

Maiden races are for horses that have never won a race recognized by that sanctioning organization for the breed.

Derby races are for 3-year-olds.

Supervision of Racing

To supervise and maintain the integrity of racing, each state has a racing commission. The commissioners' duties are to implement state rules and regulations of racing and to protect the public interest. They limit the number of racing days for each racetrack or meet, grant racing franchises to tracks, approve purse schedules, approve appointment of officials at each track, and supervise licensing of all racetrack personnel.

To protect the public, the state racing commission is also responsible for the drug testing program. Each winning horse has samples of saliva and urine tested for illegal use of drugs. The tests are made by a member laboratory of the Association of Official Racing Chemists.

At each racetrack, a number of personnel are required to supervise the racing. Three racing stewards preside over the racing at each track and supervise all other racing officials at that track. They watch each race for rule infractions. If an objection is lodged, they must determine if a foul occurred, its cause, who was responsible, and the extent of responsibility. They then take appropriate action. If a foul occurred, they may or may not disqualify the horse involved and penalize the jockey. The stewards are assisted by patrol judges, who observe the race from elevated platforms located along the racecourse. They report rule violations they observe to the stewards. Three placing judges help the stewards determine the order of finish of each race. Videotapes are made of most races to help the stewards, patrol judges, and placing judges make decisions. The videotapes are available the following day for viewing by the trainers and jockeys to analyze a horse's performance.

The racing secretary is responsible for formulating the race program for each day. He or she must determine the types of races to be run and take the entries from the trainers. The racing secretary approves stalls for racing stables, creates a purse and race program that will attract horses (condition book), and creates racing cards that will attract the public's interest. The identity of each horse is verified by its lip tattoo number and markings by the official track identifier as the horse enters the paddock area; this prevents "ringers" from being run in the race. A paddock judge is in charge of the paddock area, where the horses are saddled prior to each race. The paddock judge controls who enters the paddock area, verifies racing equipment, supervises the saddling, gives the command for the jockeys to mount, and starts the post parade. The jockey's room is under the supervision of the clerk of scales. The clerk also is responsible for seeing that each jockey rides with the proper equipment, is weighed before the race to ensure that the horse carries the prescribed weight, and is weighed at the end of the race to ensure that the horse carried the weight to the finish line. A number of employees in the jockey's room assist the clerk: assistant clerk of scales, color man (cares for and stores racing colors for each stable), number cloth and equipment custodian, porters, guards, and valets. The track veterinarian is responsible for preventing injured and disabled horses from racing so that all the horses racing are physically capable of attaining their performance capability. The starter is responsible for starting each race and ensuring a fair start. The clocker is responsible for timing the daily workouts and publishing the times for the public.

Parimutuel Betting

Parimutuel wagering means that members of the public are betting against each other instead of against some type of organization. The racing association is responsible for holding the bets and paying the winners.

There are three basic types of bets and several types of special bets. The three basic bets are win, place, and show. A win bet is for a horse to win the race; a place bet is for a horse to finish the race in first or second position; a show bet is for a horse to finish first, second, or third. Special types of bets include the daily double, quinella, perfecta, exacta, and combination. A combination bet means that a horse is bet to finish first, second, or third. There, the three basic bets are combined in one bet. If the horse wins the race, the bettor collects the payoff for win, place, and show; if the horse finishes in second place, the bettor collects the place and show bets. When the daily double is bet, the bettor must select the winners of the first and second races in order to win. A quinella wager is to select the first two horses that finish a race regardless of which of the two horses wins the race. The exacta and perfecta wagers are a variation of the quinella in that the player must select the winner and the second-place horse in the exact order of finish. Other exotic-type wagering occurs at some tracks.

The odds and the eventual payoffs are determined by the amount of money wagered on the entries. The approximate pay to win for the odds are given in Table 12-2. These are figured by the totalisator computer. The payoff

TABLE 12-2   Approximate Pay to Win (for $2) for the Odds

Odds	Pays	Odds	Pays	Odds	Pays
1–5	$2.40	5–2	$ 7.00	15	$ 32.00
2–5	2.80	3	8.00	18	38.00
1–2	3.00	7–2	9.00	20	42.00
3–5	3.20	4	10.00	25	52.00
4–5	3.60	9–2	11.00	30	62.00
Even	4.00	5	12.00	40	82.00
6–5	4.40	6	14.00	50	102.00
7–5	4.80	7	16.00	60	122.00
3–2	5.00	8	18.00	70	142.00
8–5	5.20	9	20.00	80	162.00
9–5	5.60	10	22.00	90	182.00
2	6.00	12	26.00	99	200.00

SOURCE: *American Racing Manual* (1978).

is computed according to the following scheme. The payoff for the bets on the winning horse are calculated by taking the total amount of money wagered for horses to win and deducting the percent of money held out for state taxes, racetrack operator's commission, purses paid to owners of the horses, and breeders' and stallions' awards. In California, the percentage withheld from the sum of money wagered is 15.75 percent. After this figure is determined, the amount of money bet on the winning horse is subtracted and the remainder divided by the amount of money bet on the winning horse. For example, if $150,000 is wagered on horses to win, the amount remaining after the 15.75 percent is withheld is $126,375. If the winning horse was a "long shot" and only $20,000 was bet for it to win, the next calculation will be to deduct the amount wagered on the winning horse from the win pool ($126,375− $20,000 = $106,375). The $106,375 is then divided by $20,000 to determine the payoff for each winning dollar bet ($106,375/$20,000 = $5.32). All payoffs are calculated to the lowest $.05; therefore, the $5.32 becomes $5.30. The $.02 goes into the "breakage pool" that is kept by the state and the track. The $5.30 is the odds for each dollar bet; therefore, a $2 wager returns $12.60. The $12.60 includes the $10.60 odds plus the $2 wagered.

The payoffs for place and show bets are calculated by dividing the total money bet to place into two equal pools (for the three horses finishing first, second, and third). Each pool is divided among the winning bets as outlined for the win bet.

Many states allow off-track betting. In these states, the bettor need not attend the races to place wagers. Each state governs off-track betting in that state if it is allowed. Illegal betting takes place by bettors placing their bets with "bookmakers." However, in some states like Nevada, bookmakers are licensed and the bets placed with a licensed bookmaker are legal. Simulcasting is approved for most race tracks so that people can come to the track and bet on races occurring at other tracks. Simulcast betting has saved many race tracks from bankruptcy.

In order to properly bet and handicap horses, one must be able to read the daily racing program and past performances. The results of the races for the previous day are also published. The information contained in the daily program is given in Figure 12-20. If more than 12 horses are entered in a race, the horses carrying numbers greater than 11 are considered to be field horses. By betting on the Number 12 to win, place, or show, the bettor wins if any of the field horses finishes first, second, or third, respectively. When two or more horses are entered by one trainer, they are coupled in the wagering as one entry. A bet on one horse in the entry is a bet for all the horses entered by the trainer.

In addition to the daily racing program, the Daily Racing Form publishes the daily program for all the recognized tracks in America. In the program, the past performances of each horse for each race at all the recognized tracks in America are given, as well as the conditions of the race. How to read the past performances is shown in Appendix Table 12-1.

The past performances of horses raced in America are published in the *Daily Racing Form* in the official charts for each horse entered in each race at every racetrack in America. The chart describes a race. It offers a complete, accurate, easy-to-understand word picture of the running from the time the horse is lined up at the gate to the moment the result and prices are official.

Harness Racing

All harness racing in the United States and in the Maritime Provinces of Canada is conducted under the guidance of the United States Trotting Association (USTA); the rest of Canada is under the guidance of the Canadian Trotting Association. The USTA was organized in 1938–1939 by a group of representative horsepeople from all sections of the country who previously had held membership in one of the three sponsoring or governing bodies. This move welded all Standardbred racing interests for the first time in the history of the sport and gave great impetus to the sport because it centralized authority and made administrative procedure more efficient and effective than ever before.

Before this time, various sections of the country managed their version of the sport much as they pleased. Three outstanding groups preceded the USTA organization: United Trotting Association, American Trotting Association, and National Trotting Association. Until they were combined, trainers and owners often never knew for sure just which organization they were racing under and therefore were always in doubt as to what racing rules to follow.

Harness racing on the modern parimutuel basis first was staged at Roosevelt Raceway, located at Westbury, Long Island, near New York City, in 1940, and has mushroomed into one of the nation's top spectator sports (Table 12-3). With night raceways, modern presentations, and the introduction of the starting gate, the sport changed rapidly from America's smaller

FIGURE 12-20   Daily racing program. (Courtesy Golden Gate Fields.)

towns and an essentially rural atmosphere to an attraction for metropolitan sports fans.

Major raceways are now located in or near such cities as Albany, Boston, Buffalo, Chicago, Cincinnati, Cleveland, Columbus, Dayton, Detroit, Lexington, Los Angeles, Miami, New York, Philadelphia, Pittsburgh, Portland, San

TABLE 12-3   The Growth of Harness Racing

Year	Purses	Horses racing	Colts registered	U.S. Trotting Association members	Track members	Total attendance
1950	$11,527,711.94	10,281	4386	8411	546	6,981,578
1960	31,581,922.54	17,702	6794	15,593	454	15,009,569
1970	89,280,537.00	35,465	11,981	32,725	429	26,117,742
1977	179,095,788.00	46,888	13,929	40,861	491	25,883,926
1986	387,474,750.00	57,021	17,637	50,671	464	18,397,113
1992	269,164,583.00	49,260	13,029	39,427	376	12,604,565
1998	311,961,062.00	39,005	10,881	29,350	308	7,661,998
1999	467,129,702.00	38,294	11,183	28,394	309	7,936,805

SOURCE: United States Trotting Association.

Francisco, Syracuse, Toledo, Washington, Wilmington, and many others. In 1999, 309 racetracks had Standardbred racing (Table 12-3).

Attendance at parimutuel plants skyrocketed from the year 1943 to 1975. Since 1975, however, attendance has declined. The millions who have watched racing at fairs and nonbetting meets have pushed the spectator figure up among the top five sports.

From a total of only a few thousand dollars in 1940, the wagering passed the billion-dollar mark in 1963 with $1,067,130,007 in parimutuels. In 1991, $1,741,105,821 was bet but that sum declined to $619,741,308 in 1998.

The rise of harness racing at the raceways is reflected in purses paid to horseowners and the consequent boom in the breeding industry and horses in action. Purses have reached $300 million, and over 39,000 trotters and pacers see action during a year.

The rise in wagering meetings has made harness a year-round sport with racing in California and Florida during the winter months and at northern tracks from mid-February to mid-December.

Like every other sport, harness racing has its "big league." In this case, it is the Grand Circuit. Organized back in 1873, with four member tracks "mainly for the purpose of setting up a definite itinerary for horse owners," it not only has grown to include the best of the sulky world in racing competition but also has developed into a gigantic circuit for America's top trotters and pacers. Each track sponsoring a Grand Circuit meeting is considered a member and has representation on the board of stewards. This board formulates policies, determines dates, elects officers, and conducts general affairs of the organization.

The Trotting Triple Crown for 3-year-olds is composed of three races. The first race is the Yonkers Trot, raced on the half-mile Yonkers Raceway oval at Yonkers, New York. Harness racing's counterpart to the famed Kentucky Derby is the Hambletonian, sponsored by the Hambletonian Society and first raced at Syracuse, New York. It is the second race of the sequence. The Hambletonian has been raced at Syracuse; Lexington, Kentucky; Yonkers; and

FIGURE 12-21   Giant Chill, 2-year-old Trotting Colt of the Year in 1992, driven by John Patterson, Jr. (Courtesy U.S. Trotting Association.)

Goshen, New York, where it was a fixture for many years before being moved to Du Quoin, Illinois, in 1957. Conducted on the two-in-three heat plan, the Hambletonian is the goal of all trainers and owners.

Oldest of the Trotting Triple Crown features is the Kentucky Futurity, which was first raced in 1893, a feature of the Lexington Trots meeting at Lexington each autumn and usually the grand finale for strictly 3-year-old trotting competition.

Six horses have won the trotting Triple Crown: Scott Frost, 1985; Speedy Scot, 1963; Ayres, 1964; Neveille Pride, 1968; Lindy's Pride, 1969; and Super Bowl, 1972.

The 3-year-old pacers were after their first major purse when the Little Brown Jug Classic was inaugurated at Delaware, Ohio, in 1946. Held annually since, the "Jug" now has companion attractions in the William H. Cane Futurity at Yonkers Raceway and the Messenger Stake at Roosevelt Raceway, both metropolitan New York ovals.

All the "Triple Crown" pacing events are conducted over half-mile tracks with the heat plan in effect for the Little Brown Jug and single dashes deciding the Cane Pace and the Messenger. Two of the races were named after famous horses. Little Brown Jug was a famous world champion pacer of the nineteenth century, whereas Messenger was a stallion imported in the late eighteenth century (almost all harness horses trace back to him). Certain sire lines have been dominant producers of leading money winning pacers and trotters. Speedy Crown and Super Bowl have been the leading sires of trotters and Albatross and Abercrombie have been the leaders for pacers.

Eight horses have won the Pacing Triple Crown: Adios Butler, 1959; Bret Hanover, 1965; Romeo Hanover, 1966; Rum Customer, 1968; Most Happy Fella, 1970; Niatros, 1980; Ralph Hanover, 1983; and Western Dreamer, 1997. The Harness Horse of the Year (Table 12-4) is awarded to the horse receiving the most ballots each year.

Quarter Horse Racing

Quarter Horse racing had its beginning in colonial America. The races were usually match races between two horses, and the horses ran down village streets or across small areas of cleared ground. The first recorded races were held in Enrico County, Virginia, in 1674. These types of spring races continued to be popular until the mid-1700s, when races for long distances took over. As the frontier moved westward, so did the popularity of sprint races, into the Midwest, Southwest, and West. The first organized Quarter Horse racing was held at Hacienda Moltacqua in Tucson, Arizona. Hacienda Moltacqua also had Thoroughbred, trotting, and steeplechase races, but Quarter Horse racing popularity resulted in the construction of Rillito Park, which was designed exclusively for Quarter Horse racing. During the 1900s to 1945, other racetracks were built for Quarter Horse racing and this gave birth to our modern-day Quarter Horse racing.

Today, Quarter Horse racing is conducted at over 100 racetracks. Parimutuel betting is allowed at 97 of these tracks. The total parimutuel handle at the tracks had increased rapidly until 1982, but has since declined. The number of races recognized for Quarter Horses increased until 1983, as did the total purse paid to the owners of the horses. The All-American Futurity, which is held at Ruidiso Downs in New Mexico on Labor Day, has one of the largest purse distributions of any horse race held each year. The winning horse collects over $1,000,000.

Quarter Horses race at distances of 220, 250, 300, 330, 350, 400, 440, 550, 660, 770, and 870 yards (201.2, 228.6, 274.3, 301.7, 320, 365.8, 402.3, 502.9, 603.5, 704.1, and 795.5 m). In addition to establishing world records for racing a given distance (Table 12-5), individual Quarter Horses become recognized for their speed index and for the total amount of money they win. Speed index ratings are based on an average time for horses running given distances at the track on which they race. Based on a formula, each fraction of a second is equal to one speed index point. The basis for calculation is explained in the official handbook of the American Quarter Horse Association. The leading money-earning horse since 1949 has been Refrigerator sired by Rare Jet (Appendix Table 12-2). Dash for Cash is the leading sire of money earners since 1949 (Appendix Table 12-3) and his son, First Down Dash, was 1998 leading sire of money earned by his progeny and is ranked second as the all-time leading sire.

TABLE 12-4 Harness Horse of the Year: 1975–1997

Year	Horse	Gait	Best time	Owners	Driver	Trainer
1999	Moni Maker	Trot	1:53.4	Moni Maker Stable	Wally Hennessey	Jimmy Takter
1998	Moni Maker	Trot	1:52.3	Moni Maker Stable	Wally Hennessey	Jimmy Takter
1997	Malabar Man	Trot	1:53.1	Malvern Burroughs	Malvern Burroughs	Jimmy Takter
1996	Continentalvictory	Trot	1:52.1	Continentalvictory Stable	Michel Lachance	Ron Gurfein
1995	CR Kay Suzie	Trot	1:52.4	Carl and Rod Allen Stable	Rod Allen	Carl Allen
1994	Cam's Card Shark	Pace	1:50	Jeffery S. Snyder	John Campbell	Bill Robinson
1993	Staying Togeather	Pace	1:48.2	Robert L. Hamather	Bill O'Donnell	Bob McIntosh
1992	Artsplace	Pace	1:49.2	G. Segal and B. Monieson	John Campbell	Bob McIntosh
1991	Precious Bunny	Pace	1:49.4	R. P. Heffering	Jack Moiseyev	Bill Robinson
1990	Beach Towel	Pace	1:50	Uptown Stable	Ray Remmen	Ray Remmen
1989	Matt's Scooter	Pace	1:50.1	Gordon and Illa Rumpel and Charles Juravinski	Michael Lachance	Harry Moulton
1988	Mack Lobell	Trot	1:54.4	John Erik Magnusson	John Campbell	Charles Sylvester
1987	Mack Lobell	Trot	1:52.1	One More Time Stable and FairWinds Farm	John Campbell	Charles Sylvester
1986	Forrest Skipper	Pace	1:50.3	F. L. Bartlett	Lucien Fontaine	Marc Fontaine
1985	Nihilator	Pace	1:49.3	Wall Street-Nihilator Syndicate	Bill O'Donnell	William Haught
1984	Fancy Crown	Trot	1:53.4	Fancy Crown Stable	Bill O'Donnell	Ted Andrews
1983	Cam Fella	Pace	1:53.1	J. E. F.'s Standardbred; Norm Clements and Norm Faulkner	Pat Crowe	Pat Crowe
1982	Cam Fella	Pace	1:54	Norm Clements and Norm Faulkner	Pat Crowe	Pat Crowe

(continued)

TABLE 12-4 Harness Horse of the Year: 1975–1997 (Continued)

Year	Horse	Gait	Best time	Owners	Driver	Trainer
1981	Fran Hanover	Pace	1:54.3	Dr. J. Glan Brown	Glen Garnsey	Glen Garnsey
1980	Niatross	Pace	1:49.1	Niatross Syndicate; Niagara Acres and Clint Galbraith	Clint Galbraith	Clint Galbraith
1979	Niatross	Pace	1:55.4	Niagara Acres and Clint Galbraith	Clint Galbraith	Clint Galbraith
1978	Abercrombie	Pace	1:54.3	Shirley Mitchell and L. K. Bulen	Glen Garnsey	Glen Garnsey
1977	Green Spud	Trot	1:55.3	Beverly Lloyds	William Haughton	William Haughton
1976	Keystone Ore	Pace	1:55.2	Mr. and Mrs. S. Dancer; Rose Hill Farms; R. Jones	Stanley Dancer	Stanley Dancer
1975	Savoir	Trot	1:59.2	Allwood Stable	John Chapman	Del Miller

TABLE 12-5 World Records for Quarter Horse Racing
Following are official electronically timed records for AQHA-approved distances at tracks that raced in 1998.

Name	Age at record	Year recorded	Distance (yards)	Weight (pounds)	Time (seconds)	Track condition
Junior Meyers	4	1969	220	120	11.6	fast
Dashing Scott	4	1994	250	125	12.92	fast
Taking Risks	4	1998	300	122	14.91	fast
Crash Thru Traffic	3	1998	330	120	16.33	fast
Stat Express	8	1998	350	123	17.18	fast
Bold Love	3	1980	400	120	19.18	fast
Honor Ease	3	1998	400	120	19.18	fast
Evening Snow	3	1996	440	122	20.94	fast
Tuxer	5	1995	550	122	26.33	fast
Deckum Larum[a]	5	1983	660	122	33.51	fast
Holme of the Count[b]	4	1993	660	121	32.67	fast
Miami Prince	3	1994	770	120	39.43	fast
Griswold	5	1991	870	125	43.99	fast

[a]Record around a turn.
[b]Record without a turn.

SOURCE: *Quarter Running Journal*, March 1999.

Easy Jet is the leading maternal grandsire of Register of Merit qualifiers for racing (Appendix Table 12-4). Dams of racing Quarter Horses attain fame by producing outstanding horses. Several mares have had outstanding produce records by producing fourteen or more horses that earned their Register of Merit in racing (Appendix Table 12-5). Racing Register of Merit can be achieved by obtaining a speed index of 80 or higher and/or by achieving 10 racing points.

At the conclusion of each racing year, the American Quarter Horse Association Racing Committee votes to determine the champion horses for the various classifications of racing horses. Since Shue Fly and Woven Web in the 1940s and Go Man Go in the 1950s, Dash for Cash (Figure 12-22) is the only horse to be named world champion running horse for two consecutive years (Appendix Table 12-6). Shue Fly, Woven Web, and Go Man Go were each voted the title for three consecutive years. First Down Dash has sired at least one of the division champions in each of his foal crops through 1997.

Thoroughbred Racing

Thoroughbred racing traces its foundation to the establishment of the Jockey Club in Newmarket, England, in about 1750. Prior to that, there was no stan-

FIGURE 12-22   Dash for Cash, a leading sire of racing Quarter Horses. (Courtesy Phillips Ranch.)

dardized set of rules under which races were run. However, racing was popular in England many years prior to 1750, and it developed into a sport during the reigns of the Tudor and Stuart monarchs. The oldest stakes race, Phoenix Handicap, was established at Keeneland, Kentucky, in 1831.

The first racetrack in America was established at Hempstead Plains on Long Island. From the New York area, racing spread to the other colonies. The first Jockey Club was founded in 1734, prior to the establishment of the Jockey Club in Newmarket. Over the years, two major racing centers have developed. California has the largest gross distribution in stakes and purses (Appendix Table 12-7). New York has almost the same distribution. More races are run in California than in any other state. The gross distribution of purses and stakes and number of racing days has continued to increase each year until the more than 79,000 races with a distribution of over $708 million are run each year (Appendix Table 12-8).

As a result of the sport of racing, many horses and horsepeople have become famous. The leading money-winning horses each year (Appendix Table 12-9) and for their lifetime (Appendix Table 12-10) attract considerable attention, particularly when they win the Triple Crown of Racing—Kentucky Derby, Preakness, and Belmont. In recent years, Affirmed (1978), Seattle Slew (1977), and Secretariat (1973) have accomplished this feat. Each year, the best horses of each type of race and for age are elected (Appendix Table 12-11). Of particular interest to breeders are the leading sires for the racehorses (Appendix Table 12-12). During the 1960s, Bold Ruler was the leading sire, and more recently, Mr. Prospector, Alydar, Storm Cat, Nureyev, and Danzig have been the leading sires. The owners of racehorses are interested in obtaining the best jockey to ride their horses. The leading jockeys each year have been limited to a few successful jockeys (Appendix Table 12-13). Willie Shoemaker, Eddie Arcaro, Laffite Pincay, Jerry Bailey, and Pat Day have dominated the yearly results for 35 years. Owners are also concerned about trainers for their horses. In recent years, Charlie Whittingham, Wayne Lukas, Bob Baffert, and Laz Barrera have been the leading trainers in terms of total dollars won (Appendix Table 12-14).

CHAPTER 13

Rodeo, Trail, Sports Events, and Equine-Assisted Therapy

RODEO

Rodeo, a series of contests in cowboy sport, has a colorful history tracing back to the Great Plains area and to the trail drivers. Because trail drivers seldom were able to go into town for recreation, they made a sport out of their daily skills. Each outfit developed its own riding and roping champions. History did not record the first rodeo when several outfits got together to match their champions against each other. The prize money—the cowboys' own bets—was held in a hat. At Cheyenne, Wyoming, in 1872, townsfolk gathered to watch some Texans try to ride the wild stock. In 1883, at Pecos, Texas, they penned the longhorns on the courthouse lawn and roped them down the main street. This was the first public cowboy contest for prizes. The first rodeo held for competition in front of paying spectators was held at Prescott, Arizona, in 1888. The Cheyenne Frontier Days rodeo started in 1897 and has continued ever since. The Pendleton Oregon Roundup started in 1910. Two other famous rodeos are the California Rodeo at Salinas (1911) and the Calgary Alberta Stampede (1912). Since these early days, the sport of rodeo has continued to flourish, organized by several groups such as the National Little Britches Rodeo Association, the National High School Rodeo Association, National Intercollegiate Rodeo Association, Women's Professional Rodeo

Association, Professional Rodeo Cowboys Association, and various state amateur rodeo associations. Today, the contestants compete in these contests for over $100,000 to $500,000 at the top rodeos and for over $2,600,000 at the National Finals Rodeo. Rodeos draw over 14 million spectators. Rodeo has become "big business."

Rodeo Associations

Professional Rodeo Cowboys Association

The initial organization of rodeo took place at Salinas, California, in 1926, when the Rodeo Association of America (RAA) was formed to standardize the events and rules and to name actual world champions based on the total prize money won. The first organization of the rodeo cowboys (contestants) was the Cowboys Turtle Association (CTA). The CTA was formed in late 1936 because of the payoff at the Boston Garden Rodeo. After waging a successful strike for more purse money, the CTA grew rapidly. In 1945, the CTA reorganized to form the Rodeo Cowboys Association. Later the name was changed to the Professional Rodeo Cowboys Association (PRCA). The PRCA organized a circuit system in 1975 to give professional cowboys identity on the local level. There are 12 circuits laid out on a national scale according to the number of rodeos in given areas. PROCOM, a computerized system, allows PRCA members to enter all rodeos by dialing a single phone number.

Since 1953, professional rodeo has continued to grow. Today, there are more than 8,500 contestants, who compete for over $20,000,000 in total prize money. The all-around champion may win over $250,000 per year in prize money. PRCA world champions may win $40,000 to over $100,000, depending on the event. The world champion for each event is the cowboy who wins the most money during the season. The top 15 leaders in the PRCA championship standings for each event are eligible to compete at the National Finals Rodeo. The all-around championship is awarded to the contestant winning the most money by competing in two or more events.

National Intercollegiate Rodeo Association

The National Intercollegiate Rodeo Association (NIRA) was founded in 1948 and incorporated the next year. Its primary purpose is to provide leadership in organizing and promoting college rodeos on a nationwide scale by providing rules and procedures. The NIRA is divided into 11 regions in which more than 200 junior colleges, 4-year colleges, and universities are members. During the period of 1968 to 1993, the membership increased from approximately 1,450 individual members to more than 3,000. All individual members who compete in NIRA-approved rodeos must maintain a grade-point average of C or better.

The end of each rodeo year is climaxed by the College National Finals Rodeo. Each region is represented by its top two teams and best two individuals in the five men's events, three women's events, and one men's/women's event. Bareback riding, calf roping, saddle bronc riding, steer wrestling, and bull riding comprise the men's events; the women compete in barrel racing, breakaway roping, and goat tying. Both men and women compete in team roping. The champion teams and champion all-around individuals are listed in Table 13-1.

National High School Rodeo Association

The National High School Rodeo Association sanctions rodeos for high school students in several states and one Canadian province. Claude Mullins, the father of high school rodeo, said, "It is the inherent desire of every American youth to play cowboy. They want to be good cowboys, for good cowboys made America. It is our responsibility to provide them the chance to participate in a good, clean American sport."

Little Britches Rodeo Association

Rodeos for boys and girls aged 8 to 18 are sanctioned by the Little Britches Rodeo Association. In addition to the typical rodeo events for adults, they sanction steer riding, flag race, goat tying, and dally ribbon roping for junior boys; pole bending and trail course for junior girls; and pole bending, trail course, and dally team roping for senior girls.

Women's Professional Rodeo Association

The Girl's Rodeo Association (GRA) started in 1947, during a meeting of the contestants at an all-women's rodeo at Pecos, Texas. It was incorporated in 1948 with rules similar to the PRCA. The original membership was 76, and they approved 36 rodeos for the first year. In 1981, the name was changed to Women's Professional Rodeo Association. They compete in events comparable to those described above for the men. They compete in one specialized event known as the "cloverleaf barrel race" (see below under Standard Rodeo Events). The popularity of barrel racing is evident, because it is a standard event at all PRCA-sanctioned rodeos. The GRA membership exceeds 1,400 members, who compete for $2,000,000 in prize money each year.

Standard Rodeo Events

Standard men's rodeo events are classified as timed events (steer wrestling, calf roping, and team roping) and riding events (bareback riding, saddle bronc riding, and bull riding).

TABLE 13-1 National Intercollegiate Championship Rodeo Records, 1949–1998

Year	Location	Team	All-around champion
1949	San Francisco, Calif.	Sul Ross	Harley May, Sul Ross
1950	San Francisco, Calif.	Sul Ross	Harley May, Sul Ross
1951	Fort Worth, Tex.	Sul Ross	Dick Barrett, Okla. A&M
	(Rodeo in 1951 did not have national representation, so points are based on season total.)		
1952	Rose Festival, Portland, Ore.	Sul Ross	Dick Barrett, Okla. A&M
1953	Abilene, Tex.	Hardin-Simmons	Tex Martin, Sul Ross
	(1st year All Around Girl)		Libby Prude, Sul Ross
1954	Finals Rodeo not held—based on season total	Colorado A&M	Howard Harris, Univ. of Idaho
1955	Lake Charles, La.	Texas Tech	Ira Akers, Sam Houston
1956	Colorado Springs, Colo.	Sam Houston	Ira Akers, Sam Houston
			Kathlyn Younger, Colo. A&M
1957	Colorado Springs, Colo.	McNeese State	Clyde May, McNeese State
1958	Colorado Springs, Colo.	McNeese State	Jack Burkholder, Texas
1959	Klamath, Ore.	McNeese State	Jack Roddy, Cal Poly, SLO
			Pat Dunigan, New Mexico State University
1960	Clayton, N. Mex.	Cal Poly, SLO	Ed Workman, Lubbock CC
			Karen Magnum, Sam Houston
1961	Sacramento, Calif.	Univ. of Wyoming	Ed Workman, Lubbock CC
	(Women's team)	Sam Houston	Sue Burgraff, Montana State University
1962	Littleton, Colo.	Sul Ross	Ed Workmann Lubbock CC
	(Women's team)	Sul Ross	Donna Jean Saul, Sul Ross
1963	Littleton, Colo.	Casper College	Shawn Davis, Western Montana College
	(Women's team)	Colorado State Univ.	Leota Hielscher, Colorado State University
1964	Douglas, Wyo.	Casper College	Pink Peterson, Casper College
	(Women's team)	Colorado State Univ.	Maris Mass, So. Colorado State

(continued)

TABLE 13-1 National Intercollegiate Championship Rodeo Records, 1949–1998 (Continued)

Year	Location	Team	All-around champion
1965	Laramie, Wyo.	Casper College	Pink Peterson, Casper College
	(Women's team)	Sam Houston	Becky Bergren, Sam Houston
1966	Vermillion, S.D.	Casper College	Dave Hart, Idaho State University
	(Women's team)	Arizona State Univ.	Carol O'Rourke, Montana State University
1967	St. George, Utah	Tarleton State	E. C. Ekker, University of Utah
	(Women's team)	Eastern New Mexico Univ.	Barbara Socolofsky, Kansas State University
1968	Sacramento, Calif.	Sam Houston	Phil Lyne, Southwest Texas State University
	(Women's team)	Sam Houston	Donna Kinkead, Eastern New Mexico University
1969	Deadwood, S.D.	Eastern New Mexico Univ.	Phil Lyne, Sam Houston
	(Women's team)	Tarleton State	Nancy Robinson, Cal Poly, SLO
1970	Bozeman, Mont.	Cal Poly, SLO	Tom Miller, BHSC
	(Women's team)	Tarleton State	Linda Sultemeir, Eastern New Mexico University
1971	Bozeman, Mont.	Cal Poly, SLO	Tom Miller, BHSC
	(Women's team)	Tarleton State	Jan Wagner, MSU
1972	Bozeman, Mont.	Montana State Univ.	Dave Brock, SCSC
	(Women's team)	Eastern New Mexico Univ.	Linda Munns, Utah State University
1973	Bozeman, Mont.	Cal Poly, SLO	Dave Brock, SCSC
	(Women's team)	Univ. of Arizona	Lou Ann Herstead, University of Wyoming
1974	Bozeman, Mont.	Eastern New Mexico Univ.	Dudley Little, Cal. State–Fullerton
	(Women's team)	Sam Houston	Jimmie Gibbs, Sam Houston
1975	Bozeman, Mont.	Montana State Univ.	Skip Emmett, University of Tennessee
	(Women's team)	New Mexico State Univ.	Jennifer Haynes, New Mexico State University
1976	Bozeman, Mont.	Southeastern Oklahoma State Univ.	James Ward, Southeastern Oklahoma State University
	(Women's team)	New Mexico State Univ.	Janet Crowson, New Mexico State University
1977	Bozeman, Mont.	Southeastern Oklahoma State Univ.	Tony Coleman, University of Tennessee
	(Women's team)	Utah State Univ.	Shelly Muller, University of Wisconsin–RF

1978	Bozeman, Mont.	Southeastern Oklahoma State Univ.	Hank Franzen, Casper College
	(Women's team)	Central Arizona College	Barrie Beach, Central Arizona College
1979	Lake Charles, La.	Southeastern Oklahoma State Univ.	Joe Peabody, State Fair CC
	(Women's team)	Central Arizona College	Barrie Beach, Central Arizona College
1980	Bozeman, Mont.	Southeastern Oklahoma State Univ.	Marty Melvin, South Dakota State University
	(Women's team)	Southeastern Oklahoma State Univ.	Kyle Rice, Sheridan College
1981	Bozeman, Mont.	Dawson Community College	George Mesimer, University of Tennessee
	(Women's team)	Eastern N.M.U.	Sabrina Pike, Southeastern Oklahoma State University
1982	Bozeman, Mont.	Sul Ross	Cody Lambert, Sul Ross
	(Women's team)	Southeastern Oklahoma State Univ.	Sabrina Pike, Southeastern Oklahoma State University
1983	Bozeman, Mont.	Sul Ross	Rocky Steagall, Blue Mountain CC
	(Women's team)	Eastern New Mexico Univ.	Anna Crespin, Eastern New Mexico University
1984	Bozeman, Mont.	Southwestern Texas State Univ.	John D. Opie, Blue Mountain CC
	(Women's team)	Sam Houston	Nancy C. Rea, Southern Arkansas University
1985	Bozeman, Mont.	Southwestern Oklahoma State Univ.	Kent Richard, McNeese State
	(Women's team)	Sul Ross	Lisa Scheffer, University of Montana

(continued)

TABLE 13-1 National Intercollegiate Championship Rodeo Records, 1949–1998 (*Continued*)

Year	Location	Team	All-around champion
1986	Bozeman, Mont.	West Texas College	Clay Hurst, West Hills College
	(Women's team)	Montana State Univ.	Molly McAulifee, Blue Mountain CC
1987	Bozeman, Mont.	Blue Mountain CC	Alexander Cordova, Central Arizona College
	(Women's team)	Scottsdale CC	Sherry Rosser, Southern Arkansas University
1988	Bozeman, Mont.	Montana State Univ.	Ken Lersegrav, Montana State University
	(Women's team)	Southwestern Oklahoma State Univ.	Cathy Cagliari, West Hills College
1989	Bozeman, Mont.	Odessa College	Ty Murray, Odessa College
	(Women's team)	Cal Poly, SLO	Cathy Dennis, Southern Arkansas State University
1990	Bozeman, Mont.	Montana State Univ.	Zane Davis, College of Southern Idaho
	(Women's team)	Univ. of Wyoming	Jimmi Jo Martin, University of Wyoming
1991	Bozeman, Mont.	Montana State Univ.	Shawn Vant, Montana State University
	(Women's team)	Univ. of Wyoming	Julie Adair, Cal Poly, SLO

Year	Location	School	Champion
1992	Bozeman, Mont.	Southwestern Oklahoma State Univ.	Casey Minton, West Hills College
	(Women's team)	Walla Walla CC	Penny Conforth, Walla Walla CC
1993	Bozeman, Mont.	Southwestern Oklahoma State Univ.	Zane Davis, College of Southern Idaho
	(Women's team)	Univ. of Wyoming	Shelley Johnston, Southwestern Oklahoma State University
1994	Bozeman, Mont.	Vernon Regional Jr. College Southwestern Oklahoma State University	Jason Jackson, Montana State University Tori Woodard, Southwestern Oklahoma State University
	(Women's team)		
1995	Bozeman, Mont.	Montana State University Southeastern Oklahoma State University	Jason Jackson, Montana State University Caryn Standifer, Southeastern Oklahoma State University
	(Women's team)		
1996	Bozeman, Mont.	College of Southern Idaho Southeastern Oklahoma State University	Jason Call, College of Southern Idaho Caryn Standifer, Southeastern Oklahoma State University
	(Women's team)		
1997	Rapid City, S.D.	Panhandle State University	Preston Williams, University of Nevada–Las Vegas
	(Women's team)	Weber State University	Kelli Fowers, Weber State University
1998	Rapid City, S.D.	Panhandle State University	Ross Coleman, University of Nevada–Las Vegas
	(Women's team)	Lewis-Clark State College	Lynn Wiebe, Central Wyoming College

SOURCE: National Intercollegiate Rodeo Association.

Steer Wrestling

Steer wrestling is one of the fastest events in rodeo (Figure 13-1). Winning times frequently do not exceed 4 or 5 seconds. Originally, steer wrestling was called "bull dogging" and was developed as a skill by Bill Pickett, a black cowboy. It is a team event in which two cowboys mounted on horses participate—"the dogger" and "the hazer." The event starts with a horned steer weighing 450 to 700 pounds (204 to 317.5 kg) in a chute, with the hazer positioned on the right side of the steer and the dogger on the left. Because this is a timed event, the dogger starts from behind a barrier. If the dogger breaks the barrier before it is released when the steer crosses a designated score line, the dogger receives a 10-second penalty. The hazer is responsible for keeping the steer running straight so the dogger can move into position to jump from his running horse. As the dogger moves into position, he reaches out and grabs the steer's right horn in the crook of his right elbow. Simultaneously, his left hand pushes down on the left horn while his horse veers off to the left. As the dogger leaves his horse, his heels touch the ground ahead of his body, at a 45° angle to the path the steer is traveling. The steer's head is tipped toward the center of a left-hand turn. As the steer slows down, the dogger's left hand grabs

Figure 13-1　Steer wrestling. Mike Smith, 1998 PRCA World Champion Steer Wrestler, with earnings of $161,862. (Photo by Mike Copeman, courtesy of Professional Rodeo Cowboys Association.)

the steer's upturned nose and twists the neck. The steer falls on its side with all four feet in the air. Time is signaled by a field judge.

Calf Roping

The skill of roping calves was developed on the early ranches while branding or doctoring sick animals. A skill that is still required of cowboys, it has developed into a highly competitive rodeo event (Figure 13-2). To start, a mounted cowboy is positioned on one side of a chute containing a 200- to 400-pound calf (90.7 to 181.4 kg). A rope barrier is stretched across in front of the cowboy and horse. When the calf is released and crosses a score line placed a measured distance in front of the chute, the barrier is released. The roper starts his horse so that it reaches the barrier as the calf is released. If the barrier is broken, a 10-second penalty is given. The calf is roped and the horse stops. As the horse is stopping, the roper dismounts and races to the calf. He must throw the calf on its side and tie three legs with a pigging string (a small rope about 6 feet long, or 1.8 m). While the calf is being thrown and tied, the horse must keep the rope tight to make the roper's job easier. On completing the tie, the time is over. The calf must remain tied for at least 6 seconds. Winning times usually range

FIGURE 13-2   Calf roping. Cody Ohl, 1997 and 1998 PRCA World Champion Calf Roper with earnings of $222,794. (Photo by Mike Copeman, courtesy Professional Rodeo Cowboys Association.)

between 8 and 12 seconds, depending on arena conditions. The horse plays an important role in a roper's ability to quickly rope and tie a calf.

Over the years, calf roping has been dominated at different times by Dean Oliver, winner of eight world championships; Toots Mansfield, winner of seven world championships; Don McLaughlin, five world championships; and Tom Ferguson, Joe Beaver, Fred Whitfield, and Roy Cooper. Top contestants may win over $100,000 per year roping calves.

Breakaway roping is a standard event for women in high school and collegiate competitions. To qualify for official time, the calf's head must pass through the loop, which may draw up on any part of the calf's body, providing it breaks the rope away from the saddle horn without assistance from the roper. The rope is tied to the saddle horn with a breakable string, and a handkerchief is tied to the end of the rope.

Team Roping

The art of heading and heeling steers developed out of the need to handle and restrain large cattle on the open range. The event consists of one cowboy, the header, roping a steer around the horns and his partner, the heeler, roping the hindlegs (Figure 13-3). There are two styles of team roping: in dally roping, the roper must take a turn around the saddle horn with his rope to hold the steer; in hard and fast roping, the ropes are tied to the saddle horn. Today, most team ropings are dally style (roper wraps his rope around the saddle horn after he ropes the steer). Both ropers start from a roping box as the steer is released from a chute. If he breaks the barrier before the steer crosses a score line, a 10-second penalty is given. There are three legal head catches: around both horns, around the neck, and around one horn and the neck. If the heeler catches only one hindfoot, a 5-second penalty is given.

FIGURE 13-3   Team roping. Jack Barnes and Clay O'Brien Cooper, 1985–1989 and 1992 world champion team ropers, roping a steer at the 1992 PRCA National Finals Rodeo. (Photo courtesy Professional Rodeo Cowboys Association.)

Aside from rodeo competition, team roping has become a major business and hobby for professional and amateur competitors. Ropers are classified according to their abilities and rope within their classification or higher. Major jackpot ropings are held where ropers compete for money plus saddles, belt buckles, trailers, and trucks.

A variation of team roping is team tying. After the steer is roped, the header must dismount and tie a short rope around the steer's hindlegs.

Bareback Riding

Bareback riding was never a part of daily ranch routine, but developed from the daredevil desires of one cowboy to outdo the next (Figure 13-4). This

FIGURE 13-4   Bareback riding. Mark Gomes, 1998 PRCA World Champion Bareback Rider with earnings of $142,530. (Photo by Mike Copeman, courtesy Professional Rodeo Cowboys Association.)

is the newest of the three standard riding events, started in the mid-1920s. The horse is ridden with a rigging consisting of a 10-inch-wide leather pad with a handhold cinched to the horse's back. The rider mounts the horse in a chute, and the chute gate is opened when the rider is ready. On the first jump out of the chute, the rider must spur the horse over the break of the shoulders as the horse's front feet strike the ground. Failure to do so disqualifies the rider. If successful, he is then judged on his ability to ride the horse by staying in command, maintaining proper position, and spurring properly. During the ride, the rider holds on with one hand and waves the other hand in the air. If his free hand touches the horse, the rider is disqualified. Ideally, bareback riders want to try to spur the horse on each jump, reaching as far forward as they can with their feet, then jerking their ankles upward toward the rigging. Horses are scored on how they kick, how hard they jump, how difficult they are to ride, and in how many directions they go. The ride is scored by two judges on a 25-point system for both horse and rider for a maximum of 100 points. The horse must be ridden for 8 seconds for a qualified ride.

Good bucking horses are being bred by the Flying U Rodeo Company and a number of other ranches for their athletic ability, stamina, agility, size, and personality. High Tide, 1976 World Champion Bareback Bucking Horse, is a grandson of Man o' War. Southern Pride, Sling Shot, and Joker are his full brothers, and all have been chosen for the National Finals Rodeo.

Saddle Bronc Riding

The sport of riding bucking horses with a saddle started as a form of entertainment on the great cattle drives. Therefore, saddle bronc riding is one of the classical events of rodeo (Figure 13-5). The broncs are ridden with an association saddle that meets certain specifications according to PRCA rules. The horse wears a halter with a 6-foot-long, $1\frac{1}{2}$-inch-thick rein (1.8 m long, 38.1 mm thick). The rider holds the rein and uses it to maintain balance. As the bronc leaves the chute, the rider must keep his spurs over the horse's shoulders until the first jump is completed. The rider then spurs from front to back in rhythm with the horse as it bucks. The spurring stroke must be smooth and in a long arc. The score is based on how difficult the horse is to ride, the amount of control exercised by the rider, and how he spurs. Riders are scored from 1 to 25 points and the horse is given 1 to 25 points by each of two judges.

Bull Riding

Bull riding is one of the most dangerous events in rodeo. Very seldom can the rider avoid being butted, kicked, stepped on, or hit by the bull when he gets bucked off or jumps off. Bulls are ridden by placing a rope with a handhold around the bull's chest. When the rider places his gloved hand in the handhold, another cowboy pulls the slack out of the rope. When the rope is tight enough, the free end is laid across the palm and wrapped behind the hand

FIGURE 13-5   Saddle bronc riding. Dan Mortensen, 1993–1995, 1997, and 1998 PRCA World Champion Saddle Bronc Rider earned $227,378 in 1998. (Photo by Mike Copeman, courtesy Professional Rodeo Cowboys Association.)

and across the palm. The rider clenches it with all his strength. A bell is attached to the rope to serve as a weight to pull the rope free after the rider releases it. The only rules are that the bull must be ridden for 8 seconds and that the free hand cannot touch the bull. Riders are scored by two judges who give them 1 to 25 points and the bull 1 to 25 points. Judges look for the bull's ability to jump and kick high and to change directions suddenly. Riders are scored on their ability to stay in control of the ride, remain reasonably erect, and use their legs to spur the bull.

Cloverleaf Barrel Racing

Barrel racing became a part of rodeo for young women in 1948. It consists of a race against time to make a cloverleaf pattern around three barrels (Figure 13-6). The standard pattern is to cross a score line that is 20 yards (18.3 m) from the nearest barrel. The rider races to the first barrel, turns around it, races to the second barrel 30 yards away (27.4 m), turns around it, and races to the third barrel 35 yards away (32 m). After turning around it, the rider races back across the score line. There is a 5-second penalty for each barrel knocked over.

FIGURE 13-6   Barrel racing. Mindy Morris, Texas A&M University rodeo team member, winning the 1992 Nation Intercollegiate Barrel Racing Championship at Bozeman, Montana. (Photo by Jim Polito, courtesy Mr. and Mrs. Morris.)

Goat Tying

Goat tying is a timed women's event that originated in Texas and is a standard high school and collegiate event. The contestant rides down the arena across a starting line and to the goat. As she approaches the goat, she dismounts, runs to the goat, grasps the rope to which the goat is tied, moves down the rope to the goat, throws the goat, and ties any three legs with her pigging string. Should the horse contact or run over the goat or the rope tying the goat, the contestant is penalized 10 seconds. For a qualified time, the goat must stay tied for 5 seconds after the contestant stands back 6 feet from the tied goat.

RANCH RODEOS

Ranch rodeos are competitions between ranches. Thus, ranches sponsor teams of employees that compete in bronc riding, team roping, team doctoring, wild cow milking, branding, sorting, and team penning. In the southwest, these rodeos are growing in popularity.

CUTTING HORSES

A cutting horse separates a given animal from a herd or group of cattle, whether in the contest arena or on the ranch, and prevents its return (Figure 13-7). The cutting horse came from the open-range ranches of yesteryear and was an animal born of necessity. Even in this era of modern cattle management, with its corrals and systems of pens, chutes, and gates, no superior method has been devised to separate a single animal and prevent its return with a minimum of disturbance to the remaining cattle.

In the early days, ranchers selected a cutting horse only after its ability to handle cattle had been proven. From then on, it was treated with respect and was relieved of other ranch chores. As cowboys from the various ranches got together, they talked of who had the best this or that, and they invariably discussed the merits of the top cutting horse on each ranch. These discussions led to challenges, and the cutting horse contest was on. Probably beginning around 1850, these contests increased in popularity, and on July 22, 1898, the first cutting horse contest with a record of money being posted was held in Haskell, Texas, at the Cowboy Reunion.

On March 14, 1908, the first indoor cutting horse contest was held in the Old North Side Coliseum at Fort Worth, Texas, built to house what is now known as the Southwestern Exposition and Fat Stock Show. Cutting horse contests continued through the years at the Fort Worth show, and when the first indoor rodeo appeared there in 1918, a cutting horse contest was held for the first time in connection with a rodeo.

The number of cutting horse contests continued to increase, and in March of 1946, the event was placed under a uniform set of rules with the formation of the National Cutting Horse Association (NCHA).

The NCHA has grown from 13 charter members to over 4,000 members. Purses for cutting horses in contests either approved or conducted by the NCHA went over the $1 million mark for the first time in 1976. Approved contests occur from Massachusetts in the Northeast to Florida in the South and westward to the Pacific Coast. Contests are also held in six Canadian provinces and in Australia. Cutting horse competitions offer the greatest monetary return available to a horse that does not run on a racetrack. Mr. San Peppy, owned by the King Ranch and ridden by Buster Welch, was the first horse to have lifetime earnings over $100,000 in 1978.

A cutting horse contest is conducted as follows. A herd of usually 15 to 20 cattle is held in one end of an arena by two men called "herd holders." Then, as its name is announced, the cutting horse and rider move into the herd to begin work. One animal is cut out, or separated, and driven through the herd holders toward the center of the arena. Two more riders, known as "turn back men," turn the separated animal back toward the cutting horse and toward the "safety" of the herd. Now the real action begins.

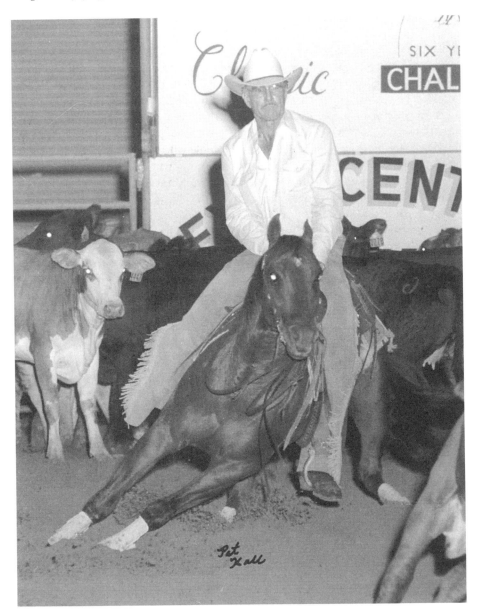

FIGURE 13-7   Sam Wilson cutting cattle with Bob Acre Doc, champion cutting horse. (Photo by Pat Hall Motion Photography, courtesy National Cutting Horse Association.)

As the calf or yearling dodges and twists to get by the cutting horse, the horse makes countermoves to hold the animal where it is. Turning on a dime, rolling out swiftly to the left and right, and all the while staying head-to-head with the stock being worked, the cutting horse demonstrates months of training and bred-in cow sense as it does its job—with no help from the rider other than the selection of the stock to work in its $2\frac{1}{2}$-minute performance. After getting the desired challenge from one head of stock, the rider signals the cutting horse to stop and to re-enter the herd for another demonstration of its ability.

While the cutting horse performs, one or more judges evaluate how hard the horse is challenged by the animal separated from the herd, how the horse handles itself in meeting its challenges, and what mistakes, if any, are made. The judge scores the horse between 60 and 80 points. Where more than one judge is used, the combined scores of the judges determine the contest winner.

TEAM PENNING

The sport of team penning has been growing at a rapid rate. It traces its roots to the ranch and feedlot work that cowboys have performed for over a century. After World War II, it became a competitive event, and numerous associations now sanction competitions. A team consists of 3 riders, who have to cut 3 head of cattle from a herd of 30 and pen them in less than 2 minutes. One end of the arena is designated the cattle holding area and the opposite end has a pen located within it. The pen is located at 75 percent of the length of the arena from the cattle holding end. The pen must be 16 feet from one side of the arena and can be on either side of the arena. The pen is 16 feet wide at one end, with a 10-foot opening on the side opposite from the cattle (Figure 13-8). It is 24 feet deep; an 8-foot panel closes off part of the 18-foot opening, and a 16-foot panel forms a wing from the opening into the pen. A starting and foul line is drawn across the arena at a distance of 60 percent of the length of the arena from the cattle end. A judge is located at the starting and foul line. The judge signals "time" when the first team member's horse's nose crosses the line and calls out the designated number the team is responsible for penning. The 30 head of cattle are marked with 10 sets of numbers so that groups of 3 have the same number. When the 3 cows with the designated number are separated from the herd, they are taken to the other end of the arena and into the pen.

When the cattle have entered the pen, one rider raises his hand to signal time to a second judge positioned outside the arena and opposite the pen. A team member can signal for time when 1 or 2 cattle are in the pen, but all times with 3 cattle in the pen are placed higher. If an undesignated cow is in the pen when a contestant calls for time, or at the end of 2 minutes, or if undesignated cows are across the foul line, the team is disqualified. No more than 4 cattle can be across the foul line at any given time or the team is disqualified. The team penning their designated cattle in the shortest period of time wins the contest.

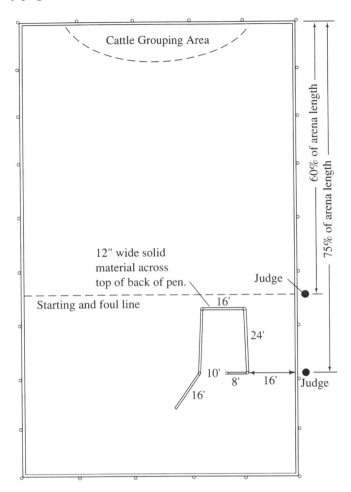

Cattle Grouping Area

60% of arena length

75% of arena length

12" wide solid
material across
top of back of pen.

Judge

16'

Starting and foul line

24'

10'   8'   16'

Judge

16'

FIGURE 13-8   Layout of team penning arena.

FOX HUNTING

Fox hunting has been a recognized sport in Great Britain, Ireland, and America for many years. By 1775, it was firmly organized in America, and even before then it was a popular sport. Packs of hounds were imported as early as 1650 by Robert Brooke of Maryland. However, they were brought over as hunting dogs. The first recorded pack of fox hunting dogs was in 1666 in England. Several packs of hounds were kept in colonial America for fox hunting. Some famous colonists with packs were Thomas Walker, George Calvert, Charles Lee, and George Washington. It was not until 1776 that the first hunting club, Gloucester Foxhunting Club, was organized in America (in Gloucester, Massachusetts). During 1781–1861, the sport was enjoyed by the wealthy landowners of Pennsylvania, Maryland, and Virginia. There were very few organized hunt clubs during this period, but after 1865, many were founded. Since 1907, when the Masters of the Foxhounds Association of America was founded, the sport has been closely regulated and has grown steadily in popularity despite organization and modern farming methods. Several hundred packs of hounds are kept by hunt clubs throughout the world so that horsepeople can enjoy a fast cross-country ride behind a pack of hounds when they so desire.

Fox hunting adheres to strict rules of protocol established in the 1900s. Most hunting clubs have a similar type of organization. The master of the foxhounds is in direct command of the field (members of the hunt). He determines if and where a hunt will be held, and makes the necessary arrangements with the farmers. The huntsman maintains the pack and kennels and is responsible for the hounds in the field. He is also responsible for giving various horn signals to the hounds and the field. The huntsman is assisted by whippers-in, who go to the woods where a fox is supposed to be. They watch for the fox to "go away" and signal its escape. The hunt then begins. Once the chase starts, the hounds are in front, followed by the master of the fox hounds and the field. The hunt usually ends when the fox "goes to earth" (disappears in its hole).

Because foxes are getting scarce and because available land is difficult to find, drag hunts are now held. Instead of chasing a live animal, the pursuers and hounds follow a scented trail laid out by touching the ground with a fox's brush or litter from the fox's den. In some areas of America, the hounds chase coyotes instead of foxes.

VAULTING

Vaulting is a gymnastic sport on a moving horse (Figure 13-9). Vaulting is also recognized as a highly effective therapeutic modality for developmental disabilities.

Dating back to Roman times, it was originally intended to develop a rider's sensitivity to the horse's movement and balance. The horse is equipped with a leather vaulting surcingle that is a wide leather strap with padded handles on either side of the horse's withers and with straps located for use in hanging exercises. The horse is worked on a longe line while exercises are performed.

The American Vaulting Association sanctions competitions. Exercises during competition include the basic seat, flag, mill, flank, free stand, and scissors. During team competition, as many as three riders may be performing on the horse at one time.

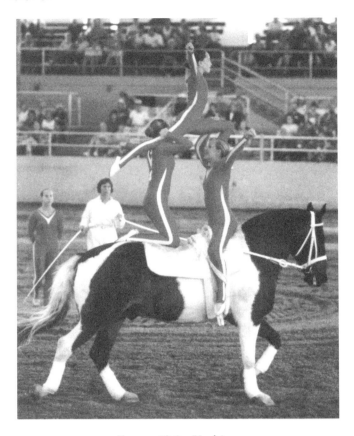

FIGURE 13-9   Vaulting.

SOCIAL, ENDURANCE, AND COMPETITIVE TRAIL RIDING

Some horsepeople enjoy the competition of endurance and competitive trail riding, whereas others enjoy social trail riding. Social rides take many forms. Small groups of friends may ride together to discuss common interests and to enjoy scenery. Horseback trips are made into the wilderness areas in and around the national parks. At pack stations, which are either privately owned or administered by the U.S. Forest Service, one may rent guides, horses, and all the necessary gear to travel into the wilderness. Many riding clubs sponsor well-organized rides; one such group is Equestrian Trails, Inc., a California organization made up of many local corrals (organizations) whose goal is to preserve and develop riding trails. Each corral has many activities, including rides, tack and tog swaps, tours, and educational meetings. Social rides, such as the Desert Caballeros, Old Spanish Trail Riders, Rancheros Visitadores, and Sonoma County Trail Blazers, are popular. These rides last for several days and cover 100 to 200 miles (160.9 to 321.8 km).

Competitive trail riding is one of the nation's popular horse activities. It is gaining popularity primarily because of the efforts of the North American Trail Ride Conference (NATRC). This body was organized in 1961 for the purpose of sanctioning competitive trail rides under a uniform judging system. The NATRC publishes an annual rule book, a riders' manual, a judges' manual, and a management manual, which are available to interested horsepeople. The objectives of the NATRC are:

1 To stimulate greater interest in the breeding and use of good horses possessed of stamina and hardiness as qualified mounts for trail use

2 To demonstrate the value of type and soundness in the proper selection of horses for a long ride

3 To learn and demonstrate the proper methods of training and conditioning horses for a long ride

4 To encourage good horsemanship in competitive trail riding

5 To demonstrate the best methods of caring for horses during and after long rides without the aid of artificial methods or stimulants

The NATRC sponsors one-day (Type B), two-day (Type A), and three-day rides. Appropriate points are given toward the annual championships, which are awarded to the finishing horses. Daily mileage in the open division is 25 to 35 miles, or 40.2 to 56.3 km a day, at a range of speed of 4 tole miles per hour (6.4 to 9.1 km per hour). Weather, terrain, season of the year, and footing on the trail are relevant factors to timing, and riders are penalized if they do not finish within certain time limits. Novice riders cover a shortened course of approximately 20 miles (32.2 km). The main object is to work all of the horses over an identical trail in the same length of time, thereby establishing a basis of fair comparison for determining the horses' soundness, condition, way of going, and manners. Although it is not a race, judgment in timing and pacing is important, because the winner usually will have ridden at a consistent pace throughout rather than "hurrying up and waiting."

One attraction of competitive trail riding is that no special type or breed of horse is necessary or favored. The prime requisite is a well-conditioned, calm horse. Riders condition their horses by following a well-planned training schedule that includes careful work over all types of terrain. Straightaway trotting, walking up and down progressively steeper hills, and working in soft sand are a few methods used to maximize development of the muscles, heart, and lungs (see Chapter 6).

The rides are judged by at least two judges, one of whom must be a practicing veterinarian and approved NATRC judge. The open division, for horses over 5 years of age, is divided into junior (riders aged 10 to 17), lightweight (rider and tack weighing less than 190 lb, or 86.2 kg), and heavyweight (rider and tack weighing more than 190 lb) categories. The novice division is primarily for young horses (aged 4 to 5) and for newcomers to the sport.

For purposes of judging, each horse starts the ride with a score of 100, evaluated as follows: soundness, 40 percent; condition, 40 percent; manners, 15 percent; and way of going, 5 percent. Although only the horses are judged, the riders also compete for horsemanship awards and are judged on the care and handling of their mounts during the entire weekend.

Competitive trail riding should not be confused with endurance riding. In contrast to competitive trail riding, where the horse must travel a fixed distance within a fixed period and is judged mainly on its soundness, condition, and manners, the endurance ride is primarily a race. It is usually 50 to 100 miles long (80.5 to 160.9 km) and must be completed within a maximum period. The horses are examined to determine that they are sound and are willing to proceed on the trail. There are three 1-hour mandatory rest stops. During the rest stops, each horse is given a thorough veterinary check, which eliminates approximately 40 percent of the entries (Figure 13-10). Awards are made to all horses that complete the ride, to the first horse to finish the ride, and to the horse that finishes in the best condition.

Several 50- to 100-mile endurance rides (80.5 to 160.9 km) are held annually. The "granddaddy" of them all is the Tevis Cup ride, which covers 100 miles in less than 24 hours (Figure 13-11). The Tevis Cup ride runs over the old Pony Express route from Lake Tahoe across the Sierra Nevada to Auburn, California.

FIGURE 13-10   Competitive trail riding horse receiving a veterinary examination at a mandatory rest stop. (Courtesy NATRC.)

FIGURE 13-11   Heather Bergantz competing in 1999 Western States Trail Ride (Tevis Cup) on "Red," who won "Haggin Cup for best of condition among top ten competitors." (Photo by Hughes Photography, courtesy American Endurance Ride Conference.)

Horse and rider encounter temperature extremes ranging from freezing in the snow-covered height to 120°F (48.9°C) in the canyons, as well as altitude extremes. The trail is rough, dusty, and rocky and includes steep inclines.

The American Endurance Ride Conference offers many award programs for horses and riders that are awarded on lifetime achievements. These programs include Rider Mileage, 1000 Mile Horse, Limited Distance, 500 Mile (LD) Horse, and National Limited Distance Mileage.

PACKING AND OUTFITTING

Packing horses and mules to carry cargo has played a role in the history of many countries. The art of packing was developed by Mongolia's Genghis Khan. Pack trains were used in Europe to transport goods in the 1700s. In America, horses were packed with cargo from the time of Cortez's landing in 1519 until the settlement of the West. In the Gold Rush days, ore, supplies, and machinery were packed into the rugged western mountain country.

Equipment

The basic equipment for packing consists of the pack saddle, saddle blanket, halter with a 10-foot lead rope (3.05 m), lash rope, lash cinch, pack cover, and panniers.

There are three types of saddles that are used for packing horses, mules, and donkeys (Figures 13-12 and 13-13). The McClellan is seldom used, and the Decker is not as popular as the sawbuck. Western stock saddles can be used for packing in cases of emergencies or when one is taking a short trip and does not want to buy or rent a pack saddle. Western stock saddles are used by

FIGURE 13-12   Sawbuck or humane pack saddle: (A) breast collar; (B) connecting strap; (C) bar of saddle tree; (D) sawbuck; (E) humane saddle tree; (F) rigging; (G) latigos; (H) ring to lead mules; (I) breeching; (J) hip straps; (K) pad; (L) billets; (M) cinches; (N) back straps. (Photos by W. Evans.)

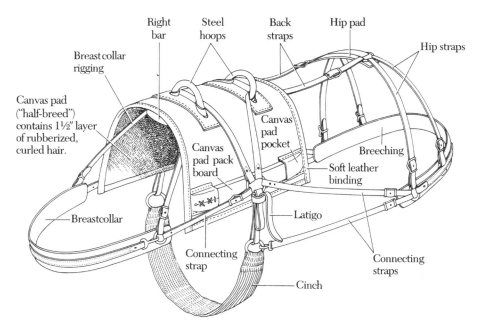

FIGURE 13-13   Decker pack saddle. (From *Horse Packing in Pictures,* by F. W. Davis. Copyright 1975 Francis W. Davis. Used by permission of Charles Scribner's Sons.)

some hunters to pack meat out of the wilderness (Figure 13-14). They ride the horse while hunting and then lead it back to camp carrying the meat. Slings are used to carry dunnage, firewood, or other things, such as bales of hay (Figure 13-15).

The saddle pad used under a pack saddle is larger than a standard western saddle pad. The pack saddle should be 30–33 × 36 inches (76.2–83.8 × 91.4 cm). It must be long enough to protect the sides of the pack animal and must extend 4 to 6 inches (10.2 to 15.2 cm) in front of the withers to protect them. If unavailable, pads can be made by placing felt carpet padding between cotton duck material.

Halters should be made of material that will not break easily. Lead ropes are usually made of $\frac{3}{4}$-inch (19-mm) cotton rope.

Lash ropes are made of $\frac{1}{2}$-inch (12.7-mm) manila rope that has had the splinters singed off and has been waxed. Nylon ropes stretch and cannot keep the load tight. Cotton rope becomes very stiff and hard when wet and/or frozen. Manila rope also stiffens when wet but is usually easier to work with. Lash ropes should be 40 to 45 feet long (12.2 to 13.7 m). They are tied to the lash cinch. Lash cinches are made of heavy cotton duck webbing with ring and hook ends reinforced with leather (Figure 13-16).

Pack covers (manta covers, manti, or manty) vary in size, depending on the type of load being packed. A general-purpose size is 6 × 8 feet (1.8 × 2.4 m), which allows the cover to double as a ground cover for a sleeping bag. They are made of waterproof canvas or rubberized, nylon-reinforced material.

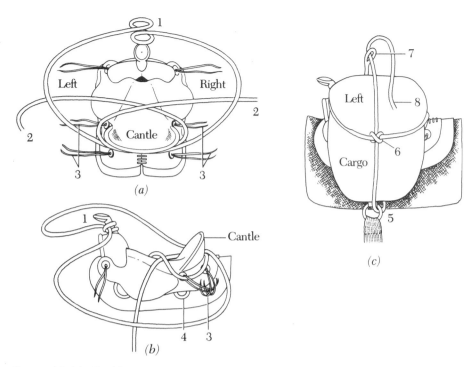

FIGURE 13-14 Packing on a western stock saddle: *(a)* top view; *(b)* side view; *(c)* side view of pack tied to saddle. Step-by-step instructions: (1) tie two half hitches on the horn; (2) run each end of the rope behind the cantle and across the seat; (3) tie these sets of saddle strings together over the rope to keep the rope from slipping over the cantle; (4) if you are riding a double-rigged saddle, tie the jockey strings over the sling rope and to the back rigging ring; (5) run the end of the rope through the cinch ring; (6) after placing the pack or cargo on the side of the saddle, pull the rope tight and tie a double half hitch; (7) tie a honda in one end of the sling rope and pass the other end through it; (8) pull the end tight and tie it off. (Adapted from *Horses, Hitches and Rocky Trails.* © 1959, Foe hack. Reprinted by permission of Swallow Press, Chicago.)

FIGURE 13-15 Set of slings for carrying dunnage, firewood, and bales of hay. (Photo by W. Evans.)

FIGURE 13-16   (A) lash rope; (B) cinch; (C) tarp. (Photo by W. Evans.)

Many types of panniers are used (Figure 13-17). Soft panniers are made of heavy duck webbing with leather-reinforced corners. Leather panniers are difficult to obtain but they wear better and protect the pack animal's sides better than cloth panniers. Rigid panniers are made of plywood and fiberglass, metal, or cowhide stretched over a rigid wood frame. A set of kitchen panniers may have drawers for utensils and staples and a fold-out work area. Canvas panniers that will slip over a western stock saddle (Figure 13-18) are also available.

In addition to the pack equipment, horse care equipment must be taken on the trip. Grooming equipment, a basic first aid kit, essential shoeing tools

FIGURE 13-17   Types of panniers: *(a)* canvas and leather; *(b)* box. (Photos by W. Evans.)

Horn slot or
fork opening

Cantle slot

Back straps

Hip straps

Tie-down
straps

Web
breeching
strap

Belly band
or cinch—front
buckled

Belly band
or cinch—
back
unbuckled

FIGURE 13-18   Canvas saddle panniers. Stirrups can be removed and carried in the panniers so they do not slap the horse.

and supplies, feed, and salt must be packed. Kitchen and camp supplies may be very elaborate or very simple. Food and personal gear must also be packed. Typical lists of equipment that are packed for trips of a week or longer are given in Table 13-2.

Saddling

To saddle a pack horse, first place the blanket on the horse's back and slide it backward into position where it extends about 4 to 6 inches (10.2 to 15.2 cm) in front of the withers (Figure 13-19). Prepare a saw buck saddle to be placed on the horse's back by folding the breeching and connecting straps on top of the saddle, folding the breastcollar and its connecting straps on top of the breechings, and folding latigos over the breastcollar (Figure 13-20). This prevents the straps and other pieces from falling down and spooking the pack animal. Place the saddle on the back, and unfold the cinches. Tighten the front cinch with the latigo first and the rear cinch last. Secure latigos with a quick-release knot (Figure 13-21) that does not form a large bump. Tighten them again just before the pack is loaded. Unfold the breastcollar and place it in position. It should be loose

TABLE 13-2   Supplies and Equipment That May Be Required on a Pack Trip (varies by number of people, length of trip, and number of pack animals)

Personal checklist	Camp equipment
To be packed in waterproof bag	*Pack on saddle*
Sleeping bag	Light rain gear
Moisture-proof ground cove	Canteen
Air mattress or foam hip pad	Tent and tent stakes
Pack in duffel bag to put in panniers	Light canvas fly
or on slings	Coleman lantern (single)
Warm jacket	Extra mantles
Light jacket	White gas (square-type can)
Shoes or boots	Axe (cover blade)
Shoes for camp	Shovel (short handle)
Shirts or blouses	50 ft $\frac{1}{2}$-in rope (15.24 m
Socks	6.35-mm rope)
Underwear	Clothespins
Pants	Saw
Bath towel and washcloth	First aid kit
Shaving kit or cosmetic kit	Toilet tissue
Toothbrush and paste	Grill
Flashlight, extra batteries and bulb	Coleman stove
Suntan lotion	Light collapsible table
Hair comb	Folding chairs
Insect bomb for tent	Whisk broom
Pack in saddle bags	Wash basin
Camera and film	Portable camp toilet
Collapsible cup or Sierra-type steel cup	Pliers
Sunglasses	Nails, assortment
Chapstick	Hammer
Insect repellent	
Lunch	
Leather gloves	
Neckerchief	
Pocket knife	

Cooking Equipment	
Utensils	Egg beater (optional)
Skillets, 10-in and 12-in cast iron	Biscuit pans
(25.4 and 30.5 cm)	Washpans, enamel
Pots, combination aluminum set,	Oven grates, use as grills
$3\frac{1}{2}$, $2\frac{1}{2}$, $1\frac{1}{2}$ qt sizes	Aluminum grill
(3.3, 2.4, and 1.4 liters)	Mixing bowls and baking pan
Dishpans	Dutch oven, medium size
Coffee pots	Can openers
Spatulas, 1 large and 1 small	

(continued)

TABLE 13-2   Supplies and Equipment That May Be Required on a Pack Trip (varies by number of people, length of trip, and number of pack animals) (*continued*)

Cooking Equipment

Silverware	Dishes (Melmac ware):
Dipper	Plates (use paper products if you
Forks, knives, spoons, in canvas holder	don't like to do dishes)
Large serving spoons and cooking forks	Bowls
Sharp knife in leather case	Cups

Other

Kitchen matches, soaked in wax and stored in waterproof container	Sandwich and lunch bags
Plastic quart bottles, with wide mouth	Paper towels, napkins
Pint Mason jars, plastic preferred	Oilcloth (tablecloth)
Plastic bread bags, to pack with, to store things, and for fish bags	Dishtowels
	Dishmop, or dishrags
	Soap and scouring pads
	Potholders

Horse Equipment

Horseshoeing equipment	Panniers
Bells	Pack covers
Hobbles	Salt
Halters	Feed and grain
Pack saddles	Tack repair items
Saddle pads	

enough so that you can run your arm between it and the pack animal. Unfold the breeching and place it about a foot below the pack animal's tail. Pull the tail out and tighten the breeching. After it is tightened, you should be able to slip your hand easily between the breeching and the hindquarters.

Packing

Next, prepare the panniers and slings for loading. A pack animal can carry a load weighing about $12\frac{1}{2}$ percent of its body weight, so a 1,000-pound animal (454 kg) can carry about 125 pounds (56.7 kg) when the animal is used daily. For shorter trips with long layovers, animals may carry a few more pounds. To determine the number of pack animals needed, weigh all the equipment and supplies to be packed. Weigh and balance the load for each pack animal; that is, each pannier in a pair must weigh the same to keep the load balanced. If the load is not balanced, it will shift to one side and make the animal's back

FIGURE 13-19   Mule with pack saddle and pad in position. (Photo by W. Evans.)

FIGURE 13-20   Pack saddle prepared for storage and saddling. (Photo by W. Evans.)

FIGURE 13-21   Quick-release latigo knot (see arrows). (Photo by W. Evans.)

sore. A small set of scales is useful. Take special precautions when packing the panniers so that supplies and equipment are not broken or the sides of the pack animal are not injured by protruding objects. Load heavy objects at the bottom of the panniers to maintain a low center of gravity. Place all breakable items in metal containers or wrap them with newspaper. Do not pack lantern fuel and other similar items with food, because the leak will ruin the food. Protect the edges of equipment such as axes, shovels, and saws to prevent cutting the pack animal. Pack personal gear in duffel bags, which are carried in slings. Sleeping bags are carried in waterproof bags and are usually packed between the sawbucks on top of the saddle.

The types of food you pack depend on your appetite and preference. Each meal must be carefully planned ahead of time. If soft-sided panniers are used, place four to five cans of food end to end and rolled in newspaper. Mark their contents in case the paper wrappers come off. Processed and canned meats are used after a few days on the trail. Hams, roast beef, chicken, stews, bacon, Spam, chili, tamales, and spaghetti are often packed. Side bacon keeps for at least 10 days if kept out of the sun. It can be kept cool by hanging it inside a damp burlap bag that is hung in the shade. If you pack frozen meat, wrap it in newspaper for insulation or pack it in a Styrofoam cooler inside a pannier. Protect the horse from the cold of the frozen meat. Keep produce cool by packing it on top of the frozen goods. Or pack the bottom of the pannier with solid goods, lay a wet burlap bag on top of them, place the produce on the wet burlap bag, and cover it with another wet burlap bag. All but the most delicate fruits and vegetables keep well if they are kept cool and out of sunlight. Eggs last for 2 weeks if kept cool. They can be packed by leaving them in their cartons and placing them in the top of the pannier. Margarine in squeeze bottles is handy. A variety of liquids, such as instant coffee, tea, and lemonade offers quick refreshment after arrival at a campsite. Pack powdered or condensed milk instead of fresh milk. Beer, pop, and liquor can also be packed. Use hard-stick processed meat, cheese, or canned meat for sandwiches. Cookies, fruit, and candy bars are also useful. Pack loaves of bread close to the top of the panniers and be careful not to mash them. Avoid packing anything in glass containers.

After making up the loads and balancing the panniers, place them on the pack animals. When both panniers are on the saddle, they should be level across the top when viewed from the side. If not, adjust the straps. Place soft dunnage on top of the saddle and panniers (Figure 13-22). Check the balance of the load by rocking the load. When released, it should stop with the sawbucks to the center of the horse's back. If not, add or remove weight from one

(a)

(b)

(c)

(d)

FIGURE 13-22   Packing a load: *(a)* sorting and weighing loads; *(b)* making dunnage loads; *(c)* dunnage load; *(d)* box load. (Photos by W. Evans.)

side. Cover the load with the pack cover to protect it from rain, tree limbs, and rocks.

A variety of hitches are used to secure a load: the most important are the diamond (Figure 13-23), double diamond (Figure 13-24), basket or box (Figure 13-25), and sling (Figure 13-26) hitches. The diamond (Figure 13-23) and double diamond (Figure 13-24) hitches are used on soft loads that are packed high. They draw the load down and close to the saddle. Use a basket hitch to lift a load up and away from a pack animal's sides when the panniers are loaded heavily. Use basket slings to carry items such as bales of hay and quarters of a deer or elk carcass (Figure 13-26). After tying the hitch with the lash rope, trace the rope and pull it tight. If the lash rope does not stay tight, the load will shift and/or fall off. Tie off the lash rope with a quick-release knot, and tuck the excess rope securely under the pack cover.

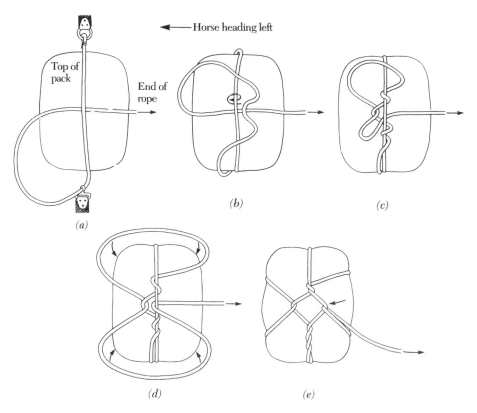

FIGURE 13-23   Tying a diamond hitch: *(a)* Lay most of the rope down behind the horse and bring up the lash rope connected to the cinch and then over the top of the pack and connect it to the cinch hook; *(b)* bring up the rope from the cinch hook and tuck it under, over, and under the part crossing the top of the pack; *(c)* pull the part of the rope lying down behind the horse through the loop formed in *(b)*; *(d)* place the rope under the corners of the pack; *(e)* tie off the rope at the point shown by the arrow.

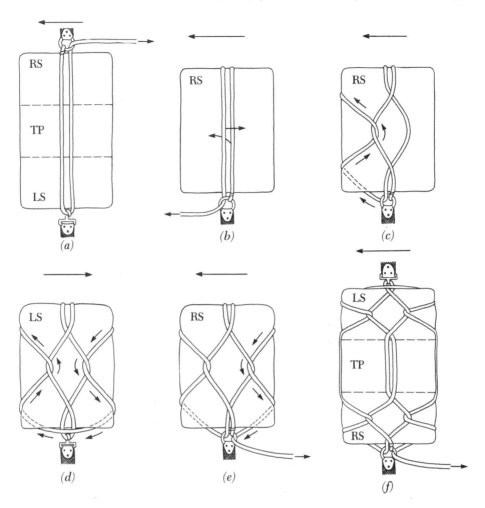

FIGURE 13-24 Tying a double diamond hitch. RS = right side. LS = left side. TP = top of the pack. ← = horse heading left. → = horse heading right. *(a)* Pass the rope from the cinch across the top of the pack, around the hook, back across the top of the pack, and through the cinch ring; *(b)* on each side of the pack, twist the two ropes and then pull them apart to form a small diamond; *(c)* run the rope from the cinch ring behind the corner of the pack and pull it through the diamond on the side of the pack and across the front of the pack; *(d)* pass the rope from across the front of the pack through the diamond formed on the left side of the pack, around the corner of the pack, across the hook, around the corner, through the diamond, and across the back of the pack; *(e)* pull the rope from across the back through the diamond, around the corner of the pack, and pass it through the cinch ring; *(f)* pull the rope tight around the pack and tie it off.

Pack animals are led down the trail by the packer. Three to five pack animals can be tied together and led. The horse that is most difficult to lead follows the packer, and the horse that can be led without any difficulties is the last in the string of horses. The packer should never lead the string by tying

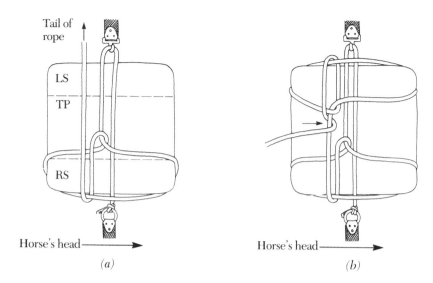

FIGURE 13-25   Tying a basket (box) hitch. RS = right side. LS = left side. TP = top of pack. *(a)* Pass the rope from the cinch ring across the top of the pack, around the hook, back across the pack, and pull it very tight. Hold the rope with your left hand next to the pack. With your right hand, lay the tail end of the rope across the top of your left hand so a loop forms on the left and the free end of rope is on the right. With your right hand, take the rope extending through the left hand and pass it under the front corner of the pack. Pull the rope tight toward the free end and pass it across the top of the pack. *(b)* Repeat the procedure on the left side. Pull the rope tight and tie it at the arrow.

FIGURE 13-26   Tying a sling hitch. Tie a clove hitch on the front sawbuck *(a)* with the center of the lash rope. Pass each lash rope around the back sawbuck *(b)* and then run through the cinch ring (right side) or cinch hook (left side).

FIGURE 13-27   Tying a string of pack animals together. Bow-line knot is around the lead mule's neck, and the rope passes through the ring hanging from the breechen. (Photo by W. Evans.)

the lead rope around the saddle horn but should hold it in his or her hand. Pack animals are tied together by passing the lead rope through a ring (2 inches, or 5.1 cm, in diameter) snapped on the left side of the breeching where the quarter strap connects, and then by tying it with a bow-line knot around the neck of the animal in front of it (Figure 13-27).

POLO

Polo developed in Persia, although it was first played in some form in China and Mongolia (Figure 13-28). The earliest historical references to polo were made in connection with Alexander the Great and Darius, King of Persia. The oldest polo club, the Silchar Club, was founded in 1859. Its rules of play were the foundation for the modern rules. International matches between Great Britain and the United States began in 1886. The game was played widely throughout the United States until the mid-1930s and is now enjoying a revival of interest in this country.

The United States Polo Association was founded in 1890 to create a uniform method of handicapping players and to standardize the rules of the game in the United States. Today, they also conduct and sanction tournaments, promote safety, and promote the sport. There are 225 member clubs and more than 3,000 registered players in the United States.

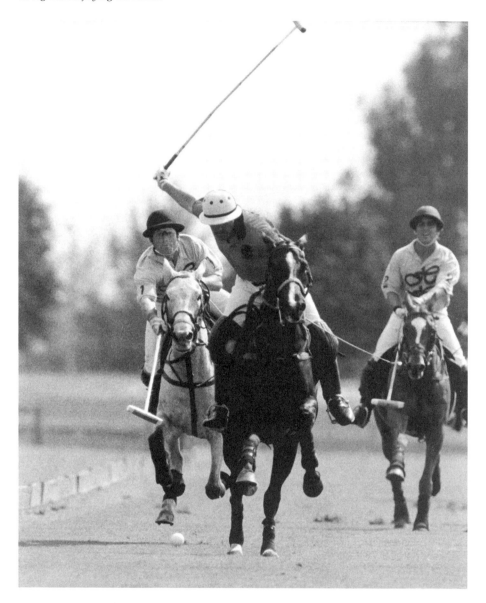

FIGURE 13-28   Polo action in a high-goal handicap polo match. (Photo by Alex Pacheco, Alex Photography.)

The game requires excellent horsemanship and balance. A successful player must have complete control of the horse, be aware of the position of every other player on the field, relate the ball to the position of teammates, and be able to hit the ball accurately at full speed while competing with a counterpart on the opposite team.

The game is played on a regulation field that is 300 yards long × 160 yards wide (274.3 × 146.3 m). The sidelines of the field may have wooden boards to deflect the ball back into play, but these boards are never more than 11 inches high (27.9 cm). If the sides are not boarded, the width of the field is 200 yards (183.9 m). The other essential pieces of equipment include the goal posts, which must be at least 10 feet high (3.05 m) and are located 8 yards apart (7.3 m) at the center of the backlines; a ball made of willow or bamboo root; polo sticks or mallets; the rider's personal equipment; and, of course, horses. Personal equipment includes blunt spurs, protective headgear, brown boots, whip, and polo saddle.

The objective of polo is to get the ball in the opposing team's goal. It is a team effort with established plans and maneuvers. A team consists of four players, two of which are forwards, one a half-back, and one a back. Number 1 is a forward and is an offensive player; number 4 is the back, responsible for defense; numbers 2 and 3 are the highest rated on the team. Number 3 serves as the field captain and number 2 has responsibility to push the play on offensive and defense. The game is played in chukkers of 7 minutes each. There are six chukkers in a match, with a 4-minute break between chukkers and a 10-minute break at halftime. The team scoring the most goals wins the game. Rules governing scoring, penalties, and method of play in America are established by the United States Polo Association.

Collegiate polo is played in an indoor arena with three players per team instead of four. The field is much smaller than the outdoor fields. Players exchange ponies during the third and fourth chukkers to keep one team from having an unfair advantage.

EQUINE-ASSISTED THERAPY

Equine-assisted therapy (therapeutic horseback riding and equine-facilitated therapy) uses equine-oriented activities to contribute positively to the cognitive, physical, emotional, and social well-being of people with disabilities (see Figure 13-29). The British Riding for the Disabled programs center around the adapted sports model. The organization's purpose is to promote mental and physical well-being through recreational sport riding. In Germany and Switzerland, a more clinical model has been developed and followed, stressing postural alignment and symmetry during medical treatment. In the United States, the two models have been integrated along with a third component emphasizing education. The North American Riding for the Handicapped Association has described three primary fields or models of therapeutic riding. The sport field is defined as equine activities adapted so that people with physical, mental, and psychological impairments can participate in sport activities with the horse. While the participant learns the skills involved in riding, driving, or vaulting,

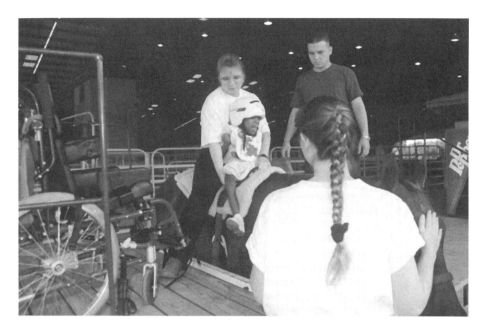

FIGURE 13-29   Equine-assisted therapy.

he or she achieves therapeutic and educational benefits. In an educational program, equine activities are used to achieve educational goals as well as therapeutic goals for people with physical, mental, and psychological impairments. The emphasis of the educational program is to incorporate cognitive, behavioral, psychological, and physical goals into the program. At the same time, the participants are learning adapted riding, driving, or vaulting. Thus, the emphasis is the reverse of that of the sport classification. Under the medical classification, therapists integrate principles of medical or psychological treatment into various uses of the horse to achieve therapy goals. The term "hippotherapy" is used to indicate direct medical treatment.

Regardless of the model or classification, a team approach is used. A therapy team consists of one or more of the following members: physician (surgeon, psychiatrist, etc.), therapist (physical, occupational, or recreational therapist, speech pathologist, etc.), educational specialist (special education instructor, adapted physical education instructor), volunteers, and a riding instructor. In a program that emphasizes sport activities, the riding instructor is the primary team member and all the participants have received approval from a physician to participate. Educational programs require leadership by educational specialists who work closely with the riding instructor. Hippotherapy requires a physician's prescription that is carried out by a physical or occupational therapist in concert with the riding instructor. The entire team works together to develop a lesson or therapy plan that includes specific goals and objectives, procedures, equipment, and type of horse for each therapy session as well as for a series of sessions. Volunteers are an important part of the team and perform a number of functions during a therapy session, serving as sidewalkers or leading the horse during most sessions.

Numerous benefits of equine-assisted therapy have been observed. For those with physical disabilities, the primary benefit is that the horse's movement provides the sensory input of a precise, repetitive pattern of movement of a person's pelvis during normal human gait. The three-dimensional movement of the horse's back simulates human gait. Other benefits include mobilization of the pelvis, lumbar spine, and hip joints; normalization of muscle tone; development of head and trunk postural control; improved symmetry; facilitation of development of righting and equilibrium reactions; improved body awareness; improved endurance; facilitated breathing; positive effect on circulation; and strong graded tactile, proprioceptive, and vestibular input that can be used to improve sensorimotor integration. Psychological benefits include improvement in self-esteem, confidence, concentration and attention span, and motivation. The effect of human–animal bonding improves group and didactic interaction, and increases responsiveness and adaptability.

There are equine-assisted therapy programs in at least 26 countries. They are associated with an international organization, the Federation of Riding for the Disabled International (FRDI), through their national organizations. The North American Riding for the Handicapped Association serves over 475 riding centers by maintaining safety standards through riding center accreditation and instructor certification programs.

Part Four

BREEDING THE HORSE

CHAPTER 14

Breeding the Stallion

The information in this chapter is mainly for those who wish to breed horses and to raise foals. However, an understanding of the reproductive processes in the mare and the stallion is a valuable aid in their care by all horse owners because horse behavior is affected by these processes. The data presented here is in sufficient detail so that the inexperienced horse breeder may conduct a successful breeding program.

REPRODUCTIVE TRACT

A diagram of the reproductive tract of the stallion is shown in Figure 14-1. Specific structures are shown in Figures 14-2, 14-3, and 14-4.

Scrotum

The scrotum, containing the two testicles, is a pouch formed by a diverticulum of the abdomen. The testes lie horizontally in the scrotum so that it is not as pendulous as the ram's or bull's. One testicle is frequently larger than the other, and one testicle is placed slightly farther back than the other, so that the scrotum is asymmetrical. The external cremaster muscle is attached to the testes (Figure 14-2) and serves to draw the testicle close to the abdominal wall for protection or to maintain the proper temperature. When the cremaster muscle is relaxed, the testicles are supported by the scrotum. Their weight tends to stretch the scrotum so that it

519

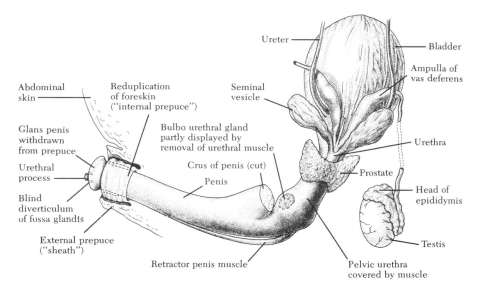

FIGURE 14-1   Reproductive tract of the stallion (lateral view). Bladder and upper urethra are twisted to expose posterior aspects. (From Eckstien and Zucherman, 1956.)

FIGURE 14-2   Testicle of a stallion: (1) cremaster muscle; (2) tunica vaginalis propria; (3) tunica albuginea; (4) gland substance. (Photo by W. Evans.)

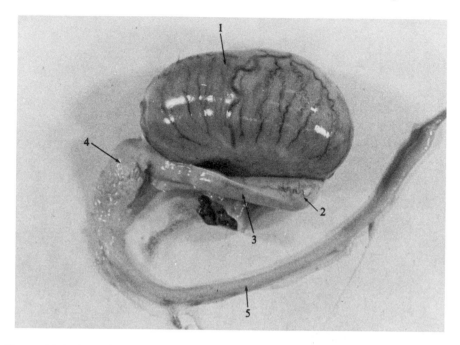

FIGURE 14-3   Testicle, epididymis, and vas deferens of the stallion: (1) testicle;
(2) head of epididymis; (3) body of epididymis; (4) tail of epididymis; (5) vas deferens.
(Photo by W. Evans.)

has a smooth appearance and is constricted above, next to the abdomen. On contraction of the external cremaster and tunica dartos muscles, the testicles are
drawn upward and the scrotum becomes wrinkled.

The blood supply to the scrotum derives from branches of the external pudic
artery. Blood drains from the scrotum via the external pudic vein. Innervation of the
scrotum derives from the ventral branches of the second and third lumbar nerves.

Testes

The testicles are shown in Figures 14-2 and 14-3. They weigh about 225 to 300 gm
and frequently the left one is slightly larger. They are about 10 to 12 cm long, 6 to
8 cm high, and 5 cm wide. The outer surface of the testicle is covered by a serosa,
the tunica vaginalis proper, which may or may not be severed during castration.
The serosa also envelops the spermatic cord except where the blood vessels and
nerves enter. The testicle is divided into lobules, each containing seminiferous
tubules, interstitial cells, and loose connective tissue. The interstitial cells produce
and secrete the male hormone, testosterone. The seminiferous tubule, the functional unit of the testicle, contains layers of spermatogenic cells in various stages of
development, and sustentacular cells extend inward from the basement membrane.

Blood in the testicle circulates via the spermatic artery and spermatic vein.

FIGURE 14-4   Accessory sex glands of the stallion: (1) ampulla; (2) vesicular glands; (3) prostate gland. The bladder is labeled 4. (Photo by W. Evans.)

Epididymis

The epididymis is composed of three areas. The head is the area where the seminiferous tubules from the lobules unite and enter the epididymis. The body is attached to the side of the testis (Figure 14-3). The tail of the epididymis leaves the body of the epididymis and is not attached to the testicle. The epididymis transports spermatozoa and other contributions of the testis to the semen, concentrates the spermatozoa by absorbing water, and provides a place for storage and maturation of the spermatozoa.

Vas Deferens

The vas deferens serves as a transport canal for the spermatozoa between the tail of the epididymis and the urethra. The tail portion of the epididymis merges into the vas deferens, which is characterized by the small diameter of its lumen and by its thick muscular wall. The size of the lumen is constant, but the muscular wall becomes enlarged approximately 15 to 20 cm prior to the entrance into the urethra. The enlarged area is the ampullar gland; many glands are located in this area. The vas deferens decreases in size as it passes under the isthmus of the seminal vesicles to open into the urethra (Figure 14-4). The excretory ducts of the seminal vesicles share the opening into the urethra with the vas deferens.

Penis

The penis of an average-size stallion is about 50 cm long in the relaxed state. The anterior 15 to 20 cm of it lies in the prepuce. It is divided into three parts: head, body, and glands (Figure 14-1). During erection, it is cylindrical in shape but the lateral sides are compressed slightly. The glans, or free end, of the penis is bell-shaped. The urethral process extends about 2 to 5 cm from the deep depression, or fossa glandis.

Prepuce

The prepuce, commonly called the *sheath*, is a double fold of skin that covers the free portion of the penis, which extends forward from the scrotum area. The external prepuce extends from the scrotum to within 5 to 7 cm of the umbilicus. Before reaching the umbilicus, it is reflected backward to form the preputial orifice. The internal prepuce starts at the preputial orifice and extends backward for 15 to 20 cm. It is reflected forward and extends almost to the preputial orifice before it is reflected backward again to form a secondary tubular invagination that contains the relaxed penis. During an erection, the increased size and length of the penis unfold the internal prepuce so that it covers the penis. The internal layers of skin contain large sebaceous glands and coil glands or preputal glands whose secretions, together with desquamated epithelial cells, form the fatty smegma. The fatty smegma and foreign substances such as dirt or wood shavings accumulate in the fossa glandis to form a round "bean." The presence of a "bean" must be checked when a stallion's or gelding's penis is being washed. The smegma also causes the prepuce and penis to accumulate dirt, so it is necessary to clean them periodically.

Accessory Sex Glands

The accessory sex glands contribute fluids of characteristic composition to stallion semen. There are three accessory sex glands: vesicular glands, bulbourethral glands, and prostate gland (Figure 14-4). The vesicular glands are paired glands. Each gland is 15 to 20 cm long and approximately 5 cm in diameter. They are reflected posteriorly so that their long axes parallel the vas deferens. The excretory duct opens into the urethra; often it has passed under the prostate gland. The bulbourethral glands are paired, ovoid-shaped, lobulated glands that lie near the ischial arch. Each gland is approximately 4 × 2.5 cm and has several ducts that open into the urethra behind the prostatic ducts. The prostate gland is composed of two lateral bulbs that are connected by a thin isthmus. Each bulb is approximately 3 × 1.5 × 0.5 cm. The isthmus covers the area where the bladder joins the urethra. Approximately 15 to 20 prostatic ducts perforate the urethra.

SEMEN PRODUCTION AND CHARACTERISTICS

Puberty for stallions varies between 11 and 15 months of age. It is the age when an ejaculate contains 1×10^8 sperm with 10 percent progressive motility. Even though the average stud colt is capable of breeding a mare by the time he is 1 year old, stallions are not usually used at stud until they are 4 to 5 years old. At 2 years, the stallion can be used at stud, but it is not recommended. If he is used, the number of services should not exceed two per week, and only 6 or 7 mares should be bred during the breeding season. The 3-year-old stallion can be used four to six times per week but his book should be limited to 10 to 12 mares. The mature stallion can be bred daily but he should get 1 day of rest every 7 to 8 days. If necessary, mature stallions can be used twice a day for 3 or 4 days each week. The effects of frequency of ejaculation on semen quality are discussed in the section on semen evaluation. During the winter, the nonbreeding season, semen production is reduced by 50 percent.

Endocrinology

Hormonal control of the reproductive processes of the stallion is not well understood. Currently, it is believed that follicle-stimulating hormone (FSH), secreted by the anterior pituitary gland, is responsible for spermatogenesis in the seminiferous tubule of the testis as well as for maintaining and repairing the tubular epithelium. Luteinizing hormone (LH) stimulates the interstitial cells to produce androgens, one of which is testosterone. Because LH is responsible for testosterone production, it is indirectly responsible for stimulating the secondary sex characteristics and accessory sex glands.

No hormonal treatment has been found that stimulates spermatogenesis. Testosterone therapy has been reported to decrease spermatogenesis. However, it is used to increase libido in stallions used for teasing purposes and can be used to elicit stallion behavior in geldings.

Estrogen (female hormone) is produced by the Sertoli cells and interstitial cells in the testes. Stallions secrete large amounts of estrogens in their urine, but their functions in the stallion are unknown. The plasma concentration of cortisol and prolactin increases in the stallion in response to sexual excitement. The physical or exercise component of sexual excitement is probably responsible for the increase.

Characteristics

Stallion semen is grayish white in appearance and consists of seminal fluid and spermatozoa. The whole semen is ejaculated in a series of 8 to 10 jets. The first 3 jets are milky in color and consistency. Approximately 80 percent of the total number of spermatozoa is ejaculated in these jets. The fluid in the jets derives mainly from the ampullar glands of the vas deferens. The later jets (4 to 10) contain very few sperm cells. The semen in these jets is mucous in appearance and is mainly derived from the seminal vesicles.

SEMEN COLLECTION, PROCESSING, EVALUATION, AND STORAGE

Evaluating stallion semen helps determine infertility and helps predict fertility. Two methods are used to evaluate a stallion's fertility based on seminal characteristics. The usual procedure is to give the stallion sexual rest for a week. Then his semen is collected two times, an hour apart, with an artificial vagina (AV). Semen is collected twice because there is a 50 percent reduction in total sperm collected between the two samples unless one of the ejaculates was incomplete; high sperm reserves were present, absent, or depleted; or the stallion was immature. If the stallion's semen does not meet minimal standards for quality, he is given at least 60 days' rest, and then the procedure is repeated. The 60-day rest period is essential, because the time required for a spermatogenic cycle is about 60 days.

The second method is used if it is necessary to determine the daily sperm output by a stallion. After sexual rest for a week, the stallion's semen is collected as discussed above for the first day and then daily for 7 or 8 days. Extensive investigations in which semen was collected daily for 2 weeks show that after 6 to 8 days, the daily sperm output becomes stable, the extra gonadal reserves have been depleted, and the stallion is ejaculating his daily production of sperm. Testicular volume estimated by ultrasonography is closely correlated with daily sperm output and is easier and quicker to determine.

Collection

The stallion semen is collected with an artificial vagina. Three basic models can be used: Japanese, Colorado, and Missouri. The Missouri and Colorado models are the most popular. Each model has advantages and disadvantages. However, the preference of the person doing the collecting usually prevails. The Colorado-style models are heavy and bulky when filled with water, but they have the advantage of maintaining the proper temperature for a longer period of time and it is easier to separate out the gel fraction. The Missouri model is much lighter and easier to handle, but during cold weather, it loses temperature at a faster rate than do the Colorado models. To collect gel-free semen with the Missouri model, a filter must be placed in the collection bottle. For collection of semen from miniature stallions, the Missouri model, miniaturized Colorado model, or standard bull AV can be used. If traditional AVs are used, the miniature stallion ejaculates into the warm part of the AV, which is deleterious to sperm, and the sperm-rich fraction may remain in the AV. Also, they are not tight enough to provide stimulation.

Preparation of the Colorado model for collection has been described in detail by Pickett and Back (1973). Prepare the Japanese model according to Figure 14-5. First, insert the donut-shaped dam made of sponge rubber and position it in the front of the aluminum casing. Then insert the rubber liner, and reflect the small end back over the small end (front end) of the casing. Secure it with cotton string to prevent any water leakage. Keeping the liner straight in the casing, reflect the large end of the liner back over the back end of the casing and secure it with cotton string. The rubber collection bulb is placed over the small (front) end of the AV. Then fill it with water through the valve. Water temperature should be 111° to 118°F (44° to 48°C) at the time of collection. If the water temperature exceeds 120°F (48.9°C), it may cause sperm damage; if it is below 100°F (37.8°C), it may cause cold shock. If the AV is filled with water that is about 120°F (48.9°C), the AV usually equilibrates at the proper temperature by the time it is used to collect the stallion. The stallion is not very sensitive to temperature, but some stallions accept the AV better if it is at the upper or lower end of the temperature range. Rather than guessing at the amount of water in the AV, it is best to weigh the AV. Filled with water, it should weigh 12 to 13 pounds (5.4 to 5.9 kg) for the average stallion. If the penis is smaller than average, more water is required (or vice versa if the stallion has a very large penis). Lubricate the open end of the AV with sterile H-R lubricant immediately prior to use. Lubricate it about one-half to three-fourths the length of the casing, applying the lubricant with a plastic glove. Use the lubricant sparingly so that it does not contaminate the semen.

Figure 14-6 shows how to collect the stallion's semen. He may be collected off a mare or off a phantom (Figure 14-7). The collector may stand on either side of the mare or phantom, but right-handed people prefer the right side. As the stallion mounts, direct the penis into the AV. Hold the AV steady by pressing it against the mare's hindquarters. Hold the AV at about a 30° angle of inclination until ejaculation occurs. As soon as the stallion begins thrusting movements, place your left hand at the base of the penis to feel the ejaculatory pulsations. As the stallion ejaculates, rotate the AV downward so that the semen drains into the collection bulb. After ejaculation is complete, remove the AV from the penis.

FIGURE 14-5 Preparing the Japanese model artifical vagina for collecting semen:
(a) Equipment: (A) aluminum casing; (B) sponge rubber dam; (C) collection bulb;
(D) rubber liner; (E) string. *(b)* Insert the sponge rubber dam. *(c)* Insert the rubber liner.
(d) Tie the ends of the rubber liner with string. *(e)* Place the collection bulb over the end.
(f) Fill with water. *(g)* Lubricate the rubber liner. (Photos by W. Evans.)

FIGURE 14-6   Collecting semen from a stallion with a Missouri model artifical vagina. (Photo by W. Evans.)

FIGURE 14-7   Collecting semen from a stallion with a Colorado model artifical vagina and using a phantom. (Photo by W. Evans.)

Care of AV Equipment

The AV equipment must be kept clean and sterile to prevent the transmission of infections and diseases. Because rubber components cannot be sterilized with heat without deterioration, rinse them in warm water and place in a Nolvasan solution (3 oz per gal, or 23.5 ml per liter). Scrub them with a brush in the antiseptic soap solution until they are clean. Next, wash them in a mild soap solution (Ivory soap is recommended), rinse them in warm water to remove any residue from the soap that would alter the pH of the semen, and finally, rinse them in 70 percent ethyl alcohol. Soap is spermicidal, so remove all of it from the rubber components as well as from the glassware that is used. Allow them to air dry in a dust-free cabinet. Rinse glassware in water, wash it in hot, soapy water (Ivory is recommended), rinse it several times to remove all soap residues, rinse it in distilled water two or three times, and dry it in an oven at 167°F (70°C). To prevent dust contamination, seal all glassware with aluminum foil and store it in a dust-free cabinet. If possible, periodically sterilize the glassware with heat. If an infected stallion is used, sterilize all equipment that his semen has touched.

Processing

Process the semen by immediately removing the collection bottle and passing the semen through an in-line milk filter or a nylon mesh filter to remove the gel if a filter was not used in the collection bottle (Figure 14-8). Collect the gel-free semen in a prewarmed, sterile plastic bottle and place it immediately in an incubator set at 100°F (37.8°C) (Figure 14-9). Insemination is discussed in Chapter 15.

Evaluation

Evaluate each seminal collection for volume and for concentration of spermatozoa per milliliter, motility, morphology, and pH. The evaluation procedure is explained in Appendix 14-1. In a clinical situation, the semen should be cultured for bacteria.

Volume

Normal values for the ejaculate volume range from 9 to 75 ml, but volumes of 300 ml have been observed. Three primary factors influence the volume: stallion, season of year, and frequency of ejaculation. The volume of semen is larger (almost twofold) during the breeding season than during winter. The absence or the amount of gel, which is influenced by stallion variability and season, is an important determinant of volume. Frequency of ejaculation influences the seminal volume. An ejaculate collected 1 hour after the first ejaculate is usually less than the first, largely because of the absence or reduced amount of gel in the second ejaculation. If the ejaculate volumes are less than 25 ml, a stallion's fertility may be questioned.

FIGURE 14-8   Filter assemblies for obtaining gel-free semen with an "in-line milk filter" or nylon mesh filter. (A) sterile plastic collection bottles; (B) nylon mesh filter; (C) cap to fold the filter in the bottle; (D) insertion of the filter in the bottle; (E) plastic insert to hold the "in-line milk filter" open; (F) "in-line milk filter."

Motility

The percentage of motile spermatozoa in an ejaculate is usually 60 to 100 percent; 70 percent is considered quite good. Motility is not influenced by season nor by collecting two consecutive ejaculates 1 hour apart. When the motility estimate is less than 50 percent, fertility may be questioned.

Concentration

The concentration is the single most important factor affecting fertility. The concentration of sperm per milliliter of gel-free ejaculate ranges between

FIGURE 14-9   Incubator for keeping semen and semen evalution supplies at proper temperature. (A) incubator; (B) microscope slides; (C) semen filters; (D) semen extender; (E) semen collection bottle; (F) microscope slide cover glasses; (G) syringe; (H) pipettes; (I) graduated cylinder.

30 and 800 million. There is a large variation between stallions, between first and second ejaculates, and according to season of the year. One study found that the average of the first ejaculate was 282×10^6 per milliliter (Pickett and Voss, 1973). The average concentration of the second ejaculate was 60 percent of the first ejaculate. During winter, the concentration is about one-half as great as during the breeding season. Stallions ejaculating with a concentration of 8×10^6 spermatozoa per milliliter or less have questionable fertility.

Total Number of Spermatozoa

The total number of spermatozoa collected can be calculated from the volume and concentration determinations. The total is usually about 15 billion per ejaculate. The second ejaculate is about 50 percent less. Season of the year affects sperm production and thus the number collected. During winter, it is about 50 percent of the total collection averaged during the breeding season.

Testicle size also influences the total number of spermatozoa collected. Scrotal width is correlated to sperm output. The equation for daily sperm production is

$$-4.88 \times 10^9 + 0.93 \times 10^9 \text{ (scrotal width in millimeters)}$$

Therefore, determine scrotal width with a set of calipers during a breeding-soundness evaluation. The average scrotal width is about 90 to 110 mm. If the width is less than 85 mm, the daily sperm output should be determined by collecting the stallion daily for seven to eight days.

Frequency of ejaculation influences the total number of spermatozoa collected. If collected from a stallion one to three times per week, the total number collected per ejaculate is about equal. When collected at more frequent intervals, the total number per ejaculate decreases. To collect the maximum number of spermatozoa each week from a stallion, collect three ejaculates per week (every other day). If collected daily, the total number collected per ejaculate is about 50 percent of the number collected per ejaculate on an every-other-day basis. Therefore, at the end of a week, the number collected for three times a week is the same as for six times per week. This is an important consideration for decreasing labor costs and chances of injury, and for preventing overuse of a stallion in an artificial insemination program.

Sexual stimulation of a stallion by teasing does not increase the total number of sperm collected per ejaculate. It does increase the seminal volume. Therefore, it is not necessary to stimulate a stallion beyond the time required for the breeding hygiene procedures.

pH

Determine the pH of the gel-free semen as a precautionary measure if the semen is evaluated. It can be measured routinely if sufficient semen is available after the mares have been inseminated. The pH of first ejaculates should be between 7.4 and 7.6, and the value for second ejaculates should be between 7.5 and 7.7. If an incomplete ejaculation is obtained, the pH will be higher, because the pH of the accessory sex gland fluid without epididymal contributions approaches 8.0. Values for the second ejaculation should be higher than the first ejaculation. Season of the year also affects pH. The lowest pH values are observed during the breeding season, and the highest values are observed during winter.

Morphology

A morphological examination is used to determine the percentage of deformed cells, which usually varies between 20 and 30 percent. The normal spermatozoan is shown in Figure 14-10. It is composed of three principal regions: head, midpiece, and tail. Because the tail is placed abaxially on the head, some normal spermatozoa look as if the tail comes out of the underside of the head. Many types of abnormalities are commonly observed (Figure 14-11). Defective

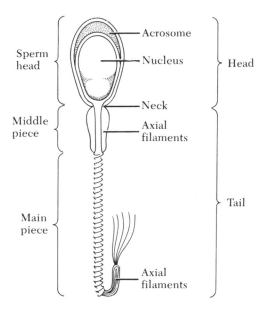

FIGURE 14-10   Morphology of stallion spermatozoan.

heads may be narrow at the base, pear-shaped, small, abnormally contoured, free heads, double heads, or giant heads. Defective midpieces may be enlarged and swollen and may have protoplasmic droplets. Tail deformities include free tails and bent, coiled, and double tails. When the percentage of abnormal spermatozoa exceeds 50 percent, fertility is questioned.

Storing Semen

The use of fresh-cooled and frozen semen has opened up a whole new realm of possibilities for mare owners. Although the use of these technologies is still limited to only a few breeds, more associations are discussing their use.

Semen can be cooled for storage on the farm to reduce the number of collections from a stallion or for shipment to other farms. The procedures for processing semen to be cooled are relatively simple for those familiar with artificial insemination. Semen is collected from stallions by normal semen-collection procedures, with careful attention to avoid contamination of the ejaculate. After collection, the gel fraction is removed and the semen is evaluated to determine the percentage of live sperm and cells with morphological defects. It is extended with a skim milk–based extender. Normally, the semen is packaged in insemination doses containing 1 billion active motile spermatozoa. This dose is twice the recommended insemination dose to account for losses during storage. After the semen is processed, it is cooled in a specially designed shipping container. Specific instructions for semen processing and storage come with each shipping container.

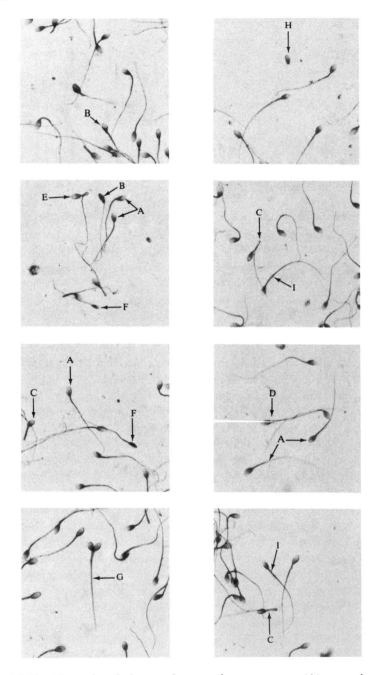

FIGURE 14-11   Normal and abnormal types of spermatozoa: (A) normal;
(B) abnormal head; (C) bent tail; (D) proximal protoplasmic droplet;
(E) looped tail; (F) microcephalic head; (G) twin heads; (H) isolated head;
(I) distal protoplasmic droplet. (Photos by W. Evans.)

There is considerable stallion variability, but most ejaculates will remain viable for 24 to 48 hours; some ejaculates can be successfully stored for over 96 hours.

There are advantages to the use of freshly cooled semen. Mares do not have to be shipped to a breeding farm and thus breeding costs are reduced; the mare owner saves transportation costs, chute fees, and board costs. There may however, be increased costs for the number of required evaluations to determine the time to inseminate the mare. And there are extra costs for shipping the container both ways, semen processing fees, and artificial insemination expenses.

With attention to detail in managing mares to be bred with fresh-cooled semen, conception rates equaling natural breeding and artificial insemination with fresh semen can be achieved.

The use of frozen semen has been approved by a limited number of breed associations, primarily the sport horse breed associations. Because of the technical requirements to freeze semen, it is not widely used—but its use is increasing. There is considerable variability among stallion ejaculates in their ability to be successfully processed.

BREEDING SOUNDNESS EVALUATION

In addition to a semen evaluation, a breeding soundness evaluation should be completed on stallions before they are bought or before the breeding season starts. If possible, the stallion's past breeding records should be examined to determine his ability to impregnate mares. These records should indicate the number of mares bred, number that conceived, average number of breedings per estrous cycle, average number of estrous cycles mares were bred per conception, and average number of breedings per conception. Fertile stallions breed each mare 1.5 to 2 times per estrous cycle, and they are bred 1 to 2 estrous cycles per conception. The conception percentage for a properly managed and fertile stallion should be greater than 90.

The stallion should be in excellent physical health, as shown by a physical examination and by his personal appearance. Injuries to the hindlegs or back may impair or prevent the stallion from mounting mares or phantoms. Overweight stallions tend to lose libido during the latter part of the breeding season, when temperatures are higher. The condition of the respiratory and circulatory systems should be evaluated, because they have a direct bearing on the longevity of the stallion. Problems such as arthritis and melanomas should also be evaluated. Heavy parasite infestations may cause colic and have other long-term effects that reduce the stallion's performance. Check for any history of colic. Palpate the reproductive tract for any abnormalities. The scrotum should contain two testicles; cryptorchids should be avoided and castrated. Detect inguinal hernias during a rectal examination. Check for hereditary imperfections such as overshot and undershot jaws.

The temperament of the stallion is important. He should be easy to handle during teasing and breeding procedures. If possible, observe him when he is breeding a mare. He should not have any stable vices. Cribbing, stall kicking, weaving, and other vices detract from the stallion's appearance to mare owners. Masturbation lowers the semen quality. Stallions that severely bite mares during copulation must be muzzled during teasing and breeding. The stallion's libido should be evaluated by determining his reaction time. Normal reaction times (from the time of seeing a mare until an attempted mount) should be about 1 to 5 minutes during breeding season. During winter, it is usually longer and may be as long as 15 minutes. Stallions with depressed libido may take as long as 30 to 60 minutes before they will mount a mare. Breeding these stallions is time-consuming. The average number of mounts per ejaculate should be about 1.5. An average of 2 to 3 is also too time-consuming. The time of copulation normally lasts from about 30 seconds to 2 or 3 minutes. The stallion usually makes 5 to 10 intravaginal thrusts prior to ejaculation, and each thrust lasts about 11 seconds. The ejaculatory reflex lasts about 15 seconds. About 5 to 12 (8 to 10 is average) ejaculation pulses can be felt on the ventral side of the base of the penis. Ejaculation can usually be determined by "tail flagging"—the stallion raises and lowers his tail several times.

Olfaction is one of the fundamental stimuli of the reproductive responses of the stallion. When the stallion smells the external genitalia of the mare or smells voided urine, he displays the olfactory or Flehman reflex, in which he extends his neck upward and curls his lip. During the reflex, he inhales and exhales air in the upper respiratory passages. During courtship or teasing, the stallion also smells the groin of the mare and bites the mare on the croup and neck. At the first approach to a mare or on removal from his stall or paddock to tease mares, the stallion snorts and continues to snort periodically during courtship.

INFERTILITY

There are many possible causes of infertility. A stallion suffering from poor health and/or poor nutrition, injury, worry, or anxiety sometimes recovers, with proper management. Another common problem is excessive masturbation. Masturbation is normal behavior in all stallions and usually occurs at night. The typical stallion masturbates an average of 3.3 bouts lasting about 3 minutes each. During the early morning hours when they arise after lying down, 50 percent of stallions will masturbate within 5 minutes. It is difficult to observe some stallions masturbating, but the presence of dried semen on the abdomen or on the back of the forelegs and a shrinkage of muscles over the loin are good indicators that the stallion has been masturbating. A couple of management practices have been tried to eliminate this vice. Turning some stallions outside where they can exercise and see other horses stops excessive masturbation, but others require that a stallion ring be placed behind the glans penis (Figure 14-12). The ring is removed before breeding a mare and is subsequently replaced. Care must be taken that a local inflammation does not develop.

Mismanagement is the most common cause of abnormal sexual behavior leading to infertility. Overuse of a stallion as a 2- or 3-year-old may lead to the development of poor breeding behavior, such as slow reaction time to breed a mare. Mature stallions that are overused during winter and fall may develop a slow reaction time. The overused young stallion often develops a bad habit of savaging (excessively biting) a mare. Disinterest may also result from excessive use of the stallion as a teaser to determine which mares are in estrus.

Infertility may develop in the latter part of the breeding season if a stallion is overused in the early part of the season; that is, before the natural breeding season. During the latter part of winter (early part of breeding season), sperm output and libido decrease. Mares are coming out of anestrus, so their estrous periods are long and irregular. It is difficult to predict ovulation during the first estrous cycle, so these mares require more breedings per conception. Also, barren and problem mares normally are the mares being bred at this time.

Unnecessary roughness while handling a stallion during breeding and teasing may reduce his libido. He may become afraid to mount and copulate. However, stallions should be trained so that they do not endanger personnel or the mare. During teasing, the young stallion should be allowed to be more aggressive than normal. After he learns how to breed mares, any overaggressiveness can be corrected.

FIGURE 14-12   *(a)* Plastic stallion rings; *(b)* stallion ring in position. (Photo by W. Evans.)

Temporary infertility will result from exposure of the testes to high temperatures that may occur during fever. The impairment lasts for 60 days, with decreased motility, poor morphology, and decreased number of spermatozoa.

Beyond 12 years of age, the number of stallions used for breeding purposes declines because of the failure to sire quality foals, health status, unsoundness, and deaths. One important factor is that some stallions develop testicular degeneration as they age. Although there is no well-defined age of onset, any stallion over 15 years of age is considered an older stallion and is at risk. It is not known why the condition develops in some stallions and not others. It is characterized by a marked, progressive shrinking and softening of the testes, and a wrinkling of the surrounding tunica albugenia. There are changes in plasma hormone concentrations prior to and during the testes changes. The hormone concentration changes can warn the stallion manager of potential decreased fertility. Characteristically, there is reduced total estrogren below 125 picograms per milliliter and increased FSH (follicle-stimulating hormone) above 25 nanograms per milliliter. The changes in hormones are usually not accompanied by changes in libido. Thus, unless the stallion manager routinely has a veterinarian palpate the testicles and obtain blood samples for hormone analysis, the first indication of testicular degeneration is a reduced conception rate and a decreased number of motile sperm in the ejaculate.

TRAINING YOUNG STALLIONS

Training the young, shy stallion takes patience and time. He is usually started by teasing a mare or mares for a few minutes. As soon as he loses interest, or after 5 to 10 minutes, teasing should be stopped. As soon as he teases a mare vigorously, he should be allowed to mount a gentle mare that is in heat. He should be guided into the proper position prior to mounting. A stallion frequently mounts on the mare's side or shoulder until he learns proper position. When he mounts correctly from behind, direct his penis into the vagina. The handler must be careful because the stallion frequently falls backward or off to the side the first few times he ejaculates. After having bred two to six times, he usually understands the process. Then train him to mount the mare by approaching her at the hip.

The stallion must be trained to accept washing procedures before breeding. For the first few times, stand the stallion next to a wall after he drops his penis while being teased. He is washed in this position so that his movements can be controlled.

CASTRATION

A castrated horse is referred to as a *gelding*. Gelding a horse has several advantages. Several geldings may be kept in a paddock, whereas each stallion must be kept by himself. Geldings are easier to care for, less prone to injury, and easier to haul because of their attitude. Many stallions tend to be lazy performers and do not perform consistently.

Age

Most horses chosen to be castrated are usually castrated between birth and 2 years of age. Several factors usually determine the age when they are gelded. Colts that have poor conformation and/or poor pedigrees are gelded as soon as the testicles descend into the scrotum. The testicles are usually in the scrotum at birth or arrive there before the tenth month after birth, but occasionally they are not fully down until the twelfth or fifteenth month after birth.

If a horse has good conformation, a good pedigree, and warrants a performance test, he is kept intact until he fails to meet specific performance criteria. Stallions that are able to perform but do not sire good foals should also be castrated. There are too many good stallions available to keep those that are poorly conformed and lack performance ability, or stallions whose progeny are of poor quality.

Procedure for Castration

Because of the possible complications that may result from castration and the need to anesthetize many colts or stallions to prevent injury, it is customary for a veterinarian to perform the castration. At least three methods of castrating a horse have been described.

1 In the *primary closure method,* the veterinarian makes an incision through the skin and vaginal tunic between the scrotum and superficial inguinal ring on each side of the scrotum. He or she ties the vessels and ductus deferens by transfixation ligatures. The testicles are removed, and all dissected planes are closed with chromic gut.

2 In the *closed technique,* the veterinarian frees each testicle and spermatic cord still contained within the parietal layer of the tunica vaginalis by blunt dissection from the surrounding tissue well into the inguinal canal. The cord structures are divided by means of an emasculator, which is left in position for approximately 1 minute.

3   In the *open technique,* the veterinarian frees the tunic vaginalis from the surrounding tissue as in the closed method. Then the tunica vaginalis communis is split with scissors so that all structures to be removed can be identified. The testicles, epididymis, and part of the cord are then removed, as previously indicated.

If the horse has been immunized against tetanus, postoperative care consists of exercise to prevent or control swelling and edema. (Otherwise, immunize immediately after castration.) The stallion libido usually subsides in 4 to 6 months but may last for 1 year.

Failure to remove the epididymis and sufficient vas deferens may cause a gelding to retain stallion behavior. Such geldings are referred to as being "proud cut." Not much can be done to correct their behavior.

Cryptorchids

An animal with one or both testes undescended into the scrotum is a cryptorchid, more commonly referred to as a ridgeling, high flanker, rig, or crypt. The testes may be descended at birth and are usually descended by the age of 10 months. Some colts may be 12 to 15 months old before the testes descend. After 15 months, colts are considered cryptorchid if the testes are not descended. A positive diagnosis can be made if the vas deferens does not pass through the inguinal canal. These horses are difficult to castrate, and many castrated ridgelings seem to retain their stallion attitude for several months after castration.

CHAPTER 15

Breeding the Mare

Mares have traditionally had a reputation for low reproductive efficiency, when compared with other domestic farm animals. On the average, about 50 percent of mares bred have live foals. The low reproductive efficiency has been related to breeding mares with reproductive problems, and placing no emphasis on conformation, which is related to reproductive success, or on the reproductive history of the mare's immediate family. Moreover, the mare has a long estrous period, during which it is difficult to determine the appropriate time to breed. Thus, it is essential for horse breeders to understand the anatomy and the physiology of reproduction in the mare and stallion if they expect high conception rates.

REPRODUCTIVE TRACT

The reproductive tract of the mare consists of two ovaries, two fallopian tubes, uterus, cervix, vagina, clitoris, and vulva. These structures are shown in Figure 15-1. The mammary gland is an accessory sex gland and is shown in Figure 15-2.

Ovaries

The ovaries of the mare perform two essential functions: the production and release of ova and hormones. In form, the ovary resembles a bean or kidney

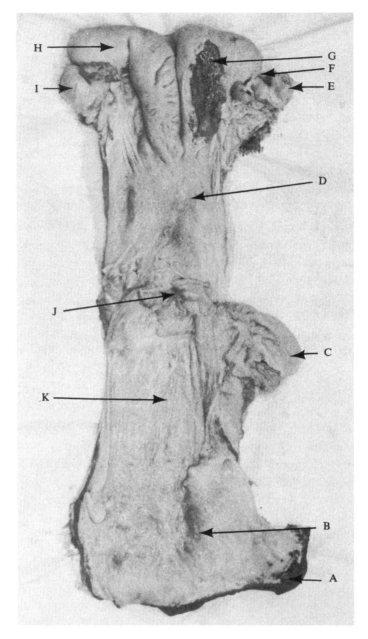

FIGURE 15-1   Reproductive organs of the mare, showing the vagina and a uterine horn opened: (A) clitoris; (B) orifice of vestibular glands; (C) bladder; (D) body of uterus; (E) ovary; (F) fallopian tube; (G) uterine horn opened to show mucosal folds; (H) uterine horn; (I) ovary; (J) external os of cervix; (K) vagina. (Photo by W. Evans.)

FIGURE 15-2   Mammary gland with one gland complex opened along the teat cistern: (A) teat; (B) teat opened along the teat cistern; (C) gland complex. (Photo by W. Evans.)

in that it has an area, the ovulation fossa, that is folded inward (Figure 15-3). This is where ovulation occurs. It is difficult to give average ovary weight or dimensions because they are influenced by many factors, such as age, breed, size, season, and reproductive state of the mare. In mature mares of average size (900 to 1100 lb), each ovary weighs approximately 50 to 75 gm and is 6 to 7 cm long and 3 to 4 cm wide.

The outer surface of the ovary is covered by a serous coat except at the hilus and ovulation fossa. The hilus is where the blood vessels and nerves enter the ovary. At the ovulation fossa, a layer of primitive germinal epithelium covers the area. The tough serous coat prevents ovulation from occurring on the surface of the ovary except at the ovulation fossa. The interior of the ovary is composed of connective tissue and follicles or corpora lutea in varying stages of growth and development or degeneration.

Follicles undergo a series of developmental events leading to the release of the ovum (see Figure 15-4) and formation of the corpus luteum. Immediately after ovulation occurs, the corpus luteum starts to develop in the area from which the follicle was released. By the sixth day after ovulation the corpus luteum is well developed and vascularized. The purpose of the corpus luteum is to produce progestin hormones. It begins secreting progestins in sufficient

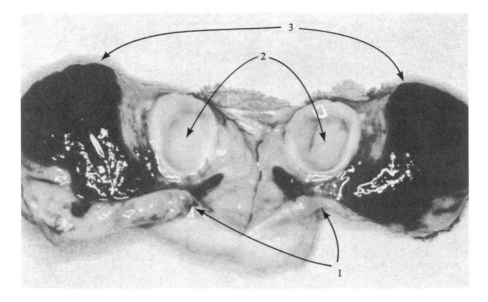

FIGURE 15-3   Cross section of a mare's ovary: (1) ovulation fossa; (2) Graafian follicles; (3) corpus hemorraghicium. (Courtesy John Hughes.)

quantities for their concentration to be measured in the blood about 48 to 79 hours after ovulation. Approximately 14 days after ovulation, the corpus luteum decreases in size, and its progestin-synthesizing capabilities decline quite rapidly if the mare is not pregnant.

In addition to the follicles that are in an active stage of growth in the ovary, there are follicles that do not complete their growth cycle and that start to undergo atresia (a degeneration process). These so-called atretic follicles are found in the ovary during or immediately after the breeding season and are in varying stages of degeneration. Corpora lutea also undergo a degeneration

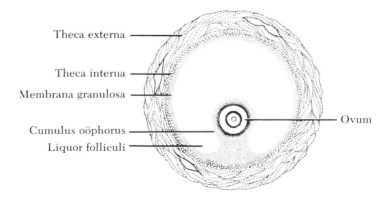

FIGURE 15-4   A Graafian follicle. (Courtesy M. Morris.)

process that may take several months. Therefore, it is common to find degenerating corpora lutea in the ovary, known as *corpus albicans,* resulting from the previous two or three estrous cycles.

The ovarian artery supplies blood to the ovaries (Figure 15-5). Several veins leave the ovary and unite to form the ovarian branch of the ovarian vein. The nerve supply is derived from the renal and aortic plexus of the sympathetic system.

Fallopian Tubes

The fallopian tubes or oviducts are the connecting links between the ovaries and the uterus. They serve two primary functions: they conduct ova from the ovaries to the uterus, and they serve as the usual site of fertilization. Each oviduct is about 30 to 70 mm long and 4 to 8 mm thick and has an inside tubal diameter of 2 to 3 mm. The oviducts are coiled and folded so that the ovary is fairly close to the uterine horn. To prevent the escape of the ovum into the abdominal cavity during ovulation, the end of each oviduct is expanded to form the ampulla and infundibulum. The infundibulum partially surrounds the ovary and has fingerlike projections (fimbrae) extending from its edge. The opening of the oviduct into the peritoneal cavity at the junction of the ampulla

FIGURE 15-5   Composite diagram of a dorsal view of the arteries and veins (shaded) of the uterus and ovaries of the mare: (1) uterine branch of vaginal vein; (2) uterine branch of vaginal artery; (3) uterine vein; (4) uterine artery; (5) ovarian artery; (6) uterine horn; (7) uterine tube; (8) uterine branch of ovarian artery; (9) ovary; (10) ovarian branch of ovarian artery; (11) uterine branch of ovarian vein; (12) ovarian branch of ovarian vein; (13) ovarian vein. (From Ginther and others, 1972.)

is called the *ostium abdominale*. The opening leading into the uterus is the *ostium uterinum* and is located at the uterotubal junction.

Uterus

The uterus of the mare consists of the left uterine horn, right uterine horn, and body. The uterine horns are located in the abdominal cavity. They are approximately 25 cm long (10 inches) and are cylindrical in shape. The horns curl downward and outward from the uterus like rams' horns. The uterine body is approximately 18 to 20 cm long and 10 cm in diameter. It is suspended in position by the broad ligament that attaches to the abdominal and pelvic walls. It is located partially in the abdominal cavity and partially in the pelvic cavity.

The wall of the uterus is composed of three muscle layers. At parturition, these muscles help expel the fetus. An inner layer of loose connective tissue contains the uterine glands.

Blood supply to the uterus is derived from three arteries: the uterine branch of the vaginal artery, the uterine artery, and the uterine branch of the ovarian artery (Figure 15-5). Blood leaves the uterus via three veins whose names correspond to those of the arteries. Nerve supply to the uterus derives from the uterine and pelvic plexus.

Cervix

The cervix is a thick, muscular sphincter that separates the body of the uterus from the vagina. It is about 5 to 7.5 cm long. The muscle layers are well developed and have extensive folds. Because of these extensive folds, there is no well-defined cervical canal. The cervix extends into the vagina, and the angle formed between the cervix and vagina is the formix. The opening into the vagina is the os cervix. Part of the mucus secreted into the vagina is derived from mucosal cells located in the mucosa layer. During estrus, these cells are very active, and a considerable amount of mucus is present in the vagina around the cervix.

Vagina

The vagina is composed of two parts. The vagina proper is located between the hymen and the cervix; the vestibulum vaginae is located between the hymen and the vulva. The hymen is located just forward of where the urethra enters the vestibulum vaginae. The vagina is about 15 to 20 cm long and 10 to 12 cm in diameter. The wall of the vagina is composed of a layer of stratified epithelium, a layer of loose connective tissue, and two layers of muscles.

Blood comes into the vagina through the internal pudic arteries and leaves via the internal pudic veins. The nerve supply is from the pelvic plexus of the sympathetic nervous system.

Vulva

The vulva is the terminal portion of the reproductive tract. It is about 10 to 12 cm in length, and the external orifice is a vertical slit approximately 12 to 15 cm long. The external urethral orifice is located 10 to 12 cm inside the vulva. The glans clitoris, homologue of the male penis, is located about 5 cm within the vulva.

Mammary Gland

The udder of the mare is composed of two gland complexes (Figure 15-2). Each complex has a broad, flat teat. Each teat has at least two streak canals, and each streak canal is connected to a teat cistern. A canal extends from each teat cistern to a gland cistern, which has a system of ducts leading to it from the secretory gland.

Blood supply to the udder is via the external pudental artery and is drained by the external pudental and subcutaneous abdominal veins. The inguinal nerve innervates the udder.

PHYSIOLOGY OF REPRODUCTION

Estrous Cycle

When the filly attains puberty at the age of 12 to 15 months, she starts to come into estrus (heat) periodically. The estrous cycle is the length of time from the first day of behavioral estrus until the first day of behavioral estrus of the next estrous cycle. For practical purposes, the estrous cycle is divided into two phases, estrus and diestrus (Figure 15-6). The average length of the estrous cycle is 21 to 23 days. Estrus lasts for about 4 to 6 days, and diestrus lasts for about 17 to 19 days. Ovulation usually occurs during the third to fifth days of

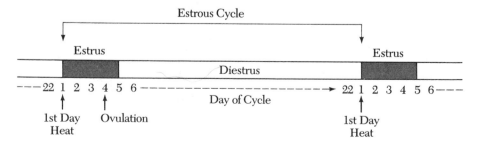

FIGURE 15-6   Estrous cycle components and time relationship.

the cycle. During the two phases, definite changes occur in the mare's behavior, in the hormone concentrations in her blood, and in her reproductive tract.

Behavioral Changes

During diestrus, the mare shows complete resentment of the stallion. She will kick, bite, and chase him. One or two days before estrus, she becomes somewhat more passive to the stallion. She may or may not object to his presence. During estrus, she is receptive to the stallion. She flexes her pelvis, raises her tail, frequently urinates, spreads her hindlegs apart, contracts and relaxes the lips of the vulva with eversion of the clitoris, and allows the stallion to bite and chew on her neck and flanks (Figures 15-7 and 15-8). The behavioral signs of the jinny (donkey) are a little different: she holds her head low, and her jaws make a chewing motion.

The end of the estrous period is closely correlated to ovulation. About 50 percent of all mares are out of estrus 24 hours after ovulation; 80 percent are out after 48 hours.

To detect when mares are in estrus, they must be teased with a stallion. The mares should be teased daily or at least every other day if they are to be bred. Several methods are used to tease mares, depending on the number of mares to be bred, physical facilities, and available labor. Each mare can be brought to the teaser, or vice versa. The teasing-rail method (Figure 15-9) and

FIGURE 15-7   Mare in estrus, showing her acceptance of the stallion. (Photo by W. Evans.)

FIGURE 15-8   Estrous mare with hindlegs spread apart, pelvis flexed, raised tail, and eversion of clitoris. (Photo by W. Evans.)

FIGURE 15-9   Teasing rail separates mare and stallion.

teasing-wall method (Figure 15-10) require the stallion handler and a mare handler. The rail or wall should be about 4 feet high, and the wall should be of solid construction. Because both the mare and stallion kick and strike, the wall should be padded. The personnel are protected by standing behind the two short padded walls. The stallion can be kept in a stall (Figure 15-11) or an outside paddock (Figure 15-12) where the mares can be brought to him. This eliminates the need for a stallion handler. The chute keeps the mare close to the stallion. By using a long lead shank, the handler can get in a position to observe the mare's perineal area. For teasing large numbers of mares, a teasing mill can be used (Figure 15-13). By the time the last mare is in her small pen, the first mare can be returned to her paddock. To tease 50 to 75 mares in a short period of time, two stallions can be placed in teasing boxes between pens (Figure 15-14). Keep exact records on each mare because some mares are timid and will not approach the teaser when they are in estrus. Any mare that does not show estrus within three weeks of teasing should be teased individually. The stallion can be taken to each mare in her paddock, pens of mares, or each pasture of mares. Teasing across a fence is dangerous for the horses. They can easily get a foot caught in the fence unless a teasing wall is built in the fence. A teasing wall is 4 feet high, about 10 to 12 feet long, and of solid construction. Mares will approach the stallion when he is brought to the teasing wall. A pony stallion can be turned into the pasture or large paddock, because he is not tall enough to breed the mares if they are in estrus.

The teaser stallion is an important part of the breeding program because he gets the mare to show behavioral signs of estrus. Most farms use a low-quality stallion for a teaser. Cryptorchid stallions whose descended testicle has been removed and vasectomized stallions make excellent teasers. A

FIGURE 15-10   Teasing a mare with a stallion across a teasing wall. Both handlers are protected from the mare and stallion's kicking and striking. (Illustration by M. Morris.)

FIGURE 15-11   Stallion teasing a mare through a window in the stall wall that is adjacent to a teasing chute. (Photo by W. Evans.)

vasectomized stallion cannot impregnate a mare if he gets loose and mounts a mare. Stallions with a genetic deformity in which the penis is reflected back between the legs are aggressive teasers. Some geldings will tease a mare and if they are given testosterone they may be suitable to use during a breeding season.

FIGURE 15-12   Paddock designed so that mares can be efficiently teased individually. (Photo by W. Evans, courtesy Taylor Ranch, Davis, California.)

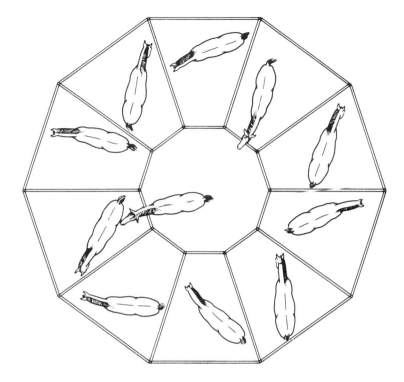

FIGURE 15-13   Diagram of a teasing mill to tease several mares simultaneously.

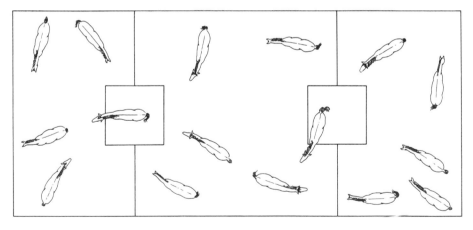

FIGURE 15-14   Large-scale teasing operation in which 50 to 75 mares can be teased simultaneously. A teaser stallion is placed in each of the two small pens.

Hormonal Changes

The endocrine changes that occur during the two phases of the estrous cycle are diagrammed in Figure 15-15. Although the changes in concentration of the hormones in the blood have been determined, the interrelationships between the hormones are not fully understood. The hormones controlling the estrous cycle originate in the brain, pituitary, and ovary.

The pituitary hormones are follicle-stimulating hormone (FSH) and luteinizing hormone (LH). FSH is responsible for the growth of follicles. Generally, FSH in the blood increases during the middiestrous phase and again during late estrus and early diestrus. It is believed that the middiestrous surge initiates the growth of follicles, and the estrous surge aids in the final growth of the dominant follicle. Inhibin, a glycoprotein synthesized in the follicle, has the capacity to decrease FSH secretion, and its blood concentration is negatively correlated to FSH concentration during the estrous cycle.

Luteinizing hormone causes ovulation and is responsible for the formation of the corpus luteum. LH concentration starts to increase 2 to 3 days prior to ovulation and reaches a maximum 1 to 2 days after ovulation. Several days after ovulation, it reaches a minimal concentration during diestrus.

FSH and LH work in a synergistic manner in the processes of follicular growth, maturation, and ovulation. Their secretion by the pituitary is primarily controlled by another hormone known as gonadotropin-releasing hormone that is secreted by the hypothalamus in the brain.

Two ovarian hormones—estrogens and progestins—participate in the control of the estrous cycle (Figure 15-15). Estradiol-17β is produced by the granulosa cells and by the interna of the Graafian follicles. As the follicle enlarges, the amount of estradiol-17β in the blood starts to increase. The increased concentration reaches a peak just prior to ovulation and then declines to a minimal concentration at 5 to 8 days after ovulation. Estrogen may facilitate the surge in LH, because it does reach a peak prior to the LH.

Within 24 hours after ovulation, the corpus luteum begins to secrete progestins, primarily progesterone. By the sixth day after ovulation, the corpus luteum is producing maximal amounts of progestins. This continues until about 12 to 14 days after ovulation, when the blood concentration of progestins rapidly declines. The cessation of corpus luteum function is caused by the release of $PGF_{2\alpha}$ by the lining of the uterus. The interval between cessation of corpus luteum function and the beginning of estrus is approximately 3 days. The blood concentration of progesterone must decline below 1 ng/ml plasma before estrus is manifested.

Reproductive Tract Changes

Characteristic changes occur in the reproductive tract of the mare during the different phases of the estrous cycle. These changes can help determine the best time to breed a mare. For mares that have silent estrous periods, these

FIGURE 15-15   Endocrine patterns during the estrous cycle of the mare. *(a)* The relationships of the gonadotropins (LH & FSH) and estradiol to estrous behavior and ovulation. *(b)* The relationship of progesterone and $PGF_{2\alpha}$ to estrous behavior and ovulation. Values for estradiol and $PGF_{2\alpha}$ are not given because of the variability of the values reported in the literature. (From Neely, Liu, and Hillman, 1983.)

changes are the only indicators used to determine when to breed the mare. The changes in weight and size of the different parts are listed in Table 15-1.

The most important changes occur on the ovary. They are determined by palpating the ovaries via the rectum (Figure 15-16) or with the aid of an ultrasonograph. During the winter anestrous period, the ovaries are usually small and inactive. However, the ovaries of some anestrous mares continually develop follicles that may or may not ovulate. As the breeding season approaches, the ovaries begin to develop. Although several follicles start to develop each estrous cycle, only one or two reach ovulatory size (Figure 15-17). The follicle that will ovulate during estrus usually becomes prominent just before estrus. It starts a rapid growth phase about 5 days prior to ovulation. Maximum follicular size attained before ovulation is about 40 to 50 mm, and the maximum size is attained the day before ovulation. Immediately before ovulation, some follicles get softer, while others do not. Therefore, a change in softness cannot be used to predict ovulation. Follicles present at the first

TABLE 15-1   Changes in Mare's Reproductive Tract During the Estrous Cycle

	Day of estrous cycle				
Structure	*2*	*4*	*7*	*11*	*17*
Anterior portion of vagina (gm)	188	216	173	194	230
Cervix (gm)	141	168	153	133	164
Uterus (gm)	696	674	558	669	849
Uterine horn (left)					
Diameter (mm)	68	55	61	58	62
Length (mm)	151	146	152	154	137
Uterine horn (right)					
Diameter (mm)	58	60	44	61	64
Length (mm)	148	155	144	160	152
Oviduct (left)					
Weight (gm)	5.57	5.72	4.85	6.17	5.20
Length (mm)	147	140	149	162	152
Oviduct (right)					
Weight (gm)	7.12	6.83	6.02	6.61	6.61
Length (mm)	154	155	147	166	143
Ovaries (gm)	136.7	128.4	122.0	111.7	116.4
Extraluteal tissue (gm)	71.9	69.6	70.5	69.0	81.8
Extraluteal fluid (gm)	62.7	54.4	42.9	25.6	22.4
Follicles 10–30 mm (no.)	6.3	6.1	7.6	4.6	3.8
Follicles 20–30 mm (no.)	3.4	2.0	1.4	1.7	1.3
Follicles > 30 mm (no.)	1.3	0.9	0.5	0.2	0.1

SOURCE: Adapted from Warszawsky and others (1972).

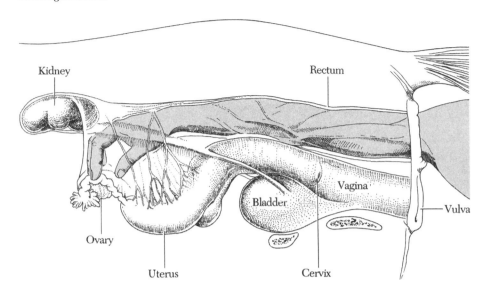

Kidney

Rectum

Vagina

Vulva

Bladder

Ovary

Uterus

Cervix

FIGURE 15-16   Palpating (feeling) the ovaries of a mare.

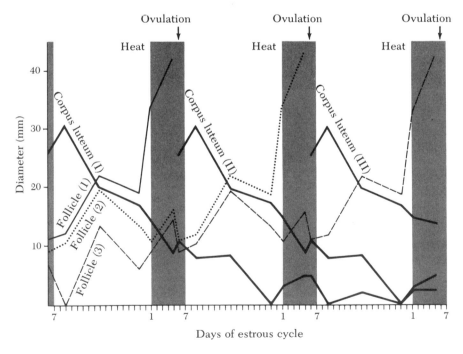

Ovulation

Ovulation

Ovulation

Heat

Heat

Heat

Diameter (mm)

40

30

20

10

Corpus luteum (I)

Follicle (1)

Follicle (2)

Follicle (3)

Corpus luteum (II)

Corpus luteum (III)

7   1   7   1   7   1   7

Days of estrous cycle

FIGURE 15-17   Curves of growth of follicle and corpus luteum during the estrous cycle. (From Hammond and Wodzicki, 1941.)

ovulation may continue to develop, and about 25 percent of the estrous cycles have a second ovulation. Some follicles become atretic, whereas others may remain for a couple of estrous cycles before they become the ovulatory follicles (Figure 15-17).

Definite changes that occur in the cervix during the estrous cycle are also quite useful in determining estrus. During diestrus, the cervix is tightly constricted, pale in color, and covered with a dry, gummy mucus. As the mare approaches estrus, the cervix begins to relax, the blood supply increases, and a clear mucus is secreted. During estrus, vascularity has increased so that the cervix is a reddish color. The cervix has relaxed so that it may lie on the floor of the vagina, and two or three fingers can be easily passed through it. A considerable amount of clean, clear, slimy mucus is secreted, covering the cervix and vagina. These changes are determined visually through a speculum (Figure 15-18).

The changes in the vagina are definite but not as dramatic as the cervical changes. During diestrus, the walls are dry and sticky and are pale in color. As the mare comes into estrus, the walls of the vagina become rosy red in color and covered with the slimy cervical mucus.

Changes that occur in the uterus are more difficult to determine and to predict. Therefore, from a practical viewpoint, they are not very useful in determining when to breed a mare. During estrus, the uterus has some muscle tone but not as much as during diestrus. During estrus, it has slight tone; during diestrus, it has good tone. Changes in vascularity also change the feel of

FIGURE 15-18　Vaginal speculums to visually examine the vagina and cervix. *(a)* A plastic speculum; *(b)* a "Caslick" speculum. (Photo by W. Evans.)

the uterus. During estrus, it is turgid but flaccid. During diestrus, tissues are not edemic, so that the uterus starts to resemble a rigid tube.

During winter anestrus, the cervix and uterus lose muscle tone and become completely flaccid in most mares that have no follicular activity. In mares with considerable ovarian activity, the uterus may have some muscle tone and the cervix may be firm and tightly constricted.

Variability in the Estrous Cycle

One of the most important aspects of managing reproduction in the mare is the extreme variability in all aspects of the estrous cycle. There is considerable variation from cycle to cycle in the same mare, and there is considerable variation from mare to mare. An understanding of these variations, of management techniques to detect variations, and of how to breed mares during the variations is necessary to prevent stallion overuse and to achieve a high conception rate.

The average length of the estrous cycle is 21 to 23 days (Table 15-2). Only about 50 percent of all mares have a normal estrous cycle length. A few are shorter but most are longer.

Winter Anestrus

A primary reason for the variability in estrous cycle is season of the year, and estrous cycle patterns are classified according to seasonal variation. Many years ago, the wild mare probably had only two or three estrous cycles per year. This restricted estrous season enabled foals to be born during favorable environmental conditions. The second general pattern is seasonal polyestrus, characterized by a period of time when the mare does not cycle (Figure 15-19). The anestrous period is usually during winter and is called winter anestrus.

TABLE 15-2   Length of Estrous Cycle and Estrous Period of Mares with One or Two Ovulations per Cycle

No. of ovulations per estrous cycle	Length of estrous cycle (days)	Length of estrus (days)	Length of diestrus (days)	Corpus luteum life span (days)
One	20.7 ± 0.2 (range 13–34)	5.4 ± 3.0 (range 1–24)	15.4 ± 3.1 (range 6–25)	12.6 ± 2.9 (range 8–18)
Two	20.2 ± 4.5 (range 13–27)	6.1 ± 2.7 (range 1–21)	14.6 ± 3.5 (range 8–25)	12.2 + 3.3 (range 5–17)

Note: All deviations are standard deviations. Same 11 mares were studied to obtain data for Tables 15-2 through 15-5.
SOURCE: Figures in last column from Stabenfeldt, Hughes, and Evans (1970). All other figures from Hughes, Stabenfeldt, and Evans, 1972b.

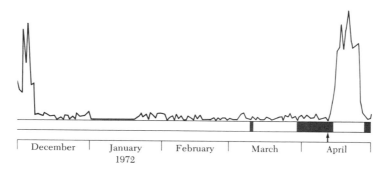

FIGURE 15-19 Reproductive history of Hi Aggie. (From Hughes, Stabenfeldt, and Evans, 1972b.)

The period of winter anestrus will vary depending on the climate. Some mares exhibit winter anestrus one year and not the following year. Normally, the more definite the seasons of the year, the higher the percentage of mares displaying winter anestrus. The third pattern is polyestrus—the mare cycles throughout the year (Figure 15-20).

Prolonged Corpus Luteum

Another type of anestrus—really, a period of irregularity in the rhythmical pattern of the estrous cycle—is the result of a spontaneously prolonged corpus luteum life-span (Figure 15-20). A spontaneously prolonged corpus luteum continues to secrete enough progestins to maintain plasma concentrations above 1 ng/ml. When the progestins are maintained above this level, signs of estrus are suppressed. The exact cause is unknown but is believed to be a failure of the uterus to synthesize or release sufficient prostaglandin to

FIGURE 15-20   Reproductive history of Paisley Star. (From Hughes, Stabenfeldt, and Evans, 1972b.)

560

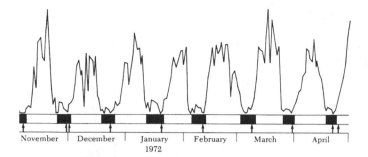

FIGURE 15-20   *Continued*

lyse the corpus luteum (make it stop functioning) at the proper stage of the cycle, or a failure of the corpus luteum to respond to prostaglandin. In some cases, it is known that the mare ovulates immediately prior to the release of prostaglandins. Because the developing corpus luteum is immature and unresponsive to prostaglandins until it is 6 to 7 days old, it fails to respond and begins to secrete progesterone. There are two methods of treatment for the anestrous condition. A warm, 0.9 percent saline solution (500 ml) can be infused into the uterus. The mare will come into estrus in about 5 to 6 days and will ovulate approximately 9 to 10 days after the infusion. Prostaglandin or an analogue of prostaglandin is the usual treatment. The mare comes into heat approximately 3 to 4 days after the injection and will ovulate during the 6- to 12-day postinjection period (Figure 15-21).

Prolonged corpus luteum function can occur at any time, and lasts for 35 to as long as 100 days or more. Therefore, the infertile period may last

FIGURE 15-21   Effect of administering prostaglandin to a mare with a prolonged corpus luteum.

beyond the length of the normal breeding season. A maiden, open, or barren mare that is not pregnant and does not come into heat at the expected time could possibly have a spontaneously prolonged corpus luteum. Actual diagnosis can be made by determining the concentration of progesterone in the blood. Concentrations over 1 ng/ml confirm the condition. It is possible for a mare to develop the condition following the estrous period in which she was bred (Figure 15-22). Because she does not come back into heat, she is assumed to be pregnant until diagnosed nonpregnant by a pregnancy check. The mare will respond to prostaglandin treatment or intrauterine saline infusion. However, be careful to determine that the mare did not conceive and abort (see section on abortion).

Diestrus Length

Aside from winter anestrus, the season of the year influences the length of the estrous cycles in other ways (Table 15-3). The average length of the diestrous period (in cycling mares) tends to be shorter in the early part of the natural breeding season and longer during winter.

Estrus Length

The estrous period is normally 5 to 6 days long (Table 15-2), but only about 50 percent of the cycles have a normal length. Some mares tend to have uniform estrous periods; others have quite variable estrous periods. Seasonal variability of the estrous period, excluding anestrus, is responsible for part of the variation. During later winter and early spring, the average estrous period is 7.6 days rather than the usual 5 to 6 days. The longest estrous periods occur when mares are going into or coming out of winter anestrus (Figure 15-19).

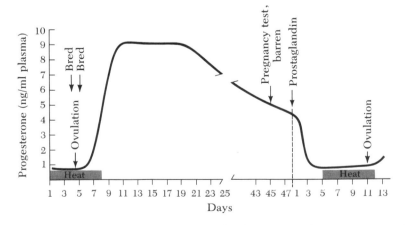

FIGURE 15-22   Effect of administering prostaglandin to a pseudopregnant mare that did not conceive or resorbed the fetus prior to 36 days of gestation.

TABLE 15-3   Effects of Seasonal Changes on Reproduction in the Mare

	Jan.	Feb.	Mar.	Apr.	May	Jun.	Jul.	Aug.	Sep.	Oct.	Nov.	Dec.
Average estrous cycle length (days)	32.3	34.4	26.1	21.9	19.5	21.1	24.6	20.4	20.6	20.5	24.8	30.4
Number of cycles observed	22	20	25	28	39	31	28	27	32	35	25	21
Number of periods of estrus	18	13	26	29	28	28	20	24	27	31	27	22
Average length of estrus (days)	5.06	6.69	8.38	7.76	5.72	4.47	4.70	4.75	4.44	4.53	5.20	7.23
Total ovulations for each month for all 11 mares	20	23	46	45	44	54	48	41	42	44	43	27
Average number of ovulations per month	0.9	1.1	2.1	2.1	2.0	2.5	2.2	1.9	1.9	2.0	2.0	1.2
Total number of diestrous periods without anestrus	16	13	21	27	24	24	21	21	26	27	22	20
Average length of diestrus without anestrus	16.3	16.3	14.2	11.8	14.0	15.8	16.2	15.4	16.1	15.3	16.0	14.3

SOURCE: Adapted from Hughes, Stabenfeldt, and Evans (1972b).

Split Estrus

Another variation in the estrous period is the split estrus: the mare is in estrus for a few days, goes out of estrus for one or more days, and returns to estrus for a few days. The total time period may last 12 to 14 days or even longer, or may be only 4 to 6 days long. There is considerable variation in the split estrus condition. Fortunately, they only occur in about 5 percent of estrous periods. They are frequently associated with estrous cycles just before or after winter anestrus.

Silent Heat

"Silent heats" are another variation of the estrous period that causes management problems in getting the mare in foal. Some mares never show estrus when teased with a stallion (Figure 15-23), or they may show estrus for a few

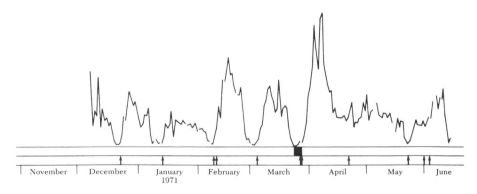

FIGURE 15-23   Reproductive history of Bashful Boots. Notice the "silent heat" periods and double ovulations. (Courtesy G. H. Stabenfeldt, J. P. Hughes, and Evans, 1972b.)

cycles and then have one or more silent heat periods (Figure 15-20). Internally, the mare is having normal estrous cycles: she ovulates and has normal plasma progesterone profiles. To breed such mares, palpate or ultrasound them two to three times per week to determine follicular growth. At the appropriate time before ovulation, they can be artificially inseminated.

Mares are sensitive to strange places, people, and horses and alter their behavior accordingly. A mare may be teased and found to be in estrus, but when she is transported to a stallion to be bred, she may not show the behavioral signs of estrus. In this situation, the mare must be palpated or ultrasonographically examined and artificially inseminated just before ovulation. Few stud managers handle this common problem properly.

A mare that is cycling and normally shows estrus can fool a stud manager just long enough to miss breeding her because she may not show estrus during one cycle (Figure 15-24). A stud manager must keep good records to detect silent heats in time for the mare to be bred. As soon as the records indicate she should be in estrus but is not, she should be examined. If necessary, she can be artificially inseminated.

Ovulation

During estrus, the mare should ovulate one follicle on the third or fourth day of estrus. Ovulation is related to the end of estrus, not the onset (see the earlier section on Behavioral Changes). Approximately 75 percent of ovulations occur when expected, about 12 percent occur 3 days before the end of estrus, and about 10 percent occur after the mare is out of estrus (Figure 15-25). Occasionally, however, a mare will ovulate before she shows signs of estrus or on the first day of estrus (Figure 15-24).

Multiple ovulations occur in 20 percent of the estrous cycles. The percentage of twin conceptions is much lower (1 to 5 percent). Usually, multiple ovulations occur in all mares if they are open (not pregnant) for a period of 2 to 3 years and if they are being closely observed. Some mares tend to have multiple ovulations. The mare in Figure 15-24 is an example of one that has frequent multiple ovulations. Most multiple ovulations are twin ovulations, but triple ovulations during a heat period have also been observed (Figure 15-24). Fortunately, multiple ovulations do not upset the rhythmicity of the estrous cycle. The total length of the cycle as well as the length of estrus and diestrus are not affected. Double ovulations are rare in pony mares.

The average interval between the multiple ovulations is about 1 day. However, they may occur on the same day or as much as 5 days apart. The ovulations may occur on one ovary or on both ovaries. The distribution between the two ovaries is about equal (Table 15-4). Multiple ovulations occur more frequently during late spring and early summer (Table 15-5).

From a management viewpoint, there is a choice of procedures. A mare having two ovulations is not bred before the first ovulation. If at least 48 hours elapse between ovulations, the mare can be bred immediately before the

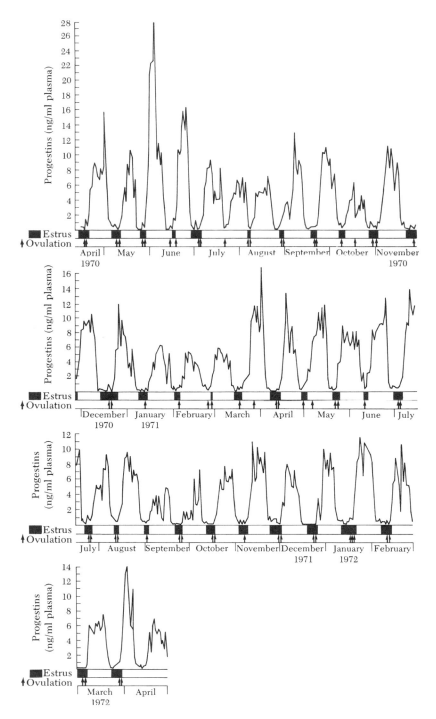

FIGURE 15-24   Reproductive history of Solid Cookie. Notice the number of double ovulations, the diestrous ovulations, the silent heat period in July 1970, the variations in estrous length, and the triple ovulation in January 1972. (From Hughes, Stabenfeldt, and Evans, 1972b.)

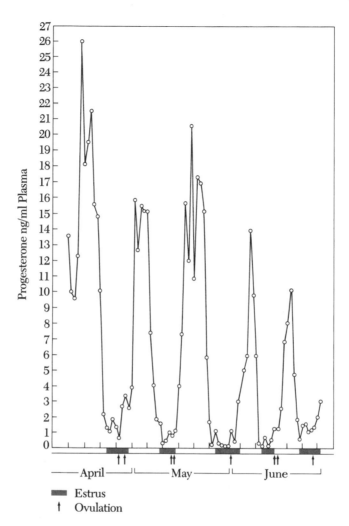

FIGURE 15-25   Reproductive history of Tule Goose. Notice the ovulation in June after the mare went out of estrus. (Courtesy J. W. Evans, J. P. Hughes, and G. H. Stabenfeldt and Evans, 1972b.)

second ovulation. If necessary, she can be bred shortly after the second ovulation. This procedure is based on the length of time the ovum is fertile. The normal period is 8 to 24 hours after ovulation. To prevent twins, one must wait until the first ovum is no longer fertile before the mare is bred. Other farm managers breed a mare regardless of the number of potential ovulations. At 13 to 15 days post-ovulation, the mare is examined for pregnancy using an ultrasound machine. If the mare has a twin pregnancy, one of the embryos is manually crushed. A skilled veterinarian can be very successful using this technique, and the remaining embryo survives.

TABLE 15-4   Incidence of Multiple Ovulation by Mare and by Ovaries, During Two-Year Period

Mare	No. of triple ovulations	No. of double ovulations	Ovulations				Average interval between ovulations (days)
			No. LL	No. RR	No. LR[a]	No. RL[a]	
Aggie Tess	0	7	1	1	2	3	0.7
Bashful Boots	0	9	2	2	1	3	1.5
Double Dark	0	5	2	2	1	0	1.6
Hi Aggie	0	1	0	0	1	0	0.0
Mr. Bruce's Miss	0	2	1	1	0	0	1.0
Paisley Star	0	6	2	1	3	0	1.2
Psychedelic Miss		4	0	2	0	2	1.2
Solid Charm	0	4	2	0	1	1	1.0
Solid Cookie	1	25	3	9	10	3	0.7
Solimistic	0	10	2	2	3	3	1.5
Tule Goose	1	11 ·	1	3	6	1	0.5
Total	2	83	16	23	28	16	1.0

[a]First letter indicates ovary in which first ovulation occurred.

SOURCE: Hughes, Stabenfeldt, and Evans (1972b).

At the opposite extreme, sometimes a mare goes through a heat period and fails to ovulate (Figure 15-19). About 25 percent of all open mares do not ovulate during at least one heat period in a year's time. Almost all the estrous periods without ovulation occur during the winter months—the mare is usually going into or coming out of the anestrous period. Others occasionally

TABLE 15-5   Multiple Ovulations, by Month

Month	No. per month	Percentage per month
January	3	23.5
February	4	22.2
March	10	40.6
April	9	25.7
May	10	32.3
June	10	25.5
July	9	25.0
August	7	21.2
September	8	24.2
October	7	20.0
November	6	17.1
December	4	18.2

SOURCE: Hughes, Stabenfeldt, and Evans (1972b).

show heat at any time during the anestrous period but the heat period is not accompanied by ovulation. Even though they show heat, very few of the mares' ovaries have any significant follicular activity during winter anestrus. Fortunately, the incidence of estrus without ovulation is not common, though it has been observed in about 3 percent of the estrous cycles, almost always in the winter anestrous period.

Mares normally ovulate only during the estrous period, but occasionally they ovulate during the diestrous period (Figure 15-24). They do not show any behavioral signs of estrus. It is doubtful that most such mares conceive if bred because the reproductive tract is probably not prepared to receive the fertilized egg. However, one mare has been reported to have conceived during a diestrous ovulation.

Foal Heat

A mare usually has her first estrous period about 7 to 9 days after foaling. However, there is considerable variation; she may show signs of estrus 1 or 2 days after foaling, or after as long as 50 days. Very seldom is the period longer than 12 days. She is in estrus normally for about 3 days but often for as long as 12 days. Ovulation is expected to occur on the eighth to twelfth day after foaling.

Mares can be successfully bred during the foal heat, but the breeder must be very careful. Only those mares that had a normal delivery should be bred. Seven days after foaling, the mare should be examined by a veterinarian. The mare should not be bred if she has a bruised cervix, lacerations, or tears in cervix or vagina, vaginal discharge, placenta retained more than 3 hours, lack of tone in the uterus or vagina, or presence of urine in the tract. If there are any other questions about breeding her, it is best to wait. In many instances, the mare can be bred if she ovulated 2 or 3 days later than the normal, expected time. The reproductive tract needs that extra time to return to a breedable condition. If time of conception is extremely important, one may use prostaglandins on the sixth day after the foal heat ovulation (see below on Estrous Cycle Manipulation).

During lactation, some mares do not show estrus to a stallion but do ovulate at the expected times. They may or may not exhibit foal heat and then may not exhibit estrus while suckling their foals. Several things may cause this lactation anestrus. Some mares are very possessive or protective of their foals so that they take the foal away from the teaser and will not approach the teaser. Such mares are usually ovulating on a regular schedule. However, a spontaneously prolonged corpus luteum may have developed after the foal heat ovulation. If so, the mares respond to prostaglandin treatment.

Estrous Cycle Manipulation

In several circumstances, the estrous cycle or some phase of it must be manipulated. Mares in anestrus must be stimulated to start cycling. Winter anestrus has been discussed, as has the spontaneously prolonged corpus luteum. The use of prostaglandins and saline infusions was discussed for the spontaneously prolonged corpus luteum condition.

Human Chorionic Gonadotrophin and
Equine Pituitary Extract

Human chorionic gonadotropin (hCG) is a hormone used to help control ovulation. hCG mimics LH activity and is commonly used to get a follicle to ovulate after it has reached ovulatory size but has failed to ovulate as expected. Following administration of hCG, most follicles ovulate within 24 to 48 hours. Some farms use hCG on an extensive basis, where each mare receives hCG on the second day of estrus and is bred the third day, and ovulation occurs 24 to 48 hours after the injection. This procedure can reduce the number of times that a mare needs to be bred. If used in conjunction with palpation, most mares are bred once each estrous cycle. Extensive use of hCG may cause antibodies to develop against it. The antibodies are specific for hCG and do not cross-react with endogenous LH. Therefore, one may not get the full benefit of an hCG injection but it will not interfere with the activity of the endogenous LH. In one study of 12 mares receiving hCG on the day when a 35-mm follicle was present for six consecutive estrous cycles, 5 mares developed antibodies against hCG, but all 12 mares ovulated each time within 48 hours after the injection (Figure 15-26).

Crude equine pituitary extract has been used to induce ovulation of a large follicle. It has the advantage in that it does not elicit an immune response, and mares with antibodies against hCG will respond to the treatment.

GnRH analogs such as deslorelin can also be used to induce ovulation (86 percent success rate) within 48 hours when a follicle greater than 30 mm in diameter is present.

Prostaglandins

Prostaglandins can be used to control the time of ovulation by controlling the life-span of the corpus luteum. Within 48 hours after the injection, the progesterone concentration in the blood is minimal. The mare comes into estrus in about 3 to 4 days and ovulates 6 to 12 days after treatment (Figure 15-27). Prostaglandins can be used to breed a mare earlier than the next estrous period following the foal heat period (Figure 15-28). If treated on the sixth day after foal heat ovulation, she comes into estrus in 3 to 4 days and ovulates within 6 to 12 days after treatment. This method is useful for mares that were not quite ready to be bred during their foal heat. The time of treatment after ovulation is important because, from the sixth day after ovulation to the endogenous release of prostaglandin, the corpus luteum is sensitive to prostaglandin treatment. Less success is achieved if prostaglandins are used on the fourth or fifth day after ovulation. After the fifth day, the success rate is approximately 65 to 80 percent. One should be aware of the six types of responses that arise after the prostaglandin treatment. Complete luteolysis (cessation of corpus luteum function) occurs for about 65 percent of the treated cycles; incomplete luteolysis occurs for 26 percent. Incomplete luteolysis, with subsequent recovery by the corpus luteum, occurs in about 6 percent of treated cycles. Very few (about 3 percent) corpora lutea fail to show any type of

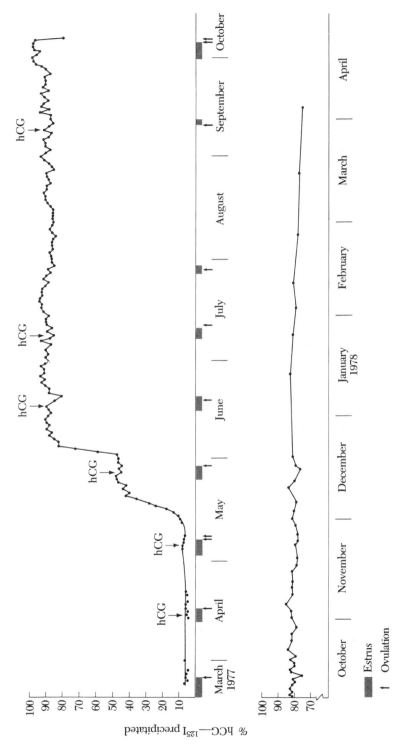

FIGURE 15-26 Time course of anti-hCG antibody development following treatments with hCG. (Courtesy J. Roser and J. W. Evans.)

571

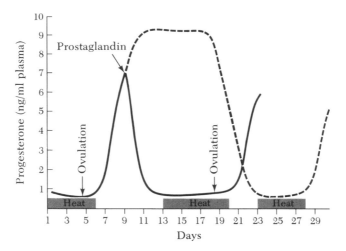

FIGURE 15-27   Effect of administering prostaglandin to shorten the length of the estrous cycle.

response. Prostaglandin treatment of a prolonged corpus luteum life-span is about 90 percent effective. Therefore, a mare may fail to respond to a treatment but usually responds to a second treatment. Prostaglandins provide ovulation within 4 days after treatment in about 32 percent of treated cycles (Figure 15-29), and about 25 percent of ovulations occur without behavioral signs of estrus (Figure 15-29). These two responses occur primarily when prostaglandin is given in the presence of a large follicle on the ovary. Therefore, it is very important to know the condition of the ovary before prostaglandin treatment and to follow very closely ovarian changes by palpation.

FIGURE 15-28   Effect of administering prostaglandin to breed the foaling mare before her normal second estrous period.

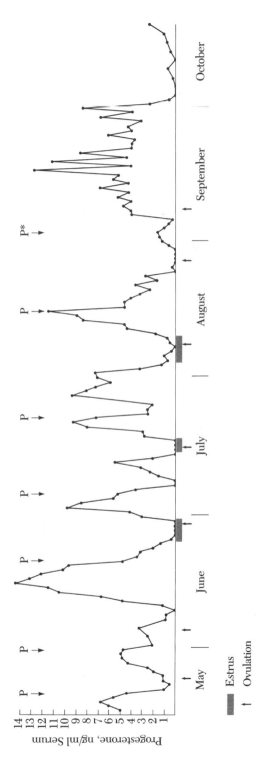

FIGURE 15-29 Luteolytic responses of a mare to sequential administration of a prostaglandin analogue (prostalene). Incomplete luteolytic responses followed prostalene injections on May 31 and August 15. Incomplete luteolysis with subsequent luteal recoveries occurred after prostalene injections on July 5 and July 22. Failure to manifest estrus was observed after prostalene treatments on May 21, May 31, and August 15. Ovulation within 4 days after treatment followed the prostalene injection on May 21. The post-treatment control cycle contained a prolonged luteal phase. P* is an injection of prostalene (4 mg). (From Kiefer and others, 1979.)

For an artificial insemination program, prostaglandins can be used to synchronize the estrous cycle of mares so that they can all be bred in a short period of time. The treatment program is to give all the mares a prostaglandin treatment on day 0, hCG on day 6, prostaglandin on day 14, hCG on day 20, and to breed on days 19 and 21. About 75 percent of the mares ovulate during the 3- to 4-day period.

Prostaglandins may not prompt the pseudopregnant mare to cycle again if the pseudopregnancy is caused by an abortion. If the mare aborts soon after the endometrial cups are stimulated to form and secrete equine chorionic gonadotropin (eCG), the eCG suppresses ovarian activity in this type of pseudopregnancy and the corpus luteum of pregnancy may regress. The mare will not come into estrus until after the eCG disappears from the blood—about 120 days. Saline infusions or prostaglandin treatments are not successful because no corpus luteum is present. If the corpus luteum is still present, prostaglandin or saline treatment will cause it to lyse but the mare may remain anestrous.

Light and Hormone Treatments for Winter Anestrus

The winter anestrous mare can be managed to have rhythmic estrous cycles before the normal breeding season by using an artificial light regime. The artificial light regime is started approximately 90 days before the beginning of the breeding season. The mares are exposed to 16 hours of light and 8 hours of darkness each day. This can be accomplished by turning the lights on at 6 A.M. and off at 10 P.M. or if there is sufficient ambient light during the day, by turning them on at 6 P.M. and off at 10 P.M. The mare responds if she is exposed to light 8.5 to 10.5 hours after darkness. Thus, if the lights go off at 10 P.M., the next morning at 8 A.M. she will be exposed to light at a time when her body recognizes the light stimulus. An automatic timer is used to prevent control failure. Lights can be fluorescent or incandescent. A 200-watt or larger incandescent bulb provides sufficient light in a 12-foot × 12-foot stall. It is not necessary to control the temperature so the mare does not need to be kept in a box stall. For outside paddocks, lights can be mounted on poles or a lighted shed can be used. About 50 percent of the mares that go into winter anestrus thus become ready to breed at the start of the breeding season. Because a few mares are polyestrous, a large percentage of the open, barren, and maiden mares are thus ready to breed at the start of the breeding season.

Hormone treatments have been developed to induce estrous cycles in the anestrous mare. Mares are treated with gonadotropin-releasing hormone (or one of its agonists) to mimic the changes in FSH and LH during a normal cycle. Continuous infusion, pulsatile infusion, implants, and twice-daily injections can initiate follicular growth and ovulation in the absence of photoperiodic stimulation. Normal corpus luteum function follows the treatments.

Other treatments are used to control duration of the first estrus as mares come out of winter anestrus. Altrenogest, a synthetic progestin given orally, or a series of injections of progesterone, estrogen, and hCG is used.

Records

One of the most important aspects of a stud manager's duties is to keep an accurate set of records for the breeding farm. It is critical for the stud manager to know the reproductive status of each mare every day. Each breed and registry association has established a specific set of records that the breeding farm must keep. The information required to complete the forms can be collected from a basic set of farm records.

When a mare is delivered to the breeding farm, fill out an arrival form and ask the person delivering the mare to sign in (Figure 15-30). The form shows information concerning the mare's name, description, age, owner's name and address, how she arrived, appearance, tattoo number, equipment with her, and any other pertinent remarks. Place a numbered neck band around the mare's neck, and enter the ID number on the arrival form. Some farms take a Polaroid

Breeding Farm Name
Address
Phone Number

ARRIVAL

Time _____   Date _____

HORSE _____   Color _____ Sex _____ Age _____

OWNER _____   Address _____

_____

Method of Arrival _____   From _____

_____

Appearance of Horse _____   Tatoo Number _____

Equipment _____

Instructions _____

_____

Remarks _____

_____

Signed _____   Signed _____
     (Owner or Agent)   *(Stud Manager)*

Copy 1–Owner   Copy 2–Horse Barn   Copy 3–Accounting   Copy 4–Farm Manager

FIGURE 15-30   "Arrival" form, to be filled out on arrival of mare to the breeding farm.

snapshot of the mare for identification purposes and to record the mare's physical condition on arrival. Send a notice of the arrival to the mare's owner (Figure 15-31), and use the same form to obtain any further needed information about the mare. When the mare leaves after the breeding season, fill out a departure form (Figure 15-32), to be signed by the person picking up the mare. It also shows information regarding her health care and treatment. Maintain a daily record of the mare's reproductive status (Figure 15-33). Record each day the mare is in estrus. When the mare is coming into estrus, enter the symbol O/H (out of heat/heat) and when the mare is in estrus enter H. As the mare goes out of heat, enter H/O (heat/out of heat). Each day the mare is bred, enter B. Mark the ovulation date with an X. Enter the results of all palpations on another form (Figure 15-34). Keep a similar set of records for the ranch-owned mares. When the mare is bred, make an entry on the stallion record form (Figure 15-35). Keep one of these forms for each stallion. To follow the health status and to maintain an accurate record of preventative medical procedures, keep a clinical record and a log of procedural activities for each mare (Figure 15-36). For ranch-owned mares, use a different form for each mare (Figure 15-37) as well as a general record (Figure 15-38). These records increase breeding efficiency and are useful when veterinary services are required. After the mare is bred and has had a positive pregnancy examination, send a postcard to notify the mare owner (Figure 15-39). If a mare is foaled out on the farm for a client, use a foal report form to notify the owner (Figure 15-40).

Computerized record systems are used by many farms. Although it takes longer to enter the data, analysis of the records is greatly improved, more efficient, and much faster. In a single entry system, filing to various accounts occurs when activity for any horse is entered. Commercially available software programs are available from several companies.

BREEDING

The procedures for naturally breeding a mare are basically the same as for artificial insemination, except for the actual act of breeding. Tease the mare to determine her receptivity and then clean her external genitalia. Clean the stallion's penis. If the mare is to be bred by artificial insemination, collect the stallion's semen with an artificial vagina.

Mare Preparation

After determining that the mare is ready to be bred, the first consideration is hygiene. Immediately before she is washed, tease her so that she will urinate and empty her bladder. Restrain the mare in a palpation or breeding chute

Breeding Farm Name
Address
Phone Number

NEW ARRIVAL REPORT

TO: _____ Date: _____

We have received _____ , a _____ _____ .
                        (Name)   (Color)   (Sex)

To facilitate our records, please fill out applicable information below and return promptly.

Age _____ Breeding: Sire/Dam _____

Sire of Foal _____ Foaling Date _____

Date of Last Service _____ Booked to _____

Shots	Yes	No	Date
Encephalomyelitis	☐	☐	
Virus Abortion	☐	☐	
Tetanus Toxoid	☐	☐	
Flu Vaccine	☐	☐	

Date Last Wormed _____

Date Last Cultured _____

Insurance _____ (Yes/No)   Who to contact? _____

Bills and reports should be mailed to: _____ Phone No. _____

Manager's or trainer's instructions _____

All due precautions will be taken, but under no circumstances will stable accept any responsibility for accident or disease.

FIGURE 15-31 "New Arrival Report," to notify owner of receipt of mare and to obtain additional information about her.

577

Breeding Farm Name
Address
Phone Number

DEPARTURE

Time _____

Date _____

HORSE _____ Color _____ Sex _____ Age _____

OWNER _____ Address _____

_____

Shots	Yes	No	Date
Encephalomyelitis	☐	☐	_____
Virus Abortion	☐	☐	_____
Tetanus Toxoid	☐	☐	_____
Flu Vaccine	☐	☐	_____
VEE	☐	☐	

Date Last Wormed _____

Oiled for Trip _____ (Yes/No)

Tranquilized for Trip _____ (Yes/No)

Veterinarian _____

Method of Departure _____ To _____

Appearance of Horse _____ Tatoo Number _____

Remarks _____

Signed _____ Signed _____

(Owner or Agent) (Stud Manager)

Copy 1–Owner   Copy 2–Horse Barn   Copy 3–Accounting   Copy 4–Farm Manager

FIGURE 15-32 "Departure" form, to be filled out when a mare departs from a breeding farm.

578

Name _____ # _____ Sire _____ Dam _____

Reg. No. _____ Reg. No. _____ Reg. No. _____

Breed _____ Year Foaled 19___ Markings _____

Characteristics _____

Date Foal	Sex	Name	No.	Sire	No

ESTROUS CYCLE RECORD

Year 19___ Bred to: _____

Mo. / Day	J	F	M	A	M	J	J	A	S	O	N	D
1												
2			O									
3			O/H									
4			H/O									
5			H									
6			H–B									
7			H–X									
8		O	H/O									
9		O/H	O/H									
10		O/H	O	Pg								
11		H										
12		H										
13		H										
14		H										
15		H										
16		H										
17		H–X										
18		H										
19		O										
20												
21												
22												
23												
24			O									
25			O/H									
26			H									
27			H–B									
28			H–X									
29			O									
30												
31												

O—out of heat. H—in heat. Pg—positive pregnancy test. B—bred to stallion. O/H—coming into heat. H/O—going out of heat. X—ovulated.

Year 19___ Bred to: _____

Mo. / Day	J	F	M	A	M	J	J	A	S	O	N	D
1												
2												
3												
4												
5												
6												
7												
8												
9												
10												
11												
12												
13												
14												
15												
16												
17												
18												
19												
20												
21												
22												
23												
24												
25												
26												
27												
28												
29												
30												
31												

FIGURE 15-33 "Estrous Cycle Record," to keep a daily record of a mare's reproductive status.

579

Date _____ 3/5 _____

Cervix _____ slightly relaxed _____

Uterus _____

Left ovary _____ active _____

Right ovary _____ 25mm anterior pole _____

Spec. _____

Treatment _____

Date _____

Cervix _____

Uterus _____

Left ovary _____

Right ovary _____

Spec. _____

Treatment _____

Date _____ 3/6 _____

Cervix _____ relaxed _____

Uterus _____ slight tone _____

Left ovary _____ 25mm follicle _____

Right ovary _____ 45mm follicle _____

Spec. _____

Treatment _____

Date _____

Cervix _____

Uterus _____

Left ovary _____

Right ovary _____

Spec. _____

Treatment _____

Date _____ 3/7 _____

Cervix _____ relaxed _____

Uterus _____ slight tone _____

Left ovary _____ 25mm _____

Right ovary _____ corpus luteum – ovulated _

Spec. _____

Treatment _____

Date _____

Cervix _____

Uterus _____

Left ovary _____

Right ovary _____

Spec. _____

Treatment _____

FIGURE 15-34   Form to record changes in the reproductive tract observed during female genital organ examinations.

to be washed (Figure 15-41). Wrap the mare's tail with a roll of 3-inch gauze or some other disposable wrapping such as a disposable, long-sleeved plastic glove, to prevent hair from being taken into the vagina by the penis during breeding. The hair may contain infectious contaminants that may cause uterine infections or abortions. Hair also causes hair burns on the penis, making it sore enough to stop the stallion from breeding. Wash the mare's external genitalia and the surrounding area with warm water and a mild soap (Figure 15-42). Use a disposable plastic bag to line the inside of the bucket, if one is used, to prevent the spread of infectious agents to other mares. Use Ivory soap or other mild antiseptic soap solutions to wash the mare. After the area is clean, rinse off all the soap. Soap is spermicidal, and it causes irritation if it is not removed. Dry off the washed area with a disposable paper towel.

STALLION RECORD   Page _____

Name _____   Breed _____ Markings _____

No. _____   Date Foaled _____

DATE	MARE	REG. NO. of MARE	BREED	COMMENTS

FIGURE 15-35   "Stallion Record," to record mares bred to a stallion.

CLINICAL RECORD

Name _____ Date Foaled _____ Markings _____

No. _____ Sex _____   _____

DATE	EXAMINATION	TREATMENT AND COMMENTS

FIGURE 15-36   "Clinical Record," to record veterinary medical services required by the horse.

**Breeding Farm Name
Address
Phone Number**

FOALING RECORD for

_____

(Mare's Name)

Year _____ : Sex _____ Color _____ Sire _____

Comments:

Year _____ : Sex _____ Color _____ Sire _____

Comments:

Year _____ : Sex _____ Color _____ Sire _____

Comments:

Year _____ : Sex _____ Color _____ Sire _____

Comments:

Year _____ : Sex _____ Color _____ Sire _____

Comments:

FIGURE 15-37   "Foaling Record" for an individual brood mare.

19____FOALING RECORD

MARE	DUE	FOALED	GESTATION LENGTH	SEX	WEANED	MARKINGS	STALLION

FIGURE 15-38   "Foaling Record" for all foals born during the year.

Breeding Farm Name
Address
Phone Number

Date _____ , 19 _____

HORSE OWNER: _____

The mare _____ bred to _____

last service date _____ was examined for

pregnancy on _____ and has been pronounced:

☐ IN FOAL   ☐ BARREN

Signed: _____

FIGURE 15-39   Notice informing an owner that a mare is pregnant or barren.

Breeding Farm Name
Address
Phone Number

FOAL REPORT

TIME FOALED _____   DATE _____

☐ Bay   ☐ Black   ☐ Chestnut   ☐ Dr. Bay or Br.   ☐ Colt   ☐ Filly

Sire/Dam _____

Owner _____

Address _____

Condition After Foaling _____

Approximate Markings _____

_____

_____

Medical Treatment _____

_____

Equipment _____

                                   Signed _____

FIGURE 15-40   "Foal Report," informing an owner that a mare has foaled.

FIGURE 15-41   Restraint chute used during reproduction examinations, breeding hygiene procedures, and medical treatments. (Photo by W. Evans.)

584

(a)

(b)

(c)

FIGURE 15-42   Breeding hygiene equipment and procedures: *(a)* Equipment: (A) a bucket lined with a disposable plastic bag and containing warm water; (B) SeptiSoft® soap; (C) squeeze bottle with SeptiSoft soap solution; (D) roll of cotton; (E) plastic cup to rinse off area with water; (F) plastic liners for bucket; (G) tail wrap; (H) paper towels. *(b)* Wrap the tail with 3-inch gauze (0.52 cm). *(c)* Tie it up tall and out of the way. *(d)* Rinse buttocks with water from a hose or with a cup of water from a bucket. *(e)* Wash buttocks with soap several times depending on how dirty the mare is. *(f)* Rinse off soap. *(g)* Remove debris from the lips of the vulva. *(h)* Dry buttocks with a paper towel. *(i)* Mare is clean. (Photos by W. Evans.)

(d)

(e)

(f)

(g)

(h)

(i)

FIGURE 15-42   *Continued*

To protect the stallion during natural breeding, the mare is usually restrained. A lip twitch may be used if the mare will not stand still when the stallion is approaching. If the mare is prone to kick, she can be restrained with a set of breeding hobbles (Figure 15-43). The hobbles should have a quick-release snap so that if the stallion steps over the rope it can be released without injuring the horse. Another method of restraint is to tie up a front leg and release it as the stallion is mounting. A mare's hindshoes should be removed if she is shod, or padded boots can be placed over her hindfeet.

Some stallions bite the neck of mares when they are breeding. A horse blanket and hood will protect the mare from being scratched and scraped. This is important if the mare is to be shown later in horse shows.

If a small maiden mare is being bred, the stallion may injure the cervix or vagina. To help prevent tears, lacerations, and bruises, a breeding roll may be used to restrict entry by the stallion (Figure 15-44). A breeding roll is a padded roll about 4 to 6 inches in diameter (10.2 to 15.2 cm) and about 18 inches long (457.2 mm). A handle on one end allows easy insertion of the roll between the mare's rump and the stallion just above the penis as the stallion mounts. To prevent the spread of infection, the roll should be covered with a disposable wrapper such as a plastic examination sleeve.

FIGURE 15-43   Preparing the mare for breeding. Hobble the mare with a set of breeding hobbles that prevent her from kicking the stallion. Use a lip twitch to prevent the mare from trying to kick or move about. Wash the area around her genital organs and wrap her tail with sterile gauze to prevent transmission of venereal diseases or infections. (Photo by W. Evans.)

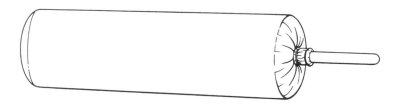

FIGURE 15-44   Breeding roll used to protect maiden mares from excessive penetration by the stallion's penis. (Illustration by M. Morris.)

As a safety precaution, where there is a marked difference in the physical size of the mare and stallion, the mare may need to stand with her hindlegs on a small mound or in a slight depression. If a stallion is too small, he may repeatedly mount and dismount the mare, which increases the chance of injury.

Stallion Preparation

Allow the stallion to tease a mare until he drops his penis. Then take him to an area a short distance away to be cleaned. Hold his penis with one hand and wash it with a mild soap and warm water (Figure 15-45). A terry washcloth or strip of sheet cotton can be used to lightly scrub the penis. The prepuce must be thoroughly cleaned. Be careful to remove all dirt, debris, and smegma. The fatty secretions from the glands in the prepuce, along with epithelial cells, form the smegma. The urethral diverticulum in the glans penis must be thoroughly cleaned, because it is common to find a small "bean" of smegma in this area. After the penis is thoroughly cleaned, remove all soap by rinsing with clean, warm water. Then dry the penis with disposal paper towels or a Turkish towel. After the stallion has bred a mare, rinse his penis with water. If the penis is relatively clean, it is best to use only clean water (no soap) during the hygiene procedures.

Before the breeding season, clean the stallion several times. If this is not done, he will usually be very dirty, and the penis will become irritated if he is thoroughly cleaned the first time. Because of the soreness, he may refuse to breed mares. The three or four cleaning sessions before breeding season also train the stallion to behave himself while he is being cleaned. Once the penis is clean, it is not necessary to use soap each time it is cleaned. Excessive use of soap may result in growth of undesirable bacteria responsible for infections of the mare's reproductive tract.

Breeding Area

The breeding area should be free from dust and have a surface that allows good footing. It can be outside, on a grassy area, or enclosed. It should be at least 40 × 40 feet (12.2 × 12.2 m) in size so that if problems develop, the mare and stallion can be safely separated. It is advisable to have the palpation or examination chute and the wash area located in another adjacent area. This prevents the breeding area from becoming too wet from the water used to wash the mare and stallion.

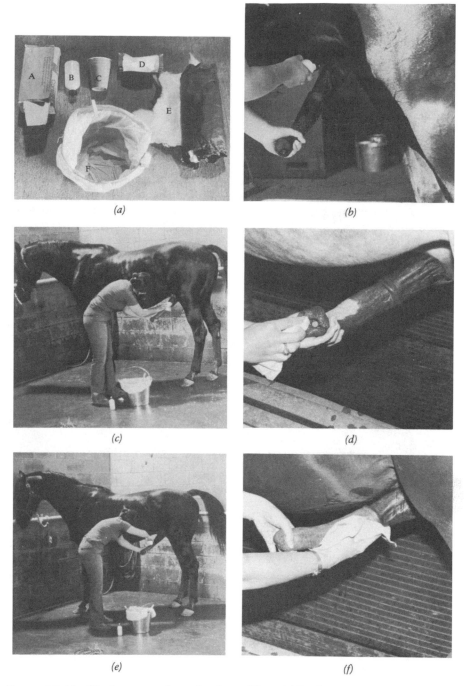

FIGURE 15-45 Hygiene procedures for the stallion: *(a)* Equipment: (A) paper towels; (B) squeeze bottle with mild soap solution (SeptiSoft®); (C) plastic water cup; (D) plastic liners for water bucket; (E) roll of cotton; (F) bucket lined with disposable plastic bag and filled with warm water. *(b)* Apply soap to the penis with the squeeze bottle. *(c)* Wash the penis with wet cotton. *(d)* Wash the end of the penis carefully. *(e)* Rinse off the soap. *(f)* Blot the penis dry with paper towels. (Photos by W. Evans.)

Natural Breeding

After preparing the stallion, mare, and breeding area, position the mare in the middle of the area. The mare's handler usually stands on the mare's left side opposite the head and facing her hindquarters (Figure 15-46). The stallion is led so that he approaches the mare at a slight angle to her hindquarters on the left side. If he is not ready to mount, he can tease the mare in the flank for a moment. This way, the mare can easily see his approach and is not startled by his presence. As the stallion mounts, the stallion handler can help guide the penis into the mare's vagina. The stallion handler should observe the stallion's tail for the characteristic "flagging movements" during ejaculation or hold the base of the penis to feel the ejaculatory pulses. After ejaculation, the stallion will dismount, and he should be immediately separated from the mare.

FIGURE 15-46   Natural breeding of a mare by a well-mannered stallion. Note the position of the mare and stallion handlers. (Courtesy William E. Jones, D.V.M.)

If a good cover was obtained, the semen was deposited in the uterus of the mare. It is not necessary to walk the mare to prevent the semen from draining out. If a considerable volume of semen runs out of the vagina after the stallion dismounts, a good cover was not obtained and the mare should be bred again in about 1 hour.

Artificial Insemination

Artificial insemination has some advantages in a breeding program. Venereal disease control is accomplished by diluting the semen with antibiotics, thereby decreasing the number of disease-producing organisms placed in the mare. The chance of injury to horses and personnel is also reduced, particularly if the stallion's semen is collected with the aid of a phantom. And overuse of the stallion can be prevented, because each collection is usually enough to breed several mares. Artificial insemination also permits evaluation of the semen for quality at periodic intervals.

When the mare is to be bred by artificial insemination, collect the semen as previously discussed. It can be processed two ways for insemination after it is collected with an artificial vagina. First, determine the volume of semen that contains sufficient spermatozoa for conception. Each mare should be inseminated with at least 100×10^6 and preferably with 500×10^6 actively motile spermatozoa. To determine the volume containing 500×10^6 actively motile spermatozoa, use the following equation:

$$\text{Milliliters} = \frac{500 \times 10^6}{\text{Concentration per ml} \times \dfrac{\% \text{ motility}}{100}}$$

A typical example for an ejaculate containing 250×10^6 spermatozoa per milliliter that is 80 percent motile is as follows:

$$\text{Milliliters} = \frac{500 \times 10^6}{250 \times 10^6 \times \dfrac{80}{100}} = 1.5$$

Fresh semen without any diluters gives excellent results even when only 1.5 to 2.0 ml are used, provided there are 500×10^6 actively motile spermatozoa.

Diluters or extenders are added to the semen to permit antibiotic and antibacterial treatment and to enhance sperm survival. One of the most popular diluters or extenders is called skim milk (see Appendix 15-1 for preparation instructions).

Prepare the mare by wrapping her tail and washing the perineal area. The fresh extended semen is contained in a disposable syringe maintained at 100°F (38°C). The syringe is connected to a sterile insemination catheter (Figure 15-47).

FIGURE 15-47   Artificial insemination equipment: (A) disposable vaginal speculum; (B) disposable plastic insemination pipette; (C) pen light; (D) disposable syringe; (E) H-R lubricant; (F) disposable sterile surgeon's glove; (G) disposable plastic sleeve. (Photo by W. Evans.)

The inseminator places his or her hand and arm in a long-sleeved plastic glove; over the plastic glove, a sterile surgeon's glove is placed over the hand. A small amount of sterile lubricant (H-R jelly) is placed on the gloves. The hand and arm are inserted in the vagina, and one finger is passed through the cervix (Figure 15-48). The hand is withdrawn slightly and the insemination catheter is inserted into the vagina under the palm of the hand. If necessary, a speculum can be used to find the cervix. The tip of the catheter is covered by the tip of a finger and passed through the cervix. The semen is deposited into the uterus and the catheter withdrawn.

Insemination or breeding should be done just before ovulation. Spermatozoa retain their capacity for fertilization for at least 72 hours after deposition in the mare's reproductive tract. There are documented cases in which breeding has preceded ovulation by 5 days and conception still occurred. However, after 72 hours the conception rate decreases rapidly. The ovum remains viable for conception for a period of 8 to 24 hours after ovulation. Therefore, from a practical standpoint, the mare should be bred every other day during estrus if she is not palpated. Breeding should begin on the second day of estrus. If the mare is bred according to palpation and follicle growth, she usually needs to be bred one time just before ovulation. If the mare ovulates just prior to breeding, her chances of conception are reduced but she still may conceive.

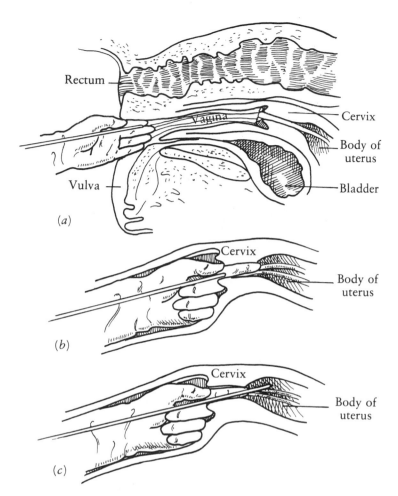

Rectum

Vagina

Vulva

Cervix

Body of
uterus

Bladder

(a)

Cervix

Body of
uterus

(b)

Cervix

Body of
uterus

(c)

FIGURE 15-48   A longitudinal-sectional diagram showing the reproductive tract and the sequential positions of the inseminator's hand and the insemination syringe when inserting the hand and syringe into the vagina *(a)*, passing the syringe into the cervix *(b)*, and when the tip of the syringe is properly positioned in the body of the uterus *(c)*, just prior to expressing semen into the body of the uterus. (From Amann and Pickett, 1983.)

Infertility Problems

The pneumovagina, or "windsucker," condition is one of the most frequently observed causes of infertility. In this conformation of the perineal area, the anus is recessed or sunken. The lips of the vulva are not almost vertical but are more horizontal (Figure 15-49). In extreme cases, the lips of the vulva are almost horizontal. This type of conformation facilitates contamination of the vagina with fecal material. During estrus when the vulva is relaxed, air is

FIGURE 15-49   Perineal conformation that is prone to cause "wind sucking," or pneumovagina.

aspirated into the vagina and uterus. These conditions are conducive to bacterial invasion of the vagina and uterus, and genital infections are common. Approximately 90 percent of mares that have a poor prognosis for a successful pregnancy have the pneumovagina condition. Therefore, evaluate perineal conformation before purchasing brood mares. To help prevent infections, the lips of the vulva can be sutured part of the way down to prevent fecal contamination and the aspiration of air. If the mare is artificially inseminated, the vulva does not have to be opened up for breeding. Care must be taken, however, to be sure the vulva is opened up before foaling.

Other infertility problems can be determined during a female genital-organ examination to evaluate breeding soundness. Inside the vagina, one may observe scars, abrasions, ulcers, and other defects of the mucosa that may cause infertility. Infections, vaginitis, and cervicitis are frequently the result of urine pooling in the anterior vagina. When urine is being pooled, there is a marked downward and forward slope of the vaginal floor, which prevents the urine from flowing out. In older mares, this occurs as the broad ligament loses elasticity. Surgical correction to allow the urine to drain out is successful in a few cases.

Damage to the cervix area can also cause infertility. If the cervical muscles are torn during foaling and if the tear does not heal properly, the cervix does not seal during pregnancy to prevent bacterial invasions, and this can cause abortion. Adhesions may develop that permanently close the vagina and prevent spermatozoa from entering the uterus.

Endometritis (infection of the uterus) is frequently found in mares that aspirate air. The air contains infectious contaminants that eventually overcome tissue resistance. The condition may become chronic and, in severe cases, pyometria (pus in the uterus) may result. The uterus may contain as much as a gallon or more of purulent discharge. In these cases, the lining of the uterus is destroyed, and no prostaglandin is released to cause the corpus luteum to stop secreting progesterone. Therefore, such mares tend to have long periods of anestrus due to prolonged corpus luteal function. The most prevalent organisms causing uterine infections are β-hemolytic streptococcus, *E. coli,* and *K. pneumoniae.* They are detected by swabbing the cervix or uterus and culturing the specimen. The streptococci are sensitive to penicillin treatment, and the *E. coli* and *K. pneumoniae* are sensitive to chloraphenicol, gentamicin, and the polymyxins. A veterinarian should select and use the appropriate pharmacological agent.

The ovaries of mares may be underdeveloped or may have become atrophied (small in size). The problem can be congenital. Ovarian cysts are numerous follicles on an enlarged ovary. The follicles fail to ovulate, so the mare is in constant estrus. Their presence requires diagnosis and treatment by a veterinarian. Tumors may be present in the uterus and block the pathway for spermatozoa. Granulosa cell tumors in the ovary cause different types of estrous behavior: anestrus, continuous sexual receptivity, or male behavior. Male behavior results from increased testosterone secretion by the tumors. Treatment is usually surgical removal of the affected ovary. The time between surgical removal of the ovary with the tumor and normal ovulation by the other ovary varies from 90 days to 2 years.

The percentage of mares that have live foals decreases as mares age, particularly after 13 years of age. Each mare is an individual case and professional help is usually required to evaluate her potential and to help her overcome her problems. As mares age, there are changes in the reproductive tract that decrease conception rate and increase embryonic loss. The veterinarian will examine the uterus for infection, uterine pooling, inflammation, trauma, damage, and scar tissue; the oviducts for infection and scar tissue; and the vulva for conformation. Hormonal relationships during the estrous cycle will also be investigated. Techniques used during the examination include ultrasonography, endoscopy, speculum, bacterial cultures, and cytology. The management of the mare is also closely examined.

Embryo Transfer

Surgical and nonsurgical methods for recovering and transferring fertilized eggs are well established by several laboratories and allow good pregnancy rates. The nonsurgical method is easy to perform. The recovery of fertilized eggs is approximately 80 percent, and an overall pregnancy rate is about 45 percent. Pregnancy rates for embryos that are transferred are about 65 percent. The initial step is to synchronize the donor and recipient mares with prostaglandins and hCG as previously described. On days 6 to 8, the embryo is collected by flushing the uterus with Dulbecco's phosphate buffered saline with 1 percent serum albumin. The medium is drained through an embryo filter cup, and the filter cup contents are poured into a gridded search dish. The embryo is located under a microscope. It is then transferred to the uterus of the recipient mare.

Embryos can be collected from mares several times during the early part of the breeding season, and the mare can be allowed to carry her own fetus later in the season. The technique offers several advantages. First, a large number of foals can be obtained from genetically superior mares. Second, the embryos from mares that chronically abort can be transferred to recipient mares. Third, mares with injuries that would endanger their lives if they remained pregnant can be used as donors. The development of methods for inducing superovulation in the mare would enhance the value of the technique.

Embryos can be stored overnight and/or shipped in a special shipping container. Storing frozen embryos has not been very successful. In-vitro fertilization has not been developed for the mare to the extent that it has been developed for humans and cattle. Only one foal has been born as a result of in-vitro fertilization.

GESTATION

Length of Gestation Period

The average length of gestation ranges between 335 and 350 days for all breeds. The length varies considerably because it is influenced by sex of the foal, month of conception, and individual traits of the mare. A range of 300 to 385 days has been observed for Morgan horses. The average was 340 days, and the median was 342 days. Colts are usually carried 2 to 7 days longer than fillies, indicating that the sire influences gestation length through the genotype. The gestation period of mares carrying a mule fetus (jack and mare) is approximately 10 days longer than the gestation period of the same mare carrying a horse fetus. Mares foaling during the spring usually have a 4- to 5-day shorter gestation. This is probably related to nutrition, because mares on a high plane of nutrition foal approximately 4 days before mares on a low plane of nutrition. Therefore, the rate of fetal development could be affected by the nutritional status of the mare.

A foal born at 300 to 320 days is classified as premature. Those born after 360 days are classified as postmature.

Hormonal Changes

After the mare conceives, a sequence of changes occurs in the blood hormone concentrations (Figure 15-50). The corpus luteum of pregnancy continues to secrete progesterone until it regresses at 150 to 210 days. Because the accessory corpora lutea developed during the second and third month and the placenta produces progesterone, the concentration is high until 120 to 150 days. Then it declines to rather low concentrations until just before parturition. About 30 days before parturition, the blood concentration increases. After the placenta is passed, it declines very rapidly. The ovaries are not essential for progesterone production after 100 days, because they can be removed without subsequent abortion.

FIGURE 15-50   Endocrine pattern during gestation of a mare.

One of the most significant hormone changes is the secretion of large quantities of equine chorionic gonadotropin (eCG) hormone that occurs between 40 and 130 days of gestation. The eCG is detectable as early as 35 days after conception. Maximum concentrations are attained at 55 to 60 days. After 130 to 170 days, it is undetectable in the blood. eCG is secreted by the endometrial cups, but its function in the mare is now known. It predominantly stimulates follicles in effect, but it also possesses a luteinizing fraction. Therefore, it is also used to stimulate follicular growth and ovulation in other species.

Estrogen starts to increase in the blood at approximately 45 days of gestation. At 80 days of gestation, it starts to increase rapidly, and maximum concentrations are attained at 200 to 210 days. A gradual decline starts after 200 to 210 days until parturition, at which time a rapid decline occurs.

The presence of the estrogens equilin and equilinen, is unique in the mare. An elevated concentration of estrone sulfate is indicative of a viable fetus.

Relaxin is produced by the equine placenta and is detectable in the blood at approximately day 70 of the pregnancy. The concentration remains high through the rest of pregnancy. It is believed to reduce uterine motility during pregnancy and to soften the pelvic ligaments at foaling. After the placenta is passed, its concentration rapidly declines because it is produced by the placenta.

Prolactin concentration gradually increases during the last few days prepartum. Its increased concentration is responsible for mammary development and initiation of milk secretion.

Concentration of cortisol does not change during gestation but does rise during the stress of foaling.

At parturition, increasing concentration of oxytocin and prostaglandin will initiate uterine contractions. Significant increases in prostaglandin $F_{2\alpha}$, produced by mare and fetus, are observed approximately 1 hour prior to foaling and are associated with rupture of the membrane. Oxytocin produced by the posterior pituitary gland leads to increased prostaglandin $F_{2\alpha}$ production. The number of uterine oxytocin receptors increases at parturition because of estrogen stimulation, and this increase enhances uterine contractility.

During the postpartum period, prostaglandin $F_{2\alpha}$ concentration declines, oxytocin concentrations increase for milk let-down, and prolactin increases for about 5 days.

There is a periodic emergence of follicular waves or periods of follicular growth characterized by an increase in diameter of a dominant follicle to 35 to 50 mm and subordinate follicles. These waves in follicle growth are preceded by an increase in FSH concentration 3 days prior to wave emergence. The successive waves occur during days 3 to 8, 16 to 23, and 29 of pregnancy. Because of these hormonal changes, management problems can arise. Pregnant mares may come into estrus and ovulate. This normally occurs between 30 and 50 days after conception. Before breeding the mare, it is advisable to give her a manual or ultrasound pregnancy examination if she skipped the expected estrus at 18 to 23 days after she was bred.

Placentation

Shortly after fertilization (4 to 6 days), the ovum migrates to the uterus. However, implantation does not occur for approximately 8 weeks. During the first 8 weeks, the chorion (Figure 15-51) is held next to the uterine mucosa by fetal fluid pressure. By 10 weeks, the uterine mucosa is penetrated by the chorionic villi, and by 14 weeks the attachment is complete. The type of attachment is epitheliochorial; that is, the chorion of the fetus is in contact with the epithelium of the mare's uterus.

The fetal placenta is formed by three membranes (Figure 15-51): chorion, allantois, and amnion. Villi, or fingerlike projections, are scattered over the surface of the chorion (outermost membrane), and for this reason the attachment is said to be "diffuse." The second membrane, allantois, lines the inside of the chorion and is fused with the amnion, thus forming the first waterbag, or *allantoic cavity.* The allantoic cavity is connected to the bladder by the urachus, which passes

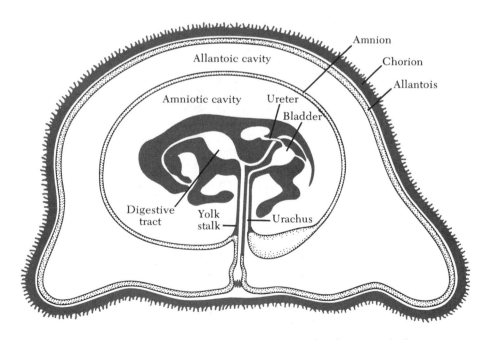

FIGURE 15-51   Fetus of the horse within the placenta. The chorion and allantois make up the chorioallantois, also often called the allantochorion. (From Frandson, 1974; after Witchi, 1956.)

through the umbilical cord. If the urachus fails to close after the umbilical cord is broken after parturition, bacteria may invade the foal. The amnion is the innermost membrane and forms the second water bag, or *amnionic cavity.*

The umbilical arteries and veins form the umbilical cord. When they reach the chorion, they spread out in the connective tissue between the allantois and chorion. The umbilical arteries and their tributaries carry unoxygenated blood and waste products from the fetus to the mare. The umbilical veins carry oxygenated blood and nutrients from the mare to the fetus. In general, blood from the two circulations do not mix, because at least six layers of tissue separate them (Figure 15-52).

The mare has a peculiar specialization: endometrial cups form from fetal cells, chorionic girdle cells, and they start development prior to implantation, which occurs on day 37. They form cup-like depressions in the chorion, which

FIGURE 15-52   Diagrammatic representation of the relationship between maternal and fetal tissues in the epitheliochorial type of placenta (for horse): (1) fetal artery; (2) fetal vein; (3) allantochorion; (4) uterine lumen; (5) maternal artery; (6) maternal vein; (7) uterine epithelium; (8) cytotrophoblast; (9) villous; (10) stroma; (11) allantoic vesicle. (From Harvey, 1959.)

becomes filled with coagulum. Coagulum is an accumulation of degenerate epithelial cells, erythroctyes, leucocytes, and eCG. The endometrial cups secrete eCG.

Fetal Growth

The growth and development of the fetus is illustrated in Figure 15-53. During the first two trimesters of pregnancy, fetal growth is slow. About 50 percent of the fetal growth (weight) occurs during the last 110 days of pregnancy.

Pregnancy Examination

Pregnancy in the mare can be determined by palpating the ovaries and uterus through the rectum, by finding the embryo with ultrasound, and by determining the presence of eCG or high concentrations of estrogen in the blood.

The quickest and most efficient method is by palpation. This is usually done by a veterinarian, but stud farm managers can learn the technique. Position of the ovaries and presence of the fetus help determine pregnancy by palpation. During the early stages of pregnancy and during a nonpregnant state, the ovaries are high in the sublumbar area. As pregnancy advances, the ovaries are displaced downward, forward, and medially. The most important indicators are the form, size, consistency, and position of the pregnant uterus and the presence of the fetus. The earliest stage that pregnancy can be positively determined is 28 to 30 days (Figure 15-54). At this stage, a bulge about 2 to

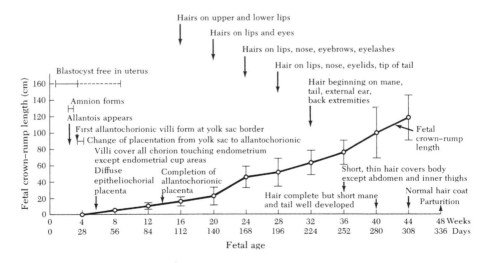

FIGURE 15-53   Fetal growth. (From Bitteridge and Laing, 1970.)

FIGURE 15-54   Left horn pregnancy, 28 to 30 days. Note the slight enlargement between the thumb and the middle fingers. (From R. Zemjanis, *Diagnostic and Therapeutic Techniques in Animal Reproduction,* 2d ed. The Williams & Wilkins Co., Baltimore. Copyright © 1970.)

3 cm in diameter is present in the uterus, usually located at the base of one horn. Transmigration of the fetus is common in the mare, so the fetus may be in the opposite horn of the uterus from the ovary in which ovulation occurred. The uterus has good muscle tone, and the cervix is tightly closed. At 5 weeks, the bulge is about 3 to 4 cm (size of a golf ball) (Figure 15-55). By 6 weeks, the bulge is 5 to 7 cm long and about 5 cm in diameter (Figure 15-56). The enlargement begins to involve the body of the uterus during the seventh week. It is 7 to 8 cm long and 6 to 7 cm in diameter. At this time, fluctuation of the fetal fluids is clearly palpable. The uterus is still in the pelvic area. At 2 months, the bulge is in the form of a football, 12 to 15 cm long, and 8 to 10 cm in diameter. About one-half of the enlargement is in the body of the uterus (Figure 15-57). The fetus continues to enlarge so that the entire uterus is involved by 3 months. The uterus starts to descend over the pelvic brim. The bulge is 20 to 25 cm long and 12 to 16 cm in diameter (Figure 15-58). To detect the fetus, use your hand with a blotting-type motion. During the 3- to 5-month period, the uterus is still partially located in the pelvic area, so the fetus can be felt without difficulty. Toward the end of the 5- to 7-month period, the uterus has completely descended. After 7 months, the pregnant uterus starts to ascend, and the fetus can be easily palpated.

FIGURE 15-55   Right horn pregnancy, 35 days. (From R. Zemjanis, *Diagnostic and Therapeutic Techniques in Animal Reproduction,* 2d ed. The Williams & Wilkins Co., Baltimore. Copyright © 1970.)

FIGURE 15-56   Right horn pregnancy, 42 to 45 days. (From R. Zemjanis, *Diagnostic and Therapeutic Techniques in Animal Reproduction,* 2d ed. The Williams & Wilkins Co., Baltimore. Copyright © 1970.)

FIGURE 15-57   Right horn pregnancy, 48 to 50 days. (From R. Zemjanis, *Diagnostic and Therapeutic Techniques in Animal Reproduction,* 2d ed. The Williams & Wilkins Co., Baltimore. Copyright © 1970.)

FIGURE 15-58   Right horn pregnancy, 60 to 65 days. (From R. Zemjanis, *Diagnostic and Therapeutic Techniques in Animal Reproduction,* 2d ed. The Williams & Wilkins Co., Baltimore. Copyright © 1970.)

The development and use of real-time ultrasonography have resulted in a very accurate means of ascertaining pregnancy. An embryo can be detected as early as 11 to 13 days of development. The principles of ultrasonography center on the ability of sound waves to be either reflected or propagated through various tissue interfaces. As the sound beam passes through a fluid-filled space, a black area appears on the screen and soft tissue appears as gray areas. Therefore, follicles on the ovary, embryonic vesicles, corpora lutea, and other structures in the equine reproductive tract can be visualized on the screen (Figure 15-59). One of the main advantages of ultrasonography is that twin fetuses can be detected very early in development, and management techniques can be used to eliminate one. Other uses of ultrasonography on the breeding farm include: determining whether a mare has entered the ovulatory season or a filly has reached puberty; detecting and differentiating single and multiple preovulatory follicles and ovulations; detecting failure of ovulation; detecting and monitoring corpora lutea; estimating the stage of the estrous cycle and evaluating the time and suitability for breeding; and detecting semen in the uterus.

The secretion of eCG during the 35- to 40-day period to about 100 to 150 days can be used for a positive pregnancy test. The immunological test for eCG is easy to perform.

Estrogen concentration in the blood is determined by a chemical assay. However, it is very seldom used. A high concentration of estrone sulfate is indicative of a viable embryo or fetus.

Abortions

Abortion is expulsion of the fetus before the time of normal foaling. There are many causes of abortions and in some instances, the cause cannot be determined. The common causes are bacteria, viruses, fungi, genetic abnormalities, injuries, and stress.

Viral abortions are caused by viruses such as herpes, which can cross the placenta and infect the fetus. The fetus dies because of the extensive damage to the liver and other organs. Herpes virus is discussed as rhinopneumonitis in Chapter 10.

Bacteria and fungi normally do not cross the placenta but cause abortions by disrupting the function of the placenta.

Bacterial abortions resulting from salmonella and streptococci occur during the latter half or during early pregnancy, respectively. Streptococci are usually introduced during breeding, so hygienic procedures are important for prevention. These bacteria account for about 25 percent of all abortions.

Genetic abortions occur when the fetus is malformed. For reasons unknown, the mare's body usually rejects the malformed fetus, and abortion occurs.

(a)

(b)

(c)

FIGURE 15-59   Ultrasound images: *(a)* three follicles on an ovary; *(b)* early pregnancy; vesicle is 2.2 cm in diameter, which is normal for day 15–16 of pregnancy; *(c)* embryo that is 34 days old.

Injury-related abortions are rare, because the fetus is well cushioned by the structure of the fetal membranes. However, it is advisable to prevent injuries caused by kicking, bumping, or squeezing.

Stress occurring during sales events or shipping can result in abortion. Shipping stress usually results from long trips during which the mare does not eat or drink water. Surgical stress can also lead to abortion. In shipping or surgical stress, endotoxins are released as a result of changes in gut bacteria resulting from dietary changes during the stressful period. The endotoxins may lyse the corpus luteum, resulting in inadequate progesterone. Use of a synthetic progestin such as Regu-Mate or progesterone injections during the stressful period and for a couple of weeks afterward is believed to help prevent abortion. Also, immunization against endotoxins helps prevent endotoxin complications.

Failure of the corpora lutea or placenta to secrete sufficient progesterone may also lead to abortion. Although this is not believed to be a common cause of abortion, many farm managers and veterinarians give progesterone to older, barren, or problem mares.

Signs

Abortions may be sudden in onset and may occur before any premonitory signs are manifest, or they may occur over a prolonged period of time. Prolonged abortions are usually accompanied by readily recognized symptoms. There is usually mammary development, and milk may stream from the udder for several days. Some mares may go through the normal symptoms exhibited prior to a normal foaling, including Stage 1 labor. The symptoms disappear for 1 to 2 days and then reappear. After two to three cycles, the fetus is expelled. Most fetuses are expelled without any difficulties, but the placenta may be retained. If so, the mare requires veterinary assistance for its removal. All abortions should be followed by a female genital organ examination by a veterinarian.

Precautions

After an abortion has occurred, the fetus should be examined by a veterinarian to determine the possible cause of abortion. During the period of time required for the analysis, the mare should be isolated to prevent the spread of a virus that may have caused the abortion. The mare's stall should be disinfected with steam or a tamed iodine solution, all contaminated bedding removed, and the afterbirth removed and disposed.

Determining Sex of Fetus

Between days 59 and 68 of pregnancy, the sex of the fetus can be accurately determined by ultrasonographic observation of the genital tubercle. The genital tubercle is the forerunner of the penis in males and the clitoris of females. Between days 48 and 54, the tubercle is visible as a hypergenic (light area) bilobulated structure about 2 mm in diameter located between the hindlegs. During differentiation, the tubercle moves from its initial position between the hindlimbs toward the umbilical cord in males and toward the tail in females. By day 63, the tubercle is immediately caudal to the umbilical cord or is under the tail. Although the optimal time of sex diagnosis is days 59 to 68, sex can be accurately determined until at least day 97. Experience of the person performing the ultrasonographic examination is a major factor in accuracy of the technique.

CHAPTER 16

Care During and After Pregnancy

Proper care of the mare during and after pregnancy is critical if she is to produce healthy and well-developed foals. Improper care can result in abortion or the presentation of a dead or deformed foal. Poor care can also result in infertility or sterility caused by damage to or infection of the reproductive tract.

FOALING

Pregnant Mare Care Immediately Before Foaling

During the last 90 to 120 days prior to foaling, the increased nutrient requirements of the pregnant mare must be met. Failure to do so will result in excessive loss of condition, and the foal's birth weight will be reduced. Her feet and teeth also need proper care, and she should be treated for external parasites.

At about 30 days before foaling, the mare should be given a booster shot for tetanus (tetanus toxoid). This results in high antibody titers, so the foal receives adequate antibodies in the colostrum for protection against tetanus. Other immunizations should be given at this time. Check the mare to determine if her vulva has been sutured. If it has, the vulva should be opened. Early removal of the sutures (opening the vulva) prevents an unexpected parturition in which the vulva is torn. Exercise should be continued if she is being exercised. However, exercise should not be strenuous during this period. Exercise maintains muscle tone.

When the mare approaches her time to foal, remove her shoes and bring her into a foaling stall or into a large, clean, grassy paddock. Mares foaled on clean grassy areas seldom have complications. They are brought into foaling stalls to receive close attention during foaling. The time to bring them into a foaling stall can be predicted within a 2- to 3-day period of foaling with the use of a water hardness test strip described below. The stall should be at least 12 × 14 feet (3.66 × 4.27 m). It should be bedded with straw or have a floor covered with synthetic material so that it can be kept clean. Straw that is clean, free of dust, and cut in long lengths is preferable. Wood shavings and other similar materials may stick to the wet nostrils of a newborn foal and suffocate it. Before the mare is placed in the stall, disinfect it with a tamed iodine disinfectant solution. The stall should be equipped with good lights and be free of any projections such as nails or broken boards.

Immediately before the mare foals, reduce her ration. This decreases the amount of material in the digestive tract and may prevent a foaling problem.

It is advisable to keep a foaling kit assembled and ready for use (Figure 16-1). It should contain two buckets, to be used for warm, clean water if trouble arises. A mild soap such as Ivory for cleaning the mare and for cleaning the attendant's hands if the mare requires help should be available. A mild disinfectant solution such as Nolvasan is desirable to keep instruments clean. Tail bandages such as 4-inch (10.2-cm) gauze bandages or leg wraps are used to wrap the tail prior to foaling during Stage 1 labor and to tie up the placenta after foaling. A cup and a solution of 2 percent iodine tincture are used to treat the navel cord. Supplies (Fleet enema) for administering an enema are essential. Towels for drying the foal are handy as are garbage bags for waste disposal. Obstetrical sleeves and a lubricant are used when it is necessary to reposition or examine the foal. Syringes and needles are used to administer antibiotics and/or tetanus antitoxin, if necessary. A small tank of oxygen that fits in the palm of the hand, obtained from an emergency medical supply store, is valuable if artificial respiration is necessary. The flow should be 2 liters per minute for 5 minutes. One must be careful to avoid lung damage. In case the foal must be bottle-fed, the kit should have a bottle fitted with a goat nipple, a wide-mouth bottle into which the mare is milked, and a funnel for pouring milk into the bottle. Keep the supplies in a box that is easy to carry to the foaling stall. A source of frozen colostrum should be available in case the mare dies.

Predicting Parturition

As a mare approaches parturition, the concentration of calcium ions in a mare's milk increases. A water hardness test strip (Figure 16-2) consisting of

FIGURE 16-1   Foaling kit: (A) storage bag; (B) portable oxygen tank; (C) water cup; (D) sterile H-R lubricant; (E) Fleet enema; (F) needles and syringes; (G) soap solution in squeeze bottle; (H) iodine solution; (I) turkish towel; (J) plastic sleeves; (K) bucket; (L) roll of cotton; (M) gauze roll (tail wrap for mare); (N) Ivory soap; (O) sterile gloves. (Photo by W. Evans.)

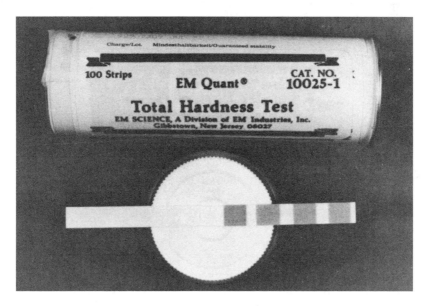

FIGURE 16-2   Total hardness water test strip used to monitor calcium ion concentration in the secretions from the udder to predict parturition.

four zones that sequentially change color from green to red-violet as the concentration of calcium increases in the milk can be used to test for calcium. Thus, a greater number of zones will change color as a mare approaches parturition.

In order to test a mare's milk or secretions from her udder, the following supplies are needed: test strips, Merckoquant total hardness test strip 10025, distilled water, 10- to 15-milliliter test tube or other cylindrical container, 10-cc syringe, and a baby bottle or other container for the milk. Commercial kits are available with all the necessary supplies and instructions for using them. After obtaining a milk sample from the mare, 6 cc of distilled water and 1 cc of the milk are thoroughly mixed in the test tube. A test strip is briefly dipped in the solution so that the four zones are immersed. The excess solution is shaken from the test strip and the number of zones changing color is noted after 1 minute.

It is recommended that a mare's milk be tested daily beginning about 3 to 4 weeks prior to the expected foaling date. When fewer than two zones change color, frequent examination of the mare for signs of stage 1 parturition is not necessary for at least 24 hours. When a color change occurs in two or more zones, mares should be examined frequently and testing should be performed twice a day, early in the morning and late in the evening. Under these conditions, a foaling attendant can be expected to watch a mare about 3 days. Extensive field testing has demonstrated that mares rarely foal unless two or more zones change color. When two zones are observed to change color for the first time, most mares will foal within 4 days. When three or four zones change color for the first time, all mares will probably foal within 3 days and a large percentage of them will foal within 24 hours.

Even though the test does not predict the exact time of parturition, it does substantially decrease the amount of time devoted to frequent examination of mares prior to foaling. This is particularly advantageous to the breeder with few mares, a small staff, and limited resources to hire foaling attendants. It will decrease the cost of bedding for foaling stalls and decrease the number of days a mare will spend in the foaling stall. When the number of foaling stalls is limited, the appropriate mares can be chosen to stay in them.

Signs of Approaching Parturition

The signs of approaching parturition are very evident in some mares, but others show few, if any, signs. Some mares merely lie down and have their foals. The general indicators are as follows. Distension of the udder is usually the first indicator, and it occurs about 2 to 6 weeks before foaling. Approximately 7 to 10 days before foaling, the muscles in the croup area shrink markedly because the muscles and ligaments in the pelvic area generally relax. The teats fill out their nipples 4 to 6 days before foaling. A waxy secretion oozes out of the end of the nipples, building up in the nipples 2 to 4 days before foaling. Within 24 hours of foaling, the wax may drop off, and milk may start to drip. Finally, the mare becomes quite nervous, frequently raises her tail and passes a small amount of urine, appears to have cramps, breaks out in a sweat, and may walk anxiously around the stall. At this time, wash the perineal area with warm water and a mild soap. Wrap the tail to help maintain cleanliness and prevent the tail from becoming entangled with the foal.

Foaling

Foaling is divided into three stages (Figure 16-3). During stage 1, the muscles in the uterine wall contract rhythmically. The contraction waves start at the anterior end of the uterus and move toward the cervix. As the contraction wave moves toward the cervix, it increases in strength. These contractions are responsible for the mare's anxious behavior. As the contraction forces get stronger, they force the allantois into the cervical canal and the vagina. Then it may appear through the vulva. Increasing pressure causes it to rupture, and 2 to 5 gallons of water (7.6 to 18.9 liters) are released. When it ruptures, stage 1 is completed. The time period for stage 1 varies from a few minutes to several hours.

Stage 2 is the actual expulsion of the fetus from the uterus. After the allantochorial membrane ruptures, the contractions continue. At this time the mare may lie down, roll, and get up several times. This is important to get the foal in the proper position for delivery. The two front feet appear, and the nose is resting just behind them (Figure 16-4). The bottoms of the feet should point downward. The forequarters pass rather easily. As the hips start to pass, the mare may have some difficulty. After a few more strong contractions, the foal is completely delivered. Stage 2 takes 10 to 20 minutes if no difficulties are encountered.

After the foal has been delivered, make sure that the membranes do not cover the foal's nostrils. If they do, the foal may suffocate. Do not disturb the mare and foal when reflecting the membranes back over the foal's body.

Stage 3 begins after the foal is completely delivered and ends with the expulsion of the afterbirth. After the foal is delivered, the mare should lie undisturbed for as long as she wants—the longer, the better. The foal will struggle to rise and will break the cord. Soon after the cord breaks, treat it with a solution of iodine (see the section on postnatal care).

The afterbirth can be tied up in a ball with a piece of string after the mare stands. This prevents her from stepping on it and tearing it off so that part of it remains in the uterus. A young mare may try to kick it, because it will slap against her legs. The weight of the placenta provides a steady pull that is usually sufficient to aid in its expulsion. It should be expelled within 30 minutes to 3 hours after foaling. If retained over 4 hours an abnormal situation exists, requiring treatment by a veterinarian. A retained placenta can cause complications such as laminitis, septicemia, and/or colic. Spread the placenta out and examine it to be sure it is intact (Figure 16-5). If a piece of it is torn off and

(a)

(b)

FIGURE 16-3   Delivery of a normal foal. Stage 1: *(a)* mare rolling; *(b)* mare looking at her side; *(c)* mare sweating and kicking at her belly; *(d)* first appearance of the placenta. Stage 2 (delivery of foal): *(e)* appearance of forelegs; *(f)* body of foal passing through the vulva. Stage 3: *(g)* forelegs tearing placenta; *(h)* placenta torn; *(i)* mare getting up; *(j)* mare up and navel cord broken. (Photos by W. Evans.)

retained in the uterus, complications arise. Also, the placenta should be weighed. A normal placenta weighs approximately 13 to 14 pounds (5.9 to 6.4 kg). If it weighs about 18 to 20 pounds (8.2 to 9.1 kg) and is very bloody, the uterus may be infected, requiring veterinary treatment.

(c)

(d)

(e)

FIGURE 16-3 *Continued*

(f)

(g)

(h)

FIGURE 16-3 *Continued*

(i)

(j)

FIGURE 16-3 *Continued*

Dystocia

Dystocia is defined as any difficulty during parturition. Fortunately, mares seldom experience dystocia. If they do, they require immediate veterinary assistance. Otherwise, the mare and/or foal will usually be critically injured. The mare should be kept up and walking around until help arrives.

When a mare starts labor, do not interfere unless she starts to have trouble. After the first water bag ruptures, people tend to try to help the mare. But

FIGURE 16-4   Normal position of a foal during foaling. The forelegs are extended, and the head and neck rest on the forelegs. The hindlegs become extended backward as the body passes out of the mare.

FIGURE 16-5   Placenta that has been spread out on the ground to be sure it is complete and that part of it has not been left in the mare: (A) point of rupture of the allantochorion; (B) allantois and amnion, which form the second water bag that immediately surrounds the foal; (C) navel cord. (Photo by H. Stokes.)

if one or both feet are visible, she requires no help at this stage. In a few minutes, and if both feet and the muzzle are visible, all will be well. Do not rush the mare, but let her continue to foal naturally. When the hips pass through the pelvis, she may encounter a slight difficulty. Let her finish and do not disturb her. If she must be helped to deliver a foal that is in the proper position, pull the foal's feet outward and slightly toward her hocks when her abdominal muscles contract. When the mare relaxes, the attendant should also relax.

The following situations may be corrected if veterinary help is unavailable. Determine them by passing an arm into the vagina and feeling the fetus forelegs and head. Most problems result from improper positioning of the limbs, body, or head: the forelegs may be bent at the knee, one foreleg bent backward, head bent backward toward the chest, head bent to the side, head and neck bent backward, buttocks presented first, hocks flexed with hindlegs under body, back against cervix, or hindleg present with forelegs. To correct these situations, push the fetus back in and reposition it with the forelegs and muzzle in the birth canal. The foal can be delivered hindlegs first without too much difficulty. However, if you are not skilled in delivering foals and do not understand fetal positions, you can easily make the conditions worse. Veterinary help is preferred.

Inducing Parturition

Mares can be induced to foal, but the procedure is generally not recommended. It may be indicated for mares that have sustained an injury, preparturient colic, prolonged gestation, or colostrum loss. Induction can alleviate the mare's condition and can allow delivery to occur when veterinary assistance is available. It may be useful on a farm in which personnel are not skilled at foaling mares or when veterinary assistance may not be easily available for urgent assistance.

Before a mare is induced, she must meet three criteria: (1) the gestational period must be greater than 320 days, (2) colostrum must be present in the udder, and the cervix should be relaxed, and (3) the fetus should be in the proper position. If the mare fails to meet these criteria, serious consequences usually develop.

To induce the mare, a veterinarian will give her oxytocin or prostaglandin. Following treatment, signs of stage 1 labor are observed within 30 minutes. The foaling process is completed by the end of 40 to 200 minutes.

Postnatal Foal and Mare Care

Foal

As soon as the foal is delivered, examine it to see if it is breathing. If no movement can be observed from a distance, inspect it closely. Artificial respiration can be given by blowing into the foal's nostrils, by pressing and releasing the rib cage, by pulling the forelegs forward and then backward, or by administering oxygen. Vigorously rubbing the foal with a towel may stimulate it to breathe. If all else fails, picking up the foal and dropping it a couple of feet may start respiration.

The navel cord should be dipped in a tincture of 2 percent iodine to prevent bacterial invasions. Failure to treat the navel cord frequently results in navel ill. Examine the stump of the cord for a few days to make sure that no urine is present. If the urachus does not close off, urine will pass from the bladder to the stump. The condition is referred to as "previous or persistent urachus." If a silver nitrate application does not cause it to close, it should be sutured, because it can easily become a route for bacterial invasions.

The foal must be protected against tetanus. This can be provided by two means. As mentioned earlier, the mare can be given a tetanus toxoid booster shot about 30 days before foaling. The foal thus receives high antibody titers against tetanus in the colostrum. These antibodies, or "passive immunity," protect the foal until it is 3 to 5 months old. The second method, which is less effective, is to give the foal a tetanus antitoxin injection. Tetanus antitoxin protects the foal for 2 to 3 weeks. The immune system does not function very well until the foal is 3 to 5 months old. One must wait to give the tetanus toxoid sequence to the foal until it is 3 to 5 months old. Therefore, it is not protected for a period of about $2\frac{1}{2}$ to 3 months unless it did receive the passive immunity.

A veterinarian should decide whether or not to administer a prophylactic dose of antibiotics. The practice is controversial. It is usually not required on farms that practice good hygiene procedures.

Normal foals usually nurse within 30 minutes to 2 hours after foaling. Before nursing, it is helpful to clean the udder with warm water and a mild soap. All soap must be washed off. If necessary, help the foal up and guide it to the mare's udder. Foals that are too weak to nurse should be fed by stomach tube. It is important for the foal to receive colostrum because it contains antibodies for disease protection, contains high levels of vitamin A, and has a laxative effect. Mares produce colostrum for about 48 hours. Therefore, if a mare streams milk from the udder for a couple of days before foaling, the foal may not get any colostrum. A colostrum bank should be kept for such emergencies. Colostrum can be milked from mares that produce a large quantity of milk. It can be stored frozen in pint containers for up to 5 years. When necessary, a pint can be warmed to body temperature and given to a foal. Place it in a soft-drink bottle fitted with a lamb's rubber nipple. The foal must receive the colostrum within 36 hours of birth and should receive it as soon as possible. The large protein molecules (antibodies) are absorbed intact from the digestive tract for up to 36 hours. Thereafter, the protein is digested and provides no benefit. By 18 to 24 hours, the ability to absorb the antibodies decreases dramatically.

Approximately 10 to 15 percent of newborn foals have a failure of passive transfer, and another 10 to 15 percent encounter partial failure of passive transfer of immunity. Failure of passive transfer can be caused by one or a combination of the following: prelactation in which there is a prepartum loss of colostrum; failure of the mare to produce adequate antibodies by natural or vaccinal exposures; failure to nurse during the first 24 hours; and failure of intestinal absorption. Because of the high percentage of foals affected, it is important to determine the immunoglobulin concentration in the blood 12 to 18 hours after birth. If a failure of protection has occurred, colostrum should be administered as soon as possible. The concentration is checked again 12 hours later. If adequate protection still has not occurred, veterinary assistance is recommended. A variety of test kits are available to determine the passive immunity status. Also, a colostrometer can be used to determine the immunoglobulin concentration in the colostrum prior to the time the foal sucks.

Meconium, the dark-colored fetal excrement, should be passed within 12 hours of birth. If it is not, the foal is constipated and should be given an enema. Give 1 or 2 pints (0.47 or 0.94 liter) of warm, soapy water. Pass the end of the hose 3 to 4 inches (7.6 to 10.2 cm) into the rectum. A 4-oz prepackaged Fleet enema is easy to obtain and use, and it gives excellent results.

Foals that are foaled in a pasture without close supervision should be watched to see if they are constipated. If they are, they frequently stop moving, squat, raise their tails, and try to defecate. These same symptoms are observed in foals that are impacted high in the colon. A veterinarian should treat them with a lubricant. Once yellow feces are passed, the digestive tract is no longer blocked.

Some foals' eyes start to water within 1 to 2 days after birth. The eyelids and lashes may be turned in (a condition called *entropion*) and should be rolled out. In such cases, rub an eye ointment in the eye.

Mare

Very few mares have complications after they foal. However, foal colic is common. This usually occurs within 10 to 15 minutes after foaling but may not occur for several hours. Foal colic is caused by continuing uterine contractions as the uterus decreases in size. The usual signs of mild colic are observed: the mare looks back at her abdomen, gets up and down, rolls, kicks at her abdomen, and bites her flanks and abdomen. Treatment is usually not necessary, but a mild sedative is helpful.

If part of the placenta is retained, the next day the mare has colic symptoms, increased temperature, increased heart and respiration rates, and possible lameness. Veterinary assistance is necessary.

Internal hemorrhaging usually results in death. It is caused by damage to the uterus or by rupture of the uterine artery, and the mare bleeds internally. At first, the condition resembles mild colic, but gets worse until, ultimately, death occurs.

Some mares are hesitant to defecate after foaling because of the pain involved. If you observe this, give the mare a wet bran mash containing mineral oil or give her a gallon of mineral oil by stomach tube.

FOAL DISEASES

It is crucial to recognize sick foals early enough so that treatment will be effective (Table 16-1). During the first few days, observe the foal frequently. It should move about normally and nurse every few minutes. Most foals nurse two to three times each hour. Failure to nurse causes the mare's udder to become swollen and sore. The presence of diarrhea or constipation, nasal discharge, difficult breathing, swelling or fluid discharges at the navel, swelling of the joints, or increased temperature (normal is 100 to 101°F, or 37.8 to 38.3°C) usually indicates a disease problem.

Diarrhea or scours may appear at any age and may or may not be serious. It is a sign of disease, not a disease itself. Diarrhea may be caused by improper management. Some common causes are foal heat in the mare, dietary upsets, coprophagy (eating feces), parasites, bacterial infections, and stress (too much exercise, excitement, or exposure). The foal can become dehydrated very quickly and die, so serious cases require immediate attention. Avoid dietary upsets such as separation of mare and foal for a few hours. When diarrhea results from coprophagy, the foal may have to be muzzled except when it is allowed to nurse. This usually occurs when the foal's digestive tract is not ready for solid materials. Digestive upsets occur when the foal is forced to exercise too long or if it runs and plays too long after it is turned out to pasture. Foals are very susceptible to ascarid and intestinal threadworm infestations, which cause diarrhea. Foals should be routinely dewormed every 2 months for the first year.

Navel ill or joint ill is a serious bacterial disease that affects foals. The organism gains entrance through the unhealed navel stump or through the placenta before birth. Symptoms of the disease include listlessness, swollen joints, reluctance to nurse, temperature, and tucked-up appearance in flanks.

About one-half of all foal deaths can be attributed to septicemias. The bacteria *Actinobacillus equuli* is usually responsible if the foal dies within a few days of birth. Death is the main symptom, but the foal may be drowsy and weak and may sleep a great deal before dying.

Convulsive syndrome is another disease of newborn foals. It is also called "barkers," "dummies," or "wanderers." The condition is caused by extreme lack of oxygen just prior to, during, or immediately after birth. Premature separation of the placenta from the uterus may be the cause in some cases. Usually, it results from unwarranted assistance at parturition. The overanxious assistant causes premature rupture of the umbilical cord, thus loss of blood that is vital to the foal. The placental blood makes up about 30 percent of blood in the lung capillaries and causes an improper inflation of the lungs, so that insufficient oxygen is transported to the brain.

The terms "barker," "dummy," and "wanderer" are descriptive of the signs of this disease. The foal may appear normal for a time after birth. Signs

TABLE 16-1   What's Wrong with My Foal? A Keeper's Guide

KEY

▭ During the perinatal period

▭ After the perinatal period

▭ Any time

Generally not life-threatening: treat and watch for complications

● Variable: foals usually respond to prompt treatment, depending on severity

◆ Not life-threatening, but not curable

★ Red alert: life-threatening

■ Most often fatal

What you see		Looking closer		Probable diagnosis	What can be done
Breathing labored, suppressed or noisy	◆	Soreness, reluctance to move		Broken ribs due to severe compression during delivery	Stall rest, gentle handling
	■	Reluctance to move or nurse, extended abdomen, "sawhorse" stance		Ruptured diaphragm, often due to trauma	Immediate corrective surgery. Prognosis grave
	★	Yellowish-stained amniotic fluid with delivery		Meconium-aspiration pneumonia	Antibiotics
	★	Depression, coughing, intermittent fever beginning at 2 weeks to 3 months		Foal pneumonia	Specific antibiotics, based on identification of bacteria from direct sample (*R. equi* a common culprit)
	■	Coughing, debility, progressive illness in spite of vigorous treatment		Combined immunodeficiency (CID): genetic lack of immune system. Virtually limited to Arabians; one Appaloosa foal has been diagnosed	Always fatal, eventually (by 3–6 months)

(continued)

TABLE 16-1 What's Wrong with My Foal? A Keeper's Guide *(Continued)*

KEY

☐ During the perinatal period
▨ After the perinatal period
▧ Any time
Generally not life-threatening: treat and watch for complications
◆ Variable: foals usually respond to prompt treatment, depending on severity
● Not life-threatening, but not curable
◀ Red alert: life-threatening
★
■ Most often fatal

What you see	Looking closer		Probable diagnosis	What can be done
Deformity	Leg joints misaligned (bowlegged or knock-kneed)	●	Angular limb deformity	Brace; surgery; stall rest
	Tight/shortened tendons force foal to "knuckle forward"	★	Contracted tendons, congenital or acquired	Surgery for moderate cases; euthanasia for severe cases
	Fetlocks on ground or windswept	◆	Ligament/tendon laxity	Rest, intermittent bracing
	Overshot or undershot jaw, parrot mouth, wry mouth, or bulldog jaw	◀	Jaw deformity	No established treatment
	Extra toes or other parts	●	Developmental error; persistence of fetal part or stage	Surgical removal
	Legs bent up, stiff, twisted; foal possibly undeliverable without surgery	■	Contracted foal	Foal usually born dead; euthanatize

Sign		Description	Cause	Treatment
Weakness—see also Incoordination/ muscle weakness; sudden loss of vigor	■	Enlarged head (hydrocephalus), "hunchback" (hemivertebra) or other severe deformity	Congenital, nongenetic defect	Survival, usefulness unlikely; euthanatize
	★	Delivery between 300 and 320 days of gestation; soft, silky haircoat; domed forehead; low birthweight; little or no suckle strength; weak fetlocks and lax pasterns	Prematurity (or dysmaturity if delivery occurred at or near term)	Oxygen, humidity, and temperature control; tube feeding; fluids
	●	Intolerance of exercise	Congenital heart defect	Cardiovascular examination; possibly surgery
	★	Will not nurse, severe diarrhea and dehydration, subnormal temperature, bluish-white third eyelid	"Sleeper foal," caused by *Actinobacillus equuli* bacteria	Antibiotics, fluids; prognosis poor
	★	Inflammation of umbilical vein, fever, depression	"Navel ill" (septicemia): systemic bacterial infection of bloodstream	Specific antibiotics, fluids, intensive nursing care; in newborn, administer 500 mg/kg plasma
Sudden loss of vigor within 12–36 hours of first nursing	★	Urine shaded pink or red; if condition persists, oral membranes and eye whites turn yellow	Neonatal isoerythrolysis (NI), also known as "yellow foal" or hemolytic icterus: due to incompatible blood types of mare and foal	Confirm with jaundiced foal agglutination (JFA) test; stop foal from nursing if diagnosed within 24 hours of birth; milk out mare's colostrum; bottle-feed foal frozen colostrum and foal milk replacer until after 36 hours old
Mare cannot nurse	★	Mare dies, does not allow nursing, or is unable to provide milk (agalactia)	Orphan or rejected foal; agalactic mare; early weaning	Supply colostrum if newborn; provide ongoing nourishment with foal milk replacer or obtain nursemare/nursegoat

(continued)

625

TABLE 16-1 What's Wrong with My Foal? A Keeper's Guide (*Continued*)

KEY

▭ During the perinatal period

▭ After the perinatal period

▭ Any time

◆ Generally not life-threatening; treat and watch for complications

● Variable: foals usually respond to prompt treatment, depending on severity

◀ Not life-threatening, but not curable

★ Red alert: life-threatening

■ Most often fatal

What you see		Looking closer	Probable diagnosis	What can be done
Bulge under skin	◆	Fluidlike oval bubble in umbilical region, easily pushed back inside body	Umbilical hernia due to compression during deliver or other trauma	Most spontaneously close; few need external support or surgical correction
	◆	Bulge of organ/tissue in scrotal area	Scrotal hernia	Surgical repair and castration
	●	Progressive enlargement behind jaw; may resonate when tapped	Tympany of the gutteral pouch	Surgery of faulty pouch opening
	●	Bulge in front of ear	Dentigerous cyst	Surgery to remove anomalous tooth
Low immunoglobulin (IgG) count	★	Less than 400 mg/dl	Failure of passive transfer (FPT); foal did not receive adequate immunity from colostrum or was unable to absorb IgG	Administer fresh/frozen colostrum if dam's colostrum is deficient and foal is less than 4 hours old; otherwise, plasma infusion
	◆	Greater than 400 mg/dl; low-risk environment	Partial failure of passive transfer	Foal probably adequately protected; but keep watching

	★	Less than 800 mg/dl; high-risk environment	Failure of passive transfer	Administer 200 mg/kg plasma; continue monitoring IgG level
Straining	●	Tail switching; meconium not passed (see also Colicky)	Simple constipation/retained meconium	Enema, fluids
	★	Distended abdomen, little or no urine produced, jaundiced membranes, toxicity, fever, progressive weakness	Ruptured bladder due to birth trauma or jerk on umbilical cord after delivery	Surgery to repair hole in bladder; drain urine from abdomen; fluids
Loose stools	◆	Mild diarrhea coinciding with dam's foal heat; foal remains bright	Transient, "9-day scours"	Gently clean foal's tail and buttock area with soapy water to prevent scalding of skin
	●	Dehydration, scalding of skin on buttocks, matting of tail	Noninfectious diarrhea (due to overeating, too-rich milk, eating manure, etc.)	Fluids, decreased/diluted rations; clean tail and buttocks as above
	★	Rapid dehydration, scalding, matting, fever, depression	Infectious diarrhea	Antibiotics, fluids; clean tail and buttocks regularly
Colicky	★	Colicky after ingesting first milk; enema ineffective	Closed colon or rectum; developmental error causes gut to end in blind pouch	Surgery: success may depend on length of missing part
	★	Rolling, thrashing, lying on back; fecal matter not passed	Severe constipation: fecal mass too large or too far forward for enema to be successful	"Blasting powder" (6 oz mineral oil, 3 oz milk of magnesia, 1 oz castor oil); fluids, sedation
	●	Lethargy, loss of appetite, diarrhea, teeth grinding, lying on back with feet in the air	Ulcer	Confirm with endoscopy; treat with cimetidine/ranitidine with sucralfate

(continued)

627

TABLE 16-1   What's Wrong with My Foal? A Keeper's Guide (*Continued*)

KEY

☐ During the perinatal period

▨ After the perinatal period

▧ Any time

◆ Generally not life-threatening; treat and watch for complications

● Variable: foals usually respond to prompt treatment, depending on severity

◀ Not life-threatening, but not curable

★ Red alert: life-threatening

■ Most often fatal

What you see	Looking closer		Probable diagnosis	What can be done
Profuse watery discharge at eyes	Blinking, avoidance of light; scratched cornea	◆	Inversion of the eyelid (entropion), dehydration; if uncorrected, can lead to blindness	Fluids; lubricate eye and lids gently; pull out eyelid as often as necessary (hourly); inject eyelid with saline and local anesthetic; surgery needed in persistent cases
Navel stump dripping urine	Wet, soiled, warm, swollen navel stump	●	"Leaky navel" (pervious urachus): failure of umbilical stump to close	Daily cauterization with silver nitrate or double strength tincture of iodine; some require surgery
Swollen joints	Joints hot, painful, lameness, fever, depression	★	"Joint ill" (septic arthritis) or bone infection (osteomyelitis); a progression of septicemia	Specific antibiotics; surgical draining; prognosis poor
Incoordination/ muscle weakness	Lack of nursing skill, delay in rising, aimless wandering or compulsive pacing, loss of maternal bond, depression, teeth grinding, "barking," seizures	★	Neonatal maladjustment syndrome (NMS)	Supportive therapy may include fluids, antibiotics, colostrum, foal milk replacer, medication to control seizures and protection from injuries

Signs		Disorder	Treatment
Head and body tremors progressively interfering with normal movements; stilted, "goose-stepping" front action	■	Cerebellar hypoplasia: genetic incompletion of cerebellum development. Diagnosed only in Arabians to date	No known treatment
Loss of appetite, progressive muscle weakness, muscle tremors causing foal's knees to quiver and give way	★	Shaker-foal syndrome (toxico-infectious botulism)	Prevent with botulism immunization; treat with antitoxin, muscle stimulants, calcium injection, penicillin, fluids
Sudden loss of muscle tone (cataplexy), "fainting," sudden sleeping spells	◆	Narcolepsy: neurological "sleep attacks"	Usually self-correcting at 1–2 weeks, up to 1 month of age
Incoordination, stiffness, gait abnormalities, "wobbler"	●	Cervical vertebral malformation (CVM): due to faulty growth of neck vertebra	Confirm with X-rays of neck; restricted diet, confinement
	★	Equine protozoal myeloencephalitis (EPM): spinal cord infection by one-celled parasites (protozoa)	Trimethoprim/sulfate
	■	Equine degenerative myeloencephalopathy (EDM): disintegration of the protective outer covering (myelin) of the spinal nerve fibers	No known treatment

SOURCE: *Modern Horse Breeding*

are often detected within minutes after birth, but they may be delayed as long as 2 hours. The barker syndrome usually is preceded by a rapid onset of signs—like jerking the head up and down in a strange fashion, aimless leg movements, colic, and muscle spasms of the limbs, body, neck, and head. These initial signs are followed by marked convulsions during which the foal may make a peculiar noise resembling the bark of a small dog.

Dummies and wanderers have less severe signs and are so-called because of apparent blindness and failure to respond to external stimuli. The dummy tends to stand or lie quietly in one place with a drowsy attitude. The wanderer moves about aimlessly, unconscious of its surroundings. If the barker survives the convulsions, it passes into the dummy or wanderer stage.

ORPHAN FOALS

Orphan foals are not difficult to raise if one has the time and patience and does not mind work and loss of sleep. Within 2 to 3 hours of birth, the foal must be fed. It is better to feed it as soon as possible. It should receive about 1 pint (0.47 liter) of colostrum, which can be freshly milked from another mare or which has been stored frozen. Follow the other standard procedures for foal care. Make arrangements for a steady supply of milk to the foal. Very seldom is a nurse mare available, but if so, the foal should be grafted to ("adopted" by) her. If no mare is available, the foal can be taught to suckle a goat. It is easy to train the goat to stand on a small platform while the foal suckles. The platform prevents the foal from standing on its knees while suckling. Goat milk is very similar to mare's milk and can be fed unaltered. Most orphan foals must be hand fed. A variety of formulas can be used. Milk substitutes such as Foal-Lac, Mare's Match Foal Milk Replacer, or milk replacers for dairy calves are excellent and easy to use. Cow's milk can be used but must be altered, because it is higher in fat and protein and lower in water and sugar. Therefore, dilute it with water ($\frac{1}{2}$ pint, or 0.24 liter, water to 2 pints, or 0.94 liter, whole milk), and add 1 ounce (28 g) of sugar and a tablespoon, or 14.3 ml, of saturated lime water. The following feeding schedule has been used successfully: during the first 2 days, the foal should be fed $\frac{1}{2}$ pint of formula (warmed to 100°F, or 37.7°C) at hourly intervals around the clock; for the next 5 days, it can be fed $\frac{1}{2}$ to 1 pint (0.24 to 0.47 liter) at 2-hour intervals. Therefore, the foal should be receiving about 8 to 9 pints (3.8 to 4.27 liters) each 24-hour period toward the end of the first week. Some foals may be able to take 10 to 12 pints (4.73 to 5.7 liters). Feed the formula in a bottle fitted with a lamb's nipple. At the end of the week or sooner, it can be trained to drink out of a bucket. Get the foal to lick the milk in the bucket by placing some milk on its lips. As soon as it starts to lick, it will start to drink.

An easier way to train an orphan foal is to let it go without milk for 4 to 6 hours so it is hungry. Mix a milk replacer in a bucket and enter the stall. Allow the foal to suckle one of your fingers and as it starts to suckle, lower your hand into the milk. After two or three attempts, the foal will usually start drinking the milk. The bucket is hung on the wall and the foal is left alone. Sufficient milk is given the foal each morning and night so that some remains in the bucket at the next feeding. It is not necessary to heat the milk, but the bucket should be cleaned at each feeding. This procedure has been used successfully to early wean (3 to 5 days of age) foals for other purposes.

Introduce the foal to a creep formula containing milk protein and a legume hay at the end of the first week. Foals will start eating it because they like to nibble on things. During the second week, feed the milk formula at 4-hour intervals; the foal should receive $1\frac{1}{2}$ to 2 pints (0.71 to 0.94 liter) at each feeding. Maintain the schedule during the third week. Intake may increase to 3 pints (1.42 liters) each feeding during the 3 weeks.

It is better to underfeed the foal than to overfeed. Overfeeding causes diarrhea. At the end of the first month, the foal can be fed twice daily and will consume about 4 pints (1.9 liters) each feeding. At this time, the foal should be receiving (daily) about 1 pint per 10 pounds (0.47 liter per 4.5 kg) of body weight. It should be eating about 3 to 4 pounds (1.4 to 1.8 kg) of hay and about 2 pounds (0.9 kg) of creep ration. When the foal is 6 weeks old, the amount of formula can be decreased to 2 pints (0.94 liter) per feeding. At 7 weeks, the formula intake can be limited to $1\frac{1}{2}$ pints (0.71 liter) per feeding, and the foal can be weaned when it is 8 weeks old. By this time, the foal will be eating 6 pounds (2.7 kg) of hay and an equal amount of creep ration.

WEANING

The stress of weaning can be reduced significantly if the foal is used to eating hay and grain. By the time it is 4 months old, it is receiving an insignificant proportion of its nutrient intake from the mare and can be weaned without a nutritional problem. If possible, wean two or more foals at the same time. A foal frets less if kept with a "buddy." Keep them in a box stall or paddock in which there is little chance of injury. Separate the mares and foals so that they are unable to see or hear each other. By the end of a week, the process should be completed.

Separate colts and fillies soon after they are 6 to 8 months of age. Puberty occurs as early as 10 months in both colts and fillies. Failure to separate them may result in an unwanted pregnancy.

The nutritional program at weaning is important (see Chapter 5).

TRAINING THE FOAL

Young foals should become accustomed to being handled if circumstances permit. They should be taught how to be led, to allow their feet to be handled, and to be groomed. This makes the horse manageable when serious training starts later in life.

If the mare is gentle, she may let people scratch the foal on the back and hindquarters while nursing. While handling the mare, take every opportunity to scratch and rub the foal. Foals that do not allow this must be caught and held. To catch the foal, crowd it against the mare or a wall. Hold it with one arm under its neck and grip the tail with the opposite hand (Figure 16-6). In this position, you can hold the foal safely or move it about. Holding the foal adjacent to the mare for a while usually calms it down. Then, after someone scratches and brushes it a few times while it is being held, it will not be afraid. It is important not to frighten the foal. As soon as it stands relaxed, place a halter on it so one person can groom it. As soon as it accepts its legs being groomed, pick them up and handle them. By gradually increasing the time the feet are held up, the feet can be cleaned with a hoof pick in a few days.

The foal should be taught to be led at an early age. There are several ways of doing so before the foal is weaned. One method is to encourage the foal (while being led) to follow its mare while she is being slowly led away. If the foal fights being led, have an assistant walk behind it to make it move forward. A butt rope can be used to encourage it to move forward (Figure 16-7). As soon as it will follow the mare, lead the foal in front of the mare, with her following behind. A few lessons and tugs on the butt rope are usually sufficient to train a foal to be led.

After a foal is weaned, it is more difficult to train to lead, because it is larger and stronger. A gentle foal can be taught by the use of a butt rope. If it is not very gentle, the foal can be taught by tying a large cotton rope around the throat latch with a bow-line knot, passing it through the halter ring, and tying the rope off about 6 feet (1.8 m) above the head. The rope should hang down about 6 to 8 inches (15.2 to 20.3 cm) below the level of normal head carriage. A foal soon learns that it must stand tied without pulling back. As soon as it stands quietly, it can be taught to lead very quickly. A rubber tire tube tied into the cotton rope teaches a foal not to pull back because it learns not to resist the tension. If the foal is tied to a stout post, tie the rope at the level of the withers and tie a piece of tire in the rope to prevent the neck from dislocating. The foal will vigorously fight being restrained, but it must remain tied until it no longer fights. At this time, it is advisable to "sack out" the weanling by rubbing a gunny sack or raincoat over it. As soon as it accepts the rubbing, slap the gunny sack or raincoat lightly all over its body until the weanling stands still and does not resist being tied. This type of training teaches the horse to accept being handled, not to be a halter puller, and not to spook.

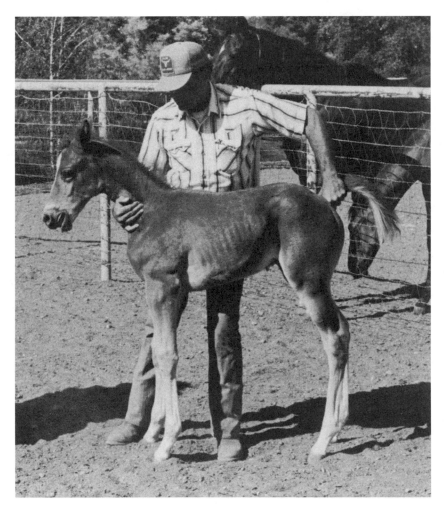

FIGURE 16-6   Restraint of a foal. Note mouth movement indicating submission. (Photo by W. Evans.)

An easier, less stressful, and safer method of training the young foal is imprint training. The advantages of imprint training include: bonding with imprint trainer so the foal is not afraid of a person; creating submissiveness by dependence, not by fear; desensitization to visual, auditory, tactile, and olfactory stimuli so that all body parts are desensitized to handling. The basic procedure for imprint training that the professional follows includes both desensitization and sensitization. The desensitization process includes rubbing the newborn foal with a towel to dry it off before it is able to get up. When the foal gets up, both the mare and the professional handle it so that it bonds with both. Next, the foal is rubbed over each body part until it relaxes and ignores the rubbing. Fingers are passed into the ear canals, the mouth, nostrils, and anus until the procedure is accepted. It usually takes 30

FIGURE 16-7   Butt rope used to teach a foal to lead. (Photo by W. Evans.)

to 100 repetitions for desensitization to occur. Next, electric clippers, crackling plastic, and other pieces of equipment such as whirling ropes and flopping flags are used to desensitize the foal. On the second day, everything is repeated to be sure that the desensitization was successful and to reinforce the acceptance. Each session is limited to 15 minutes, so several sessions each day may be necessary. The end result is that the foal will accept physical exam procedures, clippers, dogs, spray bottles, flapping objects, blankets, and saddling. Sensitization training is valuable for future performance training. The objective is opposite to desensitization in that the establishment of a conditioned response to specific stimuli is developed. One response is to move away from pressure. This is accomplished by putting pressure on the flank area with a finger. As soon as the foal moves, pressure is withdrawn. After a 20- to 30-second pause, the stimulus is applied again. After 3 to 5 sessions during the second and third day of age, the foal should readily respond. During the second day, the foal is taught to lead. Pulling on the halter to one side makes the foal step in the direction of its head to maintain balance. As the foal readily takes the step, the circle is increased and finally the foal always follows the pressure on the halter.

Considerable horse experience is required before attempting to imprint a foal. A videotape and book developed by Dr. R. M. Miller (see Bibliography) can be followed.

CONGENITAL DEFECTS IN FOALS

Congenital defects are abnormalities of structure or function present at birth. The defects are the result of disruptive events in fetal development that are genetic or environmental in origin. Many defects have no clearly established cause, while the causes of some are understood. At least 87 congenital defects have been reported for foals. Some common defects are noted below.

Malformations

Cleft palate and parrot mouth are defects of the mouth. Cleft palate is a fissure in the soft or soft and hard palates. It leads to secondary pneumonia due to inhalation of fluids into the lungs. Some can be surgically repaired. Parrot mouth is a malformation or underdevelopment of the lower jaw that hinders eating. It is believed to be caused by a dominant gene. Other dental deformities or malocclusions include lower or upper incisor teeth shifted forward but still making the lower jaw longer than the upper jaw (monkey mouth), and lower jaw much narrower than normal. These conditions require frequent "floating" of the malaligned teeth by a veterinarian to encourage correct development.

Atresia ani is an anus without an opening. Atresia coli exists when the colon ends in two blind ends. The foal develops colic shortly after birth and dies in a few days. Surgical correction is not successful because there is a lack of innervation to the area.

Interventricular septal defect is a hole or passageway between the ventricles (lower chamber) of the heart. It is the most common heart defect seen in young horses, and they usually die.

There are several eye defects as well. Complete, mature cataracts are the most common cause of blindness in young horses (the lens of the eye is opaque), but this can be surgically corrected. Iridal heterochromia is an abnormal coloration of the iris. Glass eye is nearly all-white iris (or combination of white, brown, and blue). It causes no problems for the horse.

Wobbles or equine incoordination may be inherited by a recessive process that is not understood. It causes ataxia of the rear legs. Wobblers are discussed in Chapter 2.

Umbilical hernia is an opening in the abdominal wall at the umbilicus. The hernia is present at birth or occurs within a few days. It usually corrects itself by 1 year of age. If it does not, it can be repaired surgically.

Scrotal hernia is similar to umbilical hernia except the gut protrudes through the inguinal canal into the scrotum. It also usually corrects itself.

Cryptorchidism is retention of the testicles in the inguinal canal or abdomen. It may be a unilateral or bilateral retention. The mode of inheritance is not understood.

Developmental Disorders

Developmental orthopedic diseases include noninfectious, nontraumatic conditions of the developing foal's skeletal system. Some of the conditions are rather mild conformational abnormalities that will spontaneously correct themselves as the foal develops. The more serious conditions lead to chronic lameness. A number of factors such as genetics, nutrition, and aberrations of growth have a role in developmental orthopedic diseases.

Generally, the disorders are classified as angular limb deformities, tendon problems, and osteochondroses. Angular limb deformities—crooked legs—may or may not spontaneously correct. Thus, it is important for the foal to be evaluated by an orthopedic specialist. Management of foals with these deformities may require exercise control, hoof trimming, and/or surgical intervention. Tendon problems at birth are common, and severe cases require treatment with special shoes for weak tendons and support bandages to encourage tight tendons to relax. Tendon contractures, which develop in yearling and 2-year-old horses, require careful evaluation and treatment. If the condition is treated early in development, prognosis is good; but if it progresses to the point where the fetlock knuckles forward, the prognosis is unpredictable.

Osteochondroses are a group of disorders that affect the skeleton of the young growing horse. Most often, the joint surfaces or the growth plates are affected. Osteochondritis dissecans occurs when a flap of joint cartilage becomes detached from the underlying bone. Subchondral bone cysts occur when the cartilage collapses into the underlying bone and is resorbed to form a cystic cavity. Juvenile osteoarthritis is advanced degenerative joint disease. Epiphysitis is similar to osteochondroses; the cartilage of the growth plates of the radius, tibia, and cannon bones is affected. It is characterized by enlarged and painful epiphyses. Adjustments in diet and exercise will normally lead to correction.

Incompatible Blood Groups

Neonatal isoerythrolysis (jaundice foal, isohemolytic icterus, hemolytic icterus, or NI) is a condition caused by incompatibility of blood groups. The incompatibility causes the destruction of the foal's red blood cells by serum antibodies absorbed from the colostrum. Horse blood contains factors that are inherited; if a horse fails to inherit one of the factors and receives the blood of another horse containing the factor, antibodies are formed against the factor. These antibodies destroy the red blood cells that contain the factor. When a mare that lacks one of the blood factors (usually A or Q system) is bred to a stallion that has the blood factor, the foal's blood type will be positive for the factor, because it inherits the factor from the stallion. Some of the foal's blood containing the factor passes to the mare through a faulty placenta. The mare has an antigenic response to the foal's blood and forms antibodies, which build up in the colostrum. The foal is born normal and becomes affected after it suckles and receives the colostrum. Antibodies in the colostrum are absorbed and destroy the foal's red blood cells. The foal becomes progressively anemic and dies within a few days unless treated with blood transfusions. During the first one or two pregnancies, the foal's blood sensitizes the mare's system, and subsequent pregnancies cause antibody formation. The absence of one or more of the blood factors does not occur very frequently, so the chances of the condition are not very great. During late pregnancy, the mare's blood can be tested for the presence of the antibodies.

After a mare produces one NI foal, she and the foal require special management during foaling to prevent the foal from receiving its dam's colostrum. Give the foal colostrum from another mare. Milk the mare by hand several times daily for 3 days. Feed the foal a milk formula or place it on a nurse mare until the fourth day. The foal must be muzzled and kept with the mare during this period to prevent being rejected by her after her milk becomes safe. After 3 days, the foal can be allowed to nurse the mare.

Mares bred to jacks (male donkeys) can become sensitized to blood group factors of asses. It is advisable to check all pregnant mare's serum or colostrum against the red blood cells of the jack to which she is bred.

Combined Immunodeficiency Disease

Combined immunodeficiency disease (CID) is a deficiency of the B- and T-lymphocytes found in Arabian foals. The T-lymphocytes are responsible for all cell-mediated immunity, and B-lymphocytes secrete antibodies. Because of the deficiency in the immune system, the foal dies by the time it is 5 months old, when the passive immunity is lost. CID is transmitted as an autosomal recessive genetic defect (Figure 16-8). Therefore, both the sire and dam of a CID foal carry the recessive gene. The condition has been found in Arabian and part-Arabian horses and occurs in about 2 to 3 percent of Arabian foals. It has been estimated that about 25 percent of Arabian horses are carriers. Death prior to 5 months is usually caused by an adenoviral infection in conjunction with secondary bacterial infection. Any young Arabian foal that dies should be tested for CID. The CID test offers the Arabian industry the opportunity to identify all carriers. Thus, over time, CID can be eliminated. Most important, CID carriers can be managed so that CID foals are not produced.

Other Immunity Failures

CID should not be confused with three other types of failures of the immune system. Agammaglobulinemia is a deficiency of the B-lymphocytes, but the T-lymphocytes are functional. Only one case involving a Thoroughbred foal

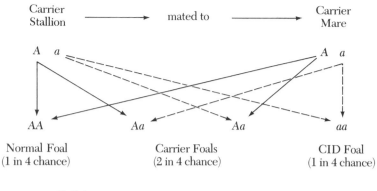

A = Normal allele
a = CID allele

FIGURE 16-8   Inheritance of combined immunodeficiency disease (CID).

has been described. Selective deficiency of IgM (specific immunoglobin) can occur and has been observed in Arabians, Thoroughbreds, and Quarter Horses. These foals may survive, but they are plagued with respiratory infections. A foal may fail to receive enough antibodies in the mare's colostrum to provide adequate immunity from diseases. It may have disease problems until its immune system becomes functional at 3 to 5 months of age. If given colostrum or a commercial immunoglobulin product at birth or protected with antibodies, it usually suffers few, if any, consequences. Commercial test kits are available to screen foals for inadequate immunoglobulin concentrations.

CHAPTER 17

Understanding Basic Genetics

Genetic principles are important to horse breeders because they are concerned about inheritance of coat color and lethal traits and about how to improve their horses for conformation and performance ability. Also, occasionally there are parentage disputes. Although our knowledge of the genetics of horses is incomplete, the basic principles used for genetic improvement of horses were developed by Mendel in the middle 1800s.

A gene map for horses is being constructed by several research groups, and will be useful to investigate the hereditary basis of behavior, performance, and diseases. Already geneticists are using the map to study the hereditary basis of muscle diseases like tying up, developmental bone diseases like osteochondrosisdessicans, and allergic diseases like culicoides hypersensitivity. As the methodology develops, geneticists will use it to gain insight to predispositions to a number of problems such as laminitis, immunity to diseases, and conformation defects. These studies should result in making better-informed decisions regarding management and treatment, and a better understanding of the contributions of genetics, environment, and chance to complex traits and diseases.

BASIC GENETICS

Genes and Chromosomes

Genetic material is passed from generation to generation in chromosomes, which are threadlike structures in the cell nucleus. Each chromosome contains a number of genes, which are DNA nucleotide sequences, and the location of a gene on a chromosome is called a locus. Genes are responsible for controlling body functions because they control the synthesis of all body proteins. Each member of a gene series is an allele; there is one allele at a locus on the chromosome. There may be several alleles for each gene, as is the case for some genes for coat color inheritance. Each equine species has a different number of chromosomes (Table 17-1). The horse has 64 chromosomes, in pairs; one chromosome from each pair is inherited from each parent. The chromosome number is reduced from 64 to 32 via meiosis, during the formation of the ovum or spermatozoan. During meiosis, a chromosome pair becomes entwined and exchanges chromosome material. The alleles are mixed randomly in the pair of chromosomes, and then the chromosome pair divides. Each germ cell receives one member of the pair of chromosomes. This prevents all the genes in a chromosome inherited from a parent from being passed intact to future generations. Therefore, each germ cell has a mixture of genes from the previous parents. Because of the mixing, the foal receives genes from all its grandparents. With the union of the ovum and spermatozoan (germ cells) at fertilization, the embryo receives 32 chromosomes from each germ cell so that it has 64 chromosomes in all its body cells.

Sex Determination

One pair of chromosomes, the sex chromosomes, determines the sex of the foal. In the female, the chromosomes are matched (same size) and called XX.

TABLE 17-1   Numbers of Chromosomes for Some Equine Species

Scientific name	Common name or names	Diploid no. of chromosomes
Equus caballus, przewalskii	Przewalski's horse	66
Equus caballus	Horse	64
Equus asinus	Donkey, ass	62
Equus hemionus onager	Asiatic wild ass	56
Equus hemionus	Transcapian wild ass	54
Equus kiang	Tibetan wild ass	52
Equus grevyi	Grevy's zebra	46
Equus burchelli boehmi	Grant's zebra	44
Equus zebra hartmannae	Hartmann's Mountain zebra	32

Therefore, during meiosis the mare's germ cells contain only the X chromosome. In males, the sex chromosomes are unmatched (unequal size) and are termed X and Y, with the Y chromosome being smaller than the X. During meiosis, half the sperm cells receive an X chromosome, and the other half receive a Y chromosome. Therefore, the male sperm cell determines the sex of the foal. Because of this situation and the unequal size of the X and Y chromosomes, a filly receives more genetic material from her sire than does a colt, and colts receive more genetic material from their dams than do fillies.

Hybrid Crosses

Hybrid crosses have been obtained among most equine species—horses, asses, and zebras. Although many crosses have been made, the most popular have been between the ass and the horse. The jackass mated to a horse mare produces a mule, and the stallion mated to the jenny produces a hinny. These two crosses produce superior, rugged work animals. The mule and the hinny are infertile. They have 63 chromosomes, because they received 32 from the horse and 31 from the donkey. During meiosis, the chromosomes are not in pairs; and as their number is halved, the sex cells usually end up without a complete set. This unbalanced condition does not allow the sex cells to function, resulting in sterility.

Genetic Infertility

Chromosomal abnormalities occur in the horse and can cause infertility. These abnormalities are verified by karyotyping, a process in which the chromosomes are spread out, viewed with a microscope, and counted. In the mare, the abnormalities usually cause abortions or the development of an abnormal foal. The foal may be phenotypically normal but may fail to reproduce after reaching maturity. Some of these abnormalities involve the sex chromosomes. The most common cases involve mares that failed to receive one X chromosome (XO genotype: 63,X gonadal dysgenesis). Their ovaries are small and firm and do not have germ cells. The result is infertility. Other causes of infertility include the failure to receive any sex chromosomes. This condition results from a failure of the X and Y chromosomes to separate out during meiosis, so one germ cell does not receive sex chromosomes. The same condition can produce a horse with an extra sex chromosome (XXX genotype; 65,XXX). Some mares having 63,X/64,XX gonadal dysgenesis have two cell lines. One line is normal and the other line is missing a sex chromosome. They rarely have foals. Some infertile mares have a male karotype (64,XY sex reversal). In males, much less is known about genetic fertility. There have been reports of karotypes of 65,XXY, XX male syndrome and XX/XY chimerism (cells within a tissue having different chromosomes—stallion sperm having XX when it should be all XY).

Parentage Disputes

Most of the major breed registries require that stallions standing at stud or all breeding animals be blood typed and/or have DNA profile on record. Other registries require that stallions used in an AI program be blood typed. The stallion, donor mare, recipient mare, and resulting foal in an embryo transfer program have to be blood typed.

At least seven blood antigen systems are responsible for 34 blood factors that characterize the red blood cell membrane of horses. Each system has alleles that are codominant (each allele causes production of a specific antigen), except for one recessive gene (the dominant allele does not allow production of the antigen specific for recessive alleles; see Table 17-2). In addition to the antigen systems, 13 loci control the formation of blood proteins (see Table 17-3). At each of these loci, there are codominant alleles, or each allele causes production of a specific protein. Both the blood antigens and the proteins can be used to settle parentage disputes. The tests are based on the exclusion principle. The blood antigens and proteins in the foal must come from the stallion and mare. If the foal has one or more alleles in the antigen system or blood proteins that are not present in the mare, they must be inherited from the stallion. All stallions that do not have the antigen(s) or protein(s) that are present in the foal and absent in the mare can be excluded as the sire. A stallion cannot be proven to be the sire because there are other stallions with the same blood type that could possibly be the sire. There are no tests to prove parentage. A typical example of a questionable parentage and the results of the blood-type tests are presented in Table 17-4. Parentage questions also occur when two mares foal in the same paddock or pasture and there is a possibility that they switched foals. Blood typing may resolve the parentage question before the owner applies for a foal's registration certificate.

TABLE 17-2   Genetic Loci That Control Blood Antigen Systems Recognized by the International Society for Animal Genetics

Blood antigen locus symbol	Factors	Known alleles
A	a, b, c, d, e, f, g	A^a, A^{adf}, A^{adg}, A^{abdf}, A^{abdg}, A^b, A^{bc}, A^{bce}, A^c, A^{ce}, A^e, A^-
C	a	C^a, C^-
D	a, b, c, d, e, f, g,	D^{adl}, D^{adllnr}, D^{adllr}, D^{bcmq}, D^{cefgmq}, $D^{cegimnq}$ D^{cfgkm}
	h, i, k, l, m, n, o,	D^{cfmqr}, D^{cgm}, D^{cgmp}, D^{cgmq}, D^{cgmqr}, D^{cgmr}, D^{deklrr}
	p, q, r	D^{deloq}, D^{delq}, D^{dfklr}, D^{dghmp}, D^{dghmq}, D^{dghmqr}, D^{dkl}, D^{dlnq}, D^{dlnqr}, D^{dlqr} D^q, D^-
K	a	K^a, K^-
P	a, b, c, d	P^a, P^{ac}, P^{acd}, P^{ad}, P^b, P^{bd}, P^d, P^-
Q	a, b, c	Q^{abc}, Q^{ac}, Q^a, Q^b, Q^c, Q^-
U	a	U^a, U^-

TABLE 17-3   Genetic Systems of Blood Proteins Used For Parentage Verification

System	Locus symbol	Recognized alleles
A1B glycoprotein	A1B	F, K, S
Albumin	ALB	A, B, I
Acid phosphatase	AP	F, S
Carbonic anhydrase	CA	E, F, I, L, O, S
Catalase	CAT	F, S
NADH-diaphorase	DIA	F, S
Carboxylesterase	ES	F, G, H, I, L, M, N, O, R, S
Group-specific component	GC	F, S
Glucose phosphate isomerase	GPI	F, I, L, S
Hemoglobin-α	HBA	A, AII, BI, BII, C, N, V
Peptidase A	PEPA	F, S
6-Phosphogluconate dehydrogenase	PGD	D, F, S
Phosphoglucomutase	PGM	F, S, V
Protease inhibitor	PI	F, G, H, I, J, K, L, L_2, N, O, P, Q, R, S, T, U, V, W, Z
Plasminogen	PLG	1, 2
Transferrin	TF	D, D_2, E, F_1, F_2, F_3, G, H_1, H_2, J, M, O, R

It is estimated that 97 percent of parentage disputes can be solved with blood-typing. However, by using DNA profiling or DNA fingerprinting, the accuracy increases to almost 100 percent. This technology utilizes sections of chromosomes called microsatellite markers, sections of DNA where the nucleic acids are arranged in a repetitive pattern. The location of the markers is the same in all horses, but the number of repeats varies with the individual horse. Another advantage is that almost any tissue can be used because all cells have the same DNA profile. Since DNA is stable, samples can be obtained long after a horse has died.

TABLE 17-4   Typical Example of Questionable Parentage, with Results of Blood-Type Tests

	Blood group systems								
Animal	A	C	D	K	P	Q	U	Alb	Pl
Dam	A^a	C^a	D^{dlnqr}	K^-	P^a	Q^{ac}	U^-	AB	LT
Foal	A^a/A^{adg}	C^a	$D^{dlnqr}D^{dkl}$	K^-	P^-	$Q^{ac}Q^a$	U^-	AB	LT
Stallion 1	A^a	C^a	D^-	K^-	P^-	Q^b	U^-	B	PQ
Stallion 2	A^{adg}	C^a	D^{dkl}	K^-	P^-	Q^a	U^-	A	LK
Stallion 3	A^a/A^{adf}	C^a	D^{deloq}	K^a	P^-	Q^b	U^-	B	NO

The foal possesses A^{adg}, D^{dkl}, and Q^a, which must have been inherited from the sire. Stallions 1 and 3 lack A^{adg}, D^{dkl}, and Q^a and are excluded as possible sires. Stallion 2 possesses all the critical blood factors in the foal's blood type and qualifies as a sire.

Coat Color Inheritance

The interest in coat color inheritance is shared by most horsepeople, and most have a favorite color pattern. In fact, several registries based on particular coat colors have been formed over the years. In most instances, the knowledge of coat color inheritance is sufficient to formulate certain guidelines for breeding horses with specific color patterns.

The inheritance of coat color in horses is very complex and is not completely understood. It is difficult to obtain the same color description for the same coat color pattern from all investigators, genetic trials are expensive, and the number of genes involved is large. Therefore, there are several theories on coat color inheritance. One of the more popular and current theories is discussed below.

The basic color pattern of horses is believed to be controlled by a limited number of genes (Table 17-5). Several other loci may modify the basic color pattern.

TABLE 17-5 Coat Colors (Phenotypes) for Genotypes

Bay	E-	A-	CC	dd
Buckskin Dun	E-	A-	CC	D-
Buckskin	E-	A-	Ccr	dd
Buckskin Dun	E-	A-	Ccr	D-
Perlino	E-	A-	crcr	dd
Perlino	E-	A-	crcr	D-
Black	E-	aa	CC	dd
Grulla	E-	aa	CC	D-
Black	E-	aa	Ccr	dd
Grulla	E-	aa	Ccr	D-
Perlino	E-	aa	crcr	dd
Perlino	E-	aa	crcr	D-
Red (sorrel/chestnut)	ee	A-	CC	dd
Red Dun	ee	A-	CC	D-
Palomino	ee	A-	Ccr	dd
Red Dun	ee	A-	Ccr	D-
Cremello	ee	A-	crcr	dd
Cremello	ee	A-	crcr	D-
Red (sorrel/chestnut)	ee	aa	CC	dd
Red Dun	ee	aa	CC	D-
Palomino	ee	aa	Ccr	dd
Red Dun	ee	aa	Ccr	D-
Cremello	ee	aa	crcr	dd
Cremello	ee	aa	crcr	D-

Note: White horse (*Ww*) genes in combination with all genotypes will be a white horse. Gray and/or roan genotypes in combination with genotypes in the table will have gray and/or roan patterns superimposed on basic coat color patterns (not visible in cremello and perlino patterns). Silver dapple (*Z-*), tobiano, overo, and leopard patterns superimposed on the genotypes in the table will result in their respective pattern superimposed on the coat color patterns.

The first step in the development of color is controlled by the alleles of the color gene (C). There are three alleles: C^C, C^c, C^{cr}. If the dominant gene (C^C) or the dilution gene (C^{cr}) is present, the hair coat, eyes, and skin will be pigmented. Any horse that is homozygous recessive (C^cC^c) would be true albino. It would have no pigment in the hair, eyes, or skin regardless of the other genes present for coat color. There are no true albino horses. Apparently, the homozygous recessive genotype (C^cC^c) is lethal in utero or the c gene does not exist. Several types of horses are classified as albinos by horsepeople, but they are not true albinos. They are white horses resulting from the action of the white gene (W) or from the C^{cr} allele. The C^{cr} allele causes the dilution of black hair to red or light brown hair. The C^{cr} allele is incompletely dominant with the allele (C^C), so both genes exert their effect. The effects of the C^{cr} gene will be discussed in the section on dilution.

There are two basic colors of horses: black (dark pigment, black or brown), due to expression of eumelanin; and red (light pigment, red or yellow), expressed by pheomelanin. Genes produce coat color by causing a switch to or from dark and light pigments, and by the presence, shape, arrangement, and number of pigment granules. At the E (extension) locus, the dominant allele (E^E) causes the production of black pigment in the hair, eyes, and skin. The recessive allele (E^e), when it is homozygous, allows the production of black pigment in the skin but not the hair. Hair appears red in response to the ee genotype, varying in shades from liver chestnut to dark chestnut to chestnut to sorrel. Control of the shades is unknown. Thercfore, $E^E E^E$ or $E^E E^e$ genotypes will have some black hair and black skin and E^eE^e genotype will have some shade of red hair and black skin. A third allele, E^D, has been postulated to increase the density of the black pigment. It is dominant to the E and e alleles and produces the so-called dominant black or jet black coat that does not fade in sunlight. Most black horses' coats will fade in the sun, especially around the muzzle and flanks, below the eyes, and on the tips of the ears. Hair appears to be brown in these areas. A postulated allele, A^B, may have a role in the chestnut series.

There is a DNA test to detect the recessive E^e allele. Thus, one can determine if the horse is homozygous for black and can only pass on the E^E allele, or if it is heterozygous, E^EE^e, and can pass on the red pigment gene.

The A locus controls the distribution pattern of eumelanin. The dominant allele, A^A, is called the agouti or bay pattern gene. It affects the distribution of black hairs by allowing them in the mane and tail and on the legs, nose, and ears. These peripheral parts of the body are referred to as "the points." The hair on the main part of the body is reddish in color but the skin is black, so the overall effect is the bay color pattern. Various shades of bay range from dark to mahogany to blood to copper to light bay. All bay horses have the allele A^A in combination with $E^E E^E$ or $E^E E^e$. The recessive allele, when homozygous (A^aA^a), allows for the uniform distribution of black hair over the body to produce the uniform black horse.

The A locus does not affect the distribution of red pigment in red E^eE^e genotype horses. Therefore, E^eE^e is epistatic to the A locus. Thus, one cannot determine which allele of A that a red-colored horse is carrying.

There are a couple of other alleles that have been hypothesized. The allele A^t has been postulated to be a mutation of allele A that causes the seal brown color in black horses. Allele A^+ may be the "wild bay pattern" gene and has been postulated to cause zebra striping (dark spinal stripe, dark vertical bar on each shoulder, and horizontal bars on the legs).

The interactions of the A and E loci are important as the base of all horse colors. Other genes are epistatic to these two loci or modify their actions.

"Dilution Genes"

The effects of dilution genes on the basic coat color patterns are very speculative, and there is little definite evidence to support the current theories. One theory is that two loci have alleles that dilute the basic patterns. At one locus, the dominant dilution allele is D^D and the recessive is D^d. The homozygous recessive, D^dD^d, allows a normal color pattern. The D^D allele in the heterozygous (D^DD^d) or homozygous (D^DD^D) condition causes the dilution of all colors on the body, but not on the points to form the dun coat color pattern. Black color patterns are diluted to produce the buckskin dun, grulla, mouse, or smoky black color. Red color patterns become pinkish-red with darkened points to produce the clay bank dun or red dun. The homozygous condition does not cause further dilution of the color patterns. A dorsal stripe, shoulder patch, and leg barring are usually associated with D^DD^D or D^DD^d.

The C^{cr} allele at the C locus causes the dilution of red pigment but not black pigment. It is partially dominant (one allele has one effect, whereas the homozygous condition has a different effect). It is referred to as the palomino gene. When heterozygous (C^cC^{cr}), the bay pattern (A^A—E^E—genotype) becomes characterized by a yellow body and black mane and tail ("buckskin" pattern). Chestnut and sorrel horses (E^eE^e genotype) would become palominos. When homozygous ($C^{cr}C^{cr}$), the red-pigmented horses are diluted to cremellos, and the bay pattern horses are diluted to perlinos. Cremellos and perlinos are white and may not always be distinguished. A DNA test can be used to determine if the horse is carrying allele E^e for red color. If it is not carrying the E^E allele, it is a cremello. If an E^E allele is detected, the horse is a perlino.

A third loci is referred to as silver dapple and is the result of the dominant gene Z^Z. The presence of the Z^Z in horses in North America is rare. When present, the Z^Z gene dilutes black body color to a chocolate or black-chocolate color with dapples. The mane and tail are diluted to silver gray or flaxen. Bay horses are diluted to a chestnut with silver gray mane and tail but they retain dark points. Horses of the E^eE^e genotype have a silver mane and tail but the body hairs are not affected.

The champagne locus is responsible for a group of colors. Allele Ch^C is dominant and dilutes black to brown, and red to yellow. Recessive allele Ch^c when homozygous has no effect. Thus, black horses become champagne (brown), bays become "amber champagne," chestnuts become "gold champagne," and palominos become "ivory champagne." The result of the Ch^C with colors other than dark colors are not well documented.

Brindle is a rare horse color characterized by vertical black stripes on any background color of the body and has no effect on dark points. The gene is dominant.

The pangar's gene is dominant and causes pale red or yellowish areas on the lower belly, flanks, behind the elbows, inside the legs, on the muzzle, and over the eyes. When present in the black horse, this gene produces the seal brown horse and dilutes chestnut to sorrel.

Modifying Genes

Several genes modify the basic coat color pattern. These genes are usually codominant to the basic coat color genes just described. Some of the modifying genes control the presence or absence of white on the face and legs.

The graying gene (G) is epistatic (masks the effect of other genes) to all other coat color genes except the W gene and is responsible for a progressive silvering of the coat. The foal is born with its basic coat color pattern. After the first hair coat is shed, white hairs start to appear. As the horse gets older, the number of white hairs increases. Some horses become gray faster and are white by the time they are old. Some never get white, but remain gray because they are turning gray slowly. The homozygous condition $(G^G G^G)$ may cause a faster rate of graying. The mane and tail may or may not become gray. Black horses with the gray gene are born black. While there is still a larger portion of black hairs, the color pattern is called an "iron" or "steel" gray. After there is a larger proportion of white hairs, the color pattern is simply referred to as gray. Bay horses with the gray pattern are called "red grays," and chestnuts with gray pattern are called "chestnut grays."

Gray horses can always be distinguished from white horses because the skin of gray horses contains black pigment. However, one must be careful not to confuse the roan gene (Rn) with the gray gene (G). The Rn gene is a simple dominant gene that causes a mixture of white and colored hairs. The white hairs are present and scattered throughout the hair coat at birth. The pattern does not change. If the white hairs are mixed with black hairs, the coat color is called "blue roan." The strawberry roan is a sorrel or chestnut color with the white hairs. A red roan is a bay with white hairs.

The homozygous dominant $(Rn^{Rn} Rn^{Rn})$ is believed to be lethal while the fetus is in utero. If so, when roans are mated to roans, the fertility rate should not exceed 75 percent, and 66.6 percent of the foals born will be roan. However, homozygous roan stallions have been identified. Other genes may control the amount of white in the coat, because it varies from horse to horse.

Breeders that are selecting for coat color patterns such as Appaloosa, paint, pinto, and palomino should avoid breeding animals that have the roan and/or gray genes. Their presence detracts from the desired color pattern. The gray gene causes the pattern to fade, and both genes cause the pattern to be without sharp definition.

The white gene (W) is epistatic to all other coat color genes. Therefore, the presence of the dominant allele causes the horse to be white. The homozygote (W^WW^W) is lethal at an early stage of pregnancy, because no true-breeding white horses have been reported. Mating white horses results in two *Ww* white foals and one *ww* nonwhite foal. White horses are not albinos, because their eyes are pigmented. These white horses are not to be confused with the perlino and cremello horses resulting from the $C^{cr}C^{cr}$ genotype. The true white horse (W^WW^w) has a much whiter coat than the off-white color of perlinos and cremellos.

A progressive silvering gene (*Sl*) has been postulated to cause a silvering effect ranging from a few white hairs to a completely white horse.

Shetland ponies have a dominant silvering gene (*S*) that causes a silver dapple color and a white mane and tail. The homozygote (S^SS^S) may have more white hairs than the heterozygote (S^SS^s). If the pony has both the S^S and G^G genes, it will turn almost white within 1 to 2 years.

One of two possible genotypes is responsible for paint and pinto horses. The tobiano pattern is white spotting that crosses over the top of the horse and extends downward. It is caused by the dominant allele at the *To* locus. The homozygote ($To^{To}To^{To}$) breeds true for the tobiano pattern. When mating a heterozygote ($To^{To}To^{to}$) to a solid-color horse, one-half of the foals should have the tobiano patterns. When one solid-colored foal is sired by a stallion or produced by a mare, the parents are proven to be heterozygotes. A genetic marker has been linked to the tobiano gene; therefore, tobiano horses can be tested to determine if they are homozygous or heterozygous. The overo "frame pattern" was once thought to be caused by the homozygous recessive genotype (O^oO^o) because the overo pattern occasionally crops up when two non-overo horses are bred. Recent evidence indicates it is more complicated and due to a dominant gene, O^OO^O. These "cropouts" produce 50 percent overos and 50 percent solid-color horses when bred to solid-color horses. The overo pattern is characterized by white that crosses under the belly and extends upward without crossing over the center line of the back. The white may also occur on the neck and flank as separate areas or merged with white under the belly. Typically, the edges of the white are a jagged pattern and at least one leg is solid colored. Head markings are usually bald-, apron-, or bonnet-faced. When some overo horses are mated and a foal with excessive white is produced, it may have *atresia coli* (a colon that ends in two blind ends and lacks nerve ganglia to the area). These foals have been found to have two copies of the mutated overo gene that is lethal when homozygous. The lethal white overo gene (*LWO*) can be detected by a new DNA test. It is advisable to have overo horses tested for the *LWO* gene prior to using them in a breeding program. If the horse has an *LWO* gene, it usually is advisable that it not be bred to another horse having an *LWO* gene. The amount of white for both patterns is probably controlled by several genes. When the tobiano and overo color patterns are on a black horse, it is called a "piebald," and when on a brown horse it is called a "skewbald."

More than one locus may be involved with the overo color pattern. Other overo patterns include the sabino and splashed-white patterns. Sabino pattern resulting from the Sb^S (dominant gene) is characterized by four white socks, a white belly and face, white on the insides of the stifles, and either the edges of the markings or the whole body will have a lot of roan coloring. Splashed-white horses generally have a continuous pattern of white on all four legs, chest, and completely over the head. The gene, Spl^S, is also dominant.

The inheritance of the Appaloosa color patterns is not very well understood. One hypothesis is that the dominant gene (*Ap*) must be present for the appaloosa pattern to be expressed. The pattern may be a white blanket extending over the hindquarters, or a combination of a blanket with dark spots. The gene *wb* is necessary for the blanket, and the gene *sp* is necessary for the dark spots in the blanket. Both genes are sex-influenced, because males may be homozygous or heterozygous for each gene. Mares must be homozygous for the pattern to be expressed. The amount of white and size of the blanket as well as the characteristics of the spots are determined by the modifier gene.

Based on the preceding hypothesis, the following genotypes may result in the corresponding phenotypes:

1　*Ap—wbwb spsp* results in blanket with spots in male and female.

2　*Ap—wbwb Spsp* results in blanket with no spots in female and blanket with spots in male.

3　*Ap—WbWb spsp* results in no blanket with spots in female and blanket with spots in male.

4　*Ap—WbWb Spsp* results in no blanket with spots in female and blanket with spots in male.

The leopard pattern, white with dark spots over the entire or most of the body (Figure 17-1), may be controlled by a dominant gene, *Lp*. Minor gene modifiers may explain the amount of white on the body.

Appaloosa horses also have particolored skin around the nostrils, nose, and anus. This is apparently caused by a dominant gene (*M*). The sclera around the eye is white and more exposed than on non-Appaloosa horses, giving the impression of a white ring around the eye. The hooves have vertical light and dark stripes. A sparse mane and tail are sometimes present. An Appaloosa horse always has one or more of these characteristics. If the color pattern is absent, the horse may still show these minor characteristics.

The basic coat color pattern of horses is also modified by genes that control the expression of white on the face and legs. Very little is known about the genes controlling the expression of white on the face and legs. A gene (*F*) has been proposed, and the dominant F^F is for solid color of the face and legs. The homozygous F^fF^f allows varying degrees of white on the face and legs. The amount of white on the face may be controlled by at least four modifying genes. A white spot on the chin is the recessive genotype, *chch*. The genes for

FIGURE 17-1   D-R Joker's Playboy, an Appaloosa stallion, and one of his leopard foals. (Courtesy L. Roberts.)

star (*st*), stripe (*sr*), and snip (*sn*) may be dominant or recessive. Genes controlling the white stocking effect are not understood. One theory is that a gene (*Pl*) is for white stockings. It is known that the spots located in the white above the coronary band are dominant.

Curly Hair

The hair on the body and tail can be curly. A recessive genotype is said to result in the kink found in the tail of many Appaloosas. The curly coat of horses in the Buckskin registry is caused by a homozygous recessive (*ctct*). The hair is in small curls over the entire body of the horse. In the Bashkir curly breed, the curly hair is believed to be inherited from either a dominant gene (CrD^C) in some horses or a recessive gene (CrR^C) in others.

Lethal Genes and Genetic Diseases

There are a number of lethal genes that result in embryonic death or death of a foal shortly after birth. The inheritance of the white (*W*), overo (*O*), and roan (*Rn*) genes were discussed in the previous section. Combined immuno-deficiency disease is discussed in Chapter 16. Hemophilia, aniridia (absence of iris in the eye), cerebellar abiotrophy, multiple exostosis (benign tumors at sites of active bone growth), epitheliogenesis imperfecta (absence of skin and hair below a knee), and collagen defect are known to occur in horses.

Hyperkalemic periodic paralysis (HYPP) is a dominant heritable condition characterized by intermittent episodes of muscle tremors, followed by weakness and/or collapse, and may result in sudden death due to paralysis of muscles in the upper respiratory tract or the heart. Some attacks are very mild and only skin rippling or localized muscle twitching is observed. Because of the various forms of the disease, however, it frequently is confused with "tying up syndrome," colic, respiratory problems, and seizures. The onset of HYPP is unpredictable but often follows stimuli such as exercise, transport, anxiety, or eating, or can occur for no apparent reason. Duration of the episodes is from 15 to 60 minutes. The condition is caused by a muscle-membrane defect and is associated with a high blood potassium concentration during an episode. It can be diagnosed by a DNA blood test and can be controlled in some affected horses by diet and, in most, by medication. Since it is caused by an autosomal dominant gene, the condition can be eliminated from a familial line of horses. It is known to occur in the descendants of one Quarter Horse stallion, Impressive.

BREEDING SUPERIOR HORSES

There are two general types of inheritance, qualitative and quantitative. In qualitative inheritance, the phenotype (physical appearance and attributes) is controlled by one or a few pairs of genes; phenotypic differences are therefore easy to distinguish. In quantitative inheritance, the phenotype is controlled by many pairs of genes; one phenotype thus tends to blend into the next one so that there is no easily recognizable, clear-cut distinction among phenotypes.

In traits affected by qualitative gene action, there are three primary types of gene action that affect the trait: dominance, codominance, and partial dominance. Dominance is defined as the ability to mask or cover up its recessive allele. Codominance in gene action results in an intermediate state between the two parents. Partial dominance also results in an intermediate state between parents, but not necessarily an exact intermediate state. The dilution gene in coat color inheritance is an example.

Most traits are influenced by quantitative gene action. For example, there is no single gene that determines the speed at which a horse can run. Instead, multiple genes are involved.

When breeding superior horses, environmental factors are involved in how well a horse performs. Training and nutrition are significant environmental factors.

Qualitative Inheritance

In any breeding program, horsepeople try to improve their horses by eliminating easily recognizable undesirable traits (phenotypes). The dominant and recessive genotype causing the phenotype may be selected to improve horses, or the breeder may choose to eliminate them. Selection for or against a dominant gene is easy because the phenotype allows recognition of the genotype. The phenotype is recognized, and the individual is kept or sold. The major difficulty in a breeding program is eliminating unwanted *recessive* genes. Animals with the recessive allele in combination with a dominant allele are termed "carrier animals," and the phenotype does not express the genotype (that is, the breeder does not know the recessive allele is present). The procedures used to detect carriers require time, effort, and money. The simplest method is to recognize and eliminate all animals that have both recessive genes (homozygous recessive); however, progress by this method is slow and never completely eliminates all carriers. For example, if the frequency of the undesirable recessive gene in the population is 0.25 (one of every four is the recessive allele), the frequency will be reduced to 0.07 after 10 generations. The generation interval in horses is 4 to 5 years; therefore, elimination would take 40 to 50 years.

The rate of progress by other methods is faster, but requires that the stallion or mare be tested. If a stallion is bred to a group of mares and one foal is produced that is homozygous recessive for the unwanted gene, the stallion is proven to carry the gene. A quick way to detect a carrier stallion is to breed him to 4 mares that are homozygous for the unwanted gene. If the foals are normal, the probability that the stallion is not a carrier is 94 percent. If 8 mares are bred without siring a homozygous recessive foal, the probability is about 100 percent that he is not a carrier. If the mares used in the test program are known carriers, more matings are needed. When 8 mares do not produce a homozygous recessive foal, the probability that the sire is not a carrier is 90 percent. When bred to 20 carrier mares without producing an undesirable foal, the probability of his not being a carrier is essentially 100 percent. However, there is always a slim chance that the stallion could be a carrier.

To determine if a mare is a carrier, she must be bred to known carriers or homozygous recessive stallions. Because the number of foals she must produce is the same as the number a stallion must sire, it is not feasible to test mares unless the embryo transfer technique is used.

To detect all the unwanted recessive genes that a stallion carries, he is bred to his own daughters. It requires 20 daughters to reach a 93 percent probability for each recessive gene, and he would have to be bred to 50 daughters to obtain almost a 100 percent probability. This would be a time-consuming and costly effort requiring at least 4 years if the mares are bred in one year and foal the next, and if the fillies are bred when they are 2 years old and foaled the next year. To obtain 50 fillies to breed, the stallion would have to initially breed about 125 mares, assuming an 80 percent foal crop, of which 50 percent were fillies.

Use of new technologies to develop tests based on DNA to recognize alleles will allow much faster progress in eliminating unwanted genes. Testing for combined immunodeficiency disease (CID) is an example of this technology.

Quantitative Inheritance

Quantitative traits are difficult to recognize, so a deliberate effort must be made to measure quantitative traits. Body weights are measured in pounds, pulling power is measured by the load the horse can pull, and speed is measured by time to race a given distance. After the measurements are made, superior animals may be identified. To identify a superior animal for a quantitative trait, one must know the average value and the variation of the horse population for that trait. The standard deviation describes the variation of a trait about the average for that trait. A standard deviation for a trait of a population is calculated as follows: find the deviation (difference) between the average for the population and each individual value, square each deviation, add all the squared deviations, divide the sum of the squared deviations by 1 less than the number of individuals, and take the square root. In a normal population, 68 percent of all the values should fall in the range of the average ±1 standard deviation. About 95 percent of all individuals are included in the range of the average ±2 standard deviations. A horse would be superior to 95 percent of the general population if its value for the trait were greater than the value of the average ±2 standard deviations. If a smaller value for the trait is desired, the horse's value would be less than the average ±2 standard deviations.

Each individual has a genetic limit for each trait, and this limit is set at fertilization. Rarely does an individual reach its genetic potential, because environmental factors influence performance. To eliminate environmental influence from performance ability, heritability estimates have been made for some traits. Heritability estimates are expressed in percentages, some examples of which are given in Table 17-6. The heritability estimates for speed range from 25 to 50 percent. For an actual value of 47 percent, that percent of the variability in speed is probably caused by heredity and 53 percent of the variability is caused by environmental influences. Low heritability estimates indicate that most of the variability is caused by the environment; that is, by training, feeding, care, and so on. Therefore, a high heritability estimate indicates to the breeder that considerable genetic progress can be made in improving a trait by mating the best to the best. A low heritability estimate means that attention should be paid to environmental influences to obtain good performances, and that not much progress can be made in improving the trait by a carefully planned breeding program.

TABLE 17-6   Heritability Estimates for Some Traits

Trait	Heritability
Speed	0.25–0.50
Wither height	0.25–0.60
Body weight	0.25–0.30
Body length	0.25
Breast circumference	0.34
Cannon bone circumference	0.19
Pulling power	0.25
Walking speed	0.40
Trotting speed	0.40
Points for movement	0.40
Points for temperament	0.25
Cow sense	0.19
Jumping	0.18
Three-day eventing	0.19
Dressage	0.17
Conformation characteristics	Medium to high
Reproductive traits	Low

Locating Animals with Superior Genotypes

The location of horses with superior genotypes depends on one's ability to eliminate or minimize environmental influences on performance. The environmental influence can never be eliminated, but it can be minimized by the examination of accurate performance records. Statistical services for some breed associations provide extensive performance records. Some records attempt to eliminate environmental influences, such as racetrack and condition of track for the race. Show ring performance records for horses shown under several different judges eliminate some environmental variation. These records may be most important for the horse being considered; with older animals, the progeny record is most important. If the horse is very young, the pedigree and appearance of the individual may be the most important. Performance records of close relatives are important, because superior breeding animals usually come from superior families. Selection is to increase the frequency of desirable genes and to increase the homozygosity of desirable gene pairs.

Linebreeding and Inbreeding Relationships

Many successful long-term horse breeding programs have used extensive culling and the breeding of closely related individuals (inbreeding), or of individuals with a common ancestor (linebreeding). Inbreeding or linebreeding raises the percentage of genes inherited from the common ancestor. For successful line-breeding or inbreeding, the common ancestor must be genetically superior.

Inbreeding increases the homozygosity of genes. There is an increased number of dominant and recessive pairs of genes. Inbreeding is accomplished by the mating of closely related individuals. The percentage of inbreeding is an estimate of the increased homozygosity of genes in the offspring as compared to the noninbred population (Table 17-7). There are advantages and disadvantages of the increased homozygosity. When inbreeding is accompanied by selection, individuals that are homozygous for desired traits are selected and used as breeding animals. They are prepotent because they pass desirable genes to the next generation. Their offspring usually resemble the prepotent parent more than the other parent. The disadvantage is that inbreeding uncovers undesirable recessive genes if they are present in the population. Homozygous recessive genes are expressed phenotypically.

There are phenotypic effects of inbreeding. Genetic defects are seen, so one must constantly be aware of this possibility. The thriftiness and vigor of the animals are usually reduced; the less vigor the animal has, the more undesirable homozygous recessive genes it probably possesses. Horses that maintain vigor probably have an increased number of heterozygous or homozygous dominant genes that cover up or mask the detrimental recessive allele. Because of the reduced vigor, they may not look as good as the noninbred population, but one must not forget that the genetically superior ones produce better offspring. Therefore, the inbreeding must have enough animals involved to be able to select a sufficient number of desirable animals and be able to cull the undesirable animals.

Linebreeding is a special form of inbreeding. In a linebreeding program, an attempt is made to keep a high relationship to a common ancestor in the pedigree. The common ancestor usually has been proven to be a genetically

TABLE 17-7   Percent of Inbreeding in the Offspring When Various Kinds of Relatives Are Mates (assuming that the parents themselves are not inbred)

Kinds of relatives mated	*Percent of inbreeding in offspring*
Parent and progeny	25.0
Full brother and full sister	25.0
Half brother and half sister	12.5
First cousins	6.3
Double first cousins	12.5
Uncle and niece or aunt and nephew	12.5
Grandparent and grandchild	12.5

Note: The percent of inbreeding is an estimate of the increased homozygosity of genes (both dominant and recessive) in the offspring as compared to their noninbred parents.
SOURCE: Adapted from Lasley (1970).

superior animal by its progeny. The common ancestor is usually at least three to four or more generations removed from the individual. However, some linebreeding programs use intensive inbreeding of closely related individuals. The purpose of linebreeding is the same as inbreeding except that it attempts to fix in the population the desirable characteristics of one or two superior ancestors. The inbreeding percentage is not as high, and the vigor is not reduced as much.

The purpose of linebreeding and inbreeding is to develop a genetically superior population of animals that can execute a particular type of performance. In many instances, the inbred or linebred families may be crossed with other similar families. If the appropriate niche is found, very superior offspring are produced. This is called *outcrossing,* and its genetic effect is to increase the number of heterozygous genes. In fact, outcrossing (or outbreeding) is a tool that many breeders use to improve their animals. Because of the increased number of heterozygous genes, many undesirable recessive alleles are masked. This system is used by most breeders because they cannot afford to develop linebred or inbred families.

There are a number of breeders who utilized linebreeding with some personal rules for success. With Thoroughbred horses, individuals have tried to use numbers derived from their rules in the hopes of finding or creating balance in the pedigree. This has been achieved by the concept of the Dosage Index (DI), the Rasmussen factor, and linebreeding to superior ancestors through a "male strain" and a "female strain." DI emphasizes stallions. The Rasmussen factor emphasizes mares and linebreeding emphasizes both.

Dosage Index has gone through a series of developments. Designed to find the proper balance between speed and stamina, the DI uses prominent stallions that represent types of racing ability to get the right gene combination. The stallions, referred to as "Chef-de-Race Stallions," are classified under five categories, according to the abilities of their progeny. Brilliant classification is for those stallions noted for siring "pure speed" for short distances. Intermediate stallions are recognized for primarily siring progeny that were successful at the mile distance. The classic category is for those whose progeny were successful at 1.25 miles, recognized as the classic distance. Stamina comes from the solid and professional categories. Some stallions are in two classifications. Each stallion's contribution to the DI is also weighted to their position in the pedigree: first generation, 16 points; second generation, 8 points; third generation, 4 points; and fourth generation, 2 points. The formula is:

$$\frac{(B \text{ points}) + (1 \text{ points}) + (C \text{ points}>2)}{(C \text{ points}>2) + (S \text{ points}) + (P \text{ points})} = DI$$

Thus, the DI is balanced when it is 1. Most American Thoroughbred race horses have a DI of greater than 1 because they have been selected for speed.

The concept of Center of Distribution (CI) has been developed as a position along the scale that corresponds to the combined influences of all the "Chef-de-Race Stallions" in the pedigree. The formula is:

$$\frac{[(2 \times \text{B-points}) + \text{I-points}] - [\text{S-points} + (2 \times \text{P-points})]}{(\text{Total points for B} + \text{I} + \text{C} + \text{S} + \text{P})} = \text{CI}$$

The Rasmussen factor is based on linebreeding to a common superior female ancestress within 5 generations through different individuals. Some of these superior ancestresses are La Troienne, Somethingroyal, and Almahmoud.

The concept of breeding horses so the pedigree traces back to a common ancestor through the sire line (sons of ancestor) and through the dam line (mares of ancestors) has been used by many successful breeders. The common ancestor is usually found in the 3rd or 4th generation. The pedigree of Peponitas Olenas Dually, 1998 National Cutting Horse Association Non-Pro Futurity Champion, has a good example in her pedigree (Figure 17-2). Doc Olena Dry,

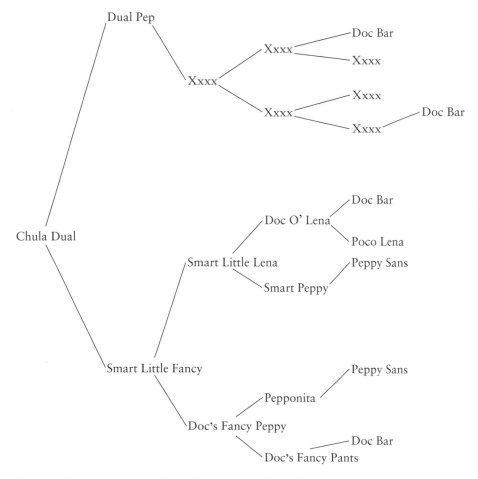

FIGURE 17-2   Pedigrees of Chula Dual, Nyoka Pep, Olenas Dually, and One Ton Dually.

FIGURE 17-2 *Continued*

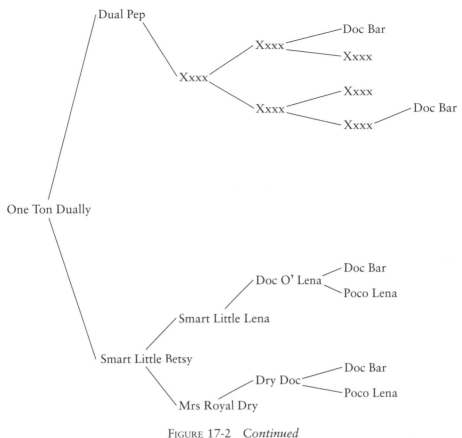

FIGURE 17-2 *Continued*

her dam, is linebred to Doc Bar and Poco Lena through a "male strain," Montana Doc, and a "female strain," Dry Doc 2. The dam of Dual Pep was sired by a son of Doc Bar and her dam was out of a daughter by Doc Bar. Thus, Dual Pep's dam is inbred to Doc Bar through a male and a female strain. One Ton Dually, another Dual Pep progeny, is bred along the same lines and has a similar example in his dam. Doc Olena Dry and Smart Little Betsy are three-quarters sisters in blood. A little different twist was used in the breeding of Smart Little Lena and Nyoka Pep, who were sired by Dual Pep. The linebreeding of Smart Little Fancy also goes back through male and female strains to Doc Bar. In the dam's pedigree of Nyoka Pep, Shesa Little Acorn, Doc's Oak, and Doc O'Lena are three-quarters brothers in blood. In summary, these four successful cutting horse progeny by Dual Pep are bred to have a "male strain" and a "female strain" to Doc Bar on the top and bottom of their pedigrees—balanced for a common ancestor (Doc Bar) and for "male and female strains."

Stallion Selection to Complement the Mare

There is no perfect horse, so horse owners are constantly trying to improve the quality of the horses they raise. In most instances, the mare owner tries to select a stallion to breed to a mare with the hope that the stallion will sire a foal with better conformation or performance potential than the mare has. Stallion owners try to select mares that will complement their stallion so that he will sire well-conformed foals.

The first step in the selection process is to find well-conformed individuals. The owner may quickly eliminate mares or stallions that have serious conformation faults, such as calf knees and offset knees, or that have too many faults. The next step is to decide which of the well-conformed stallions or mares are particularly strong where the horse to be bred is weak. Horses with poor hindleg conformation should be bred to those with very correct hindlegs and a reputation for siring or producing foals with correct hindlegs. Most breeds have sires or families that are known for certain conformation characteristics. These facts should be taken into account.

Selection is less risky if one avoids breeding to stallions during their first year as studs. To prove a stallion, do not select maiden mares but use older, proven mares.

In addition to trying to eliminate conformation faults, one must breed horses of similar size. If large stallions are bred to small mares, the foal will inherit characteristics that do not match, and the foal will be out of balance. The front end must be in balance with the hind end. The slope of the hip must complement the slope of the shoulder. Tall horses have longer necks to maintain balance. As a result of improper crosses, foals may, for example, inherit long legs from a tall parent and a short neck from a short, stocky parent. All parts are not in balance with each other.

Another tool that can be used is "nicking patterns." The term, nick, is defined as an affinity between two horses found in pedigrees which have produced more than one outstanding individual, whether those individuals find success on the race track, in performance events, or at stud. Nicks usually occur within the first few generations; beyond that realm, affinities might best be called good crosses, as their influence is somewhat diluted. In the racing industry, following nicks is quite popular among breeders. The Thoroughbred stallion Danzig has sired 18 percent stakes race winners, but when bred to daughters of Round Table, he has sired 47 percent stakes race winners. Thus, breeding a mare to a stallion according to successful nicking patterns increases the opportunity to produce a high-quality foal.

Thoroughbred breeders use several indexes to compare a stallion to all other stallions for his ability to sire successful race horses. The Average Earnings Index (AEI) ranks a sire's progeny as a ratio of earning to the average earnings of all sires for the years that the stallion has progeny racing. Since only 5 percent of Thoroughbred sires have an AEI of 2 or higher, the top 5 percent have sired progeny that average two times the earnings of progeny of all stallions. The Annual

Progeny Earning Index (APEX) is an annual index obtained when the individual earnings of all the stallion's runners is compared with average earnings of all runners by sires with ten or more foals. More precisely, the APEX is the percentage of a sire's runners that rank in the top 8 percent of all runners by money won, divided by 8. For example, if a stallion had 8 runners out of 100 runners that were in the upper 8 percent of all runners by money won, the APEX would be 1 (8/8). If the number was 20, the APEX would be 2.5 (20/8). The highest-ranked stallions usually have an index of ~2 to 3. APEX is further divided into A, B, and C runners. Runners in the top 2 percent are A runners and those in the B category are in the top 2 to 4 percent range. The C runners are in the top 4 to 8 percent range. Thus, the sum of the A, B, and C runners is actually the top 8 percent of all runners. Another breakdown of the APEX is for 2, 3, and aged runners. This breakdown allows the breeder to determine if a sire produces high-quality 2-year-olds that do not perform as well as 3-year-olds and aged horses. If the 3-year-olds' APEX is higher than the 2-year-olds' APEX, then the progeny are late developing. The Comparison Index (CI) calculates the ratio of the earnings of foals out of mares and sired by a stallion, compared with the earnings of foals out of the same mares when bred to other sires. Top sires have a CI of ~1.5 to 5.0.

Part Five

CHAPTER 18

Business Practices in the Horse Industry

The worldwide horse industry is very large and has many segments. Business practices vary from very technical and sophisticated to very simple. Likewise, the ethics of business practices range from very honest and straightforward to questionable or totally dishonest.

To be successful in the horse business, one must know and understand the segment of the horse business in which one is participating, the basic principles of business, many of the factors that influence management, and must have a business plan. Even with the best of planning and a thorough knowledge of the industry, success is not ensured because many types of horse-related businesses are very risky.

Many principles and concepts are presented in this chapter to stimulate one to think and recognize that more detailed information may be required in order to make informed decisions. In many situations, the advice of a well-informed attorney familiar with equine law is highly recommended.

SIZE AND STATUS OF HORSE INDUSTRY IN UNITED STATES

The scope, make-up, and status of the horse industry have been evaluated by the Horse Industry Alliance, which conducted a two-phase study in 1997 (household and individual surveys), and by the American Horse Council.

662

The National Agricultural Statistics Service counted 5.32 million equidae (horses, mules, and donkeys) in the U.S. in 1999. According to the American Horse Council, there are an estimated 6.9 million horses in the U.S. Of these horses, 725,000 are used for racing and breeding of race horses; 1,974,000 are used for showing; 2,970,000 are used for recreating; and 1,262,000 are used for a variety of activities including polo, rodeo, police work, and farm and ranch work. These horses are owned by 1.9 million people, but 7.1 million people are involved in the industry as owners, service providers, volunteers, and employees. The industry directly employs 619,400 people, which equates to 338,500 full-time jobs. With direct and indirect employment, it generates 1.4 million jobs. The horse industry has a major impact on the economy that is estimated at $112.1 billion on gross domestic product. It directly produces $25.3 billion in goods and services. From its activities, $1.9 billion is paid in taxes to local, state, and federal governments.

Data collected by the Horse Industry Alliance report that 33.3 percent of households make up the potential market in the U.S. Active riders are present in 10 percent of households, with another 18 percent claiming an interest in riding, while another 5 percent are former riders. Of the current riders, 97 percent ride for pleasure and 6 percent ride for competition (3 percent do both). Among current riders and those interested in riding, key positive attributes to horseback riding were entertainment, enjoyment, relaxation, relief from stress, sense of freedom, and interaction with the horse. Western style riding was favored by 80 percent of current riders, whereas only 12 percent engage in English style riding. Among riders for competition, English style riding was favored by 30 percent. Most horseback riders do so on an infrequent basis; only 10 percent ride at least once per week, and an additional 10 percent ride twice or more per month. Half of all current riders indicated they ride once per year or less. Despite this low rate of riding, they claim to be current riders. Typical riders are 31 years old and 59 percent are female. Competitive riders are younger (28 years old) and most are females (70%).

Average household income for current riders is $47,600. As the household income increases, the percentage of households participating in riding increases. Among current riders, cost as an inhibitor to riding was less significant than time, convenience, and safety. Major dislikes about riding experiences by former riders included maintenance involved, inconvenience, and risk of injury. Cost was mentioned by only 5 percent. Those not riding cite physical conditions (50%) such as age, injuries, and arthritis; no longer own a horse (36%); inconvenience (23%); and time (11%). Eighty-one percent of former riders still have an interest in riding and they would ride again if their health improved (20%), they had increased income (12%), or had more free time (7%). Former riders also claimed to have ridden more frequently than current riders—75 percent rode at least once per week and 67 percent rode twice per week or more.

In regards to horse ownership, 2 percent of households own a horse and 8 percent of non-owning households are interested in owning a horse.

Eighty-five percent of current owners live in single-family homes and the household has 3-plus members (57%). Over 70 percent have more than 1 acre of land. Two-thirds of current horse owners own more than one horse and 15 percent own 5 or more. Horse owners who ride for competition (75%) own more than one horse, and 27 percent own 5 or more. The most popular breed is the American Quarter Horse, owned by 44 percent of current owning households. Non-registered horses are owned by 18 percent of households. Seventy-five percent of current owners keep their horse on their own property or stables. The current horse owner is 33 years old and cites pleasure (87%) as the main reason for owning a horse. Other reasons include work/business (22%), investment (11%), and competition (10%). The most appealing aspect of ownership is the sense of interaction with the horse (70%), companionship, and pleasures of owning and riding. Thirty percent find the relationship with the horse and enjoyment of the outdoors and scenery most appealing. Among current owners, 66 percent cited some drawback to ownership. Expense was cited most often (39%) and specific costs mentioned were those of feed, veterinary, and shoeing. Other dislikes included cleaning up, maintenance, location inconvenience, chores, and time.

The average age of those interested in owning a horse was 28 and they cite pleasure as the reason for their interest. Cost is the most important reason for not owning (56%), followed by lack of land or place to keep a horse (42%), time (13%), and conflict with family responsibilities. If they owned a horse they would keep it on their own property (63%), at a boarding stable (20%), farm or ranch (17%), or with friends/family (12%). Most live in single-family houses (75%) and 71 percent of them own the house.

Past horse owners (89%) owned horses for pleasure; 69 percent owned two or more, would need increased income (27%) to own again, and no longer own because of lack of land (38%), cost (28%), and age (24%). The most prevalent dislikes were maintenance (27%) and cost (25%). It had been 10 years or more since 70 percent of them owned a horse.

BUSINESS PLAN

A horse business plan is any plan that allows the business to look ahead, allocate resources, focus on key points, and prepare for problems and opportunities. Business plans are developed prior to the start of a commercial horse enterprise to establish goals and procedures and costs to achieve those goals. They can be developed after a business has been in operation and needs to be analyzed. Usually revised at 2- to 3-year intervals and normally projecting at least 5 years into the future, they are vital to maintaining a focus for the business and serving as a management plan. Banks or financial institutions require them as part of a loan request procedure. At other times they can be useful, such as when applying for insurance coverage and when meeting with clients. A business plan is one of the criteria that are applied by the Internal Revenue Service to determine if an enterprise is for business purposes or for pleasure.

Components of a business plan will vary depending upon the exact business and purpose of the plan, but there are some standard components of a business plan. The Small Business Administration offers extensive advice on most business management topics, and information can be found on the World Wide Web at www.sbs.gov/starting/indexbusplans. The executive summary is essentially a condensed but powerful summary of the entire plan. A table of contents follows and is well designed to obtain detailed information in a logical, organized manner. The business section contains a description of the business and company, analysis of the market, competition and feasibility study, location of business, operating procedures, management, advertising, public relations, personnel (management team and consultants), time lines for accomplishments, projected growth, and business insurance. The financial data section includes loan applications, capital equipment list, projected balance sheet, break-even analysis, pro-forma projected income statements (profit and loss statements), and cash flow projections. The supporting documents section includes personal resumes, job descriptions, credit reports, leases, contracts, licenses, and other legal documents.

TYPES OF BUSINESS ORGANIZATIONS

A business can be organized in one of several ways. Before organizing the horse business, legal advice should be obtained and a lawyer should draft the necessary documents.

Sole Proprietorships

Sole proprietorship means one owner, the proprietor, considered to be one and the same. There are no partners, shareholders, or board of directors. The proprietor can operate the business under another name instead of the proprietor's name, but the social security number of the proprietor is the tax identification number. Sole proprietorships are the simplest and easiest form of business; however, some disadvantages of sole proprietorship are liability, taxes, and succession. Because the proprietor has responsibility for all losses, anyone with a claim against the business can go after all the assets of the proprietor. Retained earnings are taxed in the year they are earned. Sole proprietorships last as long as the owner retains ownership, but cannot continue after the owner's death. All assets are subject to estate taxes.

Corporations

Businesses can be incorporated to form one of several types of corporations. A "close corporation" limits the number of shareholders to usually 30 to 50, though this number varies according to each state. A corporation that pays taxes under the "subchapter C" IRS code is a "C" corporation; an "S" corporation operates under subchapter S. A "C" corporation pays taxes and then profits pass through to the stockholders who pay taxes on their share. The main advantage of an "S" corporation is that all profits are passed through to the stockholders, avoiding "double taxation." Only the shareholders pay taxes and none are paid by the "S" corporation. A public corporation is registered with the federal Securities and Exchange Commission, whose stock is publicly traded.

General and Limited Partnerships

General partnerships are unincorporated businesses owned by two or more persons. These owners are considered separate from individual owners, but are not tax-paying entities. Rights and responsibilities are essentially the same for each partner. Joint ventures are partnerships for a specific project. Major disadvantages are that all assets of every partner are at risk and that death of a partner can cause serious problems.

Limited partnerships have two classes of partners. The general partner(s) act(s) as manager and puts all assets at risk, whereas limited partners are not involved in management and are at risk only for their investment. Personal assets of limited partners are shielded from liability.

Limited Liability Companies

Limited liability companies combine some aspects of both partnerships and corporations. Tax obligations are passed through to owners (called members), providing liability protection. They do not issue stock and do not have a perpetual life.

LEGAL ISSUES

To obtain information about legal issues, it may be necessary to retain a lawyer familiar with equine law. When selecting a lawyer, it is important to determine his level of expertise and compare with others, to settle on a fee arrangement.

Equine Activity Statutes

These statutes have been enacted to protect horsemen, camps, stables, and other horse providers from lawsuits arising out of horse accidents that could not be avoided due to the fact that horses have their own personalities, and often act and react out of instincts that cannot be controlled by anyone. Anyone dealing with a horse should therefore be charged with the knowledge that riding or handling any horse can be dangerous, even under the best of conditions. Thus, the statutes provide that a person may not bring a lawsuit if the accident resulted from an inherent risk of equine activities. They spell out what risks are not inherent and that are therefore fair game for a lawsuit based on negligence. Most states require a notice to be posted or be included in contracts, or both, to bring the operation under the statutes' protection. Failure to follow the state's statutes will leave one open to lawsuits decided under general principles of negligence.

Attractive Nuisance

Horse owners and those who have custody of horses need to be aware that the horse can be an "attractive nuisance." Children are lured to an object on or by a condition or feature of land that is defined as an "attractive nuisance." If the landowner knows that children could trespass and become injured and has taken reasonable precautions to eliminate the hazard or protect children from harm, the attractive nuisance can be eliminated.

Livestock Laws

Livestock laws are a collection of statutes that state legislatures have enacted over the years to regulate the ownership and control over various forms of livestock, including horses. They are a complicated set of laws to define the interrelationships of livestock, people, and property. These laws vary from state to state. For example, some states require people to "fence livestock in" by a legal fence; other states require that "livestock be fenced out" to protect your property. There are laws which regulate fences along property lines, i.e., allocation of construction and maintenance.

Recreational Use Statutes

Most states have recreational use statutes that include horseback riding. These statutes protect the landowner from legal liability for any accidents that may happen when the user is on the property for recreational purposes and is paying no or a very nominal use fee. Landowners retain the right to deny access to any member of the public and to eject anyone from their property.

CONTRACTS

There are many types of contracts used in the horse business. The North American Horse Association has many common examples available to members.

Boarding Contracts

Boarding contracts generally describe the conditions under which the horse will be kept—stabling, feed, grooming, exercise—and the costs of those services. Additional information in the contract is highly desirable and can help avoid problems: instructions and authorizations regarding emergency care, information regarding mortality insurance, liability act language, health programs required by the stable and those furnished by the stable, immunization status of the horse, and possibly a release of liability. It is important for boarding-stable owners to have the contract written or reviewed by a knowledgeable attorney because statutes related to the industry vary from state to state.

Sales Transactions

It is a prudent practice to hire an equine lawyer to develop written sales or purchase contracts to protect both the buyer and seller. The minimum facts in a simple sales contract include: (1) specific horse to be sold; (2) seller owns the horse and has the right to sell it; (3) amount paid to seller; (4) date of payment; and (5) seller was paid in full. Generally, problems arise because the seller, required to disclose all known, existing defects, fails to disclose certain information. Second, if a fiduciary relationship exists, such as with agents, there is a duty to disclose. Third, the seller must disclose facts when the buyer inquires as to a specific defect. Fourth, if a seller has knowledge that a buyer is operating under mistaken or inaccurate information, the seller has a duty to affirmatively correct the buyer's misconceptions. Fifth, when a buyer is purchasing the horse for a specific purpose, a seller with such knowledge must disclose known defects related to or affecting the particular purpose for which the horse is being purchased.

One must be careful about failure to disclose and about making inaccurate statements when the horse is being sold without a written contract. Express warranties are created when the seller makes a factual statement about the condition of a horse for the purpose of inducing a buyer to make a purchase. Implied warranties are created when a buyer purchases a horse for a particular purpose that is known to the seller and the seller does not disclose that the horse may not be appropriate for the intended use.

The passing of risk of loss of a horse being sold should be included in the contract.

Despite all the items contained in a contract, the common problems that arise are related to horses that don't meet the terms of the contract, to sale of horses on approval, and when guarantees are given. Thus, it is important to have your attorney review contracts to help prevent problems. Also, contracts related to sale of stallions and syndication agreements are usually very complicated and written in detail.

Lease Agreements

Lease agreements and lease agreements with an option to purchase are common in the industry. A typical lease agreement identifies the parties concerned, horse involved with proper identification, term of lease, assignment provision, price, insurance provisions, care provisions, liability, lessor's remedies, election to terminate, representations of horse, and any additional conditions. It should also contain clauses regarding who will ride, show, or train the horse and/or specific uses for the horse. It may contain a clause giving the lessee the option to purchase the horse and, if so, how, when, and where it will be delivered, as well as consignment to sell during the lease.

Syndication Agreements

Multiple ownership of horses through syndication has been a popular trend in the horse industry to spread the liabilities of ownership; to own a percentage of a breeding stallion, or race or show horses; to increase the chances for being a winning owner; and to achieve other business objectives. In most instances, it gives owners an opportunity to own a portion of several horses, rather than sole ownership of a limited number of horses. Usually, this increases the chance of financial success in the industry, but not always. The selection and management of the syndicated horses is a critical component of success.

In stallion syndication agreements, it is advisable for the documents to outline who decides how many mares are to be bred during a season. If a stallion's book can be increased, the agreement should also cover how the additional breedings will be handled. It should include a clause about Southern Hemisphere breedings as well. Typically, extra seasons are chosen by lot or they may be sold and the income used for syndicate expenses. Extra income is then split among shareholders.

Breeding Contracts

These contracts spell out the conditions under which a stallion can be used to breed a mare, the guarantees of success, and the financial arrangements. Live foal guarantees can be quite varied in that they give conditions for the foal to be considered alive at birth. They range from live at birth, stand and suckle, alive for 24 hours, if euthanasia is necessary, etc. If a live foal does not result from the breeding, is the mare to be bred the next season or is the booking fee returned? Qualifications of the mare usually include her reproductive health status. Most misunderstandings can be avoided when the stallion owner states the expenses for which he/she is responsible.

RECORDS

Farm Records

There are a number of computerized record or farm management systems available to the horse owner. They are usually used by larger farms; many smaller farms keep their records by hand. Some computerized record systems include all aspects of farm management, such as accounting, payroll, inventory, breeding, boarding, training, and personnel. Others are specific for certain types of records. In a totally integrated system, data is entered once and goes to all parts of the program (system).

Before selecting a program, it is advisable to test the program to be sure that it will store the information you desire and generate the reports you need to manage the horses. Most programs are user friendly and have "pull down" screens for ease of use. The ability to enter batch data can save time. The reputation of the software company should be investigated to determine its support capabilities, likelihood to stay in business, and provision of updated programs.

The Jockey Club Information Systems, Inc. Windows Horse Farm Management System is a typical system. System entry is by horse or client name (Figure 18-1); when viewing the master record of a horse, there is instant access to detailed information like basic horse information, ownership, boarding information and rates, insurance policies, broodmare information, notes on characteristics, and comments allowing an unlimited amount of text (Figure 18-2). Broodmare information can be accessed either from the main menu or from a mare's master record. Detailed relevant data is displayed on the Mare Information form and from it, one can view and/or input foaling information, log teasing results, or enter/edit breeding dates (Figure 18-3). Regardless of whether the mare's breeding was "scheduled," "bred," or "canceled," there is a complete history of all breeding information. Health-record inquiry provides a quick "on-screen" snapshot of all health-related information from the horse's master record. Information within the on-screen inquiry can be filtered by date range or procedure category. Health records can be sorted according to date, with the most current information appearing at the top of the listing

Master Horse Lookup Form

FIGURE 18-1   Computer screen of Windows Horse Farm Management System® for entry into computerized record system by horse name. (Courtesy of Jockey Club Information Systems, Inc.)

Horse Information Entry/Edit Form

FIGURE 18-2   Broodmare information screen. (Windows Horse Farm Management System.® Courtesy of Jockey Club Information Systems, Inc.)

Master Mare Information Form

FIGURE 18-3   Mare information form. (Windows Horse Farm Management System.®
Courtesy of Jockey Club Information Systems, Inc.)

for each horse (Figure 18-4). In the stallion section, farms can track pertinent information such as breeding records, board billings, and stud fee billings. On the mare bookings screen, the available sessions are identified and a breeding can be scheduled. The program allows the farm manager to maintain northern and southern hemisphere breeding information. From the client information screen, everything one needs to know about a client can be seen or is a click of the mouse away. Information such as name, address, telephone numbers, account balances, charges, credits, payments received, and horse ownership is also available. This program calculates charges for horses that are owned by more than one person, based on each client's ownership percentage; all charges, including board, are divided appropriately on each client's monthly statement. Ownership changes in the middle of the month are no problem for the software either, as a complete history of this information is maintained.

This software program has over forty standard reports built into the system that can be accessed from the main menu. All the reports can be viewed on the screen, printed, or both. Because the information is stored in the Thoroughbred industry standard database structure, creating additional custom reports and queries is also possible. Some of the standard reports built into the system include: master reports by horse (Figure 18-5), client, farm horse type, arrival, and departure (Figure 18-6); procedure performed, schedule, and due reports; month-end billing reports (Figure

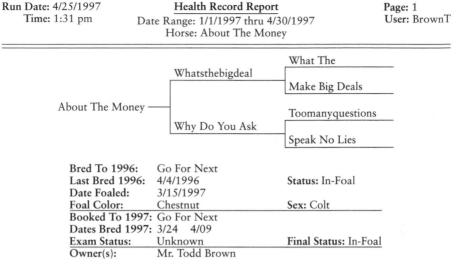

Run Date: 4/25/1997	**Health Record Report**	Page: 1
Time: 1:31 pm	Date Range: 1/1/1997 thru 4/30/1997	User: BrownT
	Horse: About The Money	

Bred To 1996:   Go For Next
Last Bred 1996:   4/4/1996   **Status:** In-Foal
Date Foaled: 3/15/1997
Foal Color: Chestnut   **Sex:** Colt
Booked To 1997: Go For Next
Dates Bred 1997: 3/24   4/09
Exam Status: Unknown   **Final Status:** In-Foal
Owner(s):   Mr. Todd Brown

Farm: Browns Farm, Inc.   **Horse Type:** Mare
Color: Chestnut   **Sex:** Mare   **YOB:** 1988

Date	Time	Procedure Description	Performed By	Results/Comments
3/15/1997		Post-Foaling Exam		Minor vulvular tear
3/15/1997		Suture		
3/20/1997		Float Teeth		
3/23/1997		Uterine Cytology		Cytology clean
3/23/1997		Uterine Culture		Slight discharge
3/23/1997		Palpation		Scheduled to breed tomorrow
3/24/1997		Bred To: Go For Next		
3/31/1997		Ivermectin		Paste Wormer
4/9/1997		Bred To: Go For Next		
4/15/1997		Rhino Vac		Booster

FIGURE 18-4   Health record report for a horse. (Windows Horse Farm Management System.® Courtesy of Jockey Club Information Systems, Inc.)

18-7); mare information by breeding, foaling, outside bookings by date, fertility analysis by stud farm or mare type, client, teasing results, and teasing worksheet; miscellaneous reports by horse characteristics, health (Figure 18-8), and farm and client mailing labels; and stallion reports by mares bred (Figure 18-9), fertility analysis and syndicate direct charges and credits, stud fee reports, syndicate master reports, and syndicate billing reports.

Automatic transfer to disk of the required information for the report of mares bred is sent to the Jockey Club for processing. In return, it is edited and returned so that the system records are updated.

Run Date: 4/25/1997
   Time: 1:35 pm

Horse Listing

Browns Farm, Inc.

Horse Name	Type	Sex	D.O.B.	Sire Name / Dam Name	Arrival Date	Departure Date	Owner(s)	Percent Owner
97–About The Money	Foal	Colt	3/15/97	Go For Next / About The Money	3/15/1997		Brown, Todd	100.00%
97–New Test Horse	Foal	Colt	3/13/97	Fuzzy Navel / New Test Horse	3/13/1997		Hall, Chris	100.00%
97–Beenthere Doneit	Foal	Filly	1/1/96	Go For Next / Beenthere Doneit	1/1/1996		Johnson, Vinicci	100.00%
97–Bubblegum Blonde	Foal	Filly	3/2/97	Go For Next / Bubblegum Blonde	3/2/1997		Adkins, Mark J.	60.00%
							Boxer, Libby	10.00%
							Ivory, Kathy	10.00%
							Johnson, Boneva	10.00%
							Johnson, Vinicci	10.00%
97–Terrible Twos	Foal	Colt	3/10/97	Black Forest / Terrible Twos	3/10/1997		Guerre, John	50.00%
							Politano, Pat	50.00%
97–Terrific Threes	Foal	Filly	2/5/97	Black Forest / Terrific Threes	2/5/1997		Boxer, Libby	50.00%
							Wagner, Glen	50.00%
A Ninetofiver	Mare	Mare		An Underestimate / Nine's Or Better	4/1/1997		Ivory, Kathy	100.00%
A Pappy's Doll	Mare	Mare		Pappy's Happy / Scared Doll	4/9/1997		Brown, Todd	100.00%
Abarah Cadabarah	Mare	Mare		Magic Derby / In A Poof	4/10/1997		Adkins, Mark J.	50.00%
							Blair, Beth	50.00%
About Bold	Mare	Mare		Bold About / Make Me Pres	4/10/1997		Courtney, Wayne	100.00%

674

Name			Year	Produce	Date	Date	Owner	Percent
About The Money	Mare	Mare	1988	Whatsthebigdeal Why Do You Ask	4/1/1997	4/16/1997	Brown, Todd	100.00%
Actors Bold	Mare	Mare		Bloody Bold Checkeredboard	4/10/1997		Blair, Beth	100.00%
Actress Bold	Mare	Mare	1990	Data Collection Collection Method	4/10/1997		Adkins, Mark J. Brown, Todd	50.00% 50.00%
All Done Now	Mare	Mare					Ivory, Kathy	100.00%
Amityville Winner	Mare	Mare		Amityville Win For the Gip	4/10/1997		Adkins, Mark J.	100.00%
And Youdidwhat	Mare	Mare		Compromising Look Smackintheface	4/1/1997		Ivory, Kathy Johnson, Boneva	50.00% 50.00%
Another Meeting	Mare	Mare		Rare Meeting Much Too Much	4/1/1997		Johnson, Vinicci	100.00%
At Another Time	Mare	Mare		Atimelikethis Another Bold One	4/1/1997		Blair, Beth Propps, Jeffrey D.	90.00% 10.00%
Aztar Is Born	Mare	Mare		Board Review Aztar Is Board	4/10/1997		Brown, Todd Ivory, Kathy Johnson, Boneva Johnson, Vinicci	20.00% 10.00% 50.00% 20.00%
Bazooka Gun	Mare	Mare	1978	Keene Grad Wildcat Fan			Brown, Todd Ivory, Kathy	25.00% 75.00%
Beenthere Doneit	Mare	Mare	1986	What The About The Money			Johnson, Vinicci	100.00%
Bold About Face	Mare	Mare		Bold About Make Me Pres	4/10/1997		Blair, Beth Ivory, Kathy	66.70% 33.30%

FIGURE 18-5 Master report for horses in computerized record system. (Windows Horse Farm Management System.® Courtesy of Jockey Club Information Systems, Inc.)

675

Run Date: 4/24/1997   Departure Form   Page: 1
Time: 2:03 pm   Horse: About The Money   User: MJA
Date Range: 1/1/1997 Thru 4/30/1997

Sire: Whatsthebigdeal	Tatoo#:	Departure Date: 4/16/1997
Dam: Why Do You Ask	Horse Type: Mare	Year of Birth: 1988
		Color: Chestnut
Owner: Mr. Todd Brown	Ship To:	Sex: Mare
Address: Manager		Vanned By: Local Haulers
Brown's Farm, Inc.	Phone:	
432 West Oak Place		
Danville, KY 40422		

Phone: (606) 224-2800

Health Record

Date Performed	Procedure	Performed By	Results
3/15/1997	Post-Foaling Exam		Minor vulvular tear
3/20/1997	Float Teeth		
3/23/1997	Uterine Cytology		Cytology clean
3/23/1997	Uterine Culture		Slight discharge
3/23/1997	Palpation		Scheduled to breed tomorrow
3/31/1997	Ivermectin		Paste Wormer
4/9/1997	Bred To: Go For Next		
4/15/1997	Rhino Vac		Booster

Booking / Breeding

Bred To 1996:	Go For Next	Booked To 1997:	Go For Next
Last Bred 1996:	4/4/1996	Last Bred 1997:	4/9/1997
Beginning Status 1997:	In-Foal	Final Status 1997:	In-Foal
Date Foaled 1997:	3/15/1997	Status After LDB:	Unknown
Foal Color 1997:	Chestnut		
Foal Sex:	Colt		

Remarks: _____

Signed By: _____ Date: _____

Run Date: 4/16/1997   Breeding Report   Page: 1
Time: 8:35 am   User: ProppsJ
Season: 1997

Times Bred	Mare Name	Last Date Bred	Double	Bred To	Days Since Last Breeding	Status
1	Actors Bold	2/12/1997	Yes	Go For Next	63	not Preg
1	Actress Bold	2/13/1997		Go For Next	62	In-Foal
1	Another Meeting	2/15/1997		Go For Next	60	In-Foal
1	A Pappy's Doll	2/18/1997		Go For Next	57	In-Foal
1	About Bold	3/1/1997		Go For Next	46	In-Foal
2	Abarah Cadabarah	3/6/1997	Yes	Go For Next	41	In-Foal
2	At Another Time	3/6/1997		Go For Next	41	In-Foal
2	A Ninetofiver	3/10/1997		Go For Next	37	In-Foal
1	Amityville Winner	3/13/1997		Go For Next	34	In-Foal
1	And Youdidwhat	3/22/1997	Yes	Go For Next	25	In-Foal
2	About The Money	4/9/1997		Go For Next	7	Unknown

FIGURE 18-6 Departure report for horses in computerized record system. (Windows Horse Farm Management System.® Courtesy of Jockey Club Information Systems, Inc.)

TJCIS Farm, Inc.
123 Main St.
Anytown, KY 15551

Mr. Todd Brown	Monthly Statement	Page: 2
Manager		
Brown's Farm, Inc.		
432 West Oak Place	Period Ending: 4/30/1997	
Danville, KY 40422		

97-About The Money

Date	Description		Total Charge	Owner Percent	Owner Portion
3/16/1997	Post Foaling Exam		$21.00	100.00%	$21.00
3/30/1997	Panacur		$10.00	100.00%	$10.00
3/30/1997	Rhino Vac		$10.50	100.00%	$10.50
			$41.50		$41.50

A Pappy's Doll

Date	Description		Total Charge	Owner Percent	Owner Portion
4/9/1997	Thru 4/11/1997	Board @ $20.00	$60.00	100.00%	$60.00
4/12/1997	Thru 4/30/1997	Board @ $35.00	$665.00	100.00%	$665.00
3/30/1997	Float Teeth		$15.00	100.00%	$15.00
3/30/1997	Palpation		$12.00	100.00%	$12.00
3/30/1997	Ivermectin		$15.00	100.00%	$15.00
			$767.00		$767.00

About The Money

Date	Description		Total Charge	Owner Percent	Owner Portion
4/1/1997	Thru 4/16/1997	Board @ $20.00	$320.00	100.00%	$320.00
			$320.00		$320.00

Actress Bold

Date	Description		Total Charge	Owner Percent	Owner Portion
4/10/1997	Thru 4/30/1997	Board @ $20.00	$420.00	50.00%	$210.00
3/30/1997	Float Teeth		$15.00	50.00%	$7.50
3/30/1997	Ivermectin		$15.00	50.00%	$7.50
3/30/1997	Rhino Vac		$10.50	50.00%	$5.25
3/30/1997	Influenza Vac		$15.00	50.00%	$7.50
			$475.50		$237.75

Aztar Is Born

Date	Description		Total Charge	Owner Percent	Owner Portion
4/10/1997	Thru 4/30/1997	Board @ $20.00	$420.00	20.00%	$84.00
3/30/1997	Float Teeth		$15.00	20.00%	$3.00
3/30/1997	Rhino Vac		$10.50	20.00%	$2.10
3/30/1997	Strangles Vac		$24.00	20.00%	$4.80
3/30/1997	Exam		$12.00	20.00%	$2.40
			$481.50		$96.30

FIGURE 18-7   Billing report. (Windows Horse Farm Management System.® Courtesy of Jockey Club Information Systems, Inc.)

TJCIS Farm, Inc.
123 Main St.
Anytown, KY 15551

Mr. Todd Brown Manager Brown's Farm, Inc. 432 West Oak Place Danville, KY 40422	**Monthly Statement** Period Ending: 4/30/1997	Page: 1

CLIENT SUMMARY

	Charges	*Credits*	*Balance*
PREVIOUS BALANCE:			$2,785.65
BEGINNING BALANCE:			$2,785.65
Current Month Horse Charges			
97-About The Money	$41.50		
A Pappy's Doll	$767.00		
About The Money	$320.00		
Actress Bold	$237.75		
Aztar Is Born	$96.30		
Total Horse Charges:	$1,462.55		
ENDING BALANCE:			$4,248.20

Please Return This Portion with Payment

Client Name	Total Due	Current Balance	Amount Past Due
Mr. Todd Brown	$4,248.20	$1,462.55	$2,785.65

FIGURE 18-7 *Continued*

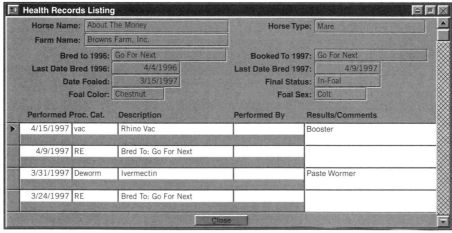

On-Screen Health Inquiry Form

FIGURE 18-8 Health record inquiry screen for horse. (Windows Horse Farm Management System.® Courtesy of Jockey Club Information Systems, Inc.)

Run Date: 4/25/1997
Time: 1:22 pm

Stallion Management Report
Stallion: Go For Next
Season: 1997

Page: 1
User: BrownT

Share	Share Holder / Mare Name / Purchaser	Dates Bred	Status	Payment Terms	Amount Due	Date Paid	Amount Paid	Date Foaled	Sex	Other Credits
02	Mr. Todd Brown A Pappy's Doll Mr. Todd Brown	100.00%								
03	Mr. Mark J. Adkins Amityville Winner Mr. Mark J. Adkins	100.00% 3/13		10/1/1997	$0.00					
04	Ms. Kathy Ivory A Ninetofiver Ms. Kathy Ivory	100.00%		10/1/1997	$0.00					
05	Mr. Mark J. Adkins Abarah Cadabarah Mr. Mark J. Adkins	100.00% 3/6 3/8		10/1/1997	$0.00					
06	Mr. Vinicci Johnson Another Meeting Mr. Vinicci Johnson	100.00% 2/15		10/1/1997	$0.00					
07	Ms. Beth Blair Actors Bold Ms. Beth Blair	100.00% 2/12		10/1/1997	$0.00					
08	Mr. Todd Brown Actors Bold Mr. Todd Brown	100.00% 2/13		10/1/1997	$0.00					
09	Ms. Kathy Ivory And Youdidwhat Ms. Kathy Ivory	100.00% 3/22			$0.00					
10	Jeffrey D. Propps At Another Time Jeffrey D. Propps	100.00% 3/6 4/16			$0.00			1/31/1997	Colt	
	Stallion Totals:				$0.00		$0.00			$0.00

FIGURE 18-9 Stallion management report. (Windows Horse Farm Management System.® Courtesy of Jockey Club Information Systems, Inc.)

TJCIS Farm, Inc.
123 Main St.
Anytown, KY 15551

Mr. Mark J. Adkins	Stud Fee Invoice	Page: 1
Links Farm		
217 Kenlock Dr.		Invoice Date 1/24/1997
Lexington, KY 40517		Invoice Number 199700004

Stallion:	Go For Next	Year: 1997	Share: 05
Mare:	Abarah Cadabarah	Last Date Bred:	3/8/1997
Terms:	Payable Sept 1	Due Date:	10/1/1997

	Stud Fee	$7,500.00
	Sales Tax	$0.00
	Total Due	$7,500.00

Barren Mare Certificate Due In Lieu Of Payment

Please Return This Portion with Payment

Name	Invoice No.	Amount Due
Mr. Mark J. Adkins	199700004	$7,500.00

FIGURE 18-9   *Continued*

ACCOUNTING

Some of the farm management record systems have accounting records built into the system, or these can be added. It is important for an accountant familiar with the business of horses to set up the accounting system, thereby saving considerable time in revising or replacing the system. Decisions will need to be made regarding the chart of accounts, depreciation methods, cash or accrual basis, and others.

The horse business accounting system should be kept separate from other business and household systems. Checking accounts should be separate and specific for the horse business.

REGISTRATION AND AWARDS PROGRAM REQUIREMENTS

Each breed association has a specific set of forms and records that must be filed by certain deadlines on an annual basis. Filing of these records is necessary to register horses and for their participation in various types of incentive programs related to performance. For state-based incentive programs, such as breeders' and owners' awards, applications to the state may be necessary. Registration forms may need to be accompanied by blood or DNA samples. If so, they require time to obtain, so one must be careful to do so in time to meet deadlines.

INSURANCE

The basic types of insurance applicable to a horse farm or horseowner are: liability, mortality, loss of use, infertility, umbrella policies, and fire. There are many variations on these themes. Liability insurance provides coverage for personal injury or property damage. Mortality compensates the owner for loss of a horse due to death. Loss of use policies are generally available only for show horses. Infertility compensates for barrenness of a mare or infertility of a stallion. Umbrella policies offer additional coverage for liabilities not covered in a normal liability policy.

When considering insurance, one should investigate the reputation of the agency that writes the policy and the underwriting company. A.M. Best rates insurance companies and an A+ rating is the highest available.

Liability Insurance

Liability insurance provides coverage for personal injury or property damage against the insured. There are three types of liability insurance used by horse owners. Farm liability covers liability on the farm property. Most farm liability policies exclude horses and activities associated with them. Thus, one must be sure that they are not excluded. A care, custody, and control liability policy covers horses that are in the care, custody, and control of the farm owner but that are owned by someone else; these horses are excluded under the farm owner's farm liability policy coverage. Generally, a farm owner boarding horses is liable only for negligence. Thus, the owner will need a boarder's liability policy to protect the property of others. A stallion liability policy provides protection from claims against the owner of the insured stallion for personal injury and property damage.

Horse-related businesses can reduce their risk by following standard practices recommended by the North American Horsemen's Association risk-reduction programs for: personal-pleasure horse owners, riders and horse enthusiasts; horse stables and farms, boarding, breeding, leasing, sales, training and lessons; horse clubs and single-day events; horse rental and trail rides, guides and outfitters, dude ranches and resorts, and horse-related camps; and pony rides and camps providing equestrian services to riders 6 years of age and younger. By requiring all employees, owners, and others associated with the business to be familiar with and understand the risk-reduction program, the chances for negligence will be greatly reduced.

Mortality Insurance

Mortality insurance covers the insured value of the horse when death occurs as a result of accident, illness, disease, and (usually) theft. There are many differences in companies offering mortality insurance and in the actual policies. Mortality insurance is available through a limited number of sources.

Annual rate will depend on the number of horses to be insured and their age and value. It is important for the policy to accept the agreed-upon value when the premium is paid. The value can be based on appraisals by qualified appraisers. Horses purchased at auction are valued at their purchase price at the fall of the hammer. If insured at a later time, the value may change. If the policy was an "actual cash value," or fair market value, the insurance company might be justified in paying less than what the horse was insured for. Thus, the horse owner should avoid paying premiums on a high value when in reality the horse's cash value is much less. Fair market value of foals is usually 2 to 3 times the stud fee. Premiums can be paid at various time intervals, such as quarterly or annually. If the stable is expanding and the purchase of additional horses is expected, and/or foals will be added at birth, the policy should include an "automatic addition clause." This clause will place a maximum value per horse to be added and age limitations. Young horses such as foals must be at least 24 hours old and the maximum age is usually 16 or 17 years. A "fall of the hammer" clause can be included so that your horse is insured the moment you purchase it at auction or at private treaty. The premiums for additions to the policy should be prorated for the time of the coverage until the renewal date. Those claiming a race horse from a claiming race can obtain "claiming insurance" so that once the race starts, they have mortality insurance during the race until the horse crosses the finish line. Once the horse finishes the race, mortality insurance will protect the owner. The contract may be such that there is no lapse in coverage as the horse finishes the race. In determining the value of a race horse, there is an important consideration. If the horse races in a claiming race, that establishes the current value for the horse. Most mortality policies will have a "claiming clause." Thus, if a horse that was purchased for a large sum of money fails to perform as entered in a claiming race, the value of the horse is established at the claiming price. If the horse returns to form and increases its value, the owner must request that the insurance company increase the value of the horse.

Veterinary certificates are required for a horse to be insured, and if the value of the horse has increased, a current veterinary certificate will be required. At renewal, veterinary certificates may or may not be necessary. It is, however, an advantage if they are not required because insurance cannot be declined by insurers on a horse at the anniversary date, regardless of its state of health until a given age (usually 16 or 17). In most policies, the insurance company will be responsible for the veterinary examination, to avoid a conflict of interest by the veterinarian.

A variety of other clauses will cover the horse under various circumstances. The cause of death may be specified but should cover all possible causes. The geographical location of the horse at death may be limited by coverage, or it may be worldwide. Use of the horse, such as for racing, breeding, rearing, and training, should be included. Some policies require that the use be declared and coverage is only valid when horses are being used for that purpose. Theft should be included. Health aspects, such as a clause for claims if the horse is a wobbler and coverage during surgery, can be part of the policy. An "L form" endorsement will cover horses that are poisoned or injured by willful and malicious circumstances. A clause for permanent infertility of males due to accident, sickness, or disease can be included.

It is also important that an "extension period" be included. If a horse is sick or injured on the day the policy expires, the horse is covered for an additional period of time before a claim must be filed. If the horse recovers, no claim would be filed; if the horse dies within the extension period, however, a claim can be filed. If the insurance company is not going to renew a policy, a clause should specify the time period before lapse of the policy that a notice of cancellation should be received.

A deductible policy will allow an owner to protect part of the investment. Another clause that can decrease the insurance cost is a "no claims bonus." The bonus occurs if no claims have been paid. Some companies will directly pay the bonus, whereas others apply it to the renewal premium.

Some states in the U.S. and some countries have a surcharge that is added to the premium.

The policy should specify in which state any litigation should be filed. It becomes much more expensive for lawyers who represent you to travel out of state. Furthermore, often lawyers cannot represent you in another state, period.

Based on the above, there are many different ways that a company can vary the quote for a premium. Thus, the horse owner or horse business owner must be careful when comparing quotes. After a decision is made regarding each clause, it may be advisable to ask for new quotes.

The horse owner has certain duties that must be performed, or a claim can be denied. The owner is required to notify the insurance company within a given time period (usually 24 hours) if an insured horse becomes injured, lame, sick, or is in an accident or changes location. Because the insurance company has a financial interest in the horse, they may review treatment with the attending veterinarian, order a new course of treatment, or send the horse to another veterinarian. They must be notified of intent to euthanize a horse and must give their consent. For humane reasons, the attending veterinarian may recommend immediate euthanasia to relieve suffering.

It is important for owners to understand all their duties and should have the agent explain them. Failure to perform the duties will give reason for the insurance company not to pay the claim. The trainer and the boarding facility should be familiar with the terms of notification and the correct protocol.

Health Insurance

Equine health insurance is available in two forms: major medical or surgical. Major medical covers veterinary treatment, medication, and surgery due to accident, injury, or illness. Surgical insurance only covers emergency and necessary surgery in a veterinary clinic. Neither form of insurance covers routine care, such as deworming and vaccinations, pre-existing conditions, or degenerative conditions.

The pre-existing condition is often misunderstood by the horse owner. It includes any condition that exists at the time a new policy is written or when the policy is renewed. Since all health insurance policies are written on an annual basis, renewals are actually a new policy.

Most policies will exclude horses based on age and some types of uses (race horses). The policy usually requires mortality insurance as well as health insurance.

Loss of Use Insurance

A loss of use policy compensates show horse owners for decreased value of an insured horse that has become ill or lame and, therefore, unable to perform its declared use in the show ring.

Infertility Insurance

The coverage of infertility policies is written many different ways. For stallions, a claim is paid if the stallion fails to achieve a certain conception percentage rate. Mares are covered against barrenness. Also, policies for coverage against embryonic death or abortion are available and are referred to as "prospective foal insurance." It expires at a specific time after the foal is born. Some contracts will convert to mortality insurance so there is no lapse of coverage.

Fire Insurance

Prevention of fire is always a concern for horse farms and facilities. Owners usually protect themselves against losses from fire with a fire insurance policy. Coverage may be included in other policies for specific horses, or in general policies. Thus, the owner needs to coordinate all policies to insure coverage and to avoid duplication of coverage.

Loss of a horse resulting directly from a fire can be covered under a "specified perils coverage" policy. Other specified perils may include floods, lightning, and collision while in transit. The horse may be covered by a mortality insurance policy that includes loss due to fire.

Fire insurance for dwellings (homes), farm personal property, and farm structures can reduce risk exposure. Dwellings on the farm and farm structures may be insured for a percentage of their value, or for their actual cash value. Some policies have clauses that automatically adjust for appreciation at specific time intervals. Farm personal property, including borrowed farm machinery and personal property of others, can also be insured.

HIRING TRAINERS

Selection of a trainer to work with a performance horse varies depending upon the type of horse.

Blood-Horse magazine provides statistical information on trainers of Thoroughbred race horses. These statistics provide information about the success of a trainer in various categories like turf and dirt surfaces, length of race, age of horse, quality of race, and number of starts. Statistics provide a glimpse of the trainer's overall performance but does not measure horsemanship, business acumen, dedication, or communication skills. After determining the ability of the trainer based on past performances, a number of other qualities and factors need to be addressed. The daily training fee varies widely as does what is included in the daily fee. Some trainers stay at a particular track and seldom travel to other race tracks. Other trainers routinely enter horses to race throughout the U.S. and Europe. Most trainers have assistants who help train various horses kept at more than one location. Thus, the knowledge and abilities of the assistants are important to consider and must be closely scrutinized. The trainer's honesty and communication with owners can be assessed by contacting references. The percentage of horses that do not finish a race or that break down gives a parameter related to ability to condition a horse at the proper pace.

Although statistics are not kept for other types of performance events, one can access a trainer's success by talking to other knowledgeable owners and examining the results from major events.

The costs for training a horse on a daily or monthly basis vary for the type of training, trainer's ability or past success, and what else is provided besides actual training—i.e., horse kept in stall or not, kept on pasture or fed hay and grain, grooming, etc. Race horse trainers' fees will vary depending on the inclusion of veterinary fees, therapist (chiropractor, acupuncture), and special stall bedding. A frank discussion with the trainer about what is included and an opportunity to examine typical bills to clients are advisable to prevent misunderstandings.

RACING HORSES

To race a horse at a recognized horse racing track, the owner must obtain an owner's license in all the states where the horse will race. Each state has different requirements. In some countries and states, an owner must establish an account at the race track. All ownership expenses are charged against the account and all purses won are deposited into the account.

Each owner must establish a set of silks that is unique to his/her stable. Some states have slightly different rules governing the basic color, diamonds on the sleeves, diamonds around the waist, logos, quarter panels on the cap, cap tassels, and cap bill. Generally, an owner or racing stable should develop the silks so they can be used in any state and any foreign country.

The purse structure of a race varies according to the size of the purse, but the winning owner gets 60 percent. Out of the owner's purse (dollars paid to the owner), the jockey gets 10 percent, trainer gets 10 percent, and sometimes, the stable help gets 2 percent. The rider or trainer of other types of performance horses is usually paid a flat fee for showing a horse, plus the purse won by the horse (or at least a high percentage of the winnings).

There are legal procedures established for disqualifying a horse in a race, and owners should be familiar with the rules. Likewise, an owner or trainer may lose track privileges for not obeying the rules. Trainers may be suspended for a number of days for not following rules of conduct. Most suspensions result from positive drug tests on the horses the trainer is racing. A trainer is totally responsible for all horses under his/her care.

State statutes vary for the relationship of the jockey riding a race horse to the owner of the horse and the trainer. In some states, they are employees; in other states, they are independent contractors. Thus, the insurance requirements for protection from liability exposure during the race vary.

EMPLOYEES AND INDEPENDENT CONTRACTORS

People with a variety of skills can be employed on staff or as independent contractors. There are major differences between an employee and an independent contractor. An independent contractor by definition is someone who carries on an independent business and contracts to do work for another according to his or her own methods, and without being subject to control of the other as to the means by which the result is accomplished but only as to the result itself. When independent contractors are contracted, the equine business will not be responsible for employeee expenses and benefits such as FICA, insurance, withholding, worker's compensation, overtime, and benefits. Another advantage of using an independent contractor is that the contractor will generally not be liable for the negligent and wrongful acts committed by the independent contractor and his/her employees. The Internal Revenue Service challenges many independent-contractor relationships, so it is prudent to use legal advice to determine whether an independent contractor meets the IRS tests.

There are many government forms that must be filed on a regular basis for employees. Knowledge of withholding requirements for income tax and social security, worker's compensation, minimum wage, insurance, overtime regulations, liability, and other benefits is essential.

PURCHASING AND SELLING HORSES

Auction Sales

Preparing to go to an auction, such as those held for many breeds and types of performance horses, to potentially purchase a horse involves several procedures. A credit application may be required, to allow the sales company to obtain certain account and credit information from the financial institution of a potential buyer. Some sales companies require an irrevocable sight letter of credit to be confirmed by the potential buyer's bank. If someone is to purchase horses for a person he/she represents, an authorization of agent form must be filed. A seat request form may be required if the potential buyer wishes to sit in the reserved section for bidders. There are conditions under which all horses are sold and the buyer and seller must thoroughly understand them to prevent any misunderstanding with the sales company. Arrangements can be made with an insurance company to insure any horse purchased at the moment the gavel falls so there is no risk exposure for the new owner.

Sales for young horses and two-year-olds in training may have a repository for x-rays and endoscopic evaluation of the larynx. Their deposition may or may not be mandatory. One must be cautious about relying on the repository x-rays, because a slight movement of the camera to a slightly different angle may disclose or fail to disclose a pathological condition. Most buyers will have their own veterinarian examine the horse prior to its sale and to secure a full set of x-rays if they are seriously interested in bidding on the horse.

Sales catalogs will give information about each individual horse to be sold. It may list the consignor, consignor's agent, barn where horse is stabled for inspection during the sale, pedigree, date of birth, conditions related to soundness and limited warranties, and nominations to specific performance events (Figure 18-10). The buyer should be familiar with all conditions stated in the front of the sales catalog.

Because the pedigree information is usually a summary, the potential buyer may want to have complete pedigree information. Computer databases are maintained by some breed and performance horse organizations, and the information can be obtained for a fee. For example, information about Thoroughbred horses can be obtained—including race records of all ancestors, previous auctions in which they were sold and their purchase price, comparison of sire's get record to other sires, nicking information for sire and dam, average prices paid for sire's and dam's produce, sire's stud fee, etc. Some buyers will study the success of horses with similar pedigrees (see the section on line breeding in Chapter 17). This information can be taken into account along with current market trends or conditions to predict the sales value of the horse. Some companies market sales guides that summarize much of the above information (Figure 18-11).

Consigned by Three Chimneys Farm, Agent for

Hip No.   Warner L. Jones Farm, Inc.   Barn
38   CHESTNUT FILLY   3
                        Foaled March 6, 1997

By MR. PROSPECTOR (1970). Stakes winner of $112,171, Gravesend H., etc. Leading sire twice, sire of 21 crops of racing age, 1031 foals, 822 starters, 161 stakes winners, 14 champions, 639 winners of 2080 races and earning $58,976,547 in N.A., including Gulch ($3,095,521, Breeders' Cup Sprint [G1], etc.), Forty Niner ($2,726,000, Travers S. [G1], etc.), Rhythm ($1,592,532, Breeders' Cup Juvenile [G1], etc.), Afleet ($995,235, Jerome H. [G1], etc.), Golden Attraction [G1] ($911,508).

1st dam
WEST TURN, by Cox's Ridge. Placed at 2, $6,040. Sister to LITTLE MISSOURI. Dam of 9 other registered foals, 8 of racing age, 5 to race, 4 winners, including—
WEST BY WEST (c. by Gone West). 10 wins, 2 to 5, $1,038,123, Nassau County H. [G1], Jamaica H. [G2], Widener H. [G3], Clarinet King S. [L] (BEL, $33,690), Whirlaway H. (FG, $18,885), 2nd Wood Memorial Invitational S. [G1], Whitney H. [G1], Saratoga Cup H. [L] (SAR, $55,000), 3rd Whitney H. [G1], Suburban H. [G1], Arlington-Washington Futurity [G2], Excelsior H. [G2], New Orleans H. [G3]. Sire.
Preston Road (c. by Miswaki). 5 wins at 3 and 5, $40,580.
Puddin Hill (f. by Afleet). Unraced. Sent to Argentina. Dam of **Mancari's Rose** (f. by Glitterman). Winner in 2 starts at 2, 1998 $32,290, 3rd Debutante S. [G3].

2nd dam
Win Nona, by Jacinto. 6 wins at 2 and 3, $53,310, 3rd Marlboro Nursery S. Sister to JA AGLO. Dam of 8 other foals, 7 to race, all winners, incl.—
LITTLE MISSOURI (c. by Cox's Ridge). 8 wins, 2 to 5, $553,025, Brooklyn H. [G1], Stuyvesant H. [G2], 2nd Ben Ali H. [G3], Louisville Breeders' Cup H. [L] (CD, $30,710), Louisville S. (CD, $7,816), 3rd Meadowlands Cup [G1], El Cajon S. [LR], 4th Razorback H. [G2]. Sire.
Winona B. (f. by Raised Socially). 4 wins at 3 and 4, $93,141, 2nd Valnor H. [L] (HAW, $10,437).

3rd dam
CONSTANCE BLACK, by On Trust. 6 wins to 5. Dam of 11 winners, incl.—
JA AGLO. 6 wins, 2 to 4, $73,530, C. B. Afflerbaugh Memorial S., etc. BLACK FLEET. 10 wins at 2 and 3, $68,314, Joliet S., Audley H. DOUBLE YOUR FUN. 4 wins, $64,490, Arlington-Washington Lassie S., etc. Win Nona. Stakes-placed winner, above.
Federal Fleet. Winner at 2. Dam of MIGHTY MIXUP ($155,786), WINKING AYE (dam of MORO-G2, $741,514; SIR NASKRA [G2]; etc.).
Vaccinated for influenza.
Engagements: Breeders' Cup.
Foaled in Kentucky. (KTDF).

                                                                    KEE 9/98

FIGURE 18-10   Catalog page from Keeneland September Yearling Sale, 1998. (Courtesy of Keeneland Association, Inc.)

21 Yring. c. by UNBRIDLED—VALID CARNAUBA (40 starts, RI 2.28) byVALID
    APPEAL. Breeder, Kinsman Farm (Ky.).
    1998 Stud Fee: $50,000; 1996 Stud Fee: $25,000. Dosage: (10-8-12-0-6); **DI:**
    2.00; **CD:** 0.44
    1997 Sales Yrigs: 30 offered, 25 sold, $159,200 avg., $140,000 med.

Unbridled w/ Valid Appeal mares: 2 fls rac age, 2 2yos, 0 strs, 0 wnrs, 0 sup rnrs, 0
Sws.
Sons of Fappiano w/ Valid Appeal mares: 14 fls rac age, 7 2yos, 7 strs, 6 wnrs (43%),
2 sup rnrs (14%), 1 SW (7%).
Sons of Fappiano w/ In Reality mares: 38 fls rac age, 5 2yos, 25 strs, 11 wnrs (29%),
0 sup rnrs, 0 SWs.

'97—B. c. by Unbridled.
'96—Meadowlake Amy, f., by Meadowlake. Unraced. 97KEESEP $35,000 Buyer:
Wexler Stables.

Valid Carnauba - (Unbridled) 96KEENOV $290,000 Buyer: Kinsman Farm.

22 Yring. c. by UNBRIDLED—VENNILA CREAM (31 starts, RI 5.18) by VALID
    APPEAL. Breeder, Brylynn Farm, Inc. (Ky.). **1998 Stud Fee: $50,000; 1996 Stud
    Fee: $25,000. Dosage:** (10-7-11-2-6); **DI: 1.67; CD:** 0.36
    1997 Sales Yrigs: 30 offered, 25 sold, $159,200 avg., $140,000 med.

Unbridled w/ Valid Appeal mares: 2 fls rac age, 2 2yos, 0 strs, 0 wnrs, 0 sup rnrs, 0
Sws.
Sons of Fappiano w/ Valid Appeal mares: 14 fls rac age, 7 2yos, 7 strs, 6 wnrs (43%),
2 sup rnrs (14%), 1 SW (7%).
Sons of Fappiano w/ In Reality mares: 38 fls rac age, 5 2yos, 25 strs, 11 wnrs (29%),
0 sup rnrs, 0 SWs.

'97—Dkbbr. c. by Unbridled.
'96—Raspberry Eggcream, f., by Time for a Change. 3 strts, 0 wins, $325 (RI 0.05).
970BSAUG $45,000 Buyer: Frank J. and Susan Moreno.

23 Yring. c. by COLONIAL AFFAIR—VENUS BOUND (15 starts, RI 1.24) by
    CONQUISTADOR CIELO. Breeder, Mr./Mrs. John Dobson (Ky.).
    1998 Stud Fee: $15,000; 1996 Stud Fee: $15,000. Dosage: (7-0-10-2-1); **DI:** 1.50;
    CD: 0.50
    1997 Sales Yrigs: 40 offered, 36 sold, $64,806 avg., $37,500 med.

Colonial Affair w/ Conquistador Cielo mares: 2 fls rac age, 2 2yos, 1 str, 0 wnrs, 0 sup
rnrs, 0 SWs.
Sons of Pleasant Colony w/ Conquistador Cielo mares: 4 fls rac age, 2 2yos, 3 strs,
1 wnr (25%), 0 sup rnrs, 0 SWs.
Sons of Pleasant Colony w/ Mr. Prospector mares: 12 fls rac age, 3 2yos, 7 strs, 4 wnrs
(33%), 2 sup rnrs (17%), 1 SW (8%).

'97—Dkbbr. c. by Colonial Affair.
'96—Hoshino Rocky, c., by Meadowlake. Unraced. 97KEESEP $115,000 Buyer:
Leading Corporation.
'95—Galaxia, f., by Relaunch. 3 strts, 0 wins, $9,620 (RI 1.55).
'94—Cherry Creek, f., by Mt. Livermore. 4 strts, 0 wins, $15,440 (RI 1.79).
'93—Paramour, h., by Wild Again. 33 strts, 5 wins, $157,955 (RI 2.71). 96KEEMAY
($60,000) RNA.
'92—No Report.
'91—Rehlat Farah, h., by Pleasant Colony. 21 strts, 7 wins, $62,856 (RI 1.48).
92KEESEP $130,000 Buyer: Darley Stud Management.
'90—Cindazanno, m., by Alleged. 14 strts, 1 win, $48,451 (RI 2.71). 91KEEJUL
$40,000 Buyer: Tom Baxter.

FIGURE 18-11 Page from *Thoroughbred Times* Buyer's Guide for Keeneland
September Yearling Sale, 1998. (Courtesy of *Thoroughbred Times, Inc.*)

Venus Bound - (Silver Hawk) 91KEENOV $77,000 Buyer: Tom Roach; Venus Bound - (Meadowlake) 95KEENOV $50,000 Buyer: Inwood Farm.

24   Yrlng. c. by HOLY BULL—VERBASLE (26 starts, RI 7.45) by SLEWPY.
    Breeder, Robert N. Clay and Stud TNT (Ky.).
    1998 Stud Fee: $25,000; **1996 Stud Fee:** $25,000. **Dosage:** (6-3-5-0-0); **DI:** 4.60;
    CD: 1.07
    1997 Sales Yrigs: 26 offered, 21 sold, $135,048 avg., $97,000 med.

Holy Bull w/ Slewpy mares: 1 fl rac age, 1 2yo, 1 str, 1 wnr (100%), 1 sup rnr (100%), 1 SW (100%).
Sons of Great Above w/ Slewpy mares: 1 fl rac age, 1 2yo, 1 str, 1 wnr (100%), 1 sup rnr (100%), 1 SW (100%).
Sons of Great Above w/ Seattle Slew mares: Not tried.

'97—Dkbbr. c. by Holy Bull.
'96—SMOKEY MIRAGE, f., by Holy Bull. 1 strt, 1 win, $24,000 (RI 10.21). 97KEESEP $70,000 Buyer: Thunderhead Farms.
'95—Rojo Warrior, c., by Kris S. Unraced. 96KEESEP $35,000 Buyer: Paula Capestro; 97BARMAY $50,000 Buyer: E. Edward Delaplane.
'94—What a Day, c., by Housebuster. 3 strts, 1 win, $28,930 (RI 4.78).

Verbasle - (Holy Bull) 96KEENOV $235,000 Buyer: Three Chimneys Farm, Agent.

25   Yrlng. f. by MEADOWLAKE—VICE ON ICE (26 starts, RI 5.20) by VICE
    REGENT. Breeder, Craig Bandoroff, S.D. Brilie and Mathew Firestone
    (Ky.).
    1998 Stud Fee: Private; **1996 Stud Fee:** $20,000. **Dosage:** (9-8-7-0-0); **DI:** 5.86;
    CD: 1.08
    1997 Sales Yrigs: 49 offered, 44 sold, $83,409 avg., $60,000 med.

Meadowlake w/ Vice Regent mares: 3 fls rac age, 0 2yos, 3 strs , 3 wnrs (100%), 1 sup rnr (33%), 1 SW (33%), 1 gr. SW. incl. MEADOW MONSTER.
Sons of Hold Your Peace w/ Vice Regent mares: 6 fls rac age, 0 2yos, 6 strs, 6 wnrs (100%), 2 sup rnrs (33%), 2 SWs (33%), 1 gr. SW. incl. MEADOW MONSTER.
Sons of Hold Your Peace w/ Northern Dancer mares: 5 fls rac age, 0 2yos, 5 strs, 4 wnrs (80%), 0 sup rnrs, 0 Sws.

'97—Ch. f. by Meadowlake.

Vice On Ice - (Carson City) 97KEENOV $460,000 Buyer: Cecil Seaman, Agent.

FIGURE 18-11   *Continued*

Upon arrival at the sale, conformation can be evaluated and health data can be obtained from the consignor. Before viewing a horse, consignors may require those inspecting the horse to fill out a request card. The number of inspections and by whom, are used by the consignor and their agent to determine the reserve bid if one is to be placed prior to the sale.

Conformation evaluation (see Chapter 2) may include actual measurements of a horse's body parts, which are entered into a computer program to determine balance. There are services that perform this evaluation and it is usually done prior to arrival at the sales facility. During the conformation evaluation, the horse is observed at the walk and trot for any suggestion of lameness and to evaluate the quality of movement (Figure 18-12).

After the initial conformation evaluation, the next step is to determine if the horse has any physical or physiological limitations. Ultrasonic examination of the heart can be used to determine heart size, thickness of the left ventricle muscle, and efficiency of contraction to move blood out of the ventricles. There are close correlations between these parameters and the horse's ability to run certain distances. Ultrasonic examination of the spleen helps predict blood volume. The larynx can be viewed with an endoscope to determine if the structures are functioning properly during inspiration and expiration. Stomach ulcers can be determined with an endoscope. During the remainder of the prepurchase process, the horse is examined from nose to tail for anything that is swollen, warm to the touch, or not normal. All the joints in the legs should be flexed. Each veterinarian has his or her own method of examination.

When horses are worked prior to the sale, for viewing by potential buyers, the quality of their performance, attitude toward work, and potential for future performances can be evaluated. Gait analysis and fatigue curves can be

Figure 18-12   Horses being inspected at Keeneland sale. (Courtesy of Keeneland Association, Inc.)

used to evaluate race horses during their workouts on the track. Complicated computerized programs are used for the analysis and consultant services are available for buyers. Very slow motion video can be used to detect defects in performance and determine if they can be overcome by proper training. Defects in movement of the feet and legs are easily recognized and can be related to potential unsoundness at a later time.

During the actual auction, buyers bid in many different ways to conceal their bid (Figure 18-13). If subtle bids are to be used, the auctioneer and/or the bid spotter must be aware of your method. For example, when the bidder looks at the bid spotter and removes his/her glasses, a bid is made. The bidder continues bidding as long as the glasses are off and quits when they are replaced. These methods only work for bidders who will place bids on several horses unless specific arrangements are made for a particular horse.

Once the final bid is recognized and the "hammer falls," the horse is sold and the successful bidder is responsible for the horse. If the horse is to remain at the sales facility overnight, arrangements must be made for it to be fed and watered. Security considerations may be important for expensive horses. Normally, horses must be removed from the sales premises within a published

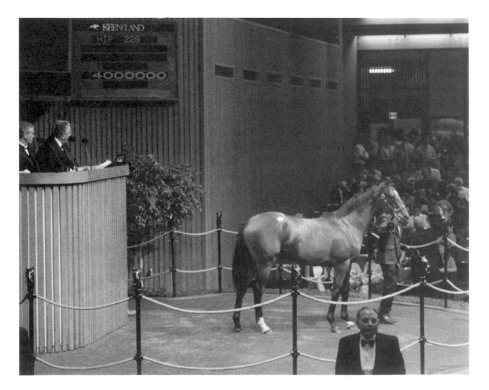

FIGURE 18-13   Thoroughbred yearling being sold in Keeneland Association sales arena. Bid is at $4,000,000. (Courtesy of Keeneland Association, Inc.)

period of time. Sales taxes may be due depending where the horse will be transported and its intended use.

To sell a horse at auction, most sales companies will require that the horse be nominated by a certain date. If it is a "select" sale, the sales company may inspect the horse prior to accepting it for the sale. The selection process usually includes a pedigree analysis, conformation analysis, and veterinary inspection. Consignment contracts will contain information regarding the owner, agent (if one is used), entry fee, commission structure, and detailed horse information like name, date foaled, color, sex, sire, dam, dam's sire, if bred and to which stallion, date of last service, pregnancy status, and what kind of prospect (broodmare, racing, weanling, yearling, stallion share, etc.). The owner must warrant title and correct identity and provide all necessary documents, blood tests, certificates for status of breeding and health, and immunizations. Other clauses may state that the auctioneer is appointed to sell the horse; the horse can be withdrawn for veterinary reasons; if sold prior to the sale, commission is due to the sales company; the date the horse is to be on the sales premises; when settlement will be made; who determines the order of sale; assignment of stabling; the date and location of sale and all information about the horse, owner, and agent are not confidential. There may be other clauses, depending on the type of sale.

To get horses properly prepared for a sale, the owner may send the horse to a person who specializes in sale preparations, hire an agent to show the horse at the sale, and purchase advertising. The person who fits the horse will make sure it is physically fit, will lead properly, and is accustomed to noise and people. The horse's muscles must be toned, proper body weight achieved, hair coat must be in proper condition, and the feet properly shod. The horse must be properly trained for a specific performance type sale. If the owner will show the horse at the sale, preparations must be made to prepare the stall, decorate the area, advertise the pedigree and other information on a summary sheet, have a stall card made to hang on the stall with the hip number, pedigree, and other information. All the necessary stall maintenance equipment, grooming equipment, tack, feed, and other supplies must be organized and taken to the sale. Someone who is competent in showing sales horses should show the horse to prospective bidders and answer questions. The process is rather complicated and it is advisable to use an agent until the owner becomes confident about handling the horse or taking care of the details for showing it at the sale.

Private Treaty

Selling horses at private treaty has many advantages and can be less expensive by avoiding the costs of selling at auction. The owner may take all responsibility or may use the services of an agent. Agents charge a commission or a flat fee for their services. The agent represents the owner and may sell the horse through an agent representing a buyer. It is unethical for an agent to get a fee from both the buyer and seller. A sales or purchase contract is used to prevent misunderstandings between the parties.

During the sale, the owner or agent must be careful not to misrepresent the horse, make statements that are implied warranties, or fail to inform or reveal the whole truth about a horse's defects, liens against the horse, behavior, and health status. Most problems that arise are related to soundness for performance or breeding, or to behavior for riding and handling. When buying a stallion, the seller implies that the horse is sound for breeding and capable of getting a mare in foal. The minimum conditions for fertility, such as the pregnancy percentage or live foal percentage, can be agreed upon and stated in the purchase contract.

Other features of a purchase contract include the terms for payment; when title and registration papers (separate properties) pass to the buyer; how, when, where, and by whom the horse will be evaluated for performance ability or soundness and the basis for rejection; where the horse is to be delivered; when risk of loss passes to buyer; who pays the stud fee for a mare in foal; who will register a foal and pay fees; agent(s) commission and who pays it; breeding rights retained by the seller or held by a third party for a stallion; who is responsible for any transaction expenses; default of payments; and other issues of concern to either party.

Agents who represent both buyer and seller are required to notify both parties and disclose any commissions that are to be paid and any other agreements. Secret commissions and markups are legal issues. Partners who purchase or sell partnership horses are required to divulge their intent to the other partners; otherwise, it is self-dealing in partnership assets.

Sales and Use Taxes

Many states have enacted a system of sales and use taxation. A thorough knowledge of each state's specific rules can help avoid or reduce the taxation. Thus, the cost of buying a horse will be less expensive. Texas and Oklahoma exclude horses from taxes while other states such as Kentucky do not permit state localities to levy a separate tax. Some states exclude certain types of horses.

INTERSTATE AND INTERNATIONAL IMPORTATION AND EXPORTATION

The horse industry is a global business and many horses are crossing interstate and international boundaries for performance events, breeding, or sale. They are transported by van or by air. When being transported by van across interstate boundaries, regulations must be met for each state the horse enters and leaves. Most regulations will be related to health, identification, and authority to transport. It is difficult and time-consuming for an individual owner to be aware of all the regulations, so an agent or the van company is usually given responsibility for ensuring that all regulations are met.

Each country has specific regulations for importation and exportation of horses, and these vary. Horses entering the United States must meet the requirements of the U.S. Department of Agriculture. These requirements periodically change and can be obtained from the Animal and Plant Health Inspection Service, Veterinary Services, National Center for Import and Export, Import Animals Staff, 4700 River Road, Unit 39, Riverdale, MD 20737-1231. Before horses can be exported from the country of origin, however, export requirements for that country must be met.

There are commercial agents like Mersant International that specialize in the importation and exportation of horses for clients. It is advisable to use an agent so that unexpected regulations are not encountered. Mersant International has recommended the following guidelines for international shipping. Be sure to give the agent at least one month to coordinate the shipment. This will give the agent time to look for other horses being shipped to the same destination so a horse does not travel alone. Shipping on a chartered flight, if one is fortunate enough to be shipping from a country that has horse charters, is usually the most economical. An attendant is required to accompany horses shipped by air. It is recommended that a professional flying attendant accompany them. Horses travel at their owner's risk, whether by van, ship, or aircraft; so it is recommended that they be insured.

Importation into United States

There are four ports of entry for animals into the United States that have USDA approved quarantine facilities (New York, Miami, Honolulu, and Los Angeles). Upon arrival in the U.S., all horses must go directly to the quarantine facility. The normal quarantine period is between 48 to 72 hours, pending the results of the blood tests done on arrival. However, the quarantine stay is determined by the country from which it is being imported. It could be as short as 2 days or as long as 60 days. All horses must meet all USDA requirements and must be cleared through U.S. Customs. This requires the use of a licensed U.S. Customs agent, and your shipping agent may or may not be licensed. One of the first things to do before shipment is to pretest the horse for piroplasmosis, dourine, glanders, and equine infectious anemia. Upon arrival, it will be tested for these diseases and will not be allowed into the country unless the results are negative. Depending on the country of origin, an import permit may be required by the USDA to enter the U.S. Upon release from quarantine, someone must be present with transportation. Frequently, a van company is used to deliver the horse to its final destination. If the horse is a Thoroughbred, the shipping agent or new owner must file the appropriate paperwork with the Jockey Club for registration purposes. If the paperwork is not submitted within 60 days, there is a penalty. Other breed associations have forms that must be filed.

Exportation from United States

The process should be started about two months prior to the shipping date to allow time to meet export requirements for the country where the horse is being shipped and give the shipping agent time to find other horses for the trip to reduce expenses. A quarantine may be required in the U.S. or at the destination or both. Taxes and/or duty may have to be paid to customs authorities upon arrival in the foreign country.

PREVENTING THEFT

Theft of horses, tack, trailers, and trucks is a common problem in the horse industry and has been for generations. To prevent theft, horse owners, boarding stables, and other places where horses and equipment are kept can take management steps to minimize the risk.

Permanently marking horses with freeze or hot iron brands or microchips discourages theft and makes it much easier to track and recover stolen horses. Tack and other equipment can be permanently identified with the owner's social security or driver's license number. Current photographs of horses and equipment can be maintained to help identify stolen items. Keeping registration papers, certificates of title, dated bills of sale, and ownership transfer papers with current photographs in special files will save valuable time in proving ownership if a theft occurs. Placement of barns and facilities away from roads or highly visible sites and behind the security of fences and locked gates will deter theft. Do not leave halters and lead ropes where they are accessible to a thief to steal a horse. The use of signs regarding trespassing, security systems, and membership in livestock associations deters theft. Use of motion detectors and other security devices is also recommended. In some areas, guard dogs, security patrols, and neighborhood watch are effective. High levels of activity reduce the chances for a thief to be successful.

If a horse is stolen, quick action to report the loss to local law enforcement agencies, state livestock inspection offices, breed associations, equine slaughter houses, livestock auctions, horse sales, race tracks, rodeos, any type of horse event being held, farriers, veterinarians, and neighbors will enhance the chances of recovery. Getting information into the local media (television, radio, and newspapers) will help spread the information quickly to a larger area.

Once the stolen horse or equipment is located, keep it under surveillance from a distance and notify the proper law enforcement agency to recover it.

MEMBERSHIPS

Memberships in breed and other types of horse organizations offer a number of benefits to the person involved in the horse industry. Benefits include interactions and networking with others having similar interests, educational programs, group insurance, product discounts, advertising, monetary rewards for owning and/or riding horses achieving certain performance goals, access to horse information data bases, publicity for type of horse owned and giving something back to the industry. There are many organizations that are specific to breeds or activities, but organizations like the American Horse Council represent all aspects of the horse industry.

SOURCES OF INFORMATION

Internet

The increasing use of the Internet has opened a means to find almost any type of information about a horse. There are a few Web sites that specialize in links to thousands of specific Web sites. Oklahoma State University Web site (www.ansi.okstate.edu/breeds/horses/horses.htm) has information about many breeds found around the world, including information on how to contact the breed organization(s) for each one. Cybersteed (www.cybersteed.com) and HayNet (www.haynet.net) also have links to numerous horse organizations. Sites such as www.thoroughbredtimes.com and horseracing.miningco. com/mlibrary.htm are extensive compendiums of links to Web sites for horse racing information like race tracks, farms, sales companies, bloodstock consultants, races, museums and parks, handicapping, media, steeplechasing, and trainers. The *Thoroughbred Times* is exclusive for Thoroughbred racing, whereas the Mining Co site covers all breeds. The Web site www.caaonline.com/sites/equine.htm is a compendium of numerous sites for a wide variety of information. Some sites are more specific about the type of information they manage but they do have links to other sites. Farriers use www.horseshoes.com. Veterinary resource links are present at many of the sites given above and on www.haynet.net. Horse publications' addresses and subscription information can be found at americanhorsepubs.org/directory.htm site. Rodeo information is at rodeo.miningco.com/mbody.htm, whereas horse show information is located at www.ahsa.org. The AHSA rule book, show dates, and other information about them are readily available on their site.

Traditional Sources

Local Cooperative Extension Service offices normally keep a collection of brochures on a variety of topics. Their horse specialists are very good sources of information. University and larger city libraries normally keep books related to horse production. Book stores are able to order books that are currently in print. Some companies specialize in out-of-print and rare horse books.

Videos have become a popular source of information because most of them are on "do it yourself" techniques.

Individual Horse

The American Quarter Horse Association and the Jockey Club Information Systems (EquineLine) keep detailed records for each horse registered with AQHA and the Jockey Club, respectively. Some of the available information includes pedigree information going back several generations, race and/or show records, and get of sire and dam produce records. By establishing an account with the service, records can be viewed on the computer screen, downloaded, printed, or sent by e-mail. In addition to individual horse records, jockey and trainer statistics can be obtained. The National Cutting Horse Association keeps performance records of horses shown in their approved contests. Many other associations keep specific performance records. These data bases can be accessed with a password issued by the organization after a fee is paid.

APPENDIX 3-1

Addresses of Breed Associations and Registries, Business Associations, Magazines, and State Horse Councils

Breed Associations and Registries

Akhal Teke Registry of America. 21314 129th Ave., SE, Snohomish, WA 98296-7843.

American Association of Breeders of Holsteiner Horses, Inc. Y. Wallem. Woodman Rd., S. Hampton, NH 03827.

American Association of Owners and Breeders of Peruvian Paso Horses. P.O. Box 189, Ramona, CA 92065-0189.

American Bashkir Curly Registry. P.O. Box 246, Ely, NV 89301.

American Bay Horse Association. P.O. Box 844F, Wheeling, IL 60090.

American Buckskin Registry Association. P.O. Box 3850, Redding, CA 96049.

American Connemara Pony Society. R.D. #1, Goshen, CT 06756.

American Council of Spotted Asses. P.O. Box 121, New Mule, MO 62365.

American Donkey and Mule Society, Inc. 2901 N. Elm St., Denton, TX 76201.

American Fox Trotting Horse Breed Association. Box 666, Marshfield, MO 65706.

American Gotland Horse Association. R.R. #2, Box 181, Elkland, MO 65644.

American Hackney Horse Society. P.O. Box 174, Pittsville, IL 62363.

American Holsteiner Horse Association, Inc., 222 E. Main St., Suite 1, Georgetown, KY 40324.

American Hunter and Jumper Association. P.O. Box 1174, Fort Wayne, IN 46801.

American Indian Horse Registry. Route 3, Box 64, Lockhart, TX 78644.

American Miniature Horse Association, Inc. 5601 South IH 35W, Alvarado, TX 76009.

American Miniature and Shetland Horse Registry. P.O. Box 3415, Peoria, IL 61614.

American Morgan Horse Association. P.O. Box 960, Shelburne, VT 05482-0906.

American Mustang Association. P.O. Box 338, Yucaipa, CA 92399.

American Mustang and Burro Association. P.O. Box 7, Benton City, WA 99320.

American Paint Horse Association. P.O. Box 961023, Fort Worth, TX 76161-0023.

American Part-Blooded Horse Registry. 4120 South East River Dr., Portland, OR 97222.

American Paso Fino Pleasure Horse Association. P.O. Box 2363, Pittsburgh, PA 15219.

American Pony. 926 Summit Ave., Gainesville, TX 76240.

American Quarter Horse Association. 2701 I-40 East, Amarillo, TX 79168.

American Quarter Pony Association. Route 1, Box 585, Marengo, OH 43334.

American Saddlebred Horse Association, Inc. 4093 Ironworks Pike, Lexington, KY 40511.

American Saddlebred Pony Association. 801 South Court St., Scott City, KS 67871.

American Saddle Horse Breeders' Association. 929 South Fourth St., Louisville, KY 40203.

American Shetland Pony Club. P.O. Box 3415, Peoria, IL 61614.

American Suffolk Horse Association. 4240 Goehring Road, Ledbetter, TX 78946-9707.

American Trakehner Association. 1520 West Church Street, Newark, OH 43081.

American Vaulting Association. P.O. Box 3663, Saratoga, CA 95070-1663.

American Walking Pony Association. Route 5, Box 88, Upper River Road, Macon, GA 31201.

American Warmblood Registry, Inc. Box 395, Hastings, NY 10706.

American Warmblood Society. 6801 W. Romley, Phoenix, AZ 85043.

Andalusian Horse Registry of the Americas. P.O. Box 1290, Silver City, NM 88061.

Appaloosa Horse Club. P.O. Box 8403, Moscow, ID 83843.

Appaloosa Horse Club of Canada. P.O. Box 940, Claresholm, Alberta, Canada T0L 0T0.

Arabian Horse Registry of America. 12000 Zuni St., Westminster, CO 80234-2300.

Azteca Horse Association of the United States. 2613 Camino De Verdad, Mercedes, TX 78570.

Belgian Draft Horse Corporation of America. P.O. Box 335, Wabash, IN 46992.

Canadian Arabian Horse Registry. R.R. 1, Bowden, Alberta, Canada T0M 0K0.

Canadian Buckskin Association. P.O. Box 135, Okotoks, Alberta, Canada T0L 1T0.

Canadian Icelandic Horse Federation. P.O. Box 5, Site 9, R.R. #8 Edmonton, Alberta T5L 4H8.

Canadian Percheron Association. P.O. Box 200, Crossfield, Alberta, Canada T0M 050.

Canadian Pinto Horse Association. P.O. Box 297, Spruce Grove, Alberta, Canada T0E 2C0.

Canadian Walking Horse Association. P.O. Box 56, Site 2, R.R. #8, Calgary, Alberta, Canada T2J 2T9.

Capitol Quarter Horse Association. 25302 Edison Rd., Box 594, South Bend, IN 46624.

Chickasaw Horse Association. Mrs. J.A. Barker, Jr., secretary. Box 607, Love Valley, NC 28677.

Cleveland Bay Horse Society of America. P.O. Box 221, South Windham, CT 06266.

Clydesdale Breeders Association of the United States. 17378 Kelly Road, Pecatonica, IL 61063.

Colorado Ranger Horse Association, Inc. R.D. 1, Box 1290, Wampum, PA 16157-9610.

Cross-Bred Pony Registry. P.O. Box M, Andover, NJ 07821.

Endurance Horse Registry, P.O. Box 63, Agoura, CA 91301.

Galiceño Horse Breeders Association. P.O. Box 219, Godley, TX 76044.

Gotland Russ Association of North America. Road 1, Box 174, Wheeling, WV 26059.

Haflinger Association of America. 153 South St., Rockport, MA 01966.

Haflinger Registry of North America. 14640 Star Route 83, Coshocton, OH 43812.

Hanovarian Society. 3090 Old San Jose Rd., Soquel, CA 95073.

Hungarian Horse Association. Bitterrott Stock Farm, Hamilton, MT 59840.

Hunter Club of America. P.O. Box 274, Washington, MI 48094.

International American Albino Association. P.O. Box 79, Crabtree, OR 97335.

International Andalusian Horse Association. 256 So. Robertson, #9378F, Beverly Hills, CA 90211.

International Andalusian and Lusitano Horse Association. 101 Carnoustie N. #200, Shoal Creek, AL 35242.

International Arabian Horse Association. P.O. Box 33696, Denver, CO 80233. (Half-Arab and Anglo-Arab Registries)

International Buckskin Horse Association. P.O. Box 357, St. John, IN 46373.

International Miniature Horse Registry. 3 Malaga Cove Plaza, Palos Verdes Peninsula, CA 90274.

International Morab Registry. R.R. 3, Box 235, Ava, MO 65608-9553.

Jockey Club. 380 Madison Ave., New York, NY 10017. (Thoroughbred horses)

Missouri Fox Trotting Horse Breed Association. P.O. Box 1027, Ava, MO 65608.

Model Quarter Horse Association. P.O. Box 127, Monument, OR 97864.

National Appaloosa Pony. P.O. Box 206, Gaston, IN 47342.

National Association of Paso Fino Horses of Puerto Rico. Aptdo. 253, Guaynabo, PR 00657.

National Chickasaw Horse Association. R.R. #2, Clarinda, IA 51632.

National Miniature Donkey Association. R.D. 1, Box 472, Dewey Rd., Rome, NY 13440.

National Palomino Breeders Association. P.O. Box 146, London, KY 40741.

National Pinto Horse Registry. P.O. Box 486, Oxford, NY 13830.

National Quarter Horse Registry. Box 235, Raywood, TX 77582.

National Quarter Pony Association, Inc. 5135 County Rd. 25, Rt. #1, Marengo, OH 43334.

National Show Horse. 11700 Commonwealth Drive, Suite 200, Louisville, KY 40299.

North American Mustang Association and Registry. P.O. Box 850906, Mesquite, TX 75185-0906.

North American Single-Footing Horse Association. P.O. Box 1079, Three Forks, MT 59752.

North American Trakehner Association. 1660 Collier Rd., Akron, OH 44320.

Norwegian Fjord Association of North America. 24570 Chardon Rd., Grayslake, IL 60030.

Norwegian Fjord Horse Registry. 1203 Appian Dr., Webster, NY 14580-9129.

Original Half Quarter Horse Registry. Hubbard, OR 97032.

Palomino Horse Association. P.O. Box 324, Jefferson City, MO 65102.

Palomino Horse Breeders of America. 15253 E. Shelly Dr., Tulsa, OK 74116-2620.

Palomino Horse Club of Canada. R.R. #5 Wetaskiwin, Alberta, Canada T9A 1X2.

Paso Fino Horse Association, Inc. J. Knight. P.O. Box 600, Bowling Green, FL 33834.

Percheron Horse Association of America. P.O. Box 141, Fredericktown, OH 43019.

Peruvian Horse Association of Canada. Lyalta, Alberta, Canada T0J 1Y0.

Peruvian Paso Horse Registry of North America. 3077 Wiljan Court, Suite A, Santa Rosa, CA 95407.

Pinto Horse Association of America. 1900 Samuels Ave., Fort Worth, TX 76102-1141.

Pony of the Americas Club. 5240 Elmwood Ave., Indianapolis, IN 46203.

Purebred Hanoverian Association of American Breeders & Owners, Inc. 250 Miller Rd., Lakewood, NJ 08701.

Racking Horse Breeders Association of America. 67 Horse Center Road, Decatur, AL 35603.

Rocky Mountain Horse Association. 2805 Lancaster Road, Danville, KY 40422.

Shetland Pony Identification Bureau. 1108 Jackson St., Omaha, NE 68102.

Southwest Spanish Mustang Association. Box 148, Finley, OK 74543.

Spanish-Barb Breeders Association. P.O. Box 641, Lyons, CO 80540.

Spanish Mustang Registry. 8328 Stevenson Ave., Sacramento, CA 95828.

Standard Jack and Jennet Registry of America. P.O. Box 1155, Pulaski, TN 38478-1155.

Standard Quarter Horse Association. 4390 Fenton St., Denver, CO 80212.

Swedish Gotland Breeders Society. Rt. 3, Box 134, Corinth, KY 41010.

Tarpan Stud Association. Rt. 3, Box 314F, Hampton, GA 30228.

Tennessee Walking Horse Breeders' and Exhibitors' Association of America. P.O. Box 286, Lewisburg, TN 37091.

United States Dressage Federation, Inc. P.O. Box 80668, Lincoln, NE 68501.

United States Icelandic Horse Federation. 38 Park St., Montclair, NJ 07042.

United States Lipizzan Registry. 707 13th Street SE, Suite 275, Salem, OR 97301.

United States Saddle Donkey Club. P.O. Box 244, Tularosa, NM 88352.

United States Trotting Association. 750 Michigan Ave., Columbus, OH 43215. (Standardbred horses)

United States Trotting Pony Association. P.O. Box 468, Fowler, IN 47944.

Warmblood Paardenstambock in Nederland. 6208 Reba Dr., Roseville, CA 95678.

Welsh Pony and Cob Society of America, Inc. P.O. Box 2977, Winchester, VA 22604.

White Horse Registry. P.O. Box 79, Crabtree, OR 97335.

World Akhal Tekke Horse Association, Inc. 1837 West County Rd. 76, Willington, CO 80549.

Business Associations

American Association of Equine Practioners. 4075 Iron Works Pike, Lexington, KY 40511.

American Driving Society. P.O. Box 160, Metamora, MI 48455.

American Endurance Ride Conference. 701 High St., Suite 203, Auburn, CA 95603.

American Farriers Association. Kentucky Horse Park, 4809 Ironwood Pike, Lexington, KY 40511.

American Horse Council. 1700 K St. Northwest, Number 300, Washington, DC 20006-3805.

American Horse Shows Association. 220 East 43rd St., New York, NY 10017.

American Thoroughbred Breeders and Owners Association. 36 Ozone Park, Jamaica, NY 11417.

American Vaulting Association. 20066 Glen Brae Dr., Saratoga, CA 98070.

American Veterinary Medical Association. 1931 No. Meacham Rd., #100, Shaumburg, IL 60173.

Animal Poison Control Center. University of Illinois, 2001 S. Lincoln Ave., Urbana, IL 61801.

Arabian Horse Racing Association of America. 66 South Riversdale Dr., Batavia, OH 45103.

Carriage Association of America. 117 Pointers-Auburn Rd., Salem, NJ 08079.

CHA. P.O. Box 188, Lawrence, MI 49064.

Driving for the Disabled, Inc. 4246 Madonna Rd., Jarrettsville, MD 21084.

Food and Drug Administration Center for Veterinary Medicine. 5600 Fishers Lane, Rockville, MD 20857.

Intercollegiate Horse Show Association. Smoke Run Farm, Hollow Road, Stony Brook, NY 11790.

International Side-Saddle Organization. R.D. 2, Box 2055, Mt. Holly, NJ 08060.

International Team Penning Association. P.O. Box 54, Tyler, TX 75710.

Jockey Club Information Systems. 821 Corporate Drive, Lexington, KY 40503-2794.

National Cutting Horse Association. 4704 Highway 377 South, Fort Worth, TX 76116-8805.

National High School Rodeo Association. 128 North 2nd St., Douglas, WY 82633.

National Intercollegiate Rodeo Association. 2925 Isaacs Ave., Walla Walla, WA 99362.

National Little Britches Rodeo Association. 1045 W. Rio Grande, Colorado Springs, CO 80906.

National Reining Horse Association. 28881 SR 83, Coshocton, OH 43812.

National Senior Pro Rodeo Association. P.O. Box 419, Roundup, MT 59072.

National Thoroughbred Racing Association. 2343 Alexandria, Lexington, KY 40504.

North American Riding for the Handicapped Association. P.O. Box 3310, Denver, CO 80233.

North American Trail Ride Conference. P.O. Box 20315, El Cajon, CA 92021.

Polocrosse Association of the United States. 2716 E. Bell Rd., Phoenix, AZ 85032.

Professional Rodeo Cowboy's Association. 101 Pro Rodeo Dr., Colorado Springs, CO 80919.

Thoroughbred Owners and Breeders Association. P.O. Box 4367, Lexington, KY 40544-4367.

Thoroughbred Racing Association of North America, Inc. 3000 Marcus Ave., Suite 2W4, Lake Success, NY 11042.

United Professional Horsemen's Association. 4059 Iron Works Pike, Lexington, KY 40511.

USDA Animal and Plant Health Inspection Service. Federal Building, 6505 Belcrest Rd., Hyattsville, MD 20782.

USDA Extension Service. 14th St. and Independence Ave. S.W., Washington, D.C. 20250.

USDA National Agricultural Library. 10301 Baltimore Blvd., Beltsville, MD 20750.

United States Dressage Federation, Inc., 1212 O St., Lincoln, NE 68501.

United States Driving for the Disabled. S. & M. Bowen, Jarrettsville, MD 21084.
United States Equine Marketing Association. P.O. Box 178, Philomont, VA 22131.
United States Polo Association. 4059 Iron Works Parkway, Suite 1, Lexington, KY 40511-8483.
United States Pony Clubs. S. Gidings. 893 S. Matlack St., Suite 110, West Chester, PA 19382.
United States Saddle Donkey Club. P.O. Box 244, Tularosa, NM 88352.
Women's Professional Rodeo Association. L. Moore. Route 5, Box 698, Blanchard, OK 73010.

Magazines

(See americanhorsepubs.org/directory.htm for other publications.)

American Connemara Pony Society News. American Connemara Pony Society. Hoshiekon Farm. R.D. #1, Goshen, CT 06756.
American Farriers Journal. P.O. Box 624, Brookfield, WI 53008-0624.
American Hanoverian. 3401 St. John's Dr., Dallas, TX 75205.
American Morgan Horse Association. P.O. Box 960, Shelburne, VT 05482-0960.
American Saddlebred. 4093 Iron Works Pike, Lexington, KY 40511-8434.
American Trakehner. 1520 West Church Street, Newark, OH 43055.
America's Horse. 1600 Quarter Horse Dr., Amarillo, TX 79104.
Appaloosa Journal. Appaloosa Horse Club. 5070 Highway 8 West, Moscow, ID 83843.
Arabian Horse Times. 1050 8th Street, N.E., Waseca, MN 56093.
Arabian Horse World. 1316 Tamson Drive, #101, Cambria, CA 93428.
Arizona Thoroughbred. P.O. Box 41774, Phoenix, AZ 85080.
Aside World. P.O. Box 1104, Bucyrus, OH 44820.
Backstretch. P.O. Box 7065, Louisville, KY 40257-0065.
Blood-Horse. P.O. Box 4038, Lexington, KY 40544-4038.
Brayer. 2901 N. Elm, Denton, TX 76201-7632.
Buckskin Horses Magazine. P.O. Box 2347, Waldron, AR 72958.
California Thoroughbred. P.O. Box 60018, Arcadia, CA 91066-6018.
Carriage Journal. 177 Pointers-Auburn Road, Salem, NJ 08079-4312.
Chronicle of the Horse. Box 46, Middleburg, VA 20118.
Cutting Horse Chatter. 4704 Highway 377 South, Fort Worth, TX 76116-8805.
Daily Racing Form. 315 Hudson St., 9th Floor, New York, NY 10013.
Draft Horse Journal. Box 670, Waverly, IA 50677.
Dressage Today. 656 Quince Orchard Rd. #600, Gaithersberg, MD 20878-1472.
Endurance News. 11960 Heritage Oak Place, Suite 9, Auburn, CA 95603-4727.
Equestrian Trails. 13741 Foothill Blvd., Suite 220, Slymar, CA 91342-3015.
Equus. 656 Quince Orchard Rd., Gaithersburg, MD 20878-1472.
Florida Horse. P.O. Box 2106, Ocala, FL 34478-2106.
Hackney World. Box W, East Granby, CT 06026.
Hoofbeats. United States Trotting Association, 750 Michigan Ave., Columbus, OH 43215-1191.
Horse Circuit News. 8098 E. 400 S., New Castle, IN 47362.
Horse and Rider. 1597 Cole Blvd., Suite 350, Golden, CO 80401.
Horse Show. American Horse Shows Association, 4047 Iron Works Pkwy., Lexington, KY 40511-8483

Horse World. P.O. Box 1007, Shelbyville, TN 37162-1007.

Horseman's Journal. P.O. Box 202290, Austin, TX 78720-2290.

Horseman's Yankee Pedlar. 83 Leicester St., North Oxford, MA 10537.

International Arabian Horse. 10805 E. Bethany Dr., Aurora, CO 80014-2605.

The Journal. P.O. Box 1027, Ava, MO 65608-1027.

Lariat. P.O. Box 229, Beaverton, OR 97045-0029.

Miniature Donkey Talk. 1338 Hughes Shop Road, Westminster, MD 21158.

Miniature Horse Voice. P.O. Box 857, Loris, SC 29569.

Mules. P.O. Box 2736, Chino, CA 91708.

NARHA Strides. P.O. Box 33150, Denver, CO 80233.

National Horseman. P.O. Box 43397, Middletown, KY 40243.

NRHA Reiner. P.O. Box 94, Minster, OH 45865-0094.

Paint Horse Journal. American Paint Horse Association, P.O. Box 961023, Fort Worth, TX 76161-0023.

Palomino Horse. 2626 East 21st Street, Suite 2, Tulsa, OK 74114.

Performance Horse. P.O. Box 7426, Eugene, OR 97401.

POA Magazine. 5240 Elmwood Ave., Indianapolis, IN 46203-5990.

Polo Player's Edition. 3500 Fairlane Farms Rd., Suite 9, Wellington, FL 33414.

Practical Horseman. P.O. Box 589, Unionville, PA 19375.

Prorodeo Sports News. 101 Pro Rodeo Dr., Colorado Springs, CO 80919.

Quarter Horse Journal. P.O. Box 32470, Amarillo, TX 79120-2470.

Quarter Racing Journal. P.O. Box 32470, Amarillo, TX 79120.

Saddle and Bridle. 375 No. Jackson, St. Louis, MO 63130-4243.

Southern Horseman. P.O. Box 71, Meridian, MS 39302-0071.

Spanish-Barb Journal. 13862 Gulf Haven Rd., Gulfport, MS 39503.

Tack 'n' Togs. Miller Publishing Company, P.O. Box 67, Minneapolis, MN 55440.

Texas Thoroughbred. P.O. Box 14967, Austin, TX 78761.

Thoroughbred Daily News. 811 River Rd., Fair Haven, NJ 07704.

Thoroughbred Record. 367 W. Short St., Lexington, KY 40507.

Thoroughbred Times. 496 Southland Dr., Lexington, KY 40533-8237.

Trail Rider. 147 Sun Ridge Rd., Alexandria, LA 76302.

Trottingbred. 575 Broadway, Hanover, PA 17331.

Turf and Sport Digest. 511-513 Oakland Ave., Baltimore, MD 21212.

USCTA News / Eventing USA. 525 Old Waterford Rd., NW, Leesburg, VA 20176.

USPC News. 4071 Iron Works Pkwy., Lexington, KY 40511-8462.

Vaulting World. 11845 Skyline Blvd., Los Gatos, CA 95030.

Voice of the Tennessee Walking Horse. P.O. Box 286, Lewisburg, TN 37091-0286.

Western Horseman. P.O. Box 7980, Colorado Springs, CO 80933-7980.

Whip. P.O. Box 160, Metamora, MI 48455-0160.

Women's Pro Rodeo News. 2112 Montgomery St., Fort Worth, TX 76107.

State Horse Councils

Arizona State Horsemen's Association
P.O. Box 131758
Phoenix, AZ 85046-1758
(602) 867-6814

Arkansas Horse Council
P.O. Box 737
Jasper, AR 72641
(870) 446-6226

California State Horsemen's Association
P.O. Box 1228
Clovis, CA 93613-1228
(559) 325-1055

Colorado Horsemen's Council
220 Livestock Exchange Building
Denver, CO 80216
(303) 292-4081

Connecticut Horse Council
P.O. Box 905
Cheshire, CT 06410-0905
(203) 250-8842

Delaware Equine Council
853 Raughley Hill Rd.
Harrington, DE 19952
(302) 398-4682

Georgia Horse Foundation
P.O. Box 736
Dahlonega, GA 30533-0736
(706) 542-1852

Horse Council of Nevada, Inc.
4175 W. Wigwam Avenue
Las Vegas, NV 89139-7759
(702) 896-5084

Horsemen's Council of Illinois
P.O. Box 1605
Springfield, IL 62705-1605
(217) 483-3235

Idaho Horse Council
5000 Childen Blvd.
Boise, ID 83714
(208) 323-8148

Indiana Horse Council
225 South East St., Suite 738
Indianapolis, IN 46202-4059
(317) 692-7115

Iowa Horse Industry Council
1817 E. 30th St.
Des Moines, IA 50317-8613
(515) 266-4734

Kansas Horse Council
P.O. Box 201
Sabetha, KS 66534-0201

Kentucky Horse Council
P.O. Box 11706
Lexington, KY 40577-1706
(800) 459-4677

Maine Equine Advisory Council
RFD #1, Box 700
Litchfield, ME 04350-9711
(207) 268-4604

Maryland Horse Council
P.O. Box 4891
Timonium, MD 21093-4891
(301) 948-8585

Michigan Horse Council
P.O. Box 22008
Lansing, MI 48909-2008
(517) 223-7248

Minnesota Horse Council
13055 Riverdale Dr.
Coon Rapids, MN 55448
(612) 576-1757

Mississippi Horse Council
1924 McCullough Blvd.
Tupelo, MS 38801
(601) 842-9346

Missouri Equine Council, Inc.
P.O. Box 681
Republic, MO 65738-0681
(417) 732-4062

Nebraska Horse Council
R.R. 1, Box 70 A2
Denton, NE 68501
(402) 797-5865

New Hampshire Horse Council
273 Poor Farm Road
New Ipswich, NH 03071
(603) 878-1694

New Jersey Horse Council
25 Beth Drive
Moorestown, NJ 08057-3021
(609) 231-0771

New Mexico Horse Council
Box 10206
Albuquerque, NM 87184-0206
(505) 344-8548

New York State Horse Council
760 Webster Rd.
Webster, NY 14580
(716) 872-3178

North Carolina Horse Council
P.O. Box 12999
Raleigh, NC 27605-2999
(919) 821-1030

Ohio Horseman's Council
15620 Mt. Olive Road
Rockbridge, OH 43149
(704) 385-0111

Oklahoma Horse Industry Council, Inc.
P.O. Box 423
Claremore, OK 74018-0423
(918) 343-1772

Oregon Horse Council
P.O. Box 234
Cheshire, OR 97419

Pennsylvania Equine Council
P.O. Box 570339
Boaldsburg, PA 16827-0570
(717) 469-7517

South Carolina Horsemen's Council
P.O. Box 11280
Columbia, SC 29211
(803) 734-2210

South Dakota Horse Council
P.O. Box 25
Hayi, SD 57241
(605) 783-3832

Sunshine State Horse
    Council, Inc.
P.O. Box 4158
North Fort Meyers,
    FL 33918-4158
(941) 731-2999

Tennessee Horse Council
P.O. Box 69
College Grove, TN 37046-0069
(615) 395-9294

Utah Horse Council
3259 S. Bluff Rd.
Syracuse, UT 84075
(801) 776-0420

Vermont Horse Council
P.O. Box 105
Montpelier, VT 05601-0105
(800) 722-1419

Virginia Horse Council
P.O. Box 6099
Charlottesville, VA 22906-6099
(804) 975-2010

Washington State Horse Council
2363 Mt. View Road E.
Port Orchard, WA 98366
(360) 769-8083

West Virginia Horse Council
418 Little Sandy Road
Elkview, WV 25071
(304) 965-5912

Wisconsin State Horse Council
132A South Ludington Street
Columbus, WI 53925-1516
(920) 623-0393

APPENDIX 5-1

Ration Formulation

Rations are used to demonstrate the method, using rules of thumb refined by the National Research Council recommendations.

Example 1

The first sample ration formulated is for a 500-kg (1100-lb) gelding that is ridden occasionally for ½ hour at a time; that is, a gelding fed a maintenance ration. Calculations are given in both the metric and avoirdupois weight systems.

Step 1. Determine the daily nutrient requirements. These requirements are given in Appendix Table 5-3.

Digestible energy	16.4 Mcal
Total protein	656 gm, or 1.44 lb
Calcium	20 gm, or 0.04 lb
Phosphorus	14 gm, or 0.031 lb
Vitamin A	15,000 IU

Step 2. From Table 5-7A on rules of thumb, we can make a tentative decision to feed the horse a roughage ration. The limiting factor for its ration should be the energy content. Therefore, the amount of a particular roughage that will provide the necessary energy is determined by the equation:

$$\frac{\text{Mcal digestible energy required by horse}}{\text{Mcal digestible energy per kg (or lb) of dry matter in roughage}} = \begin{array}{l} \text{weight of roughage} \\ \text{on a dry matter} \\ \text{basis that is} \\ \text{necessary} \end{array}$$

If we decide to use alfalfa hay (hay, s-c, early-bloom), its nutrient content is given in Appendix Table 5-9, entry 005. This alfalfa hay contains 90.5 percent dry matter. The dry matter contains 2.48 Mcal/kg, or 1.13 Mcal/lb; 19.9 percent crude protein; 1.41 percent Ca; and 0.21 percent P. This hay contains about 139.8 mg carotene/kg, or 11.86 mg carotene/lb (Appendix Table 5-10). Therefore, from Appendix Table 5-10 the vitamin A equivalent is 55,918 IU per kg, or 4,744 IU per pound.

The amount of energy required by the horse is contained in 6.77 kg (14.9 lb) dry matter:

$$\frac{16.4 \text{ Mcal}}{2.48 \text{ Mcal/kg}} = 6.61 \text{ kg of dry matter}$$

or

$$\frac{16.4 \text{ Mcal}}{1.13 \text{ Mcal/lb}} = 14.5 \text{ lb of dry matter}$$

Step 3.   The ration must be checked to see if the remainder of the nutrient requirements is met by feeding 6.61 kg (14.5 lb) of dry matter (alfalfa hay). The nutrient content for alfalfa hay is given in Appendix Tables 5-6 and 5-7.

Total protein = weight × CP content:

$$6.61 \text{ kg} \times .199 \quad = 1.315 \text{ kg}$$

or

$$1.45 \text{ lb} \times .199 \quad = 2.89 \text{ lb}$$

Calcium = weight × calcium content:

$$6.61 \text{ kg} \times .141 \quad = 0.093 \text{ kg}$$

or

$$1.45 \text{ lb} \times .141 \quad = 0.204 \text{ lb}$$

Phosphorus = weight × phosphorus content:

$$6.61 \text{ kg} \times .0021 \quad = 0.014 \text{ kg}$$

or

$$1.45 \text{ lb} \times .0021 \quad = 0.030 \text{ lb}$$

Vitamin A = weight × Vitamin A content:

$$6.61 \text{ kg} \times 55,918 = 369,618 \text{ IU}$$

or

$$1.45 \text{ lb} \times 25,417 = 368,547 \text{ IU}$$

Then compare the daily requirements with the ration contents:

	Requirements	Ration contents	Comments
Digestible energy	16.4 Mcal	16.4 Mcal	Ration meets requirement.
Total protein	656 gm *or* 1.44 lb	1315 gm *or* 2.89 lb	Ration has excessive protein, and it may be possible to reduce amount of ration since some protein will be used for energy.
Calcium	20 gm *or* 0.04 lb	93 gm *or* 0.204 lb	Ration has fivefold requirement.
Phosphorus	14 gm *or* 0.031 lb	14 gm *or* 0.030 lb	Ration meets requirement.
Vitamin A	15,000 IU	369,618 IU	Ration has twenty-five-fold requirement.

Therefore, the ration meets the daily nutrient requirements. The other necessary questions are (1) Will the horse consume the ration? and (2) Is the Ca:P ratio acceptable? The horse will consume up to 1.5 to 2.0 percent of its body weight (Table 5-8), which is 7.5 to 10 kg (16.5 to 22 lb) and is greater than the weight of the ration. The Ca:P ratio is 6.6 (93 gm Ca/14 gm P, or 0.204 lb Ca/0.030 lb P), which is more than 6:1. Therefore, it would be advisable to mix a phosphorus supplement with the trace-mineralized salt.

Step 4.　The final step is to convert the ratio to an "as fed" basis, because the calculations were based on 100 percent dry matter. Alfalfa is 90.5 percent dry matter; therefore, the equation for conversion is

$$\frac{\text{Weight in dry matter}}{\%\ \text{dry matter}} = \text{weight "as fed"}$$

$$\frac{6.61\ \text{kg}}{0.95} = 6.95\ \text{kg} \quad or \quad \frac{14.5\ \text{lb}}{0.95} = 15.26\ \text{lb}$$

Example 2

The calculations for a more difficult ration are used to demonstrate how to use a combination of roughage and grain. The calculations are taken from the National Academy of Sciences, National Research Council (1989) bulletin, *Nutrient Requirements for Horses.*

The basic idea is to compare the animal's needs to the amount supplied and, if the nutrients are not adequate, to determine what feedstuffs should be added and how much is needed to correct the deficiency. All of the calculations in the example are on a dry-matter basis.

Calculate ration for yearling, 12 months old, being fed for moderate growth, weighing 325 kg (715 lb), with expected mature weight of 500 kg (1,100 lb). The hay available is timothy, s-c early-bloom (Appendix Table 5-9, entry 230).

Step 1. Compare the nutrient content of the forage with the requirements of the horse. Use actual analysis if available; if not, use Appendix Tables 5-9 and 5-10 for the forage content. The approximate horse requirements for the ration are from Table 5-7A in the text.

	Digestible energy		Crude Protein (%)	Calcium (%)	Phos- phorus (%)	Vitamin A	
	(Mcal/kg)	(Mcal/lb)				(IU/kg)	(IU/lb)
Forage supplies	2.06	0.94	10.8	0.5	0.29	57,680	1543
Horse needs	2.8	1.3	12.6	0.43	0.24	2160	980

Timothy hay alone lacks energy and protein concentration. Therefore, a grain supplement rich in these nutrients must be added. According to Table 5-7A in the text, the yearling will eat 6.5 to 9.75 kg (14.3 to 21.45 lb) of a ration containing 2.8 Mcal of DE per kg (1.3 Mcal/lb). A mixture of equal parts of hay containing 2.06 Mcal/kg (0.94 Mcal/lb) and grain with 3.54 Mcal/kg (1.6 Mcal/lb) would provide 2.8 Mcal/kg (1.27 Mcal/lb); that is,

$$\frac{2.06 + 3.54}{2} = 2.8$$

Corn (Appendix Table 5-9, entry 096) and oats (Appendix Table 5-9, entry 148) in equal parts would provide 3.6 Mcal per kilogram (1.64 Mcal/lb); that is,

$$\frac{3.84 + 3.36}{2} = 3.6$$

Step 2. Calculate the crude protein. The yearling required 12.6 percent crude protein in the total ration. One part of hay with 10.8 percent crude protein plus 1 part of grain (corn and oats, equal parts) with 12.25 percent crude protein will contain 11.5 percent protein in the total ration.

$$11.5 = \frac{10.8 + \left(\dfrac{10.4 + 14.0}{2}\right)}{2}$$

The "square" method can be used to calculate what level of protein is required in the grain ration in order to correct the protein deficiency of the hay and corn–oats ration:

The difference between the percent crude protein in the hay and the desired level (12.6 percent) is 1.8 percent, which is equivalent to 1 part of the ration. Therefore, 1.8 percent (1 part) added to 12.6 percent gives 14.4 percent, the required percentage of crude protein in the grain ration. That is, 14.4 percent plus 10.8 percent divided by 2 = 12.6 percent in the total ration.

The same "square" method can be used to determine how much protein supplement should be added to the grain in order to attain a mixture with 14.4 percent protein. Soybean meal (Appendix Table 5-9, entry 212) contains 50.9 percent protein.

Subtracting diagonally, we determine that a mixture of 39.6 parts of grain and 2.2 parts of soybean meal would result in a concentrate containing 14.4 percent protein or, in other words, 94.7 percent (39.6 parts grain/41.8 parts total) corn–oats and 5.3 percent (2.2 parts soybean meal/41.8 parts total) soybean meal is needed. Check to be certain that the protein level is adequate. According to Appendix Table 5-3, the yearling needs 0.75 kg (1.65 lb) of crude protein daily. Multiply the amount fed in the hay and the concentrate mix by the concentration:

$$3.25 \text{ kg } (7.15 \text{ lb}) \text{ of hay} \times 10.8\% = 0.351 \text{ kg } (0.77 \text{ lb}) \text{ of protein}$$

$$3.25 \text{ kg } (7.15 \text{ lb}) \text{ of grain} \times 14.4\% = 0.468 \text{ kg } (1.03 \text{ lb}) \text{ of protein}$$

The total of 0.819 kg (1.8 lb) is a little more than the requirement of 0.75 kg (1.65 lb).

Step 3. Now determine the calcium and phosphorus status. Again multiply amount fed by concentration. The grain concentration of 0.067 percent Ca was determined by corn containing 0.05 percent Ca; oats, 0.06 percent Ca; and soybean meal, 0.29 percent Ca. Therefore, $(0.73 \times 0.05) + (0.73 \times 0.06) + (0.053 \times 0.29) = 0.067$ percent Ca in the mixture.

For total calcium,

$$3.25 \text{ kg of hay} \times 0.51\% \text{ Ca} = 0.016 \text{ kg} \times 1000 \text{ gm/kg} = 16 \text{ gm}$$

or

$$7.15 \text{ lb of hay} \times 0.51\% \text{ Ca} = 0.036 \text{ lb}$$

$$3.25 \text{ kg of grain} \times 0.067\% \text{ Ca} = 0.0022 \text{ kg} \times 1000 \text{ gm/kg} = 2.2 \text{ gm}$$

or

$$7.15 \text{ lb of grain} \times 0.067\% \text{ Ca} = 0.005 \text{ lb}$$

The total is 18.2 g (or 0.04 lb).

The grain concentration of 0.364 percent P was determined by corn containing 0.31 percent P; oats, 0.38 percent P; and soybean meal, 0.71 percent P. Therefore, $(0.473 \times 0.31) + (0.473 \times 0.38) + (0.053 \times 0.71) = 0.364$ percent P in the mixture.

For total phosphorus,

$$3.25 \text{ kg of hay} \times 0.29\% \text{ P} = 0.0094 \text{ kg} \times 1000 \text{ gm/kg} = 9.4 \text{ gm}$$

or

$$7.15 \text{ lb of hay} \times 0.29\% \text{ P} = 0.021 \text{ lb}$$

$$3.25 \text{ kg of grain} \times 0.364\% \text{ P} = 0.012 \text{ kg} \times 1000 \text{ gm/kg} = 12.0 \text{ gm}$$

or

$$7.5 \text{ lb of grain} \times 0.364\% \text{ P} = 0.026 \text{ lb}$$

The total is 18.5 g (0.04 lb).

Subtract the amount of calcium and phosphorus supplied from the amount needed:

	Ca	P
Yearling requires	29 gm (0.064 lb) of Ca	16 gm (0.035 lb) of P
Hay and grain supply	−18.2 gm (0.040 lb)	−21.4 gm (0.047 lb)
Additional needed	10.8 gm (0.024 lb)	− 5.4 gm (0.0008 lb)

When calcium is supplied by calcium carbonate containing 39.4 percent calcium (Table 5-3 in the text), divide amount needed by concentration: 10.8 gm Ca needed/0.394 = 27.4 gm, *or* 0.024 lb/0.394 = 0.061 lb, of calcium carbonate needed. Therefore, there is 0.83 percent calcium carbonate in the grain mixture (0.0274 kg/3.25 kg grain, *or* 0.061 lb/7.15). Now, all the requirements have been met.

APPENDIX TABLE 5-1 Daily Nutrient Requirements of Ponies (200-kg mature weight)

	Weight (kg)	Daily gain (kg)	DE (Mcal)	Crude protein (gm)	Lysine (gm)	Calcium (gm)	Phosphorus (gm)	Magnesium (gm)	Potassium (gm)	Vitamin A (10^3 IU)
Mature horses										
Maintenance	200		7.4	296	10	8	6	3.0	10.0	6
Stallions (breeding season)	200		9.3	370	13	11	8	4.3	14.1	9
Pregnant mares	200									
9 months			8.2	361	13	16	12	3.9	13.1	12
10 months			8.4	368	13	16	12	4.0	13.4	12
11 months			8.9	391	14	17	13	4.3	14.2	12
Lactating mares										
foaling to 3 months	200		13.7	688	24	27	18	4.8	21.2	12
3 months to weaning	200		12.2	528	18	18	11	3.7	14.8	12
Working horses										
light work[a]	200		9.3	370	13	11	8	4.3	14.1	9
moderate work[b]	200		11.1	444	16	14	10	5.1	16.9	9
intense work[c]	200		14.8	592	21	18	13	6.8	22.5	9
Growing horses										
Weanling, 4 months	75	0.40	7.3	365	15	16	9	1.6	5.0	3
Weanling, 6 months										
moderate growth	95	0.30	7.6	378	16	13	7	1.8	5.7	4
rapid growth	95	0.40	8.7	433	18	17	9	1.9	6.0	4
Yearling, 12 months										
moderate growth	140	0.20	8.7	392	17	12	7	2.4	7.6	6
rapid growth	140	0.30	10.3	462	19	15	8	2.5	7.9	6

(continued)

APPENDIX TABLE 5-1 (Continued)

	Weight (kg)	Daily gain (kg)	DE (Mcal)	Crude protein (gm)	Lysine (gm)	Calcium (gm)	Phosphorus (gm)	Magnesium (gm)	Potassium (gm)	Vitamin A (10^3 IU)
Growing horses										
Long yearling, 18 months										
not in training	170	0.10	8.3	375	16	10	6	2.7	8.8	8
in training	170	0.10	11.6	522	22	14	8	3.7	12.2	8
2-year-old, 24 months										
not in training	185	0.05	7.9	337	13	9	5	2.8	9.4	8
in training	185	0.05	11.4	485	19	13	7	4.1	13.5	8

NOTE: Mares should gain weight during late gestation to compensate for tissue deposition. However, nutrient requirements are based on maintenance body weight.

[a] Examples are horses used in Western and English pleasure, bridle path hack, equitation, etc.

[b] Examples are horses used in ranch work, roping, cutting, barrel racing, jumping, etc.

[c] Examples are horses in race training, polo, etc.

SOURCE: *Nutrient Requirements of Horses*, 5th ed., National Research Council (1989).

Appendix Table 5-2 Daily Nutrient Requirements of Ponies (400-kg mature weight)

	Weight (kg)	Daily gain (kg)	DE (Mcal)	Crude protein (gm)	Lysine (gm)	Calcium (gm)	Phosphorus (gm)	Magnesium (gm)	Potassium (gm)	Vitamin A (10³ IU)
Mature horses										
Maintenance	400		13.4	536	19	16	11	6.0	20.0	12
Stallions (breeding season)	400		16.8	670	23	20	15	7.7	25.5	18
Pregnant mares										
9 months	400		14.9	654	23	28	21	7.1	23.8	24
10 months			15.1	666	23	29	22	7.3	24.2	24
11 months			16.1	708	25	31	23	7.7	25.7	24
Lactating mares										
foaling to 3 months	400		22.9	1,141	40	45	29	8.7	36.8	24
3 months to weaning	400		19.7	839	29	29	18	6.9	26.4	24
Working horses										
light work[a]	400		16.8	670	23	20	15	7.7	25.5	18
moderate work[b]	400		20.1	804	28	25	17	9.2	30.6	18
intense work[c]	400		26.8	1,072	38	33	23	12.3	40.7	18
Growing horses										
Weanling, 4 months	145	0.85	13.5	675	28	33	18	3.2	9.8	7
Weanling, 6 months										
moderate growth	180	0.55	12.9	643	27	25	14	3.4	10.7	8
rapid growth	180	0.70	14.5	725	30	30	16	3.6	11.1	8
Yearling, 12 months										
moderate growth	265	0.40	15.6	700	30	23	13	4.5	14.5	12
rapid growth	265	0.50	17.1	770	33	27	15	4.6	14.8	12

(continued)

APPENDIX TABLE 5-2 (Continued)

	Weight (kg)	Daily gain (kg)	DE (Mcal)	Crude protein (gm)	Lysine (gm)	Calcium (gm)	Phosphorus (gm)	Magnesium (gm)	Potassium (gm)	Vitamin A (10^3IU)
Growing horses										
Long yearling, 18 months										
not in training	330	0.25	15.9	716	30	21	12	5.3	17.3	15
in training	330	0.25	21.6	970	41	29	16	7.1	23.4	15
2-year-old, 24 months										
not in training	365	0.15	15.3	650	26	19	11	5.7	18.7	16
in training	365	0.15	21.5	913	37	27	15	7.9	26.2	16

NOTE: Mares should gain weight during late gestation to compensate for tissue deposition. However, nutrient requirements are based on maintenance body weight.

[a] Examples are horses used in Western and English pleasure, bridle path hack, equitation, etc.

[b] Examples are horses used in ranch work, roping, cutting, barrel racing, jumping, etc.

[c] Examples are horses in race training, polo, etc.

SOURCE: *Nutrient Requirements of Horses*, 5th ed., National Research Council (1989).

APPENDIX TABLE 5-3 Daily Nutrient Requirements of Horses (500-kg mature weight)

	Weight (kg)	Daily gain (kg)	DE (Mcal)	Crude protein (gm)	Lysine (gm)	Calcium (gm)	Phosphorus (gm)	Magnesium (gm)	Potassium (gm)	Vitamin A (10^3IU)
Mature horses										
Maintenance	500		16.4	656	23	20	14	7.5	25.0	15
Stallions (breeding season)	500		20.5	820	29	25	18	9.4	31.2	22
Pregnant mares										
9 months	500		18.2	801	28	35	26	8.7	29.1	30
10 months			18.5	815	29	35	27	8.9	29.7	30
11 months			19.7	866	30	37	28	9.4	31.5	30
Lactating mares										
foaling to 3 months	500		28.3	1,427	50	56	36	10.9	46.0	30
3 months to weaning	500		24.3	1,048	37	36	22	8.6	33.0	30
Working horses										
light work[a]	500		20.5	820	29	25	18	9.4	31.2	22
moderate work[b]	500		24.6	984	34	30	21	11.3	37.4	22
intense work[c]	500		32.8	1,312	46	40	29	15.1	49.9	22
Growing horses										
Weanling, 4 months	175	0.85	14.4	720	30	34	19	3.7	11.3	8
Weanling, 6 months										
moderate growth	215	0.65	15.0	750	32	29	16	4.0	12.7	10
rapid growth	215	0.85	17.2	860	36	36	20	4.3	13.3	10

(continued)

	Weight (kg)	Daily gain (kg)	DE (Mcal)	Crude protein (gm)	Lysine (gm)	Calcium (gm)	Phosphorus (gm)	Magnesium (gm)	Potassium (gm)	Vitamin A (10³IU)
Growing horses										
Yearling, 12 months										
moderate growth	325	0.50	18.9	851	36	29	16	5.5	17.8	15
rapid growth	325	0.65	21.3	956	40	34	19	5.7	18.2	15
Long yearling, 18 months										
not in training	400	0.35	19.8	893	38	27	15	6.4	21.1	18
in training	400	0.35	26.5	1,195	50	36	20	8.6	28.2	18
2-year-old, 24 months										
not in training	450	0.20	18.8	800	32	24	13	7.0	23.1	20
in training	450	0.20	26.3	1,117	45	34	19	9.8	32.2	20

NOTE: Mares should gain weight during late gestation to compensate for tissue deposition. However, nutrient requirements are based on maintenance body weight.

[a]Examples are horses used in Western and English pleasure, bridle path hack, equitation, etc.

[b]Examples are horses used in ranch work, roping, cutting, barrel racing, jumping, etc.

[c]Examples are horses in race training, polo, etc.

SOURCE: Nutrient Requirements of Horses, 5th ed., National Research Council (1989).

APPENDIX TABLE 5-4 Daily Nutrient Requirements of Horses (600-kg mature weight)

	Weight (kg)	Daily gain (kg)	DE (Mcal)	Crude protein (gm)	Lysine (gm)	Calcium (gm)	Phos-phorus (gm)	Magne-sium (gm)	Potas-sium (gm)	Vitamin A (10³IU)
Mature horses										
Maintenance	600		19.4	776	27	24	17	9.0	30.0	18
Stallions (breeding season)	600		24.3	970	34	30	21	11.2	36.9	27
Pregnant mares	600									
9 months			21.5	947	33	41	31	10.3	34.5	36
10 months			21.9	965	34	42	32	10.5	35.1	36
11 months			23.3	1,024	36	44	34	11.2	37.2	36
Lactating mares										
foaling to 3 months	600		33.7	1,711	60	67	43	13.1	55.2	36
3 months to wearing	600		28.9	1,258	44	43	27	10.4	39.6	36
Working horses										
light work[a]	600		24.3	970	34	30	21	11.2	36.9	27
moderate work[b]	600		29.1	1,164	41	36	25	13.4	44.2	27
intense work[c]	600		38.8	1,552	54	47	34	17.8	59.0	27
Growing horses										
Weanling, 4 months	200	1.00	16.5	825	35	40	22	4.3	13.0	9
Weanling, 6 months										
moderate growth	245	0.75	17.0	850	36	34	19	4.6	14.5	11
rapid growth	245	0.95	19.2	960	40	40	22	4.9	15.1	11
Yearling, 12 months										
moderate growth	375	0.65	22.7	1,023	43	36	20	6.4	20.7	17
rapid growth	375	0.80	25.1	1,127	48	41	22	6.6	21.2	17

(*continued*)

	Weight (kg)	Daily gain (kg)	DE (Mcal)	Crude protein (gm)	Lysine (gm)	Calcium (gm)	Phos-phorus (gm)	Magne-sium (gm)	Potas-sium (gm)	Vitamin A (10³ IU)
				Growing horses						
Long yearling, 18 months										
not in training	475	0.45	23.9	1,077	45	33	18	7.7	25.1	21
in training	475	0.45	32.0	1,429	60	44	24	10.2	33.3	21
2-year-old, 24 months										
not in training	540	0.30	23.5	998	40	31	17	8.5	27.9	24
in training	540	0.30	32.3	1,372	55	43	24	11.6	38.4	24

NOTE: Mares should gain weight during late gestation to compensate for tissue deposition. However, nutrient requirements are based on maintenance body weight.

[a]Examples are horses used in Western and English pleasure, bridle path hack, equitation, etc.

[b]Examples are horses used in ranch work, roping, cutting, barrel racing, jumping, etc.

[c]Examples are horses in race training, polo, etc.

SOURCE: Nutrient Requirements of Horses, 5th ed., National Research Council (1989).

APPENDIX TABLE 5-5 Daily Nutrient Requirements of Horses (700-kg mature weight)

	Weight (kg)	Daily gain (kg)	DE (Mcal)	Crude protein (gm)	Lysine (gm)	Calcium (gm)	Phosphorus (gm)	Magnesium (gm)	Potassium (gm)	Vitamin A (10^3IU)
Mature horses										
Maintenance	700		21.3	851	30	28	20	10.5	35.0	21
Stallions (breeding season)	700		26.6	1,064	37	32	23	12.2	40.4	32
Pregnant mares	700									
9 months			23.6	1,039	36	45	34	11.3	37.8	42
10 months			24.0	1,058	37	46	35	11.5	38.5	42
11 months			25.5	1,124	39	49	37	12.3	40.9	42
Lactating mares										
foaling to 3 months	700		37.9	1,997	70	78	51	15.2	64.4	42
3 months to weaning	700		32.4	1,468	51	50	31	12.1	46.2	42
Working horses										
light work[a]	700		26.6	1,064	37	32	23	12.2	40.4	32
moderate work[b]	700		31.9	1,277	45	39	28	14.7	48.5	32
intense work[c]	700		42.6	1,702	60	52	37	19.6	64.7	32
Growing horses										
Weanling, 4 months	225	1.10	19.7	986	41	44	25	4.8	14.6	10
Weanling, 6 months										
moderate growth	275	0.80	20.0	1,001	42	37	20	5.1	16.2	12
rapid growth	275	1.00	22.2	1,111	47	43	24	5.4	16.8	12
Yearling, 12 months										
moderate growth	420	0.70	26.1	1,176	50	39	22	7.2	23.1	19
rapid growth	420	0.85	28.5	1,281	54	44	24	7.4	23.6	19

(continued)

APPENDIX TABLE 5-5 (Continued)

	Weight (kg)	Daily gain (kg)	DE (Mcal)	Crude protein (gm)	Lysine (gm)	Calcium (gm)	Phos-phorus (gm)	Magne-sium (gm)	Potas-sium (gm)	Vitamin A (10³IU)
Growing horses										
Long yearling, 18 months										
not in training	525	0.50	27.0	1,215	51	37	20	8.5	27.8	24
in training	525	0.50	36.0	1,615	68	49	27	11.3	36.9	24
2-year-old, 24 months										
not in training	600	0.35	26.3	1,117	45	35	19	9.4	31.1	27
in training	600	0.35	36.0	1,529	61	48	27	12.9	42.5	27

NOTE: Mares should gain weight during late gestation to compensate for tissue deposition. However, nutrient requirements are based on maintenance body weight.

[a]Examples are horses used in Western and English pleasure, bridle path hack, equitation, etc.

[b]Examples are horses used in ranch work, roping, cutting, barrel racing, jumping, etc.

[c]Examples are horses in race training, polo, etc.

SOURCE: *Nutrient Requirements of Horses*, 5th ed., National Research Council, 1989.

APPENDIX TABLE 5-6 Daily Nutrient Requirements of Horses (800-kg mature weight)

	Weight (kg)	Daily gain (kg)	DE (Mcal)	Crude protein (gm)	Lysine (gm)	Calcium (gm)	Phosphorus (gm)	Magnesium (gm)	Potassium (gm)	Vitamin A (10³IU)
Mature horses										
Maintenance	800		22.9	914	32	32	22	12.0	40.0	24
Stallions (breeding season)	800		28.6	1,143	40	35	25	13.1	43.4	36
Pregnant mares										
9 months	800		25.4	1,116	39	48	37	12.2	40.6	48
10 months			25.8	1,137	40	49	37	12.4	41.3	48
11 months			27.4	1,207	42	52	40	13.2	43.9	48
Lactating mares										
foaling to 3 months	800		41.9	2,282	81	90	58	17.4	73.6	48
3 months to weaning	800		35.5	1,678	60	58	36	13.8	52.8	48
Working horses										
light work[a]	800		28.6	1,143	40	35	25	13.1	43.4	36
moderate work[b]	800		34.3	1,372	48	42	30	15.8	52.1	36
intense work[c]	800		45.7	1,829	64	56	40	21.0	69.5	36
Growing horses										
Weanling, 4 months	250	1.20	21.4	1,070	45	48	27	5.3	16.1	11
Weanling, 6 months										
moderate growth	305	0.90	22.0	1,100	46	41	23	5.7	18.0	14
rapid growth	305	1.10	24.2	1,210	51	47	26	6.0	18.6	14
Yearling, 12 months										
moderate growth	460	0.80	28.7	1,291	55	44	24	7.9	25.4	21
rapid growth	460	0.95	31.0	1,396	59	49	27	8.1	25.9	21

(continued)

	Weight (kg)	Daily gain (kg)	DE (Mcal)	Crude protein (gm)	Lysine (gm)	Calcium (gm)	Phos-phorus (gm)	Magne-sium (gm)	Potas-sium (gm)	Vitamin A (10³IU)
Growing horses										
Long yearling, 18 months										
not in training	590	0.60	30.2	1,361	57	43	24	9.6	31.3	27
in training	590	0.60	39.8	1,793	76	56	31	12.6	41.2	27
2-year-old, 24 months										
not in training	675	0.40	28.7	1,220	49	40	22	10.6	35.0	30
in training	675	0.40	39.1	1,662	66	54	30	14.5	47.6	30

NOTE: Mares should gain weight during late gestation to compensate for tissue deposition. However, nutrient requirements are based on maintenance body weight.

[a]Examples are horses used in Western and English pleasure, bridle path hack, equitation, etc.

[b]Examples are horses used in ranch work, roping, cutting, barrel racing, jumping, etc.

[c]Examples are horses in race training, polo, etc.

SOURCE: *Nutrient Requirements of Horses*, 5th ed., National Research Council (1989).

APPENDIX TABLE 5-7 Daily Nutrient Requirements of Horses (900-kg mature weight)

	Weight (kg)	Daily gain (kg)	DE (Mcal)	Crude protein (gm)	Lysine (gm)	Calcium (gm)	Phosphorus (gm)	Magnesium (gm)	Potassium (gm)	Vitamin A (10³IU)
				Mature horses						
Maintenance	900		24.1	966	34	36	25	13.5	45.0	27
Stallions (breeding season)	900		30.2	1,207	42	37	26	13.9	45.9	40
Pregnant mares	900									
9 months			26.8	1,179	41	51	39	12.9	42.9	54
10 months			27.3	1,200	42	52	39	13.1	43.6	54
11 months			29.0	1,275	45	55	42	13.9	46.3	54
Lactating mares										
foaling to 3 months	900		45.5	2,567	89	101	65	19.6	82.8	54
3 months to weaning	900		38.4	1,887	66	65	40	15.5	59.4	54
Working horses										
light work[a]	900		30.2	1,207	42	37	26	13.9	45.9	40
moderate work[b]	900		36.2	1,448	51	44	32	16.7	55.0	40
intense work[c]	900		48.3	1,931	68	59	42	22.2	73.4	40
				Growing horses						
Weanling, 4 months	275	1.30	23.1	1,154	48	53	29	5.8	17.7	12
Weanling, 6 months										
moderate growth	335	0.95	23.4	1,171	49	44	24	6.2	19.6	15
rapid growth	335	1.15	25.6	1,281	54	50	28	6.5	20.2	15
Yearling, 12 months										
moderate growth	500	0.90	31.2	1,404	59	49	27	8.6	27.7	22
rapid growth	500	1.05	33.5	1,509	64	54	30	8.8	28.2	22

(continued)

APPENDIX TABLE 5-7 (Continued)

	Weight (kg)	Daily gain (kg)	DE (Mcal)	Crude protein (gm)	Lysine (gm)	Calcium (gm)	Phos-phorus (gm)	Magne-sium (gm)	Potas-sium (gm)	Vitamin A (10^3 IU)
Growing horses										
Long yearling, 18 months										
not in training	665	0.70	33.6	1,510	64	49	27	10.9	35.4	30
in training	665	0.70	43.9	1,975	83	64	35	14.2	46.2	30
2-year-old, 24 months										
not in training	760	0.45	31.1	1,322	53	45	25	12.0	39.4	34
in training	760	0.45	42.2	1,795	72	61	34	16.2	53.4	34

NOTE: Mares should gain weight during late gestation to compensate for tissue deposition. However, nutrient requirements are based on maintenance body weight.

[a]Examples are horses used in Western and English pleasure, bridle path hack, equitation, etc.

[b]Examples are horses used in ranch work, roping, cutting, barrel racing, jumping, etc.

[c]Examples are horses in race training, polo, etc.

SOURCE: *Nutrient Requirements of Horses*, 5th ed., National Research Council (1989).

APPENDIX TABLE 5-8 Other Minerals and Vitamins for Horses and Ponies
(on a dry-matter basis)

	Adequate concentrations in total rations				
	Maint-enance	Pregnant and lactating mares	Growing horses	Working horses	Maximum tolerance levels
Minerals					
Sodium (%)	0.10	0.10	0.10	0.30	3[a]
Sulfur (%)	0.15	0.15	0.15	0.15	1.25
Iron (mg/kg)	40	50	50	40	1,000
Manganese (mg/kg)	40	40	40	40	1,000
Copper (mg/kg)	10	10	10	10	800
Zinc (mg/kg)	40	40	40	40	500
Selenium (mg/kg)	0.1	0.1	0.1	0.1	2.0
Iodine (mg/kg)	0.1	0.1	0.1	0.1	5.0
Cobalt (mg/kg)	0.1	0.1	0.1	0.1	10
Vitamins					
Vitamin A (IU/Kg)	2,000	3,000	2,000	2,000	16,000
Vitamin D (IU/kg)[b]	300	600	800	300	2,200
Vitamin E (IU/kg)	50	80	80	80	1,000
Vitamin K (mg/kg)[c]					
Thiamin (mg/kg)	3	3	3	5	3,000
Riboflavin (mg/kg)	2	2	2	2	—
Niacin (mg/kg)					
Pantothenic acid (mg/kg)					
Pyridoxine (mg/kg)					
Biotin (mg/kg)					
Folacin (mg/kg)					
Vitamin B_{12} (μg/kg)					
Ascorbic acid (mg/kg)					
Choline (mg/kg)					

[a]As sodium chloride.

[b]Recommendations for horses not exposed to sunlight or to artificial light with an emission spectrum of 280–315 mm.

[c]Blank space indicates that data are insufficient to determine a requirement or maximum tolerable level.

SOURCE: *Nutrient Requirements of Horses*, 5th ed., National Research Council (1989).

APPENDIX TABLE 5-9   Composition of Feeds (Excluding Vitamins) Commonly Used in Horse Diets

Entry no.	Feed name	International feed number[a]	Dry matter (%)	DE[b] (Mcal/kg)	DE[b] (Mcal/lb)	Crude protein (%)	Lysine (%)	Ether extract (%)	Fiber (%)	NDF (%)	ADF (%)	Ash (%)
						Alfalfa (*Medicago sativa*)						
001	fresh, late vegetative	2-00-181	23.2	0.68	0.31	5.1	0.29	0.7	5.6	7.2	5.6	2.4
002			100.0	2.94	1.34	22.2	1.24	2.9	24.2	30.9	24.0	10.2
		N	14			17	1	4	4	14	12	6
		SD	3.39			2.00		0.947	2.29	4.79	3.66	0.826
003	fresh, full bloom	2-00-188	23.8	0.55	0.25	4.6		0.6	7.2	9.2	8.6	2.6
004			100.0	2.32	1.05	19.3		2.8	30.4	38.6	35.9	10.9
		N	8			8		2	2	12	2	8
		SD	3.88			3.70		0.565	1.83	6.14	2.82	2.35
005	hay, sun-cured, early-bloom	1-00-059	90.5	2.24	1.02	18.0	0.81	2.6	20.8	35.6	28.9	8.4
006			100.0	2.48	1.13	19.9	0.90	2.9	23.0	39.3	31.9	9.2
		N	43			63	1	28	29	14	15	36
		SD	1.92			2.25		1.35	3.98	3.58	2.40	1.61
007	hay, sun-cured, midbloom	1-00-063	91.0	2.07	0.94	17.0		2.4	25.5	42.9	33.4	7.8
008			100.0	2.28	1.03	18.7		2.6	28.0	47.1	36.7	8.5
		N	60			56		23	22	22	26	41
		SD	1.88			2.93		1.82	4.25	6.53	2.58	1.48
009	hay, sun-cured, full-bloom	1-00-068	90.9	1.97	0.89	15.5	0.79	1.8	27.3	44.3	35.2	7.1
010			100.0	2.17	0.98	17.0	0.87	2.0	30.1	48.8	38.7	7.8
		N	21			20	1	12	14	10	9	16
		SD	2.06			2.50		1.73	4.27	3.49	2.42	1.07
011	meal, dehydrated, 15% protein	1-00-022	90.4	2.00	0.91	15.6	0.63	2.2	26.2	50.1	33.9	8.9
012			100.0	2.21	1.00	17.3	0.69	2.4	29.0	55.4	37.5	9.9
		N	23			21	4	13	18	1	2	12
		SD	2.18			1.75	0.077	0.438	3 17		1.47	0.934
013	meal, dehydrated, 17% protein	1-00-023	91.8	2.16	0.98	17.4	0.85	2.8	24.0	41.3	31.5	9.8
014			100.0	2.36	1.07	18.9	0.92	3.0	26.2	45.0	34.3	10.6
		N	72			50	24	37	46	1	2	21
		SD	1.50			0.677	0.169	0.493	2.25		0.951	0.613
						Alyceclover (*Alysicarpus vaginalis*)						
015	hay, sun-cured	1-00-361	89.7	1.64	0.75	10.9		1.6	36.2			5.7
016			100.0	1.83	0.83	12.2		1.7	40.3			6.4
		N	4			3		2	3			2
		SD	0.901			0.464		0.068	1.30			0.147
						Bahiagrass (*Paspalum notatum*)						
017	fresh	2-00-464	28.7	0.61	0.26	3.6		0.5	8.7	21.0	10.2	32
018			100.0	2.03	0.92	12.6		1.6	30.4	73.1	35.5	11.1
		N	9			6		2	3	3	3	2
		SD	1.91			4.14		0.047	1.83	0.233	0.493	1.27
019	hay, sun-cured	1-00-462	90.0	1.75	0.79	8.5		1.8	28.1	66.6	33.9	5.7
020			100.0	1.94	0.88	9.5		2.0	31.2	73.9	37.7	6.3
		N	4			6		2	6	3	3	1
		SD	0.420			2.30		0.141	2.33	1.67	2.86	
021	hay, sun-cured, late-vegetative	1-20-787	91.0	1.70	0.77	8.9		2.1	29.7	66.4	37.9	7.1
022			100.0	1.87	0.85	9.8		2.3	32.7	73.0	41.6	7.8
		N	1			2		2	2	1	2	2
		SD				0.424		0.848	0.495		5.09	2.54
023	hay, sun-cured, early-bloom	1-06-138	91.0	1.61	0.73	6.4		1.4	30.9	69.2	38.2	8.5
024			100.0	1.77	0.80	7.0		1.5	34.0	76.0	42.0	9.3
		N	1			1		1	1	1	1	1
		SD										
						Barley (*Hordeum vulgare*)						
025	grain	4-00-549	88.6	3.26	1.49	11.7	0.40	1.8	4.9	16.8	6.2	2.4

Entry no.	Calcium	Phosphorus	Magnesium	Potassium	Sodium	Sulfur	Copper	Iodine	Iron	Manganese	Selenium	Zinc	Cobalt
			Macrominerals (%)						Microminerals (mg/kg)				
						Alfalfa (*Medicago sativa*)							
001	0.40	0.07	0.08	0.53	0.05	0.08	2.5		26	9			0.04
002	1.71	0.30	0.36	2.27	0.21	0.36	10.8		111	41			0.17
	10	10	10	10	2	9	1		1	2			1
	0.488	0.038	0.105	0.507	0.015	0.097				18			
003	0.28	0.06	0.10	0.86	0.04	0.07	3.6		70	10		8	0.12
004	1.19	0.26	0.40	3.62	0.16	0.31	14.9		293	41		32	0.49
	6	6	6	6	6	1	5		6	6		6	5
	0.242	0.036	0.106	0.892	0.069		2.3		232	35.2		16.2	0.057
005	1.28	0.19	0.31	2.32	0.14	0.27	11.4	0.15	205	33	0.50	27	0.26
006	1.41	0.21	0.34	2.56	0.15	0.30	12.7	0.17	227	36	0.55	30	0.29
	98	91	93	96	7	1	93	1	97	95	86	97	9
	0.394	0.047	0.100	0.617	0.135		3.0		137	25.5	0.395	7.6	0.238
007	1.24	0.22	0.32	1.42	0.11	0.26	16.1	0.15	204	25		28	0.36
008	1.37	0.24	0.35	1.56	0.12	0.28	17.7	0.16	225	28		31	0.39
	9	13	7	8	5	3	3	1	4	4		3	2
	0.287	0.047	0.111	0.510	0.053	0.028	5.6		182	7.7		14.1	0.047
009	1.08	0.22	0.25	1.42	0.06	0.25	9.0	0.12	141	38		24	0.21
010	1.19	0.24	0.27	1.56	0.07	0.27	9.9	0.13	155	42		26	0.23
	6	7	6	7	3	1	6	1	8	6		4	4
	0.144	0.078	0.112	0.758	0.073		4.2		28.1	8.6		2.8	0.280
011	1.25	0.23	0.26	2.22	0.07	0.19	9.5	0.12	280	28	0.28	19	0.17
012	1.38	0.25	0.29	2.46	0.08	0.21	10.5	0.13	309	31	0.31	21	0.19
	5	5	5	6	4	4	2	1	3	2	2	2	1
	0.073	0.026	0.047	0.143	0.006	0.019	1.7		54.7	2.5	0.320	1.4	
013	1.38	0.23	0.29	2.40	0.10	0.22	8.6	0.15	405	31	0.33	19	0.30
014	1.51	0.25	0.32	2.61	0.11	0.24	9.3	0.16	441	34	0.36	21	0.33
	25	28	12	11	10	8	6	1	7	7	2	5	3
	0.132	0.024	0.041	0.292	0.050	0.029	1.7		76.4	3.7	0.396	7.5	0.041
						Alyceclover (*Alysicarpus vaginalis*)							
015													
016													
						Bahiagrass (*Paspalum notatum*)							
017	0.13	0.09	0.08	0.44			2.1		24	21	0.02	8	
018	0.44	0.30	0.27	1.53			7.2		85	75	0.06	29	
	3	3	2	2			2		1	1		1	
	0.040	0.173	0.028	0.106			1.8						
019	0.45	0.20	0.17						54.01				
020	0.50	0.22	0.19						60.00				
	1	1	1						1				
021	0.25	0.19	0.25	1.64									
022	0.28	0.21	0.27	1.80									
	1	1	1	1									
023	0.24	0.18	0.23	1.46									
024	0.26	0.20	0.25	1.60									
	1	1	1	1									
						Barley (*Hordeum vulgare*)							
025	0.05	0.34	0.13	0.44	0.03	0.15	8.2	0.04	73.53	16	0.18	17	0.17

(continued)

APPENDIX TABLE 5-9   Composition of Feeds (Excluding Vitamins) Commonly Used in Horse Diets (*Continued*)

Entry no.	Feed name	International feed number[a]	Dry matter (%)	DE[b] (Mcal/kg)	DE[b] (Mcal/lb)	Crude protein (%)	Lysine (%)	Ether extract (%)	Fiber (%)	NDF (%)	ADF (%)	Ash (%)
		Barley (*Hordeum vulgare*)										
026		100.0	3.68	1.67	13.2	0.45	2.0	5.6	19.0	7.0	2.7	
		N	237			304	67	208	210	25	13	217
		SD	2.08			1.90	0.099	0.465	1.09	3.33	5.22	0.335
027	grain, Pacific coast	4-07-939	88.6	3.17	1.48	9.7	0.27	2.0	6.0	18.6	8.0	2.4
028		100.0	3.58	1.67	11.0	0.30	2.2	6.8	21.0	9.0	2.7	
		N	17			14	10	9	11	3	4	8
		SD	0.773			0.640	0.052	0.135	1.25	0.503	0.997	0.139
029	hay, sun-cured	1-00-495	88.4	1.78	0.81	7.8		1.9	23.6			6.6
030		100.0	2.01	0.92	8.8		2.1	26.7			7.5	
		N	10			6		6	5			4
		SD	2.17			0.426		0.120	0.694			0.206
031	straw	1-00-498	91.2	1.47	0.67	4.0		1.7	37.8	66.1	44.5	6.8
032		100.0	1.62	0.73	4.4		1.9	41.5	72.5	48.8	7.5	
		N	29			35		7	26	2	3	8
		SD	3.31			0.907		0.269	4.03	1.83	4.65	1.40
		Beet, sugar (*Beta vulgaris altissima*)										
033	pulp, dehydrated	4-00-669	91.0	2.33	1.06	8.9	0.54	0.5	18.2	40.5	25.0	4.9
034		100.0	2.56	1.16	9.8	0.60	0.6	20.0	44.6	27.5	5.3	
		N	47			31	6	25	29	2	5	22
		SD	1.37			1.04	0.151	0.151	2.40	20.4	6.79	1.29
		Bermudagrass, coastal (*Cynodon dactylon*)										
035	fresh	2-00-719	30.3	0.72	0.33	3.8		1.1	8.6	22.2	11.1	2.4
036		100.0	2.38	1.08	12.6		3.7	28.4	73.3	36.8	8.1	
		N	15			48		10	11	41	41	34
		SD	6.91			2.88		0.954	1.77	5.10	4.64	1.86
037	hay, sun-cured, 15–28 days' growth	1-09-207	88.4	1.92	0.87	10.6	0.38	2.4	26.7	64.5	30.0	6.7
038		100.0	2.17	0.98	12.0	0.45	2.7	30.2	73.0	34.0	7.5	
		N	4			17		16	16	6	6	16
		SD	0.326			1.84		0.380	2.30	2.54	1.84	0.860
039	hay, sun-cured, 29–42 days' growth	1-09-209	93.0	1.96	0.89	10.9		2.4	28.0	68.0	32.7	6.2
040		100.0	2.10	0.95	12.0		2.6	31.0	75.0	36.2	6.9	
		N	4			22		18	18	5	5	18
		SD	1.61			3.05		0.68	2.59	1.60	1.40	1.18
041	hay, sun-cured, 43–56 days' growth	1-09-210	93.0	1.74	0.79	7.3	0.28	2.5	30.4	71.3	35.7	7.5
042		100.0	1.87	0.85	7.8	0.30	2.7	32.6	76.6	38.3	8.0	
		N	1			4		2	2	3	3	2
		SD				1.19		1.83	4.73	2.45	4.18	1.34
		Bluegrass, Kentucky (*Poa pratensis*)										
043	fresh, early vegetative	2-00-777	30.8	0.64	0.29	5.4		1.1	7.8			2.9
044		100.0	2.09	0.95	17.4		3.5	25.2			9.4	
		N	4			2		2	2			1
		SD	0.694			0.144		0.070	0.211			
045	fresh, milk stage	2-00-782	42.0	0.75	0.34	4.9		1.5	12.7			3.1
046		100.0	1.78	0.81	11.6		3.6	30.3			7.3	
		N	1			1		1	1			1
		SD										
047	hay, sun-cured, full-bloom	1-00-772	92.1	1.58	0.72	8.2		3.0	29.9			5.4
048		100.0	1.71	0.78	8.9		3.3	32.5			5.9	
		N	2			1		1	1			1
		SD										

Entry no.	Macrominerals (%)						Microminerals (mg/kg)						
	Calcium	Phosphorus	Magnesium	Potassium	Sodium	Sulfur	Copper	Iodine	Iron	Manganese	Selenium	Zinc	Cobalt
Barley (*Hordeum vulgare*)													
026	0.05	0.38	0.15	0.50	0.03	0.17	9.2	0.05	83.02	18	0.20	19	0.19
	117	134	73	71	19	14	45	1	59	60	54	65	6
	0.018	0.073	0.018	0.132	0.017	0.009	4.1		30.2	3.7	0.152	18.0	0.229
027	0.05	0.34	0.12	0.51	0.02	0.14	8.1		86.14	16	0.19	15	0.09
028	0.05	0.38	0.14	0.58	0.02	0.16	9.1		97.19	18	0.11	17	0.10
	12	12	3	5	4	3	2		3	3	1	3	1
	0.013	0.045	0.003	0.056	0.001	0.012	0.65		32.5	0.4		0.27	
029	0.21	0.25	0.14	1.30	0.12	0.15	3.9		265.31	35			0.06
030	0.24	0.28	0.16	1.47	0.14	0.17	4.4		299.96	39			0.07
	5	5	2	3	1	2	1		1	3			1
	0.039	0.028	0.042	0.025		0.002				0.3			
031	0.27	0.06	0.21	2.16	0.13	0.16	4.9		183.09	15		7	0.06
032	0.30	0.07	0.23	2.36	0.14	0.17	5.40		200.78	16		7	0.07
	34	40	22	22	5	5	18		20	4		17	1
	0.088	0.032	0.052	0.480	0.003	0.012	1.3		72.0	0.7		0.583	
Beet, sugar (*Beta vulgaris altissima*)													
033	0.62	0.09	0.26	0.20	0.18	0.20	12.5		266.69	34	0.11	1.0	0.07
034	0.68	0.10	0.28	0.22	0.20	0.22	13.8		293.00	38	0.12	1.0	0.08
	18	23	21	12	8	9	5		13	10	1	3	3
	0.069	0.012	0.047	0.073	0.073	0.010	0.07		62.8	1.3		0.03	0.041
Bermudagrass, coastal (*Cynodon dactylon*)													
035	0.15	0.08											
036	0.49	0.27											
	8	8											
	0.072	0.033											
037	0.35	0.24	0.18	1.90									
038	0.40	0.27	0.21	2.20									
	1	1	1	1									
039	0.30	0.19	0.11	1.58									
040	0.32	0.20	0.16	1.70									
	1	1	1	1									
041	0.24	0.17	0.12	1.21									
042	0.26	0.18	0.13	1.30									
	1	1	1	1									
Bluegrass, Kentucky (*Poa pratensis*)													
043	0.15	0.14	0.05	0.70	0.04	0.05			92				
044	0.50	0.44	0.18	2.27	0.14	0.17			300				
	2	2	2	2	1	1			1				
	0.091	0.042	0.007	0.014									
045													
046													
047	0.24	0.25		1.40									
048	0.26	0.27		1.52									
	1	1		1									

(*continued*)

APPENDIX TABLE 5-9   Composition of Feeds (Excluding Vitamins) Commonly Used in Horse Diets (*Continued*)

Entry no.	Feed name	International feed number[a]	Dry matter (%)	DE[b] (Mcal/ kg)	DE[b] (Mcal/ lb)	Crude protein (%)	Lysine (%)	Ether extract (%)	Fiber (%)	NDF (%)	ADF (%)	Ash (%)
						Brewer's grains						
049	dehydrated	5-02-141	92.0	2.53	1.15	23.4	0.88	5.9	13.7	42.3	22.1	4.4
050			100.0	2.75	1.25	25.4	0.96	6.5	14.9	46.0	24.0	4.8
						Brome, smooth (*Bromus inermis*)						
051	fresh, early	2-00-956	26.1	0.66	0.31	5.6		1.0	6.0	12.5	8.1	2.7
052	vegetative		100.0	2.59	1.17	21.3		4.0	23.0	47.9	31.0	10.4
		N	8			6		3	3	4	5	6
		SD	6.39			2.47		0.351	0.530	3.63	3.16	0.459
053	fresh, mature	2-08-364	54.9	0.89	0.40	3.4		1.3	19.1	35.4		3.8
054			100.0	1.62	0.73	6.1		2.4	34.8	64.5		6.9
		N	5			4		3	3	1		3
		SD	1.69			0.577		0.078	1.39			0.120
055	hay, sun-cured,	1-05-633	87.6	1.87	0.85	12.6		1.9	28.0	50.5	32.2	9.5
056	midbloom		100.0	2.13	0.97	14.4		2.2	31.9	57.7	36.8	10.9
		N	2			4		3	3	1	3	3
		SD				3.22		0.157	3.21		4.58	1.75
057	hay, sun-cured,	1-00-944	92.6	1.57	0.71	5.6		1.8	29.8	65.3	41.5	6.7
058	mature		100.0	1.69	0.77	6.0		2.0	32.2	70.5	44.8	7.2
		N	6			2		1	2	1	1	2
		SD	0.539			0.283			2.82			1.41
						Canarygrass, reed (*Phalaris arundinacea*)						
059	fresh	2-01-113	22.8	0.58	0.26	3.9		0.9	5.6	10.6	6.5	2.3
060			100.0	2.54	1.15	17.0		4.1	24.4	46.4	28.3	10.2
		N	4			3		2	2	1	1	3
		SD	4.89			3.65		0.494	3.39			1.85
061	hay, sun-cured	1-01-104	89.3	1.78	0.81	9.1		2.7	30.2	62.9	32.7	7.3
062			100.0	2.00	0.91	10.2		3.0	33.9	70.5	36.6	8.1
		N	10			14		10	10	6	6	10
		SD	2.08			2.06		0.639	3.80	1.14	0.783	0.804
						Canola (*Brassica napus-Brassica campestris*)						
063	seeds, meal solvent-	5-06-146	90.8	2.83	1.28	37.1	2.08	2.8	11.0	21.8	15.8	6.4
064	extracted		100.0	3.11	1.41	40.9	2.29	3.0	12.1	24.0	17.4	7.1
		N	13			33	25	28	19	16	2	26
		SD	2.41			2.02	0.169	1.04	2.16	1.46	1.62	0.416
						Carrot (*Daucus spp.*)						
065	roots, fresh	4-01-145	11.5	0.43	0.20	1.2		0.2	1.1	1.4	1.3	1.0
066			100.0	3.78	1.72	10.0		1.3	9.5	12	11	8.4
		N	9			5		6	6	1	1	5
		SD	1.21			0.842		0.501	1.32			1.95
						Citrus (*Citrus spp.*)						
067	pomace without	4-01-237	91.1	2.56	1.16	6.1	0.20	3.4	11.6	21.0	21.0	6.0
068	fines, dehydrated		100.0	2.81	1.27	6.7	0.22	3.7	12.8	23.0	23.0	6.6
		N	275			365	4	260	314	1	1	335
		SD	1.52			0.398	0.000	0.862	1.19			0.808
						Clover, alsike (*Trifolium hybridum*)						
069	fresh, early	2-01-314	18.9	0.47	0.21	4.5		0.6	3.3			2.4
070	vegetative		100.0	2.49	1.13	24.1		3.2	17.5			12.8

Entry no.	Macrominerals (%)						Microminerals (mg/kg)						
	Calcium	Phosphorus	Magnesium	Potassium	Sodium	Sulfur	Copper	Iodine	Iron	Manganese	Selenium	Zinc	Cobalt
Brewer's grains													
049	0.30	0.50	0.15	0.08	0.21	0.29	21.2	0.06	245	37	0.70	28	0.07
050	0.33	0.55	0.16	0.09	0.23	0.32	23.0	0.07	266	40	0.76	30	0.08
Brome, smooth (*Bromus inermis*)													
051	0.14	0.12	0.08	0.82		0.05						6	
052	0.55	0.45	0.32	3.16		0.20						21	
	2	2	1	1		1						1	
	0.098	0.176											
053	0.14	0.09					1.2						
054	0.26	0.16					2.2						
	2	3					1						
	0.009	0.036											
055	0.25	0.25	0.09	1.74	0.01		21.9		80	35		26	0.51
056	0.29	0.28	0.10	1.99	0.01		25.0		91	40		30	0.58
	1	1	1	1	1		1		1	1		1	1
057	0.24	0.20	0.11	1.71	0.01		9.6		74	68		22	0.17
058	0.26	0.22	0.12	1.85	0.01		10.4		80	73		24	0.19
	3	2	3	3	2		2		2	2		1	2
	0.149	0.007	0.066	0.803			5.1		28.2	45.8			0.061
Canarygrass, reed (*Phalaris arundinacea*)													
059	0.08	0.08		0.83									
060	0.36	0.33		3.64									
	2	2		1									
	0.056	0.042											
061	0.32	0.21	0.19	2.60	0.01	0.12	10.6		134	82		16	
062	0.36	0.24	0.22	2.91	0.02	0.14	11.9		150	92		18	
	12	12	8	8	2	1	1		1	1		1	
	0.095	0.040	0.062	0.471	0.007								
Canola (*Brassica napus-Brassica campestris*)													
063	0.63	1.18	0.55	1.22	0.01	1.23	77		85	49	0.91	73	
064	0.69	1.30	0.61	1.34	0.01	1.35	85		94	54	1.00	81	
	14	3	2	13	1	1	1		2	2	1	2	
	0.085	0.269	0.048	0.096					26.2	5.3		12.5	
Carrot (*Daucus spp.*)													
065	0.05	0.04	0.02	0.32	0.06	0.02	1		14	3.6			
066	0.40	0.35	0.20	2.80	0.48	0.17	10		120	31			
	4	4	4	4	2	2	2		4	1			
	0.058	0.055	0.053	0.948	0.118	0.001	1.0		57.0				
Citrus (*Citrus spp.*)													
067	1.71	0.12	0.16	0.70	0.08	0.07	5.6		328	7		14	0.17
068	1.88	0.13	0.17	0.77	0.08	0.08	6.1		360	7		15	0.19
	20	16	9	14	5	6	6		11	8		6	3
	0.418	0.020	0.018	0.174	0.021	0.042	0.42		335	0.7		2.6	0.097
Clover, alsike (*Trifolium hybridum*)													
069	0.22	0.08	0.06	0.44	0.08	0.03	1.1		86	13			
070	1.19	0.42	0.34	2.31	0.46	0.17	6.0		455	67			

(*continued*)

APPENDIX TABLE 5-9   Composition of Feeds (Excluding Vitamins) Commonly Used in Horse Diets (*Continued*)

Entry no.	Feed name	International feed number[a]	Dry matter (%)	DE[b] (Mcal/ kg)	DE[b] (Mcal/ lb)	Crude protein (%)	Lysine (%)	Ether extract (%)	Fiber (%)	NDF (%)	ADF (%)	Ash (%)
						Clover, alsike (*Trifolium hybridum*)						
		N	3			1		1	1			1
		SD	0.116									
071	hay, sun-cured	1-01-313	87.7	1.71	0.78	12.4		2.4	26.2			7.6
072			100.0	1.95	0.89	14.2		2.8	29.9			8.7
		N	9			2		3	3			3
		SD	1.32			0.770		0.381	0.488			0.087
						Clover, ladino (*Trifolium repens*)						
073	fresh, early vegetative	2-01-380	19.3	0.48	0.22	5.0		0.9	2.7			2.3
074			100.0	2.50	1.14	25.8		4.6	13.9			11.9
		N	4			3		3	3			3
		SD	1.44			1.21		1.87	0.404			1.38
075	hay, sun-cured	1-01-378	89.1	1.96	0.89	20.0		2.4	18.5	32.1	28.5	8.4
076			100.0	2.20	1.00	22.4		2.7	20.8	36.0	32.0	9.4
		N	5			4		3	3	1	1	2
		SD	2.71			1.18		0.750	2.90			0.161
						Clover, red (*Trifolium pratense*)						
077	fresh, early-bloom	2-01-428	19.6	0.50	0.22	4.1		1.0	4.6	7.8	6.1	2.0
078			100.0	2.53	1.15	20.8		5.0	23.2	40.0	31.0	10.2
		N	5			3		2	3	1	1	2
		SD	0.464			3.06		0.070	4.25			0.567
079	fresh, full-bloom	2-01-429	26.2	0.66	0.27	3.8		0.8	6.8	11.3	9.2	2.0
080			100.0	2.25	1.02	14.6		2.9	26.1	43.0	35.0	7.8
		N	4			3		2	2	1	1	2
		SD	3.00			0.461		1.55	5.02			0.705
081	fresh, regrowth, early vegetative	2-28-255	24.0	0.77	0.35	5.4				6.4	4.8	
082			100.0	3.19	1.45	22.3				26.7	19.9	
		N	8			8					8	8
		SD	2.58			2.12					2.80	2.91
083	hay, sun-cured	1-01-415	88.4	1.96	0.89	13.2		2.5	27.1	41.4	31.8	6.7
084			100.0	2.22	1.01	15.0		2.8	30.7	46.9	36.0	7.5
		N	21			13		11	11	2	2	9
		SD	1.91			1.91		0.322	3.96	12.9	9.19	0.889
						Corn, dent yellow (*Zea mays indentata*)						
085	aerial part with ears, sun-cured (fodder)	1-28-231	81.0	1.67	0.76	7.2		1.9	20.4	38.9	20.2	5.5
086			100.0	2.06	0.94	8.9		2.4	25.2	48.0	25.0	6.8
		N	1			1		1	1	1	1	1
		SD										
087	aerial part without ears, without husks, sun-cured (stover, straw)	1-28-233	87.7	1.42	0.65	4.1		1.1	30.3	69.5	44.0	6.2
088			100.0	1.62	0.74	4.6		1.3	34.6	79.3	50.1	7.0
		N	4			3		1	1	3	3	2
		SD	2.43			1.38				8.34	6.65	0.374
089	cobs, ground	1-28-234	90.1	1.22	0.56	2.5		0.6	31.9	78.4	35.6	1.6
090			100.0	1.36	0.62	2.8		0.6	35.4	87.0	39.5	1.8
		N	3			3		3	3	2	2	1
		SD	0.246			0.278		0.148	0.405	2.82	6.36	
091	distiller's grains, dehydrated	5-28-235	92.0	3.21	1.46	27.8	0.81	6.6	11.3	39.6	15.6	3.1
092			100.0	3.49	1.59	30.3	0.88	7.1	12.3	43.0	17.0	3.4
		N	3			4	2	3	4	1	1	2
		SD	2.00			1.20	0.063	3.51	1.67			1.41
093	ears, ground (corn and cob meal)	4-28-238	86.2	2.83	1.29	7.8	0.17	3.2	8.1	24.1	9.5	1.6
094			100.0	3.29	1.50	9.0	0.20	3.7	9.4	28.0	11.0	1.9
		N	2			1	1	1	1	1	1	1
		SD	1.13									

Entry no.	Calcium	Phosphorus	Magnesium	Potassium	Sodium	Sulfur	Copper	Iodine	Iron	Manganese	Selenium	Zinc	Cobalt
							Macrominerals (%)		*Microminerals (mg/kg)*				

Macrominerals (%) — Calcium, Phosphorus, Magnesium, Potassium, Sodium, Sulfur.
Microminerals (mg/kg) — Copper, Iodine, Iron, Manganese, Selenium, Zinc, Cobalt.

Clover, alsike (*Trifolium hybridum*)

Entry no.	Calcium	Phosphorus	Magnesium	Potassium	Sodium	Sulfur	Copper	Iodine	Iron	Manganese	Selenium	Zinc	Cobalt
	1	1	1	1	1	1	1		1	1			
071	1.14	0.22	0.39	1.95	0.40	0.17	5.3		228	61			
072	1.30	0.25	0.45	2.22	0.46	0.19	6.00		260	69			
	2	2	1	2	1	2	1		1	1			
	0.011	0.006		0.738		0.028							

Clover, ladino (*Trifolium repens*)

Entry no.	Calcium	Phosphorus	Magnesium	Potassium	Sodium	Sulfur	Copper	Iodine	Iron	Manganese	Selenium	Zinc	Cobalt
073	0.25	0.07	0.08	0.50	0.02	0.03						4	
074	1.27	0.35	0.42	2.40	0.12	0.16						20	
	1	1	1	1	1	1						1	
075	1.20	0.30	0.42	2.17	0.12	0.19	8	0.27	419	110		15	0.14
076	1.35	0.33	0.47	2.44	0.13	0.21	9	0.30	470	123		17	0.16
	3	3	3	3	1	3	3	1	4	3		1	1
	0.228	0.060	0.067	0.275		0.010	1.2		211.0	60.9			

Clover, red (*Trifolium pratense*)

Entry no.	Calcium	Phosphorus	Magnesium	Potassium	Sodium	Sulfur	Copper	Iodine	Iron	Manganese	Selenium	Zinc	Cobalt
077	0.44	0.07	0.10	0.49	0.04	0.03	1.7	0.05	59	10		4	0.03
078	2.26	0.38	0.51	2.49	0.20	0.17	9.0	0.25	300	50		19	0.16
	1	1	1	1	1	1	1	1	1	1		1	1
079	0.26	0.07	0.13	0.51	0.05	0.04	2.6	0.07	79	12		4	0.03
080	1.01	0.27	0.51	1.96	0.20	0.17	10.0	0.25	300	47		16	0.12
	1	1	1	1	1	1	1		1	1		1	1
081	0.41	0.06	0.11	0.46		0.05							
082	1.71	0.26	0.48	1.90		0.21							
	8	8	8	8		8							
	0.181	0.029	0.098	0.531		0.014							
083	1.22	0.22	0.34	1.60	0.16	0.15	9.7	0.22	211	95		15	0.14
084	1.38	0.24	0.38	1.81	0.18	0.16	11.0	0.25	238	108		17	0.16
	11	11	7	11	2	2	4	1	8	4		3	1
	0.226	0.055	0.134	0.584	0.038	0.008	12.6		121.0	46.5		17.1	

Corn, dent yellow (*Zea mays indentata*)

Entry no.	Calcium	Phosphorus	Magnesium	Potassium	Sodium	Sulfur	Copper	Iodine	Iron	Manganese	Selenium	Zinc	Cobalt
085	0.41	0.20	0.23	0.75	0.02	0.11	6.5		81	55			
086	0.50	0.25	0.29	0.93	0.03	0.14	8.0		100	68			
	1	1	1	1	1	1	1		1	1			
087	0.46	0.09	0.27	1.39	0.07	0.15	4.0		138	40		17	
088	0.52	0.10	0.31	1.59	0.08	0.17	4.5		158	46		19	
	2	2	2	2	2	1	2		2	1		1	
	0.028			0.106	0.431	0.012	0.7		60.1				
089	0.11	0.04	0.06	0.80	0.07	0.42	6.3		207	5	0.07	4	0.12
090	0.12	0.04	0.07	0.89	0.08	0.47	7.0		230	6	0.08	5	0.13
	2	2	2	2	1	2	1		1	1	1	1	1
	0.001	0.003	0.002	0.021		0.002							
091	0.10	0.41	0.06	0.17	0.09	0.42	44.2	0.05	205	21	0.24	32	0.08
092	0.10	0.45	0.07	0.18	0.10	0.46	48.0	0.05	223	23	0.27	35	0.09
	2	2	1	1	1	1	1	1	1	1	2	1	1
	0.006	0.433									0.190		
093	0.06	0.23	0.13	0.44	0.02	0.16	6.9	0.03	78	20	0.06	12	0.27
094	0.07	0.27	0.15	0.51	0.02	0.19	8.0	0.03	91	23	0.07	14	0.31
	1	1	2	2	1	2	1	1	1	1	2	1	1
			0.008	0.027		0.0.35					0.028		

(*continued*)

APPENDIX TABLE 5-9   Composition of Feeds (Excluding Vitamins) Commonly Used in Horse Diets (*Continued*)

Entry no.	Feed name	International feed number[a]	Dry matter (%)	DE[b] (Mcal/ kg)	(Mcal/ lb)	Crude protein (%)	Lysine (%)	Ether extract (%)	Fiber (%)	NDF (%)	ADF (%)	Ash (%)
						Corn, dent yellow (*Zea mays indentata*)						
095	grain	4-02-935	88.0	3.38	1.54	9.1	0.25	3.6	2.2	9.5	3.6	1.3
096			100.0	3.84	1.75	10.4	0.28	4.1	2.5	10.8	4.1	1.5
		N	545			527	440	89	72	3	5	64
		SD	2.44			1.42	0.045	0.620	1.17	2.10	0.844	0.306
097	silage	3-02-912	30.4	0.82	0.37	2.4	0.13	1.0	7.2	14.8	8.4	1.6
098			100.0	2.68	1.22	7.9	0.43	3.3	23.8	48.9	27.8	5.1
		N	8			12	1	5	7	2	8	5
		SD	5.05			0.590		0.044	1.25	3.04	4.24	1.13
						Cotton (*Gossypium spp.*)						
099	hulls	1-01-599	90.4	1.71	0.78	3.8		1.5	43.2	79.8	59.0	2.6
100			100.0	1.89	0.86	4.2		1.7	47.8	88.3	65.3	2.9
		N	22			28		26	27	2	4	20
		SD	1.34			0.744		1.19	3.07	2.41	4.31	0.487
101	seeds, oil residue, solvent-extracted, ground, 41% protein	5-01-621	91.0	2.74	1.25	41.3	1.68	1.5	12.2	25.4	17.5	6.5
102			100.0	3.01	1.37	45.4	1.85	1.7	13.4	27.9	19.2	7.1
		N	65			52	18	41	40	3	7	31
		SD	1.36			0.926	0.074	0.566	1.06	1.95	2.85	0.397
						Fats and oils						
103	fat, animal hydrolyzed	4-00-376	99.2	7.94	3.61			98.4				
104			100.0	8.00	3.64			99.2				
		N	5					3				
		SD	0.277					1.04				
105	oil, vegetable	4-05-077	99.8	8.98	4.08		99.7					
106			100.0	9.00	4.09			99.9				
		N	5					6				
		SD	0.289					0.104				
						Fescue, Kentucky 31 (*Festuca arundinacea*)						
107	fresh	2-01-902	31.3	0.70	0.32	4.7	0.18	1.7	7.7	19.4	10.8	2.2
108			100.0	2.2	1.01	15.0	0.57	5.5	24.6	62.2	34.4	7.2
		N	5			51	2	18	18	8	8	2
		SD	3.76			2.02	0.077	0.757	2.39	8.36	4.39	3.60
109	hay, sun-cured, full-bloom	1-09-188	91.9	1.89	0.86	11.8		5.1	23.9	61.6	35.7	7.6
110			100.0	2.06	1.01	12.9		5.6	26.0	67.1	39.2	8.3
		N	3			11		9	8	4	4	9
		SD	3.01			3.35		0.591	2.91	4.51	4.77	1.08
111	hay, sun-cured, mature	1-09-189	90.0	1.76	0.80	9.8		4.2	28.1	63.0	35.1	6.1
112			100.0	1.95	0.89	10.8		4.7	31.2	70.0	39.0	6.8
		N	1			13		13	10	1	1	13
		SD				3.58		0.846	2.36			0.920
						Fish, Anchovy (*Engraulis ringen*)						
113	meal, mechanically extracted	5-01-985	92.0	2.76	1.25	65.5	5.03	4.2	1.0			14.7
114			100.0	3.00	1.36	71.2	5.47	4.6	1.1			16.0
		N	67			58	40	36	9			47
		SD	1.19			2.24	0.429	1.62	0.015			1.54
						Fish, Menhaden (*Brevoortia tyrannus*)						
115	meal, mechanically extracted	5-02-009	91.7	2.93	1.33	62.2	4.74	9.8	0.7			18.9
116			100.0	3.20	1.45	67.9	5.17	10.7	0.8			20.6
		N	79			91	64	96	38			87
		SD	1.18			2.65	0.252	1.84	0.206			2.12

| | Macrominerals (%) | | | | | | Microminerals (mg/kg) | | | | | | |
Entry no.	Calcium	Phosphorus	Magnesium	Potassium	Sodium	Sulfur	Copper	Iodine	Iron	Manganese	Selenium	Zinc	Cobalt
	Corn, dent yellow (Zea mays indentata)												
095	0.05	0.27	0.11	0.32	0.03	0.11	3.7		31	5	0.12	19	0.13
096	0.05	0.31	0.12	0.37	0.03	0.13	4.2		35	6	0.14	22	0.14
	48	47	41	35	26	7	33		29	31	17	33	6
	0.070	0.039	0.031	0.033	0.014	0.017	1.3		12.6	1.5	0.125	5.5	0.177
097	0.09	0.07	0.06	0.36	0.02	0.03	1.8		98	11	0.02	13	0.03
098	0.31	0.23	0.20	1.17	0.06	0.12	5.8		321	36.4	0.06	42	0.10
	8	7	9	7	5	2	9		8	8	6	8	1
	0.126	0.034	0.089	0.126	0.052	0.007	1.6		261	17.7	0.035	31.0	
	Cotton (Gossypium spp.)												
099	0.13	0.08	0.13	0.79	0.02	0.08	12.0		119	108	0.08	20	0.02
100	0.15	0.09	0.14	0.88	0.02	0.08	13.3		131	119	0.09	22	0.02
	16	16	10	11	7	6	4		5	3	1	3	3
	0.016	0.018	0.001	0.055	0.001	0.062	4.0		49.7	2.2		0.1	0.005
101	0.17	1.11	0.54	1.30	0.04	0.26	19.5		188	21	0.90	61	0.48
102	0.18	1.22	0.59	1.40	0.05	0.29	21.4		206	23	0.98	67	0.53
	23	26	14	15	13	6	8		9	10	1	4	4
	0.029	0.100	0.068	0.164	0.007	0.095	2.0		99.5	0.9		4.3	0.785
	Fats and oils												
103													
104													
105													
106													
	Fescue, Kentucky 31 (Festuca arundinacea)												
107	0.16	0.12	0.09	0.72		0.06							7
108	0.51	0.37	0.27	2.30		0.18							22
	25	27	24	24		24							1
	0.105	0.076	0.055	0.489		0.036							
109	0.40	0.29	0.16	2.17		0.24	25.7		174	95			35
110	0.43	0.32	0.17	2.30		0.26	28.0		190	103			38
	1	1	1	1		1	1		1	1			1
111	0.37	0.27	0.14	1.76	0.02		19.8		119	87		32	
112	0.41	0.30	0.16	1.96	0.02		22.0		132	97		35	
	2	2	2	2	1		2		2	2		2	
	0.127	0.070	0.021	0.190			12.7		9.2	22.6		1.4	
	Fish, Anchovy (Engraulis ringen)												
113	3.74	2.47	0.25	0.72	0.88	0.72	9.1	3.14	215	11	1.35	105	0.17
114	4.06	2.69	0.27	0.79	0.96	0.78	9.9	3.41	234	12	1.47	114	0.19
	51	52	32	35	32	4	27	2	28	31	27	31	1
	0.537	0.446	0.052	0.277	0.329	0.235	1.8	3.49	63.2	5.9	0.254	16.7	
	Fish, Menhaden (Brevoortia tyrannus)												
115	5.01	2.87	0.15	0.71	0.41	0.53	10.3	1.09	545	37	2.15	144	0.15
116	5.46	3.14	0.16	0.77	0.44	0.58	11.3	1.19	594	40	2.34	157	0.17
	68	67	19	21	22	4	20	2	21	21	16	18	2
	0.800	0.314	0.028	0.160	0.131	0.259	3.5	1.41	271	17.7	0.690	19.0	0.068

(continued)

APPENDIX TABLE 5-9   Composition of Feeds (Excluding Vitamins) Commonly Used in Horse Diets (*Continued*)

Entry no.	Feed name	International feed number[a]	Dry matter (%)	DE[b] (Mcal/ kg)	DE[b] (Mcal/ lb)	Crude protein (%)	Lysine (%)	Ether extract (%)	Fiber (%)	NDF (%)	ADF (%)	Ash (%)
						Flax, common (*Linum usitatissimum*)						
117	seeds	5-02-052	93.6	3.40	1.54	21.1	0.86	36.0	6.2		7.5	4.9
118			100.0	3.63	1.65	22.5	0.92	38.4	6.6		8.0	5.2
		N	4			12	1	4	3		1	3
		SD	0.643			2.42		1.48	0.178			1.38
119	seeds, meal, solvent-	5-02-048	90.2	2.74	1.25	34.6	1.16	1.4	9.1	22.6	17.4	5.9
120	extracted		100.0	3.04	1.38	38.4	1.28	1.6	10.1	25.0	19.0	6.5
		N	25			16	9	18	13	1	1	10
		SD	1.12			1.52	0.082	0.752	0.597			0.257
						Lespedeza, common (*Lespedeza striata*)						
121	fresh, late vegetative	2-07-093	25.0	0.55	0.25	4.1		0.5	8.0			3.2
122			100.0	2.20	1.00	16.4		2.0	24.0			12.8
		N	2			1		1	1			1
		SD										
123	hay, sun-cured, midbloom	1-02-554	90.8	1.93	0.88	11.4		2.3	26.2			4.5
124			100.0	2.13	0.97	12.6		2.5	30.0			4.9
		N	3			2		2	2			2
		SD	2.93			2.82		0.692	1.30			1.14
						Lespedeza, Kobe (*Lespedeza striata*)						
125	hay, sun-cured, midbloom	1-02-574	93.9	1.96	0.89	10.0		2.8	26.?			3.8
126			100.0	2.08	0.95	10.6		3.0	27.9			4.1
		N	1			1		1	1			1
		SD										
						Meadow plants, intermountain						
127	hay, sun-cured	1-03-181	95.1	1.60	0.73	8.2		2.4	31.2			8.2
128			100.0	1.69	0.77	8.7		2.5	32.7			8.6
		N	72			219		9	9			4
		SD	1.37			2.25		0.442	1.27			1.04
						Milk						
129	fresh (horse); see											
130	Appendix Table 1											
131	skimmed, dehydrated	5-01-175	94.1	3.81	1.73	33.4	2.54	1.0	0.2	0.0	0.0	7.9
132	(cattle)		100.0	4.05	1.84	35.5	2.70	1.0	0.2	0.00	0.0	8.4
		N	57			30	15	27	12	1	1	25
		SD	1.35			2.11	0.249	1.48	0.081			0.398
						Millet, pearl (*Pennisetum glaucum*)						
133	fresh	2-03-115	20.7	0.35	0.16	2.1		0.6	6.5			1.9
134			100.0	1.70	0.77	10.1		2.9	31.1			9.2
		N	4			2		2	2			2
		SD	0.190			0.137		0.079	0.092			0.088
135	hay, sun-cured	1-03-112	87.4	1.34	0.61	7.3		1.8	32.2			8.9
136			100.0	1.53	0.70	8.4		2.0	36.9			10.2
		N	3			2		2	2			2
		SD	0.407			1.00		0.106	1.37			0.155

Entry no.	Macrominerals (%)						Microminerals (mg/kg)						
	Calcium	Phosphorus	Magnesium	Potassium	Sodium	Sulfur	Copper	Iodine	Iron	Manganese	Selenium	Zinc	Cobalt
Flax, common (*Linum usitatissimum*)													
117	0.22	0.54	0.40	0.74		0.23			90	61			
118	0.23	0.58	0.43	0.79		0.25			100	65			
	2	10	1	10		1			1	1			
	0.003	0.088		0.090									
119	0.39	0.80	0.60	1.38	0.14	0.39	25.7		319	38	0.82		0.19
120	0.43	0.89	0.66	1.53	0.15	0.43	28.5		354	42	0.91		0.21
	12	12	8	8	7	5	6		7	6	1		3
	0.022	0.034	0.007	0.015	0.003	0.026	0.33		12.2	0.15			0.018
Lespedeza, common (*Lespedeza striata*)													
121	0.30	0.07		0.32									
122	1.20	0.28		1.28									
	1	1		1									
123	1.07	0.17	0.22	0.94					282	211			
124	1.18	0.19	0.24	1.04					310	232			
	2	2	2	2					2	2			
	0.076	0.030	0.040	0.024					42.0	113			
Lespedeza, Kobe (*Lespedeza striata*)													
125	1.11	0.32	0.27	0.89					291	193			
126	1.18	0.34	0.29	0.95					310	206			
	1	1	1	1					1	1			
Meadow plants, intermountain													
127	0.58	0.17	0.16	1.50	0.11								
128	0.60	0.18	0.17	1.58	0.12								
	216	216	209	209	196								
	0.238	0.041	0.088	0.530	0.118								
Milk													
129													
130													
131	1.28	1.02	0.12	1.60	0.51	0.32	11.7		8	2	0.12	38	0.11
132	1.36	1.09	0.13	1.70	0.54	0.34	12.4		8	2	0.13	41	0.12
	16	14	11	15	8	5	4		2	6	1	4	2
	0.027	0.018	0.014	0.102	0.085	0.004	0.28		2.6	0.1		4.1	0.003
Millet, pearl (*Pennisetum glaucum*)													
133													
134													
135													
136													

(*continued*)

APPENDIX TABLE 5-9 Composition of Feeds (Excluding Vitamins) Commonly Used in Horse Diets (*Continued*)

Entry no.	Feed name	International feed number[a]	Dry matter (%)	DE[b] (Mcal/ kg)	DE[b] (Mcal/ lb)	Crude protein (%)	Lysine (%)	Ether extract (%)	Fiber (%)	NDF (%)	ADF (%)	Ash (%)
						Molasses and Syrup						
137	beet, sugar,	4-00-668	77.9	2.65	1.20	6.6		0.2	0.0	0.0	0.0	8.9
138	molasses,more		100.0	3.40	1.55	8.5		0.2	0.0	0.0	0.0	11.4
	than 48% invert	N	21			12		3				9
	sugar, more	SD	1.71			1.11		0.105				1.34
	than 79.5 degrees brix											
139	citrus, syrup	4-01-241	66.9	2.27	1.03	5.7		0.2	0.0	0.0	0.0	5.1
140	(citrus molasses)		100.0	3.40	1.55	8.5		0.3	0.0	0.0	0.0	7.7
		N	12			8		7				5
		SD	3.42			2.18		0.012				1.22
141	sugarcane,	4-04-695	94.4	3.21	1.46	9.0		0.8	7.1			12.0
142	molasses,		100.0	3.40	1.55	9.5		0.9	7.5			12.7
	dehydrated	N	7			7		8	7			4
		SD	2.73			2.36		0.638	3.01			5.74
143	sugarcane,	4-04-696	74.3	2.60	1.18	4.3		0.2	0.4		0.3	9.9
144	molasses, more		100.0	3.50	1.59	5.8		0.2	0.5		0.4	13.3
	than 46%	N	84			64		6	1		1	52
	invert sugar,	SD	3.27			2.03		0.240				2.34
	more than 79.5 degrees brix (blackstrap)											
						Oats (*Avena sativa*)						
145	grain	4-03-309	89.2	2.85	1.30	11.8	0.39	4.6	10.7	24.4	14.2	3.1
146			100.0	3.20	1.45	13.3	0.44	5.2	12.0	27.3	15.9	3.4
		N	97			110	18	108	99	14	2	91
		SD	1.80			1.25	0.061	1.00	1.35	4.52	1.55	0.507
147	grain, grade 1,	4-18-520	89.0	2.99	1.36	12.5	0.44	5.1	10.8	25.8		3.0
148	heavy, 51.5		100.0	3.36	1.53	14.0	0.49	5.7	12.1	29.0		3.4
	kg/hl	N				35	4	36	31	4		36
		SD				1.56	0.038	0.728	1.29	0.735		0.292
149	grain, Pacific	4-07-999	90.9	2.91	1.32	9.1	0.33	5.0	11.2			3.8
150	coast		100.0	3.20	1.45	10.0	0.37	5.5	12.3			4.2
		N	13			7	4	6	6			3
		SD	0.426			0.377	0.063	0.386	0.508			0.257
151	groats	4-03-331	89.6	3.09	1.40	15.5	0.55	6.1	2.5			2.0
152			100.0	3.45	1.57	17.3	0.62	6.8	2.8			2.3
		N	41			43	18	35	35			14
		SD	1.55			1.70	0.077	0.924	0.833			0.230
153	groats by-product,	1-08-316	91.4	1.66	0.76	4.3	0.15	1.5	29.0			5.8
154	less than 30%		100.0	1.82	0.83	4.7	0.16	1.6	31.7			6.4
	fiber	N	29			27	4	27	27			12
		SD	1.33			1.04	0.062	0.456	2.93			0.451
155	hay, sun-cured	1-03-280	90.7	1.75	0.79	8.6		2.2	29.1	57.1	34.8	7.2
156			100.0	1.92	0.87	9.5		2.4	32.0	63.0	38.4	7.9
		N	27			32		13	17	1	1	11
		SD	2.55			2.26		0.885	3.57			0.850
157	hulls	1-03-281	92.4	1.59	0.72	3.8	0.18	1.4	30.6	66.7	36.5	6.1
158			100.0	1.72	0.78	4.1	0.20	1.5	33.2	72.2	39.6	6.6
		N	26			17	4	15	15	4	4	12
		SD	1.14			1.33	0.042	0.813	3.44	5.72	2.06	0.699
159	straw	1-03-283	92.2	1.49	0.68	4.1		2.0	37.2	68.6	44.2	7.2
160			100.0	1.62	0.74	4.4		2.2	40.4	74.4	47.9	7.8
		N	71			74		16	64	4	5	14
		SD	2.10			1.09		0.424	2.98	2.70	2.48	1.85

Entry no.	Macrominerals (%)						Microminerals (mg/kg)						
	Cal-cium	Phos-phorus	Mag-nesium	Potas-sium	So-dium	Sul-fur	Cop-per	Io-dine	Iron	Man-ganese	Sele-nium	Zinc	Co-balt
						Molasses and Syrup							
137	0.12	0.02	0.23	4.72	1.16	0.46	16.8		68	4		14	0.36
138	0.15	0.03	0.29	6.06	1.48	0.60	21.6		87	6		18	0.46
	13	11	10	10	8	9	7		8	7		1	5
	0.054	0.007	0.014	0.290	0.079	0.048	1.3		25.2	0.3			0.032
139	1.18	0.09	0.14	0.09	0.28	0.14	72.2		339	26		92	0.11
140	1.76	0.14	0.21	0.14	0.41	0.21	107.9		507	38		137	0.16
	8	7	7	7	5	7	4		4	4		2	2
	0.323	0.035	0.010	0.006	0.029	0.022	3.5		10.9	1.2		0.22	0.002
141	1.03	0.14	0.44	3.39	0.19	0.43	74.9		236	54		31	1.14
142	1.10	0.15	0.47	3.59	0.20	0.46	79.3		250	57		33	1.21
	5	3	1	2	1	1	1		1	1		1	1
	0.347			0.601									
143	0.74	0.08	0.31	2.98	0.16	0.35	48.8	1.56	196	44		15	1.18
144	1.00	0.10	0.42	4.01	0.22	0.47	65.7	2.10	263	59		21	1.59
	32	31	12	16	9	9	8	1	11	11		5	4
	0.182	0.017	0.098	0.885	0.020	0.025	26.0		34.4	6.4		6.0	0.752
						Oats (*Avena sativa*)							
145	0.08	0.34	0.14	0.40	0.05	0.21	6.0	0.11	65	36	0.21	35	0.06
146	0.09	0.38	0.16	0.45	0.06	0.23	6.7	0.13	73	40.5	0.24	39	0.06
	64	71	48	47	15	13	27	1	38	37	32	40	8
	0.030	0.048	0.031	0.117	0.026	0.010	1.8		25.2	10.0	0.146	10.9	0.016
147	0.05	0.34	0.12	0.38			5.8		83	37	0.20	35	
148	0.06	0.38	0.14	0.43			6.5		93	41	0.23	39	
	36	36	32	32			26		31	32	32	32	
	0.010	0.066	0.018	0.039			2.7		14.9	7.9	0.220	11.5	
149	0.10	0.31	0.17	0.38	0.06	0.20			73	38	0.08		
150	0.11	0.34	0.19	0.42	0.07	0.22			80	42	0.08		
	3	3	1	2	1	3			1	1	1		
	0.006	0.016		0.007		0.019							
151	0.08	0.42	0.11	0.36	0.03	0.20	6.0	0.11	71	31	0.45	33	
152	0.09	0.47	0.13	0.40	0.04	0.22	6.7	0.12	79	34	0.51	37	
	21	21	12	13	5	6	8	1	9	9	2	2	
	0.029	0.033	0.034	0.038	0.026	0.001	0.9		20.9	7.3	0.233	3.5	
153	0.15	0.17	0.13	0.50	0.05	0.18	3.0		100	18			
154	0.16	0.19	0.14	0.54	0.06	0.19	3.3		110	20			
	7		8	2	2	2	1		1	1			
	0.034	0.050	0.087	0.031	0.017	0.040							
155	0.29	0.23	0.26	1.35	0.17	0.21	4.4		369	90		41	0.07
156	0.32	0.25	0.29	1.49	0.18	0.23	4.8		406	99		45	0.07
	7	26	23	11	16	3	4		5	4		1	3
	0.092	0.059	0.268	0.655	0.060	0.058	1.5		160./	48.2			0.002
157	0.15	0.14	0.12	0.55	0.06	0.09	6.6		128	25	0.40	27	
158	0.16	0.15	0.13	0.59	0.07	0.10	7.1		138	27	0.43	29	
	9	9	6	8	6	2	4		3	5	1	3	
	0.041	0.048	0.038	0.058	0.088	0.066	3.2		48.4	9.68		8.0	
159	0.22	0.06	0.16	2.33	0.39	0.21	9.5		151	29		5	
160	0.23	0.06	0.17	2.53	0.42	0.22	10.3		164	31		6	
	68	66	18	16	5	6	4		15	5	11		
	0.094	0.038	0.041	0.255	0.072	0.018	0.54		47.1	11.8		1.1	

(*continued*)

APPENDIX TABLE 5-9 Composition of Feeds (Excluding Vitamins) Commonly Used in Horse Diets (*Continued*)

Entry no.	Feed name	International feed number[a]	Dry matter (%)	DE[b] (Mcal/kg)	DE[b] (Mcal/lb)	Crude protein (%)	Lysine (%)	Ether extract (%)	Fiber (%)	NDF (%)	ADF (%)	Ash (%)
						Orchardgrass (*Dactylis glomerata*)						
161	fresh, early bloom	2-03-442	23.5	0.54	0.24	3.0		0.9	7.5	12.9	7.2	1.9
162			100.0	2.29	1.04	12.8		3.7	32.0	55.1	30.7	8.1
		N	8			7		5	5	3	2	6
		SD	3.87			2.37		0.801	2.93	8.31	1.98	1.68
163	fresh, midbloom	2-03-443	27.4	0.55	0.25	2.8		1.0	9.2	15.8	9.8	2.1
164			100.0	2.02	0.92	10.1		3.5	33.5	57.6	35.6	7.5
		N	3			4		2	2	1	1	4
		SD	5.36			3.89		0.368	2.25			0.535
165	hay, sun-cured, early-bloom	1-03-425	89.1	1.94	0.88	11.4		2.6	30.2	53.1	30.1	7.6
166			100.0	2.17	0.99	12.8		2.9	33.9	59.6	33.8	8.5
		N	7			9		6	5	4	4	6
		SD	3.30			3.51		0.826	1.72	5.28	1.25	1.60
167	hay, sun-cured, late-bloom	1-03-428	90.6	1.72	0.78	7.6		3.1	33.6	58.9	34.2	9.1
168			100.0	1.90	0.87	8.4		3.4	37.1	65.0	37.8	10.1
		N	7			1		1	1	3	3	3
		SD	1.51							2.77	0.207	3.10
						Pangolagrass (*Digitaria decumbens*)						
169	fresh	2-03-493	20.2	0.39	0.10	1.8		0.5	6.6		7.5	1.5
170			100.0	1.95	0.89	9.1		2.3	32.6		36.9	7.6
		N	9			11		9	10		1	9
		SD	2.37			1.34		0.423	1.39			1.12
171	hay, sun-cured, 15–28 days' growth	1-10-638	91.0	1.72	0.78	9.2		2.2	29.1	63.7	37.1	7.7
172			100.0	1.89	0.86	10.1		2.4	32.0	70.0	40.8	8.5
		N	1			8		2	8	8	8	1
		SD				2.04		0.282	2.57	4.38	3.96	
173	hay, sun-cured, 29–42 days' growth	1-26-214	91.0	1.62	0.74	6.7		1.8	29.5	66.2	38.1	7.3
174			100.0	1.78	0.81	7.4		2.0	32.4	72.7	41.8	8.0
		N	1			8		2	8	8	8	1
		SD				1.45			3.01	3.73	4.12	
175	hay, sun-cured, 43–56 days' growth	1-29-573	91.0	1.41	0.64	5.7		1.6	29.3	70.0	41.9	6.9
176			100.0	1.55	0.70	6.3		1.8	32.2	77.0	46.0	7.6
		N	1			8		2	8	8	8	1
		SD				1.79		0.283	3.67	2.33	3.89	
						Pea (*Pisum spp.*)						
177	seeds	5-03-600	89.1	3.07	1.40	23.4	1.65	0.9	5.6	17.3	8.0	2.8
178			100.0	3.45	1.57	26.3	1.86	1.0	6.3	19.5	9.0	3.2
		N	19			18	11	14	14	2	1	13
		SD	0.822			3.05	0.136	0.195	0.666	2.64		0.187
						Peanut (*Arachis hypogaea*)						
179	hay, sun-cured	1-03-619	90.7	1.74	0.79	9.9		3.3	30.3		37.2	8.2
180			100.0	1.91	0.87	10.9		3.6	33.4		41.0	9.0
		N	18			14		13	14		1	13
		SD	1.04			0.800		0.963	6.92			1.99
181	hulls (pods)	1-08-028	90.7	1.13	0.52	7.3	0.36	1.9	57.1	65.1	60.6	4.0
182			100.0	1.25	0.57	8.1	0.40	2.1	63.0	71.7	66.8	4.7
		N	17			18	2	14	15	3	2	8
		SD	1.74			1.51	0.021	1.33	6.72	7.17	1.98	1.84
183	seeds without coats, meal, solvent extracted	5-03-650	92.4	3.00	1.36	48.9	1.45	2.1	7.7			5.8
184			100.0	3.25	1.48	52.9	1.57	2.3	8.4			6.3
		N	16			12	2	10	10			7
		SD	1.82			3.93	0.062	0.997	1.19			1.02

Entry no.	Calcium	Phosphorus	Magnesium	Potassium	Sodium	Sulfur	Copper	Iodine	Iron	Manganese	Selenium	Zinc	Cobalt
	Macrominerals (%)						Microminerals (mg/kg)						

Orchardgrass (*Dactylis glomerata*)

Entry no.	Calcium	Phosphorus	Magnesium	Potassium	Sodium	Sulfur	Copper	Iodine	Iron	Manganese	Selenium	Zinc	Cobalt
161	0.06	0.09	0.07	0.80	0.01	0.06	7.8		185	24			
162	0.25	0.39	0.31	3.38	0.04	0.26	33.1		785	104			
	1	1	1	1	1	1	1		2	1			
									21.2				
163	0.06	0.05	0.09	0.57	0.07		13.7		19	37		7	0.03
164	0.23	0.17	0.33	2.09	0.26		50.1		68	136		25	0.10
	1	2	1	1	1		1		1	1		1	1
		0.079											
165	0.24	0.30	0.10	2.59	0.01	0.23	16.9		83	140		36	0.38
166	0.27	0.34	0.11	2.91	0.01	0.26	19.0		93	157		40	0.43
	1	1	1	1	1	1	1		1	1		1	1
167	0.24	0.27	0.10	2.42	0.01		18.1	18.00	76	151	0.03	34	0.27
168	0.26	0.30	0.11	2.67	0.01		20.0	20.00	84	167	0.03	38	0.30
	1	1	1	1	1		1	1	1	1	1	1	1

Pangolagrass (*Digitaria decumbens*)

Entry no.	Calcium	Phosphorus	Magnesium	Potassium	Sodium	Sulfur	Copper	Iodine	Iron	Manganese	Selenium	Zinc	Cobalt
169	0.08	0.04	0.04	0.29									
170	0.38	0.22	0.18	1.42									
	8	8	5	4									
	0.078	0.064	0.046	0.284									
171	0.53	0.19	0.18	1.55									
172	0.58	0.21	0.20	1.70									
	1	1	1	1									
173	0.42	0.21	0.14	1.27									
174	0.46	0.23	0.15	1.40									
	1	1	1	1									
175	0.35	0.16	0.13	1.00									
176	0.38	0.18	0.14	1.10									
	1	1	1	1									

Pea (*Pisum spp.*)

Entry no.	Calcium	Phosphorus	Magnesium	Potassium	Sodium	Sulfur	Copper	Iodine	Iron	Manganese	Selenium	Zinc	Cobalt
177	0.12	0.41	0.12	0.95	0.22				64	3		23	
178	0.14	0.46	0.14	1.06	0.25				72	3		26	
	6	7	2	2	2				2	1		1	
	0.054	0.107	0.004	0.117	0.000				22.3				

Peanut (*Arachis hypogaea*)

Entry no.	Calcium	Phosphorus	Magnesium	Potassium	Sodium	Sulfur	Copper	Iodine	Iron	Manganese	Selenium	Zinc	Cobalt
179	1.12	0.14	0.44	1.25		0.21							0.07
180	1.23	0.16	0.49	1.38		0.23							0.08
	5	5	4	4		1							1
181	0.23	0.06	0.14	0.83	0.08	0.09	14.4		278	47		22	0.11
182	0.26	0.07	0.15	0.92	0.09	0.09	15.9		306	51		24	0.12
	6	6	4	5	3	2	2		3	2		2	2
	0.012	0.009	0.045	0.068	0.101	0.008	2.7		15.8	24.5		0.1	0.002
183	0.29	0.61	0.15	1.18	0.03	0.30	15.0	0.06	143	27		33	0.11
184	0.32	0.66	0.17	1.28	0.03	0.33	16.0	0.07	155	29		36	0.12
	2	3	1	2	1	2	1	1	1	1		1	1
	0.247	0.048		0.038		0.002							

(continued)

APPENDIX TABLE 5-9   Composition of Feeds (Excluding Vitamins) Commonly Used in Horse Diets (*Continued*)

Entry no.	Feed name	International feed number[a]	Dry matter (%)	DE[b] (Mcal/ kg)	DE[b] (Mcal/ lb)	Crude protein (%)	Lysine (%)	Ether extract (%)	Fiber (%)	NDF (%)	ADF (%)	Ash (%)
				Prairie plants, Midwest								
185	hay, sun-cured	1-03-191	91.0	1.48	0.67	5.8		2.1	30.7			7.2
186			100.0	1.62	0.74	6.4		2.3	33.7			8.0
		N	8			5		5	5			4
		SD	1.42			1.63		0.647	1.94			1.07
				Redtop (Agrostis alba)								
187	hay, sun-cured midbloom	1-03-886	92.8	1.83	0.83	11.1		2.4	29.0			6.0
188			100.0	1 97	0 90	12.0		2.6	31.2			6.5
		N	1			1		1	1			1
		SD										
				Rice (Oryza sativa)								
189	bran with germs	4-03-928	90.5	2.62	1.19	13.0	0.57	13.6	11.7	30.0	18.0	10.4
190			100.0	2.90	1.30	14.4	0.63	15.0	12.9	33.0	20.0	11.5
		N	37			34	19	29	25	8	1	27
		SD	0.744			1.42	0.120	2.14	1.46	6.57		2.16
191	grain, ground	4-03-938	89.0	3.38	1.54	7.5	0.24	1.6	8.6			5.3
192			100.0	3.80	1.75	8.4	0.28	1.8	9.7			6.0
		N	9			5	4	4	4			2
		SD	0.755			0.604	0.047	0.162	0.597			0.214
193	hulls	1-08-075	91.9	1.15	0.52	2.8	0.08	1.0	39.2	75.7	66.1	19.0
194			100.0	1.25	0.57	3.1	0.09	1.1	42.7	82.4	72.0	20.6
		N	21			22	3	18	18	3	2	12
		SD	1.45			1.10	0.025	1.07	3.59	4.95	1.54	1.51
195	mill run	1-03-941	91.6	0.63	0.28	6.3	0.26	5.2	28.9			15.7
196			100.0	0.68	0.31	6.9	0.29	5.6	31.5			17
		N	22			23	5	18	20			9
		SD	0.907			0.740	0.061	0.816	2.79			1.53
				Rye, grain (Secale cereale)								
197		4-04-047	87.5	3.36	1.53	12.0	0.41	1.5	2.2	16.3	3.7	1.6
198			100.0	3.84	1.74	13.7	0.47	1.7	2.5	18.6	4.2	1.9
		N	93			70	10	61	64	1	1	66
		SD	1.49			1.05	0.048	0.245	0.595			0.171
				Ryegrass, Italian (Lolium multiflorum)								
199	fresh	2-04-073	22.6	0.51	0.23	4.0		0.9	4.7	13.8	8.6	3.9
200			100.0	2.20	1.02	17.9		4.1	20.9	61.0	38.0	17.4
		N	5			2		2	2	1	1	2
		SD	2.35			2.26		0.141	1.27			2.33
201	hay, sun-cured, late vegetative	1-04-065	85.6	1.57	0.71	8.8		2.1	20.4	54.8	36.0	9.4
202			100.0	1.84	0.83	10.3		2.4	23.8	64.0	42.0	11.0
		N	2			1		1	1	1	1	1
		SD	4.81									
				Sorghum (Sorghum bicolor)								
203	grain	4-04-383	90.1	3.21	1.46	11.5	0.26	2.7	2.6	20.7	8.3	1.7
204			100.0	3.56	1.62	12.7	0.29	3.0	2.8	23.0	9.3	1.9
		N	220			230	94	64	43	2	2	59
		SD	2.33			1.97	0.067	0.681	0.989	7.00	0.353	0.445
				Sorghum, Johnsongrass (Sorghum halepense)								
205	hay, sun-cured	1-04-407	90.5	1.50	0.68	6.7		2.0	30.4			7.7

Entry no.	Macrominerals (%)						Microminerals (mg/kg)						
	Calcium	Phosphorus	Magnesium	Potassium	Sodium	Sulfur	Copper	Iodine	Iron	Manganese	Selenium	Zinc	Cobalt
Prairie plants, Midwest													
185	0.32	0.12	0.24	0.98					80			31	
186	0.35	0.14	0.26	1.08					88			34	
	3	3	2	1					1			1	
	0.008	0.063	0.023										
Redtop (*Agrostis alba*)													
187	0.58	0.32		1.57									
188	0.63	0.35		1.69									
	1	1		1									
Rice (*Oryza sativa*)													
189	0.09	1.57	0.88	1.71	0.03	0.18	11.0		207	358	0.40	30	1.38
190	0.10	1.73	0.97	1.89	0.03	0.20	12.2		229	396	0.44	33	1.53
	21	21	13	18	6	9	6		9	8	1	7	2
	0.064	0.401	0.246	0.220	0.027	0.001	3.8		80.6	125		23.8	0.257
191	0.07	0.32	0.13	0.44	0.06	0.04	2.7	0.04	50	18		15	0.04
192	0.07	0.36	0.14	0.49	0.07	0.05	3.0	0.05	57	20		17	0.05
	4	4	4	5	3	3	1	1	1	1		1	1
	0.021	0.080	0.027	0.359	0.033	0.007							
193	0.11	0.07	0.34	0.60	0.02	0.07	3.1		91	294	0.14	22	
194	0.12	0.07	0.37	0.65	0.02	0.08	3.4		99	320	0.15	24	
	15	14	3	8	1	5	1		1	4	1	1	
	0.067	0.016	0.401	0.622		0.033			27.1				
195	0.15	0.46	0.10	0.52		0.18	9.9		228	9		105	
196	0.17	0.50	0.11	0.57		0.19	10.8		250	10		115	
	10	10	1	2		1	1			1		1	
	0.086	0.071		0.333									
Rye, grain (*Secale cereale*)													
197	0.06	0.32	0.11	0.45	0.02	0.15	7.6		63	72	0.38	28	
198	0.07	0.36	0.12	0.51	0.03	0.17	8.6		72	82	0.44	32	
	19	17	10	9	8	8	5		8	5	1	6	
	0.020	0.047	0.039	0.020	0.008	0.008	0.2		25.7	6.8		3.0	
Ryegrass, Italian (*Lolium multiflorum*)													
199	0.15	0.09	0.08	0.45	0.00	0.02			226				
200	0.65	0.41	0.35	2.00	0.01	0.10			1,000				
	2	2	1	1	1	1			1				
	0.007	0.007											
201	0.53	0.29		1.34					274				
202	0.62	0.34		1.56					320				
	1	1		1					1				
Sorghum (*Sorghum bicolor*)													
203	0.04	0.32	0.15	0.37	0.01	0.13	5.4		57	12	0.41	27	0.27
204	0.04	0.36	0.17	0.41	0.01	0.15	6.0		63	14	0.46	30	0.30
	27	26	24	15	14	3	13		23	21	3	21	1
	0.052	0.076	0.049	0.099	0.015	0.035	2.4		19.2	3.8	0.583	22.3	
Sorghum, Johnsongrass (*Sorghum halepense*)													
205	0.80	0.27	0.31	1.22	0.01	0.09			534				

(continued)

APPENDIX TABLE 5-9   Composition of Feeds (Excluding Vitamins) Commonly Used in Horse Diets (*Continued*)

Entry no.	Feed name	International feed number[a]	Dry matter (%)	DE[b] (Mcal/ kg)	DE[b] (Mcal/ lb)	Crude protein (%)	Lysine (%)	Ether extract (%)	Fiber (%)	NDF (%)	ADF (%)	Ash (%)
						Sorghum, Johnsongrass (*Sorghum halepense*)						
206			100.0	1.66	0.75	7.5		2.2	33.6			8.6
		N	6			2		2	2			2
		SD	0.313			0.349		0.083	0.365			0.343
						Soybean (*Glycine max*)						
207	seed coats	1-04-560	90.3	1.69	0.77	11.0	0.47	1.9	36.0	59.9	44.3	4.4
208			100.0	1.88	0.85	12.2	0.53	2.1	39.9	66.3	49.0	4.9
		N	28			27	2	17	23	6	6	10
		SD	3.43			2.51	0.246	0.567	4.79	2.03	2.85	0.481
209	seeds, meal,	5-20-637	89.1	3.14	1.43	44.5	2.87	1.4	6.2	13.3	8.9	6.4
210	solvent		100.0	3.52	1.60	49.9	3.22	1.6	7.0	14.9	10.0	7.2
	extracted,	N	119			111	38	87	92	2	3	66
	44% protein	SD	1.22			1.25	0.242	0.672	0.955	1.27	0.057	0.581
211	seeds without	5-04-612	89.9	3.36	1.53	48.5	3.09	1.0	3.5	6.9	5.5	6.0
212	hulls, meal,		100.0	3.73	1.70	54.0	3.44	1.1	3.8	7.7	6.1	6.7
	solvent-	N	78			75	18	41	55	1	3	34
	extracted	SD	1.72			1.72	0.168	0.386	0.557		0.750	0.678
						Sunflower, Common (*Helianthus annuus*)						
213	seeds without	5-04-739	92.5	2.59	1.17	45.2	1.68	2.7	11.7	37.0	27.8	7.5
214	hulls, meal,		100.0	2.80	1.27	48.9	1.82	2.9	12.7	40.0	30.0	8.1
	solvent-	N	21			22	11	19	20	1	1	14
	extracted	SD	1.73			3.96	0.148	0.625	2.18			0.347
						Timothy (*Phleum pratense*)						
215	fresh, late vegetative	2-04-903	26.7	0.70	0.29	3.3		1.0	8.6	14.9	7.7	2.0
216			100.0	2.37	1.08	12.2		3.8	32.1	55.7	29.0	7.5
		N	5			8		2	2	6	1	8
		SD	1.86			3.87		0.251	1.93	3.65		0.970
217	fresh, midbloom	2-04-905	29.2	0.58	0.27	2.7		0.9	9.8			1.9
218			100.0	2.00	0.91	9.1		3.0	33.5			6.6
		N	6			2		2	2			2
		SD	1.76			0.727		0.171	0.262			0.755
219	hay, sun-cured	1-04-822	89.1	1.83	0.83	9.6		2.5	30.0	54.7	31.4	5.1
220	early-bloom		100.0	2.06	0.94	10.8		2.8	33.6	61.4	35.2	5.7
		N	13			12		10	8	5	5	9
		SD	1.72			3.35		0.545	1.36	1.22	2.38	0.918
221	hay, sun-cured	1-04-883	88.9	1.77	0.80	8.6		2.3	30.0	56.6	32.3	5.4
222	midbloom		100.0	1.99	0.90	9.7		2.6	33.8	63.7	36.4	6.1
		N	10			20		11	11	13	13	8
		SD	1.93			1.95		0.344	1.36	2.32	2.19	1.13
223	hay, sun-cured	1-04-884	89.4	1.73	0.78	7.2		2.6	31.5	57.4	33.5	4.6
224	full-bloom		100.0	1.94	0.88	8.1		2.9	35.2	64.2	37.5	5.2
		N	8			15		7	7	8	8	8
		SD	2.43			1.03		0.729	1.20	2.19	2.27	0.813
225	hay, sun-cured	1-04-885	88.3	1.59	0.72	6.9		2.4	31.5	61.0	36.9	4.8
226	late-bloom		100.0	1.80	0.82	7.8		2.7	35.6	69.1	41.8	5.4
		N	6			6		6	4	2	2	3
		SD	0.609			0.692		0.360	0.853	1.55	1.76	1.15
						Trefoil, birdsfoot (*Lotus corniculatus*)						
227	fresh	2-20-786	19.3	0.42	0.19	4.0		0.8	4.1	9.0		2.2
228			100.0	2.18	0.99	20.6		4.0	21.2	46.7		11.2
		N	9			12		3	3	11		7
		SD	4.28			3.97		1.30	7.74	11.7		3.25

Entry no.	Calcium	Phosphorus	Magnesium	Potassium	Sodium	Sulfur	Copper	Iodine	Iron	Manganese	Selenium	Zinc	Cobalt
	Macrominerals (%)						Microminerals (mg/kg)						
Sorghum, Johnsongrass (*Sorghum halepense*)													
206	0.89	0.30	0.35	1.35	0.01	0.10			590				
	2	2	2	2	1	1			2				
	0.109	0.015	0.004	0.002					14.1				
Soybean (*Glycine max*)													
207	0.48	0.17	0.20	1.17	0.02	0.10	16.1		369	10	0.13	43	0.11
208	0.53	0.18	0.22	1.29	0.03	0.11	17.8		409	11	0.14	48	0.12
	10	8	2	5	4	2	1		2	3	1	2	1
	0.134	0.069	0.070	0.258	0.020	0.028			120	5.0		33.7	
209	0.35	0.63	0.27	1.98	0.03	0.41	19.9		165	31	0.45	50	0.11
210	0.40	0.71	0.31	2.22	0.04	0.46	22.4		185	35	0.51	57	0.12
	26	29	19	21	12	6	15		15	15	10	13	1
	0.109	0.043	0.029	0.245	0.031	0.046	7.9		39.0	3.5	0.281	7.5	
211	0.26	0.64	0.29	2.12	0.01	0.44	20.2	0.11	130	37	0.19	57	0.11
212	0.29	0.71	0.33	2.36	0.01	0.48	22.5	0.12	145	41	0.22	63	0.12
	19	19	6	9	4	2	6	1	2	5	2	7	1
	0.053	0.053	0.026	0.152	0.012	0.003	5.0		35.3	8.66	0.147	7.7	
Sunflower, Common (*Helianthus annuus*)													
213	0.42	0.94	0.65	1.17	0.03	0.31	3.7		31	19	2.12	97	
214	0.45	1.02	0.70	1.27	0.03	0.33	4.0		33	20	2.30	105	
	11	11	7	7	2	2	1		1	2	1	1	
	0.083	0.248	0.120	0.333	0.006	0.140				6.0			
Timothy (*Phleum pratense*)													
215	0.11	0.07	0.04	0.73	0.03	0.03	2.4		35	34		10	0.04
216	0.40	0.26	0.16	2.73	0.11	0.13	8.9		132	127		36	0.15
	4	4	4	4	4	2	2		4	2		2	2
	0.123	0.076	0.037	0.401	0.092		2.5		78.2	32.7		7.1	0.082
217	0.11	0.09	0.04	0.60	0.06	0.04	3.3		52	56			
218	0.38	0.30	0.14	2.06	0.19	0.13	11.2		179	192			
	2	2	2	2	2	2	1		2	1			
	0.173	0.067	0.016	0.484	0.000	0.002			29.1				
219	0.45	0.25	0.11	2.14	0.01	0.12	9.8		181	92		55	
220	0.51	0.29	0.13	2.41	0.01	0.13	11		203	103		62	
	3	3	2	2	1	1	1		2	1		1	
	0.077	0.065	0.021	2.10					4.24				
221	0.43	0.20	0.12	1.61	0.01	0.12	14.2		132	50		38	
222	0.48	0.23	0.13	1.82	0.01	0.13	16.0		149	56		43	
	2	2	3	3	1	1	2		3	2		1	
	0.077	0.056	0.046	0.401			15.5		47.5	13.9			
223	0.38	0.18	0.08	1.78	0.07	0.12	25.9		125	83		48	
224	0.43	0.20	0.09	1.99	0.07	0.14	29.0		140	93		54	
	3	4	3	4	3	3	2		2	2		1	
	0.095	0.014	0.038	0.518	0.092	0.010	33.9		24.9	16.9			
225	0.34	0.13	0.08	1.42	0.06	0.14			203				
226	0.38	0.15	0.09	1.61	0.07	0.16			230				
	1	2	1	2	1	1			2				
		0.049		0.035					98.9				
Trefoil, birdsfoot (*Lotus corniculatus*)													
227	0.33	0.05	0.08	0.63	0.02	0.05	2.5		34	16		6	0.09
228	1.74	0.26	0.40	3.26	0.11	0.25	12.8		176	83		31	0.49
	8	8	6	8	6	1	5		5	5		5	6
	0.398	0.046	0.124	1.66	0.053		3.4		125	13.6		7	0.211

(continued)

APPENDIX TABLE 5-9   Composition of Feeds (Excluding Vitamins) Commonly Used in Horse Diets (*Continued*)

Entry no.	Feed name	International feed number[a]	Dry matter (%)	DE[b] (Mcal/kg)	DE[b] (Mcal/lb)	Crude protein (%)	Lysine (%)	Ether extract (%)	Fiber (%)	NDF (%)	ADF (%)	Ash (%)
						Trefoil, birdsfoot (*Lotus corniculatus*)						
229	hay, sun-cured	1-05-044	90.6	1.99	1.19	14.4		1.9	29.3	42.6	32.6	6.7
230			100.0	2.20	1.00	15.9		2.1	32.3	47.5	36.0	7.4
		N	9			8		7	7	1	1	5
		SD	1.46			2.31		0.524	5.32			0.797
						Wheat (*Triticum aestibum*)						
231	bran	4-05-190	89.0	2.94	1.33	15.4	0.56	3.8	10.0	38.1	12.5	5.9
232			100.0	3.30	1.50	17.4	0.63	4.3	11.3	42.8	14.0	6.6
		N	86			64	21	56	6	6	37	
		SD	1.23			1.13	0.100	0.805	1.28	8.68	1.46	0.606
233	flour by-product,	4-05-205	88.9	3.04	1.38	16.4	0.68	4.2	7.8	31.1	10.5	4.6
234	less than 9.5% fiber		100.0	3.42	1.55	18.5	0.76	4.7	8.8	35.0	11.8	5.2
		N	65			59	19	48	49	1	2	24
		SD	1.41			1.15	0.084	0.662	1.00		1.13	1.17
235	fresh, early	2-05-176	22.2	0.64	0.29	6.1		1.0	3.9	10.2	6.3	3.0
236	vegetative		100.0	2.88	1.31	27.4		4.4	17.4	46.2	28.4	13.3
		N	2			2		1	1	1	1	1
		SD	0.988			1.62						
237	grain, hard, red	4-05-268	88.9	3.43	1.56	13.0	0.40	1.6	2.5	10.4	3.4	1.7
238	winter		100.0	3.86	1.75	14.6	0.45	1.8	2.8	11.7	3.9	2.0
		N	26			22	9	15	13	3	3	14
		SD	1.38			1.35	0.043	0.261	0.377	3.99	1.05	0.249
239	grain, soft, red	4-05-294	88.4	3.41	1.55	11.4	0.36	1.6	2.4	12.4	3.5	1.8
240	winter		100.0	3.86	1.75	12.9	0.40	1.8	2.7	14.0	4.0	2.1
		N	15			22	2	8	4	1	1	8
		SD	1.68			0.669	0.015	0.208	0.564			0.252
241	hay, sun-cured	1-05-172	88.7	1.68	0.76	7.7		2.0	25.7	60.3	36.4	7.0
242			100.0	1.90	0.86	8.7		2.2	29.0	68.0	41.0	7.9
		N	12			8		6	9	1	1	4
		SD	3.09			2.22		0.903	2.01			2.05
243	mill run, less than	4-05-206	89.9	3.12	1.42	15.6	0.57	4.1	8.2		9.9	5.1
244	9.5% fiber		100.0	3.47	1.57	17.3	0.64	4.6	9.1		11.0	5.7
		N	31			17	17	17	18		1	13
		SD	0.740			0.731	0.081	0.319	0.464			0.212
245	straw	1-05-175	91.3	1.48	0.67	3.2		1.8	38.0	72.1	50.2	7.1
246			100.0	1.62	0.74	3.5		2.0	41.7	78.9	55.0	7.7
		N	37			68		15	25	14	16	46
		SD	3.12			1.29		1.10	5.81	4.82	4.95	2.61
						Wheat, soft, white winter (*Triticum aestivum*)						
247	grain	4-05-337	90.2	3.54	1.61	10.6		1.5	2.2	8.7	2.4	1.5
248			100.0	3.92	1.78	11.8		1.6	2.5	9.7	2.7	1.7
		N	13			16		13	7	12	1	10
		SD	1.05			1.69		0.201	0.359	2.00		0.566
						Wheatgrass, crested (*Agropyron desertorum*)						
249	fresh, early	2-05-420	28.5	0.72	0.33	6.0		0.6	6.2			2.9
250	vegetative		100.0	2.54	1.16	21.0		2.2	21.6			10.0
		N	6			11		22	22			20
		SD	2.68			4.50		0.641	3.10			1.82
						Whey (*Bos taurus*)						
251	dehydrated	4-01-182	93.2	3.78	1.72	13.1	0.94	0.7	0.2	0.0	0.0	8.7
252	(cattle)		100.0	4.06	1.84	14.0	1.00	0.8	0.2	0.0	0.0	9.4
		N	68			50	17	38	11	1	1	23
		SD	1.58			2.00	0.147	0.491	0.071			2.03

Entry no.	Calcium	Phosphorus	Magnesium	Potassium	Sodium	Sulfur	Copper	Iodine	Iron	Manganese	Selenium	Zinc	Cobalt
	Macrominerals (%)						Microminerals (mg/kg)						
Trefoil, birdsfoot (*Lotus corniculatus*)													
229	1.54	0.21	0.46	1.74	0.06	0.23	8.4		206	26		70	0.10
230	1.70	0.23	0.51	1.92	0.07	0.25	9.3		227	29		77	0.11
	3	3	3	4	1	1	1		3	1		1	1
	0.088	0.011	0.200	0.253					149.7				
Wheat (*Triticum aestibum*)													
231	0.13	1.13	0.56	1.22	0.05	0.21	12.6	0.07	145	119	0.51	98	0.07
232	0.14	1.27	0.63	1.37	0.06	0.24	14.2	0.07	163	134	0.57	110	0.08
	30	29	17	17	13	8	8	1	10	8	5	6	3
	0.031	0.211	0.065	0.097	0.019	0.023	1.8		55.7	14.2	0.254	36.0	0.034
233	0.13	0.89	0.34	0.98	0.02	0.17	15.9	0.11	90	114	0.74	97	0.10
234	0.14	1.00	0.38	1.10	0.02	0.19	17.9	0.12	101	128	0.83	109	0.11
	30	31	16	17	5	11	11	1	12	10	1	6	8
	0.047	0.079	0.089	0.047	0.011	0.056	6.0		18.8	3.35		47.3	0.035
235	0.09	0.09	0.05	0.78	0.04	0.05			22				
236	0.42	0.40	0.21	3.50	0.18	0.22			100				
	1	1	1	1	2	2							
					0.148	0.035							
237	0.04	0.38	0.13	0.43	0.02	0.13	4.9		36	35	0.25	33	0.14
238	0.05	0.42	0.14	0.48	0.02	0.15	5.5		41	39	0.28	37	0.16
	13	13	11	12	6	3	7		9	9	5	8	4
	0.007	0.045	0.031	0.052	0.023	0.020	1 1		6.7	12.4	0.185	13.1	0.069
239	0.03	0.36	0.12	0.35	0.01	0.13	5.7		40	32	0.04	34	0.10
240	0.04	0.41	0.13	0.40	0.01	0.14	6.5		45	37	0.05	38	0.12
	16	17	16	16	2	15	16		16	16	1	15	1
	0.017	0.027	0.008	0.026	0.001	0.009	1.3		5.6	2.4		2.8	
241	0.13	0.18	0.11	0.88	0.19	0.19			177				
242	0.15	0.20	0.12	0.99	0.21	0.22			200				
	8	8	1	5	2	2			1				
	0.022	0.077		0.440	0.098	0.035							
243	0.10	1.02	0.47	1.20	0.22	0.17	18.5		95	104	0.63		0.21
244	0.11	1.13	0.53	1.33	0.24	0.19	20.6		105	116	0.70		0.23
	16	16	11	10	1	3	5		6	5	1		3
	0.007	0.058	0.093	0.269		0.026	0.5		5.9	3.8			0.027
245	0.16	0.04	0.11	1.28	0.13	0.17	3.3		143	37		6	0.04
246	0.17	0.05	0.12	1.40	0.14	0.19	3.6		157	41		6	0.05
	51	48	37	39	5	5	34		35	34		30	2
	0.065	0.024	0.024	0.709	0.005	0.005	1.2		39.5	13.7		0.774	0.008
Wheat, soft, white winter (*Triticum aestivum*)													
247	0.06	0.30	0.10	0.39	0.02	0.12	7.0		36	36	0.05	27	0.14
248	0.07	0.33	0.11	0.43	0.02	0.13	7.8		40	40	0.05	30	0.15
		10	1	1	1	2	1		1	1	1	1	1
		0.063				0.001							
Wheatgrass, crested (*Agropyron desertorum*)													
249	0.12	0.09	0.08										
250	0.44	0.33	0.28										
	22	22	1										
	0.177	0.141											
Whey (*Bos taurus*)													
251	0.85	0.76	0.13	1.16	0.62	1.04	46		194	6	0.06	5	0.11
252	0.92	0.81	0.14	1.25	0.66	1.11	49.9		208	6	0.08	5	0.12
	24	26	11	10	6	8	6		9	8	1	2	4
	0.144	0.128	0.012	0.237	0.272	0.006	4.15		94.8	2.2		2.4	0.002

(continued)

APPENDIX TABLE 5-9   Composition of Feeds (Excluding Vitamins) Commonly Used in Horse Diets (*Continued*)

Entry no.	Feed name	International feed number[a]	Dry matter (%)	DE[b] (Mcal/ kg)	DE[b] (Mcal/ lb)	Crude protein (%)	Lysine (%)	Ether extract (%)	Fiber (%)	NDF (%)	ADF (%)	Ash (%)
						Whey (*Bos taurus*)						
253	low lactose,	4-01-186	93.7	3.37	1.53	16.8	1.40	1.0	0.2	0.0	0.0	16.0
254	dehydrated (dried		100.0	3.61	1.64	17.9	1.50	1.1	0.2	0.0	0.0	17.1
	whey product)	N	28			21	15	20	3			1[4]
	(cattle)	SD	1.75			0.958	0.122	0.166	0.119			2.78
						Yeast, brewer's (*Saccharomyces cerevisiae*)						
255	dehydrated	7-05-527	93.1	3.07	1.40	43.4	3.23	1.0	3.2		3.7	6.7
256			100.0	3.30	1.50	46.6	3.47	1.1	3.5		4.0	7.2
		N	65			46	24	32	30			26
		SD	1.09			3.11	0.351	0.619	1.11			1.00

Stage of Maturity Terms Used in Appendix Table 5-9

Preferred term for plants that bloom	Definition	Comparable terms
Germinated	Stage in which the embryo in a seed resumes growth after a dormant period	Sprouted
Early vegetative	Stage at which the plant is vegetative and before the stems elongate	Fresh new growth, before heading out, before inflorescence emergence, immature, prebud stage, very immature, young
Prebloom	Stage at which stems are beginning to elongate to just before blooming; first bud to first flowers	Before bloom, bud stage, budding plants, heading to in bloom, heads just showing, jointing and boot (grasses), prebloom, preflowering, stems elongated
Early-bloom	Stage between initiation of bloom and stage in which 1/10 of the plants are in bloom; some grass heads are in anthesis	Early anthesis, first flower, headed out, in head, up to 1/10 bloom
Midbloom	Stage in which 1/10 to 2/3 of the plants are in bloom; most grass heads are in anthesis	Bloom, flowering, flowering plants, half-bloom, in bloom, mid-anthesis
Full-bloom	Stage in which 2/3 or more of the plants are in bloom	Three-fourths to full bloom, late anthesis
Late-bloom	Stage in which blossoms begin to dry and fall and seeds begin to form	Fifteen days after silking, before milk, in bloom to early pod, late to past anthesis
Milk stage	Stage in which seeds are well formed but soft and immature	After anthesis, early seed, fruiting, in tassel, late bloom to early seed, past bloom, pod stage, post anthesis, post bloom, seed developing, seed forming, soft, soft immature
Dough stage	Stage in which the seeds are of doughlike consistency	Dough stage, nearly mature, seeds, dough seeds well developed, soft dent
Mature	Stage in which plants are normally harvested for seed	Dent, dough to glazing, fruiting, fruiting plants, in seed, kernels ripe, ripe seed
Post ripe	Stage that follows maturity; seeds are ripe and plants have been cast and weathering has taken place (applies mostly to range plants)	Late seed, over ripe, very mature
Stem-cured	Stage in which plants are cured on the stem; seeds have been cast and weathering has taken place (applies mostly to range plants)	Dormant, mature and weathered, seeds cast
Regrowth early vegetative	Stage in which regrowth occurs without flowering activity; vegetative crop aftermath; regrowth in stubble (applies primarily to fall regrowth in temperate climates); early dry season regrowth.	Vegetative recovery growth

Entry no.	Macrominerals (%)						Microminerals (mg/kg)						
	Cal-cium	Phos-phorus	Mag-nesium	Potas-sium	So-dium	Sul-fur	Cop-per	Io-dine	Iron	Man-ganese	Sele-nium	Zinc	Co-balt
Whey (*Bos taurus*)													
253	1.50	1.11	0.22	2.86	1.45	1.07	7.0	9.89	245	8	0.05	8	
254	1.60	1.18	0.23	3.05	1.54	1.15	7.5	10.55	262	9	0.06	8	
	15	16	8	10	10	2	1	1	2	3	1	1	
	0.128	0.180	0.079	0.682	0.418	0.056			39.5	0.9			
Yeast, brewer's (*Saccharomyces cerevisiae*)													
255	0.14	1.36	0.24	1.68	0.07	0.44	38.4	0.36	83	6	0.91	39	0.51
256	0.15	1.47	0.26	1.81	0.08	0.47	41.3	0.38	89	7	0.98	42	0.54
	26	29	23	21	17	7	15	1	17	17	3	16	4
	0.040	0.149	0.062	0.232	0.029	0.061	29.3		50.0	5.5	0.476	19.1	0.696

NOTE: The following abbreviations were used: DE, digestible energy; NDF, neutral detergent fiber; ADF, acid detergent fiber; CP, crude protein. A blank space indicates that data are not available for that nutrient.

[a]The following variables appear below the feed number: N is the number of observations; SD is the standard deviation.

[b]The following equations were used to calculate DE: for class 1 and 2 feeds, DE (Mcal/kg) = 4.22 − 0.11 (% ADF) + 0.0332 (% CP) + 0.00112 (% ADF)^2; for class 4 and 5 feeds, DE (Mcal/kg) = 4.07 − 0.055 (% ADF) (Fonnesbeck, 1981).

SOURCE: *Nutrient Requirements of Horses*, 5th ed., National Research Council (1989).

Abbreviations Used		*Abbreviations Used*	
			mechanically extracted,
dehy	dehydrated	mech extd	expeller extracted,
extd	extracted		hydraulic extracted,
extn	extraction		or old process
extn unspecified	extraction unspecified	μg	microgram
gm	gram	mg	milligram
gr	grade	mt	more than
grnd	ground	s-c	sun-cured
IU	International Units	solv extd	solvent extracted
kcal	kilocalories	spp	species
kg	kilogram(s)	w	with
lt	less than	wo	without

Appendix Table 5-10 Vitamin Composition of Feeds Commonly Used in Horse Diets

Entry no.	Feed name	International feed number[a]	Dry matter (%)	Carotene (mg/kg)	A equivalent[b] (IU/kg)	D (IU/kg)	E (mg/kg)	Biotin (mg/kg)	Choline (mg/kg)	Folate (mg/kg)	Niacin (mg/kg)	Pantothenic acid (mg/kg)	Riboflavin (mg/kg)	Thiamin (mg/kg)	B_6 (mg/kg)	B_{12} (µg/kg)
							Alfalfa (Medicago Sativa)									
001	fresh, late vegetative	2-00-181	23.2			51	39.7									
002			100.0			221	171.5									
	N		14			1	1									
	SD		3.39													
003	fresh, full-bloom	2-00-188	23.8									7.5				
004			100.0									31.3				
	N		8									1				
	SD		3.88													
005	hay, sun-cured, early-bloom	1-00-059	90.5	126.5	50,608	1,806	23.5									
006			100.0	139.8	55,918	2,000	26.0									
	N		43	3	3	1	1									
	SD		1.92	61.9	24,775											
007	hay, sun-cured, midbloom	1-00-063	91.0	30.3	41,900	1,810	10.0						9.6			
008			100.0	33.3	46,000	2,000	11.0						10.6			
	N		60	1	1	1	1						1			
	SD		1.88													
009	hay, sun-cured, full-bloom	1-00-068	90.9	59.1	23,631	1,810	10.0									
010			100.0	65.0	26,000	2,000	11.0									
	N		21	2	2	1	1									
	SD		2.06	56.5	22,627											
011	meal, dehydrated, 15% protein	1-00-022	90.4	74.5	29,787		81.9	0.25	1,573.1	1.56	41.6	20.7	10.6	2.99	6.28	
012			100.0	82.3	32,934		90.6	0.28	1,739.3	1.73	46.0	22.9	11.7	3.31	6.94	
	N		23	3	3		3	1	1	1	2	2	4	2	1	
	SD		2.18	23.8	9,540		29.8				1.39	0.619	0.256	0.089		
013	meal, dehydrated, 17% protein	1-00-023	91.8	120.3	48,132		105.9	0.33	1,349.6	4.37	37.0	29.8	12.9	3.39	7.19	
014			100.0	131.1	52,433		115.3	0.36	1,470.2	4.76	40.3	32.4	14.1	3.69	7.83	
	N		72	3	3		7	6	18	12	18	18	14	9	7	
	SD		1.50	37.5	15,013		28.9	0.027	280	2.57	12.5	2.35	1.20	0.196	1.52	
							Alyceclover (Alysicarpus vaginalis)										
015	hay, sun-cured	1-00-361	89.7													
016			100.0													
	N		4													
	SD		0.901													

754

Bahiagrass (Paspalum notatum)

No.	Item	IFN		DM	2	3	4	5	6	7	8	9	10	11	12	13
017	fresh	2-00-464		28.7	20,973		52.4									
018				100.0	72,994		182.5									
			N	9	1		1									
			SD	1.91												
019	hay, sun-cured	1-00-462		90.0												
020				100.0												
			N	4												
			SD	0.420												
021	hay, sun-cured, late vegetative	1-20-787		91.0												
022				100.0												
			N	1												
			SD													
023	hay, sun-cured, early-bloom	1-06-138		91.0												
024				100.0												
			N	1												
			SD													

Barley (Hordeum vulgare)

No.	Item	IFN		DM	2	3	4	5	6	7	8	9	10	11	12	13
025	grain	4-00-549		88.6	817		2.0	23.2	0.15	1,037.1	0.57	78.5	8.1	1.6	4.52	6.48
026				100.0	922		2.3	26.2	0.17	1,170.9	0.64	88.6	9.1	1.8	5.11	7.32
			N	237	3		3	10	12	19	13	64	68	68	60	59
			SD	2.08	789		1.97	14.3	0.039	76.4	0.058	15.8	2.84	0.343	0.697	2.23
027	grain, Pacific coast	4-07-939		88.6				26.2	0.15	976.3	0.50	46.7	7.1	1.5	4.19	2.85
028				100.0				29.6	0.17	1,101.6	0.56	52.7	8.0	1.7	4.72	3.26
			N	17				3	1	4	1	5	4	4	2	1
			SD	0.773				19.2		90.2		6.38	0.410	0.382	0.250	
029	hay, sun-cured	1-00-495		88.4	18,574	975	46.4									
030				100.0	21,000	1,102	52.5									
			N	10	1	1	1									
			SD	2.17												
031	straw	1-00-498		91.2	843	603	2.1									
032				100.0	924	661	2.3									
			N	29	1	1	1									
			SD	3.31												

Beet, sugar (Beta vulgaris altissima)

No.	Item	IFN		DM	2	3	4	5	6	7	8	9	10	11	12	13
033	pulp, dehydrated	4-00-669		91.0	88		0.2	580		820.9		16.8	1.4	0.7	0.39	
034				100.0	97		0.2	637		901.9		18.4	1.5	0.8	0.42	
			N	47	2		2	2		6		6	7	7	4	
			SD	1.37	0.323		0.000	4.34		14.4		1.69	0.356	0.232	0.121	

(continued)

APPENDIX TABLE 5-10   Vitamin Composition of Feeds Commonly Used in Horse Diets (*Continued*)

Entry no.	Feed name	International feed number [a]	Dry matter (%)	Caro-tene (mg/kg)	A equi-valent [b] (IU/kg)	D (IU/kg)	E (mg/kg)	Bio-tin (mg/kg)	Cho-line (mg/kg)	Fol-ate (mg/kg)	Niacin (mg/kg)	Panto-thenic acid (mg/kg)	Ribo-flavin (mg/kg)	Thia-min (mg/kg)	B$_6$ (mg/kg)	B$_{12}$ (µg/kg)
	Bermudagrass, coastal (*Cynodon dactylon*)															
035	fresh	2-00-719	30.3	100.0	39,993											
036			100.0	330.5	132,198											
		N	15	4	4											
		SD	6.91	56.6	22,642											
037	hay, sun-cured, 15–28 days' growth	1-09-207	88.4													
038			100.0													
		N	4													
		SD	0.326													
039	hay, sun-cured, 29–42 days growth	1-09-209	93.0													
040			100.0													
041	hay, sun-cured, 43–56 days' growth	1-09-210	93.0													
042			100.0													
		N	1													
		SD														
	Bluegrass, Kentucky (*Poa pratensis*)															
043	fresh, early vegetative	2-00-777	30.8	148.5	59,420		47.8									
044			100.0	481.9	192,770		155.0									
		N	4	1	1		1									
		SD	0.694													
045	fresh, milk stage	2-00-782	42.0													
046			100.0													
		N	1													
		SD														
047	hay, sun-cured, full-bloom	1-00-772	92.1													
048			100.0													
		N	2													
		SD														

	Brewer's grain												
049	dehydrated	5-02-141	92.0	26.7	0.63	1,652	0.20	44.0	8.2	1.5	0.6	0.7	0.004
050			100.0	29.0	0.68	1,795	0.22	47.8	8.91	1.6	0.7	0.8	0.004
	Brome, smooth (*Bromus inermis*)												
051	fresh, early vegetative	2-00-956	26.1			60,854				152.1			
052			100.0			233,158				582.9			
N			8			1				1			
SD			6.39										
053	fresh, mature	2-08-364	54.9										
054			100.0										
N			5										
SD			1.69										
055	hay, sun-cured, midbloom	1-05-633	87.6										
056			100.0										
N			2										
SD													
057	hay, sun-cured, mature	1-00-944	92.6										
058			100.0										
N			6										
SD			0.539										
	Canarygrass, reed (*Phalaris arundinacea*)												
059	fresh	2-01-113	22.8										
060			100.0										
N			4										
SD			4.89										
061	hay, sun-cured	1-01-104	89.3	16.9		6,762						8.5	3.57
062			100.0	18.9		7,576						9.5	4.00
N			10	7		7						1	1
SD			2.08	31.5		12,631						1	1
	Canola (*Brassica napus-Brassica campestris*)												
063	seeds, meal, solvent-extracted	5-06-146	90.8		0.82	6,082.8			2.09	183.1	12.4	3.0	4.72
064			100.0		0.90	6,700.0			2.03	201.6	13.6	3.3	5.20
N			13		1	1			1	2	2	2	1
SD			2.41							58.8	5.80	0.634	1

APPENDIX TABLE 5-10 Vitamin Composition of Feeds Commonly Used in Horse Diets (Continued)

Entry no.	Feed name	International feed number[a]	Dry matter (%)	Carotene (mg/kg)	A equivalent[b] (IU/kg)	D (IU/kg)	E (mg/kg)	Biotin (mg/kg)	Choline (mg/kg)	Folate (mg/kg)	Niacin (mg/kg)	Pantothenic acid (mg/kg)	Riboflavin (mg/kg)	Thiamin (mg/kg)	B6 (mg/kg)	B12 (µg/kg)
	Carrot (Daucus spp.)															
065	roots, fresh	4-01-145	11.5	77.9	31,160		6.9	0.01		0.14	6.7	3.5	0.6	0.67	1.39	
066			100.0	677.5	271,000		60.2	0.07		1.20	58.0	30.1	4.9	5.79	12.05	
	N		9	2	2		1	1		1	3	1	3	3	1	
	SD		1.21	166	66,468						12.3		1.01	1.24		
	Citrus (Citrus spp.)															
067	pomace without	4-01-237	91.1	0.2	85				790.0		22.2	14.0	2.1	1.47		
068	fines, dehydrated		100.0	0.2	93				867.0		24.4	15.4	2.3	1.61		
	N		275	2	2				7		6	6	7	3		
	SD		1.52	0.016	6.49				59.7		0.342	1.08	0.475	0.134		
	Clover, alsike (Trifolium hybridum)															
069	fresh, early vegetative	2-01-314	18.9	72.4	28,977											
070			100.0	384.0	153,600											
	N		3	1	1											
	SD		0.116													
071	hay, sun-cured	1-01-313	87.7	163.2	65,285									15.1	4.21	
072			100.0	186.0	74,400									17.2	4.80	
	N		9	1	1									1	1	
	SD		1.32													
	Clover, ladino (Trifolium repens)															
073	fresh, early vegetative	2-01-380	19.3	68.1	27,249											
074			100.0	352.5	141,006											
	N		4	1	1											
	SD		1.44													
075	hay, sun-cured	1-01-378	89.1	143.7	57,475						9.8	1.0	15.2	3.74		
076			100.0	161.2	64,480						11.0	1.1	17.0	4.20		
	N		5	1	1						1	1	1	1		
	SD		2.71													

Clover, red (Trifolium pratense)

Entry	Feed	Int'l Feed No.												
077	fresh, early-bloom	2-01-428	19.6	48.5				19,402						
078			100.0	247.5				98,994						
	N		5	1				1						
	SD		0.464											
079	fresh, full-bloom	2-01-429	26.2	54.4				21,744						
080			100.0	207.5				82,994						
	N		4	1				1						
	SD		3.00											
081	fresh, regrowth, early vegetative	2-28-255	24.0											
082			100.0											
	N		8											
	SD		2.58											
083	hay, sun-cured	1-01-415	88.4	24.3	9,727		0.09	1,700	37.7	9.9	15.7			1.97
084			100.0	27.5	11,005		0.11	1,900	42.6	11.2	17.8			2.22
	N		21	2	2		2	1	2	2	2			2
	SD		1.91	13.1	5,252		0.007		0.571	0.027	0.056			0.033

Corn, dent yellow (Zea mays indentata)

Entry	Feed	Int'l Feed No.												
085	aerial part with ears, sun-cured (fodder)	1-28-231	81.0											
086			100.0											
	N		1											
	SD													
087	aerial part without ears, without husks, sun-cured (stover, straw)	1-28-233	87.7	3.5	1,403									
088			100.0	4.0	1,600									
	N		4	1	1									
	SD		2.43											
089	cobs, ground	1-28-234	90.1	0.9	361				7.2					
090			100.0	1.0	400				8.0					
	N		3	1	1				1					
	SD		0.246											
091	distiller's grains, dehydrated	5-28-235	92.0	2.8	1,104	0.86	0.48	1,161.0	36.8	11.5	5.2		1.66	7.17
092			100.0	3.0	1,200	0.94	0.52	1,262.0	40.0	12.5	5.6		1.80	7.79
	N		3	1	1	1	1	1	1	1	1		1	2
	SD		2.00											4.36
093	ears, ground (corn and cob meal)	4-28-238	86.2	3.4	1,379	0.24	0.03	355.1	17.2	17.2	4.1	0.9	2.84	5.95
094			100.0	4.0	1,600	0.28	0.04	412.0	20.0	20.0	4.8	1.0	3.30	6.90
	N		2	1	1	1	1	1	1	1	1	1	1	1
	SD		1.13											
095	grain	4-02-935	88.0	5.4	2,162	0.31	0.07	496.0	20.9	22.5	5.1	1.1	3.73	6.16
096			100.0	6.1	2,458	0.35	0.08	563.8	23.8	25.6	5.8	1.2	4.24	7.01
	N		545	4	4	4	3	8	2	6	5	6	3	4
	SD		2.44	2.39	958	0.056	0.012	56.5	1.69	2.43	0.993	0.200	0.341	2.27

(continued)

APPENDIX TABLE 5-10   Vitamin Composition of Feeds Commonly Used in Horse Diets (*Continued*)

Entry no.	Feed name	International feed number[a]	Dry matter (%)	Carotene (mg/kg)	A equivalent[b] (IU/kg)	D (IU/kg)	E (mg/kg)	Biotin (mg/kg)	Choline (mg/kg)	Folate (mg/kg)	Niacin (mg/kg)	Pantothenic acid (mg/kg)	Riboflavin (mg/kg)	Thiamin (mg/kg)	B6 (mg/kg)	B12 (µg/kg)
						Corn, dent yellow (*Zea mays indentata*)										
097	silage	3-02-912	30.4	13.2	5,285	133					14.2					
098			100.0	43.5	17,406	439					46.6					
		N	8	2	2	1					2					
		SD	5.05	12.0	4,816						5.13					
						Cotton (*Gossypium spp.*)										
099	hulls	1-01-599	90.4										3.7			
100			100.0	100.0									4.1			
		N	22										3			
		SD	1.34										0.054			
101	seeds, oil residue,	5-01-621	91.0				14.6	0.56	2,783.5	2.55	40.9	13.7	4.7	7.32	5.41	
102	solvent-extracted, ground, 41% protein		100.0				16.1	0.61	3,058.0	2.81	44.9	15.1	5.2	8.04	5.95	
		N	65				4	3	14	4	14	14	14	9	4	
		SD	1.36				3.13	0.000	107	0.333	3.23	3.26	0.337	0.773	0.771	
						Fats and oils										
103	fat, animal hydrolyzed	4-00-376	99.2													
			100.0													
		N	5													
		SD	0.277													
105	oil, vegetable	4-05-077	99.8				57.0									
106			100.0				57.0									
		N	5				1									
		SD	0.289													
						Fescue, Kentucky 31 (*Festuca arundinacea*)										
107	fresh	2-01-902	31.3	68.2	27,279											
108			100.0	218.0	87,208											
		N	5	1	1											
		SD	3.76													
109	hay, sun-cured, full-bloom	1-09-188	91.9													
110			100.0													
		N	3													

Table (rotated 90°). Column headers appear on the preceding page; data columns are shown here numbered (1)–(11). For each feed the four stacked values are: as‑fed mean, 100% dry‑matter mean, N (number of samples), and SD.

Entry	Feed (IFN)	Stat	(1)	(2)	(3)	(4)	(5)	(6)	(7)	(8)	(9)	(10)	(11)
111	hay, sun-cured, mature (1-09-189)	mean	90.0										
112		100% DM	100.0										
		N	1										
		SD	3.01										

Fish, anchovy (*Engraulis ringen*)

Entry	Feed (IFN)	Stat	(1)	(2)	(3)	(4)	(5)	(6)	(7)	(8)	(9)	(10)	(11)
113	meal, mechanically extracted (5-01-985)	mean	92.0	5.0	0.20	4,408.0	0.16	100.0	15.0	7.3	0.52	4.71	352.0
114		100% DM	100.0	5.4	0.21	4,791.0	0.17	108.7	16.3	8.0	0.57	5.12	382.0
		N	67	3	5	10	5	11	10	10	4	4	8
		SD	.19	1.96	0.069	720	0.055	29.2	4.19	2.31	0.304	1.48	178

Fish, menhaden (*Brevoortia tyrannus*)

Entry	Feed (IFN)	Stat	(1)	(2)	(3)	(4)	(5)	(6)	(7)	(8)	(9)	(10)	(11)
115	meal, mechanically extracted (5-02-009)	mean	91.7	5.8	0.18	3,114.5	0.15	54.6	8.6	4.8	0.57	3.81	122.1
116		100% DM	100.0	6.2	0.20	3,398.0	0.17	59.6	9.4	5.3	0.62	4.15	133.2
		N	79	3	3	5	2	7	6	8	5	3	6
		SD	1.18	2.06	0.076	256	0.070	1.85	0.454	0.230	0.223	2.06	46.4

Flax, common (*Linum usitatissimum*)

Entry	Feed (IFN)	Stat	(1)	(2)	(3)	(4)	(5)	(6)	(7)	(8)	(9)	(10)	(11)
117	seeds (5-02-052)	mean	93.6										
118		100% DM	100.0										
		N	4										
		SD	0.643										
119	seeds, meal, solvent-extracted (5-02-048)	mean	90.2	7.5		1,393.0	1.26	33.0	14.7	2.9	7.54	8.60	
120		100% DM	100.0	8.3		1,544.1	1.40	36.5	16.3	3.2	8.36	9.53	
		N	25	3		7	1	9	7	9	6	1	
		SD	1.12	1.57		263		7.56	1.17	0.881	2.98		

Lespedeza, common (*Lespedeza striata*)

Entry	Feed (IFN)	Stat	(1)	(2)	(3)	(4)	(5)	(6)	(7)	(8)	(9)	(10)	(11)
121	fresh, late vegetative (2-07-093)	mean	25.0										
122		100% DM	100.0										
		N	2										
		SD											
123	hay, sun-cured, midbloom (1-02-554)	mean	90.8										
124		100% DM	100.0										
		N	3										
		SD	2.93										

(continued)

APPENDIX TABLE 5-10 Vitamin Composition of Feeds Commonly Used in Horse Diets (*Continued*)

Entry no.	Feed name	International feed number[a]	Dry matter (%)	Carotene (mg/kg)	A equivalent[b] (IU/kg)	D (IU/kg)	E (mg/kg)	Biotin (mg/kg)	Choline (mg/kg)	Folate (mg/kg)	Niacin (mg/kg)	Pantothenic acid (mg/kg)	Riboflavin (mg/kg)	Thiamin (mg/kg)	B6 (mg/kg)	B12 (µg/kg)
Lespedeza, Kobe (*Lespedeza striata*)																
125	hay, sun-cured, midbloom	1-02-574	93.9													
126			100.0													
		N	1													
		SD														
Meadow plants, intermountain																
127	hay, sun-cured	1-03-181	95.1	31.9	12,744											
128			100.0	33.5	13,393											
		N	72	2												
		SD	1.37	13.1	5,251											
Milk																
129	fresh (horse)	5-02-401	10.6		42.4					0.00	0.5	2.8	0.2	0.28	0.28	1.3
130			100.0		401					0.01	4.4	26.7	1.8	2.65	2.65	12.1
		N	42		1					1	1	1	1	1	1	1
		SD	0.656													
131	skimmed, dehydrated	5-01-175	94.1			420	9.1	0.33	1,393.2	0.62	11.5	36.4	19.1	3.72	4.09	50.9
132	(cattle)		100.0			446	9.6	0.35	1,479.8	0.66	12.2	38.6	20.3	3.95	4.35	54.1
		N	57			1	3	6	11	6	11	20	22	6	5	5
		SD	1.35				0.743	0.009	47.2	0.023	0.598	4.77	3.37	0.484	0.437	10.0
Millet, pearl (*Pennisetum glaucum*)																
133	fresh	2-03-115	20.7	37.8	15,128											
134			100.0	182.5	72,994											
		N	4	1	1											
		SD	0.190													
135	hay, sun-cured	1-03-112	87.4													
136			100.0													
		N	3													
		SD	0.407													

(continued)

Molasses and syrup

137 / 138 — beet, sugar, molasses, more than 48% invert sugar, more than 79.5 degrees brix — 4-00-668

Stat								
as-fed	77.9	4.0	827.5		41.0	4.5	2.3	
100% DM	100.0	5.1	1,062.4		52.7	5.8	2.9	
N	21		2		6	6	6	
SD	1.71	1	116		5.55	0.437	0.249	

139 / 140 — citrus, syrup (citrus molasses) — 4-01-241

Stat				
as-fed	66.9	26.9	12.7	6.2
100% DM	100.0	40.3	19.0	9.3
N	12	4	4	4
SD	3.42	1.58	0.746	0.349

141 / 142 — sugarcane, molasses, dehydrated — 4-04-695

Stat		
as-fed	94.4	5.2
100% DM	100.0	5.5
N	7	2
SD	2.73	0.158

143 / 144 — sugarcane, molasses, more than 46% invert sugar, more than 79.5 degrees brix (blackstrap) — 4-04-696

Stat										
as-fed	74.3	5.4	0.69	763.4	0.11	36.4	37.4	2.8	0.86	4.21
100% DM	100.0	7.3	0.92	1,027.1	0.15	49.0	50.3	3.8	1.16	5.67
N	84	2	3	15		19	18	20	7	2
SD	3.27	0.848	0.036	149	1	6.81	2.42	0.664	0.081	4.24

Oats (Avena sativa)

145 / 146 — grain — 4-03-309

Stat											
as-fed	89.2	0.1	15.0	44	967.6	0.27	14.0	9.7	1.4	6.13	2.61
100% DM	100.0	0.1	16.8	49	1,084.4	0.30	15.7	10.9	1.6	6.87	2.93
N	97		6		4	10	47	49	34	29	
SD	1.80	1	8.04	1	72.6	0.050	3.33	0.338	0.886	1.04	

147 / 148 — grain, grade 1, heavy, 51.5 kg/hl — 4-18-520

Stat								
as-fed	89.0	13.6	3.69	6.3	1.6	13.3		
100% DM	100.0	15.3		7.1	1.8			
N	48	32		32	32	2		
SD		2.60		2.19	0.196	0.164		

149 / 150 — grain, Pacific coast — 4-07-999

Stat					
as-fed	90.9	20.2	916.9	14.4	11.7
100% DM	100.0	22.2	1,008.7	15.8	12.8
N	13	1	2	2	2
SD	0.426		12.3	0.100	2.42

151 / 152 — groats — 4-03-331

Stat							
as-fed	89.6	14.8	1,131.6	0.20	9.6	13.8	6.49
100% DM	100.0	16.5	1,263.7	0.22	10.7	15.4	7.25
N	41	1	1	1	9	11	6
SD	1.55		58.1		3.55	2.21	1.23

153 / 154 — groats by-product, less than 30% fiber — 1-08-316

Stat							
as-fed	91.4	0.2	87	410.6	9.9	3.4	2.8	1.23	1.00
100% DM	100.0	0.2	95	449.1	10.8	3.7	3.1	1.35	21.12
N	29						7		5
SD	1.33	1	1	70.7	0.877	0.233	1.42	0.538	0.175

155 — hay, sun-cured — 1-03-280

Stat		
as-fed	90.7	27.0
100% DM		
N		1,400
SD		10,792

APPENDIX TABLE 5-10 Vitamin Composition of Feeds Commonly Used in Horse Diets (*Continued*)

Entry no.	Feed name	International feed number[a]	Dry matter (%)	Carotene (mg/kg)	A equivalent[b] (IU/kg)	D (IU/kg)	E (mg/kg)	Biotin (mg/kg)	Choline (mg/kg)	Folate (mg/kg)	Niacin (mg/kg)	Pantothenic acid (mg/kg)	Riboflavin (mg/kg)	Thiamin (mg/kg)	B6 (mg/kg)	B12 (µg/kg)
							Oats (*Avena sativa*)									
156			100.0	29.7	11,898	1,543										
		N	27	2	2	1										
		SD	2.55	32.0	12,826											
157	hulls	1-03-281	92.4						260.0	0.96	9.2	3.1	1.5	0.61	2.19	
158			100.0						281.3	1.04	10.0	3.4	1.7	0.66	2.37	
		N	26						4	1	3	2	4	1	1	
		SD	1.14						129		1.58	0.257	0.563			
159	straw	1-03-283	92.2	3.5	1,401	610										
160			100.0	3.8	1,520	661										
		N	71	11	11	1										
		SD	2.10	2.03	815											
							Orchardgrass (*Dactylis glomerata*)									
161	fresh, early-bloom	2-03-442	23.5													
162			100.0													
		N	8													
		SD	3.87													
163	fresh, midbloom	2-03-443	27.4													
164			100.0													
		N	3													
		SD	5.36													
165	hay, sun-cured, early-bloom	1-03-425	89.1	33.4	13,336											
166			100.0	37.5	15,000											
		N	7	1	1											
		SD	3.30													
167	hay, sun-cured, late bloom	1-03-428	90.6	18.1	7,247											
168			100.0	20.0	8,000											
		N	7	1	1											
		SD	1.51													
							Pangolagrass (*Digitaria decumbens*)									
169	fresh	2-03-493	20.2													
170			100.0													
		N	9													
		SD	2.37													

764

		Ref. No.												
171 172	hay, sun-cured, 15–28 days' growth	1-10-638 N SD	91.0 100.0 1											
173 174	hay, sun-cured, 29–42 days' growth	1-26-214 N SD	91.0 100.0 1											
175 176	hay, sun-cured, 43–56 days' growth	1-29-573 N SD	91.0 100.0 1											

Pea (Pisum spp.)

		Ref. No.												
177 178	seeds	5-03-600 N SD	89.1 100.0 0.822	0.7 0.8 1	285 320 1	3.0 3.3 1	0.18 0.20 1	545.8 612.4 1	0.22 0.25 1	30.5 34.3 2 0.401	27.7 31.1 1	1.8 2.0 2 1.80	4.61 5.17 2 4.53	1.96 2.20 1

Peanut (Arachis hypogaea)

		Ref. No.												
179 180	hay, sun-cured	1-03-619 N SD	90.7 100.0 18 1.04	31.5 34.8 2 21.8	12,618 13,911 2 8,759	3,260.0 3,600.0 1				8.8 9.7 2 0.037				
181 182	hulls (pods)	1-08-028 N SD	90.7 100.0 17 1.74	0.8 0.9 1	320 353 1									
183 184	seeds without coats, meal, solvent-extracted	5-03-650 N SD	92.4 100.0 16 1.82			2.9 3.2 1	0.33 0.36 1	1,893.8 2,048.9 1	0.65 0.70 1	177.5 192.0 1	36.8 39.8 1	9.1 9.8 1	5.70 6.20 1	5.95 6.43 2 2.15

Prairie plants, Midwest

		Ref. No.												
185 186	hay, sun-cured	1-03-191 N SD	91.0 100.0 8 1.42		865 950 1									

Redtop (Agrostis alba)

		Ref. No.												
187 188	hay, sun-cured, midbloom	1-03-886 N SD	92.8 100.0 1	4.6 5.0 1	1,856 2,000 1									

(continued)

APPENDIX TABLE 5-10   Vitamin Composition of Feeds Commonly Used in Horse Diets (*Continued*)

Entry no.	Feed name	International feed number[a]	Dry matter (%)	Carotene (mg/kg)	A equivalent[b] (IU/kg)	D (IU/kg)	E (mg/kg)	Biotin (mg/kg)	Choline (mg/kg)	Folate (mg/kg)	Niacin (mg/kg)	Pantothenic acid (mg/kg)	Riboflavin (mg/kg)	Thiamin (mg/kg)	B6 (mg/kg)	B12 (µg/kg)
	Rice (*Oryza sativa*)															
189	bran with germs	4-03-928	90.5				85.3	0.42	1,243.8	1.60	305.9	25.0	2.6	21.94	16.21	
190			100.0				94.2	0.47	1,373.7	1.77	337.9	27.6	2.8	24.23	17.90	
N			37				3	6	8	2	11	10	12	6	2	
SD			0.744				47.6	0.021	78.8	0.925	25.5	7.73	0.142	1.30	4.66	
191	grain, ground	4-03-938	89.0				14.0	0.80	926.5	0.25	40.0	7.1	0.7	2.90	4.40	
192			100.0				15.7	0.90	1,041.5	0.28	45.0	8.0	0.8	3.20	5.00	
N			9				1	1	3	1	3	2	2	1	1	
SD			0.755						123		9.40	6.02	0.309			
193	hulls	1-08-075	91.9				7.5	0.62	1,010.0	0.62	28.1	7.9	0.5	2.21	0.07	
194			100.0				8.1	0.67	1,100.0	0.67	30.6	8.6	0.6	2.41	0.08	
N			21				1		1		3	1	2	2	1	
SD			1.45								14.3		0.129	0.023		
195	mill run	1-03-941	91.6				5.3				36.0		0.6	2.17		
196			100.0				5.8				39.3		0.6	2.37		
N			22				2				1		1	1		
SD			0.907				3.08									
	Rye (*Secale cereale*)															
197	grain	4-04-047	87.5	0.1	35		14.5	0.05	419.1	0.58	14.1	7.2	1.8	4.51	2.97	
198			100.0	0.1	40		16.6	0.06	479.0	0.66	16.1	8.3	2.0	5.16	3.40	
N			93	1	1		4	4	2	5	7	8	9	7	1	
SD			1.49				1.16	0.010	19.1	0.100	1.52	1.42	0.406	1.13		
	Ryegrass, Italian (*Lolium multiflorum*)															
199	fresh	2-04-073	22.6													
200			100.0													
N			5													
SD			2.35													
201	hay, sun-cured, late vegetative	1-04-065	85.6	248.2	99,287											
202			100.0	290.2	116,000											
N			2	1	1											
SD			4.81													

(continued)

Sorghum (*Sorghum bicolor*)

No.	Feed	IFN / N / SD												
203	grain	4-04-383	90.1	1.2	468	10.0	0.26	0.22	692.5	46.6	10.2	1.2	4.52	5.40
204			100.0	1.3	520	12.0	0.29	0.24	768.9	51.8	11.3	1.4	5.02	5.00
		N	220		1	1	1	1	2	4	2	5	4	1
		SD	2.33						9.69	14.2	1.77	0.213	0.940	
205	hay, sun-cured	1-04-407	90.5	35.3	14,102									
206			100.0	38.9	15,579									
		N	6	3	3									
		SD	0.313	8.53	3,414									

Sorghum, Johnsongrass (*Sorghum halepense*)

Soybean (*Glycine max*)

No.	Feed	IFN / N / SD												
207	seed coats	1-04-560	90.3	6.6					586.5	24.8	13.4	3.6	1.59	1.70
208			100.0	7.3					649.4	27.4	14.8	4.0	1.76	1.88
		N	28	1					3	1	1	1	1	1
		SD	3.43						148					
209	seeds, meal, solvent-extracted, 44% protein	5-20-637	89.1	3.0			0.69	0.36	2,704.6	26.1	13.8	3.0	6.59	5.90
210			100.0	3.4			0.77	0.41	3,036.0	29.3	15.5	3.4	7.40	6.62
		N	119	2			6	2	12	12	12	12	3	3
		SD	1.22	0.055			0.161	0.003	75.4	1.54	0.796	0.412	0.045	1.08
211	seeds without hulls, meal, solvent-extracted	5-04-612	89.9	3.3			0.74		2,746.5	21.5	14.8	2.9	3.10	4.92
212			100.0	3.7			0.82		3,053.9	23.9	16.4	3.3	3.45	5.47
		N	78	2			1		2	1	1	8	5	2
		SD	1.72	0.014					26.9	0.387	4.09	0.517	2.20	0.255

Sunflower, common (*Helianthus annuus*)

No.	Feed	IFN / N / SD												
213	seeds without hulls, meal, solvent-extracted	5-04-739	92.5	11.1					3,627.7	242.1	40.6	3.5	3.10	13.67
214			100.0	12.0					3,923.3	261.9	43.9	3.8	3.30	14.78
		N	21	2					5	5	3	6	1	2
		SD	1.73	0.298					1,076	66.8	1.14	1.52		3.42

Timothy (*Phleum pratense*)

No.	Feed	IFN												
215	fresh, late vegetative	2-04-903	26.7	62.6	25,028									

APPENDIX TABLE 5-10 Vitamin Composition of Feeds Commonly Used in Horse Diets (*Continued*)

Entry no.	Feed name	International feed number[a]	Dry matter (%)	Carotene (mg/kg)	A equivalent[b] (IU/kg)	D (IU/kg)	E (mg/kg)	Biotin (mg/kg)	Choline (mg/kg)	Folate (mg/kg)	Niacin (mg/kg)	Pantothenic acid (mg/kg)	Riboflavin (mg/kg)	Thiamin (mg/kg)	B6 (mg/kg)	B12 (μg/kg)
							Timothy (*Phleum pratense*)									
216			100.0	234.0	93,600											
	N		5	1	1											
	SD		1.86													
217	fresh, midbloom	2-04-905	29.2	56.7	22,672											
218			100.0	194.0	77,600											
	N		6	1	1											
	SD		1.76													
219	hay, sun-cured, early-bloom	1-04-882	89.1	46.8	18,719		11.6									
220			100.0	52.5	21,000		13.0									
	N		13	1	1		1									
	SD		1.72													
221	hay, sun-cured, midbloom	1-04-883	88.9	47.4	18,964	1,763										
222			100.0	53.3	21,340	1,984										
	N		10	1	1	1										
	SD		1.93													
223	hay sun-cured, full-bloom	1-04-884	89.4	42.5	17,000											
224			100.0	47.5	19,000											
	N		8	1	1											
	SD		2.43													
225	hay, sun-cured, late-bloom	1-04-885	88.3	39.7	15,897											
226			100.0	45.0	18,000											
	N		6	1	1											
	SD		0.609													
							Trefoil, birdsfoot (*Lotus corniculatus*)									
227	fresh	2-20-786	19.3													
228			100.0													
	N		9													
	SD		4.28													
229	hay, sun-cured	1-05-044	90.6	130.6	52,250	1,398							14.6	6.16		
230			100.0	144.2	57,680	1,543							16.1	6.80		
	N		9	1	1	1							1	1		
	SD		1.46													

Wheat (Triticum aestivum)

No.	Item	IFN	(1)	(2)	(3)	(4)	(5)	(6)	(7)	(8)	(9)	(10)	(11)	(12)	(13)
231	bran	4-05-190	89.0	2.6	1,048		14.3	1,201.1	0.38	1.77	196.7	27.9	3.6	8.36	10.33
232			100.0	2.9	1,177		16.0	1,349.2	0.42	1.98	221.0	31.4	4.0	9.39	11.61
	N		86	3	3		7	20	4	9	15	20	20	7	6
	SD		1.23	0.023	9.37		3.97	423	0.202	0.667	44.8	4.11	1.93	2.13	3.43
233	flour by-product,	4-05-205	88.9	3.1	1,227		23.9	1,227.8	0.24	1.24	94.9	17.8	2.0	14.17	9.15
234	less than 9.5%		100.0	3.5	1,380		26.9	1,381.1	0.27	1.39	106.8	20.0	2.3	15.94	10.29
	fiber (middlings) N		65	3	3		5	13	2	7	10	13	11	8	5
	SD		1.41	0.017	7.16		4.89	360	0.211	0.893	4.15	2.14	0.340	1.97	2.73
235	fresh, early vegetative	2-05-176	22.2	115.4	46,180						12.6	4.7	6.1		
236			100.0	520.1	208,026						56.9	21.2	27.6		
	N		2	1	1						1	1	1		
	SD		0.988												
237	grain, hard, red	4-05-268	88.9				11.1	1,007.2	0.11	0.38	53.0	10.2	1.3	4.52	3.02
238	winter		100.0				12.5	1,133.2	0.12	0.43	59.7	11.4	1.5	5.09	3.40
	N		26				4	6	1	5	7	6	7	5	5
	SD		1.33				2.56	197		0.044	6.09	2.44	0.298	1.33	1.55
239	grain, soft, red	4-05-294	88.4				15.6	891.7		0.41	53.4	10.1	1.5	4.71	3.21
240	winter		100.00				17.7	1,008.9		0.46	60.4	11.4	1.7	5.33	3.63
	N		15				1	2		2	2	2	1	2	2
	SD		1.68					186		0.025	5.88	1.97		0.800	2.35
241	hay, sun-cured	1-05-172	88.7	75.8	30,304	1,370							15.1		
242			100.0	85.4	34,147	1,543							17.0		
	N		12	2	2	1									
	SD		3.09	37.0	14,803										
243	mill run, less than	4-05-206	89.9	2.0			31.9	1,004.7	0.31	1.08	115.6	13.7	2.1	15.25	11.09
244	9.5% fiber		100.0	2.2			35.5	1,117.9	0.34	1.20	128.7	15.2	2.4	16.97	12.33
	N		31				1	9	1	2	9	9	8	4	2
	SD		0.740					48.5		0.034	10.4	1.08	0.648	0.123	0.122
245	straw	1-05-175	91.3	2.0	805	604							2.2		
246			100.0	2.2	882	661							2.4		
	N		37		1	1									
	SD		3.12												

Wheat, soft, white winter (Triticum aestivum)

No.	Item	IFN	(1)	(2)	(3)	(4)	(5)	(6)	(7)	(8)	(9)	(10)	(11)	(12)	(13)
247	grain	4-05-337	90.2				18.0	978.0	0.11	0.40	53.0	11.1	1.2	4.70	4.77
248			100.0				20.0	1,097.0	0.12	0.40	59.0	12.3	1.3	5.30	5.29
	N		13				1	1	1	1	1	1	1	1	1
	SD		1.05												

(continued)

APPENDIX TABLE 5-10 Vitamin Composition of Feeds Commonly Used in Horse Diets (*Continued*)

Entry no.	Feed name	International feed number[a]	Dry matter (%)	Caro-tene (mg/kg)	A equi-valent[b] (IU/kg)	D (IU/kg)	E (mg/kg)	Bio-tin (mg/kg)	Cho-line (mg/kg)	Fol-ate (mg/kg)	Niacin (mg/kg)	Panto-thenic acid (mg/kg)	Ribo-flavin (mg/kg)	Thia-min (mg/kg)	B6 (mg/kg)	B12 (µg/kg)
								Wheatgrass, crested (*Agropyron desertorum*)								
249	fresh, early vegetative	2-05-420	28.5	123.4	49,377											
250			100.0	433.6	173,458											
	N		6	1	1											
	SD		2.68													
								Whey (*Bos taurus*)								
251	dehydrated (cattle)	4-01-182	93.2		48.8		0.2	0.35	1,790.7	0.85	10.6	46.2	27.4	4.00	3.22	18.9
252			100.0		52.4		0.2	0.38	1,920.8	0.91	11.4	49.6	29.4	4.29	3.45	20.3
	N		68		1		1	7	11	8	12	26	18	8	6	7
	SD		1.58					0.055	285	0.117	1.13	6.86	3.09	0.474	0.978	4.38
253	low lactose, dehydrated (dried whey product) (cattle)	4-01-186	93.7					0.51	4,109.2	0.90	17.8	74.7	24.2	5.06	4.49	36.0
254			100.0					0.54	4,387.3	0.96	19.0	79.8	25.8	5.40	4.79	38.4
	N		28					9	11	9	11	11	12	7	6	4
	SD		1.75					0.164	676	0.499	0.979	4.90	12.3	0.337	1.61	3.91
								Yeast, brewer's (*Saccharomyces cerevisiae*)								
255	dehydrated	7-05-527	93.1				2.1	1.04	3,847.0	9.69	443.3	81.5	33.6	85.21	36.66	1.1
256			100.0				2.3	1.12	4,133.9	10.41	476.4	87.6	36.1	91.56	39.40	1.1
	N		65				2	13	21	18	21	31	31	14	16	3
	SD		1.09				0.145	0.123	378	2.49	46.3	25.6	6.05	23.2	8.61	0.14

NOTE: A blank space indicates that data are not available for that nutrient.

The following variables appear below the feed number: N = number of observations; SD = standard deviation.

[a] The vitamin A equivalent was calculated as carotene × 400 except values for fresh horse milk (IFN, 5-02-401) and dehydrated whey (IFN, 4-01-182), which represent actual amounts of vitamin A.

SOURCE: *Nutrient Requirements of Horses*, 5th ed., National Research Council (1989).

APPENDIX TABLE 5-11 Weight-Unit Conversion Factors

Units given	Units wanted	For conversion, multiply by	Units given	Units wanted	For conversion, multiply by
lb	gm	453.6	μg/kg	μg/lb	0.4536
lb	kg	0.4536	Mcal	kcal	1000.
oz	gm	28.35	kcal/kg	kcal/lb	0.4536
kg	lb	2.2046	kcal/lb	kcal/kg	2.2046
kg	mg	1,000,000.	ppm	μg/gm	1.
kg	gm	1000.	ppm	mg/kg	1.
gm	mg	1000.	ppm	mg/lb	0.4536
gm	μg	1,000,000.	mg/kg	%	0.0001
mg	μg	1000.	ppm	%	0.0001
mg/g	mg/lb	453.6	mg/gm	%	0.1
mg/kg	mg/lb	0.4536	gm/kg	%	0.1

SOURCE: National Research Council (1978).

APPENDIX TABLE 5-12 Weight Equivalents

1 lb = 453.6 gm = 0.4536 kg = 16 oz
1 oz = 28.35 gm
1 kg = 1000 gm = 2.2046 lb
1 gm = 1000 mg
1 mg = 1000 μg = 0.001 gm
1 μg = 0.001 mg = 0.000001 gm
1 μg per mg or 1 mg per kg is the same as ppm

SOURCE: National Research Council (1978).

APPENDIX 12-1

Racing Tables

Past performance information for racehorses gives a detailed analysis of performance in previous races. The information is used by bettors to handicap the horses and determine which one should win a race. It is used by trainers, owners, and breeders to compare horses' racing abilities.

APPENDIX TABLE 12-1 How to Read Past Performances of Racehorses

Labels (pointing to the sample line):

- Day →
- Month →
- Year →
- Number of Race →
- Track Raced On →
- Distance →
- Fractional Times of Horse in Lead at Each of These Points
- Time of Winner →
- Track Condition →
- Closing Odds →
- Denotes Favorite →
- Weight Carried →
- Apprentice Allowance →
- First Call →
- Second Call →
- In Stretch →
- At Finish →
- Winning Margin →
- Jockey →
- Post Position →
- Denotes Claim →
- Type of Race or Claiming Price →
- Speed Rating →
- ‹ Race Exclusively for Fillies or Fillies & Mares
- First Two Horses in Order of Finish (With Weight Carried by First Horse)
- Number of Starters →

27 Jun 74² AP 6f :22⁴ :46 1:11³ ft 9-5 ▲ 117⁵ 5³ 4² 2ʰ 1¹½ Jones J⁵ c5000 87 ⊕ Donnie 117 Lovely Day 8

EVERYTHING YOU WANT TO KNOW IS IN THE P.P.'s!

27Jun 74² AP 6f :22⁴ :46 1:11³ ft 9-5 ▲ 117⁵ 5³ 4² 2ʰ 1¹½ Jones J⁵ c5000 87 ⊕ Donnie 117 Lovely Day 8

DATE RACE WAS RUN—The day, month, and year. This race was run June 27, 1974.

27Jun 74² AP 6f :22⁴ :46 1:11³ ft 9-5 ▲ 117⁵ 5³ 4² 2ʰ 1¹½ Jones J⁵ c5000 87 ⊕ Donnie 117 Lovely Day 8

NUMBER OF RACE AND TRACK RACED ON—This was the second race at Arlington Park (AP). See the past performances section of Daily Racing Form for a complete list of track abbreviations.

27Jun 74² AP 6f :22⁴ :46 1:11³ ft 9-5 ▲ 117⁵ 5³ 4² 2ʰ 1¹½ Jones J⁵ c5000 87 ⊕ Donnie 117 Lovely Day 8

DISTANCE OF RACE—The race was at six furlongs, or ¾ of a mile (there are 8 furlongs to a mile). An "a" before the distance (a6f) denotes an "about" or inexact distance (about six furlongs). A circled ⊕ before the distance denotes the race was run on the main turf course; a squared ⊡ a race run on the track's inner turf course.

27Jun 74² AP 6f :22⁴ :46 1:11³ ft 9-5 ▲ 117⁵ 5³ 4² 2ʰ 1¹½ Jones J⁵ c5000 87 ⊕ Donnie 117 Lovely Day 8

FRACTIONAL TIMES—The first fraction (:22 4/5) is the time of the horse in front at the ¼; the second fraction (:46) is the time of the horse in front at the ½. For a listing of the fractions at other distances, see Fractional Times explanation below.

27Jun 74² AP 6f :22⁴ :46 $\underline{1:11^3}$ ft 9-5 ▲ 117⁵ 5³ 4² 2ʰ 1¹¹⁄₂ JonesJ⁵ c5000 87 Ⓔ Donnie 117 Lovely Day 8

FINAL TIME OF FIRST HORSE TO FINISH—This is the winner's final time (the six furlongs were run in 1:11 3/5). In all cases, this is the time of the first horse to finish (when the winner is disqualified, this is HIS time, not the time of the horse awarded first money).

27Jun 74² AP 6f :22⁴ :46 1:11³ $\underline{ft}$ 9-5 ▲ 117⁵ 5³ 4² 2ʰ 1¹¹⁄₂ JonesJ⁵ c5000 87 Ⓔ Donnie 117 Lovely Day 8

TRACK CONDITION—The track was fast (ft).

27Jun 74² AP 6f :22⁴ :46 1:11³ ft $\underline{9\text{-}5}$ ▲ 117⁵ 5³ 4² 2ʰ 1¹¹⁄₂ JonesJ⁵ c5000 87 Ⓔ Donnie 117 Lovely Day 8

APPROXIMATE CLOSING ODDS—The horse was approximately 9-5 in the wagering. A triangle ▲ following the odds indicates the horse was approximately 9-5 in the wagering; an "e" that he was part of an entry (two or more horses coupled in the wagering); an "f" that he was in the mutuel field.

27Jun 74² AP 6f :22⁴ :46 1:11³ ft 9-5 ▲ $\underline{117}^5$ 5³ 4² 2ʰ 1¹¹⁄₂ JonesJ⁵ c5000 87 Ⓔ Donnie 117 Lovely Day 8

WEIGHT CARRIED IN THIS RACE—The horse carried 117 pounds. The small figure following the weight indicates the amount of the apprentice allowance claimed. When an apprentice allowance is claimed, the exact amount of the claim is listed.

27Jun 74² AP 6f :22⁴ :46 1:11³ ft 9-5 ▲ 117⁵ $\underline{5}^3$ 4² 2ʰ 1¹¹⁄₂ JonesJ⁵ c5000 87 Ⓔ Donnie 117 Lovely Day 8

FIRST CALL—The horse was running fifth, three lengths behind the leader, at this stage of the race (at the ¼ mile in this instance). The larger figure indicates the horse's running position; the small one, his total margin behind the first horse. If he was in front at this point (1²), the superior figure would indicate the margin by which he was leading the second horse.

27Jun 74² AP 6f :22⁴ :46 1:11³ ft 9-5 ▲ 117⁵ 5³ $\underline{4}^2$ 2ʰ 1¹¹⁄₂ JonesJ⁵ c5000 87 Ⓔ Donnie 117 Lovely Day 8

SECOND CALL—The horse was fourth at this stage of the race (at the ½ mile in this case) a total of two lengths behind the leader.

27Jun 74² AP 6f :22⁴ :46 1:11³ ft 9-5 ▲ 117⁵ 5³ 4² $\underline{2}^h$ 1¹¹⁄₂ JonesJ⁵ c5000 87 Ⓔ Donnie 117 Lovely Day 8

STRETCH CALL—The horse was second at this stage of the race, a head behind the leader.

(continued)

775

Appendix Table 12-1 (*Continued*)

27Jun 74² AP 6f :22⁴ :46 1:11³ ft 9-5 ▲ 117⁵ 5³ 4² 2ʰ 1¹¹⁄₂ JonesJ⁵ c5000 87 ⊕ Donnie 117 Lovely Day 8

FINISH—The horse finished first, 1½ lengths in front of the second horse. If second, third, or unplaced, the superior figure indicates his margin behind the winner.

27Jun 74² AP 6f :22⁴ :46 1:11³ ft 9-5 ▲ 117⁵ 5³ 4² 2ʰ 1¹¹⁄₂ JonesJ⁵ c5000 87 ⊕ Donnie 117 Lovely Day 8

JOCKEY AND POST POSITION—J. Jones rode the horse, who started from post position number 5.

27Jun 74² AP 6f :22⁴ :46 1:11³ ft 9-5 ▲ 117⁵ 5³ 4² 2ʰ 1¹¹⁄₂ JonesJ⁵ c5000 87 ⊕ Donnie 117 Lovely Day 8

CLAIMING PRICE OR TYPE OF RACE—The horse was entered to be claimed for $5,000 and the "c" indicates he was claimed. See reverse side for a complete list of the race classification abbreviations used in this portion of the past performance line.

27Jun 74² AP 6f :22⁴ :46 1:11³ ft 9-5 ▲ 117⁵ 5³ 4² 2ʰ 1¹¹⁄₂ JonesJ⁵ c5000 87 ⊕ Donnie 117 Lovely Day 8

SPEED RATING—The horse's speed rating was 87. See reverse side for an explanation of speed ratings.

27Jun 74² AP 6f :22⁴ :46 1:11³ ft 9-5 ▲ 117⁵ 5³ 4² 2ʰ 1¹¹⁄₂ JonesJ⁵ c5000 87 ⊕ Donnie 117 Lovely Day 8

FIRST TWO FINISHERS—These are the first two finishers in the race, with the weight carried by the first horse. The ⊕ preceding the first horse's name indicates the race was exclusively for fillies or fillies and mares.

27Jun 74² AP 6f :22⁴ :46 1:11³ ft 9-5 ▲ 117⁵ 5³ 4² 2ʰ 1¹¹⁄₂ JonesJ⁵ c5000 87 ⊕ Donnie 117 Lovely Day 8

NUMBER OF STARTERS—Eight horses started in this race.

POINTS OF CALL IN PAST PERFORMANCES

The points of call in the past performances vary according to the distance of the race. The points of call of the running positions for the most frequently raced distances are:

Distance	1st Call	2nd Call	3rd Call	4th Call
2 Furlongs	Start	–	Stretch	Finish
5/16 Mile	Start	–	Stretch	Finish
3 Furlongs	Start	–	Stretch	Finish
3½ Furlongs	Start	–	Stretch	Finish
4 Furlongs	Start	¼ mile	Stretch	Finish
4½ Furlongs	Start	¼ mile	Stretch	Finish
5 Furlongs	$1/18$ mile	$3/8$ mile	Stretch	Finish
5½ Furlongs	¼ mile	$3/8$ mile	Stretch	Finish
6 Furlongs	¼ mile	½ mile	Stretch	Finish
6½ Furlongs	¼ mile	½ mile	Stretch	Finish
7 Furlongs	¼ mile	½ mile	Stretch	Finish

Distance	1st Call	2nd Call	3rd Call	4th Call
1 Mile	½ mile	¾ mile	Stretch	Finish
1 Mile, 70 Yds	½ mile	¾ mile	Stretch	Finish
$1^1/_{16}$ Miles	½ mile	¼ mile	Stretch	Finish
$1^3/_8$ Miles	½ mile	¼ mile	Stretch	Finish
$1^3/_{16}$ Miles	½ mile	¼ mile	Stretch	Finish
$1^1/_4$ Miles	½ mile	1 mile	Stretch	Finish
$1^5/_{16}$ Miles	½ mile	1 mile	Stretch	Finish
$1^3/_8$ Miles	½ mile	1 mile	Stretch	Finish
$1^1/_2$ Miles	½ mile	$1^1/_4$ mile	Stretch	Finish
$1^5/_8$ Miles	½ mile	$1^3/_8$ mile	Stretch	Finish
$1^3/_4$ Miles	½ mile	$1^1/_2$ mile	Stretch	Finish

NOTE: The second call in most races is made ¼ mile from the finish; the stretch call ⅛ mile from the finish.

FRACTIONAL TIMES

In races at less than one mile, fractional times are given for the horse in the lead at the quarter-mile and half-mile. In races at one mile or more, fractional times are given for the half-mile and three-quarter mile.

NOTE: In races at the shorter distances, only the fraction for the quarter-mile is used, except for races at three and one-half furlongs, in which the fractions are given for the quarter-mile and three-eighths mile.

(continued)

KEY TO SYMBOLS, ABBREVIATIONS IN PAST PERFORMANCES

FOREIGN-BRED HORSES

An asterisk(*) preceding the name of the horse indicates foreign-bred. (No notation is made for horses bred in Canada and Cuba).

MUD MARKS

*—Fair mud runner X—Good mud runner
⊗—Superior mud runner

COLOR

B.—Bay Blk.—Black Br.—Brown Ch.—Chestnut
Gr.—Gray Ro.—Roan Wh.—White
Dk. b. or br.—Dark bay or brown
(Lt. before color denotes Light)

SEX

c—colt h—horse g—gelding rig—ridgling
f—filly m—mare

PEDIGREE

Each horse's pedigree lists, in the order named, color, sex, year foaled, sire, dam and grandsire (sire of dam).

BREEDER

Abbreviation following breeder's name indicates the state, place of origin, or foreign country in which the horse was foaled.

TODAY'S CLAIMING PRICE

Claiming prices for horses entered today appear in bold face type to right of trainer's name.

RECORD OF STARTS AND EARNINGS

The horse's racing record for his most recent two years of competition appears to the extreme right of the name of the breeder. This lists the year, number of starts, wins, seconds, thirds, and earnings. The letter "M" in the win column of the upper line indicates the horse is a maiden. If the letter "M" is in the lower line only, it indicates the horse was a maiden at the end of that year.

RACE CLASSIFICATIONS

10000 – Claiming race (eligible to be claimed for $10,000). Note: The letter c preceding claiming price (c10000) indicates horse was claimed.

M10000 – Maiden claiming race (non-winners–eligible to be claimed).

10000H – Claiming handicap (eligible to be claimed).

o10000 – Optional claiming race (entered **NOT** to be claimed).

10000o – Optional claiming race (eligible to be claimed).

Mdn – Maiden race (non-winners).

AlwM – Maiden allowance race (for non-winners with special weight allowance for those having started in a claiming race).

Alw – Allowance race.

HcpO – Overnight handicap race.

SplW – Special weight race.

Wfa – Weight-for-age race.

Mtch – Match race.

A10000 – Starter allowance race (horses who have started for claiming price shown, or less, as stipulated in the conditions).

H10000 – Starter handicap (same restriction as above).

S10000 – Starter special weight (restricted as above). Note: Where no amount is specified in the conditions of the "starters" race dashes are substituted, as shown below:

A—— H—— S——

DISTANCE

a – preceding distance (a6f) denotes "about" distance (about 6 furlongs in this instance.)

TURF COURSES

Ⓣ – before distance indicates turf (grass) course race.

▣ – before distance indicates inner turf course.

TRACK CONDITIONS

ft–fast	fr–frozen	gd–good	sl–slow
sy–sloppy	m–muddy	h–heavy	

Turf course races, including steeplechase and hurdles:

hd–hard	fm–firm	gd–good	yl–yielding	sf–soft

Note: SC in place of track condition indicates Synthetic Course in use at various tracks. The condition of this synthetic course is fast at all times.

CLOSING ODDS

2▲–favorite   2e–entry   15f–mutuel field

APPRENTICE OR RIDER WEIGHT ALLOWANCES

Allowance (in pounds) indicated by superior figure following weight–117[5].

ABBREVIATIONS USED IN POINTS OF CALL

no–nose   h–head   nk–neck

POST POSITION

Horse's post position appears after jockey's name–WilsonR[4]

STEEPLECHASE AND HURDLE RACES
[S–Steeplechase]   [H–Hurdle race]

STAKES RACES

AlwS – Allowance stakes.
HcpS – Handicap stakes.
ScwS – Scale weight stakes.
SpwS – Special weight stakes.
WfaS – Weight-for-age stakes.
50000S – Claiming stakes (eligible to be claimed).

INVITATIONAL RACES

InvH – Invitational handicap.
InvSc – Invitational scale weight
InvSp – Invitational special weights.
InvW – Invitational weight-for-age.

RACES EXCLUSIVELY FOR FILLIES, MARES

ⓕ–Immediately following the speed rating indicates races exclusively for fillies or fillies and mares.

SPEED RATINGS

This is a comparison of the horse's time with the track record established prior to the opening of the meeting. The track record is given a rating of 100 and one point is deducted for each one-fifth second slower than the record. When a horse breaks the track record, one point is added to the par 100 for each one-fifth second faster than the record. One-fifth of a second is considered the equivalent of one length.

(continued)

No ratings are given for hurdle or steeplechase events, for races of less than three furlongs, for races where the horse's speed rating is less than 25.

NOTE: Speed ratings for new distances are computed and assigned when adequate time standards are established. At Caliente, Mexico, which operates throughout the year, rating changes are made whenever a track record is broken.

EACH HORSE'S MOST RECENT WORKOUTS APPEAR DIRECTLY UNDER THE PAST PERFORMANCES

For example, July 30 Bel 3f ft : 38b indicates the horse worked on July 30 at Belmont Park. The distance of the trial was 3 furlongs over a fast track and the horse was timed in 38 seconds, breezing. The following abbreviations are used to describe how each horse worked:

b–breezing	d–driving	e–easily	g–worked from stall gate	h–handily	bo–bore out
trt following track abbreviation indicates horse worked on training track.		tc–turf course	TR–Trial race
		HC–Hillside Course	

SOURCE: Copyright © 1974 Triangle Publications

Rank	Horse/sire	Starts	Wins (SW)	2d (SP)	3d (SP)	S.I.	Earnings	Owner	Breeder
1	Refrigerator by RareJet	36	22 (11)	8 (7)	3 (3)	115	$2,126,309	James E. Helzer	Sonny Vaughn
2	Winalota Cash by Light On Cash	31	19 (10)	8 (5)	1 (1)	111	1,952,848	Andra D. Meridyth	O. S. Carlton III
3	Eastex by Texas Dancer (TB)	31	13 (4)	4 (1)	5 (3)	106	1,869,406	Speedhorse Inc.	Dr. and Mrs. H. D. Hall
4	Mr. Master Bug by Master Hand (TB)	25	17 (5)	4 (2)	3 (2)	110	1,793,718	Marvin Barnes	Marvin Barnes
5	Ronas Ryon by Windy Ryon	23	18 (5)	4 (2)	0 (0)	105	1,777,977	B. Benham	James Floyd Plummer
6	Dashingly by Dash for Cash	25	18 (5)	5 (4)	0 (0)	104	1,754,323	J. Baxter Brinkman	Muriel E. Hyland
7	Higheasterjet by Pine's Easter Jet	30	20 (8)	2 (0)	2 (0)	107	1,633,035	G.D. Highsmith	D. McMull and J. Highsmith
8	A Delightful Dasher	7	6 (3)	1 (0)	0 (0)	95	1,504,154	Gwendolyn Eaves	Gwendolyn Eaves
9	Corona Cash by First Down Dash	26	16 (10)	6 (2)	1 (1)	101	1,484,480	Henry E. Brown	Robert D. Etchandy Estate
10	Merganser by Duck Dance (TB)	23	13 (4)	3 (0)	2 (0)	105	1,373,704	Bobby D. Cox	McKinnerney/Doering/Shaw
11	Strawberry Silk by Beduino (TB)	17	11 (2)	3 (2)	0 (0)	105	1,266,264	Jackie Spencer	T. K. Partnership
12	Dash For Speed by Dash for Cash	30	22 (12)	3 (1)	2 (2)	107	1,225,337	Clarence Scharbauer, Jr.	Phillips/McRae Int. Inc.
13	Special Effort by Raise Your Glass (TB)	14	13 (4)	0 (0)	1 (1)	104	1,219,950	Burnett Ranches Ltd.	Allen Moehring

(continued)

APPENDIX TABLE 12-2 Leading Money-Earning Quarter Horses, 1949–1999 (Continued)

Rank	Horse/sire	Starts	Wins (SW)	2d (SP)	3d (SP)	S.I.	Earnings	Owner	Breeder
14	Falling In Love Again by First Down Dash	20	8 (1)	1 (0)	3 (2)	108	1,188,375	David F./Susan Mackie	Cindy/Luke Knox
15	Elans Special by Special Effort	22	11 (2)	4 (1)	3 (3)	98	1,186,540	Edward C. Allred	Dr. Lindsey Burbank, Sr.
16	On a High by Dash for Cash	22	9 (3)	6 (1)	4 (1)	113	1,167,234	On a High Joint Venture	Jerry Rheudasil
17	Toltac by Beduino (TB)	18	12 (5)	4 (1)	0	113	1,143,043	Vessels' Stallion Farm/ D/E. Payne	Mrs. Catherine Richardson
18	Make Mine Cash by Dash for Cash	26	7 (3)	5 (1)	5 (2)	110	1,142,428	Jan Stith/Penny Hoeft	Ted Bruce/Floyd Jackson
19	Streaking Flyer by Strawfly Special	14	5 (1)	3 (1)	1 (1)	96	1,141,128	Southern Rose Ranch	Dan/Terry Lovingier
20	Noblesse Six by Streakin Six	52	13 (6)	12 (6)	3 (1)	110	1,125,024	Steve Chavez	Phillips Ranch

Note: Money earned at official distances only. S.I. = speed index, TB = Thoroughbred, SW = stakes winners, SP = stakes placed.

SOURCE: *Quarter Racing Journal,* March, 1999.

Appendix Table 12-3 Leading Quarter Horse Sires of Money Earners, 1949–1999

Rank	Sire	Racing age foals	Starters	Winners (SW)	Wins (SW)	ROM	S.I. 90 & Up	Total earnings	Earnings/ starter	Leading earner	Earnings
1	Dash For Cash	1,369	1,154	824(143)	2,843(329)	958	646	$39,377,264	$34,122	Dashingly	$1,754,323
2	First Down Dash	979	789	597(123)	1,814(237)	712	498	30,926,442	39,197	Corona Cash	1,484,480
3	Easy Jet	2,505	2,019	1,382(145)	3,971(243)	1,563	864	26,223,538	12,988	Mr. Trucka Jet	1,033,115
4	Special Effort	1,353	1,064	714(66)	1,975(114)	819	489	15,918,109	14,961	Elans Special	1,186,540
5	Streakin Six	1,043	781	537(67)	1,780(134)	599	363	15,066,554	19,291	Noblesse Six	1,125,024
6	Beduino (TB)	706	598	435(40)	1,331(80)	496	293	13,089,592	21,889	Strawberry Silk	1,266,264
7	Merridoc	1,361	1,075	664(53)	2,069(121)	738	385	12,850,099	11,954	Solvency	632,422
8	Chicks Beduino	1,118	736	475(65)	1,252(113)	573	350	11,709,807	15,910	Separatist	599,931
9	Moon Lark	1,141	933	575(52)	1,935(106)	660	381	10,225,215	10,960	Spring Lark	793,025
10	Raise Your Glass (TB)	1,288	981	648(49)	1,914(91)	699	360	10,217,723	10,416	Special Effort	1,219,950
11	Rocket Wrangler	1,628	1,221	762(56)	2,297(83)	835	414	9,407,803	7,705	Dash For Cash	507,688
12	Easily Smashed	1,667	1,187	718(63)	2,075(109)	792	426	9,257,914	7,799	Chrises Smash	276,529
13	The Signature	798	600	391(43)	1,195(81)	446	274	8,988,421	14,981	Heza Fast Man	801,356
14	Zevi	983	772	530(61)	1,695(92)	585	330	8,626,851	11,175	Hiclass Girl	398,455
15	Pass 'Em Up	1,640	1,250	741(45)	2,327(74)	801	365	8,197,060	6,558	Pass Over	521,172
16	Reb's Policy	502	440	326(31)	1,348(72)	347	188	8,173,981	18,577	Town Policy	862,180
17	Runaway Winner	847	636	433(40)	1,049(58)	500	290	7,718,996	12,137	Treacherously	622,004
18	Top Moon	1,829	1,340	795(74)	2,768(114)	804	348	7,704,102	5,749	Moon Lark	859,356
19	On A High	754	579	387(34)	1,147(77)	455	266	7,657,740	13,226	See Me Do It	912,214
20	Go Man Go	942	775	552(83)	2,063(171)	552	312	7,631,518	9,847	Vim and Vigor	309,831

Note: Money earned at official distances only; includes every horse that has been indexed since 1945. S.I. = speed index, TB = Thoroughbred, ROM = Register of Merit. SW = stakes race winners.

Source: *Quarter Racing Journal,* March, 2000.

Appendix Table 12-4 All-Time Leading Maternal Grandsires of Register of Merit Qualifiers

Rank	Broodmare/sire	Dams[a]	Racing age foals	Starters	Avg. per starter	ROM	S.I. 90 & Up	Winners	Wins	Earnings	Leading Earner	Earnings
1	Easy Jet	960	5,543	3,499	11,693	2,408	1,304	2,126(193)	6,497(367)	$40,912,973	Eastex	$1,869,406
2	Go Man Go	436	3,278	2,211	8,066	1,419	714	1,372(107)	4,591(173)	17,834,502	Ettago Chickie	534,465
3	Dash For Cash	502	2,695	1,803	14,592	1,352	795	1,165(130)	3,281(224)	26,308,996	Elans Special	1,186,540
4	Top Moon	720	4,252	2,113	4,449	1,133	477	1,036(72)	2,882(113)	9,400,128	Jaimie Jay	313,172
5	Azure Te (TB)	460	2,791	1,719	6,528	1,113	527	1,007(64)	2,841(94)	11,222,300	Hot Idea	374,616
6	Lady Bug's Moon	416	2,891	1,733	7,536	1,043	485	935(57)	2,706(95)	13,060,213	Mr. Master Bug	1,793,718
7	Jet Deck	253	2,078	1,486	10,136	1,040	549	957(91)	3,323(154)	15,061,711	Rule The Deck	522,165
8	Rocket Wrangler	575	3,076	1,574	6,907	1,011	517	904(70)	2,504(115)	10,871,952	Rock 'N' Rona	230,113
9	Pass 'Em Up	558	2,678	1,461	6,515	972	434	811(68)	2,265(111)	9,518,682	Joanna Kate	505,942
10	Three Bars (TB)	259	1,988	1,272	5,498	793	374	800(88)	2,895(189)	6,933,957	Easy Jet	445,723
11	Raise Your Glass	449	2,172	1,213	10,754	766	407	679(75)	2,066(140)	13,044,636	Noblesse Six	1,125,074
12	Leo	290	2,809	1,378	4,461	754	364	811(95)	2,877(223)	6,146,643	Little Blue Sheep	389,854
13	Tiny Charger	288	1,932	1,159	9,386	723	369	669(59)	2,254(89)	10,878,483	Solvency	632,422
14	Hempen	345	1,798	1,081	9,648	718	419	648(65)	1,815(104)	10,429,935	Way Maker	617,444
15	Rebel Cause	353	2,066	1,173	6,417	708	342	672(41)	2,108(72)	7,527,453	Denim 'N' Diamonds	731,118
16	Beduino (TB)	283	1,431	946	16,394	695	406	597(72)	1,712(129)	15,508,825	Dash Thru Traffic	1,056,943
17	Alamitos Bar	297	1,810	1,037	11,894	677	347	621(53)	2,065(94)	12,334,433	Higheasterjet	1,633,035
18	Three Oh's	340	2,010	1,090	5,868	668	310	629(43)	1,850(65)	6,395,940	Magics Mighty Man	305,210
19	Rocket Bar	176	1,464	986	8,209	637	298	613(46)	2,183(115)	3,093,817	Charger Bar	495,437
20	Pacific Bailey	1,036	4,653	1,316	2,505	636	257	612(27)	1,783(40)	3,296,790	Thanks to Cute Bar	134,618

[a]With racing age foals.

Note: ROM = Register of Merit, S.I. = speed index, TB = Thoroughbred. The numbers in parentheses are number of stakes winners and number of stakes race wins.

Source: Quarter Racing Journal, March, 2000.

APPENDIX TABLE 12-5   Leading Quarter Horse Dams of Register of Merit Qualifiers, 1945–1998.

Rank	Dam	Racing age foals	Starters	Winners (SW)	Wins (SW)	ROM	S.I. 90 & Up	Total earnings	Leading earner	Earnings
1	Jet Effort	17	16	14(2)	76(6)	15	10	$ 196,781	Jeff Effort Jet	$ 64,591
2	Deckella	17	16	14(7)	73(12)	15	9	225,286	Break Dancer Hodge	49,667
3	Star Brandy	19	17	14(3)	62(4)	15	10	122,929	Reber	22,087
4	Miss Snazzy Bar	18	15	11(3)	57(4)	15	11	187,029	Snafols	71,808
5	Sugar Antique	18	15	14(1)	82(1)	14	8	115,565	Gatling Gun	27,673
6	Queen Chloe	15	15	13(3)	51(6)	14	7	295,244	Pie Prince	106,872
7	Jet Yet Joan	16	15	14(1)	48(2)	14	4	172,827	Brazos Thunder	84,941
8	Devildidit	15	15	13(6)	105(18)	14	12	520,077	Devil Who	254,389
9	Camptown Girl	17	16	13(1)	65(8)	14	10	985,062	Town Policy	862,100
10	Ginger Baker	18	15	13(1)	54(6)	14	7	112,177	Little Pana Bar	66,178
11	Casco Charge	16	15	12(1)	52(4)	14	5	451,035	Heza Charger	300,916
12	Easy Secret	17	15	12(2)	35(3)	14	9	763,757	Meganette	657,620
13	Callmecutie	18	17	11(4)	65(10)	14	7	1,407,133	Justanold Love	949,836

Note: ROM = Register of Merit, S.I. = speed index, TB = Thoroughbred. The numbers in parentheses are number of stakes race winners and number of stakes race wins. There are 26 mares with 13 ROM qualifiers.

SOURCE: *Quarter Racing Journal*, March, 2000.

APPENDIX TABLE 12-6 Champion Quarter Running Horses, 1940–1998

Year	World champion	Champion stallion	Champion mare	Champion gelding
1940–1941	Clabber	Clabber		
1941–1942	Shue Fly	Nobodies Friend	Shue Fly	
1942–1943	Shue Fly	Joe Reed 11	Shue Fly	
1943–1944	Shue Fly	Piggin String (TB)	Shue Fly	
		Texas Lad		
1944–1945	(no award)	Dee Dee	Queenie	
1945–1946	Queenie	Piggin String (TB)	Queenie	
1946–1947	Woven Web (TB)	Hard Twist	Woven Web (TB)	
1947	Woven Web (TB)	Pelican	Woven Web (TB)	
1948	Woven Web (TB)	Scotter W	Woven Web (TB)	
1949	Maddon's Bright Eyes	Diamond Bob	Maddon's Bright Eyes	
1950	Blob Jr	Blob Jr	Maddon's Bright Eyes	
1951	Monita	Bart B S	Monita	
	Maddon's Bright Eyes	Hard Twist	Maddon's Bright Eyes	
		Clabbertown G		
1952	Johnny Dial	Johnny Dial	Stealla Moore	Brigand (TB)
1953	Miss Meyers	Rukin String	Miss Meyers	Brigand (TB)
1954	Josie's Bar	Palleo Pete	Josie's Bar	Brigand (TB)
1955	Go Man Go	Go Man Go	Posey Vandy	Arizonan
1956	Go Man Go	Go Man Go	Vanetta Dee	Vannevar
1957	Go Man Go	Go Man Go	Vanetta Dee	Vannevar
1958	Mr Bar None	Mr Bar None	Vanetta Dee	Vandy's Flash
1959	(no award)	Double Bid	Miss Louton	Pulp
			Triple Lady	

Year				
1960	Vandy's Flash	Tonto Bars Hawk	Triple Lady	Vandy's Flash
1961	Pap	Breeze Bar	First Call	Pap
1962	No Butt	Jet Deck	No Butt	Caprideck
1963	Jet Deck	Jet Deck	Anna Dial	Dariman
1964	Goetta	Pasamonte Paul	Goetta	Dari Star
1965	Go Josie Go	Tiny Watch	Go Josie Go	Joe Sherry
1966	(no award)	Duplicate Copy / Tiny Watch	Go Josie Go	Cee Bar Deck
1967	Laico Bird	Duplicate Copy	Laico Bird	Brad Len
1968	Kaweah Bar	Mighty Deck	Top Rockette	Kaweah Bar
1969	Easy Jet	Easy Jet	Go Derussa Go	Kaweah Bar
1970	Kaweah Bar	EasyJet	Go Together	Kaweah Bar
1971	Charger Bar	Bunny Bid	Charger Bar	Kaweah Bar
1972	Mr Jet Moore	Mr Jet Moore	Charger Bar	Kaweah Bar
1973	Truckle Feature	Truckle Feature	Charger Bar	Come Six
1974	Tiny's Gay	Tiny's Gay	Charger Bar	Flight 109
1975	Easy Date	Bugs Alive in 75	Easy Date	Wanta Go
1976	Dash for Cash			
1977	Dash for Cash			
1978	Miss Thermolark			
1979	Moon Lark			
1980	Super Sound Charge			
1981	Special Effort			
1982	Sgt. Pepper Feature			
1983	Dashingly			
1984	Dash's Dream			
1985	Cash Rate			
1986	Gold Coast Express			

(continued)

APPENDIX TABLE 12-6 Champion Quarter Running Horses, 1940–1998 (Continued)

Year	World champion	Champion stallion	Champion mare	Champion gelding
1987	First Down Dash			Mighty Deck Three
1988	Merganser			The Plan
1989	See Me Do It			Dynamo Victory
1990	Dash for Speed			Face in the Crowd
1991	Special Leader			Eastex
1992	Refrigerator			Solvency
1993	Refrigerator			Elliptical
1994	Down With Debt			Easy Go Effort
1995	Winalota Cash			Liberty Coin
1996	Dashing Folly			
1997	SLM Big Daddy			
1998	SLM Big Daddy			

	Champion 2-year-old			
Year	Horse	Filly	Colt	Gelding
1980	Mighty Deck Three	Ettago Chickie	Jet View	Mighty Deck Three
1981	Special Effort	Dashingly	Special Effort	The Plan
1982	Mr. Master Bug	Yankee Win	Mr. Master Bug	Dynamo Victory
1983	Tolltac	Indigo Illusion	Tolltac	Face in the Crowd
1984	Eastex	Sixy Chick	Spring Lark	Eastex
1985	Brigand Silk	Dashing Phoebe	Brigand Silk	Solvency
1986	Ronas Ryon	Cash Perks	Ronas Ryon	Elliptical
1987	(no award)	(no award)	Shoot Yeah	Easy Go Effort
1988	Merganser	See Me Do It	Merganser	Liberty Coin

Year	Horse	Filly	Colt	Gelding
1989	Strawberry Silk	Strawberry Silk	Power Train	Way Maker
1990	Refrigerator	Quick Fun	Taking on the Cash	Refrigerator
1991	Corona Chick	Corona Chick	Royal Quick Dash	Ed Grimley
1992	Deceptively	Deceptively	Dash Thru Traffic	Mega Dash
1993	A Classic Dash	Jumping Tac Flash	A Classic Dash	Treacherously
1994	Mr. Jess Perry	Ah Sigh	Mr. Jess Perry	Heza Fast Man
1995	Winalota Cash	Shake The Bank	Splash Bac	Winalota Cash
1996	Toast To Dash	Haulin Pass	Toast To Dash	Uncas
		Speedy Empress		
1997	Corona Cash	Corona Cash	This Snow Is Royal	Artesias Special Chic
1998	First Sovereign	Deelish	First Sovereign	He's My Dasher

Champion 3-year-old

Year	Horse	Filly	Colt	Gelding
1980	Jamie Jay	Jamie Jay	Extra Easy	Native Gambler
1981	Sgt. Pepper Feature	Queen for Cash	Easily Smashed	Sgt. Pepper Feature
1982	Leading Star	Leading Star	Special Effort	My Startime
1983	Mr. Master Bug	Bartendress	Mr. Master Bug	Call Caleb
1984	Dash's Dream	Dash's Dream	Tolltac	Rise N High
1985	Prissy Fein	Prissy Fein	Spring Lark	Easy Austin
1986	Gold Coast Express	Dashing Phoebe	Six Fortunes	Gold Coast Express
1987	First Down Dash	Florentine	First Down Dash	Hold All Tickets
1988	Dash For Speed	Dash For Speed	Dashing Val	Shawnes Favorite
1989	See Me Do It	See Me Do It	Sig Hanson	Rambac
1990	Special Project	Sweet 'N' Special	Special Project	Apprehend
1991	Taking on the Cash	See Me Gone	Taking on the Cash	Refrigerator
1992	Rare Form	Corona Chick	Rare Form	Femmes Frolic

(continued)

APPENDIX TABLE 12-6   Champion Quarter Running Horses, 1940–1998 (Continued)

		Champion 3-year-old		
Year	Horse	Filly	Colt	Gelding
1993	Royal Down Dash	Royal Down Dash	Some Dasher	For Forty Blast
1994	I Hear A Symphony	I Hear A Symphony	Heza Fast Man	Develop A Plan
1995	Ah Sigh	Ah Sigh	Meter Be Gone	Mars Blackman
1996	Dashing Folly	Dashing Folly	Now I Know	Winalota Cash
1997	Dashing Perfection	Fabulous Form	Especially Rare	Dashing Perfection
1998	Corona Cash	Corona Cash	Dashin Is Easy	The Casanova

		Champion aged			
Year	Horse	Mare	Stallion	Gelding	Distance Horse[a]
1980	Super Sound Charge	Lady Juno	Super Sound Charge	Town Policy	
1981	Denim N Diamonds	Denim 'N' Diamonds	Oh Shiney	Vespero	
1982	Sgt. Pepper Feature	Denim 'N' Diamonds	Luck's Gay Chick	Sgt. Pepper Feature	
1983	Dashingly	Dashingly	Johnny Vittoro	The Black Alliance	
1984	Mr. Master Bug	Staunch's Velvet	Mr. Master Bug	The Black Alliance	
1985	Cash Rate	Dash's Dream	Zellions	Cash Rate	
1986	Cash Rate	Heavenly	Sir Alibi	Cash Rate	
1987	Gold Coast Express	St. Willa	New Year's Special	Gold Coast Express	Calyx
1988	Florentine	Florentine	Bully Bullion	Chingaderos	Truly a Pleasure
1989	Dash for Speed	Dash for Speed	Cash Legacy	Chingaderos	Movin' Brown Jug
1990	Dash for Speed	Dash for Speed	Jazzing Hi	Tee Roy Reb	Baychaino
1991	Special Leader	Isaw's Sugar Bear	Special Leader	Apprehend	Griswold
1992	Refrigerator	Juno's Request	Six to Five	Refrigerator	Griswold

1993	Refrigerator	Sound Dash	Six to Five	Refrigerator	Griswold
1994	Down With Debt	Down With Debt	Make Mine Bud	Refrigerator	Better Than Never
1995	My Debut	Special Phoebe	Rare Bar	My Debut	Speedy Lunch
1996	Kool Kue Baby	Kool Kue Baby	Roll Into Mischief	IB Quick	Sign It Super
1997	SLM Big Daddy	Dashing Folly	Now I Know	SLM Big Daddy	I've Been Blessed
1998	SLM Big Daddy	Kool Kue Baby	Dean Miracle	SLM Big Daddy	Windville

[a]First awarded in 1987.

NOTE: TB = Thoroughbred.

SOURCE: *Quarter Racing Journal*, March, 1999.

Appendix Table 12-7   Breakdown of the Total Gross Distribution in Stakes and Purses in 1991 for Thoroughbreds by States, including Canada and Mexico.

Locality	Racing days	Races run	Gross distribution
Arizona	194	1,901	$ 7,184,387
Arkansas	65	633	11,293,375
California	622	5,714	133,444,336
Delaware	150	1,407	7,160,800
Florida	378	3,842	48,953,388
Georgia	2	10	335,000
Idaho	51	371	595,829
Illinois	441	4,305	48,901,201
Iowa	105	693	1,640,430
Kansas	74	536	2,395,085
Kentucky	283	2,715	57,016,053
Louisiana	520	5,566	36,656,177
Maryland	270	2,778	41,945,800
Massachusetts	27	273	735,650
Michigan	209	1,938	12,139,149
Minnesota	124	1,024	7,489,342
Montana	50	453	689,019
Nebraska	199	1,985	9,342,528
New Hampshire	260	2,793	16,883,700
New Jersey	297	3,026	37,143,990
New Mexico	408	2,868	10,114,168
New York	480	4,518	101,402,640
Ohio	471	4,588	23,241,876
Oklahoma	315	2,031	12,174,757
Oregon	116	1,009	1,893,061
Pennsylvania	523	4,815	30,582,380
Texas	249	1,273	4,127,933
Washington	292	2,831	15,041,477
West Virginia	466	4,659	12,153,939
Wyoming	33	218	291,790
Canada	817	7,614	72,090,545
Mexico	73	694	2,099,600
Grand Totals	8,605	79,305	$770,358,135

source: *American Racing Manual* (1992).

APPENDIX TABLE 12-8   Annual Statistics for Thoroughbred Racing, 1907–1998

Year	Racing days	No. races	Starters	Gross distribution
1907	1,004	6,252	5,662	$ 5,375,554
1908	921	5,699	5,405	4,351,691
1909	724	4,510	4,890	3,146,695
1910	1,063	6,501	4,180	2,942,333
1911	1,037	6,289	4,038	2,337,957
1912	926	5,806	3,553	2,391,625
1913	969	6,136	3,541	2,920,963
1914	906	5,849	3,632	2,994,525
1915	839	5,454	3,700	2,853,037
1916	1,035	6,098	3,754	3,842,471
1917	902	5,899	4,200	4,066,253
1918	610	3,968	3,575	3,425,347
1919	686	4,408	3,531	4,642,865
1920	1,022	6,897	4,032	7,773,407
1921	1,074	7,250	4,623	8,435,083
1922	1,182	8,045	5,049	9,096,215
1923	1,319	8,991	5,437	9,675,811
1924	1,456	10,007	5,906	10,825,446
1925	1,656	11,579	6,438	12,577,270
1926	1,713	12,065	7,218	13,884,820
1927	1,680	11,832	7,794	13,935,610
1928	1,613	11,465	8,171	13,332,361
1929	1,599	11,133	8,332	13,417,817
1930	1,653	11,477	8,791	13,674,160
1931	1,660	11,690	9,128	13,084,154
1932	1,518	10,835	9,017	10,082,757
1933	1,746	12,680	9,176	8,516,326
1934	1,959	14,261	9,470	10,445,495
1935	2,133	15,830	10,544	12,794,418
1936	2,033	15,344	10,757	12,994,605
1937	2,140	16,250	11,515	14,363,562
1938	2,140	16,243	12,185	14,946,609
1939	2,199	16,967	12,804	15,312,839
1940	2,096	16,401	13,257	15,911,167
1941	2,162	16,912	13,683	17,987,225
1942	2,228	17,593	12,614	18,136,118
1943	2,052	16,094	11,258	18,555,680
1944	2,396	19,228	12,959	29,159,099
1945	2,480	19,587	14,307	32,300,060
1946	3,020	23,940	17,601	49,291,024
1947	3,134	24,884	19,063	53,932,141

(continued)

APPENDIX TABLE 12-8   Annual Statistics for Thoroughbred Racing, 1907–1998 (*Continued*)

Year	Racing days	No. races	Starters	Gross distribution
1948	3,183	25,388	20,254	54,436,063
1949	3,309	26,832	21,616	52,317,078
1950	3,290	26,932	22,554	50,102,098
1951	3,394	27,856	22,819	55,551,124
1952	3,515	29,051	23,813	63,950,236
1953	3,635	30,069	24,417	72,870,819
1954	3,685	30,467	25,294	74,255,611
1955	3,827	31,757	26,056	76,643,696
1956	3,979	33,445	26,507	81,311,581
1957	4,120	34,982	27,355	85,300,966
1958	3,910	33,325	28,099	85,467,082
1959	4,218	36,579	28,623	92,848,541
1960	4,304	37,661	29,773	93,741,552
1961	4,641	40,744	30,381	98,846,843
1962	4,772	41,766	33,579	103,525,712
1963	5,203	45,449	35,828	113,122,209
1964	5,326	46,922	37,812	121,777,847
1965	5,284	47,335	38,502	126,463,984
1966	5,254	46,814	39,604	130,653,813
1967	5,344	47,811	41,853	139,170,738
1968	5,553	49,777	43,710	150,644,478
1969	5,825	52,315	45,808	168,713,911
1970	6,242	56,676	49,087	185,625,110
1971	6,394	57,467	50,470	201,435,894
1972	6,624	59,410	52,488	210,607,082
1973	6,888	62,272	54,813	233,936,153
1974	7,201	65,312	56,520	263,951,376
1975	7,488	68,210	58,816	292,583,798
1976	7,593	69,480	61,084	318,963,255
1977	7,525	68,822	61,970	336,022,495
1978	7,579	69,499	62,950	367,637,193
1979	7,515	69,407	70,914	415,414,224
1980	7,443	68,243	64,519	451,195,968
1981	7,661	70,882	65,844	508,361,268
1982	7,729	71,516	65,510	527,958,549
1983	7,617	71,007	74,609	547,008,364
1984	7,995	74,395	78,267	608,458,129
1985	8,143	75,687	82,594	652,475,303
1986	8,273	77,733	86,119	672,783,639
1987	8,539	80,382	89,511	711,782,767

Year	Racing days	No. races	Starters	Gross distribution
1988	8,488	79,593	90,517	742,144,444
1989	8,858	82,705	91,441	775,708,145
1990	8,641	79,971	89,724	779,358,135
1991	8,605	80,736	79,036	770,358,135
1992		79,249	84,755	791,600,000
1993		73,969	80,238	769,700,000
1994		72,344	76,539	797,200,000
1995		69,985	73,870	852,200,000
1996		66,308	71,982	897,000,000
1997		65,421	70,370	938,400,000
1998		62,912	70,291	993,500,000

NOTE: The following number of horses started in 1902, 5271; 1903, 5525; 1904, 5962; 1905, 6232; and 1906, 5962. All statistics include United States, Canadian, Mexican, Cuban, and Puerto Rican racing with the following exceptions:

1. Cuba: not included after 1957.
2. Mexico: Caliente, only through 1943; 1958 through 1960. Including Mexico City, 1944 through 1957; 1961 through 1970.
3. Puerto Rico: 1963 and 1964 only.
4. 1992–1998: U.S., Canada, and Puerto Rico.

SOURCE: *American Racing Manual* (1992).

SOURCE: Equibase Company, LLC.

APPENDIX TABLE 12-9   Thoroughbred Horses That Were Annual Money-Winning
Leaders Since 1902

Year	Horse	Age	Starts	1st place	2d place	3d place	Amount won
1902	Major Dangerfield	3	7	4	2	1	$ 57,685
1903	Africander	3	15	8	3	1	70,810
1904	Delhi	3	10	6	2	0	75,225
1905	Sysony	3	9	9	0	0	144,380
1906	Accountant	3	13	9	1	1	83,570
1907	Colin	2	12	12	0	0	131,705
1908	Sir Martin	2	13	8	4	0	78,590
1909	Joe Madden	3	15	5	9	1	44,905
1910	Novelty	2	16	11	2	7	72,630
1911	Worth	2	13	10	1	0	16,645
1912	Star Charter	4	17	6	7	5	14,655
1913	Old Rosebud	2	14	12	2	0	19,057
1914	Roamer	3	16	12	1	7	29,105
1915	Borrow	7	9	4	1	1	20,195
1916	Campfire	2	9	6	2	0	49,735
1917	Sun Briar	2	9	5	1	2	59,506
1918	Eternal	2	8	6	1	0	56,173
1919	Sir Barton	3	13	8	3	2	88,250
1920	Man O' War	3	11	11	0	0	166,140
1921	Morvich	2	11	11	0	0	115,234
1922	Pillory	3	7	4	1	1	95,564
1923	Zev	3	14	12	1	0	272,008
1924	Sarzen	3	12	8	1	1	95,640
1925	Pompey	2	10	7	2	0	121,630
1926	Crusader	2	15	9	4	0	166,033
1927	Anita Peabody	2	7	6	0	1	111,905
1928	High Strung	2	6	5	0	0	153,590
1929	Blue Larkspur	3	6	4	1	0	153,450
1930	Gallant Fox	3	10	9	1	0	308,275
1931	Gallant Flight	2	7	7	0	0	219,000
1932	Gusto	3	16	4	3	2	145,940
1933	Singing Wood	2	9	3	2	2	88,050
1934	Calvacade	3	7	6	1	0	111,235
1935	Omaha	3	9	6	1	2	142,255
1936	Granville	3	11	7	3	0	110,295
1937	Seabiscuit	4	15	11	2	2	168,580
1938	Stagehand	3	15	8	2	3	189,710
1939	Challedon	3	15	9	2	3	184,535
1940	Bimelech	3	7	4	2	1	110,005
1941	Whirlaway	3	20	13	5	2	272,386
1942	Shutout	3	12	8	2	0	238,872

1943	Count Fleet	3	6	6	0	0	174,055
1944	Pavot	2	8	8	0	0	179,040
1945	Busher	3	13	10	2	1	273,735
1946	Assault	3	15	8	2	3	424,195
1947	Armed	6	17	11	4	1	376,325
1948	Citation	3	20	19	1	0	709,470
1949	Ponder	3	21	9	5	2	321,825
1950	Noor	5	12	7	4	1	346,940
1951	Counterpoint	3	15	7	2	1	250,525
1952	Crafty Admiral	4	16	9	4	1	277,225
1953	Native Dancer	3	10	9	1	0	513,425
1954	Determine	3	15	10	2	3	328,700
1955	Nashua	2	12	10	1	1	752,550
1956	Needles	3	8	4	2	0	440,850
1957	Round Table	3	22	15	1	3	600,383
1958	Round Table	4	20	14	4	0	662,780
1959	Sword Dancer	3	13	8	4	0	537,004
1960	Bally Ache	3	15	10	3	1	455,045
1961	Carry Back	3	16	9	1	3	565,349
1962	Never Bend	2	10	7	1	2	402,969
1963	Candy Spots	3	12	7	2	1	604,481
1964	Gun Bow	4	16	8	4	2	580,100
1965	Buckpasser	2	11	9	1	0	568,096
1966	Buckpasser	3	14	13	1	0	669,078
1967	Damascus	3	16	12	3	1	817,941
1968	Forward Pass	3	13	7	2	0	546,674
1969	Arts and Letters	3	14	8	5	1	555,604
1970	Personality	3	18	8	2	1	444,049
1971	Riva Ridge	2	9	7	0	0	503,263
1972	Droll Role	4	19	7	3	4	471,633
1973	Secretariat	3	12	9	2	1	860,404
1974	Chris Evert	3	8	5	1	2	551,063
1975	Foolish Pleasure	3	11	5	4	1	716,278
1976	Forego	6	8	6	1	1	491,701
1977	Seattle Slew	3	7	6	0	1	641,370
1978	Affirmed	3	11	8	2	0	901,541
1979	Spectacular Bid	3	12	10	1	1	1,279,334
1980	Temperance Hill	3	17	8	3	1	1,130,452
1981	John Henry	6	10	8	0	0	1,798,030
1982	*Perrault	5	8	4	1	2	1,197,400
1983	*All Along	4	7	4	1	1	2,138,963
1984	Slew o' Gold	4	6	5	1	0	2,627,944
1985	Spend A Buck	3	7	5	1	1	3,552,704
1986	Snow Chief	3	9	6	1	1	1,875,200
1987	Alysheba	3	10	3	3	1	2,511,156
1988	Alysheba	4	9	7	1	0	3,808,600

(continued)

APPENDIX TABLE 12-9   Thoroughbred Horses That Were Annual Money-Winning Leaders Since 1902 (*continued*)

Year	Horse	Age	Starts	1st place	2d place	3d place	Amount won
1989	Sunday Silence	3	9	7	2	0	$4,578,454
1990	Unbridled	3	11	4	3	2	3,718,149
1991	Dance Smartly	3	8	8	0	0	2,876,821
1992	A.P. Indy	3	7	5	0	1	2,622,560
1993	Bertrando	4	9	3	4	1	2,217,800
1994	Concern	3	14	3	5	6	2,541,670
1995	Cigar	5	10	10	0	0	4,819,800
1996	Cigar	6	8	5	2	1	4,910,000
1997	Skip Away	4	11	4	5	2	4,089,000
1998	Silver Charm	5	9	6	2	0	4,696,506
1999	Almutawakel	4	4	1	1	1	3,290,000

*Foreign bred

SOURCE: *American Racing Manual* (1992) and Jockey Club Information Systems.

APPENDIX TABLE 12-10   Leading Money-Winning Thoroughbred Horses of North America with Earnings of at Least $3 million, through 1998.

Horse	Starts	1st place	2d place	3d place	Amount won
Cigar	33	19	4	5	$9,999,815
Skip Away	38	18	10	6	9,616,360
Silver Charm	24	11	7	2	6,683,006
Alysheba	26	11	8	2	6,679,242
John Henry	83	39	15	9	6,591,860
Sunday Silence	14	9	5	0	4,968,554
Easy Goer	20	14	5	1	4,873,770
Spend a Buck	15	10	3	2	4,220,689
Creme Fraiche	64	17	12	13	4,024,727
Unbridled	24	8	6	6	4,489,475
Ferdinand	29	8	9	6	3,777,978
Slew o' Gold	21	12	5	1	3,533,534
Precisionist	46	20	10	4	3,485,393
Snow Chief	24	13	3	5	3,383,210
Cryptoclearance	44	12	10	7	3,376,327
Black Tie Affair	45	18	9	6	3,370,694
Bet Twice	26	10	6	4	3,308,599
Steinlen	45	20	10	7	3,300,100
Gulch	32	13	8	4	3,095,521
Dance Smartly (F)	13	11	1	1	3,083,456
Lady's Secret (F)	45	25	9	3	3,021,425
All Along (F)	21	9	4	2	3,015,764

NOTE: F = filly.

SOURCE: *Blood-Horse*, Feb. 27, 1999.

Appendix Table 12-11 Annual Thoroughbred Champions

Year	2-year-old colt or gelding	2-year-old filly	Best 2-year-old	3-year-old colt or gelding	3-year-old filly	Best 3-year-old
1957	Nadir	Idun	Idun	Bold Ruler	Bayou	Bold Ruler
1958	First Landing	Quill	First Landing	Tim Tam	Idun	Tim Tam
1959	Warfare	My Dear Girl	Warefare	Sword Dancer	Royal Native	Sword Dancer
1960	Hail to Reason	Bowl of Flowers	Hail to Reason	Kelso	Berlo	Kelso
1961	Crimson Satan	Cicada	Crimson Satan	Carry Back	Bowl of Flowers	Carry Back
1962	Never Bend	Smart Deb	Never Bend	Jaipur	Cicada	Jaipur
1963	Hurry to Market	Tosmah	Hurry to Market	Chateaugay	Lamb Chop	Chateaugay
1964	Bold Lad	Queen Empress	Bold Lad	Northern Dancer	Tosmah	Northern Dancer
1965	Buckpasser	Mocassin	Buckpasser	Tom Rolfe	What A Treat	Tom Rolfe
1966	Successor	Regal Gleam	Successor	Buckpasser	Lady Pitt	Buckpasser
1967	Vitriolic	Queen of the Stage	Vitriolic	Damascus	Furl Sail	Damascus
1968	Top Knight	Gallant Bloom	Top Knight	Stage Door Johnny	Dark Mirage	Dark Mirage
1969	Blent Screen	Fast Attack	Silent Screen	Arts and Letters	Gallant Bloom	Arts and Letters
1970	Hoist the Flag	Forward Gal	Hoist the Flag	Personality	Office Queen	Personality

Year	2-year-old colt or gelding	2-year-old filly	3-year-old colt or gelding	3-year-old filly	Older colt, horse, or gelding
1971	Riva Ridge	Numbered Account	Canonero II	Turkish Trouser	Ack Ack
1972	Secretariat	La Prevoyante	Key to the Mint	Susan's Girl	Autobiography
1973	Protagonist	Talking Picture	Secretariat	Desert Vixen	Riva Ridge
1974	Foolish Pleasure	Ruffian	Little Current	Chris Evert	Forego
1975	Honest Pleasure	Dearly Precious	Wajima	Ruffian	Forego
1976	Seattle Slew	Sensational	Bold Forbes	Revidere	Forego
1977	Affirmed	Lakeville Miss	Seattle Slew	Our Mims	Forego

(continued)

APPENDIX TABLE 12-11 Annual Thoroughbred Champions (*Continued*)

Year	2-year-old colt or gelding	2-year-old filly	3-year-old colt or gelding	3-year-old filly	Older colt, horse, or gelding
1978	Spectacular Bid	Candy Eclair and It's In the Air	Affirmed	Tempest Queen	Seattle Slew
1979	Rockhill Native	Smart Angle	Spectacular Bid	Davona Dale	Affirmed

Year	Handicap horse	Handicap mare	Sprinters	Grass horse	Steeplechaser or hurdler	Horse of year
1957	Dedicate	Pucker Up	Decathalon	Round Table	Neji	Bold Ruler
1958	Round Table	Barnastar	Bold Ruler	Round Table	Neji	Round Table
1959	Sword Dancer	Tempted	Intentionally	Round Table	Ancestor	Sword Dancer
1960	Bold Eagle	Royal Native			Benguala	Kelso
1961	Kelso	Airman's Guide		TV Lark	Peal	Kelso
1962	Kelso	Primonetta			Barnaby's Bluff	Kelso
1963	Kelso	Cicada		Mongo	Amber Driver	Kelso
1964	Kelso	Tosmah			Bon Nouvel	Kelso
1965	Roman Brother	Old Hat	Affectionately	Parka	Bon Nouvel	Roman Brother
1966	Buckpasser	Open Fire	Impressive	Assaagai	Tuscalee and Mako	Buckpasser
1967	Damascus	Straight Deal	Dr. Fager	Fort Marcy	Quick Pitch	Damascus
1968	Dr. Fager	Gamely	Dr. Fager	Dr. Fager	Bon Nouvel	Dr. Fager
1969	Arts and Letters	Gallant Bloom	Ta Wee	Hawaii	L'Escargot	Arts and Letters
1970	Fort Marcy	Shuvee	Ta Wee	Fort Marcy	Top Bid	Fort Marcy

Year	Older filly or mare	Grass horse	Sprinter	Steeplechaser or hurdler	Horse of year
1971	Shuvee	Run the Gauntlet	Ack Ack	Shadow Brook	Ack Ack
1972	Typecast	Cougar II	Chou Croute	Soothsayer	Secretariat
1973	Susan's Girl	Secretariat	Shecky Greene	Athenian Idol	Secretariat
1974	Desert Vixen	Dahlia	Forego	Gran Kan	Forego
1975	Susan's Girl	Snow Knight	Gallant Bob	Life's Illusion	Forego
1976	Proud Delta	Youth	My Juliet	Fire Control and Straight and True	Forego
1977	Cascapedia	Johnny D.	What A Summer	Cafe Prince	Seattle Slew
1978	Late Bloomer	Mac Diaimida	Dr. Patches and J. O. Tobin	Cafe Prince	Affirmed
1979	Waya	Bowl Game (M) Trillion (F)	Star De Naskra	Martie's Anger	Affirmed

Year	2-year-old colt or gelding	2-year-old filly	3-year-old colt or gelding	3-year-old filly	Older colt, horse, or gelding
1980	Lord Avie	Heavenly Cause	Temperance Hill	Genuine Risk	Spectacular Bid
1981	Deputy Minister	Before Dawn	Pleasant Colony	Wayward Lass	John Henry
1982	Roving Boy	Landaluce	Conquistador Cielo	Christmas Past	Lemhi Gold
1983	Devil's Bag	Althea	Slew o' Gold	Heartlight No. One	Bates Motel
1984	Chief's Crown	Outstandingly	Swale	Life's Magic	Slew o' Gold
1985	Tasso	Family Style	Spend a Buck	Mom's Command	Vanlandingham
1986	Capote	Brave Raj	Snow Chief	Tiffany Lass	Turkoman
1987	Forty Niner	Epitome	Alysheba	Sacahuista	Ferdinand
1988	Easy Goer	Open Mind	Risen Star	Winning Colors	Alysheba
1989	Rhythm	Go for Wand	Sunday Silence	Open Mind	Blushing John
1990	Fly So Free	Meadow Star	Unbridled	Go for Wand	Criminal Type

(continued)

Year	2-year-old colt or gelding	2-year-old filly	3-year-old colt or gelding	3-year-old filly	Older colt, horse, or gelding
1991	Arazi	Pleasant Stage	Hansel	Dance Smartly	Black Tie Affair
1992	Gilded Time	Eliza	A. P. Indy	Saratoga Dew	Pleasant Tap
1993	Dehere	Phone Chatter	Prairie Bayou	Hollywood Wildcat	Bertrando
1994	Timber Country	Flanders	Holy Bull	Heavenly Prize	The Wicked North
1995	Maria's Man	Golden Attraction	Thunder Gulch	Serena's Song	Cigar
1996	Boston Harbor	Storm Song	Skip Away	Yanks Music	Cigar
1997	Favorite Trick	Countess Diana	Silver Charm	Ajina	Skip Away
1998	Answer Lively	Silverbulletday	Real Quiet	Banshee Breeze	Skip Away

Year	Older filly or mare	Grass horse	Sprinter	Steeplechaser or hurdler	Horse of year
1980	Glorious Song	John Henry (M) Just A Game II (F)	Plugged Nickle	Zaccio	Spectacular Bid
1981	Relaxing	John Henry (M) De La Rose (F)	Guilty Conscience	Zaccio	John Henry
1982	Track Robbery	Perrault (M) April Run (F)	Gold Beauty	Zaccio	Conquistador Cielo
1983	Ambassador of Luck	John Henry (M) All Along (F)	Chinook Pass	Flatterer	All Along
1984	Princess Rooney	John Henry (M) Royal Heroine (F)	Eillo	Flatterer	John Henry
1985	Life's Magic	Cozzene (M) Pebbles (F)	Precisionist	Flatterer	Spend a Buck
1986	Lady's Secret	Manila (M) Estrapade (F)	Smile	Flatterer	Lady's Secret

1987	North Sider	Theatrical (M) Miesque (F)	Groovy	Inlander	Ferdinand
1988	Personal Ensign	S'nshine F've (M) Miesque (F)	Gulch	Jimmy Lorenzo	Alysheba
1989	Bayakoa	Steinlen (M) Brown Bess (F)	Safely Kept	Highland Bud	Sunday Silence
1990	Bayakoa	Itsalgrktome (M) Laugh and Be Merry (F)	Housebuster	Morley Street	Criminal Type
1991	Queena	Tight Spot (M) Miss Alleged (F)	Housebuster	Morley Street	Black Tie Affair
1992	Paseana	Sky Classic (M) Flawlessly (F)	Rubiano	Lonesome Glory	A. P. Indy
1993	Paseana	Kotashaan (M) Flawlessly (F)	Cardmania	Lonesome Glory	Kotashaan
1994	Sky Beauty	Paradise Creek (M) Hatoof (F)	Cherokee Run	Warm Spell	Holy Bull
1995	Inside Information	Northern Spur (M) Possibly Perfect (F)	Not Surprising	Lonesome Glory	Cigar
1996	Jewel Princess	Singspiel (M) Wandesta (F)	Lit de Justice	Corregio	Cigar
1997	Hidden Lake	Chief Bearheart (M) Ryafan (F)	Smoke Glacken	Lonesome Glory	Favorite Trick
1998	Escena	Buck's Boy (M) Fiji (F)	Reraise	Flat Top	Skip Away

NOTE: M = mare, F = filly. Beginning with 1971, the annual champions were determined in a combined poll of the staff members of the *Daily Racing Form*, the Board of Selection of the Thoroughbred Racing Associations, and members of the National Turf Writers Association.

SOURCE: *American Racing Manual* (1992) and Jockey Club Information Services.

APPENDIX TABLE 12-12   Annual Leading Thoroughbred Sire, Money Won, 1955–1999

Year	Horse	Performers sired	Races won	Amount
1955	Nasrullah	40	69	$1,433,660
1956	Nasrullah	50	106	1,462,413
1957	Princequillo	75	147	1,698,427
1958	Princequillo	65	110	1,394,540
1959	Nasrullah	69	141	1,434,543
1960	Nasrullah	64	122	1,419,683
1961	Ambiorix	73	148	936,976
1962	Nasrullah	62	107	1,474,831
1963	Bold Ruler	26	56	917,531
1964	Bold Ruler	44	88	1,457,156
1965	Bold Ruler	51	90	1,091,924
1966	Bold Ruler	51	107	2,306,523
1967	Bold Ruler	63	135	2,249,272
1968	Bold Ruler	57	99	1,988,427
1969	Bold Ruler	59	90	1,357,144
1970	Hail to Reason	53	82	1,400,839
1971	Northern Dancer	44	93	1,288,580
1972	Round Table	65	98	1,199,933
1973	Bold Ruler	41	74	1,488,622
1974	TV Lark	90	101	2,011,878
1976	What a Pleasure	85	108	1,622,159
1977	Dr. Fager	79	124	1,593,079
1978	Exclusive Native	63	106	1,969,867
1979	Exclusive Native	71	104	2,872,605
1980	Raja Baba	108	149	2,483,352
1981	Nodouble	92	115	2,800,884
1982	His Majesty	56	86	2,675,823
1983	Halo	69	86	2,773,637
1984	Seattle Slew	46	49	5,361,259
1985	Buckaroo	49	50	4,145,272
1986	Lyphard	50	49	4,051,985
1987	Mr. Prospector	81	104	5,877,385
1988	Mr. Prospector	82	106	8,986,790
1989	Halo	93	114	7,520,142
1990	Alydar	98	111	6,378,760
1991	Danzig	68	109	6,214,669
1992	Danzig	107	74	6,940,248
1993	Danzig	114	72	7,198,561
1994	Broad Brush	92	72	5,400,326
1995	Palace Music	50	23	5,333,576
1996	Cozzene	105	60	5,173,595
1997	Deputy Minister	103	60	8,588,905
1998	Deputy Minister	96	46	8,567,723
1999	Storm Cat	120	71	10,374,436

SOURCE: *American Racing Manual* (1992) and Jockey Club Information Systems.

APPENDIX TABLE 12-13   Annual Stakes, Winning Jockey Riding Thoroughbreds, Money Won (total winners' value)

Year	Jockey	Stakes won	Total win value
1935	Wright, W. D.	18	$ 122,150
1936	Richards, H.	14	173,470
1937	Kurtsinger, C.	16	259,820
1938	Wall, N.	19	286,170
1939	Stout, J.	15	231,985
1940	Arcaro, E.	16	170,165
1941	Arcaro, E.	15	229,975
1942	Woolf, G.	23	341,680
1943	Longden, J.	20	290,222
1944	Woolf, G.	14	338,135
1945	Longden, J.	24	528,220
1946	Arcaro, E.	21	404,380
1947	Dodson, D.	35	899,915
1948	Arcaro, E.	35	1,082,585
1949	Brooks, S.	26	728,335
1950	Arcaro, E.	30	689,035
1951	Arcaro, E.	18	531,250
1952	Arcaro, E.	40	1,172,404
1953	Arcaro, E.	20	839,734
1954	Arcaro, E.	29	895,690
1955	Arcaro, E.	34	1,226,657
1956	Hartack, W.	26	1,037,077
1957	Hartack, W.	43	1,718,231
1958	Shoemaker, W.	36	1,600,503
1959	Shoemaker, W.	29	1,034,422
1960	Ussery, R.	20	931,441
1961	Shoemaker, W.	25	1,156,470
1962	Shoemaker, W.	38	1,474,516
1963	Shoemaker, W.	32	996,785
1964	Shoemaker, W.	34	1,243,827
1965	Baeza, B.	24	1,085,661
1966	Shoemaker, W.	37	1,303,787
1967	Shoemaker, W.	38	1,629,874
1968	Baeza, B.	25	1,181,745
1969	Rotz, J. L.	20	931,565
1970	Rotz, J. L.	24	1,031,548
1971	Shoemaker, W.	46	1,567,295
1972	Turcotte, R.	21	1,226,282
1973	Turcotte, R.	16	1,087,397
1974	Pincay, L., Jr.	38	1,427,407
1975	Shoemaker, W.	29	1,353,655

APPENDIX TABLE 12-13   Annual Stakes, Winning Jockey Riding Thoroughbreds, Money Won (total winners' value) (*continued*)

Year	Jockey	Stakes won	Total win value
1976	Shoemaker, W.	30	$ 1,569,960
1977	Shoemaker, W.	30	1,590,920
1978	McHargue, D. G.	37	1,662,595
1979	Pincay, L., Jr.	44	2,720,006
1980	Shoemaker, W.	35	2,381,656
1981	Shoemaker, W.	31	2,723,656
1982	Pincay, L., Jr.	45	3,598,505
1983	Pincay, L., Jr.	40	3,031,664
1984	McCarron, C. J.	54	5,171,280
1985	Velasquez, J.	57	7,777,864
1986	Day, P.	55	6,606,225
1987	Day, P.	50	8,842,944
1988	McCarron, C. J.	39	10,286,220
1989	Day, P.	50	8,763,556
1990	Perret, C.	57	9,170,233
1991	Day, P.	60	8,887,080
1992	Desormeau, K.	46	7,784,868
1993	Smith, M.	62	7,835,559
1994	Smith, M.	67	9,985,703
1995	Bailey, J.	40	10,116,581
1996	Bailey, J.	56	10,507,395
1997	Stevens, G.	47	10,452,816
1998	Stevens, G.	54	12,059,492
1999	Day, P.	48	18,094,195

SOURCE: *American Racing Manual* (1996), and Jockey Club Information Systems.

APPENDIX TABLE 12-14   Annual Leading Trainer of Thoroughbreds, Money Won

Year	Trainer	Starts	Number of wins	Amount won
1908	Rowe, J.		50	$ 284,335
1909	Hildreth, S. C.		73	123,942
1910	Hildreth, S. C.		84	148,010
1911	Hildreth, S. C.		67	49,418
1912	Schorr, J. F.		63	58,110
1913	Rowe, J.		18	45,936
1914	Benson, R. C.		45	59,315
1915	Rowe, J.		19	75,596
1916	Hildreth, S. C.		39	70,750
1917	Hildreth, S. C.		23	61,698
1918	Bedwell, H. G.		53	80,296
1919	Bedwell, H. G.		63	208,728

Year	Trainer	Starts	Number of wins	Amount won
1920	Feustal, L.		22	186,087
1921	Hildreth, S. C.		85	262,768
1922	Hildreth, S. C.		74	247,014
1923	Hildreth, S. C.		75	392,124
1924	Hildreth, S. C.		77	255,608
1925	Tompkins, G. R.		30	199,245
1926	Harlan, S. P.		21	205,681
1927	Bringloe, W. H.		63	216,563
1928	Schorr, J. F.		65	258,425
1929	Rowe, J., Jr.		25	314,881
1930	Fitzsimmons, J.		47	397,335
1931	Healy, J. W.		33	297,300
1932	Fitzsimmons, J.		68	266,650
1933	Smith, R. A.		53	135,720
1934	Smith, R. A.		43	249,938
1935	Stotler, J. H.		87	303,005
1936	Fitzsimmons, J.		42	193,415
1937	McGarvey, R.		46	209,925
1938	Sande, E. H.		15	226,495
1939	Fitzsimmons, J.		45	266,205
1940	Smith, T.		14	269,200
1941	Jones, B. A.		70	475,318
1942	Gaver, J. M.		48	406,547
1943	Jones, B. A.		73	267,915
1944	Jones, B. A.		60	601,660
1945	Smith, T.		52	510,655
1946	Jacobs, H.		99	560,077
1947	Jones, H. A.		85	1,334,805
1948	Jones, H. A.		81	1,118,670
1949	Jones, H. A.		76	978,587
1950	Burch, P. M.		96	637,754
1951	Gaver, J. M.		42	616,392
1952	Jones, B. A.		29	662,137
1953	Trotsek, H.		54	1,028,873
1954	Molter, W.		136	1,107,860
1955	Fitzsimmons, J.		66	1,270,055
1956	Molter, W.		142	1,227,402
1957	Jones, H. A.		70	1,150,910
1958	Molter, W.		69	1,116,544
1959	Molter, W.		71	847,290
1960	Jacobs, H.		97	748,349
1961	Jones, H. A.		62	759,856
1962	Tenney, M. A.		58	1,099,474
1963	Tenney, M. A.	192	40	860,703

(continued)

APPENDIX TABLE 12-14   Annual Leading Trainer of Thoroughbreds, Money
Won (*Continued*)

Year	Trainer	Starts	Number of wins	Amount won
1964	Winfrey, W. C.	287	61	$ 1,350,534
1965	Jacobs, H.	610	91	1,331,528
1966	Neloy, E. A.	282	93	2,456,250
1967	Neloy, E. A.	262	72	1,776,089
1968	Neloy, E. A.	212	52	1,233,101
1969	Burch, E.	156	26	1,067,936
1970	Whittingham, C.	551	82	1,302,354
1971	Whittingham, C.	393	77	1,737,115
1972	Whittingham, C.	429	79	1,734,028
1973	Whittingham, C.	423	85	1,865,385
1974	Martin, F.	846	166	2,408,411
1975	Whittingham, C.	487	93	2,437,244
1976	Van Berg, J.	2,362	496	2,976,196
1977	Barrera, L. S.	781	127	2,715,848
1978	Barrera, L. S.	592	100	3,314,564
1979	Barrera, L. S.	492	98	3,608,517
1980	Barrera, L. S.	559	99	2,969,151
1981	Whittingham, C.	376	74	3,993,302
1982	Whittingham, C.	410	63	4,587,457
1983	Lukas, D. W.	595	78	4,267,261
1984	Lukas, D. W.	805	131	5,835,921
1985	Lukas, D. W.	1,140	218	11,155,188
1986	Lukas, D. W.	1,510	259	12,344,595
1987	Lukas, D. W.	1,735	343	17,502,110
1988	Lukas, D. W.	1,500	318	17,842,358
1989	Lukas, D. W.	1,398	305	16,103,998
1990	Lukas, D. W.	1,396	267	14,508,871
1991	Lukas, D. W.	1,497	289	15,942,223
1992	Lukas, D. W.	1,349	230	9,806,436
1993	Frankel, R.	346	79	8,880,000
1994	Lukas, D. W.	693	147	9,250,000
1995	Lukas, D. W.	840	194	12,858,429
1996	Lukas, D. W.	1,008	192	15,967,609
1997	Lukas, D. W.	854	175	10,351,397
1998	Baffert, B.	538	139	15,000,870
1999	Baffert, B.	735	169	16,934,607

NOTE: No starts records exist prior to 1963.
SOURCE: *American Racing Manual* (1992) and Jockey Club Information Systems.

APPENDIX TABLE: 12-15 A History of Standard-Bred Record Speed: 1890–1998

	2-year-old		3-year-old		Aged		2:00 miles
	C & G	F	C & G	F	S & G	M	
Pacers							
1890	2:16 ½	2:24 ½	2:14 ¼	2:14	2:06 ¼	2:10	None
1900	2:07 ¾	2:10 ½	2:05 ½	2:09 ¼	2:00 ½	2:04 ½	None
1910	2:07 ¾	2:08 ¾	2:05 ½	2:06 ¼	1:55 ¼	2:00 ¼	5
1920	2:07 ¾	2:08 ¾	2:01 ¼	2:00 ¾	1:55 ¼	1:58 ¼	5
1930	2:04 ¼	2:04 ¾	1:59 ½	2:00 ¾	1:55 ¼	1:58 ¼	5
1940	2:00 ¾	2:02 ¾	1:57 ¾	1:59 ¾	1:55	1:56 ¾	8
1950	2:00 ⅘	2:00 ⅘	1:57 ¾	1:59 ¾	1:55	1:56 ¾	22
1960	1:57	1:58 ½	1:55 ⅗	1:57	1:54 ⅗	1:56 ¾	106
1970	1:57	1:57 ½	1:54	1:56 ⅖	1:53 ⅗	1:56 ¾	287
1980	1:54	1:56 ½	1:49 ⅘	1:53 ⅗	1:52	1:52 ⅖	3,760
1986	1:53	1:53 ⅗	1:49 ⅘	1:51 ⅗	1:51 ½	1:52 ⅗	14,761
1998	1:50	1:51.2	1:48.2	1:49.4	1:46.1	1:49.2	38,724
Trotters							
1890	2:20 ¾	2:18	2:12	2:10 ½	2:10	2:08 ¾	None
1900	2:10 ¾	2:14	2:10 ½	2:08 ¾	2:03 ¼	2:08 ¾	None
1910	2:09 ½	2:07 ¾	2:04 ¾	2:06 ½	1:58 ¾	1:58 ½	1
1920	2:04 ½	2:04 ¼	2:03 ½	2:02 ¼	1:58	1:58 ½	None

(continued)

APPENDIX TABLE: 12-15   A History of Standard-Bred Record Speed: 1890–1998 (*Continued*)

	2-year-old		3-year-old		Aged		2:00 miles
	C & G	F	C & G	F	S & G	M	
Trotters							
1930	2:02 ¾	2:02	1:59 ¾	1:59 ½	1:56 ¾	1:58 ½	4
1940	2:02	2:02	1:58 ½	1:59 ¼	1:55 ¼	1:58 ¼	2
1950	2:00	2:02	1:58	1:59 ¼	1:55 ¼	1:56 ¾	4
1960	2:00	1:59 ⅘	1:58	1:58	1:55 ¼	1:56 ¾	14
1970	1:58 ⅖	1:58 ⅗	1:56 ⅖	1:58	1:54 ⅘	1:56 ¾	19
1980	1:57	1:56 ⅗	1:55	1:56 ⅗	1:54 ⅘	1:56 ¾	138
1986	1:55 ⅗	1:56 ⅘	1:53 ⅖	1:53 ⅘	1:54	1:55 ⅖	711
1998	1:53.2	1:55	1:52.1	1:52.1	1:51	1:51.4	3,784

NOTE: The fastest mile (whether a time trial or a race mile) for each age and sex, by gait, is charted. In addition, the chart shows the total number of 2:00 miles for each of year shown. C = colt, G = gelding, F = filly, S = stallion, and M = mare.

SOURCE: United States Trotting Association.

APPENDIX TABLE 12-16 Harness Racing Records through 1986

Fastest mile:	Cambest, Springfield, Ill, August, 1993, T1:46.1
Fastest race mile:	Jenna's Beach Boy, The Meadowlands, June, 1996, 1:47.3
Fastest trotting mile:	Pine Chip, The Red Mile, October, 1994, TT1:51
Most money won (pacer):	Nihilator, $3,225,653
Most money won (trotter):	Peace Corps, $4,137,737
Most money won (driver):	John Campbell, $166,153,825
Most 2:00 Lifetime miles (horse):	Sharp Kosmos, 86
Most 2:00 Lifetime miles (driver):	John Campbell, 7,372
Most 2:00 All-time miles (track):	The Meadowlands, 42,096
Most lifetime wins (horse):	Symbol Allen, 241 (modern record)
Most lifetime wins (horse):	Goldsmith Maid, 350 (historic record)
Most lifetime wins (driver):	Herve Filion, 14,783
Record attendance (night):	Roosevelt Raceway, 54,861, August 20, 1960
Record attendance (day):	Delaware County Fair, 56,129, September 18, 1997
Record handle:	The Meadowlands, $6,771,449, July 15, 1995
Record auction price (yearling):	Laugh A Day, $625,000, 1983
Record auction price (racehorse):	Bree's Brief, $505,000, 1985
Record auction price (broodmare):	Winkys Gill, $800,000, 1986
Top Purse:	$2,161,000, Woodrow Wilson Pace, The Meadowlands, 1984 (won by Nihilator)

SOURCE: United States Trotting Association.

APPENDIX 12-2

Glossary of Dressage Terms

Change of leg   Change of leading leg at the canter.

Collected gait   Remaining on the bit, the horse moves forward with its neck raised and arched as a result of energetic impulsion. Lightness of forehand, engagement of hindquarters are called for. Shorter strides, but lighter and more mobile.

Counter-canter   A suppling movement deliberately asking for the opposite of the normal lead, such as right lead on a circle to the left.

Extended gait   Covering as much ground as possible, lengthening strides to the utmost while maintaining the same rhythm.

Free walk   A relaxed gait in which the horse is allowed complete freedom to stretch out and lower its head and neck.

Half-pass   A variation of travers, executed on the diagonal instead of along the wall. The horse, slightly bent round the inside leg of the rider, should be as close as possible parallel to the long sides of the arena, the forehand slightly in advance of the quarters.

Lateral movement   Work on two tracks, in which the horse is bent uniformly from poll to tail and moves with the forehand and quarters on two different tracks. Shoulder-in, haunches-in (travers), haunches-out (renvers), and half-passes are the lateral movements.

Medium gait   Between the collected and extended.

Passage   A measured, very collected, very elevated, and very cadenced trot, characterized by a pronounced engagement of the quarters, a more accentuated flexion of the knees and hocks, and the graceful elasticity of the movements.

Piaffe   A highly measured, collected, elevated, and cadenced trot on the spot.

Pirouette   Circle executed on two tracks, with a radius equal to the length of the horse, the forehand moving around the haunches, and maintaining the exact rhythm and sequence of footfalls of the gait being used.

Rein back   Backward movement in which hooves are raised and set down almost simultaneously by diagonal pairs.

Renvers (haunches-out)   The inverse movement in relation to travers, with the tail instead of the head to the wall.

Serpentine   Series of equal curves from one side of the centerline to the other, changing the direction of the turn each time the horse passes over the center line.

Shoulder-in   The horse is slightly bent round the inside leg of the rider, and its inside legs pass and cross in front of the outside legs. The horse is looking away from the direction in which it is moving.

Transition   Change of gait or speed.

Travers (haunches-in)   The horse is lightly bent around the inside leg of the rider. Its outside legs pass and cross in front of the inside legs. The horse is looking in the direction in which it is moving. Performed along the wall or on the center line, at an angle of about 30° to the direction in which the horse is moving.

Volte   Circle of 6 meters diameter (20 feet).

Working gait   Regular and unconstrained, energetic but calm, with even, elastic steps.

APPENDIX 12-3

Glossary of Racing Terms

Acey-Deucey   Jockeys with their stirrups at uneven levels, the inside or left iron lower than the right, ride *acey-deucey*.

Age   The age of a racehorse is recorded as beginning on January 1 of the year in which the horse is foaled (born). Even if a horse is foaled December 31, it is considered 1 year old on January 1 (breeding is planned to avoid this).

Backside   The stable and training area of a racetrack.

Bleeder   A horse that bleeds after or during a workout or race; the result of a nasal hemorrhage caused from a ruptured throat vein.

Blowout   A brief final drill (usually 3 to 4 furlongs, or 0.6 to 0.8 km) two days or the day before a race designed to further sharpen or maintain an edge of conditioning for the impending contest.

Bolt   When a horse swerves sharply from the regular course, it is said to have *bolted*.

Brace bandages   Resilient bandages on the legs of horses worn in some cases in an effort to support lame legs, worn in other cases to protect a horse from cutting and skinning its legs while racing.

Breaking   When a horse leaves its gait and breaks into a gallop, it is *breaking*. A trotter or pacer must remain on that gait in a race. If it makes a *break*, the driver must immediately pull it back to its gait.

Breeder   The breeder of a horse is considered to be the owner of its dam, at the time of service.

Breeze, Breezing   An easy workout under stout restraint by the exercise rider to stabilize an already sharp horse's condition between engagements.

Bug boy   An apprentice jockey, so-called because of the "bug" or asterisk denoting the 5-pound weight allowance in the official program.

Chalk   The favorite or most heavily played horse in a race. The term originated in the days of bookmakers, when the odds were written on slates with chalk.

814

Check rein A line running from the bit to the top of the horse's head, then to the saddle hook to keep a horse's head up. Trotters and pacers commonly race with heads high to maintain a balanced, reaching stride.

Chute The straightaway entering onto the main oval track for races at 6 furlongs (1.2 km) (starting on backstretch) and 10 furlongs (2 km) (beginning at left of grandstand).

Climbing A Thoroughbred is said to be *climbing* when striding in an unnatural, upward fashion, not reaching out forward as in a coordinated gait.

Clocker The clocker times a horse's workouts, and these times are published for the benefit of the public. Almost all workouts are taken early in the morning during training hours.

Colors The jockey's silk or nylon jacket and cap provided by the owner.

Colt (c) A male horse between 2 and 3 years of age.

Coupled entry Two or more horses belonging to the same owner or trained by the same person are said to be *coupled*, and they run as an *entry* comprising a single betting unit. Their program number, regardless of post position, would be "1" and "1A." A second entry in the race would be listed in the program as "2" and "2B." A bet on one horse of a coupled entry is a bet on both.

Crab bit A bit with prongs extending at the horse's nose. Its purpose is to tip the horse's head up and help prevent it from ducking its head, bowing its neck, and pulling hard on the rein.

Cross Where a jockey joins the reins is his or her "cross." American riders generally ride with a shorter "cross" than elsewhere in the world.

Cushion The loose top surface of the racetrack.

Darby A stakes race exclusively for 3-year-olds.

Dash A race decided in a single trial.

Dead heat When the photofinish camera shows two horses inseparable at the finish, the race is declared a *dead heat,* or tie.

Declaration Withdrawing an entered horse from a race before the closing of overnight entries. A horse that has been withdrawn is said to have been *declared.*

Driving An all-out effort by horse and/or jockey.

Elbow boots Sheepskin-lined pads worn high on front legs to protect elbows (points at rear and bottom of shoulders) from the front feet as they are folded back in top stride. Needed on high-gaited trotters.

Field The entire group of starters in a race is known collectively as the *field.*

Field horses Two or more horses coupled as one betting interest. A *field* appears when there are more than ten entries in a race. Horse number 10 on the program and over are the *field.* A bet on one field horse is bet on all field horses.

Filly (f) A female horse between 2 and 3 years of age.

Foul Any action by any jockey that tends to hinder another jockey or any horse in the proper running of the race.

Free-for-all Horses (or races for such horses) that have won considerable money and must race in fast classes. Means "free for all to enter and open to all horses, regardless of earnings."

Free-legged pacer A pacer that races without hobbles.

Futurity A stakes race exclusively for 2-year-olds.

Gaiting strap Strap strung inside shafts of sulky to keep the horse from swinging the rear end to the right and left and traveling sideways on its gait.

Green horse A horse that has never trotted or paced in a public race or against time.

Handle   The aggregate amount of money passing in and out of the parimutuel machines for a given period—a race, a day, a meeting, or a season.

Head pole   A cue (usually a billiard cue with a hole bored in the handle to accommodate a leather thong) fastened alongside horse's head and neck to keep its head straight.

Heat   One trip in a race that will be decided by winning two or more trials.

Hind shin boots   Leather protecting guards on the lower hindlegs prevent cuts and bruises from the front shoes, which graze the hindlegs of some trotters.

Hobbles   Leather straps encircling the front and hind legs of a pacer on the same side to keep those legs moving in unison and to help the horse maintain gait. The straps running over the horse's back and to the haunches are known as *hobble hangers*.

Horse (h)   A male horse 4 years of age or older.

Impost   Weight assessment.

In the money   A horse finishing first, second, or third is *in the money*. To horsepeople, fourth and fifth are also included because the fourth- and fifth-place finishers also receive purse money.

Inquiry   In some races, even though the numbers of the first four horses to cross the finish line are posted on the tote (totalisator) board, the *official sign* (located on the tote board) is delayed due to the posting of the *inquiry sign*. The inquiry can originate from the stewards or an objection can be lodged by a jockey. Until the objection is resolved by the stewards, the result of the race is not official. The order of finish may stay the same or be revised to penalize a finisher that interfered with another horse during the running of a race. Once a decision is reached by the stewards, the *official sign* will replace the *inquiry sign*.

Irons   Stirrups.

Jog cart   A cart longer and heavier than a racing sulky, used in warm-up miles because it is more comfortable for the rider than a sulky.

Jogging   A slow warm-up or exercise for several miles, with the horse going the wrong way on the track.

Knee boots   Boots fitted around the knees and held up by suspenders (usually white) over the horse's withers. They protect the knees from blows from the opposite foot, especially on turns where a horse is more likely to break stride if it "brushes its knees."

Lead pad   A piece of equipment under the saddle in which thin slabs of lead may be inserted to bring the rider's weight up to that assigned a horse, in a specific race.

Lugging and pulling   Some horses pull on the reins, "lug" on one rein, or bear out or in with the driver or jockey, making it hard to drive or ride them and rate the race.

Lugging in or out   A horse is said to be "lugging in" or "lugging out" if it is pulling toward the inside or outside, respectively. A jockey or driver must make every effort to keep his mount on a straight course to prevent interference with other entrants.

Maiden   Horse, mare, or gelding that has never won a heat or race.

Mare (m)   A female horse 4 years of age or older.

Martingale   A strap running from the girth between the horse's front legs to the reins, which are threaded through the rings at the end of the martingale. Helps prevent the horse from tossing and raising its head.

Minus pool   When an outstanding horse is so heavily played that, after the deduction of the state tax and commission, not enough money remains in the pool to pay off the legally prescribed minimum, it is called a *minus pool*, and the racetrack or racing association makes up the difference.

Morning glory   A horse that performs well in morning workouts but fails to race to its potential in the afternoon.

Morning line   The approximate odds usually printed in the program and posted on the totalisator board prior to any betting. The morning line is a forecast of how it is believed the betting will go on a particular race.

Mutuel pool   The total amount wagered on a race in each ticket category (win-place-show). The total number of winning tickets in the *win* category share the entire pool equally. The same is true of the daily double and quinella pool. The *place* pool is divided into two parts, and the *show* pool into three parts, and divided among the holders with winning tickets on the horse involved.

Official   The designation given to the result of a race by the stewards when no occurrence has happened during the running that in their judgment would revise the actual order of finish, in terms of purse distribution to owners, and parimutuel payoffs paid to winning bettors.

Open bridle   A bridle without blinds or blinkers covering the eyes. Some bridles are rigged with blinds that shut off vision to the rear and side, and a few horses are raced with goggles or "peekaboo" blinds.

Overlay or underlay   A horse is called an *overlay* or an *underlay* in wagering parlance when its odds are, respectively, greater or less than those estimated by the track's official morning line maker.

Overnight   A race for which entries close 72 hours or less before the post time for the race on the day the race is to be run. Also, the mimeographed sheet available to horsepeople at the racing secretary's office showing the entries for the following day.

Overweight   Depending on the conditions of a race, each horse carries an assigned weight. When the jockey cannot make the weight, overweight is allowed, but not more than 5 pounds.

Owner   This includes sole owner, part owner, or lessee of a horse. An interest in the winnings of a horse does not constitute part ownership. The owner makes one of the greatest contributions to the sport of horse racing—he or she pays the bills! In all states, the owner must be licensed, of good reputation, and financially responsible.

Paddock   The area where the horses are saddled and viewed prior to the race. The paddock is always adjacent to the jockeys' quarters.

Parked out   Lapped on horses at the pole or rail so that there is no chance to get in. A horse parked out, or "on the limb," has farther to go and usually tires and falls back, unless it is far superior to the other horses in the race. The parked-out symbol is used in many past performance charts.

Post   The starting point for the race.

Post parade   The time before the race when the horses leave the paddock, come on the racetrack, and walk in front of the stands in order for everyone to have a look at them. The duration of the post parade is usually 10 minutes.

Post position   A horse's position in the starting gate from the inside rail outward is decided by a drawing at the close of entries, before the race. In Quarter Horse racing, every horse must maintain its position as nearly as possible in the lane in which it starts, from the gate down the straightaway to the finish.

Post time   The official time set by the stewards at which a race will start and at which horses are required to be at the post and ready to start.

Quarter boots   Close-fitting boots on the front heel to protect the tender quarter (heel of the foot) from being cut by the hind shoes.

Racing secretary   The official who writes the conditions for the races and assigns the weights for handicap races.

Racing strip   The track surface itself, which is made up of two parts. The bottom layer, called the *base*, is a mixture of sand and (mostly) clay. It supports the *cushion*, which is generally a 3-inch (76-mm) layer of topsoil mixed with sand. The cushion serves as a shock absorber to ease the intense striking force to which a horse's forelegs are subject when in full stride.

Router   A horse at its best over a "distance of ground" or more than a mile.

Scoring   Preliminary warming up of horses before the start. The horses are turned near the starting point and hustled away as they will be in the race.

Scratch   Racing's idiom for indicating that a horse is declared out of a race in which it was entered, after the entries were drawn.

Shadow roll   A large sheepskin-type roll worn just above a horse's nose and just below its eyes. It cuts off the horse's view of the track so that it will not shy at shadows, pieces of paper, or other objects.

Short   A Thoroughbred not advanced enough in its conditioning to run the complete distance of a race at its fastest often is termed a "short" horse.

Silks   Jockey's or driver's silks. *See* Colors.

Standardbred   Pure-bred trotting or pacing horses. A nonstandard horse is a crossbred horse or one that cannot be traced in breeding far enough to qualify for standard registration.

Starter   The starter is one of the track officials. He or she has complete jurisdiction over the starting of the horses and has the authority to give orders necessary to ensure a fair start. He or she directs the assistant starters, who lead each horse into the stall gate according to the post position corresponding to the draw made when the horses were entered. These people must know the horses and do any special handling required to get each horse safely into the gate.

Starting gate   Generally, an electromechanical device in which Quarter Horses and Thoroughbred horses are loaded. When they are all in and standing in an alert manner with their heads up, the starter presses a button that throws open all the stall doors simultaneously, a bell clangs, and the field is dispatched. Opening the gate activates the electric timer, which records the time of the race in 1/100ths of a second.

Stewards   Racetrack officials. A minimum of three stewards preside over the racing at all tracks, one of whom is a representative of the respective state racing commission. The word of the stewards in all matters is law. It is their duty to see that the race meeting is run according to the rules of racing. They rule on claims of foul or any protests and impose fines and suspensions. All fines and suspensions are reported by them to the state racing commission and in turn to the National Association of State Racing Commissioners, so that offenders may be barred from taking part in other race meetings in that state or any other during the period of suspension. The stewards have complete jurisdiction over a race meeting.

Stick   The jockey's whip (sometimes called a *bat*).

Sulky or bike   A light racing rig with bicycle-type wheels used in harness races. The sulkies weigh from 29 to 37 pounds (13.2 to 16.8 kg) and usually have hardwood shafts. Aluminum and steel sulkies have been introduced recently.

Tack   The saddle and other equipment worn by a horse during a race or exercise.

Toe weights   Brass or lead weights weighing from 2 to 4 ounces (56.7 to 113.4 gm). They are clipped to the edge of the front hoofs to extend a horse's stride.

Totalisator   An intricate piece of electronic equipment that records each wager and total wagering in the win, place, and show pools, and in other pools, as the parimutuel tickets are sold by a manually operated vending machine. This equipment also calculates the odds on each horse at given intervals, according to the amount wagered.

Totalisator, or "Tote," board   A display board in the infield, on which is posted, electronically, data essential to the racegoer, such as the approximate odds, total amount bet in each pool, track condition, post time, time of day, result of race, official sign or inquiry sign (if a foul is claimed), running time of each race, and the mutual payoff prices, after each race is declared official.

Track conditions

Fast   A track that is thoroughly dry and at its best. Footing is even.

Sloppy   During or immediately after a heavy rain; water has saturated the cushion and there may be puddles, but the base is still firm. Footing is splashy but even, and the running remains fast.

Muddy   Water has soaked into the base and it is soft and wet. Footing is deep and slow.

Heavy   A drying track that is muddy and drying out. Footing is heavy and sticky.

Slow   Still wet, between heavy and good. Footing is heavy.

Good   Rated between slow and fast. Moisture remains in the strip but footing is firm.

Off   An off track is anything other than fast. The usual progression of track conditions before and after a heavy rain is fast—sloppy—muddy—heavy—slow—good—fast.

Trainer   The person who conditions and prepares horses for racing; the coach.

Valet   An employee who takes care of a jockey's equipment, sees to it that the correct silks are at his or her locker, that the rider has the proper weight in his or her lead pad, carries the saddle and equipment to the paddock, helps the trainer saddle the horse, meets the rider after the race, and carries the saddle and equipment back to the jockey's room.

Walkover   A race from which all entrants but one have been withdrawn. Thus, the remaining horse need but "walk over" the prescribed course to win.

Weigh out   The procedure in which the racing official known as the clerk of the scales, before the race, checks the weights of jockeys and their riding equipment (saddle, pommel pad, girth) against the officially assigned weights to be carried by each horse in the race. These weights must agree. After the race, the jockeys and their riding equipment are weighed in. This procedure assures that the assigned weights are carried to the post and throughout the race.

Wheel   A horse, turning around suddenly, without guidance by its rider, is said to *wheel*.

APPENDIX 13-1

Glossary of Rodeo Terms

Added money   The purse, or the part of the total money put up by the committee.

All-Around World Champion   To be eligible for the title All-Around World Champion, a cowboy must compete in two events. The top money winner who competed in two or more events is the world champion.

Average   When a rodeo has more than one go-round in an event, the contestants are paid off for the best ride or time in each go-round and for the best average of all go-rounds. The winner of the average is the event winner.

Barrier   In the timed events, the stock is given a predetermined head start, depending on arena conditions, called the score and marked by the shoreline. A rope is stretched across the front of the box from which the contestant's horse will come out. The barrier rope is released by a measured length of twine that is pulled loose from the calf or steer as it crosses the score line.

Breaking the barrier   If the contestant rides through and breaks the barrier, before it is released, a penalty of 10 seconds is added to the contestant's total time.

Champion   Many rodeos award buckles or saddles to the champions of each event and to the all-around winner of the rodeo. The top 15 money winners in each event after the year's-end rodeo, the Grand National at the Cow Palace in San Francisco, are eligible to compete in the National Finals Rodeo (NFR), held in Las Vegas in early December.

Day money   The amount of prize money paid to the winners of each go-round.

Entry fee   The money paid by the contestant before he can compete at a rodeo. This is added to the prize money in that event. The size of the fee varies with the amount of the purse, ranging from $10 at the smallest rodeos to $200. Contestants must pay a separate entry fee for each event entered.

Hazer   The cowboy who rides on the opposite side of the steer to keep the steer from running away from the steer wrestler's horse.

Honda   The eye in one end of a rope through which the other end is passed to form the loop in a lariat.

Jackpot　An event for which no purse is put up by the rodeo. Winners split all or part of the entry fees.

No time　When a flag fieldman waves "no time," it means that the contestant has not caught or thrown the animal properly and receives no time on that animal in that go-round, but is still entitled to compete in the next go-round.

Pickup man　A mounted cowboy who helps the rider off a bronc when a ride is complete. The pickup man then pulls off the flank strap from the bronc and removes the bronc from the arena.

PRCA Champions　The top money winners in each event were called PRCA Champions during 1976–1978. (PRCA stands for Professional Rodeo Cowboys Association.)

Prize money　Money paid to the winners of the various events in a rodeo. It comprises the purse and the entry fees paid by the contestants. The split of the prize money depends on the total monies in a go-round. If it is under $2,000, it is split four ways: 40, 30, 20, and 10 percent. There is a fixed ratio for the number of monies paid and a set percentage, depending on total go-rounds and amount of prize money.

Pulling leather　When a saddle bronc rider touches any part of the saddle with a free hand, he or she is said to be pulling leather and is disqualified.

Reride　Another ride is given to a bronc or bull rider in the same go-round when the first ride was unsatisfactory for any of several reasons.

Rough stock events　The riding events: bareback riding, saddle bronc riding, and bull riding.

Score　The distance between the box opening and the score line, or head start, given the stock in the timed events.

Timed events　Calf roping, team roping, and steer wrestling.

World Champion　In 1976, under new championship regulations, the top 15 contestants in an event had an equal chance to become the World Champion of the event. The winner of the NFR was the World Champion. In 1979, the rules were changed, and the World Champion in each event is the largest money winner for the year.

APPENDIX 13-2

Glossary of Polo Terms

Appealing   Claims by players for a foul, generally expressed by the raising of mallets above the head or by a helicoptering motion.

Backshot   One of the basic strokes requiring a backhand swing, changing the flow of play by sending the ball in the opposite direction.

Ball   A polo ball is 3 to $3^1/_2$ inches in diameter and weighs $3^1/_2$ to $4^1/_2$ ounces.

Bump   A player is permitted to ride into another player so as to spoil his shot. The angle of the collision should not exceed 45°. The faster the horse travels, the smaller the angle must be.

Chukker   Also called a period. There are 6 chukkers in a game, each lasting 7 minutes, plus up to 30 seconds in overtime.

Field   The ground is 300 yards long and 160 yards wide.

Goal   Anytime a ball crosses the line between the goal posts, it is considered a goal.

Goal posts   Posts placed 8 yards apart and collapsible upon impact.

Handicap   All registered players are rated on a scale of minus 2 to 10 (higher means better player). The handicap of a team is the sum total rating of its players; in handicap matches, the team with the higher handicap gives the difference in rating to the other team.

Hook   A player may spoil another's hit by putting his mallet in the way of the striking player. A cross hook occurs when the player reaches over his opponent's mount in an attempt to hook. A cross hook is a foul.

Knock-in   Should a team in an offensive drive hit the ball across the opponents' back line, the defending team resumes the game with a free hit from their back line.

Line of the ball   This is the concept governing traffic on the field: the ball creates an imaginary line as it travels, and the other player or players established in this line have the right of way on the play.

Mallet   Also known as the stick, varies in length from 48 to 54 inches and is flexible. The shaft is made from bamboo cane and the head from either the bamboo root or a hard wood. The broadside of the head is used to strike the ball.

Near side   The left side of the horse.

Neck shot   A ball which is hit under the horse's neck from either side.

Off side   The right side of a horse.

Out-of-bounds   When a ball crosses the sidelines or goes over the sideboards, it is considered out-of-bounds and the umpire throws in another ball between the two teams at that point.

Penalty   A free hit toward the goal from a set distance. The severity of the foul committed determines what penalty will be awarded. The range is as follows:
  1) an automatic goal,
  2) a free hit from 30 yards to an undefended goal,
  3) a free hit from 40 yards to an undefended goal,
  4) a free hit from 60 yards to an undefended goal,
  5) a free hit from the point of the infraction or from midfield,
  6) safety.

Polo ponies   There is no height limit, but most are between 15 and 15.3 hands. Each player uses an average of six horses per match and rides a different one in each chukker.

Pony goal   A goal scored as the result of being deflected across the goal line by a pony's legs or feet.

Positions   Each of the four team members plays a distinctly different position. The players may momentarily change positions but will try and return to their initial assignments. Number one is the most forward offensive player. Number two is just as aggressive but plays deeper and harder. Number three is the pivot player between offense and defense and tries to run all plays to the offense. Number four, or the *back,* is the defensive player whose role is principally to protect the goal.

Ride-off   This occurs when two riders make contact and attempt to push each other off the line of the ball to prevent the other from striking.

Safety   Also known as penalty number 6. When a defending player hits the ball across his own back line, the other team is awarded a free hit 60 yards from the back line, with the ball placed at the same distance from the sidelines where it went out.

Sideboards   A nine- to eleven-inch board along the sidelines only. They are optional.

Sudden death   If a match is tied at the end of the sixth chukker, an overtime period(s) will be played until one of the teams scores, thus determining a winner.

Tail shot   Hitting the ball behind and across the horse's rump.

Teams   There are four players on a team.

Third man   The referee sitting at the sidelines. If and when the two umpires on the field are in disagreement, the third man makes the final decision.

Throw-in   A chukker and many plays begin at midfield, with the umpire bowling the ball between the two ready teams.

Time-out   An umpire calls time-out when a foul is committed, an accident occurs, or at his own discretion. A player may call time-out only if he has broken track or is injured. No time-out is allowed for changing horses or replacing a broken mallet.

Umpire   The two mounted officials on the field during the game.

APPENDIX 14-1

Semen Evaluation Procedures

To prepare for the semen evaluation, turn on all equipment and allow it to equilibrate to temperature or voltage. Place all glassware and supplies that will come in contact with the semen in an incubator set at 100°F (38°C). Remove from the freezer extenders to be used during the evaluation and thaw them. Then place them in the incubator. Prepare colorimetric tubes for concentration determinations. If the semen is to be used to inseminate a mare, prewarm all necessary supplies to 100°F (38°C) in the incubator.

Volume

The first step in evaluating semen is to determine the gel-free volume. Gently pour the semen into a graduated cylinder (Appendix Figure 14-1). To determine the gel volume, turn the filter upside down in a beaker until it all drains out. Then measure it in a graduated cylinder. After reading the volume, immediately return the cylinder to the incubator and record the volume on the semen evaluation record (Appendix Figure 14-2). Be sure that all the equipment that the semen touches is at the proper temperature and on a slide warmer to maintain the proper temperature.

Motility

As soon as the volume is determined, estimate motility. Stallion spermatozoa usually move in a straight line, but because of their abaxial midpieces, they may move in circles.

(a)

(b)

APPENDIX FIGURE 14-1 Semen volume determination: *(a)* semen is poured from the collection bulb into the filter; *(b)* gel-free semen is poured into a volumetric cylinder to determine volume and filter is placed in a beaker to collect gel. (Photos by W. Evans.)

Breeding Farm Name
Address
Phone Number

SEMEN EVALUATION RECORD

Stallion _____   Date _____

Collector _____   Time _____

Number of Mounts _____

Volume: gel-free semen   _____

          gel   _____

          semen (total volume) _____

Motililty: _____ % using extended semen

Concentration (gel-free):

          _____ % transmittance = _____ × 10⁶/ml

          _____ spermatozoa in hemocytometer × 10⁶ = _____ = 10⁶/ml

Total spermatozoa:

          _____ × 10⁶/ml × _____ ml (gel-free) = _____ × 10⁹

pH: _____

Motile sperm/ml gel-free: _____ concentration/ml

          × _____ % motility

          = _____ motile sperm

Morphology (number of spermatozoa per 100 observed):

    abnormal head   _____   abnormal tail _____   normal _____

    isolated head   _____   droplets   _____

    abnormal mid piece _____   other   _____

APPENDIX FIGURE 14-2   Semen evaluation record.

Motility estimates can be made by placing a drop of semen with a prewarmed Pasteur pipette on a prewarmed slide, covering the drop with a prewarmed cover slip and observing the spermatozoa with a 100 or 400× microscope that has a slide warmer (Appendix Figure 14-3). It is important to use a slide warmer to keep the spermatozoa from experiencing cold shock. To estimate motility, a series of yes/no decisions is made; for example, are 2 of 3, 3 of 4, 4 of 5, 5 of 6, or 9 of 10 motile? Three to five fields should be observed for each drop. If the spermatozoa are clumping together, which prevents a good estimate, the semen can be extended by pipetting 0.25 ml of semen into 4.75 ml of an extender in a vial. Then observe a drop of the extended semen for motility. One of the most popular extenders is the dried skim milk extender, prepared by placing 50 ml of sterile water in a sterile 100-ml

(a)

(b)

(c)

(d)

APPENDIX FIGURE 14-3 Semen motility evaluation: *(a)* Equipment: (A) microscope slides; (B) semen extender; (C) cover slips for microscope slides; (D) Pasteur pipette with rubber bulb and a slide warmer. *(b)* Semen is pipetted into warm extender with a warm pipette. *(c)* Drop of extended semen is placed on warm microscope slide. *(d)* A warm cover slip is placed over the drop of extended semen. (Photos by W. Evans.)

graduated cylinder. Then add 5 gm of nonfortified dried skim milk, 5 gm of glucose, 50,000 units of penicillin, and 50 mg of streptomycin to the cylinder. After they are dissolved, fill the cylinder to 100 ml with sterile distilled water. Freeze vials containing 4.5 ml of the extender until they are needed. This extender must be clearly labeled, because it is not suitable for extending semen for artificial insemination. A disadvantage of the extender is that it is opaque and the spermatozoa are hard to see.

Concentration

There are three ways to determine concentration. The less expensive method is to use a hemocytometer (Appendix Figure 14-4). Prepare semen by pipetting 0.2 and 0.4 ml of gel-free semen into 7.8 and 7.6 ml, respectively, of a 10-percent formalin solution; place a rubber stopper in the test tube; and slowly invert 8 to 10 times. If you shake the tubes, air bubbles will be trapped in the solution, thus resulting in a false value. You can make 1 liter of the formalin solution, because it can be stored. Mix it by placing 500 ml of distilled water in a 1-liter volumetric flask or graduated cylinder. Then add 9.0 gm of sodium chloride and mix until it dissolves. Add 100 ml of a 37-percent formaldehyde solution (formalin) and mix thoroughly. Add distilled water, to a final volume of 1 liter. Store the solution in a bottle that prevents evaporation.

The tip of a pasteur pipette is filled with the diluted semen. It is used to fill the hemocytometer chambers (Appendix Figure 14-4). Both sides of the chamber are covered with a hemocytometer cover slip and filled by capillary action. The spermatozoa in the five squares (illustrated in Appendix Figure 14-5) are counted. For a 1:20 dilution (0.2 ml of semen in a 7.8-ml formalin solution), the number of spermatozoa counted in the five squares is equivalent to that number of million spermatozoa per ml of undiluted semen. Count each square under 400× magnification, and take care to count each spermatozoan once. Therefore, as you count the spermatozoa in the square that has 16 smaller squares, count the spermatozoa on the lines of the smaller squares at the top and right for each row of spermatozoa. Count those on the bottom and left lines when you count across the next row.

After use, wash the hemocytometer and cover slip by squirting them with distilled water and rinsing with ethanol. They must not be scratched.

If several stallions are being evaluated on a frequent basis, it is advisable to use a spectrophotometer (Appendix Figure 14-6) or an automated system such as the Densimeter produced by Animal Reproduction Systems. Set the spectrophotometer at a wavelength of 550 mμ and to 0 percent transmittance without a tube. Place a colorimetric tube containing formalin solution in the spectrophotometer and adjust it to read 100-percent transmittance. Remove the tube and readjust the spectrophotometer to 0 percent. Return the formalin tube and readjust the spectrophotometer to 100 percent. Continue this until it reads 0 percent without a tube and 100 percent for the formalin tube without further adjustments. Prepare semen as for the hemocytometer method, except prepare it in colorimeter tubes. Record the percent transmittance for the 1:20 and 1:40 dilution of semen. The concentration of spermatozoa per ml is obtained from a standard curve (Appendix Figure 14-7), previously prepared by serially diluting a 1:10 dilution of spermatozoa in formalin solution, recording the percent transmittance, and determining the number of spermatozoa in a hemocytometer. The percent transmittance should be between 20 and 80 percent for accurate determination.

When a spectrophotometer is used, the colorimeter tubes must be clean and free from scratches. Wash them with a soft test tube brush and store them in a rubberized test tube rack. Immediately before insertion into the spectrophotometer, wipe the colorimeter tube with a tissue to remove any dust or fingerprints. Each time the light bulb is changed, a new standard curve must be made. Also, the calibration should be checked every few months to maintain accuracy.

The Densimeter is easy to use and has an advantage in that it will calculate the insemination volume based on the concentration, motility, and number of motile

(a)   *(b)*

(c)   *(d)*

Appendix figure 14-4   Determining spermatozoa concentration with a hemocytometer.
(a) Equipment consists of formalin solution, paper wipes, pipette bulb, pipettes, test tubes, test tube stoppers, and a test tube rack; *(b)* additional equipment consists of microscope, mechanical counter, and hemocytometer; *(c)* formalin and semen are pipetted into test tubes; *(d)* both sides of hemocytometer chamber are filled with diluted semen. (Photos by W. Evans.)

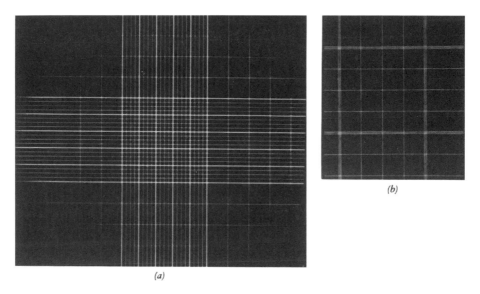

(a)

(b)

APPENDIX FIGURE 14-5   Hemocytometer field: *(a)* entire field; *(b)* one of the five fields that are counted. (Photos by W. Evans.)

APPENDIX FIGURE 14-6   Spectrophotometer used to determine concentration of spermatozoa. (Photo by W. Evans.)

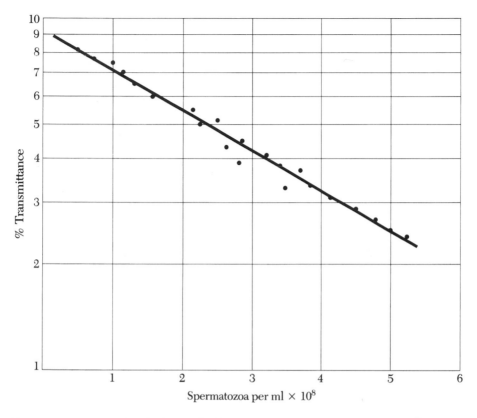

APPENDIX FIGURE 14-7 Standard curve for determining spermatozoa concentration using a spectrophotometer.

spermatozoa to be inseminated. Automated pipettes are supplied with the Densimeter so that the semen aliquant (.18 ml) and diluting fluid (3.42 ml) are accurately pipetted into the cuvette.

pH

Determine the pH with a pH meter (Appendix Figure 14-8). Digital pH meters are inexpensive and easy to use: simply rinse the electrode with distilled water, dry with tissue paper, and submerge in a small portion of the semen.

Morphology

Prepare the slide for morphological examination carefully, because the spermatozoa can be easily damaged, increasing the percentage of abnormal sperm. To prepare the slide, place a small drop of gel-free semen and a small drop of Hancock's stain on one end of a slide (Appendix Figure 14-9). Prepare Hancock's stain by dissolving

APPENDIX FIGURE 14-8   Equipment for determining pH of semen. (A) pH meter; (B) paper wipes; (C) distilled water to wash electrodes of pH meter; (D) beaker to hold semen; (E) pH standards. (Photo by W. Evans.)

6 gm of nigrosin in 60 ml of deionized water. After the nigrosin dissolves, add 1 gm of eosin.

After mixing, filter the solution. Mix the two drops with a small glass rod or the corner of another slide. Holding the slide at a 45° angle, allow the edge of another slide to touch the drop and then pull it across the slide with zigzag motions to form the smear. Use very little pressure to pull the slide. A common mistake is to get the layer of stained spermatozoa too thick, which makes it difficult to observe the spermatozoa. After making the smear, dry the stained slide on a slide warmer or in an incubator before using it. Using the microscope at 400×, count and classify at least 100 spermatozoa.

Another procedure that stains the spermatozoa for morphological evaluation is as follows:

1   Prepare a thin, uniform smear of fresh semen on a clean, dry microscope slide.

2   Dry the smear fast over an open flame (match).

3   Submerge the slide for 3 minutes in a solution of one part ethyl alcohol and one part ethyl ether.

4   Remove the slide and dry it in air.

5   Add two or three drops of stain to the smear and place the slide over a steam bath for 6 minutes. Prepare the stain by mixing 200 ml (5 gm/100 ml) of aniline, 100 ml of a 5 percent solution (5 gm/100 ml) of Eosin B, and 100 ml of a 1-percent solution (1 gm/100 ml) of phenol. After mixing, filter the strain through filter paper and store it in a bottle with an eyedropper.

APPENDIX FIGURE 14-9 Morphological examination of spermatozoa: *(a)* Equipment: applicator sticks, semen, microscope slides, stain, and Pasteur pipette with rubber bulb; *(b)* a drop of stain is placed on the slide; *(c)* a drop of semen is placed adjacent to the drop of stain and mixed; *(d)* the microscope slide is used to make a smear. (Photos by W. Evans.)

6   Remove the slide and wash it with distilled water to remove excess stain.

7   Dry in air.

8   Examine in the microscope. The head of the spermatozoa will be pale bluish-gray, the neck outlined in dark blue and colorless inside, and the tail components dark blue.

APPENDIX 15-1

Preparation of Semen Extenders

Cream-Gel

Prepare cream-gel semen extender by dissolving 1.3 grams of unflavored Knox gelatin in 10 milliliters of deionized water (available at grocery stores). Autoclave the solution and add half-and-half (light cream) to make 100 milliliters. Prepare the half-and-half by heating it in a double boiler at 92°C for 10 minutes. If a scum forms, remove it. Add 1 million units of crystalline penicillin and 1 gram of crystalline streptomycin. Freeze the 100 milliliters of extender in containers of 10-milliliter doses. Before collecting the stallion, thaw enough extender and warm it to 100°F (38°C). Extend semen to a ratio of 1:1 to 1:3 (semen:extender) in the extender storage vial. Usually, it is made in 1-liter batches and stored in 25- to 50-milliliter aliquants. Sterile Whirl-Pak bags are good storage containers.

Skim Milk

Dissolve 12 grams of nonfortified, nonfat dried skim milk powder in 500 milliliters of 5 percent dextrose solution (5 grams per 100 milliliters). Heat at 92°C for 10 minutes. Upon cooling, add 200 milligrams of gentamicin sulfate. Package in 25- to 50-milliliter aliquants and freeze.

Bovine Serum Albumin—Sucrose

Mix 100 grams of sucrose in 700 milliliters of deionized water, stirring the sugar into the solution. Once in the solution, gently pour 30 grams of bovine serum albumin

(BSA, Sigma A4503) on top of the liquid. Let it stand for several hours, allowing the BSA to dissolve. Do not shake or stir the BSA into the solution. Add an antibiotic (200 milligrams gentamicin sulfate) and dilute to 1 liter with deionized water. The pH should be 7.0. Package and freeze. (*Caution*: Each lot of albumin must be tested to be sure that it does not negatively affect motility. Because of the difficulty in obtaining lots that are usable, this extender is seldom used. If the albumin is okay, it is an excellent extender.)

Bibliography

Introduction: Owning a Horse

American Horse Council Industry Directory. 1999. American Horse Council. Washington, D.C.

Baird, B. 1976. The remarkable rider: Horse-related activities for the handicapped. *Proceedings, First National Horsemen's Seminar.* Fredericksburg, Va.: Virginia Horse Council.

Donald, A. F., P. G. Gibbs, and V. Mason. 1999. What to do if your horse is stolen L-5244. College Station, Tex.: Texas Agricultural Extension Service.

Gibbs, P. G., and L. H. Wall. 1998. *15 steps to minimize theft of horses, facilities and equipment* L-5210. College Station, Tex.: Texas Agricultural Extension Service.

Gibbs, P. G., L. H. Wall, and D. Householder. 1998. Permanent identification of horses L5211. College Station, Tex.: Texas Agricultural Extension Service.

Horses and Land-Use Planning. 1973. Washington, D.C.: National Horse and Pony Youth Activities Council.

Howard, H. A. 1978. Horses help the handicapped. *Horseman* 23:13–20.

Jacobson, P., and M. Hayes. 1972. *A Horse Around the House.* New York: Crown.

Kohler, C. F. 1976. Livestock insurance—all breeds of horses. *Proceedings, First National Horsemen's Seminar.* Fredericksburg, Va.: Virginia Horse Council.

Lopez, J. 1974. Demographic survey. *American Horseman.*

McCowan, L. L. 1977. Riding for the handicapped. *Proceedings, Second National Horsemen's Seminar.* Fredericksburg, Va.: Virginia Horse Council.

Rhulen, P. 1977. Liability in respect to the horse business. *Proceedings, Second National Horsemen's Seminar.* Fredericksburg, Va.: Virginia Horse Council.

Wood, K. A. 1973. *The Business of Horses.* Chula Vista, Cal.: Wood.

———. 1987. *Law for the Horse Breeder.* Rancho Santa Fe, Cal.: Wood.

Chapter 1: Selecting and Buying a Horse

Adams, O. R. 1974. *Lameness in Horses.* Philadelphia, Pa.: Lea & Febiger.

Barbalace, R. C. 1977. *An Introduction to Light Horse Management.* Minneapolis, Minn.: Burgess.

Bradley, M. 1971. Determining the Age of Horses by Their Teeth. Columbia, Mo.: *University of Missouri Science and Technology Guide* 2842.

Care and Training of the Trotter and Pacer. 1997. Columbus, Ohio: U.S. Trotting Association.

Drevemo, S., G. Dalin, I. Fredricson, and G. Hjerten. 1980. Equine locomotion 1: The analysis of linear and temporal gait characteristics of trotting Standardbreds. *Equine Veterinary J.* 12:60–65.

Drevemo, S., I. Fredricson, G. Dalin, and K. Bjorne. 1980. Equine locomotion 2: The analysis of coordination between limbs of trotting Standardbreds. *Equine Veterinary J.* 12:66–70.

Drevemo, S., G. Dalin, I. Fredricson, and K. Bjorne. 1980. Equine locomotion 3: The reproducibility of gait of Standardbred trotters. *Equine Veterinary J.* 12:71–73.

Ensminger, M. E. 1969. *Horses and Horsemanship.* Danville, Ill.: Interstate.

Evans, J. W. 1992. Gaits. In J. W. Evans (ed.), *Horse Breeding and Management.* World Series Animal Science C. Production-System Approach, Vol. 7. Amsterdam: Elsevier Scientific Publishers.

Fox, R. 1999. How to shop for a horse. *America's Horse* 1(6):27–30.

Frederickson, J., S. Drevemo, G. Dalin, G. Hjerten, and K. Bjorne. 1980. The application of high speed cinematography for the quantitative analysis of equine locomotion. *Equine Veterinary J.* 12(2):54–59.

Getty, R., ed. 1953. *Sisson and Grossman's The Anatomy of Domestic Animals.* Philadelphia, Pa.: Saunders.

Gorman, J. A. 1967. *The Western Horse: Its Types and Training.* Danville, Ill.: Interstate.

Harrison, J. C. 1968. *Care and Training of the Trotter and Pacer.* Columbus, Ohio: U.S. Trotting Association.

Heglund, N. C., and R. C. Taylor. 1974. Scaling stride frequency and gait to animal size: Mice to horses. *Science* 186:1112–1113.

Hildebrand, M. 1965. Symmetrical gaits of horses. *Science* 150:701–708.

Kobluk, C. N. 1988. New concepts in gait analysis. *Equine Sports Medicine News* 8:118–119.

Kobluk, C. N., D. Schnurr, F. D. Horney, G. Summer-Smith, R. A. Willoughby, V. S. Dekleer, and T. C. Hearn. 1989. Use of high-speed cinematography and computer-generated gait diagrams for the study of equine hind limb kinematics. *Equine Veterinary J.* 21:48–58.

Littlejohn, A., and R. Munro. 1972. Equine recumbency. *Veterinary Record* 90:83–85.

Mal, M. E., C. A. McCall, C. Newland, and K. Cummings. 1993. Evaluation of a one-trial learning apparatus to test learning ability in weanling horses. *Applied Animal Science* 35(4):305–311.

McCall, A. 1990. A review of learning behavior in horses and its application to horse training. *J. Animal Science* 68(1):75–81.

Mellin, J. 1961. *The Morgan Horse.* Brattleboro, Vt.: Greene Press.

Messemer, G. 1978. Choosing your child's trainer. *Horseman* 22:14–19.

Miller, R. W. 1974. *Western Horse Behavior and Training.* New York: Doubleday.

Mills, D., and K. Nankervis. 1999. *Equine Behavior: Principles and Practice.* London: Blackwell Science.

Montgomery, G. G. 1957. Some aspects of the sociality of the domestic horse. *Transactions, Kansas Academy of Sciences* 60:419–424.

Official Guide for Determining the Age of the Horse. No date. American Association of Equine Practitioners, 14 Hillcrest Circle, Rt. 3, Golden, Colo. 80401.

Ohlde, B. 1999. Home on the web. *America's Horse* 1(6):22–23.

Potter, G. D. 1976. Horse behavior and management. *Proceedings, First National Horsemen's Seminar.* Fredericksburg, Va.: Virginia Horse Council.

Pratt, G. W. 1977. Remarks on lameness and breakdown. *Thoroughbred Record* 209:1486–1489.

Pratt, G. W., and J. T. O'Conner. 1978. A relationship between gait and breakdown. *American J. Veterinary Research* 39:249–253.

Ratzlaff, M. H., R. M. Shindell, and K. K. White. 1985. The interrelationships of stride lengths and stride times to velocities of galloping horses. *Equine Veterinary J.* 5:279–283.

Ruckebush, Y. 1972. The relevance of drowsiness in the circadian cycle of farm animals. *Animal Behavior* 20:637–643.

Sappington, B. F., and L. Goldman. 1994. Discrimination learning and concept formation in the Arabian. *Journal Animal Science* 72(12):3080–3087.

Stoneridge, M. A. 1968. *A Horse of Your Own.* New York: Doubleday.

Waring, G. H., S. Wierzbowski, and E. S. E. Hafez. 1975. The behavior of horses. In E. S. E. Hafez (ed.), *The Behavior of Domestic Animals.* Baltimore, Md.: Williams & Wilkins.

Chapter 2: Evaluating Conformation and Soundness

Adams, O. R. 1974. *Lameness in Horses.* 3d ed. Philadelphia, Pa.: Lea & Febiger.

American Horse Shows Association Rule Book. Annual. New York: American Horse Shows Association.

Ball, M. A., M. Wildenstein, and S. Shin. 1998. Examining white line disease. *American Farriers J.*, July/August 79–83.

Baum, J. L. 1974. Navicular disease. *Iowa State University Veterinarian* 36:34–36.

Beeman, M. 1972. The relationship of form to function. *Quarter Horse J.* 12:82–128.

Borton, A. 1977. Selection of the horse. In J. W. Evans, A. Borton, H. F. Hintz, and L. D. Van Vleck, *The Horse.* New York: W. H. Freeman and Company.

Bradley, M. 1971. Determining the Age of Horses by Their Teeth. Columbia, Mo.: *University of Missouri Science and Technology Guide* 2842.

Dial, S. E. 1977. Conformation is the key to Secretariat's greatness. *Horseman* 21:51–54.

Edwards, G. B. 1971. *Know the Arabian Horse.* Omaha, Neb.: Farnam Horse Library.

———. 1973. *Anatomy and Conformation of the Horse.* Croton-on-Hudson, N.Y.: Dreenan Press.

4-H Horse Judging Guide. No date. University Park, Pa.: Cooperative Extension, Pennsylvania State University.

Gay, C. W. 1932. *Lippincott's Farm Manuals: Productive Horse Husbandry.* Greenville, Tex.: Green.

Harnson, J. C., ed. 1968. *Care and Training of the Trotter and Pacer.* Columbus, Ohio: U.S. Trotting Association.

Harper, M. W. 1913. *Management and Breeding of Horses.* New York: Orange Judd.

Hayes, M. H. 1972. *Veterinary Notes for Quarter Horses.* New York: Arco.

Householder, D. D., et al. 1992. Freeze-branding of horses. 1992 *Texas A&M Horse Short Course Proceedings,* 65–70.

Miller, R. M. 1970. Cancer of the eyelid and photosensitization. *Western Horseman* 35:48–49, 152.

Official Guide for Determining the Age of the Horse. No date. American Association of Equine Practitioners, 14 Hillcrest Circle, Rt. 3, Golden, Colo. 80401.

Redden, R. 1998. *Understanding Laminitis.* Lexington, Ky.: The Blood-Horse.

Roberts, S. J. 1969. Comments on equine leptospirosis. *J. American Veterinary Medical Association* 155:442–445.

Rossdale, P. D. 1975. *The Horse from Conception to Maturity.* London: Allen.

Runciman, B. 1940. Roaring and whistling in Thoroughbred horses. *Veterinary Record* 53:37.

Van Pelt, R. W. 1969. Inflammation of the tarsal synovial sheath (thoroughpin) in horses. *J. American Veterinary Medical Association* 155:1481–1488.

Van Vleck, L. D. 1977. Breeds in the United States. In J. W. Evans, A. Borton, H. F. Hintz, and L. D. Van Vleck, *The Horse.* New York: W. H. Freeman and Company.

Chapter 3: Choosing the Breed

American Stud Book. Published every four years. New York: Jockey Club.

Briggs, H. M. 1969. *Modern Breeds of Livestock.* 3d ed. New York: Macmillan.

Conn, G. H. 1957. *The Arabian Horse in America.* New York: Barnes.

Davenport, H. 1909. (Republished 1947.) My quest for the Arabian horse. In H. Davenport, *Arabian Horse Registry of America.* Denver, Colo.: Arabian Horse Registry of America.

Denhardt, R. M. 1948. *The Horse of the Americas.* Norman, Okla.: University of Oklahoma Press.

Dinsmore, W. 1935. *Judging Horses and Mules.* Chicago, Ill.: Horse and Mule Association of America.

Estes, J. A., and J. H. Palmer. 1942. *An Introduction to the Thoroughbred Horse.* 1st rev. ed. 1949, A. Bower (ed.); 2d rev. ed., 1972, C. H. Stone (ed.). Lexington, Ky.: The Blood-Horse.

Eustis-Cross, B., and N. Bowker. 1992. *The Wild Horse: An Adopter's Manual.* New York: Howell Book House.

Fletcher, J. L. 1945. A genetic analysis of the American Quarter Horse. *J. Heredity* 36:346.

———. 1946. A study of the first fifty years of Tennessee Walking Horse breeding. *J. Heredity* 37:369.

Gazder, P. J. 1954. The genetic history of the Arabian horse in the United States. *J. Heredity* 45:95.

Gilbey, W. 1900. *Ponies: Past and Present.* London: Vinton.

Glyn, R. 1971. *The World's Finest Horses and Ponies.* New York: Doubleday.

Goodall, D. M. 1965. *Horses of the World.* London: Country Life.

Griffen, J. 1966. *The Pony Book.* New York: Doubleday.

Haines, F. 1963. *Appaloosa: The Spotted Horse in Art and History.* Fort Worth, Tex.: Amon Carter Museum of Western Art.

Haines, F., R. L. Peckinpah, and G. B. Hatley. 1957. *The Appaloosa Horse.* Lewiston, Idaho: Bailey.

Harper, M. W. 1913. *Management and Breeding of Horses*. New York: Orange Judd.

Hervey, J. 1947. *The American Trotter*. New York: Coward-McCann.

Miller, R. W. 1969. *Appaloosa Coat Color Inheritance*. Bozeman, Mont.: Montana State University.

Nye, N. 1964. *The Complete Book of the Quarter Horse*. New York: Barnes.

Osborne, W. D. 1967. *The Quarter Horse*. New York: Grosset & Dunlap.

Patten, J. W. 1960. *The Light Horse Breeds*. New York: Barnes.

Reese, H. H. 1956. *Horses of Today: Their History, Breeds, and Qualifications*. Pasadena, Cal.: Wood and Jones.

Sanders, A. H., and W. Dinsmore. 1917. *A History of the Percheron Horse*. Chicago, Ill.: Sanders.

Savitt, S. 1966. *American Horses*. New York: Doubleday.

Sires and Dams Book. Annual. Columbus, Ohio: U.S. Trotting Association.

Speelman, S. R. 1941. *Breeds of Light Horses*. USDA Farmers' Bulletin No. 952. Washington, D.C.: U.S. Department of Agriculture.

Taylor, L. 1961. *The Horse America Made: The Story of the American Saddle Horse*. New York: Harper & Row.

Telleen, M. 1972. The draft breeds. *Western Horseman* 37:80.

Trotting and Pacing Guide. Annual. Columbus, Ohio: U.S. Trotting Association.

Wentworth, L. 1945. *The Authentic Arabian Horse and His Descendants*. London: Allen & Unwin.

Widmer, J. 1959. *The American Quarter Horse*. New York: Scribner's.

Zahre, A. 1959. *The genetic history of the Arabian horse in America*. Unpublished doctoral thesis, Michigan State University, East Lansing.

Zarn, M., T. Keller, and K. Collins. 1977a. *Wild, Free-Roaming Horses, Status of Present Knowledge*. U.S. Departments of Interior and Agriculture Technical Note 294. Denver, Colo.: U.S. Department of Interior and U.S. Department of Agriculture.

———. 1977b. *Wild, Free-Roaming Burros, Status of Present Knowledge*. U.S. Departments of Interior and Agriculture Technical Note 296. Denver, Colo.: U.S. Department of Interior and U.S. Department of Agriculture.

Chapter 4: Providing Physical Facilities

Ambrosiano, N., and M. Harcourt. 1992. *Horse Barns Big and Small*. Millwood, N.Y.: Breakthrough Publications.

Bingham, B. H., and A. Huff. 1968. *Horseman's Handbook: Barns and Related Equipment*. Publication No. 147. Blacksburg, Va.: Virginia Polytechnic Institute.

Blickle, J. D., R. L. Maddex, L. T. Windling, and J. H. Pedersen. 1971. *Horse Handbook Housing and Equipment*. Midwest Plan Service Series. Ames, Iowa: Iowa State University.

Borton, A. 1977. Fences, buildings, and equipment for horses. In J. W. Evans, A. Borton, H. F. Hintz, and L. D. Van Vleck, *The Horse*. New York: W. H. Freeman and Company.

Burton, D. W., and H. F. Hintz. 1974. Feeding facilities. *American Horseman* 5:1416, 54–55.

Chastain, J., and L. Jacobson. 1992. *Farm Buildings Wiring Handbook*. St. Paul, Minn.: University of Minnesota.

Dunn, N. 1972. *Horse handling facilities*. In M. E. Ensminger (Ed.), Stud Managers Handbook, Vol. 8. Clovis, Cal.: Agriservices Foundation.

Ensminger, M. E. 1969. *Horses and Horsemanship*. Danville, Ill.: Interstate.

Evans, J. W. 1977. *Management of a horse farm*. In J. W. Evans, A. Borton, H. F. Hintz, and L. D. Van Vleck, *The Horse*. New York: W. H. Freeman and Company.

Fallon, E. 1967. Breeding farm hygiene. *Lectures: Stud Managers Course*. Lexington, Ky.: Grayson Foundation.

Gaines, D. 1977. Build that fence to last. *Horseman* 21:54–58.

Harvey, H. M. 1968. Stock farm management. In J. C. Harrison (ed.), *Care and Training of the Trotter and Pacer*. Columbus, Ohio: U.S. Trotting Association.

Hollingsworth, K. 1971. New-design sheds serve very well. In *A Barn Well Filled*. Lexington, Ky.: The Blood-Horse.

Kelley, L. J. 1992. Fasteners. *Equus* 179:49–53.

Lakin, R. 1987. The great muck off. *Equus* 119:57.

Lieberman, R., et al. 1992. Details that make a difference. *Modern Horse Breeding* 9(3):1117.

Mallagren, R. 1999. *The Equine Arena Handbook*. Loveland: Alpine Publications.

Martin, G. A. 1981. *Fences, Gates and Bridges: A Practical Manual*. New York: Viking Penguin.

O'Dea, J. C. 1966. Veterinarian's view of farm layout. *The Blood Horse* 92:3790–3791.

Parsons, R. A. 1970. *Riding, Horse Barns, and Equipment*. M-25. Davis, Cal.: University of California Cooperative Extension Service.

Smith, P. C. 1967. *The Design and Construction of Stables*. London: Allen.

Stone, C. H. 1971. Good fences make good neighbors and good horse farms. In *A Barn Well Filled*. Lexington, Ky.: The Blood-Horse.

Sutton, H. H. 1963. The veterinarian and horse farm management. In J. F. Bone and others (eds.), *Equine Medicine and Surgery*. Wheaton, Ill.: American Veterinary Publications.

Umstadter, L. W. 1976. Do's and don'ts for horse farm facilities. *The Morgan Horse* 33:1409–1414.

Valliere, D. W. 1971. A barn for all seasons. In *A Barn Well Filled*. Lexington, Ky.: The Blood-Horse.

Vivian, J. 1987. *Building Fences of Wood, Stone, Metal, and Planks*. Charlotte, Vt.: Williamson Publishing.

Watson, M. G. 1988. *Fields and Fencing*. Putney, Vt.: Threshold Books.

Willis, L. C. 1973. *The Horse Breeding Farm*. New York: Barnes.

Young, J. R. 1986. Mucking out. *Horseman* 31(6):74.

———. 1988. Facility Considerations for Horse Farms (video). Available from Department of Agricultural Communications, 102 Public Information Building, Oklahoma State University, Stillwater, Okla. 74078.

Chapter 5: Feeding

Alexander, F., and M. E. Davies. 1969. Studies on vitamin B_{12} in the horse. *British Veterinary J.* 125:169.

Argenzio, R. A., J. E. Lowe, D. W. Pickard, and C. E. Stevens. 1974. Digesta passage and water exchange in the equine large intestine. *American J. Physiology* 226:1035.

Aronson, A. L. 1972. Lead poisoning of cattle and horses following long-term exposure to lead. *American J. Veterinary Research* 33:627.

Baalsrud, K. J., and G. Overnes. 1986. The influence of vitamin E and selenium supplements on antibody production in horses. *Equine Veterinary J.* 18:472.

Baker, H. J., and J. R. Lindsey. 1968. Equine goiter due to excess dietary iodine. *J. American Veterinary Medical Association* 153:1618.

Baker, J. P. 1971. Horse nutritive requirements. *Feed Management* 22:10–15.

Barth, K. M., J. W. Williams, and O. G. Brown. 1977. Digestible energy requirement of working and non-working ponies. *J. Animal Science* 44:585.

Battle, G. H., S. G. Jackson, and J. P. Baker. 1988. Acceptability and digestibility of preservative-treated hay by horses. *Nutrition Reports International* 37:83.

Baucus, K. L., S. L. Ralston, V. A. Rich, and E. L. Squires. 1987. The effect of dietary copper and zinc supplementation on composition of mare's milk. *Proceedings, Tenth Equine Nutrition and Physiology Symposium*, pp. 174–184.

Bille, N. 1971. Vitamin D excess and calciphylaxis in domestic animals. *Nutrition Abstracts Rev.* 41:758.

Boren, S. R., D. R. Topliff, D. W. Freeman, R. J. Bahr, D. G. Wagner, and C. V. Maxwell. 1987. Growth of weanling Quarter Horses fed varying energy and protein levels. *Proceedings, Tenth Equine Nutrition and Physiology Symposium*, p. 43.

Bradbury, P., and S. Werk. 1974. *Horse Nutrition Handbook*. Houston, Tex.: Cordovan.

Breuer, L. H. 1975. Effects of mare diet during late gestation and lactation, supplemental feeding of foal and early weaning on foal development. *Proceedings, Fourth Equine Nutrition Symposium*. Pomona, Cal.: California State Polytechnic University.

Breuer, L. H., and D. L. Golden. 1971. Lysine requirement of the immature equine. *J. Animal Science* 33:227.

Caliuk, E. A. 1961. Water metabolism and water requirements of horses. *Tr. Vses. Inst. Konevodstso.* 23:195. (As cited in *Nutrition Abstracts Rev.* 32:574, 1962.)

Carroll, F. D. 1950. B vitamin content in the skeletal muscle of the horse fed a B vitamin low diet. *J. Animal Science* 9:139.

Carroll, F. D., H. Goss, and C. E. Howell. 1949. The synthesis of B vitamins in the horse. *J. Animal Science* 8:290.

Cello, R. M. 1962. Recent findings in periodic ophthalmia. *Proceedings, Eighth Annual Convention of American Association of Equine Practitioners*.

Cheeke, P. R., and L. R. Shull. 1985. *Natural Toxicants in Feeds and Poisonous Plants*. Westport, Conn.: AVI Pub.

Christensen, C. 1987. Blister beetles and alfalfa. *Equine Data Line*, September. Lexington, Ky.: University of Kentucky Cooperative Extension Service.

Coger, L. S., H. F. Hintz, H. F. Schryver, and J. E. Lowe. 1987. The effect of high zinc intake on copper metabolism and bone development in growing horses. *Proceedings, Tenth Equine Nutrition and Physiology Symposium*, p. 173.

Cymbaluk, N. F., and D. A. Christensen. 1986. Nutrient utilization of pelleted and unpelleted forages by ponies. *Canadian J. Animal Science*, 66:237.

Dawson, F. L. M. 1977. Recent advances in equine reproduction. *Equine Veterinary J.* 9:4–11.

Dill, S. G., and W. C. Rebhun. 1985. White muscle disease in foals. *The Compendium on Continuing Education for the Practicing Veterinarian* 7:S627.

Dorsett, D. J. 1983. *Hay Judging Guidelines.* D-1079. College Station, Tex.: Texas Agriculture Extension Service.

Drew, B., W. P. Barber, and D. G. Williams. 1975. The effect of excess dietary iodine on pregnant mares and foals. *Veterinary Record* 97:93.

Duren, S. E., S. G. Jackson, J. P. Baker, and D. K. Aaron, 1987. Effect of dietary fat on blood parameters in exercised Thoroughbred horses. In J. R. Gillespie and W. E. Robinson (eds.), *Equine Exercise Physiology* II, pp. 674–685. Davis, Cal.: ICEEP Pub.

Fonnesbeck, P. V. 1968. Consumption and excretion of water by horses receiving all hay and hay-grain diets. *J. Animal Science* 27:1350.

———. 1969. Partitioning of the nutrients of forage for horses. *J. Animal Science* 28:624.

Fonnesbeck, P. V., and L. D. Symons. 1967. Utilization of carotene of hay by horses. *J. Animal Science* 26:1030.

Fowler, M. E. 1963. Poisonous plants. In J. F. Bone, et al. (eds.), *Equine Medicine and Surgery.* Wheaton, Ill.: American Veterinary Publications.

Gabel, A. A., D. A. Knight, S. M. Reed, J. A. Pultz, J. D. Powers, I. R. Bramlage, and W. J. Tyznik. 1988. Comparison of incidence and severity of developmental orthopedic disease on 17 farms before and after adjustment of ration. *Proceedings Thirty-third Annual Convention of American Association of Equine Practitioners.* pp. 163–170.

Garton, C. I., G. W. Vander Noot, and P. V. Fonnesbeck. 1964. Seasonal variation in carotene and vitamin A concentration of the blood of brood mares in New Jersey. *J. Animal Science* 23:1233. (Abstract.)

Gibbs, P. G., and G. D. Potter. 1993. *Feeding young horses for sound development B-5043.* College Station, Tex.: Texas Agricultural Experiment Station.

Gibbs, P. G., D. H. Sigler, and T. B. Goehring. 1987. Influence of diet on growth and development of yearling horses. *Proceedings, Tenth Equine Nutrition and Physiology Symposium,* p. 37.

Glade, M. J. 1988. The role of endocrine factors in equine developmental orthopedic disease. *Proceedings, Thirty-third Annual Convention of American Association of Equine Practitioners,* pp. 171–190.

Guenthner, H. R. 1974. *Horse Pastures.* Cooperative Extension Service Bull. C.151. Reno, Nev.: University of Nevada.

Harrington, D. D., and E. H. Page. 1983. Acute vitamin D_3 toxicosis in horses: Case reports and experimental studies of the comparative toxicity of vitamin D_2 and D_3. *J. American Veterinary Medical Association* 182:1358.

Hartley, W. J., and A. B. Grant. 1961. A review of selenium responsive diseases of New Zealand livestock. *Federation Proceedings* 20:678.

Hintz, H. F. 1968. Energy utilization in the horse. *Proceedings, Cornell Nutrition Conference.* Ithaca, N.Y.: Cornell University, pp. 47–50.

———. 1975. Digestive physiology of the horse. *J. South African Veterinary Association* 46:1316.

———. 1977. Feeds and feeding. In J. W. Evans, A. Borton, H. F. Hintz, and L. D. Van Vleck, *The Horse.* New York: W. H. Freeman and Company.

———. 1983. *Horse Nutrition—A Practical Guide.* New York: Arco.

Hintz, H. F., J. E. Lowe, A. J. Clifford, and W. J. Visek. 1970. Ammonia intoxication resulting from urea ingestion by ponies. *J. American Veterinary Medical Association* 157:963.

Hintz, H. F., S. J. Roberts, S. Sabin, and H. F. Schryver. 1971. Energy requirements of light horses for various activities. *J. Animal Science* 32:100.

Hintz, H. F., and H. F. Schryver. 1972. Nitrogen utilization in ponies. *J. Animal Science* 34:592.

Hintz, H. F., H. F. Schryver, J. Doty, C. Lakin, and R. A. Zimmerman. 1984. Oxalic acid content of alfalfa hays and its influence on the availability of calcium, phosphorus, and magnesium to ponies. *J. Animal Science* 58:939.

Hintz, H. F., H. F. Schryver, and J. E. Lowe. 1971. Comparison of a blend of milk products and linseed meal as protein supplements for young growing horses. *J. Animal Science* 33:1274.

Hintz, H. F., H. F. Schryver, J. E. Lowe, J. King, and L. Krook. 1973. Effect of vitamin D on Ca and P metabolism in ponies. *J. Animal Science* 37:282. (Abstract.)

Houpt, T. R., and K. A. Houpt. 1965. Urea utilization by the pony. *Federation Proceedings* 24:628.

Howell, C. E., G. H. Hart, and N. R. Ittner. 1941. Vitamin A deficiency in horses. *American J. Veterinary Research* 2:60.

Jackson, S. A., V. A. Rich, S. L. Ralston, and E. W. Anderson. 1985. Feeding behavior and feed efficiency of horses as affected by feeding frequency and physical form of hay. *Proceedings, Ninth Equine Nutrition and Physiology Symposium,* 9:78.

Jarrett, S. H., W. A. Shurg, and B. L. Reid. 1987. Plasma tractions of vitamin A alcohol, palmitate, and acetate in horses fed deficient and excess dietary vitamin A. *Proceedings, Tenth Equine Nutrition and Physiology Symposium,* pp. 1–4. Soc. Symp. Fort Collins, Colo.: Colorado State University.

Jefferies, N. E. 1970. *Better Pastures for Horses and Ponies.* Cooperative Extension Service Circular 294. Bozeman, Mont.: Montana State University.

Johnson, R. J., and J. W. Hart. 1974. Utilization of nitrogen from soybean meal, biuret and urea by equine. *Nutrition Report International* 9:209.

Jordan, R. M., V. S. Myers, B. Yoho, and F. A. Spurrell. 1975. Effect of calcium and phosphorus levels on growth, reproduction and bone development of ponies. *J. Animal Science* 40:78.

Joyce, T. R., K. R. Pierce, W. M. Romain, and J. G. Baker. 1971. Clinical study of nutritional secondary hyperparathyroidism in horses. *J. American Veterinary Medical Association* 158:2033.

Kelley, L. J. 1992. Reducing fescue's risks. *Equus* 183:66–67.

Kingsbury, J. 1964. *Poisonous Plants of the United States and Canada.* Englewood Cliffs, N.J.: Prentice-Hall.

Knight, D. A., S. E. Weisbrode, L. M. Schmall, and A. A. Gabel. 1988. Copper supplementation and cartilage lesions in foals. *Proceedings, Thirty-third Annual Convention of American Association of Equine Practitioners,* pp. 191–194.

Krook, L., and J. E. Lowe. 1964. Nutritional secondary hyperparathyroidism in the horse. *Veterinary Pathology* 1: Supplement 1.

Krzak, W. E., H. W. Gonyou, and L. M. Lawrence. 1991. Wood chewing by stabled horses: Diurnal pattern and effects of exercise. *J. Animal Science* 69:1053–1058.

Lawrence, L., K. J. Moore, H. F. Hintz, E. H. Jaster, and L. Wischover. 1987. Acceptability of alfalfa hay treated with an organic acid preparation. *Canadian J. Animal Science* 67:217.

Lawrence, L. A., E. A. Ott, R. L. Asquith, and G. J. Miller. 1987. Influence of dietary iron on growth, tissue mineral composition, apparent phosphorus absorption, and chemical properties of bone. *Proceedings, Tenth Equine Nutrition and Physiology Symposium,* p. 563.

Linerode, P. A. 1966. Studies on the synthesis and absorption of B complex vitamins in the equine. Unpublished doctoral thesis, Ohio State University, Columbus.

McCann, J. S., and C. S. Hoveland. 1991. Equine grazing preferences among winter annual grasses, and clovers adapted to the southeastern United States. *Equine Veterinary J.* 11:275–277.

McNeely, G. H., and others. 1975. *Feed Requirements of the Light Horse.* Cooperative Extension Publication 75-FS/4005. Davis, Cal.: University of California.

Martin, A. A. 1975. Nigro pallidal encephalomalacia in horses caused by chronic poisoning with yellow star thistle. *Nutrition Abstracts Rel.* 45:85.

Mayhew, I. G., C. M. Brown, H. D. Stowe, A. L. Trapp, F. J. Derksen, and S. F. Clement. 1987. Equine degenerative myeloencephalopathy: A vitamin E deficiency that may be familial. *J. Veterinary Internal Medicine* 1:45.

Meyers, M. C., G. D. Potter, L. W. Greene, S. F. Crouse, and J. W. Evans. 1987. Physiological and metabolic response of exercising horses to added fat. *Proceedings, Tenth Equine Nutrition and Physiology Symposium,* p. 107.

Moxon, A. L. 1937. Alkali disease or selenium poisoning. *South Dakota Agricultural Experiment Station Technical Bull.* 311:1.

National Research Council. 1989. *Nutrient Requirements for Horses.* Washington, D.C.: National Academy of Sciences.

Nelson, A. W. 1961. *Nutrient Requirements of the Light Horse.* Amarillo, Tex.: American Quarter Horse Association.

Nelson, D. D., and W. J. Tyznik. 1971. Protein and non-protein nitrogen utilization in the horse. *J. Animal Science* 32:68.

Nickel, R., A. Schummer, E. Seiferle, and W. O. Sack. 1973. *The Viscera of Domestic Animals.* New York: Springer-Verlag.

Olsson, N., and A. Ruudvere. 1955. The nutrition of the horse. *Nutrition Abstracts Rev.* 25:1.

Ott, E. A. 1971. Energy and protein for reproduction in the horse. *Proceedings, Second Equine Nutrition Symposium.* Ithaca, N.Y.: Cornell University.

Ott, E. A., and R. L. Asquith. 1986. Influence of level of feeding and nutrient content of the concentrate on growth and development of yearling horses. *J. Animal Science* 62:290.

Pagan, J. D., B. Essen-Gustavsson, A. Lindholm, and J. Thornton. 1987a. The effect of exercise and diet on muscle and liver glycogen repletion in Standardbred horses. *Proceedings, Tenth Equine Nutrition and Physiology Symposium,* pp. 431–435.

———. 1987b. The effect of dietary energy sources on performance in Standardbred horses. In J. R. Gillespie and W. E. Robinson (eds.), *Equine Exercise Physiology* II, pp. 686–700. Davis, Cal.: ICEEP Pub.

Pagan, J. D., and H. F. Hintz. 1986b. Equine energetics. I. Relationship between body weight and energy requirements in horses. *J. Animal Science* 63:815.

———. 1986c. Equine energetics. II. Energy expenditure in horses during submaximal exercise. *J. Animal Science* 63:822.

Pagan, J. D., H. F. Hintz, and T. R. Rounsaville. 1984. The digestible requirements of lactating pony mares. *J. Animal Science* 58:1382.

Platt, H. 1984. Growth of the equine foetus. *Equine Veterinary J.* 16:247.

Potter, G. D., J. W. Evans, G. W. Webb, and S. P. Webb. 1987. Digestible energy requirements of Belgian and Percheron horses. *Proceedings, Tenth Equine Nutrition and Physiology Symposium,* p. 133.

Potter, G. D., and J. D. Huchton. 1975. Growth of yearling horses fed different sources of protein with supplemental lysine. *Proceedings, Fourth Equine Nutrition Symposium.* Pomona, Cal.: California State Polytechnic University.

Pratt, J. N. 1973. Let's grow better pastures. *Quarter Horse J.* 27:162, 192.

Prior, R. L., H. F. Hintz, J. E. Lowe, and W. J. Visek. 1974. Urea recycling and metabolism of ponies. *J. Animal Science* 38:565.

Quinn, C. R. 1975. Isobutylidene diurea as a protein substitute for horses. Unpublished doctoral thesis, Colorado State University, Fort Collins.

Ralston, S. L. 1988. Nutritional management of horses competing in 160 km races. *Cornell Veterinarian* 78:53.

Ralston, S. L., S. A. Jackson, V. A. Rich, and E. L. Squires. 1985. Effect of vitamin A supplementation on the seminal characteristics and sexual behavior of stallions. *Proceedings, Ninth Equine Nutrition and Physiology Symposium,* p. 74.

Reed, K. R., and N. K. Dunn. 1977. Growth and development of the Arabian horse. *Proceedings, Fifth Equine Nutrition and Physiology Symposium,* p. 76.

Romane, W. M., and others. 1966. Cystitis syndrome of the equine. *Southwest Veterinarian* 19:95–99.

Roneus, B. O., R. V. J. Hakkarianen, C. A. Lindholm, and J. L. Tyopponen. 1986. Vitamin E requirements of adult Standardbred horses evaluated by tissue depletion and repletion. *Equine Veterinary J.* 18:50.

Rusoff, L. L., R. B. Lank, T. E. Spillman, and H. B. Elliot. 1965. Non-toxicity of urea feeding to horses. *Veterinary Medicine* 60:1123.

Schryver, H. F., P. H. Craig, and H. F. Hintz. 1970. Calcium metabolism in ponies fed varying levels of calcium. *J. Nutrition* 100:955.

Schryver, H. F., H. F. Hintz, and P. H. Craig. 1971a. Calcium metabolism in ponies fed a high phosphorus diet. *J. Nutrition* 101:259.

————. 1971b. Phosphorus metabolism in ponies fed varying levels of phosphorus. *J. Nutrition* 101:1257.

Schryver, H. F., D. W. Meakim, J. E. Lowe, J. Williams, L. V. Soderholm, and H. F. Hintz. 1987. Growth and calcium metabolism in horses fed varying levels of protein. *Equine Veterinary J.* 19:280.

Schryver, H. F., O. T. Oftedal, J. Williams, L. V. Soderholm, and H. F. Hintz. 1986. Lactation in the horse: The mineral composition of mare's milk. *J. Nutrition.* 116:2142.

Schryver, H. F., M. T. Parker, P. D. Daniluk, K. I. Pagan, J. Williams, L. V. Soderholm, and H. F. Hintz. 1987. Salt consumption and the effect of salt on mineral metabolism in horses. *Cornell Veterinarian* 77:122.

Scott, B. D., G. D. Potter, J. W. Evans, J. C. Reagor, G. W. Webb, and S. P. Webb. 1987. Growth and feed utilization by yearling horses fed added dietary fat. *Proceedings, Tenth Equine Nutrition and Physiology Symposium,* pp. 101–106.

Slade, L. M., L. D. Lewis, C. R. Quinn, and M. L. Chandler. 1975. Nutritional adaptations of horses for endurance performance. *Proceedings, Fourth Equine Nutrition Symposium.* Pomona, Cal.: California State Polytechnic University.

Slade, L. M., D. W. Robinson, and K. E. Casey. 1970. Nitrogen metabolism in non-ruminant herbivores. I. The influence of non-ruminant herbivores. 1. The influence of non-protein nitrogen and protein quality on the nitrogen retention of adult mares. *J. Animal Science* 30:753.

Snow, D. H., and C. J. Vogel. 1987. *Equine Fitness: The Care and Training of the Athletic Horse.* Devon, England: David and Charles Pub.

Stillions, M. C., and W. E. Nelson. 1972. Digestible energy during maintenance of the light horse. *J. Animal Science* 34:981.

Stillions, M. C., S. M. Teeter, and W. E. Nelson. 1971. Ascorbic acid requirements of mature horses. *J. Animal Science* 32:249.

Stover, S. M. 1992. Crooked legs and growing pains. *Quarter Horse J.* February: 74–75.

Stowe, H. D. 1967. Reproductive performance of barren mares following vitamins A and E supplementation. *Proceedings, Thirteenth Annual Convention of American Association of Equine Practitioners,* pp. 81–93.

————. 1968. Alpha-tocopherol requirements for equine erythrocyte stability. *American J. Clinical Nutrition* 21:135.

Tyznik, W. J. 1975. Feeding the foal. Paper presented to May 1975 *California Livestock Symposium,* Fresno, Cal.

Ullrey, D. E., R. D. Struthers, D. G. Hendricks, and B. E. Brent. 1966. Composition of mare's milk. *J. Animal Science* 25:217.

Van Niekerk, C. H., and J. S. van Heerden. 1972. Nutrition and ovarian activity of mares early in the breeding season. *J. South African Veterinary Association* 43:351–360.

Wagoner, D. W. 1973. Feeding to Win. Grapevine, Tex.: *Equine Research Publications.*

Watkins, J. 1992. Developmental Disorders of Young Growing Horses. Presentation at Texas A&M Horse Short Course.

Webb, S. P., G. D. Potter, and J. W. Evans. 1987. Physiologic and metabolic response of race and cutting horses to added dietary fat. *Proceedings, Tenth Equine Nutrition and Physiology Symposium,* p. 115.

Weeks, P. J. 1975. Good pastures. *Horseman* 19:21–27.

White, H. E. 1976. Establishing and maintaining horse pasture. *Proceedings, First National Horsemen's Seminar.* Fredericksburg, Va.: Virginia Horse Council.

————. 1977. Hay for horses. Cooperative Extension Service, *Horse Facts,* Vol. 2, No. 5. Blacksburg, Va.: Virginia Polytechnic Institute and State University.

Wooden, G., K. Knox, and C. L. Wild. 1970. Energy metabolism in light horses. *J. Animal Science* 30:544.

Wysocki, A. A., and J. P. Baker. 1975. Utilization of bacterial protein from the lower gut of the equine. *Proceedings, Fourth Equine Nutrition Symposium.* Pomona, Cal.: California State Polytechnic University.

Chapter 6: Handling

Anonymous. 1998. Homeward bound. *Blood-Horse* (Sept.):5024–5030.

Barbalace, R. C. 1974. *Light Horse Management.* Minneapolis, Minn.: Burgess.

Beach, F. A., and J. Jaynes. 1954. Effects of early experience upon the behavior of animals. *Psychol. Bull.* 51:239–263.

Beck, D., and S. Sidles. 1975. Trailering. *The Morgan Horse* 35:1400–1403; 35: 1631–1633.

Carlson, T. 1975. Taking the burden out of trailer loading. *Horseman* 29:72–82.

Denenberg, V. H. 1962. The effects of early experience. In E. S. E. Hafez (ed.), *The Behaviour of Domestic Animals,* London: Baillier, Tindall & Cox, pp. 109–138.

Gorman, J. A. 1967. *The Western Horse.* Danville, Ill.: Interstate.

Hinchcliff, K. 1998. Exercise induced pulmonary hemorrhage (EIPH): Is it a disease? 1998 WAES Convention.

Kaplan, S. 1976. Trailering tips. *Horseman* 22:36–39.

King, J. A. 1958. Parameters relevant to determining the effects of early experience upon the adult behavior of animals. *Psychol. Bull.* 55:46–58.

Leahy, J. R., and P. Barrow. 1953. *Restraint of Animals.* Ithaca, N.Y.: Cornell Campus Store.

Marx, Melvin H. 1969. *Learning: Processes.* London: Collier-Macmillan Limited.

Miller, R. W. 1975. *Western Horse Behavior and Training.* New York: Doubleday.

Newton, G., and S. Levine, eds. 1968. *Early Experience and Behavior.* Springfield, Ill.: Thomas.

Porter, M. 1998. Sports medicine: Avoiding travel fatigue. *The Horse Interactive* (April).

Rondum, K. 1973. Teach your horse to load. *Practical Horseman* 74:41–45.

Trailer Towing Guide. 1975. Wausaw, Wis.: Hammer Blow Company.

Yeates, B. F. 1987. Application of psychological principles to horse training. 1987. *Horse Short Course Proceedings,* Texas Agricultural Extension, pp. l–17.

Chapter 7: Grooming

Grooming. 1973. *Practical Horseman* 74:19–24, 37.

Hackney, S. B. 1999. Tip top grooming tips. *Horse Illustrated* 23(6): 106–122.

How to Clip Your Horse. 1976. Temple, N.H.: Derbyshire.

Jennings, J., and S. Vaughn. 1976. Body clipping. *Quarter Horse J.* 28:172–180.

McHam, D. 1975. Groom your horse if you can't ride him. *Horseman* 43:60–63.

Meek, N. 1978. Grooming: How professionals do it. *Horse Lovers National* 74:42, 43, 46.

Chapter 8: Caring for the Feet

Adams, O. R., ed. 1974. *Lameness in Horses.* 3d ed. Philadelphia, Pa.: Lea & Febiger.

Ball, M. A., M. Wildenstein, and S. Shin. 1998. Examining white line disease. *American Farriers Journal,* July/August pp. 79–83.

Butler, K. D. 1974. *The Principles of Horseshoeing.* Ithaca, N.Y.: Butler.

———. 1977a. The hoof's role in competitive trail riding. *Saddle Action* 1:18–21, 50.

———. 1977b. Practical hoof physiology. *Proceedings. Second National Horsemen's Seminar.* Fredericksburg, Va.: Virginia Horse Council.

———. 1985. *The Principles of Horseshoeing II.* Maryville, Mo.: Doug Butler Publisher.

Canfield, D. M. 1968. *Elements of Farrier Science.* Albert Lea, Minn.: Enderes Tool Co.

Carlson, C., B. Pich, and J. Wrigley. 1989. Shoe sizing comparison chart. *American Farriers J.* January/February: 56–60.

Emery, L., J. Miller, and N. Van Hoosen. 1977. *Horseshoeing Theory and Hoof Care.* Philadelphia, Pa.: Lea & Febiger.

Evans, J. W. 1977. Anatomy and care of the foot. In J. W. Evans, A. Borton, H. F. Hintz, and L. D. Van Vleck, *The Horse.* New York: W. H. Freeman and Company.

Getty, R., ed. 1953. *Sisson and Grossman's The Anatomy of Domestic Animals.* Philadelphia, Pa.: Saunders.

Greeley, R. G. 1970. *The Art and Science of Horseshoeing.* Philadelphia, Pa.: Lippincott.

Harrison, J. C. 1968. *Care and Training of the Trotter and Pacer.* Columbus, Ohio: U.S. Trotting Association.

The Horseshoer. 1941. Technical manual TMA-220. Washington, D.C.: War Department.

Kays, D. J. 1969. *How to Save a Horse.* New York: Barnes.

O'Connor, J. T., and J. C. Briggs. 1971. Feet: Conformation and motion. *The Morgan Horse* 364:27–32.

Springhall, J. A. 1964. *Elements of Horseshoeing.* Brisbane, Australia: University of Queensland Press.

Wiseman, R. F. 1968. *The Complete Horseshoeing Guide.* Norman, Okla.: University of Oklahoma Press.

Chapter 9: Recognizing Illness and Giving First Aid

Brown, C. M. 1978. Bandage the forearm. *Horseman* 2.3:34.

Hewett, D. K. 1973. Leg wraps. *Quarter Horse J.* 25:170–171.

Hoeppner, G. 1976. Keeping your horse sound: Therapy for lameness. *Horse of Course* 5:36–39.

McHam, D. 1976. Emergency first aid. *Horseman* 21:35–38.

———. 1978. First aid: Do it right. *Horseman* 23:31–34.

MacKay-Smith, M., and L. DeButts. 1977. Locating lameness. *Equus* 12:47–55.

Naviaux, J. L. 1974. First aid. In J. L. Naviaux, *Horses in Health and Disease.* New York: Arco.

Nesbitt, C. 1977. A bandaging primer: The right way to bandage a horse. *Horse of Course* 6:26–28.

Rossdale, P. D. 1971. Diagnosis of lameness. *Thoroughbred of California* 62:780–792.

The wrap session I. 1978. *Equus* 4:51–55.

The wrap session II. 1978. *Equus* 9:29–33.

Chapter 10: Knowing About Parasites and Diseases

Abbott, E. M. 1998. Larval cyathostomosis—Part I: The disease, its diagnosis and treatment. *Equine Practice* 20(5):6.

———. 1998. Larval cyathostomosis—Part II: Prevention. *Equine Practice* 20(6):6.

Bello, T. R. 1985. *The Control and Treatment of Internal Equine Parasites.* Sommerville, N.J.: Hoechst-Roussel Agri-Vet Company.

Bello, T. R., and J. E. T. Laningham. 1992. Evaluation of daily pyrantel tartrate treatment of horses for prevention of intestinal penetration and development of small strongyle larvae resulting from experimentally induced infections. *Equine Veterinary J.* 12:280–286.

Bradlcy, R. E. 1986. Distribution and frcqucncy of bcnzimidazolc rcsistancc in cquinc small strongyles. *Equine Practice* 8:7–11.

Bushnell, R. B., D. P. Furman, E. C. Loomis, and L. A. Riehl. 1976. *Control of External Parasites of Livestock.* Division of Agricultural Sciences, Leaflet 2854. Davis, Cal.: University of California.

Catcott, E. J., and J. F. Smithcors, eds. 1972. *Equine Medicine and Surgery.* Wheaton, Ill.: American Veterinary Publications.

Cernick, S. L. 1977. *Preventative Medicine and Management for the Horse.* New York: Barnes.

Deal, A. S., E. C. Loomis, G. G. Gurtle, and W. C. Fairbanks. 1969. *Fly Control on the Horse Ranch*. Cooperative Extension Service Bull. AXT-307. Davis, Cal.: University of California.

Dengri, G. M. 1993. Review of oribatid mites as intermediary hosts of tapeworm of the anaplacephalidae. *Experimental and Applied Acarology* 17:567–580.

DiPietro, J. A., et al. 1989. Efficacy of ivermectin in the treatment of induced *Parascares equorum* infection in pony foals. *J. American Veterinary Medical Association* 12:1712–1714.

Do it yourself fecal egg count—step by step. 1979. *Equus* 23:51.

Donawick, W. J. Colics of the horse. Unpublished. Veterinary Clinic, New Boltons, Pa.

Drudge, J. H. 1978. *Internal Parasites of Horses*. Sommerville, N.J.: American Hoechst Corporation.

Drudge, J. H., and E. T. Lyons. 1996. *Internal Parasites of Equids with Emphasis on Treatment and Control*. Sommerville, N.J.: Hoechst-Roussel Agri-Vet Company.

Equine Infectious Anemia. 1977. Gaithersburg, Md.: Equine Health Publications.

Georgi, J. R. 1977. Parasites of the horse. In J. W. Evans, A. Borton, H. F. Hintz, and L. D. Van Vleck, *The Horse*. New York: W. H. Freeman and Company.

Granstom, D. 1997. *Understanding Equine Protozoal Myeloencephalitis*. Lexington, Ky.: The Blood-Horse.

Hayes, M. H. 1972. *Veterinary Notes for Horse Owners*. New York: Arco.

Hintz, H. F., and J. E. Lowe. 1977. Diseases of the horse. In J. W. Evans, A. Borton, H. F. Hintz, and L. D. Van Vleck, *The Horse*. New York: W. H. Freeman and Company.

Hollett, B. 1990. Equine parasite—tapeworms. *Veterinary Report* 1(10):80.

Kivipelto, J., C. Nicklin, and R. L. Asquith. 1998. A comparison of two programs (pyrantel tartrate administered daily and 3× pyrantel pamoate administrative at 8-week intervals) for the reduction of tapeworm EPG in the horse. *J. Equine Veterinary Science* 18:125–128.

Loomis, E. C., J. P. Hughes, and E. L. Bramhall. 1975. *The Common Parasites of Horses*. Cooperative Extension Service Publication 4006. Davis, Cal.: University of California.

Masri, M. D. 1991. Anhidrosis. *Equine Veterinary Data* 12(15):282–283.

Proctor, D. L. 1969. Internal parasites of the horse. *Proceedings, Fifteenth Annual Convention of American Association of Equine Practitioners*, pp. 351–363.

Rossdale, P. D. 1971. Colic. *Thoroughbred of California* 61:770–779.

———. 1976. *Inside the Horse*. Arcadia, Cal.: California Thoroughbred Breeders Association.

Schroeder, W. G. 1969. Suggestions for handling horses exposed to rabies. *J. American Veterinary Medical Association* 155:1842–1843.

Thompson, D. 1979. They kill while you wait. *Equus* 23:35.

Uhlinger, C. 1990. Effects of three anthelmentic schedules on the incidence of colic. *Equine Veterinary J.* 22:251–254.

———. 1991. Equine small strongyles: Epidemiology, pathology, and control. *The Compendium on Continuing Education for the Practicing Veterinarian* 13:863–869.

Wise, W. E., J. H. Drudge, and E. T. Lyons. 1972. *Controlling Internal Parasites of the Horse*. Lexington, Ky.: University of Kentucky Cooperative Extension Booklet Vet-1.

Ziker, S. C. 1992. Tick insecticide approved. *Equine Veterinary Data* 13:165.

Chapter 11: Riding and Driving

About bits. 1973. *Practical Horseman* 74:30–33, 50–51.

Barbalace, R. C. 1974. *Light Horse Management.* Minneapolis, Minn.: Burgess.

Barron, J. 1999. In Position to Win. *Quarter Horse J.* 51(8):46–49.

Bradley, M. 1973. *Western Equitation: Mounting, Correct Seat, Dismounting.* Science and Technology Guide 2876. Columbia, Mo.: University of Missouri Cooperative Extension.

Bradley, M., and S. D. Hardwicke. 1971. *English Equitation: Mounting, Correct Seat, Dismounting.* Science and Technology Guide 2875. Columbia, Mo.: University of Missouri Cooperative Extension.

Chamberlain, H. D. 1937. *Training Hunters, Jumpers, and Hacks.* New York: Surrydale Press.

Christopher, R. 1978. Saddle seat: Who says it's English? *Horse Lovers National* 43:8–15.

Close, P. 1977. Les Corbett: Saddle seat equitation. *Western Horseman* 42:32–34.

Davis, J. A. *The Reins of Life.* Plant City, Fla.: Kimbal Horse Books.

DeRomasskan, G. 1964. *Fundamentals of Riding.* New York: Doubleday.

———. 1968. *Riding Problems.* Brattleboro, Vt.: Greene Press.

Dillon, J. 1960. *A School for Young Riders.* New York: Arco.

———. 1961. *Form over Fences.* New York: Arco.

DuPont, J. 1973. From egg butt to billet strap. *Quarter Horse J.* 25:84.

Edwards, R. H. 1965. *Saddlery.* New York: Barnes.

Ensminger, M. E. 1972. *Breeding and Raising Horses.* U.S. Department of Agriculture Handbook No. 394. Washington, D.C.: Agricultural Research Service.

Evans, J. W. 1990. The recreational use of the horse. In J. W. Evans, A. Borton, H. F. Hintz, and L. D. Van Vleck, *The Horse.* New York: W. H. Freeman and Company.

Felton, S. W. 1967. *The Literature of Equitation.* London: Allen.

Ferguson, B. 1971. An explanation of the aids as used at the walk, trot, and canter. *The Morgan Horse* 31:32.

Floyd, J. 1979a. Mounting and dismounting. *Side-Saddle News* 6:3.

———. 1979b. Ready to ride. *Side-Saddle News* 6:3.

Forbes, J. 1972. *So Your Kids Want a Pony.* Brattleboro, Vt.: Greene Press.

Foreman, M. 1983. *Horse Handling Science.* Vols. 1, 2, and 3. Fort Worth, Tex.: Horse Handling Science (P.O. Box 9371).

Gianoli, L. 1969. *Horses and Horsemanship Through the Ages.* New York: Crown.

Gorman, J. A. 1967. *The Western Horse: Its Types and Training.* Danville, Ill.: Interstate.

Greenall, J. 1976. Hitching a single horse to an antique carriage. *The Morgan Horse* 36:509–512.

———. 1977. Appointments for driving antique carriages. *The Morgan Horse* 37:554–566.

Hamilton, S. 1977. Before you saddle up. *Equus* 11:36–42.

Hyland, A. 1971. *Beginner's Guide to Western Riding.* London: Pelham Books.

Jones, S. N. 1966. *The Art of Western Riding.* Portales, N.M.: Bishop.

Kaiser, N. W. 1975. Sidesaddle—the past revisited. *The Morgan Horse* 35:346–347.

Kiser, J. J. 1972. *What Judges Look for in Equitation Classes.* Science and Technology Guide 2838. Columbia, Mo.: University of Missouri Cooperative Extension.

Kulesza, S. 1965. *Modern Riding.* New York: Barnes.

Levings, N. P. 1968. *Training the Quarter Horse Jumper.* New York: Barnes.

Littauer, V. S. 1963. *Common Sense Horsemanship*. Rev. ed. New York: Arco.

——. 1967. *The Development of Modern Riding*. London: Allen.

——. 1973. *How the Horse Jumps*. London: Allen.

McCowan, L. L. 1972. *It Is Ability That Counts*. Augusta, Mich.: Cheff Center for the Handicapped (Rural Route 1, P.O. Box 171).

Mason, B. S. 1940. *Roping*. New York: Ronald Press.

Morris, G. 1971. *Hunter Seat Equitation*. New York: Doubleday.

Powell, M. D. 1970. Who owns horses? *Arabian Horse World* 11:66.

Santini, P. 1967. *The Caprilli Papers*. London: Allen.

Saunders, G. C. 1966. *Your Horse*. Rev. ed. New York: Van Nostrand Reinhold.

Shannon, E. 1970. *Manual for Teaching Western Riding*. Washington, D.C.: American Association for Health, Physical Education, and Recreation.

Stoneridge, M. A. 1968. *A Horse of Your Own*. New York: Doubleday.

Tree talk. 1969. *Appaloosa News* 26:8–9.

Trench, C. C. 1970. *A History of Horsemanship*. Norwich, England: Jarrold.

Tuke, D. 1965. *Bit by Bit*. New York: Barnes.

Williamson, C. O. 1965. *Breaking and Training for Stock Horses*. 5th ed. Hamilton, Neb.: Williamson School of Horsemanship (P.O. Box 506).

Wright, G. 1966. *Learning to Ride, Hunt and Show*. New York: Doubleday.

Yeates, B. F., and M. Bradley. 1972. *Pre-Bit Hackamore Training*. Science and Technology Guide 2864. Columbia, Mo.: University of Missouri Cooperative Extension.

Young, J. R. 1954. *The Schooling of the Western Horse*. Norman, Okla.: University of Oklahoma Press.

Chapter 12: Showing and Racing

Abby, H. C. 1970. *Show Your Horse*. New York: Barnes.

American Horse Shows Association Rule Book. Annual. New York: American Horse Shows Association.

American Racing Manual. Annual. Lexington, Ky.: Daily Racing Form, Inc.

Essary, D. 1974. *Quarter Horse Racing*. Amarillo, Tex.: American Quarter Horse Racing Association.

Evans, J. W. 1990. The recreational use of the horse. In J. W. Evans, A. Borton, H. F. Hintz, and L. D. Van Vleck, *The Horse*. New York: W. H. Freeman and Company.

Evans, L. T. 1964. *Standardbred Sport*. Columbus, Ohio: U.S. Trotting Association.

Jockey Club Fact Book. 1999. New York: The Jockey Club.

Mercer, T., ed. *Quarter Running Horse Chart Book*. Annual. Amarillo, Tex.: American Quarter Horse Racing Association.

Racing's leading earners. 1979. *Thoroughbred Record* 211:64.

Third Level Test 1 (Revised). 1977. New York: American Horse Shows Association.

Chapter 13: Rodeo, Trail, Sports Events, and Equine-Assisted Therapy

Back, J. 1959. *Horses, Hitches and Rocky Trails*. Chicago, Ill.: Swallow Press.

Barsaleau, R. B. 1977. Initiating the schedule. *Saddle Action* 1:39, 58.

Beacon, N. 1970. Competitive trail riding. *The Morgan Horse* 30:25.

Bradley, M. 1973. *Intermediate Trail Riding*. Science and Technology Guide 2883. Columbia, Mo.: University of Missouri Cooperative Extension.

Campion, L. 1990. *The Cutting Horse.* New York: Prentice-Hall.

Casewell, L. F. 1976. *Packing and Outfitting.* Cooperative Extension Service Publication No. 622. Blacksburg, Va.: Virginia Polytechnic Institute.

Clevenger, B. 1975. Cowboy polo. *Horseman* 19:26–28.

Davis, F. W. 1975. *Horse Packing in Pictures.* New York: Scribner's.

Distance Riding Manual. 1972. San Martin, Cal.: North American Trail Ride Conference.

Engel, B. T. 1988. *A Bibliography for Therapeutic Riding in Sports, Education and Medicine.* Durango, Colo.: B. Engel Therapy Services.

———. 1992. *Therapeutic Riding Programs, Instruction, and Rehabilitation.* Durango, Colo.: B. Engel Therapy Services.

Engel, B. T., M. L. Galloway, and M. P. Bull. 1989. *The Horse, the Handicapped, and the Riding Team in a Therapeutic Riding Program.* Durango, Colo.: B. Engel Therapy Services.

Evans, J. W. 1977. The recreational use of the horse. In J. W. Evans, A. Borton, H. F. Hintz, and L. D. Van Vleck, *The Horse.* New York: W. H. Freeman and Company.

For Our Fans. 1972. Special Events Directory for Golden Gate Fields and Bay Meadows Race Track. Albany, Calif.: Tanforan Racing Association.

Hannan, L. T. 1977. Menu for a horse camper's feast. *Horseman* 21:64–68.

Harrison, S. 1992. *Cutting: A Guide for the Nonpro Rider.* New York: Howell/Book House.

Hill, O. C. 1976. *Packing and Outfitting Field Manual.* Cooperative Extension Service Bull. 636. Laramie: University of Wyoming.

Jennings, J. 1978. Three-day eventing. *Quarter Horse J.* 30:162–171.

Jones, C. 1973. Fox hunting in America. *American Heritage* 24:62–68, 101.

Joswick, F., M. Kittredge, and L. McCowan. 1986. *Aspects and Answers.* Augusta, Mich.: Cheff Center for the Handicapped.

Miles, H. T. 1974. The three-day event. *American Horseman* 5:57–66.

Official Pro Rodeo Media Guide. 1999. Denver, Colo.: Professional Rodeo Cowboys Association.

Rider's Manual. 1976. Gilroy, Cal.: North American Trail Ride Conference.

Saare, S. 1972. *Endurance Riding and Management.* Santa Rosa, Cal.: Northwest Printing.

———. 1973. *Distance Riding Manual.* Moscow, Idaho: Appaloosa Horse Club.

Wiggins, W. 1978. *The Great American Speedhorse.* New York: Sovereign Books.

Yearbook of the United States Polo Association. 1978. Oak Brook, Ill.: U.S. Polo Association.

Chapter 14: Breeding the Stallion

Amann, R. P., and B. W. Pickett. 1984. *An Overview of Frozen Semen: Procedures for Thawing and Insemination of Frozen Equine Spermatozoa.* Special Series 33. Ft. Collins, Colo.: Colorado State University Experiment Station.

Asbury, A. C., and J. P. Hughes. 1964. Use of the artificial vagina for equine semen collection. *J. American Veterinary Medical Association* 144:879–882.

Berndtson, W. E., B. W. Pickett, and T. M. Nett. 1974. Reproductive physiology of the stallion. IV: Seasonal changes in the testosterone. *J. Reproduction and Fertility* 39:115–118.

Bielanski, W. 1960. Reproduction in horses. Vol. 1: Stallions. *Instytut Bull.* 116. Krakow, Poland: Instytut Zootechniki.

Bowen, J. M., N. Tobin, R. B. Simpson, W. B. Ley, and M. M. Ansari. 1982. Effects of washing on the bacterial flora of the stallion's penis. *J. Reproduction and Fertility* 32:41.

Card, C. E. 1997. Pregnancies from imipramine and zylazine induced ex-copula ejaculation in a disabled stallion. *Canadian Veterinary Medical Association* 38(3):171–174.

Chenoweth, P. J., R. R. R. Pascoe, H. L. McDougal, and P. J. McCosker. 1970. An abnormality of the spermatozoa of a stallion (Equus caballus). *British Veterinary J.* 126:476–481.

Colborn, D. R., D. L. Thompson, T. L. Roth, J. S. Capehart, and K. L. White. 1991. Responses of cortisol and prolactin to sexual excitement and stress in stallions and geldings. *J. Animal Science* 69:2556–2562.

Eckstein, P., and S. Zuckerman. 1956. Morphology of the reproductive tract. In A. S. Parkes (ed.), *Marshall's Physiology of Reproduction.* 3d ed. Boston, Mass.: Little, Brown.

El Wishy, A. B. 1975. Morphology of epididymal spermatozoa in the ass (Equus asinus) and stallion (Equus caballus). *Zeitschrift für Tierzuchtung und Zuechtungsbiologie* 92:67–72.

Fraser, A. F. 1968. *Reproductive Behavior in Ungulates.* New York: Academic Press.

Gebauer, M. R., B. W. Pickett, and E. E. Swierstra. 1974a. Reproductive physiology of the stallion. II: Daily production and output of sperm. *J. Animal Science* 39:732–736.

———. 1974b. Reproductive physiology of the stallion. III: Extragonadal transit time and sperm reserves. *J. Animal Science* 39:737–742.

Gebauer, M. R., B. W. Pickett, J. L. Voss, and E. E. Swierstra. 1974. Reproductive physiology of the stallion: Daily sperm output and testicular measurements. *J. American Veterinary Medical Association* 165:711–713.

Getty, R., ed. 1953. *Sisson and Grossman's The Anatomy of Domestic Animals.* Philadelphia, Pa.: Saunders.

Hafez, E. S. E. 1968. *Reproduction in Farm Animals.* Philadelphia, Pa.: Lea & Febiger.

Haner, E. P., H. C. Dellgren, S. E. McCraine, and C. K. Vincent. 1970. Pubertal characteristics of Quarter Horse stallions. *J. Animal Science* 30:321.

Hansen, J. C. 1965. Artificial insemination. *The Blood Horse* 90:3368.

Heinze, C. D. 1966. Methods of equine castration. *J. American Veterinary Medical Association* 148:428.

Hughes, J. P., and R. G. Loy. 1970. Artificial insemination in the equine: A comparison of natural breeding and artificial insemination of mares using semen from six stallions. *Cornell Veterinarian* 60:463.

Johnston, P. F., and J. L. Deluca. 1998. Chemical ejaculation of stallions after the administration of oral imipramine followed by intravenous xylazine. *Proceedings American Association Equine Practioneers,* pp. 12–15.

Julian, L. M., and W. S. Tyler. 1959. Anatomy of the male reproductive organs. In H. H. Cole and P. T. Cupps (eds.), *Reproduction in Domestic Animals.* Vol. 1. New York: Academic Press.

Kenny, R. M., and W. L. Cooper. 1974. Therapeutic use of a phantom for semen collection from a stallion. *J. American Veterinary Medical Association* 165:706–707.

Kenny, R. M., R. S. Kingston, A. H. Rajamannon, and C. F. Ramberg. 1971. Stallion semen characteristics for predicting fertility. *Proceedings, Seventeenth Annual Convention of American Association of Equine Practitioners* 17:53.

Klem, M. E., J. L. Kreider, J. B. Pruitt, and G. D. Potter. 1986. Motility and fertility of equine spermatozoa extended in bovine serum albumin and sucrose. *Theriogenology* 26:569.

Klug, E., E. Deegen, B. Lazarz, L. Rojem, and H. Merkt. 1982. Effect of adrenergic neurotransmitters upon the ejaculatory process in the stallion. *J. Reproduction and Fertility* 32:31.

Kosniak, K. Characteristics of the successive jets of ejaculated semen of stallions. *J. Reproduction and Fertility* 23:59–61.

Lowe, J. E., and R. Dougherty. 1972. Castration of horses and ponies by a primary closure method. *J. American Veterinary Medical Association* 160:183.

McKinnon, A. O. 1996. Artificial insemination of cooled, transported and frozen semen. In *Equine Stud Medicine,* Sydney: Post-Graduate Foundation in Veterinary Science 319–337.

McKinnon, A. O., and J. L. Voss. *Equine Reproduction.* Philadelphia, Pa.: Lea & Febiger.

McKinnon, A. O., and J. B. Walker. 1998. Effect of ambient temperature and container on temperature of extended equine semen. *World Equine Veterinary Review* 3:5–11.

Morel, M. D. 1999. *Equine Artificial Insemination.* Wallingford: CABI Publishing.

Nishikawa, Y. 1959. *Studies on Reproduction in Horses.* Tokyo: Japan Racing Association.

Paccamonti, D. L., A. V. Beisten, J. M. Parlevliat, and B. Colenbrander. 1999. Reproductive parameters of miniature stallions. *Theriogenology* 51: 1343–1349.

Pickett, B. W. 1974. Evaluation of stallion semen. In O. R. Adams (ed.), *Lameness in Horses,* 3d ed. Philadelphia, Pa.: Lea & Febiger.

———. 1976. Stallion management with special reference to semen collection, evaluation, and artificial insemination. *Proceedings, First National Horsemen's Seminar.* Fredericksburg, Va.: Virginia Horse Council.

Pickett, B. W., and D. G. Back. 1973. *Procedures for preparation, collection, evaluation, and insemination of stallion semen.* General Series 935. Fort Collins: Colorado State University, Experimental Station.

Pickett, B. W., D. G. Back, L. D. Burwash, and J. L. Voss. 1971. The effect of extenders, spermatozoal number and rectal palpation on equine fertility. *Proceedings, Fifth Technology Conference on Artificial Insemination and Reproduction.*

Pickett, B. W., and G. Marvin Beeman. 1975. The arguments for artificial insemination. *The Morgan Horse* 35:38–40.

Pickett, B. W., L. C. Faulkner, and T. M. Sutherland. 1970. Effect of month and stallion on seminal characteristics and sexual behaviors. *J. Animal Science* 31:713.

Pickett, B. W., and J. L. Voss. 1973. *Reproductive management of the stallion General Series 934.* Fort Collins, Colo.: Colorado State University, Experimental Station.

Pickett, B. W., J. L. Voss, and E. W. Anderson. 1976. Are you managing your stallion for maximum reproductive efficiency? *The Morgan Horse* 36:145–151.

Pickett, B. W., J. L. Voss, and E. L. Squires. 1977. Impotence and abnormal sexual behavior in the stallion. *Theriogenology* 8:329–347.

Skinner, J. D., and J. Bowen. 1968. Puberty in the Welsh stallion. *J. Reproduction and Fertility* 16:133.

Swierstra, E. E., M. R. Gebauer, and B. W. Pickett. 1974. Reproductive physiology of the stallion. I: Spermatogenesis and testis composition. *J. Reproduction and Fertility* 40:113–123.

Tischner, M., K. Kosniak, and W. Bielanski. 1974. Analysis of the patterns of ejaculation in stallions. *J. Reproduction and Fertility* 39:329–335.

Transported Semen Handbook for the Stallion Owner and Veterinarian. Beverly, Mass.: Hamilton Thorne Research.

Varner, D. D., et al. 1990. *Diseases and Management of Breeding Stallions*. Goleta, Cal.: American Veterinary Publications.

Voss, J. L., and B. W. Pickett. 1976. Reproductive management of the broodmare. *General Series* 961. Fort Collins, Colo.: Colorado State University, Experimental Station.

Wierzbowski, S. 1958. Ejaculatory reflexes in stallions following natural stimulation and the use of the artificial vagina. *Animal Breeding Abstracts* 26:367.

Wilcox, S., K. Dusza, and K. Houpt. 1991. The relationship between recumbent rest and masturbation in stallions. *J. Equine Veterinary Science* 11:23–26.

Chapter 15: Breeding the Mare

Allen, W. R. 1977. *Ova Transfer: Techniques and Results in Horses*. Canadian Agricultural Monograph No. 16.

Allen, W. R., and D. R. Antczak. 1985. Equine embryo transfer. *Equine Veterinary J.*, Supplement 3.

Allen, W. R., and L. E. A. Rowson. 1973. Control of the mares oestrous cycle by prostaglandins. *J. Reproduction and Fertility* 33:539.

———. 1975. Surgical and nonsurgical egg transfer in horses. *J. Reproduction and Fertility* 23:525–530.

Arthur, G. H. 1970. The induction of oestrus in mares by uterine infusion of saline. *Veterinary Record* 86:554.

Arthur, G. H., and W. E. Allen. 1972. Clinical observations on reproduction in a pony stud. *Equine Veterinary J.* 4:109.

Bergfelt, D. R., B. G. Mann, N. B. Schwartz, and O. J. Ginther. 1991. Circulating concentrations of immunoreactive inhibin and FSH during the estrous cycle of mares. *Equine Veterinary J.* 11:319–322.

Berliner, V. R. 1959. The estrous cycle of the mare. In H. H. Cole and P. T. Cupps (eds.), *Reproduction in Domestic Animals*. Vol. 1. New York: Academic Press.

Bitteridge, K. J, and J. A. Laing. 1970. The diagnosis of pregnancy. In J. A. Laing (Ed.), *Fertility and Infertility in Domestic Animals*. Baltimore: Williams & Wilkins.

Braselton, W. E., and W. H. McShan. 1970. Purification and properties of follicle-stimulating and luteinizing hormones from horse pituitary glands. *Archives of Biochemical Biophysics* 139:56.

Burkhardt, J. 1949–1950. Sperm survival in the genital tract of the mare. *J. Agricultural Science* 39–40:201–203.

———. 1947. Transition from anoestrus in the mare and the effects of artificial lighting. *J. Agricultural Science* 37:64.

Cole, H. H., and P. T. Cupps, eds. 1959. *Reproduction in Domestic Animals*. New York: Academic Press.

Eckstein, P., and S. Zuckerman. 1956. Morphology of the reproductive tract. In A. A. Parkes (ed.), *Marshall's Physiology of Reproduction*. 3d ed. Boston, Mass.: Little, Brown.

Evans, J. W., J. P. Hughes, D. P. Neely, G. H. Stahellfeldt, and C. M. Winget. 1979. Episodic LH secretion patterns in the mare during the oestrus cycle. *J. Reproduction and Fertility* 27:143–150.

Fitzgerald, B. F. 1986. Use of a GnRH analogue to induce ovulation in mares: A preliminary study. *Modern Veterinary Practice*. March:247.

Frandson, R. D., ed. 1974. *Anatomy and Physiology of Farm Animals*. Philadelphia, Pa.: Lea & Febiger.

Geschwind, I. I., R. Dewey, J. P. Hughes, J. W. Evans, and G. H. Stahenfeldt. 1978. Circulating luteinizing hormone levels in the mare during oestrus cycle. *J. Reproduction and Fertility* 23:207–212.

Getty, R., ed. 1953. *Sisson and Grossman's The Anatomy of Domestic Animals*. Philadelphia, Pa.: Saunders.

Ginther, O. J. 1992. *Reproductive Biology of the Mare*. Cross Plains, Wis.: Equiservices.

———. 1986. *Ultrasonic Imaging and Reproductive Events in the Mare*. Cross Plains, Wis.: Equiservices.

Ginther, O. J., and N. L. First. l971. Maintenance of the corpus luteum in hysterectomized mares. *American J. Veterinary Research* 32:1687.

Ginther, O. J., M. C. Garcia, E. L. Squires, and W. P. Steffenhagen. 1972. Anatomy of vasculature of uterus and ovaries in the mare. *American J. Veterinary Research* 33:1561.

Hammond, J., and K. Wodzicki. 1941. Anatomical and histological changes during the oestrus cycle in the mare. *Proceedings of the Royal Society* 130(B):1.

Hansen, J. C. 1965. Artificial insemination. *The Blood-Horse* 90:3368–3370.

———. 1966. Artificial insemination. *Modern Vet Practice* 47:4.

Harrison, R. J. 1946. The early development of the corpus luteum in the mare. *J. Anatomy* 80:160.

Harvey, E. B. 1959. Implantation, development of the fetus and fetal membranes. In H. H. Cole and P. T. Cupps (eds.), *Reproduction in Domestic Animals*. Vol. 1. New York: Academic Press.

Householder, D. D., J. L. Fleeger, Y. H. Clamann, and A. M. Sorenson. 1974. Criteria for detecting ovulation in the mare. *J. Animal Science* 39:212.

Hughes, J. P., G. H. Stabenfeldt, and J. W. Evans. 1972a. Clinical and endocrine aspects of the estrous cycle in the mare. *Proceedings, American Association of Equine Practitioners* 1:119.

———. 1972b. Estrous cycle and ovulation in the mare. *J. American Veterinary Medical Association* 161:1367.

Irvine, D. S., B. R. Downey, W. G. Parker, and J. J. Sullivan. 1975. Duration of oestrus and time of ovulation in mares treated with synthetic Gn-Rh (AY-24,031). *J. Reproduction and Fertility* 23:279–283.

Johnson, A. L. 1986. Pulsatile administration of gonadotropin-releasing hormone advances ovulation in cycling mares. *Biology of Reproduction* 35:113.

———. 1987. Gonadotropin-releasing hormone treatment induces follicular growth and ovulation in seasonally anestrous mares. *Biology of Reproduction* 36:1199.

Kiefer, B. L., J. F. Roser, J. W. Evans, D. P. Neely, and C. A. Pachezo. 1979. Progesterone patterns observed with multiple injections of a $PGR_{2\alpha}$ analogue in the cyclic mare. *J. Reproduction and Fertility* 27:237–244.

Kubiak, J. R., and J. W. Evans. 1986. Predicting the time of parturition. *Equine Veterinary Data* 7(28):350.

Loy, R. G. 1970. The reproductive cycle of the mare. *Lectures of the Stud Managers Course* 9:20.

Loy, R. G., and J. P. Hughes. 1966. The effects of human chorionic gonadotropin on ovulation, length of estrus and fertility in the mare. *Cornell Veterinarian* 61:41.

McCue, P. M. 1992. Breeding the older mare. *Texas Thoroughbred* 17:38, 40–41.

McCue, P. M., M. M. LeBlanc, G. Y. Akita, J. R. Pascoe, D. M. Whitherspoon, and G. H. Stabenfeldt. 1991. Granulosa cell tumors in two cycling mares. *Equine Veterinary J.* 11:281–282.

McDowell, K. J., D. G. Powell, and C. B. Baker. 1992. Effect of book size and age of mare and stallion on foaling rates in Thoroughbred horses. *J. Equine Veterinary Science* 12:364–367.

McGee, W. R., and H. D. McGee. *Veterinary Notes for the Standardbred Breeder.* Columbus, Ohio: U.S. Trotting Association.

Matthews, R. G., R. T. Ropiha, and R. M. Butterfield. 1967. The phenomenon of foal heat in mares. *Australian Veterinary J.* 43:579–582.

Meacham, T., and C. Hutton. 1968. Reproductive efficiency on 14 horse farms. *J. Animal Science* 27:434.

Nishikawa, Y. 1959. *Studies on Reproduction in Horses.* Tokyo: Japan Racing Association.

Noden, P.A., H. D. Hafs, and W. D. Oxender. 1973. Progesterone, estrus and ovulation after prostaglandin F-2 alpha in horses. *Federation Proceedings* 32:229.

Nuti, L. C., H. J. Grimek, W. E. Braselton, and W. H. McShan. 1972. Chemical properties of equine pituitary follicle-stimulating hormone. *Endocrinology* 91:1418.

Palmer, E., M. A. Draincourt, and R. Ortavant. 1982. Photoperiodic stimulation of the mare during winter anestrous. *J. Reproduction and Fertility* 32:275.

Pattison, M. L., C. L. Chen, and S. L. King. 1972. Determination of LH and estradiol-17$_\beta$ surge with reference to the time of ovulation in mares. *Biology of Reproduction* 7:136.

Penida, M. H., O. J. Ginther, and W. H. McShan. 1972. Regression of the corpus luteum in mares treated with an antiserum against equine pituitary fraction. *American J. Veterinary Research* 33:1767.

Rogers, T. 1971. *Mare Owner's Handbook.* Houston, Tex.: Cordovan.

Rosborough, J. P. 1960. Breeding hygiene, procedures and practices. *Proceedings, Illinois Short Courses for Horse Breeders,* p. 30.

Roser, J. F., B. L. Kiefer, J. W. Evans, D. P. Neely, and C. A. Pacheco. 1979. The development of antibodies to human chorionic gonadotropin following its repeated injection in the cyclic mare. *J. Reproduction and Fertility* 27:173–179.

Rossdale, P. D. 1973. Mares in breeding season. *Thoroughbred of California* 61:42.

Rowlands, I. W., W. R. Allen, and P. D. Rossdale. 1982. Equine Reproduction III: Proceedings of Third International Symposium on Equine Reproduction. *J. Reproduction and Fertility,* Supplement 32.

———. 1987. Equine Reproduction IV: Proceedings of Fourth International Symposium on Equine Reproduction. *J. Reproduction and Fertility,* Supplement 35.

Ryan, R. J., and R. V. Short. 1965. Formation of estradiol-17$_\beta$ by granulosa and theca cells of the equine ovarian follicle. *Endocrinology* 76:108.

Stabenfeldt, G. H., J. P. Hughes, and J. W. Evans. 1970. Ovarian activity during the estrous cycle of the mare. *Endocrinology* 90:1379.

Stabenfeldt, G. H., J. P. Hughes, J. D. Wheat, J. W. Evans, P. C. Kennedy, and P. T. Cupps. 1974. The role of the uterus in ovarian control in the mare. *J. Reproduction and Fertility* 37:343.

Turner, C. W. 1952. The Mammary Gland. Vol. 1: *The Anatomy of the Udder of Cattle and Domestic Animals.* Columbia, Mo.: Lucas.

Warszawsky, L. F., W. G. Parker, N. L. First, and O. J. Ginther. 1972. Gross changes of internal genitalia during the estrous cycle in the mare. *American J. Veterinary Research* 33:19.

Webel, S. K., and E. L. Squires. 1982. Control of the oestrous cycle in mares with altrenogest. *J. Reproduction and Fertility* 32:193.

Witchi, E. 1956. *Development of Vertebrates.* Philadelphia, Pa.: Saunders.

Wood, K. A. 1973. *The Business of Horses.* Chula Vista, Cal.: Wood.

Chapter 16: Care During and After Pregnancy

Allen, W. R. 1970. Endocrinology of early pregnancy in the mare. *Equine Veterinary J.* 2:64.

———. 1970. *Equine gonadotropins.* Unpublished doctoral thesis, Cambridge University, England.

Amoroso, E. C. 1955. Endocrinology of pregnancy. *British Medical Bull.* 11:117.

Andrist, F. 1962. *Mares, Foals and Foaling.* London: Allen.

Bain, A. M. 1969. Foetal losses during pregnancy in the Thoroughbred mare: A record of 2,562 pregnancies. *New Zealand Veterinary J.* 17:155.

Ball, B. A., T. V. Little, J. A. Weber, and G. L. Woods. 1989. Survival of day-4 embryos from young, normal mares and aged, subfertile mares after transfer to normal recipient mares. *J. Reproduction and Fertility* 85:187–194.

Bergfeldt, O. R., and O. J. Ginther. 1992. Relationships between circulating concentration of FSH and follicular waves during early pregnancy in mares. *Equine Veterinary J.* 12:274–279.

Bitteridge, K. J., and J. A. Laing. 1970. The diagnosis of pregnancy. In J. A. Laing (ed.), *Fertility and Infertility in Domestic Animals.* Baltimore, Md.: Williams & Wilkins.

Brown, S. 1978. Raising an orphan foal. *Horse of Course* 7:29–32.

Cole, H. H., and H. Goss. 1943. The source of equine gonadotropin. In *Assays in Biology.* No. 107. Berkeley, Cal.: University of California Press.

Cole, H. H., and G. H. Hart. 1942. Diagnosis of pregnancy in the mare by hormonal means. *J. American Veterinary Medical Association* 101:124.

Fowler, M. E. 1973. Diarrhea in foals. *Quarter Horse of the Pacific Coast* 10:13.

Frandson, R. D., ed. 1974. *Anatomy and Physiology of Farm Animals.* Philadelphia, Pa.: Lea & Febiger.

Harvey, E. B. 1959. Implantation, development of the fetus, and fetal membranes. In H. H. Cole and P. T. Cupps (eds.), *Reproduction in Domestic Animals.* Vol. 1. New York: Academic Press.

Jeffcott, L. B., J. G. Atherton, and J. Mingay. 1969. Equine pregnancy diagnosis. *Veterinary Record* 84:80.

Jeffcott, L. B., and P. D. Rossdale. 1977. A critical review of current methods for induction of parturition in the mare. *Equine Veterinary J.* 9:208–215.

Laing, J. A., ed. 1970. *Fertility and Infertility in Domestic Animals.* Baltimore, Md.: Williams & Wilkins.

LeBlanc, M. M. 1985. Colostrometer: Methods of evaluating immunoglobulin content in mare colostrum. *American Association of Equine Practitioners Newsletter* 2:14.

Lovely, J. D., G. H. Stabenfeldt, J. P. Hughes, and J. W. Evans. 1975. Endocrine patterns of the mare at term. *J. Reproduction and Fertility* 23:449–456.

McMullen, W. C. 1975. Foal doctoring. *Horseman* 19:22–24.

Madigan, J. E. 1987. *Manual of Equine Neonatal Medicine.* Woodland, Cal.: Live Oak Publishing.

Mahaffey, Leo W. 1968. Abortion in mares. *Veterinary Record* 82:681.

Miller, R. M. 1989. *Imprint Training of the Foal* (video). Available from Equivad, 83 East Shaw, Suite 250, Fresno, California 93710.

———. 1991. *Imprint Training of the Newborn Foal.* Colorado Springs, Colo.: Western Horseman.

Murphy, B. D., and S. D. Martinuk. 1991. Equine chorionic gonadotropin. *Endocrine Reviews* 12:27–44.

Nett, T. M., D. W. Holtan, and V. L. Estergreen. 1972. Plasma estrogens in pregnant mares. *Proceedings, Western Section of the American Society of Animal Science* 23:509.

Papkoff, H. 1969. Chemistry of the gonadotropin. In H. H. Cole and P. T. Cupps (eds.), *Reproduction in Domestic Animals.* Vol. 2. New York: Academic Press.

Paul, R. R. 1973. Foaling date. *The Morgan Horse* 33:40.

Pugh, D. G., and S. L. White. 1987. Commercially available tests for identification of the colostrum-deficient foal. *Equine Practice* 9(4):8.

Rogers, T. 1971. *Mare Owner's Handbook.* Houston: Cordovan.

Rollins, W. C., and C. E. Howell. 1951. Genetic sources of variation in the gestation length of the horse. *J. Animal Science* 10:797.

Ropiha, R. T., R. G. Matthews, R. M. Butterworth, F. M. Moss, and W. J. McFadden. 1969. The duration of pregnancy in Thoroughbred mares. *Veterinary Record* 84:552.

Sisson, S., and J. D. Grossman. 1953. *The Anatomy of Domestic Animals.* Philadelphia, Pa.: Saunders.

Zemianis, R. 1970. Examination of the mare. In R. Zemjanis, *Diagnostic and Therapeutic Techniques in Animal Reproduction.* Baltimore, Md.: Williams & Wilkins.

Chapter 17: Understanding Basic Genetics

Adalsteinsson, S. 1974. Inheritance of the palomino color in Icelandic horses. *J. Heredity* 65:15.

———. 1977. Inheritance of yellow dun and blue dun in the Icelandic Trotter horse. *J. Heredity* 69:146–148.

Anthony, E. 1998. Making nicks work for you. *Market Watch.* Aug. 6, 1998.

Archer, R. K. 1972. True haemophilia in horses. *Veterinary Record* 91:655.

Aurich, R. 1959. *A contribution to the inheritance of umbilical hernia in the horse.* Berliner and Munchener Tierartzliche Wochenschrift 72:420.

Basrur, P. K., H. Kanagawa, and J. P. W. Gilman. 1969. An equine intersex with unilateral gonadal agenesis. *Canadian J. Comparative Medicine* 33:297–305.

Basrur, P. K., H. Kanagawa, and L. Podliachouk. 1970. Further studies on the cell populations of an intersex horse. *Canadian J. Comparative Medicine* 34:294.

Bayley, W. 1991. Hyperkalemic periodic paralysis. *Equine Veterinary Data* 12:13.

Bengtsson, S., B. Gahne, and J. Rendel. 1968. Genetic studies on transferring albumins, prealbumins, and esterases in Swedish horses. *Acta Agriculturae Scandinavia* 18:60.

Bengtsson, S., and K. Sandberg. 1972. Phosphoglucomutase polymorphism in Swedish horses. *Animal Blood Groups and Biochemical Genetics* 3:115.

Benirschke, K., L. E. Brownhill, and M. M. Beath. 1962. Somatic chromosomes of the horse, the donkey, and their hybrids, the mule and hinny. *J. Reproduction and Fertility* 4:319.

Benirschke, K., and N. Malouf. 1957. Chromosome studies of equidae. In H. Dathe (ed.), *Equus.* Vol. 1, No. 2. Berlin: Tierpark.

Bielanski, W. 1946. The inheritance of shortening of the lower jaw (brachygnathia inferior) in the horse. *Przeglad Hodowlany* 14:24.

Blakeslee, L. H., R. S. Hudson, and R. H. Hunt. 1943. Curly coat of horses. *J. Heredity* 34:115–118.

Blunn, C. T., and C. E. Howell. 1936. The inheritance of white facial markings in Arabian horses. *J. Heredity* 27:393.

Bornstein, S. 1967. The genetic sex of two intersexual horses and some notes on the karotypes of normal horses. *Acta Veterinaria Scandinavia* 8:291.

Bouters, R., M. Vandeplassche, and A. De Moor. 1972. An intersex (male pseudohermaphrodite) horse with 64,XX/65,XXY mosaicism. *Equine Veterinary J.* 4:150.

Bowling, A. T. 1996. *Horse Genetics.* Wallingford: CAB International.

Bowling, A. T., and A. Ruvinsky. 2000. *The Genetics of the Horse.* Wallingford: CAB International.

Braend, M. 1964. Serum types of Norwegian horses. *Nordisk Veterinary Medicine* 16:363.

———. 1967. Genetic variation of horse hemoglobin. *J. Heredity* 58:385.

———. 1970. Genetics of horse acidic prealbumins. *Genetics* 65:495.

Braend, M., and C. Stormont. 1964. Studies on hemoglobin and transferrin types of horses. *Nordisk Veterinary Medicine* 16:31.

Briquet, R., Jr. 1957. So-called "albino horses." *Boletin de Industria Animal* 16:243.

———. 1959. Investigations on the relationship between markings on face and limbs in horses. *Revista de Ramonta Veterinaria* 19 (entire issue).

Britton, J. W. 1945. An equine hermaphrodite. *Cornell Veterinarian* 35:373.

———. 1962. Birth defects in foals. *Thoroughbred* 34:288.

Buckingham, J. 1936. Hermaphrodite horses. *Veterinary Record* 48:218.

Butz, H., and H. Meyer. 1957. Epitheliogenesis imperfecta neonatorium equi (incomplete skin formation in the foal). *Deutsche Tierarztliche Wochenschrift* 64:555.

Castle, W. E. 1946. Genetics of the Palomino horse. *J. Heredity* 37:35.

———. 1948. The ABC of color inheritance in horses. *Genetics* 33:22.

———. 1951a. Dominant and recessive black in mammals. *J. Heredity* 42:48.

———. 1951b. Genetics of the color variety of horses. *J. Heredity* 42:297.

———. 1953. Note on the silver dapple mutation of Shetland ponies. *J. Heredity* 44:224.

———. 1954. Color coat inheritance in horses and other mammals. *Genetics* 39:35.

———. 1960. Fashion in the color of Shetland ponies and its genetic basis. *J. Heredity* 51:247.

———. 1961. Genetics of the Claybank dun horse. *J. Heredity* 51:121.

Castle, W. E., and W. R. Singleton. 1961. The Palomino horse. *Genetics* 46:1143.

Castle, W. E., and W. H. Smith. 1953. Silver dapple, a unique color variety among Shetland ponies. *J. Heredity* 44:139.

Clegg, M. T., J. M. Boda, and H. H. Cole. 1954. The endometrial cups and allantochorionic pouches in the mare with emphasis on the source of equine gonadotropin. *Endocrinology* 54:448.

Cradock-Watson, J. E. 1967. Immunological similarity of horse, donkey, and mule haemoglobins. *Nature* 215:630.

Cronin, N. T. I. 1956. Hemolytic disease of newborn foals. *Veterinary Record* 67:474.

Cross, R. S. N. 1966. Equine periodic ophthalmia. *Veterinary Record* 78:8.

Crowe, M. W., and T. W. Swerczak. 1985. Equine congenital defects. *American Journal of Veterinary Research* 46:353.

Dimock, W. W. 1950. "Wobbles"—an hereditary disease in horses. *J. Heredity* 41:319.

Dreux, P. 1970. The degree of expression on limited piebaldness in the domestic horse. *Annales de Génétique et de Sélection Animale* 2:119.

Dungsworth, D. I., and M. E. Fowler. 1966. Cerebral hypoplasia and degeneration in a foal. *Cornell Veterinarian* 56:17.

Dunn, H. O., J. T. Vaughan, and K. McEntee. 1974. Bilaterally cryptorchid stallion with female karyotype. *Cornell Veterinarian* 64:265.

Dusek, J. 1965. The heritability of some characters in the horse. *Zivocisna Vyroha* 10:449.

———. 1970. Heritability of conformation and gait in the horse. *Zeitschrift für Tierzuchtung und Zuchtbiologie* 87:14.

———. 1971. Some biological factors and factors of performance in the study of heredity in horse breeding. *Scientia Agriculturae Bohemoslovaca* 3:199.

Emik, L. O., and C. E. Terrill. 1949. Systematic procedures for calculating inbreeding coefficients. *J. Heredity* 40:51.

Eriksson, K. 1955. Hereditary aniridia with secondary cataract in horses. *Nordisk Veterinary Medicine* 7:773.

Fischer, H., and K. Helbig. 1951. A contribution to the question of the inheritance of patella dislocation in the horse. *Tierzuchter* 5:105.

Flechsig, J. 1950. Hereditary cryptorchidism in a depot stallion. *Tierzuchter* 4:208.

Foye, D. B., H. C. Dickey, and C. J. Sniffen. 1972. Heritability of racing performance and a selection index for breeding potential in the Thoroughbred horse. *J. Animal Science* 35:1141.

Franks, D. 1962a. Differences in red-cell antigen strength in the horse due to gene interaction. *Nature* 195:580.

———. 1962b. Horse blood groups and hemolytic disease of the newborn foal. *Annals of the New York Academy of Sciences* 97:235.

Fraser, W. 1966. Two dissimilar types of cerebellar disorders in the horses. *Veterinary Record* 78:608.

Gahne, B. 1966. Studies of the inheritance of electrophoretic forms of transferring albumins, prealbumins, and plasma esterases of horses. *Genetics* 53:681.

Gahne, B., S. Bengtsson, and K. Sandberg. 1970. Genetic control of cholinesterase activity in horse serum. *Animal Blood Groups and Biochemical Genetics* 1:207.

Gluhovski, N., H. Bistriceanu, A. Sucui, and M. Bratu. 1970. A case of intersexuality in the horse with type 2A + XXXY chromosome formula. *British Veterinary J.* 126:522.

Hadwen, S. 1931. The melanomata of gray and white horses. *Canadian Medical Association J.* 21:519.

Hamori, D. 1940. Inheritance of the tendency to hernia in horses. *Allatorvosi Lapok* 63:136.

———. 1941. Parrot mouth and hog mouth as inherited deformities. *Allatorvosi Lapok* 64:57.

Hartwig, W., and U. Reichardt. 1958. The heritability of fertility in horse breeding. *Zuchtungskunde* 30:205.

Hintz, R. L. 1980. Genetics of performance in the horse. *J. Animal Science* 51:582.

Hitenkov, G. G. 1941. Stringhalt in horses and its inheritance. *Vestnik Sel'jskohozyaist-vennoi Nauki Zivotn* 2:64.

Hsu, T. C., and K. Benirschke. 1957. *An Atlas of Mammalian Chromosomes.* New York: Springer-Verlag.

Hughes, J. P., and A. Trommershausen-Smith. 1977. Infertility in the horse associated with chromosomal abnormalities. *Australian Veterinary J.* 53:253–257.

Hultgren, B. D., and D. Duffield. 1986. Spotted horse research: An update. *Paint Horse Journal.* March:116.

Huston, R., G. Saperstein, and H. W. Leipold. 1977. Congenital defects in foals. *J. Equine Medical Surgery* 1:146–161.

Hutchins, D. R., E. E. Lepherd, and L. G. Crook. 1967. A case of equine haemophilia. *Australian Veterinary J.* 43:83.

Jeffcott, L. B., and K. E. Whitehall. 1973. Twinning as a cause of foetal and neonatal loss in the Thoroughbred mare. *J. Comparative Pathology* 73:83.

Jones, T. C., and F. D. Maurer. 1942. Heredity in periodic ophthalmia. *J. American Veterinary Medical Association* 101:248.

Jones, W. E. 1970. Cytogenetics of the horse. *Quarter Horse J.* 22:38–46, 78.

———. 1979. Overo white foal syndrome. *J. Equine Medicine and Surgery* 3:54.

Jones, W. E., and R. Bogart. 1971. *Genetics of the Horse.* East Lansing, Mich.: Caballus.

Junnell, J. A., J. O. Sanders, J. D. Williams, and G. D. Potter. 1988. Pedigree analysis of four decades of Quarter horse breeding. *J. Animal Science* 57:585.

Kieffer, N. 1973. Inheritance of racing ability in the thoroughbred. *Thoroughbred Record* 204:50.

Kieffer, N. M. 1981. Linebreeding. *Thoroughbred Record* 15 April:1711.

Kieffer, N. M., N. Judge, and S. Burns. 1971. Some cytogenetic aspects of an equus caballus intersex. *Mammalian Chromosome News Letter* 12:18.

King, J. M., R. V. Short, O. E. Mutton, and J. L. Hammerton. 1965. The reproductive physiology of male zebra–horse and zebra–donkey hybrids. *J. Reproduction and Fertility* 9:391.

Lasley, J. F. 1970. *Genetic principles in horse breeding.* (Available from J. F. Lasley, 2207 Bushnell Drive, Columbia, MO 65201.)

———. 1972. *Genetics of Livestock Improvement.* Englewood Cliffs, N.J.: Prentice-Hall.

McGuire, T. C., M. J. Poppie, and K. L. Banks. 1974. Combined (B- and T-lymphocyte) immunodeficiency: A fatal genetic disease in Arabian foals. *J. American Veterinary Medical Association* 164:70.

Miller, R. W. *Appaloosa Coat Color Inheritance.* Moscow, Ida.: Montana State University, Bozeman and Appaloosa Horse Club.

Miser, M. 1951. Observation and discussion of variation and inheritance of white markings in horses. *Japanese J. Zootechnical Science* 22:23.

Naylor, J. M., J. A. Robinson, and J. Bertone. 1992. Familial incidence of hyperkalemic periodic paralysis in Quarter Horses. *J. American Veterinary Medical Association* 3:340–343.

Niece, R. L., and D. W. Kracht. Genetics of transferrins in burros *(Equus asinus). Genetics* 57:837.

Odriozola, M. 1948. Agouti color in horses: Change of dominance in equine hybrids. *Proceedings, Eighth International Congress of Genetics,* p. 635.

———. 1951. *A Los Colores del Caballo.* Madrid: National Syndicate of Livestock.

O'Ferral, G. J., and E. P. Cunningham. 1974. Heritability of racing performance in Thoroughbred horses. *Livestock Production Science* 1:87.

Osterhoff, D. R. 1967. Haemoglobin, transferrin, and albumin types in equidae (horses, mules, donkeys, and zebras). *Proceedings, Tenth European Conference on Animal Blood Groups and Biochemical Polymorphism.* Paris, 1966, p. 345.

Osterhoff, D. R., and L. S. Ward-Box. 1972. Quantitative studies on horse hemoglobins. *Proceedings, Twelfth European Conference on Animal Blood Groups and Biochemical Polymorphism,* Budapest, 1970, p. 541.

Osterhoff, D. R., D. O. Schmid, and L. S. Ward-Box. 1970. Blood group and serum type studies in Basuto ponies. *Proceedings, Eleventh European Conference on Animal Blood Groups and Biochemical Polymorphism.* Warsaw, 1968, p. 453.

Payne, H. W. 1968. Aneuploidy in an infertile mare. *J. American Veterinary Medical Association* 153:1293–1299.

Pern, E. M. 1970. The heritability of speed in Thoroughbred horses. *Genetika Moskva* 6:110.

Pirri, J., and D. G. Steele. 1952. The heritability of racing capacity. *The Blood Horse* 63:976.

Poppie, M. J., and T. C. McGuire. 1977. Combined immunodeficiency the foals of Arabian breeding: Evaluation of mode of inheritance and estimation of prevalence of affected foals and carrier mares and stallions. *J. American Veterinary Medical Association* 170:31–33.

Prawochenski, R. T. 1936. A case of lethal genes in the horse. *Nature* 137:689.

Pulos, W., and F. B. Hutt. 1969. Lethal dominant white in horses. *J. Heredity* 60:59.

Rooney, F. R., and M. E. Prickett. 1966. Foreleg splints in horses. *Cornell Veterinarian* 53:411.

Sandlberg, K. 1970. Blood group factors and erythrocytic protein polymorphism in Swedish horses. *Proceedings, Eleventh European Conference on Animal Blood Groups and Biochemical Polymorphism.* Warsaw, 1968, p. 447.

———. 1974. Blood typing of horses: Current status and application to identification problems. *Proceedings, First World Congress Applied to Livestock Production* 1:253.

Sangor, V. L., R. E. Mairs, and A. L. Trapp. 1964. Hemophilia in a foal. *J. American Veterinary Medical Association* 142:259.

Scekin, V. A. 1973. The inheritance of stringhalt (cock gait) in the horse. *Konevodstru* 2:20.

Schwark, H. J., and E. Neisser. 1971. Breeding of English Thoroughbred Horses in the G.D.R. Vol. 2: Results of estimates of heritability and breeding value. *Archiv Tierzuchter* 14:69.

Scott, A. M. 1972. Improved separation of polymorphic esterases in horse. *Proceedings, Twelfth European Conference on Animal Blood Groups and Biochemical Polymorphism.* Budapest, 1970, p. 527.

Searle, A. G. 1968. *Comparative Genetics of Coat Colour in Mammals.* London: Logo Press.

Severson, B. D. 1917. Cloven hoof in Percherons. *J. Heredity* 8:466.

———. 1918. Extra toes in horses and steers. *J. Heredity* 9:39.

Singleton, W. R., and Q. C. Bond. 1966. An allele necessary for dilute coat color in horses. *J. Heredity* 57:75.

Smith, A. T. 1972. Inheritance of chin spot markings in horses. *J. Heredity* 63:100.

Speed, J. G. 1958. A cause of malformation of the limbs of Shetland ponies with a note on its phylogenic significance. *British Veterinary J.* 114:18.

Spence, S. E. 1967. Can you tell tobiano from overo? *Paint Horse J.* 1:17.

Spier, S. J., G. P. Carlson, and T. A. Holliday. 1990. Hyperkalemic periodic paralysis in horses. *J. American Veterinary Medical Association* 197:1009–1017.

Sponseller, J. L. 1967. Equine cerebellar hypoplasia and degeneration. *Proceedings, Annual Meeting of American Association of Equine Practitioners,* pp. 123–126.

———. 1996. *Equine Color Genetics.* Ames, Iowa: Iowa State University Press.

Stormont, C. 1972. Genetic markers in the blood of horses. *Proceedings, Horse Identification Seminar.* Pullman, Wash.: Washington State University.

Stormont, C., and Y. Suzuki. 1963. Genetic control of albumin phenotypes in horses. *Proceedings, Society for Experimental Biology and Medicine* 114:673.

———. 1964. Genetic systems of blood groups in horses. *Genetics* 50:915.

———. 1965. Paternity tests in horses. *Cornell Veterinarian* 55:365.

Stormont, C., Y. Suzuki, and J. Rendel. 1965. Application of blood typing and protein tests in horses. *Proceedings, Ninth European Conference on Animal Blood Groups and Biochemical Polymorphism.* Prague, 1964, p. 221.

Stormont, C., Y. Suzuki, and E. A. Rhode. Serology of horse blood groups. *Cornell Veterinarian* 54:439.

Theile, H. 1958. Polydactyly in a foal. *Monatshefte Veterinary Medicine* 13:342.

Thornton, L. 1999. Balancing the pedigree. *Southern Horseman.* April:34–37, 40, 42, 44, and 46.

Tolksdorff, E., W. Jochle, D. R. Lamond, E. Klug, and H. Merkt. 1976. Induction of ovulation during the post partum period in the Thoroughbred mare with a prostaglandin analogue, Synchrocept. *Theriogenology* 6:403–412.

Trommershausen-Smith, A. 1972. Inheritance of chin spot markings in horses. *J. Heredity* 63:100.

———. 1977. Lethal white foals in matings of overo spotted horses. *Theriogenology* 8:303–311.

Trujillo, J. M., C. Stenius, L. Christian, and S. Ohno. 1962. Chromosomes of the horse, the donkey, and the mule. *Chromosoma* 13:243.

Trujillo, J. M., B. Walden, P. O'Neil, and H. B. Anstall. 1965. Sex–linkage of glucose-6-phosphate dehydrogenase in the horse and donkey. *Science* 148:1603.

———. 1967. Inheritance and subunit composition of haemoglobin in the horse, donkey, and their hybrids. *Nature* 213:88.

Tuff, P. 1948. The inheritance of a number of defects in the joints, bones, and ligaments of the foot of the horse. *Norske Veterinaertidsstrift* 60:385.

Van Vleck, L. D. 1977a. Principles of Mendelian inheritance. In J. W. Evans, A. Borton, H. F. Hintz, and L. D. Van Vleck, *The Horse.* New York: W. H. Freeman and Company.

———. 1977b. Principles of selection for quantitative traits. In J. W. Evans, A. Borton, H. F. Hintz, and L. D. Van Vleck, *The Horse.* New York: W. H. Freeman and Company.

———. 1977c. Relationships and inbreeding. In J. W. Evans, A. Borton, H. F. Hintz, and L. D. Van Vleck, *The Horse.* New York: W. H. Freeman and Company.

———. 1977d. Some Mendelian traits: Blood factors, colors, lethals. In J. W. Evans, A. Borton, H. F. Hintz, and L. D. Van Vleck, *The Horse.* New York: W. H. Freeman and Company.

Van Vleck, L. D., and M. Davitt. 1977. Confirmation of a gene for dominant dilution of horse colors. *J. Heredity* 68:280–282.

Varo, M. 1965a. On the relationship between characters for selection in horses. *Annales Agriculturae Fenniae* 4:38.

———. 1965b. Some coefficients of heritability in horses. *Annales Agriculturae Fenniae* 4:223.

Weber, W. 1947a. Congenital cataract, a recessive mutation in the horse. *Schweizerische Archiv Tierheilkunde* 89:244.

Weisner, E. 1955. The importance of inherited eye defects in horse breeding. *Tierzuchter* 4:310.

Werk, J. 1997. Inbreeding to females: Putting the Rasmussen Factor to the test. *Owner-Breeder* 10(5):1–7.

Wheat, J. D., and P. C. Kennedy. 1953. Cerebellar hypoplasia and its sequelae in a horse. *J. American Veterinary Medical Association* 131:241.

White, D. J., and D. A. Farebrother. 1969. A case of intersexuality in the horse. *Veterinary Record* 85:203.

Chapter 18: Business Practices in the Horse Industry

Fershtman, J. I. 1998. Independent contractor or employee: It pays to know the difference. www.horseadvice.com.

The Insider's Guide to Buying Thoroughbreds at Auction. 1998. Lexington, Ky.: The Blood-Horse.

Paulick, P. 1998. Shedrow success—leading trainers. *The Market Watch*, May 14, 1998.

Tharp, T. K. 1998. What you don't know might hurt you. *Thoroughbred Times.* May 30, pp. 46–47.

Vernon, T. M. 1999. The equine liability laws and the lessons to be learned (part 1). *Cutting Horse Chatter* 52(7):116–118.

Index